The Roman Catholic Church and the
Home Rule Movement in Ireland, 1870-1874

Paul Cardinal Cullen

The Roman Catholic Church and the Home Rule Movement in Ireland, 1870–1874

by Emmet Larkin

The University of North Carolina Press

Chapel Hill and London

Manufactured in the United States of America

The paper in this book meets the guidelines for permanence and durability
of the Committee on Production Guidelines for Book Longevity
of the Council on Library Resources.

94 93 92 91 90   5 4 3 2 1

Library of Congress Cataloging-in-Publication Data

Larkin, Emmet J., 1927–
The Roman Catholic Church and the Home Rule movement
in Ireland, 1870–1874 / by Emmet Larkin.
p.   cm.
Includes bibliographical references.
ISBN 0-8078-1886-0 (alk. paper)
1. Home rule (Ireland) 2. Ireland—Politics and
government—1837–1901. 3. Catholic Church—Ireland—
History—19th century. 4. Christianity and
politics. I. Title.
DA957.9.L36   1990
322'.1'0941509034—dc20
89-36347
CIP

Publication of this work was assisted by grants from the American Ireland Fund,
the Council on National Literatures, and the University of Chicago.

Chapter I of this work appeared in somewhat different form in
The Recorder: A Journal of the American Irish Historical Society,
and is reproduced here by permission of the journal.

To my daughter, Heather

Contents

Preface

In the first published volume of this work I explained how and why I embarked on writing a history of the Roman Catholic Church in Ireland in the nineteenth century;[1] I will not, therefore, burden the reader again on that score. I have once again adopted techniques of style and scholarly apparatus that are not quite orthodox, and I think it would be helpful again to repeat to some extent what I said in my earlier volumes about technique. The richness in the quality and quantity of both the general archival materials and the personal papers of the principal characters in this study is still very impressive. In presenting the evidence, therefore, I have again used a technique that I call "mosaic." The many varied and colored bits and pieces of evidence have been selected and arranged to create a portrait of the Church between 1870 and 1874. There are, I believe, a number of advantages in using the mosaic technique when the materials are appropriate. Because the writing of history can never result in more than a representation of what was "true," a historical portrait in mosaic is perhaps more "realistic" than might at first be supposed. The technique of mosaic allows for the inclusion of a great deal more of the evidence in its original form and contributes, therefore, not only to the immediacy of the actual experience but also to the authority of the representation, thereby enhancing the reality of the portrait. In all representations, and perhaps even more so in a mosaic, appreciation has a great deal to do with the proper relationship of the elements to the mind's eye—in a word, the achievement of perspective. If I have been successful, then, in constructing my mosaic, the numerous details should integrate and the various parts should harmonize when the volume is read as a whole.

Because the system of footnoting in this volume also is somewhat unorthodox, I think an explanation to the reader is again in order. Most of the ecclesiastical as well as the lay correspondence quoted here has not been catalogued in any more systematic way than by date. The correspondence, therefore, has been noted in the text simply as K (Kirby), C (Cullen), B (Butt), and so forth, with the dates and correspondents also indicated in the text. The problem of showing a break or omission in any particular letter quoted has been resolved by using the word "then" in parenthetical interpolation: for example, "The Home Rule movement," Cullen explained to Kirby on May 19, "is dominated by Protestants and Fenians"

---

1. *The Roman Catholic Church and the Creation of the Modern Irish State, 1878–1886* (Philadelphia, 1975).

(K). "I am determined, therefore," he then added, "to have nothing to do with it for the present," indicates that between the last quotation and the previous one there has been a break in the original text. Sometimes the letter used for quotation was a copy rather than the original, as is revealed in the designation. For example, if Cullen wrote Kirby and the designation is C rather than K, the letter quoted is obviously a copy. If there has been any variation from this procedure, it has been noted. The various abbreviations used for the correspondence are listed on page xv.

Given the fact that this volume is the sixth published in my now projected twelve-volume history of the Roman Catholic Church in Ireland in the nineteenth century (1780–1918), it may not be out of place here to explain that the previous volumes so far published are III (1850–60), IV (1860–70), VII (1878–86), VIII (1886–88), and IX (1888–91). I am presently finishing the sequel, VI (1874–78), to this present volume, V (1870–74), and when it is done I shall have completed that portion of my history from 1850 to 1891 in seven volumes. There are then two volumes projected for the period 1780–1850, I (1780–1829) and II (1829–50); and two for the period 1891–1918, X (1891–1905) and XI (1906–18). Because these projected eleven volumes are primarily concerned with the high politics of the Church in Ireland in the nineteenth century, and though they are certainly the necessary preliminary to grasping the basic frame of what was fundamentally a hierarchical institution, they are not sufficient in themselves to understanding the social and pastoral role of the Irish Church in the nineteenth century. If vouchsafed the necessary longevity, therefore, I also propose to write a companion volume, "The Devotional Revolution in Ireland, 1830–1880," in order to explain how the Irish people became that uniquely pious and practicing religious phenomenon they have essentially remained down to the present day, and thus provide, in some measure at least, a social dimension to my history of the Irish Church.

In turning to the many obligations I have incurred in the research and writing of this volume, I must again explain that there is no one I am more indebted to than the late Dr. Donal Herlihy, Bishop of Ferns, and formerly Rector of the Irish College in Rome. I also sincerely thank the Most Reverend Dr. Dominic Conway, present Bishop of Elphin, and formerly Spiritual Director and then Rector of the Irish College in Rome, for all his help and kindness. I am also under considerable obligation to the late Most Reverend Dr. Dermot Ryan, Pro-Prefect of Propaganda, and former Archbishop of Dublin, and the late Most Reverend Dr. Kevin McNamara, Archbishop of Dublin, for their permission to research in the Dublin Diocesan Archives. I must once again thank the Most Reverend Dr. Thomas Morris, Archbishop of Cashel, for his permission to read the Leahy correspondence on microfilm in the National Library of Ireland, and I am also under obligation to the late Bishop of Elphin, the Most Reverend Dr. Vincent J. Hanly, for his permission to read the Gillooly correspondence on microfilm. Dom Mark Tierney, O.S.B., who has arranged and catalogued the Leahy papers in the Cashel archives, Reverend John J. Silke, former archivist of the Irish College in Rome, and Reverend Kevin Kennedy, former archivist of the Dublin Diocesan Archives, were all most helpful. My debt to the late Mina Carney for all her help in the researching of this volume is still very considerable. To the staffs of the Dublin Diocesan Archives and the National Library of Ireland, I offer my sincere thanks for their unvarying kindness, patience, and help. I must particularly thank, however, Miss Mary Purcell, and the present archivist, David Sheehy, of the Dublin Diocesan Archives, and the two former Directors and the Assistant Keeper of Manuscripts of the National Library, Ailfred MacLochlainn, Michael Hewson, and Gerald Lyne, respectively, for their generous help. I must also thank the Rt. Rev. Mgr. Míceál Ledwith, President of St. Patrick's College, Maynooth, for his kind permission to read the Minutes of the Board of Trustees for that College, and the Rt. Rev. Mgr. Patrick J. Corish, professor of modern history at St. Patrick's College, Maynooth, for all his help in making my visits to the College fruitful and productive. Finally, I should like to thank my good friend and former colleague, Karl F. Morrison, for having read portions of this book and his wise advice and counsel in regard to them.

For all the various opportunities to continue my research through numerous grants-in-aid, I thank the American Irish Foundation, the American Philosophical Society, the Social Science Research Council, the American Council for Learned Societies, and the National Endowment for the Humanities. I must also especially thank Mr. William J. McNally, Executive Director of the American Ireland Fund, and Dr. Anne Paolucci, President of the Council on National Literatures, and the division of Social Sciences at the University of Chicago, without whose generous aid the publication of this volume would have been impossible. I am also very grateful to the editor of *The Recorder: A Journal of the American Irish Historical Society* for permission to reproduce the first chapter of this book. In conclusion, I should like to take this opportunity, inadequate as it is, to express my thanks to all those who had a hand or part in the making of this book, and indeed of my history of the Church in Ireland over the years, and especially my graduate assistant, Miss Julie Rogers, as well as our hardworking and hard-pressed secretarial staff, Mrs. Marnie Veghte and Mrs. Elizabeth Bitoy. No one but myself, of course, is responsible for any of the errors that may yet be found in this volume.

The Roman Catholic
Archbishops and Bishops in Ireland,
1870–1874

Archbishops of Ireland

Armagh: Daniel McGettigan, 1870–87
Dublin: Paul Cullen, 1852–78
Cashel: Patrick Leahy, 1857–75
Tuam: John MacHale, 1834–81

Bishops of the Province of Armagh

Ardagh and Clonmacnoise: Neal MacCabe, C.M., 1867–70;
George Conroy, 1871–78
Clogher: James Donnelly, 1864–93
Derry: Francis Kelly, 1864–89
Down and Connor: Patrick Dorrian, 1865–85
Dromore: John Pius Leahy, O.P., 1860–90
Kilmore: Nicholas Conaty, 1865–86
Meath: Thomas Nulty, 1866–98
Raphoe: Daniel McGettigan, 1856–70; James MacDevitt, 1871–79

Bishops of the Province of Dublin

Ferns: Thomas Furlong, 1857–75
Kildare and Leighlin: James Walshe, 1856–88;
James Lynch, C.M. (Coadjutor), 1869–96
Ossory: Edward Walsh, 1846–72;
Patrick F. Moran (Coadjutor), 1871–84

Bishops of the Province of Cashel

Cork: William Delany, 1847–86
Cloyne: William Keane, 1857–74
Kerry: David Moriarty, 1854–77
Killaloe: Michael Flannery, 1858–91; Nicholas Power (Coadjutor), 1865–71;
James Ryan (Coadjutor), 1872–89
Limerick: George Butler, 1864–86
Ross: Michael O'Hea, 1858–76
Waterford: Dominic O'Brien, 1855–73; John Power, 1873–86

Bishops of the Province of Tuam

Achonry: Patrick Durcan, 1852–75;
Francis MacCormack (Coadjutor), 1871–87
Clonfert: John Derry, 1847–70; Patrick Duggan, 1871–96
Elphin: Laurence Gillooly, C.M., 1856–95
Galway: John MacEvilly, 1856–78
Killala: Thomas Feeny, 1847–73; Hugh Conway (Coadjutor), 1871–93
Kilmacduagh and Kilfenora: John MacEvilly (Administrator), 1866–83

Abbreviations

A	*Acta Sacrae Congregationis*, Propaganda
B	Butt Papers
C	Cullen Papers
D	Daunt Papers
F.O.	Foreign Office Papers
G	Gillooly Papers
K	Kirby Papers
L	Leahy Papers
M	Monsell Papers
Ma	Manning Papers
S.R.C.	*Scritture Riferite Nei Congressi*, Propaganda
W	Woodlock Papers

Prologue

This is the story of the part played by the Roman Catholic Church in the first stage of the emergence of the modern Irish political system. That system, at the national level, had been actually created by Daniel O'Connell nearly a half century before in his struggle for Catholic Emancipation during the 1820s. Indeed, as long as O'Connell lived, his extraordinary political presence had been sufficient to sustain that system, but the system was never able, independent of its creator, to take on a life of its own. Though O'Connell had been able to create and sustain a system, he had not been able to institutionalize it. The constituent elements of this system— the leader, the party, and the bishops as a body—had survived the death of the great man in 1847, but they had survived more as attenuated than as concrete political realities. The concept of leader, for example, would not be realized again in any vital way until more than a generation later, when Isaac Butt emerged in the early 1870s, and the crystallization of the bishops as a body would not finally take place until the meeting of the first Vatican Council in Rome during 1870. Though the party had fared somewhat better than either the leader or the bishops in the intervening years, it was even slower to reemerge as a concrete political reality. The party, in fact, did not begin to take on its final shape and form until after the general election of 1874.

Whatever may be said, however, about the timing of the reemergence of the constituent elements of the modern Irish political system at the national level, there is little doubt that the most forceful and confident of those elements between 1870 and 1874 was the bishops as a body. This renewed vitality on the part of the bishops was largely the result of their having met and successfully resolved in the decade of the 1860s a formidable series of challenges—political, educational, pastoral, and constitutional. The confidence of the bishops was then enormously increased when their corporate will as a national hierarchy finally crystallized at the first Vatican Council, where they fraternized as a body almost on a daily basis for nearly eight months between December 1869 and July 1870. In the long history of their body, the Irish bishops had never experienced so prolonged and so sustained an intimacy as when they met formally and informally on a regular basis at the Irish College where apparently the greater number of them resided. Shortly after the Irish bishops left Rome in late July, their confidence was further enhanced by a series of episcopal appointments that infused much youthful vigor and energy into a body that had been rapidly aging. Between February 1871 and May 1873, eight episcopal appointments were made in a regular hierarchy of twenty-seven bishops, or nearly one-third of their number in the short period of something over two years. In this rapid refurbishing of the national hierarchy, moreover, the procedures that had come to govern the Irish episcopal appointments in the 1860s were carried into the 1870s, and for the next sixty years the Irish bishops remained essentially a co-opting body.

Though the bishops began the decade of the 1870s as a bristling and bustling body, the other elements in the Irish political system, the leader and the party, still faced some very stiff up-hill work before they could begin to vie with their lordships on equal terms. Isaac Butt, who eventually emerged as leader in late 1873, was professionally and intellectually an extraordinarily endowed man. He was perhaps the most gifted and certainly the most eloquent barrister at the Irish bar since Daniel O'Connell. In more recent years, Butt had also demonstrated his considerable political astuteness by drawing nearly all the threads of Irish nationalist life into his own hands. He had, for example, early won the confidence and gratitude of the Fenian, or Irish Republican Brotherhood, by his very able defence of their leaders during the celebrated State Trials of 1865–66. Three years later, in 1869, he was elected president of both the Amnesty Association, which demanded that all of those Fenians still in jail should be set free, and the Tenant Right League, which advocated fixity of tenure at a fair rent and free sale for the Irish tenant farmer. As president of the league, moreover, Butt maintained that the final solution to the Irish land question was the establishment of a peasant proprietorship which would allow the tenants to purchase their holdings from their landlords under a long-term program financed by the state. Finally, in May 1870, Butt founded the Home Government Association through which he tried to enlist in a political consensus every shade of Irish public opinion, from the Fenians on the extreme left to his fellow Irish Protestants on the extreme right.

In the next two and a half years, Butt bent himself to the dual task of becoming the leader of the Irish people and creating a party committed to Home Rule in the House of Commons. Between May 1870 and the end of 1872, with the support of some half a dozen members of Parliament and the more advanced constitutional Nationalists in the country, Butt began to establish his leadership and to build a party. In a series of twelve by-elections during this period, Butt achieved very considerable success in making Home Rule the vital issue in the constituencies and increasing his following in the House of Commons to some dozen of the 103 Irish members. By December 1872, it had become evident that Home Rule had not only captured the political imagination of the country, and that the next general election would probably result in a Home Rule sweep outside of Ulster, but that Butt had also emerged as the dominant personality in the movement.

What was perhaps even more impressive, however, was that Butt had achieved all of this in the face of the most determined opposition on the part of the leader of the Irish Church, Paul Cardinal Cullen. The cardinal's dislike of Butt and Home

Rule was both personal and political. On the personal side, he had developed a deep distrust and antipathy for Butt, and he was very suspicious of the Home Rule movement because he thought it was at once too Fenian and too Protestant in its leadership. On the political side, the problem was that Cullen and the great majority of the Irish bishops had committed themselves in the general election of 1868 to an Irish-Liberal alliance under the leadership of William Gladstone on the basis of the Liberal leader's promise to do justice to Ireland by legislating for its needs according to Irish ideas. The emergence of the Home Rule movement, therefore, threatened not merely to subvert that recently made alliance but more particularly to wreck the promise of a settlement of the question of university education for Irish Catholics, on which the Irish bishops in general, and Cullen in particular, had set their hearts and hopes.

When indeed those hopes were wrecked in February 1873 by Gladstone's inability to meet the bishops' expectations in the Irish University bill he introduced in the House of Commons, the consequent advice of the bishops to their members of Parliament to vote against the measure resulted in the defeat of the government and the crippling of Gladstone's ministry. Ironically, the wreck of the Irish-Liberal alliance also eventuated in a deep political crisis for the Home Rule movement and its leader. Though the Irish-Liberal alliance was then in ruins, the anticipated political rapprochement between the bishops and the Home Rule movement did not take place in spite of Butt's best efforts to conciliate the bishops. Indeed, Cullen proved to be more adamant than ever in regard to Butt and Home Rule, and his very great personal influence among the bishops allowed him to carry the body with him in continuing to hold aloof. In the next several months, this unexpected political reversal resulted in the movement losing a great deal of its momentum in the country. The decline became especially evident in the two by-elections that took place in counties Roscommon and Waterford respectively in June and July, when no Home Rule candidates contested the seats, and two Liberals were returned unopposed.

A consensus began to emerge among Home Rulers during the summer of 1873 that a national conference should be called to give the movement renewed purpose and vigor by establishing it on a broader base in the country. The conference was called for November 1873 in Dublin by a requisition in October that was signed by 3 bishops, 26 M.P.'s, and 24,000 local worthies. The achievement of the conference, which was attended by some eight hundred delegates, was that it provided the movement with a program, an organization, and a leader. All the various factions—Fenians, advanced Nationalists, Repealers, moderate Nationalists, and Whigs—subsumed their political views in Home Rule and adopted as their means to that end the newly formed Home Rule League in place of the old Association. The great question, of course, was what the response of the country would be to the work of the conference. That reaction, in fact, was not long delayed, for two months later almost to the day, on January 24, 1874, Gladstone announced that there would be an immediate general election.

The result of this snap election, however, proved to be not only a dreadful defeat for Gladstone and his Liberal party but also a very mixed blessing for the Home Rule movement. In the new House of Commons, the Liberals' seats were reduced to 247 of a total of 658, as the Conservatives, lead by Disraeli, won 351 seats and the Home Rulers returned 60 members. The Liberal rout in Ireland was even greater as they were only able to hold 11 of the 103 Irish seats. By gaining some 50 seats in Ireland, the Home Rulers had apparently won a great political victory, but the appearance belied the reality. Given the overall Conservative majority of 44 against the Liberals and Home Rulers combined, the latter had really very little political leverage in the new House. In Ireland, moreover, in spite of the overwhelming vote of confidence in Home Rule by the electors in the constituencies, Cardinal Cullen and the great majority of the bishops still refused to endorse in any formal way either the Home Rule movement or its leader.

In the meantime, the bishops as a body were having considerably more success in dealing with a question that was not only much closer to their hearts but also potentially was much less divisive than popular politics—the education question. By 1870, in fact, the bishops were virtually at one on that question. They were both agreed and determined that Irish education on all its levels—primary, inter-mediate, and university—should be not only denominational but also under their absolute control. Between 1870 and 1874, therefore, the differences about educa-tional matters that emerged among the Irish bishops were concerned with tactics rather than principles. During this period the bishops had to face basically three challenges in regard to education, and as a body they responded well to them all. The first challenge had to do with their ongoing struggle of more than a quarter of a century with the Board of National Education, which was administratively responsible for the primary system, and which the bishops thought was con-tinually attempting to encroach on their rights in regard to the system. The second was what was to be done about their national seminary, St. Patrick's College, Maynooth, since this institution in the summer of 1869 had been disendowed by the state as part of the disestablishment and disendowment of the Protestant Church in Ireland. The third and most serious of the educational challenges was the perennial problem posed by the Catholic University of Ireland, which was crippled both financially by lack of money and academically by the need for a charter of incorporation from the state to allow it to grant degrees to its students.

Though the bishops succeeded in containing the national board and reforming Maynooth, they had greater difficulty in sustaining the Catholic University. In 1870, the University was once again in very serious difficulties. Over the previous decade its income had declined by nearly a fifth and its student body by about a third. In the next four years worse was to follow as both income and the student body shrunk by nearly another forty percent. The great irony of this accelerating decline was that it was in large part the result of the Irish-Liberal alliance. One of the expected fruits of that alliance was an Irish University bill, which the Irish bishops hoped would provide both an endowment and a charter for the Catholic University. Between 1870 and 1873, therefore, the will of the bishops in particular, and the Catholic body in general, to sustain the University was gradually sapped because the boon annually expected from the Liberal ministry was always postponed. When Gladstone finally introduced his University bill in February 1873, the bishops were bitterly disappointed because it did not provide for an endowment, and worse, it appeared to introduce the principle of non-denominational or mixed education at the university level. The bishops rejected the bill and the Irish-Liberal alliance was wrecked. With the Catholic University on the verge of collapse, the bishops pulled themselves together and made saving the University their educational priority during 1873–74. They doubled the income of the University, attempted to revitalize the student body, especially in the arts and science faculty, and refurbished the faculty by filling vacancies and making new appointments. By March 1874, therefore, in spite of all the vicissitudes, political and educational, it was evident that the bishops were a united and confident body and that any political initiative taken at the national level absolutely required their support as a body for its eventual success.

Part I
The Bishops

Pope Pius IX

I

The First Vatican Council
December 1869–July 1870

The first Vatican Council of 1869–70 was one of the crucial events in the development of the modern Irish Church. It was at the Vatican Council that the Irish bishops as a body finally crystallized as a national hierarchy and, thus, set the seal to the consolidation of the modern Irish Church.[1] Indeed, one of the significant ironies of the Council was that what was originally intended as a profound ecumenical experience for the Universal Church also resulted in a real deepening of the national consciousness of many of the hierarchies that assisted at the Council from all over the world. During the Council, for example, the national hierarchies were early obliged to meet as distinct bodies in order to formulate their views on the issues to be discussed and the procedures to be followed at the Council. This preliminary caucusing, of course, was absolutely necessary if any business was to be done when some 750 prelates each had a voice and a vote. A number of national hierarchies, especially those in the English-speaking world, because of the missionary nature of their churches were also encouraged by the Roman authorities to meet regularly to settle their outstanding problems. And the Irish, English, Scottish, American, Canadian, and Australian bishops all took advantage of the Roman solicitude. Of them all, however, perhaps none profited more from this novel experience as a body than did the Irish, and certainly none returned from the Council with greater confidence in their ability to meet all the various challenges in the relationship between Church and state than did the Irish.

The first Vatican Council had been originally called by Pius IX on June 26, 1867 to address the many evils by which he felt the Roman Catholic Church was oppressed in the modern world and of which he had given an outline in his celebrated *Syllabus of Errors* in 1865. However, by the time the Council was

---

1. Emmet Larkin, *The Consolidation of the Roman Catholic Church in Ireland, 1860–1870* (Chapel Hill, 1987), pp. 693–94.

convened formally on December 8, 1869, the feast of the Immaculate Conception of the Blessed Virgin Mary, the issue that had come to transcend all others in the Church was whether the Council would proceed to a dogmatic definition of papal infallibility.[2] In the minds of the vast majority of the some one thousand bishops who governed the Universal Church in 1869, the question was not whether the doctrine of papal infallibility was true, which apparently most of them accepted, but rather whether it was opportune at that moment in time to have it proclaimed as a dogmatic truth of the Church. Both before and at the Council, therefore, the great division of opinion was between the infallibilists, who thought it should be defined as truth, and the inopportunists, who did not believe the times were propitious for such a definition. Of the some 750 prelates and dignitaries who eventually attended the Council, and who were entitled to a voice and vote in the proceedings, about 600 were infallibilists, and about 150 were inopportunists. Among the infallibilists, moreover, two further groups may be distinguished: the moderates and the *zelante*. The moderates, who numbered about 500, were inclined to a more modest and restricted formula in the formal definition of infallibility, while the *zelante*, who numbered something less than 100, were prepared to extend the definition to include virtually every formal utterance of the pope, whether it was about politics, faith, or morals.

Of the twenty-one Irish bishops, representing a hierarchy of thirty, who attended the Council, seventeen were staunch infallibilists, and four were inopportunists, thus reflecting the general proportion of about four to one at the Council in favor of defining infallibility. The leading figure among the Irish bishops, and the man who set the pace among them on the issue of infallibility, was Paul Cardinal Cullen, the archbishop of Dublin, and the formal head of the national hierarchy. Though Cullen had been a convinced infallibilist and an uncompromising ultramontanist all his ecclesiastical life, he adopted a moderate line at the Council in regard to infallibility. The key to understanding Cullen's role at the Council is an appreciation of the fact that in the matter of ecclesiastical politics he was above all a Roman. Not only had he been trained in Rome and spoke and wrote Italian fluently, but also he had lived and worked in Rome for some thirty years before being appointed the formal head of the Irish Church, by Pius IX in 1849. He was, moreover, both devoted to the person of Pius IX, who had rewarded

2. The best account of the first Vatican Council in English is still Cuthbert Butler, O.S.B., *The Vatican Council* (London, 1930). See also James Hennesey, S.J., *The First Council of the Vatican: The American Experience* (New York, 1963). For an authoritative view of the Council in its historical context, see Roger Aubert et al., *The Church in the Age of Liberalism* (New York, 1981), volume 8 of *History of the Church,* ed. Hubert Jedin and John Dolan. The complete *Acta* of the Council, and the documents, reports, petitions, minutes, congregations, and committees, as well as the stenographic reports of all the speeches made, are printed in the continuation of J. D. Mansi, *Sacrorum Conciliorum, Nova et Amplissima Collectio* (Arnhem and Leipzig, 1923–27), vols. 49–53, ed. L. Petit and J. -B. Martin.

his loyalty by making him the first Irish cardinal in the history of the Church, and had a keen appreciation of the subtleties and nuances of Roman ecclesiastical politics as well as a perceptive understanding of the ways and means of the Roman Curia. In short, Cullen's line at the Council would be the line taken by the Roman authorities.

The Roman authorities had early manifested their cautious and moderate line regarding the introduction of infallibility. The subject was not included, for example, among the eighty-three schemata of the agenda drawn up by the various preparatory committees for the eventual consideration of the Fathers of the Council. The pope, however, in a brief outlining the procedure to be followed at the Council, had prudently arranged for this question, or any other, to be introduced, by inviting the bishops to submit their proposals in writing to a special congregation, the *deputatio de postulatis,* appointed by him for the purpose. This congregation, which consisted of twelve cardinals (one of whom was Cullen) and fourteen bishops, was to review the proposals submitted and then make its recommendations to the pope, who reserved for himself the right to decide whether to place them on the agenda of the Council. This seems to suggest that the Roman authorities were of the opinion that infallibility would emerge in its own good time and only after a basis for mutual confidence and collegial action had been laid by the Fathers of the Council as they mastered and approved less controversial matters.

Cullen's own moderation and respect for regular procedure were well illustrated shortly before the Council met, when the *Univers,* a French Catholic paper edited by a layman, Louis Veuillot, the most intransigent of ultramontanes and zealous of infallibilists, published a call by several bishops to carry infallibility at the Council by acclamation. "I hope," Cullen explained to Tobias Kirby, rector of the Irish College in Rome, on November 2, 1869, "it will not be done. It will be better to define it after the usual routine, as was done with the divinity of our Lord at Nice, and with so many doctrines in Trent."[3] "I think," he added, for good measure, "the Bishops in France who are calling out for this or that definition wd. do better to leave the whole matter to the Council." Indeed, shortly after he arrived in Rome on December 4, Cullen must have been greatly relieved to learn that the pope had precluded the possibility of any such extravagance at the Council by laying down the rules of procedure in his brief, and he had also set up a number of committees besides that of the *deputatio de postulatis* to facilitate the smooth functioning of business. In his brief the pope had directed that four committees—those for faith, discipline, regular clergy, and eastern churches—should be elected by secret ballot of all the prelates entitled to vote at the Council. The pope had also appointed five cardinal presidents from the Roman Curia to

3. Kirby Papers (K), Archives of the Irish College, Rome.

preside over the Council in his name. The first president, in company with the four other presidents, was to chair the general congregations, or meetings, of all the prelates, and each of the four other presidents was also to preside over one of the four working committees. Thus, Cardinal Reisach was appointed first president, and Cardinals Bilio, Capalti, Bizzarri, and De Luca, respectively, presided over the four above-mentioned committees.

The purpose of each of the four committees was to consider the criticisms and amendments proposed by the bishops after their discussion of the various schemata submitted by the preparatory committees. Each of the committees was to redraft the particular schema pertinent to them in the light of the bishops' suggestions and resubmit it to the bishops for their further consideration and, if found satisfactory, approval. This ordinary business, as distinguished from the committee work, was to be conducted in general congregations of all the prelates, and when a schema was finally approved, it was to be promulgated formally by the pope at a public session of the Council. Each of the four committees was to consist of twenty-four prelates. Cardinals, however, were not eligible for committee membership. It was immediately realized, of course, that the crucial committee, if and when the question of infallibility should be introduced, was that on faith, and both the infallibilists and inopportunists quickly geared themselves up to secure control of that committee. The initiative among the infallibilists quickly fell to the *zelante,* who were both well organized and well led, and who, with the archbishop of Westminster, Henry Edward Manning, in the vanguard, were determined not to allow the inopportunists a single place on the *deputatio de fide.* Manning and his friends proceeded to draw up a list of twenty-four infallibilists, which was circulated to all of the prelates under the name of the influential Cardinal de Angelis, who would soon succeed on the death of Cardinal Reisach as the first president of the Council. The inopportunists, led by the bishop of Orléans, Felix Dupanloup, also drew up their list, and, though that list gave them a working majority, it was not exclusive, as some seven infallibilists of moderate views were included and several places were left open. In the December 14 election, however, the result was virtually a clean sweep for the *zelante* candidates. Only one inopportunist was elected, and he, the archbishop of Esztergom and primate of Hungary, Janos Simor, had been placed on the list by mistake because before he had left home he had written an infallibilist pastoral, but by the time of the election he no longer supported that position.

Shortly before the election to the *deputatio de fide,* the Irish bishops caucused to nominate one of their number, the archbishop of Cashel, Patrick Leahy, who was an ardent infallibilist, as their candidate. He was adopted by the *zelante* for their list and was duly elected. The English bishops had also caucused before the election, but much to the mortification of their primate, Archbishop Manning, they selected Thomas Grant, the bishop of Southwark, their best theologian and a moderate infallibilist, as their candidate. The *zelante,* however, adopted Manning for their list, and he was elected rather than Grant. Flushed with success, the *zelante,* under the continued patronage of Cardinal de Angelis, also attempted to pack the remaining three committees on discipline, regular clergy, and eastern churches with their adherents, but they were apparently somewhat less successful in their efforts. Shortly before the election to the *deputatio de disciplina,* for example, the Irish bishops caucused again to nominate their candidate, and to the great consternation of Cullen they proceeded to choose his worst enemy in the Irish Church, the archbishop of Tuam, John MacHale. "The Irish bishops," Cullen reported to his secretary, George Conroy, in Dublin, on the day of the election, December 20, "have elected [i.e., nominated] Dr. MacHale as their candidate, and have presented him to the French, American, and Italian bishops as their choice."4 What rankled Cullen the most was the apparent inconsistency of the bishops, who as a body had just formally denounced to Propaganda a few days before the conduct of Patrick Lavelle, a Tuam priest, long favored and protected by Mac-Hale, who, in a recent letter in the press addressed to them as a body, had maintained that the notorious secret society, the Fenian Brotherhood, was not condemned according to the canons of the Church and challenged the bishops to contradict him if what he said was not so.5 "Many of our bishops," Cullen complained to Conroy, "denounced his Grace [MacHale] most heartily for his conduct regarding Lavelle and his conduct towards the Propaganda and on the very same day put him forward to represent Ireland in disciplinary matters in facie universae ecclesiae [in the face of the Universal Church]. I do not know whether the fact will be animadverted on in Rome, but I suppose if the Fenians get hold of it they will proclaim it as a great victory for their sect." "It is better," he advised Conroy, "not to speak of this unless it be published in the papers."

When the results of the election to the *deputatio de disciplina* were finally announced several days later, MacHale, who was eventually to be numbered among the inopportunists at the Council, was greatly complimented by the very large number of votes he received, placing third on the list of twenty-four prelates elected. This *succès d'estime* on the part of MacHale apparently annoyed Cullen very much, for he did his best to find out how the Irish bishops had come to nominate MacHale in the first place. "I have," he finally reported to Conroy on January 11, 1870, "learned how Dr. MacHale was elected by the bishops; they made no previous choice [i.e., there was no caucusing in his favor]; four or five voted for him: the others scattered their votes in 1s, 2s, or 3s for different other bishops, and as Dr. MacH. had more votes than any other, the scrutator declared him elected" (C). "This was not right," Cullen further maintained, "as there

4. Cullen Papers (C), Dublin Diocesan Archives.
5. Larkin, pp. 647–61.

should have been an absolute majority. However, the matter is over and it is not worthwhile to speak of it. Pass it over in silence." Cullen's account of MacHale's nomination is at once unconvincing and revealing. It is unconvincing because a plurality of five among twenty-one bishops, if the other sixteen votes were distributed in ones, twos, and threes, would have produced some nine or ten candidates besides MacHale, the probability of which was highly unlikely. Indeed, Cullen undoubtedly received this account from one of his adherents in the episcopal body, and it is psychologically very interesting as a mark of both his pique and his gullibility as far as MacHale was concerned. The account, however, is also very revealing in what it tells about the corporate consciousness of the bishops as a body, especially when it is considered in the context of the Irish bishops' nominations to all four of the Council's committees.

In fact, MacHale's nomination was not, as Cullen would have Conroy believe, some random statistical accident, but it was rather the conscious choice of the Irish bishops, as appropriate to their dignity as a body. Because the papal brief governing the procedures of the Council had precluded Cullen because he was a cardinal from being elected to any of the committees, and because the recent death of the archbishop of Armagh had resulted in that see being vacant, there were in the Irish Church only two archbishops, those of Cashel and Tuam, eligible for the four committees. In terms of ecclesiastical precedence, Cashel was senior to Tuam, and, therefore, it was most natural that Cashel should be nominated to the first committee—on faith—and Tuam to the second—on discipline. That the Irish bishops were making their choices based on what they felt were the needs of the body rather than on either the politico-ecclesiastical views of those nominated or, especially, the personal desires of Cullen, was even more evident in their choices for the remaining two committees. For the committee on regular clergy they nominated John Derry, the bishop of Clonfert and MacHale's most loyal supporter in the episcopal body for more than twenty years. Technically, Derry was not the senior Irish suffragan bishop attending the Council. Both he and the bishop of Cork, William Delany, had been provided for their sees by the pope on the same day, but Delany had been consecrated a month before Derry. Since his consecration, however, Derry had played a much more prominent role in the affairs of the episcopal body than had Delany, and given that the question of precedence was more technical than real, he was therefore honored by the body as their choice for the third committee and was duly elected.[6]

Finally, the Irish bishops' nomination for the committee on eastern churches was an even more striking example of their conception of their own needs as a body. Their choice, Daniel McGettigan, the bishop of Raphoe, shortly before the bishops had arrived in Rome, had been commended by the clergy of Armagh as

6. Butler, 1:185.

the first name, or *dignissimus,* on their *terna* for their widowed archdiocese. Before leaving for Rome, the bishops of the province of Armagh had made their customary report on the clergy's commendation of three names to the congregation of Propaganda, and they had unanimously recommended McGettigan. Cullen, however, had other ideas about who should be appointed to Armagh. He favored his thirty-six-year-old secretary and protégé, George Conroy, who had received five votes in the election for Armagh, and who, though he had tied for third place on the *terna,* had been excluded by the Armagh clergy from the three names they forwarded to Rome. In Rome, McGettigan had informed Cullen he would not accept the dignity if offered, and Cullen was led to hope, therefore, that when the cardinals of Propaganda met to consider the clergy's commendation and the bishops' report, he, as a member of that congregation, would persuade the cardinals to recommend to the pope that Conroy be appointed. When the Irish bishops then proceeded to nominate McGettigan as their candidate for the committee on eastern churches, therefore, they were intent on making it perfectly clear to both Cullen and the Roman authorities that McGettigan was their choice for Armagh rather than Conroy. By their nomination, moreover, the bishops were also making it evident to McGettigan that in their view he should not refuse the dignity if offered. As events occurred, McGettigan not only was elected to the committee on eastern churches, but he was also, in spite of Cullen's strenuous efforts on behalf of Conroy, appointed, by Pius IX early in March 1870, archbishop of Armagh. The lesson to be learned from all this, of course, is not simply that the Irish bishops as a body were able to contain Cullen, or even that they were able to contain him in Rome—the source of his real power and influence in the Irish Church—but rather in what it reveals about the developing self-confidence of the body that allowed them to make their corporate will effective in the Irish Church.

In the meantime, while the procedural preliminaries were being completed, the Council had begun on December 28, 1869, to consider the first of the schemata drawn up by the preparatory committees. The discussion of the first schema on the Catholic faith, or *de fide Catholica,* continued through six general congregations, until January 10, 1870, when it was referred to the *deputatio de fide* for revision according to the amendments suggested by the prelates. The prelates then began on January 14 to discuss the first of the four schemata on the Church, or *de Ecclesia.* They completed their discussion of the first two schemata, on the office of a bishop and episcopal vacancies, on January 25, and referred them to the *deputatio de disciplina* for revision and resubmission; they then took up the third schema, on the clergy. That schema occupied the prelates until February 8, when they forwarded it to the same committee and began to discuss the fourth schema, on the catechism. This discussion lasted until February 22, when it was also referred to the *deputatio de disciplina,* and the Council was suspended for a month to attempt to resolve the very serious accoustical problems posed by the right transept in St. Peter's Basilica, which served as the great hall, or *Aula Maxima,* of the Council.

Throughout the month of January, meanwhile, a great number of petitions and counterpetitions were submitted to the pope about the introduction of the question of infallibility. At the end of January, the pope referred all of the petitions to the *deputatio de postulatis,* which on February 8 recommended that the question be placed on the agenda of the Council, and on March 1, the pope confirmed the recommendation. This confirmation was publicly announced on March 6, and the formula for defining the primacy and infallibility of the pope was distributed to the prelates, who were given until March 25 to submit their comments on it in writing. The general congregations, meanwhile, had been resumed on March 18, and the *deputatio de fide's* revisions of the schema on the Catholic faith were submitted to the prelates, who then proceeded in fifteen Congregations to discuss the revised text, which took nearly a month's time. On April 12, the prelates finally proceeded to a trial vote on the revised schema, and 510 voted *placet,* or approval, while 85 voted *placet juxta modum,* or approval with a reservation. Those who had voted with a reservation then submitted the amendments they thought necessary, and their reasons for them, in writing to the *deputatio de fide.* The amendments, which numbered 148, were considered by the *deputatio,* and on April 19, it announced it had rejected all but two as being inappropriate. Finally, on April 24, Low Sunday, in the third public session, the Dogmatic Constitution on the Catholic Faith, or the *Constitutio Dogmatica de Fide Catholica,* was approved unanimously by the 667 prelates present. The pope then confirmed the proem, four decrees, and the seventeen canons appropriate to the decrees, which made up the first of two parts of the projected "Dogmatic Constitution," called the *Dei Filius,* or "The Son of God," and anathematized those who denied them.

However, by early March, and even after it had been publicly announced on March 6 that the question of infallibility would be put on the agenda of the Council, it became increasingly evident to the supporters of infallibility that the volume of business facing the Council would postpone the consideration of the vital question for at least a year. "The only misfortune here," Cullen reported to Conroy on March 3, "is that we go on too slowly" (C). "I am urging them," he added, referring to the Roman authorities, "to bring on the Church and the Infallibility without delay. They are for waiting." "Were the Infallibility once decided," he assured Conroy, "all disputes would cease." A week later, Cullen returned to the same theme, writing on March 10 again to Conroy, "I am now persuaded that we shall not get through our business of the Council for a full year. Everything is so slow. I am urging those in power to bring on Infallibility before Easter. They are timid" (C). Shortly after, and apparently with Cullen's tacit approval, eleven of the Irish bishops, headed by the archbishop of Cashel, presented a petition to have the question of infallibility brought on immediately after the pope's promulgation in the third public session of the *Dei Filius*.7 Indeed, during March, eight such petitions, including some two hundred signatures, had been submitted to the cardinal presidents or the pope.

These petitions provoked a number of counterpetitions, even from those who wanted infallibility defined but did not think it prudent to bring the question up in the normal order of business. The majority of the cardinal presidents were reluctant to change the order of business; they preferred to proceed with the second part of the Constitution on the Catholic Faith until the Council was prorogued for the summer and then to resume in the fall and winter with the Constitution on the Church. After the first parts of this were considered, the question of infallibility would arise in its natural turn. During Holy Week, April 10–17, however, the *zelante,* headed by Manning and Ignaz von Senestréy, the bishop of Regensburg, pleaded with Cardinal Bilio, the president of the *deputatio de fide,* to bring the question immediately before that *deputatio* in order that it might be introduced in the Council. In refusing, Bilio told Senestréy that he was so worried about the possibility of provoking a schism that he could not sleep.8 Undeterred, a delegation of the *zelante* appealed to the first president of the Council, Cardinal de Angelis, on Easter Monday, April 18, but he too demurred, saying that Cardinal de Luca agreed with Bilio, though Cardinals Capalti and Bizzarri, the other presidents, were favorable to its introduction. The next day, April 19, Manning and Senestréy appealed to the pope, who gave them to understand that he would direct the cardinal presidents to bring the matter immediately before the *deputatio de fide* to prepare for its introduction in the Council. At the meetings of the *deputatio de fide* on April 21–23, however, Bilio kept the members hard at work on the second part of the Constitution on the Catholic Faith. In exasperation, Manning and Senestréy circulated a petition on April 23, which was signed by 150 prelates and presented that same evening to the pope, asking him to have the question introduced at once. The pope agreed, and, at the meeting of the *deputatio de fide* on April 27, Bilio introduced the question by submitting for consideration the schema for the Constitution on the primacy and infallibility of the pope.

Cullen, meanwhile, was not in Rome to witness these exciting events. He had

---

7. Ibid., 2:37. See also Mansi, 51:710–11. The eleven Irish bishops were Leahy (Cashel), Keane (Cloyne), Donnelly (Clogher), Gillooly (Elphin), MacEvilly (Galway), Dorrian (Down and Connor), Butler, (Limerick), Conaty (Kilmore), Power (Coadjutor to Killaloe), MacCabe (Ardagh), and O'Hea (Ross). For Cullen's speech, see Mansi, 52:112–15.

8. Hennesey, p. 220.

secured permission in an audience with the pope on April 6 to return to Ireland for Easter because of the very unsettled state of the country in the aftermath of the Roman condemnation of the Fenian Brotherhood and the refusal of William Gladstone, the prime minister, to grant amnesty to any more Fenian prisoners. Cullen left Rome on Thursday, April 7, for Marseilles by boat via Civita Vecchia. "On board," he reported from Marseilles on April 9 to Kirby in Rome, "we met Mgr. Trioche, Archbishop of Babylon—we were greatly amused with his Gallicanism" (K). "Mgr. Trioche," Cullen then explained, "sits in the council next to Dr. McHale, and when asked his opinion about him he said that he was a prudent and wise man, and that he would not let himself be dictated to by a neophyte like Dr. Manning." "I entered," he added, "into a defence of the Roman doctrines with the good bishop. After discussing them for a while he became more reasonable, but we lost the benefit of his attacks on the ultramontani, with which he amused us at first. I hope Dr. McHale does not deserve the praises which he gave him." Cullen continued his journey via Paris and London and arrived in Dublin on Monday evening, April 11, where he remained for nearly three weeks. When he left Dublin on Sunday evening, May 1, he departed in a happier frame of mind about the condition of the country than when he had arrived. He returned to Rome by the same route that he had come, and on his way from Liverpool to London he had occasion to read some extracts from Disraeli's latest novel, *Lothair.* "On the road yesterday," he reported to Conroy from Paris on May 3, "we saw some extracts of Disraeli's new novel in which he has some sneers at Dr. Manning and myself and hits the Catholic Church very hard" (C).

When he arrived again in Rome on Friday evening, May 6, Cullen was distressed to learn that not all of the Irish bishops at home and abroad were sound on the question of infallibility. "I am sorry," he reported to Conroy on May 10, "that *i nostri* [ours] from America and even Ireland *non sono tali come doverebbero essere* [are not such as they ought to be]" (C). "Dr. Kenrick," he explained, referring to the archbishop of St. Louis in the United States and to the bishop of Kerry in Ireland, "is in Naples publishing a treatise *adversus infallib.* Dr. Moriarty has come out strongly [against infallibility]." "Dr. Leahy," he added, referring to the bishop of Dromore in Ireland, who had also been opposed to defining infallibility, "has adopted the opinion of St. Thomas and come round." "The discussions next week," he then predicted, "will be very long and stormy. I hope, however, it will be *post nubila Phoebus* [sunny after the clouds]." But the following day, Cullen was even more gloomy. "We shall," he reported again to Conroy on May 11, "have a *bella horrida bella* [a war, a frightening war]" (C). "Dr. Kenrick and Dr. Purcell [the archbishop of Cincinnati]," he explained, "published a very strong letter against Dr. Spalding [the archbishop of Baltimore]. Dr. Kenrick has been in Naples and has brought out a little treatise on Infallibility. Its teaching appears to be liable to the charge of *suspecta de haeresi.* He appears to have lost his head altogether. He seems even to call in to question the legitimacy of the Vatican Council, and he thinks that cardinals without Sees, bishops who are only vicars-apostolic, and heads of religious orders ought to be expelled from the Council or not to get a vote." "He, Dr. Purcell, Dr. Connolly [archbishop of Halifax]," Cullen noted, who were all of Irish birth, "and some others, several indeed, do little credit to Ireland." "The young American-Irish bishops," he added in conclusion, "both in the States and Canada, nearly all seem wrong. The old teaching of Maynooth has left its traces."

Meanwhile, the *deputatio de fide,* which had been instructed by its president on April 27 to proceed to consider the question of the primacy and infallibility of the papacy, had been hard at work on both revising the constitution to be proposed and preparing a report about the suggestions and amendments on the subject that the prelates had submitted in response to the pope's early March request that the matter be on the Council's agenda. The revised constitution and report were finally ready on May 8 and were distributed to the prelates the following day. The constitution and report were then introduced at the general congregation on May 13, and the great debate, which was to last some two months, began the next day. The debate may be divided into four parts. The first, which lasted from May 14 to June 3, was crucial because it was concerned with the constitution as a whole and the opportuneness of its definition. The second, which began on June 6 and ended on June 14, was devoted to a discussion of the first three chapters, on the primacy. The third, which lasted from June 15 through July 4, involved discussions about amending the last chapter, on infallibility. Finally, between July 5 and July 13, the amendments that had been proposed by the prelates in regard to the first three chapters were discussed and voted on.

Though the Irish bishops as a national hierarchy made a very respectable contribution to all of these debates, it was Cullen who proved once again that he was the most gifted man amongst them. His first intervention, on May 19, was a memorable one, and it has been aptly described by an eminent historian as "one of the great speeches of the Council."[9] It is all the more impressive because in the two previous general congregations several very fine speeches had been made against defining infallibility. On May 17, the learned German church historian, Karl Josef von Hefele, bishop of Rothenburg, had cited the condemnation of Pope Honorius I (625–38) by the Third Council of Constantinople in 680 A.D. as a formal heretic for his approval of monothelitism as a historical instance of how a pope could err in matters of faith. The following day, May 18, Cardinals Schwarzenberg and Rauscher, the archbishops of Prague and Vienna, both had made very effective and able speeches against the definition. That evening Manning apparently called on Cullen and informed him that the pope was anxious that the two cardinals be

9. Butler, 2:48.

replied to *nominatim,* and because of their exalted rank it would have to be done by a cardinal. Indeed, several days after his triumph Cullen explained Manning's role to Conroy. "I must say," he noted on May 21, "I owe my success to Dr. Manning. He called on me and begged of me to answer Schwarzenberg and Rauscher. Only for the encouragement he gave me, I would not have mentioned them" (C).

On the afternoon of the day of his speech, Cullen was still so exhilarated that he wrote Conroy a long letter describing the whole episode. "I made," he reported on May 19, "a sort of parliamentary speech. Two cardinals and Dr. Hefele spoke yesterday and the day before. I took down the heads of what they said, and I came out on them like an Irishman in Donnybrook Fair and I knocked them to pieces."

> Hefele was standing fair under the pulpit whilst I read from his own history of Councils a couple of pages in which he fully acquitted Honorious. I fear I killed the poor man, for ere yesterday he contradicted in his speech what he said in his history. I had no mercy at all on my own colleagues Schwarzenberg and Rauscher, but the bishops were so well pleased to see a note of truth administered to cardinals that half the Council came to congratulate me when I was done.
>
> You know my voice is not strong, yet I believe I made everyone in the great hall hear me. What is more strange that so long without speaking Latin I spoke without any assistance of papers, except where I had to read some few long passages from Irish writers. Still I scarcely ever had to stop for a word. If I could speak two or three times I think all my Latin would return. Tomorrow Dr. MacHale and Dr. Leahy speak. About 60 have given in their names to speak pro or contra.[10]

"I dare say one hundred bishops," Cullen then noted in conclusion, referring to the personal visits made by prelates to the Irish College where he was residing, "have congratulated me on the onslaught I made on my colleagues. No Italian would have done it, but I have heard that the Pope was anxious that some cardinal should answer them. Don't publish any of this except to priests."

---

10. See Mansi, 52:113–16, for Cullen's discussion of Hefele in regard to Honorius. I have not been able to obtain a copy of the edition of Hefele's history from which Cullen quoted in his speech. In a later edition of his history, however, Hefele was definitely of the opinion that Honorius was a heretic and that the opinions he expressed in his celebrated two letters were his formal teaching as pope, or *ex cathedra.* See Charles Joseph Hefele, *Histoire des Conciles* (Paris, 1909), trans. H. Leclercq, O.S.B., 3:386–87. "If one now asks: are or are not the two letters which were published by Honorius, *ex cathedra,* to use the accepted expression? The advocates themselves differ in opinion on this subject. Pennachi is of the opinion that they have been published *auctoritate apostolica,* Schneeman upholds the opposite view. For my part I confess I am of the opinion of Pennachi; for Honorius wished to impart a regulation of doctrine and of faith on the first occasion to the church of Constantinople and implicitly to the whole Church; in his second letter he even used the following expression: *Ceterum, quantum ad dogma ecclesiasticum pertinet . . . non unam vel duas operationes in mediatore Dei et hominum definire debemus.*"

The next day, May 20, MacHale spoke, but Cullen could find nothing good in the form or substance of his presentation. "Dr. MacHale," Cullen reported to Conroy, "spoke to-day against Infallibility and the opportuneness of the definition. His voice was so weak and he could do nothing but give a compendium of Delahogue" (C). "He complained of me," Cullen explained, "for yesterday I said that I was sure he would bear testimony to the Pope's Infallibility as he had signed the Synod of Thurles. All he could say was that he had not given me any authority to speak in his name. His speech was quite lame and undecided. He defended Gallicanism, appearing almost ashamed to do what he was doing. Dr. Leahy will answer him to-morrow." "I write one line," Cullen reported again the next day, May 21, "to say that Dr. Leahy of Cashel made a magnificent speech. He tore Dr. MacHale to pieces, and he extinguished the Primate of Hungary [Simor], both of whom spoke yesterday. Dr. MacHale will scarcely ever speak again" (C). "Dr. Leahy," he explained, "spoke for an hour and a half. He did not read, but spoke and he was heard by everyone. I think Ireland has now established its primacy in the Council, *quod omnium aequum est* [that it is the equal of all]." "The only thing," he noted in concluding, "I now have to say is save us from our friends; all the Irish bishops are on their metal [*sic*] to speak." While Cullen was certainly right about Leahy's very fine effort, he was less than fair to MacHale, who was then in his eightieth year. The English bishop of Birmingham, William Ullathorne, for example, noted in a letter written on May 20, to the bishop of Newport, Thomas Brown, who had remained at home because of his age, that among the very able speakers that day was MacHale.[11] The following day, May 21, he also reported Leahy's effort to Brown. "To-day the Archbishop of Cashel," he noted, "made one of the most clear, solid, and luminous speeches yet heard in the Council."[12] Perhaps the last word on the relative efforts of the leaders of the Irish Church should be left to the discriminating American bishop of Rochester, Bernard J. McQuaid. "The Archbishop of Cashel," he reported to his secretary, James Early, on May 24, "threw Cardinal Cullen into the shade. Tuam did well considering his age."[13]

As the debate wore on, however, Cullen and those in the majority became concerned that those opposed to a definition would talk the question to death. "I fear," he informed Conroy on May 27, "we are in a mess. An opposition backed up by France, Austria, Bavaria, and Prussia, to say nothing of Italy, is rather formidable. They will be able I fear to keep the debate going on for months" (C). "I dare say," he explained, "we have had already more than 30 speeches. How we are to get over this difficulty it is hard to see, and in the meantime disturbances may arise

---

11. Butler, 2:65. Mansi, 52:144–51.
12. Butler, 2:65. Mansi, 52:163–70.
13. Hennesey, p. 233.

or the City become unhealthy, or something happen to the Pope." "Any of these circumstances," he concluded gloomily, "would put an end to the Council and the Pope's authority would be greatly diminished." The debate dragged into the next week, and on June 3, at the end of that day's debate, after some sixty-five prelates had spoken (thirty-nine *pro* and twenty-six *con*) during fifteen general congregations, totalling more than sixty hours, the secretary to the Council, Joseph Fessler, the bishop of St. Polten in Austria, mounted the *ambo,* or pulpit, and announced that the presidents of the Council had received a petition from more than 150 prelates to bring the general debate to a close in order that the text on the primacy and infallibility of the pope might be introduced. The great majority of the prelates, over the strenuous protests of the minority, agreed to the closure, and the presidents, under the standing orders of the Council, declared the general discussion at an end.

The discussion of the first three chapters, on the primacy of the pope, therefore, began on Monday, June 6. The first and second chapters were concerned respectively with the institution of the primacy by Christ in St. Peter's person and the perpetuation of it in the Bishops of Rome as the successors of St. Peter. These chapters caused little difficulty, and the discussion of them took only a single day, June 7. After the general congregation that day, Cullen was so heartened by the great despatch with which business was now being done that he wrote Conroy, explaining that he hoped that the public session at which the pope's infallibility would be proclaimed would take place, appropriately enough, on June 29, St. Peter's day (C). Shortly after the discussion of the third chapter, on the nature and power of the primacy, began, however, Cullen was a good deal less optimistic about the progress being made. "When last writing," he explained to Conroy on June 9, "I thought we were likely to go on rapidly and to have everything regarding the Pope's primacy and infallibility ready for S. Peter's Day. I fear I was then too sanguine, and I now return to my former views that we shall be much longer than we wish before anything can be done" (C). "The opposition got a check last week," he reported further, referring to the closure of debate by the cardinal presidents, "and seemed to have become reasonable, but to-day they have rallied again, and they threaten to fight us at every step. With the liberty of speaking which they enjoy, they can detain us two months longer." "However, everything is uncertain," he concluded in a more optimistic vein, "and perhaps we may be more successful than we imagine. We have had a congregation to-day (Thursday) and we shall meet to-morrow and Saturday."

The reason that the minority among the prelates had rallied for the discussion of the third chapter was that it focused on what they believed to be the heart of the matter. They felt that the whole tendency of the theology in the Constitution *de Ecclesia Christi,* "concerning the Church of Christ," presented to the Council was to eliminate the role of the episcopate and Ecumenical Councils and reduce all to merely the Church and the pope.[14] The minority among the prelates was most particularly concerned that the declaration that the pope had "ordinary and immediate" jurisdiction in the whole Church be defined so as not to impinge on the "immediate and ordinary" jurisdiction of individual bishops in their dioceses. The minority wanted it to be made clear that the bishops received their spiritual jurisdiction and power as the successors of the Apostles and not as vicars or delegates of the pope. Indeed, an amendment to the third chapter to that effect, proposed by Cardinal Rauscher, was accepted by the *deputatio de fide* and eventually incorporated into the final text of the definition. "We have," Cullen meanwhile reported to Conroy on June 14, "the Council every day. We have got over three Chapters about the Pope, and to-morrow we commence the last on infallibility. The battle will be sharp, but we are six or eight to one, or perhaps ten to one."

The discussion of the final chapter of the Constitution *de Ecclesia Christi,* on the infallibility of the pope, began on Wednesday, June 15, and did not end until July 4. The purpose of the discussion, as on that of the primacy, was to offer amendments to the text of the proposed definition. Cullen spoke at the next general congregation on Saturday, June 18, and offered as an amendment a new form of the definition of infallibility than that which had been under discussion. This amendment was most significant because it was the form, with a few minor modifications, that eventually would be adopted and proclaimed as doctrine. Some question has been raised, however, as to who the real author of the new form of definition was. Though the bishop of Regensburg, Ignaz von Senestréy, maintained in his diary that Cardinal Bilio suggested it to Cullen, Cullen's own correspondence throws little light on the matter except to make it clear that, before he introduced the new form of definition, he had cleared it with the cardinal presidents of the Council, of whom Bilio was one. In any case, on June 18, Cullen was preceded in the *ambo* by three of his fellow cardinals—Jean Baptiste Pitra, a French Benedictine, Henri Marie de Bonnechose, archbishop of Rouen, and Felippo Maria Guidi, archbishop of Bologna. The sensations of the day, and perhaps of the Council, were the amendments proposed, and the arguments supporting them made by Guidi. He was a Dominican who had a very considerable reputation as a theologian, and because he had not spoken before at the Council, he was received with very great interest and attention.

To the great consternation of the more intransigent of the infallibilists, however,

14. Butler, 2:74.

he argued very ably that the pope was not personally infallible in defining dogma, but rather that his dogmatic definitions were infallible and that the title of chapter four, therefore, should be "The Infallibility of the Pope's Dogmatic Definitions," rather than "The Infallibility of the Pope." Guidi then also pointed out, to the even greater dismay of the infallibilists, that in issuing dogmatic decrees the pope cannot act merely of himself, independently of the Church, but is obliged to take counsel with the bishops who manifest the tradition of the churches, and he proposed a canon that would anathematize those who thought differently. Cullen, who spoke after Guidi, not only was appalled by his colleague's remarks, but he was also taken very much unawares. "I am after speaking for an hour," he informed Conroy on June 18, "on infallibility. An Italian cardinal spoke before me. I was persuaded he was all right but he went over almost completely to Gallicanism" (C). "I ventured," Cullen then explained, "to answer his arguments *ex abrupti* [on the spur of the moment] and doing so, I spoiled the speech I had prepared. However, the cardinal legates [the cardinal presidents] thanked me and said I had refuted my predecessor in the pulpit completely. The last part of my speech I had studied, so it went off very well. I spoke all through from memory, and otherwise I could not have answered my opponent." "In my speech," Cullen then added, "I produced a new form for the definition, in which I made the matter clear and simple. The legates approved of it, but it is hard to know what the Council will do. I think we shall have the question settled by the middle of July. Unfortunately I did not sleep last night, and my lips were so parched that I could scarcely say a word. Having got a drop of water, I got strong and was heard by all." "It is said," he reported finally, "that the opposition is reduced very low, but the Italian cardinal will give them a new impulse."

Cullen's temper did not improve over the weekend, and when, on Monday, June 20, he returned to the Irish College, after listening to MacHale for more than an hour, he was even more annoyed. "I am after returning," he reported to Conroy, "from the Council. Dr. MacHale made a long speech; it was really childish, answering what I said about having admitted infallibility at the Council of Thurles. He said: *non pensavimus de ea re* [We haven't thought about that matter]. He could not recall the Latin word *cogitavimus* [we did not consider]. One of the Spanish bishops cried out *vergognen—subscripisti et non pensavisti*! [shame—you have subscribed and not thought!]" (C). "He then spoke of the evidence before Parliament," Cullen noted, referring to some testimony given by his predecessor in the see of Dublin, Daniel Murray, and the late celebrated bishop of Kildare and Leighlin, "of the archbishop of Dublin whom he mentioned several times, and of Dr. Doyle, which proves, said he, that the Irish are not *ultra montani*. In the end he read a letter he sent several years ago to the Pope, acknowledging the Pope's supreme authority. Whilst he was reading the letter one of the bishops said loudly, *proprio pugione te confodisti* [you have stabbed yourself with your own dagger].

At the end no one knew whether he was *pro* or *contra* the infallibility, but all appeared satisfied that he had made a fool of himself."

Even for Cullen, who when he was not complaining about MacHale was usually denigrating him, this ridicule involved a new level of pettiness. In the next part of his letter, however, Cullen finally revealed what was really troubling him. "I spoke last Saturday," he confessed, "under a very great disadvantage."

> In the first place I was the last among the speakers, and had been listening to others for about 3 hours; in the second place I was sick and had slept scarcely five minutes the previous night; in the third place I was vexed with the Cardinal Archbishop of Bologna who made a dangerous speech. In the fourth place I undertook to answer that speech without a moment's preparation. You see I was in a bad position; still I got on very well, and all the cardinals thanked me, and the Pope said he was much obliged to me for having administered castigation to one who had corresponded so badly to his favours. It was the Pope who made this bishop cardinal and had made him Archbishop of Bologna. His speech was full of contradictions, but it was applauded by the opposition.[15]

"The famous Strossmayer," Cullen noted, referring to the Croatian bishop of Bosnia, "said to Guidi: *Habebis meritum in aeternum* [You will have an eternal reward] when he got out of the pulpit. I think we lose a whole fortnight by this unfortunate speech." "Dr. MacHale," he assured Conroy in conclusion, and coming full circle in his long letter, "does no harm to anyone. Very few can understand him."

Apparently what was really disturbing Cullen was that Guidi's remarkable presentation had spoiled, in effect, what was to be his own crowning moment in the Council and in the Church. Cullen obviously hoped that by presenting the formula on which all could unite, he would earn the honor and glory that would be eternally his. The day after his ridicule of MacHale, and his explanation of why he had been so disadvantaged in his presentation, however, he was more hopeful about his formula for defining infallibility. "Probably," he informed Conroy on June 21, "it will be accepted. The Cardinal Legates approve of it and Mgr. Dupanloup is reported to have said that he will consent to it. If this be true (and we shall know tomorrow) we may get away early in July" (C). "My amendment," he added most revealingly, "was accepted by the legates, before I proposed It. There may still be opposition, but we are in an enormous majority." Cullen's informa-

---

15. Cullen was apparently so annoyed by what Guidi had done that he became confused about what he was attempting to say to Conroy. Guidi, as the archbishop of Bologna, had been created a cardinal priest by Pius IX in 1863, and on the recent death of the cardinal bishop of Frascati, which was one of the six suburban sees of Rome, he was promoted to the prestigious rank of a cardinal bishop. Guidi was, therefore, not only the archbishop of Bologna, but, as the bishop of Frascati, he was also a suffragan bishop of the pope.

tion, however, with regard to Dupanloup and the minority was not quite accurate. What had actually happened was that the archbishop of Malines, Victor Dechamps, a leading infallibilist representing a number of the majority prelates, had met with the archbishop of Paris, Georges Darboy, and the bishop of Mayence, Wilhelm von Ketteler, who were two of the chief inopportunists, to see if some accommodation could be reached.[16] Dechamps, however, had declared himself in favor of Guidi's formula rather than Cullen's as an appropriate basis for accommodation, and Darboy and Ketteler agreed. Darboy then suggested to Cardinal de Luca, one of the presidents of the Council, that a new schema on infallibility framed in terms of Guidi's recent presentation be introduced. The cardinal presidents, apparently because the pope did not approve of what Guidi had proposed, decided not to withdraw the schema then under consideration and substitute another formula, either Guidi's or Cullen's, but rather to let the debate run its course and, when it ended, to choose an appropriate formula from all of those that had been proposed.

The debate, meanwhile, dragged on. "I fear our return home," Cullen reported disconsolately to Conroy on SS. Peter's and Paul's day, June 29, "is adjourned *sine die* [without a day being appointed for resumption]. The speakers are determined to wear us out."

> Dr. Moriarty spoke yesterday for one hour and a half. His speech was a very tiresome web of sophistry and quotations from theologians of the 14th or 15th century, men whose opinions are of no weight. Among others he attached great importance to some sentences of Cardinal de Cusa, who was a mere astronomer and diplomatist. He said very offensive things but not in very offensive language. He was interrupted by the bishops crying Oh! Oh! once or twice. Towards the end he got completely bewildered, and though he did nothing but read, he was not able to make out what he had in his papers. Dr. MacHale, contrary to his custom, waited till the very end of the discourse which finished after one o'clock. Dr. Moriarty did a great deal to lower the character of Ireland. He and Dr. MacHale are looked upon as great failures (C).

"We have now," Cullen then noted sadly, "a long list of Irish on the wrong side. Dr. Kenrick, Dr. Connolly, Dr. MacHale, Dr. Moriarty and some American bishops *minorum gentium* [of Irish descent]."

Meanwhile, in order to give a lift to both his own morale and the cause of infallibility, Cullen had invited a large number of his friends in Rome to dine with him the following day in the Irish College. "Yesterday, S. Paul's Day," he informed Conroy on July 1, "we had all the *orthodox* Irish bishops to dine with me, also Dr. Spalding [Baltimore], Dr. McCloskey [New York], Dr. Manning [Westminster],

---

16. Butler, 2:98–99.

Dr. Eyre [Glasgow], Dr. Scandela [Gibraltar] and the four new bishops whom I consecrated since I came to Rome."[17] There were nearly forty"(C). "We drank the Pope's health and infallibility most enthusiastically," he assured Conroy. "We had from the United States only two archbishops as above, and Dr. O'Connell of Grassville, California. We excluded only two Irish bishops, nempe [of course], Dr. MacHale and Dr. Moriarty. It was well to show that we condemn them. All those present were strong for the infallibility, so we have a strong vote after all." There were, in fact, only seventeen Irish bishops remaining in Rome because four had returned to Ireland. Toward the end of May, the bishop of Clonfert, John Derry, and the bishop of Ferns, Thomas Furlong, had secured permission to return home for health reasons, and in early June the bishop of Dromore, John Pius Leahy, was also excused for the same reason, while the bishop of Kilmore, Nicholas Conaty, secured a two-month leave of absence to settle some diocesan business. Derry, who was seriously ill, died on June 28, but before his death he asked his brother to write to the archbishop of Armagh, Daniel McGettigan, requesting that he assure the pope that he had always been a believer in infallibility and also to convey that assurance to MacHale and Cullen.[18] Furlong and Leahy, however, had, toward the end of January, signed a petition along with MacHale and Moriarty protesting the opportuneness of defining papal infallibility.[19] Furlong apparently agreed with that opinion on leaving Rome, but Leahy had been reported by Cullen as having changed his mind before his departure.[20] Conaty, on the other hand, had been from the beginning a determined supporter of infallibility.

The discussion about amending chapter four, on the pope's infallibility, concluded on July 4, and the recommendations by the *deputatio de fide* on the amendments to chapter three, on the primacy, were introduced and acted on in general congregation the following day. "To-day," Cullen reported to Conroy on July 5, "we voted the 3rd Chapter and the Pope with very little opposition. Now we have only to vote on the 4th Chapter, i.e. on Infallibility. At the voting no speeches are made, so it is a very short business" (C). "However," he further explained, "it is very hard to get a good form for the definition. The one I proposed was approved by a great many but some bishops have proposed amendments on it and probably some of them will be adopted. It is hard to find words that please so many people, even when they agree on the substance." "It is now expected," he added more hopefully, "that we shall be let off in ten days." It took some six days, however, for

17. The four bishops were Thomas W. Croke, bishop of Auckland, New Zealand; Martin Griver, apostolic administrator of the bishop of Perth, Australia; Henry Carfagnini, bishop of Harbor Grace, Canada; and Thomas J. Power, bishop of St. John's, Newfoundland.
18. C, Cullen to Conroy, July 17, 1870.
19. Butler, 1:207. See also C, Cullen to Conroy, January 21, 1870, for list of Irish infallibists.
20. C, Cullen to Conroy, May 29, 1870.

the *deputatio de fide* to prepare its recommendation for the amendments to the fourth chapter. Finally, on July 11, the Tyrolese bishop of Brixen, Vincent Gasser, in his nearly four-hour presentation of the recommendations of the *deputatio*, made what was perhaps the most impressive speech yet made in the Council. "I am after returning," Cullen wrote Conroy that same day, "from the General Congregation. We voted the chapter *De Infallibilitate Rom. Pontificis* [correctly, *De Romani Pontificis Infallibili Magisterio*] paragraph by paragraph and amendment by amendment. Everything was carried by our friends most triumphantly. There were about 600 voters. I think the opposition never had 40 votes" (C). "The form of Definition," he added, referring to his own formula, "was substantially adopted. Some few words were added to explain matters which however did not change the sense, for example the word[s] "cathedra loquens" [speaking from the throne—correctly—*ex cathedra loquens*, i.e., the pope speaking as teacher of the Universal Church] which I did not put in were added."

Two days later, on July 13, a formal vote was finally taken on "The First Dogmatic Constitution of the Church of Christ," which included the proem and the four chapters. The voting of the 601 prelates present took nearly two hours, with 451 voting *placet,* 88 *non placet,* and 62 *placet juxta modum.* Some 71 prelates then in Rome did not attend the general congregation. The 62 prelates who voted approval with modifications were required by custom to submit their amendments in writing, and these were then printed and distributed to the prelates for their consideration at the next general congregation, which took place on July 16. Of the 163 amendments submitted, all but two were rejected by the *deputatio de fide* in their recommendation to the prelates. The first was the omission of some words of St. Augustine and was carried almost unanimously. The second was the addition of the clause "*non autem ex consensue Ecclesiae,*" or "not from the consent of the Church," to Cullen's form of definition. "My form of definition," Cullen explained to Conroy on July 16, "has passed through all the congregations with the addition of ex cathedra, and *sine consensu episcoporum* [without the consent of the bishops] which the Spaniards insisted to add to the words *constitutiones Pontificum ex sese esse infallibiles* [Pontifical decrees are of themselves infallible]. The sense was not changed" (C). What is curious in this letter to Conroy is Cullen's version in Latin as to what was amended, and it is especially interesting if it is compared to the final version of the definition, for he made a number of mistakes, which are a revealing indication of how he interpreted, at least, the form of his definition and the changes made in it.[21] Appar-

---

21. The final paragraph of chapter four, "Concerning the Infallible Magisterium of the Roman Pontiff," reads: "Itaque Nos traditioni a fidei Christianae exordio perceptae fideliter inhaerendo, ad Dei Salvatoris nostri gloriam, religionis Catholicae exaltationem et Christianorum populorum salutem, sacro approbante Concilio, docemus et divinitus revelatum dogma esse definimus: Romanum Pontificem, cum ex Cathedra loquitur, id est, cum omnium Chris-

ently, he subconsciously substituted, in writing Conroy, the word *episcoporum,* "of the bishops," for *Ecclesiae,* "of the Church," and he misread the word *constitutiones,* "decrees," for *definitiones,* "definitions," and *irreformabiles,* "irreformable," for *infallibiles,* "infallible"—all of which tended toward a stricter interpretation, in favor of infallibility, of the form of definition adopted by the Council.[22]

The fourth, and what was to be the final public session of the first Vatican Council, was held on Monday, July 18, and, amidst very great pomp and circumstance punctuated by thunder and lightning, the pope defined and confirmed by virtue of his supreme apostolic authority the First Dogmatic Constitution of the Church of Christ, *Pastor Aeternus.* "The great Session is over," the bishop of Birmingham, William Ullathorne, reported to the bishop of Newport, Thomas Brown, on that same day. "The decree was voted by 533 '*placet*s' to 2 'non *placet*s' amidst a great storm. The lightning flashed into the aula, the thunder rolled over the roof, and glass was broken by the tempest in a window nearly over the pontifical throne and came rattling down."[23] "After the votes were given," he further explained, "the Pope confirmed it at once, and immediately there was a great cheering and clapping from the bishops, and cheers in the body of St. Peter's. Then the 'Te Deum' began, the thunder forming the diapason." "The Council," he noted in conclusion, "is to go on with those who remain, and we are all to return by St. Martin's Day, November 11. But by that time no one knows what may be going on in Italy, or what may happen to suspend the Council."

Cullen's report of the proceedings to Conroy, the next day, was a good deal more prosaic. "We had the public session yesterday," he explained. "The Bishop of Fabriano read the Decrees from the pulpit, then all the cardinals and the bishops were asked one by one whether they agreed to the statutes or not. 533 gave their *placet*s, two said *non placet:* one Neopolitan, the other Fitzgerald of Little Rock, U.S." (C). "Four cardinals," he added, obviously scandalized, "Schwartzenb, Rau-

---

tianorum Pastoris et Doctoris munere fungens, pro suprema sua apostolica auctoritate doctrinam de fide vel moribus ab universa Ecclesia tenendem definit, per assistentiam divinam, ipsi in beato Petro promissam, ea infallibilitate pollere, qua divinus Redemptor Ecclesiam suam in definienda doctrina de fide vel moribus instructam esse voluit; ideoque eiusmodi Romani Pontificis definitiones ex sese, non autem ex consensu Ecclesiae irreformabiles esse." Butler, 2:294.

22. Cullen's proposed form of definition presented to the fathers of the Council on June 18 read: "Itaque nos, traditioni a fidei christianae exordio perceptae fideliter inhaerendo, ad Dei Salvatoris nostri gloriam, fidei catholicae exaltationem et christianorum populorum salutem, sacro approbante concilio, docemus et divinitus revelatum dogma esse definimus, Romanum pontificem, cui in persona Petri a Christo Domino dictum est: Tu es Petrus, et super hanc petram aedificabo ecclesiam meam, et iterum: Ego rogavi pro te ut non deficiat fides tua, cum doctrinum de fide et moribus, ad aedificationem Spiritus sancti ea infallibilitate gaudere, qua divinus Redemptor ecclesiam suam instructam esse voluit; ideoque haec Romani pontificis decreta ex sese irreformabilia esse." Mansi, 52:751-52.

23. Butler, 2:166.

scher, Hohenloe, and Matthieu of Besancon, stayed away, so did Mérode, the Pope's elemosinire. The Germans and Hungarians remained away." "Dr. Clifford, Dr. Errington, Dr. MacHale, and Dr. Moriarty," Cullen then noted, referring to those English and Irish bishops who had voted *non placet* at the trial vote on July 13, "did not answer to their names; all the other Irish, Scottish, and English bishops voted right. At the first meeting [July 13] Dr. Vaughan said *non placet,* but yesterday he was all right. Twenty-four bishops of the United States said *placet.* Five others were absent." "Twenty-six Irish bishops," he then observed finally, referring to his colleagues of Irish birth, "presented me with an address yesterday, thanking me for the way I had acted in the Council. It is very short. I will tell Dr. Moran to send it to you so that it may be inserted in the *Freeman.* Of course, Dr. MacHale and Dr. Moriarty did not sign. The address was got up after the public session in a hurry."

That same day, July 19, war was declared between France and Prussia, and because of that calamity, as well as the oppressive heat of the Roman summer, the great majority of the bishops, most of whom had now been absent from their dioceses for more than eight months, made rapid preparations to return home. Most of the bishops, including the Irish, had already left Rome when, on August 4, Napoleon III withdrew the French garrison, which had been the main support for some ten years of what was left of the pope's temporal power, in order to strengthen his military position against the Prussians on the eastern frontier. For the rest of August and early September the Roman authorities made an effort to carry on the Council, and general congregations were held on August 13 and 23 and September 1, with about 120 prelates in attendance. Shortly after the Prussians' disastrous defeat of the French at Sedan on September 1, however, where Napoleon III was captured with 100,000 of his troops, the Italian government declared its intention to occupy Rome and the territory adjacent to it. After about ten days of fruitless appeals to surrender peaceably from the Italian government to Pius IX, Italian troops assaulted Rome, on September 20, and, after a brief struggle of a few hours, the pope ordered his troops to lay down their arms. A month later, on October 20, the pope announced in an Apostolic letter that the Council was adjourned *sine die.*

The great work of the first Vatican Council was undoubtedly defining the primacy and the infallibility of the pope. As far as the modern Irish Church was concerned, however, the most significant result of the Council was that in the more than eight months that the Irish bishops spent together in Rome, they finally crystallized as a body. This was the first time that the bishops had spent any considerable time together as a body since the the national synod of Thurles had convened in the late summer of 1850. In the intervening nineteen years, the bishops had met formally and informally on the average of something more than once a year in Dublin and Maynooth. Their meetings, however, seldom lasted more than three or four days, and because of the great amount of work to be done, they were generally hectic and hurried, with little time allowed for either informal discussions or the exchange of ideas.[24] Soon after their arrival in Rome, the bishops began to meet formally at least once or twice a week both to discuss outstanding Irish business and to attend to the necessary preliminaries of their work for the Council. "The Propaganda," Cullen reported to his vicar general, Edward McCabe, on December 11, "has recommended the Irish Bishops to hold private meetings to discuss our own affairs and to see what reforms we require. If you recollect anything that requires change be so good as to mention it in your next" (C). During December 1869, the bishops met formally on three successive Thursdays (16, 23, and 30) to discuss what was to be done about Father Lavelle and Fenianism before finally deciding to ask the Holy Office of the Inquisition to condemn the Brotherhood *nominatim*. Apparently, in early December, Cardinal Barnabò also had suggested to the various English-speaking hierarchies that they meet together to discuss their common problems.[25] "I had a long talk," William Ullathorne, the English bishop of Birmingham, reported to a correspondent at home on December 23, "with two American archbishops deputed by their body, this morning, about a scheme for all the English-speaking bishops preparing what they have to propose to the Council for their special requirements, and have been moving in other directions for the same end."[26] "Our plan," he explained, "likely to be realized, is this. The bishops of Ireland, England, Scotland, America, Australia, India, etc., will each meet separately and draw up their proposals, then two delegates of each country will meet together and settle what we shall bring together jointly. It is only by contrivances of this kind that in so large a multitude things can be brought to bear in action."

No sooner had the Irish and other English-speaking hierarchies begun to meet in late December, however, than rumors began to be circulated in the press that already parties and factions were being formed in the Council. "The stories in the *Times*," Cullen explained to Conroy on December 28, "about the bishops being divided into parties is all moonshine. The Irish bishops come here on Wednesday to talk about Irish customs and discipline, but there is nothing like a party. Other bishops do the same in regard to their own affairs. This is done to see whether anything from any particular country is to be brought before the Synod" (C). The Irish bishops continued their Wednesday meetings well into January,[27] but they apparently backed away from pursuing any English-speaking union because, as Ullathorne had noted earlier, "the higher Irish prelates" were evidently "a little shy of the go-ahead Americans."[28] The English and American delegates continued to

---

24. Larkin, p. 662.
25. Butler, 1:160.
26. Ibid., 1:177.
27. C, Cullen to Conroy, January 11, 1870.
28. Butler, 1:168. Ullathorne to Mother Imelda Poole (?), December 16, 1869. In a note on his "Sources" (1:xv), Butler explains that most of the letters written by Ullathorne from the first

meet together during January, but by the end of the month, their efforts to arrive at any concerted action had broken down.[29] Indeed, by the end of January it had become apparent that the American, Canadian, and English bishops were deeply divided on the question of infallibility, and the issues at the Council had begun to transcend national identities and language groups. The differences between the Americans and the Irish had been further aggravated, moreover, by the Roman decision to condemn Fenianism, about which the Americans, though deeply concerned, were not consulted by either the Irish bishops or the Roman authorities. In effect, then, the Irish bishops played a lone and a strong hand as a body during the early months of the Council, and because of the differences on the question of infallibility in the other English-speaking hierarchies, which deepened as the Council continued, the Irish, virtually united and determined on the question, eventually emerged as the dominant group among the English-speaking bishops. Because, therefore, of their intense common experiences in Rome, confronting and resolving difficult issues, the Irish bishops had at the Council finally crystallized as a body, and they returned home better prepared corporately than they had ever been to meet the challenges they would face in Church and state in the decade of the seventies.

Vatican Council were to Mother Imelda, but in quoting them Butler does not designate which were written to her or to others.
29. Hennesey, p. 55.

II

The Bishops as a Body
April 1870–May 1873

By 1870, the appointments to Irish bishoprics were obviously the single most important factor in maintaining the harmony and unity of the episcopal body. In the decade of the 1860s, the *sine qua non* governing the eleven episcopal appointments made to Irish sees was that none of those appointed should be supporters of the archbishop of Tuam. Given that basic requirement, the priorities governing Irish episcopal appointments were mainly three. First, the candidate above all should be sound on the education question. That is, he should be an avowed opponent of mixed education of Protestants and Catholics on all levels, primary, secondary, and university; he should be determined to further the control of the bishops as a body over Irish education at every level; and he should brook no interference from the laity on educational issues. Second, he should be a zealous pastoral reformer, prepared to enforce the Acts and Decrees of the Synod of Thurles of 1850, as well as those of the various national and provincial synods since then which governed such matters. Finally, he should be a determined opponent of Fenianism and, also, be prepared to exercise a tight control over the political propensities of his clergy even in constitutional politics. It is not too great a claim to say that by 1870 the Irish bishops as a body were virtually in consensus on all these issues. Within less than three years after the Irish bishops returned from the first Vatican Council, however, there were eight appointments made to Irish sees, in a regular hierarchy that numbered twenty-seven. In view of such a rapid turnover in so short a period of time, it is important to examine those appointments in some detail, to determine their significance for the ongoing harmony and unity of the Irish bishops as a body.

During the Council, in a long and confidential memorandum written on April 22, 1870, to Cardinal Barnabò, the prefect of Propaganda, Laurence Gillooly, the bishop of Elphin, recommended that the bishops of Killala and Achonry be provided with coadjutors because of their advanced age and the infirm state of

Provinces and Dioceses of Ireland

their health.[1] Barnabò consulted with Cullen in early May and learned that all that Gillooly had reported about the necessity of providing the two bishops with coadjutors was only too true.[2] On May 22, therefore, Barnabò formally applied to the pope for permission to write to the two bishops in the pope's name, exhorting them to proceed to the selection of a coadjutor according to the customary procedure, and the pope authorized him to do so.[3] Barnabò wrote to both bishops on May 27, and in early June they arranged to assemble their senior clergy and commend the customary three names, or *terna,* to Rome. The bishop of Killala convened his clergy on July 7, in the cathedral town of Ballina in county Mayo.[4] Of the eighteen votes cast that day, Thomas MacHale, a nephew of the archbishop of Tuam and professor of theology at the Irish College in Paris, was returned first on the list as *dignissimus,* or worthiest, with eight votes, and Hugh Conway, the parish priest of Skreen, was second as *dignior,* or more worthy, with seven votes, and three others tied for third place, as *dignus,* or worthy, with one vote each; these were Bartholomew Costello, the parish priest of Crossmolina, Patrick Malone, the parish priest of Belmullet, and Peter Nolan, a native of the diocese of Killala, who had lately become an Oblate father and was resident in that community's house in Sligo, in the diocese of Elphin.

The formal procedure in Irish episcopal appointments, which had been in force since 1829 by virtue of a Roman decree, or rescript, was that the *terna* was to be reviewed and reported on by the bishops of the province concerned. They would then forward their report to the Propaganda, and the cardinals of that congregation would consider both the commendation of the clergy and the report of the bishops in making their own recommendation for the pope's final and authoritative approval. The bishops of the province of Tuam, however, were somewhat embarrassed about holding the usual meeting because two of their number, the ailing bishops of Killala and Achonry, were in Ireland, and three others, the archbishop of Tuam and the bishops of Elphin and Galway, were in Rome attending the Council. The customary procedure, of course, would have been to have the three bishops in Rome meet, soliciting in the meantime the proxies or the views of the two ailing bishops in writing or, failing that, to postpone the meeting until all could gather more conveniently in Ireland after the Council. On July 10, however, shortly after the Killala clergy had met, and before the news of their *terna* could have reached Rome, John MacEvilly, the bishop of Galway, wrote

---

1. *Scritture Riferite nei Congressi, Irlanda* (S.R.C.), vol. 36, fols. 692–93, Archives of the Sacred Congregation for the Evangelization of the People.

2. Ibid.

3. *Acta Sacrae Congraegationis* (A), vol. 237 (1871), fol. 80, "Ristretto con Sommario sulla elezione dei Vescovi Coadiutori per le Diocesi di Achonry e Killala, non che dei Vescovi di Raphoe, Ardagh e Clonfert in Irlanda, Gennaio, 1871" (fols. 79-108).

4. Ibid., fol. 92.

Barnabò and proposed that the procedure for appointing Irish bishops, as outlined in the rescript of 1829, be modified.[5] After explaining that he had taken counsel with the bishops of Kerry and Limerick, as well as the coadjutor to Killaloe, who all belonged to the province of Cashel and were then also in Rome, MacEvilly suggested that the bishops be allowed to submit their views about the candidates to the Propaganda separately rather than collectively. When the bishops of a province met together, MacEvilly explained, it very often occurred that in spite of their different opinions on the merits of the several candidates, they expressed a single point of view in their collective report to the Propaganda, and generally the point of view of one or another of the prelates enjoyed greater influence in the province. In fact, to avoid differences among the bishops, the greater part yielded to other people's opinions, and hence the Propaganda was not fully informed on the quality and fitness of the ecclesiastics who were commended. MacEvilly pointed out that the bishops often had to undergo a sort of moral violence because the candidates were related to a bishop or the archbishop of the province, and often that prelate insisted that preference be given to his relative. Thus, when the commendation of the Killala clergy arrived in Rome shortly after MacEvilly had presented his letter, he apparently asked Barnabò to secure a special dispensation from the pope to present their reports separately, while awaiting the formal decision of the Propaganda on his and the other bishops' request to modify the customary procedure in general. The pope approved the request in the case of Killala, and the three bishops of the province of Tuam then submitted their separate reports and, shortly afterward, left Rome.

In submitting his views, on July 16, Archbishop MacHale clearly understood that the appointment to Killala was a choice between his nephew, who had received eight votes, and Conway, who had received seven, and he did his best, or perhaps his worst, to impugn Conway's good name.[6] MacHale began by explaining the virtues and attainments of his nephew. He reported that Thomas was forty-eight years of age and had been educated in Rome at the Irish and Roman colleges, where he had earned doctorates in philosophy and theology. Since 1850 he had been a professor of sacred scripture and canon law at the Irish College in Paris and had taken no part in the great disturbances which had taken place in that institution in the late 1850s, which had resulted in the Propaganda turning the College over to the Irish Vincentians. Indeed his nephew had lived since then in great peace and concord in that community. Moreover, he knew Hebrew, Latin, Greek, Italian, French, Spanish, and English, had been secretary to the two

---

5. Ibid., fol. 97. The results of the voting could, of course, have been forwarded to MacEvilly by telegram, and given his charge that there was a very real danger of nepotism on the part of MacHale, they probably were. See also unsigned and apparently misdated memorandum in Italian on this subject, S.R.C., vol. 36, fols. 988–89.

6. Ibid., fols. 93–94.

provincial synods of Tuam held in recent years, and had also received seven votes from the body of Irish bishops when he had been the unsuccessful candidate for rector of the Catholic University some ten years before. MacHale then reviewed Conway's career. He noted that he was about fifty-five years of age and had completed his studies with sufficient credit at the national seminary at Maynooth, where he was promoted to the priesthood. He knew Latin, Greek, Hebrew, English, and perhaps the rudiments of French. As a parish priest he had erected, not without difficulty, a comfortable enough church, but at one time he seemed to be a man too much concerned with secular affairs. MacHale, moreover, saved his worst for last, noting that he felt it was due the honor of the episcopate to report that a servant had recently given birth to a child shortly after leaving Conway's house and that this had given rise to some suspicion in regard to Conway's character. No one, however, MacHale added, should judge Conway entirely on the basis of what he, MacHale, felt obliged to report and, as far as he knew, Conway had always exercised his office as a priest in a praiseworthy manner. In referring to the three priests tied for third place on the *terna,* MacHale did little more than note that they were good priests.

The bishops of Elphin and Galway, respectively, submitted their reports to Propaganda on July 16 and 17, and though they were technically separate, certainly they were not conceived independently of each other.[7] The joint message of these letters was that, though Thomas MacHale was a learned, pious, and moral priest, he really did not have the qualities necessary to be a bishop. Not only was his health bad, which would prevent him from pursuing the active, pastoral life expected of an Irish bishop, but he was also a hypochondriac who was more zealous about the state of his own physical health than he was about the healthy spiritual state of others. Moreover, if appointed a bishop, he would be, in politico-religious matters, a determined follower of his uncle, who for so many years had proved to be disruptive of the peace and concord of the bishops as a body in Ireland. In his letter, the bishop of Elphin also pointed out that the eight votes that Thomas MacHale had received were obtained for him by Bartholomew Costello, one of those tied for third place on the *terna* and leader of the MacHale faction in the diocese of Killala. Indeed, the bishop of Galway went further, asserting that the eight votes were really a species of moral violence because the priests who had voted for MacHale were all related to each other and the candidate. The bishop of Elphin also maintained that, in his considered opinion, no appointment that could be made to an Irish diocese could be more damaging to the care of souls than the appointment of MacHale.

When the bishops of Elphin and Galway then turned to a discussion of the merits of Conway, they were as positive about him as they had been negative about

7. Ibid., fols. 94–96.

MacHale. They found in Conway, for example, whom they both claimed they knew well, prudence, active zeal, serious mien, learning, and a sterling reputation among the clergy and the people, all qualities requisite for being a good bishop. They also noted that he had always been loyal to the Holy See and its teachings and most especially in regard to what was in Ireland the crucial issue—the education question. Both bishops believed also that if Conway were appointed, he would be able to bring to an end the divisions that had disturbed the diocese for more than thirty years. In referring to the three candidates tied for third place, both bishops were unequivocal in maintaining that none of them could be considered worthy of the episcopal dignity. Shortly after the three bishops had submitted their individual reports, on July 16 and 17, the cardinal prefect wrote to the bishop of Killala requesting his report on the *terna* and, apparently, also asking him about Conway's alleged moral lapse, as mentioned in MacHale's report.

In his reply, which was undated, the bishop of Killala was very cautious about who he actually preferred as his coadjutor.[8] He chose, in fact, to answer *seriatim* the customary list of points, circulated by Propaganda, thought to be important in helping the authorities make up their minds. There were some fourteen points to be attended to in the formal list—age, nationality, education, degrees, teaching, pastoral experience, languages, etc.—and Feeny pointed out that since he did not know MacHale very well, he could not answer the more qualitative questions having to do with piety, morality, judgment, determination, health, administrative abilities, etc. His report on MacHale, therefore, was necessarily somewhat attenuated, while the one on Conway, who had been one of his priests for nearly thirty years, was not only very full but also very laudatory. When Feeny finally came to the delicate point raised in the cardinal prefect's letter, he pointed out that Conway not only enjoyed an honorable reputation but also there was nothing that could be said against his morals. As far as the whisperings referred to by the cardinal, which were occasioned by envy and jealousy, Feeny added, the just and terrible retribution of canon law against false accusers should immediately be visited upon those who cannot prove what they say. Finally, in regard to the three other names on the *terna,* Feeny chose not to dignify them with even an abbreviated consideration of their qualifications. In concluding this discussion of the various reports of the bishops of the province of Tuam, it should also be noted that the cardinal prefect apparently did not write Patrick Durcan, the bishop of Achonry, asking for his views on the Killala *terna.*

In the meantime, while most of the Irish bishops were leaving Rome, the senior clergy of the diocese of Achonry, under the presidency of their bishop, met on July 21, in the town of Ballaghdereen in county Mayo, to commend three names

8. Ibid., fols. 96–97.

to Rome for a coadjutor with the right of succession to their venerable bishop.[9] Of the eighteen votes cast, Terence O'Rorke, archdeacon of the diocese and parish priest of Ballysodare, was chosen *dignissimus* with nine votes, while Matthew Finn, parish priest of Kilmovee, and John McDermott, parish priest of Cloonacool, each received three votes. The remaining three votes were cast for James (Pius in religion) Devine, a priest of the Passionist order and rector of the order's house at Harold's Cross near Dublin, Bernard Goodman, prior of the Dominican house in Sligo, and Bernard Durcan, brother of the bishop of Achonry and vicar general of the diocese. The bishop of Elphin, who was on his way home, wrote to the rector of the Irish College in Rome, Tobias Kirby, from Paris on July 28. The substance of his letter asked the rector to speak to Cardinal Barnabò and to request that he secure once again the permission of the pope to dispense the bishops of the province of Tuam from the obligation of meeting together to report on the candidates commended for the coadjutorship of Achonry, as well as on those candidates about to be commended for the vacancy in the diocese of Clonfert (created by the death of the bishop), and to allow the bishops to present their reports separately.[10] The bishop of Elphin also assured Kirby that he also was writing in the name of the bishop of Galway. "In case your Eminence deigns to agree," Kirby advised Barnabò, in presenting Gillooly's request, on August 1, "in the prudence of this suggestion, it would be enough to write a line to the archbishop or to the bishops, saying that given the age and infirmity of the two bishops [i.e., Killala and Achonry] and the actual circumstances, the bishops are dispensed from the obligation of meeting together for the said elections, seeing that the Sacred Congregation will be pleased with a separate report from each bishop. Thus the motive or the occasion for some grave dissension will be removed, and the inconvenience of exposing the prelates to saying one thing in the meeting for some reason, and to be obliged afterwards to contradict themselves."[11]

The pope agreed to dispense the bishops' obligation in regard to the *ternae* for Achonry and Clonfert, and, upon the election of the *terna* for Clonfert on August 18, at which the customary memorial mass for the deceased bishop was celebrated, the bishops of Galway, Elphin, and Achonry, who assisted, met informally and discussed the preferred names for Achonry. "Drs. Durkan [*sic*] & Gillooly & myself," the bishop of Galway reported to Cullen the next day, "have agreed to recommend Father Pius Devine of Harold's Cross for Achonry" (C). "We could not possibly recommend Fr. O'Rorke," MacEvilly added, alluding to the alleged immorality of that priest in sexual matters, "who obtained a majority of the votes.

9. Ibid., fols. 81–82.
10. Ibid., fols. 97–98.
11. Ibid.

From what I hear he is *utterly unfit* to be made a Bishop." "Fr. McDermott, who was third on the list," he noted, "seems to be *devoid of common sense,* everlastingly roving about. The only one of the three who could be recommended is Fr. Finn. But even he would I fear be hardly competent from the state of his health to manage that Diocese." "Fr. Pius," MacEvilly further explained to Cullen, "who is an Achonry man & knows the Diocese well, & the Irish language which is indispensible in that Diocese (O'Rorke don't know a word of Irish) who moreover has given several Missions in that Diocese, seems to me the man who would best promote the salvation of the people, and enforce discipline, which, I fear, is much needed in that Diocese." "He got one vote, and I have reason to believe that he would have got more only for his bold denunciation of Fenianism which made the young P. Priests rally round O'Rorke. Some of these Achonry people (the younger PP's) are a good deal bitten by the principles of a *neighbouring* Diocese. They brought them from Maynooth with them, and hence they require some vigour & firmness combined with due prudence to set things right." "Your Eminence is aware," MacEvilly finally noted, "that the H. See has allowed us to give our views separately on the three vacancies in the Province."

Though the bishops of Elphin and Galway once again wrote separate letters, on August 20 and 26, to the cardinal prefect, they covered much the same ground in their reports.[12] They agreed that O'Rorke, the first on the list, was impossible because of the public scandal associated with his name, that Finn, though a good priest, was incapacitated by failing health, and that McDermott was simply not up to episcopal mark. They also eliminated, in effect, two of the three other names that had received one vote, namely, Bernard Goodman, the Dominican, and Bernard Durcan, the bishop's brother, because both were physically incapacitated. In the end, Gillooly and MacEvilly recommended Pius Devine. When the archbishop of Tuam and the bishop of Achonry jointly wrote the cardinal prefect on August 25, after meeting in Tuam, however, they expressed that not only were they very unhappy that their colleagues of Elphin and Galway had refused to attend their meeting, but also they had not been advised why their colleagues had been dispensed of the obligation to make the collective report prescribed in the Roman decree, or rescript, of 1829.[13] After expressing their dissatisfaction with this breach of procedure, MacHale and Durcan proceeded to explain why none of the three names on the Achonry *terna* were fit to be promoted to the episcopal dignity. They maintained that O'Rorke, the first on the list, though clever could not be recommended because he had been publicly accused of the crime that had been ascribed to Hugh Conway, one of the two candidates for coadjutor to Killala, which previously had been referred to Barnabò and the rumor of which

12. Ibid., fols. 89–91.
13. Ibid., fols. 91–92.

had spread to the adjacent dioceses of Achonry and Elphin. For the honor and good name of the episcopacy, therefore, they recommended that O'Rorke positively be excluded. They also vetoed the second and third names on the list because these men, they felt, were not episcopal material. The only remaining name, then, was Pius Devine, the Passionist, who was thirty-two years old and rector and professor of theology at St. Paul's College near Dublin. He knew Greek, Latin, Italian, and French very well, and he was a learned and pious preacher in both English and Irish. MacHale and Durcan united, therefore, in recommending him very highly for the coadjutorship to Achonry. It should be also noted that the cardinal prefect did not ask the bishop of Killala to submit his views in regard to the Achonry *terna*.

In any case, MacHale and Durcan's very questionable and gratuitous reference to Conway's alleged crime against a former servant was a good measure of the lengths to which MacHale was prepared to go to preserve what was left of his episcopal power base in his province. That MacHale succeeded in involving Durcan in the unfortunate innuendo was yet another indication of his astuteness and unscrupulousness when he wanted to have his own way. He well understood that his suffragans, the bishops of Elphin and Galway, with the covert support and encouragement of Cullen, were attempting to undermine what was left of his power and influence. He must have been greatly heartened, therefore, by the choice made by the clergy of the diocese of Clonfert for their *terna,* when he presided over their meeting on August 18 at Ballinasloe in county Galway.[14] Of the sixteen votes cast, William Derry, the parish priest of Clonfert (Eyrecourt) and brother of the late bishop, received eleven votes, while Thomas Burke, the parish priest of Kilmalanogue (Portumna), received three, and Matthew Walsh, the parish priest of Lusmagh (Banagher), rounded out the *terna* with one vote.

In his letter of the following day, August 19, to Cullen, MacEvilly explained why MacHale, indeed, must have been very pleased by the *terna.* "I must confess," MacEvilly reported, "that I am myself greatly puzzled what to do in the case. Frs. Burke and Walsh are out of the question. The latter who is a very excellent man is beyond 72 years of age, but in every other respect a most excellent man. Father Burke never had [*sic*] been remarkable for his piety. But altho' a man of very great abilities, I would consider his appointment as Bishop a great misfortune. I fear his ideas on Education and cognate subjects are not the most correct" (C). "Fr. Derry," he admitted, "is the best of the three. But I must candidly tell your Eminence, if I had a choice, I would not think of him."

He is said to be *exceedingly rich,* and I believe he dealt very extensively in the late Bishop's time in farming and dealing in cattle. He has been always a very

14. Ibid., fols. 85–86.

taciturn kind of man, & it is hard to know what his views may be on the great
Ecclesiastical Questions of the day. If I thought he was disposed to follow the
example of his brother in his adhesion to Dr. MacHale through thick and thin,
I would consider it to be an undoubted disqualification in the present temper
of the times & state of the Irish Church. I believe, however, nothing can be
alleged against his character & his literary acquirements are, I believe, pass-
able.

"Before giving my opinion to the Holy See," he assured Cullen finally, "I will
enquire more on the subject. But my present feeling is not to incur any responsibility by recommending even him."

In the same letter, dated August 25, in which they had reported on the Achonry
terna, MacHale and Durcan also had incorporated their views on the commendation of the Clonfert clergy.[15] They reported on the candidates in reverse order,
noting that Walsh was not very remarkable for his gifts and was more than sixty-
five years of age, while Burke, though they did not wish to exclude him, was not
very worthy of the episcopal dignity. As for Derry, he was fifty-five years of age,
and, after finishing his course of studies with honors at Maynooth, he spent a year
in Rome at the Irish College and earned a doctorate in theology. In addition to
Greek and Latin, he was skilled in Italian, French, and English. He had been
ordained in Rome in 1843, and as a parish priest he had been a wise and faithful
pastor. In view of his outstanding knowledge, prudence, and piety, therefore,
MacHale and Durcan recommended that he be appointed to the vacant see of
Clonfert. MacHale must have been very pleased with the turn things had taken in
regard to the three appointments to be made in his province. The Achonry report
had given him not only another opportunity to raise questions about Conway's
moral fitness for Killala, and thereby to strengthen his nephew's claim to that
appointment, but also it had given him the opportunity to mend his fences with
the bishop of Achonry by acceding to his desire to have Pius Devine, a relative of
his, as his coadjutor. Who Devine would eventually take his lead from in eccle-
siastico-political matters, moreover, was still an open question. Finally, the patent
superiority of Derry to the other two candidates on the Clonfert *terna,* and his
presumed loyalty to MacHale and the principles he espoused in Church and
nation, all augured well for the ability of the archbishop to sustain himself in the
province of Tuam, in spite of all the machinations of his ecclesiastical enemies at
home and in Rome.

The bishops of Elphin and Galway, on the other hand, were very much perplexed about how to proceed with their reports to Propaganda. They were faced
with the problem that they could recommend none of the three names on the
terna, but because the diocese was so small, asking Propaganda to order a new
terna, which would exclude the three names just commended, would make the

---

15. Ibid., fol. 103.

choice of the Clonfert clergy even more narrow than it had been, given the obvious lack of episcopal material available in the diocese. Apparently Gillooly and Mac-Evilly consulted Cullen about what was to be done, and either he advised them to consult Barnabò or he did so himself. Barnabò then suggested that the two bishops, of themselves, nominate a priest whom they thought had the requisite qualities to be appointed to Clonfert. The priest that they eventually decided to recommend, interestingly enough, Hugh O'Rourke, professor of *belles lettres* at Maynooth and a native of the diocese of Tuam, was suggested to them by Cullen. Because the search for an appropriate candidate took nearly a month, Gillooly and MacEvilly were not able to forward their reports until the middle of September. "I forgot to mention," Gillooly explained to Cullen on September 14, "to your Eminence in Dublin that in my report on the Election for Clonfert I intended to recommend the Maynooth Professor whom your Eminence named to me. I have made inquiries about him and I have just now sealed a letter to Card. Barnabò—in which I strongly approve of him and say of the others what I learned regarding them" (C). "Dr. McEvilly [*sic*] will follow the same course," he assured Cullen in conclusion, "and I hope Dr. Durcan, whom I expect to see in a few days."

The individual reports of Gillooly and MacEvilly to Barnabò on September 14 and 15 are less interesting for their praise of O'Rourke than for their condemnation of Derry.[16] The points that both of them made were essentially three: first, that Derry was exceedingly rich and had made his money in farming and dealing in cattle; second, that he had the reputation for being miserly and very avaricious; and third, that he had a tendency toward insobriety. In his letter, Gillooly added salt to the soup by maintaining that Derry also had the reputation of being neglectful of his spiritual duties because of his temporal interests. Neither bishop, however, said a word about what was undoubtedly uppermost in their minds in regard to Derry's unfitness for Clonfert, namely, that he would prove to be, as his late brother had been, a loyal and devoted follower of the archbishop of Tuam. Both Gillooly and MacEvilly also explained to Barnabò that the other two names on the list were not fit to be promoted and that O'Rourke was everything that could be desired in a bishop (except, MacEvilly indicated, for some question about his health). Once again, as in the case of the Achonry *terna,* it should be noted that Barnabò did not ask the bishop of Killala for his views on the commendation of the Clonfert clergy.

In the meantime, in the two vacancies that had occurred in the province of Armagh since the beginning of the year, namely, Raphoe and Ardagh, the pro-

16. Ibid., fols. 103-5.

cedural wheels had been allowed to turn in their customary way. The vacancy in Raphoe had been the result of the translation of its bishop, Daniel McGettigan, to the archbishopric of Armagh in early March, while that of Ardagh had occurred when its bishop, Neal McCabe, died suddenly, apparently from an internal hemorrhage, on July 24, in Marseilles, while he was returning to Ireland from the Council. In regard to the Raphoe vacancy, the pope had given his permission in late March for the clergy of that diocese to assemble to commend a *terna,* and appointed James Lynch, the coadjutor of the bishop of Kildare and Leighlin, to preside because he was the only able-bodied bishop in Ireland while everyone else was at the Council.[17] When the clergy of Raphoe assembled on May 11 in Stranorlar in county Donegal, they cast their twenty-two votes for four candidates. Charles O'Donnell, parish priest of Ardara, on the west coast, received nine votes as *dignissimus,* James MacDevitt, professor of logic and metaphysics at the missionary College of All Hallows in Dublin, was returned as *dignior* with five votes, while John MacMenamin, parish priest of Stranorlar, and James MacFadden, parish priest of Tallaghbegly East and Tory Island on the north coast, tied for *dignus* with four votes each. Of course, Lynch, who had presided, was a complete stranger to Raphoe, and he did not know any of the northern clergy. It took him some time, therefore, to answer to the questionnaire regarding the abilities and qualities of the candidates that Barnabò had forwarded to him on March 27 with the pope's rescript, authorizing him to preside at the meeting. Indeed, Lynch did not forward his comments on the *terna* for more than a month, and when he did, on June 16, they proved to be somewhat perfunctory, as was also his earlier, apparently undated, letter announcing the results of the voting.[18] Barnabò then wrote Lynch again to ask him for a more formal letter about the meeting at which the Raphoe clergy had commended their *terna.* By the time Lynch's reply of July 12 reached Rome, most of the Irish bishops were preparing to return home, and apparently the bishops of the province of Armagh decided to defer their report on the Raphoe *terna* until after they had returned to Ireland.

Cullen, meanwhile, had written to his secretary in Dublin, George Conroy, asking him to find out what he could about the candidates proposed for Raphoe. "Give us your opinion," Cullen noted briefly at the end of a letter written on May 29, "of the three [*sic*] candidates for Raphoe and especially of McDevitt" (C). "Dr. Woodlock," he added, referring to the rector of the Catholic University, "praises this last very highly." A short time later, Conroy replied in an undated note to Cullen marked "private."

As I do not myself know the ecclesiastics named for Raphoe (excepting Dr.

17. Ibid., fols. 83–84.
18. Ibid., fols. 98–99.

McDevitt) I have learned the following details concerning them from a reliable source:

1. Fr. O'Donnell, the first on the list, is described as having *great energy* and *remarkable prudence*. Of these qualities he gave proof on occasion of the evictions in Donegal some years ago. He is said to be much beloved by the priests and by the laity of the Diocese.

2. Fr. McFadden is said to be superior to many in talent etc; but not so much liked by some. He too was energetic at the time of the evictions.

3. Of Fr. McMenamin I have not heard anything remarkable.

4. Fr. McDevitt I know very well, but I am inclined to distrust my own judgement in his case as I did not always find his views to agree with mine when in All Hallows. He is in most things a Maynooth man *pur sang* [pure-blooded]. I once endeavoured a good deal to have the course of studies at All Hallows conformed ["replaced" crossed out] to the Roman model; but Fr. McDevitt's opposition made my attempt almost entirely fruitless.

"He is much esteemed," Conroy noted pointedly in conclusion, "by Dr. McGettigan."

The bishops of the province of Armagh, however, were not able to meet until some six weeks after they had all returned from Rome. When they did meet on September 15, at Maynooth, they were unanimous in recommending the second on the list, MacDevitt, to succeed McGettigan in Raphoe.[19] In their report, the bishops, although admitting that the other three candidates on the *terna* were to be praised for their very considerable gifts and attainments, eliminated them, in effect, because of their individual shortcomings and defects. MacFadden, who had tied with MacMenamin for third place on the list, suffered from vertigo, and because the dizziness rendered him subject to falling, he sometimes had to abstain from celebrating mass. This, the bishops explained, made it impossible for them to recommend him. MacMenamin, had not only lost the use of one eye, but it was to be feared that shortly he would be deprived of the other. He did not, moreover, know any Irish, which was absolutely necessary in the diocese of Raphoe in order to fulfill the pastoral charge of a bishop. As far as O'Donnell, the first on the list, was concerned, though he had many laudable qualities, he had not given evidence of pastoral zeal and did not seem concerned for the education of the young or for the reform of the people confided to his care, though he had been given various opportunities to do so. Turning finally to MacDevitt, the bishops admitted that his one failing was that he had not had any pastoral experience as either a parish priest or curate because he had been, since his ordination at Maynooth, teaching in the College of All Hallows in Dublin. He was, however, a priest distinguished for his eloquence, learning, and piety, and he had given, moreover, undoubted evidence of his pastoral zeal by preaching and hearing confessions during his

19. Ibid., fols. 100–101.

vacation time when he visited his native diocese of Raphoe. They, therefore, unanimously recommended him for the appointment to Raphoe.

The remains of the late bishop of Ardagh, meanwhile, had been returned to Paris for burial with his Vincentian brethren, and as was customary on the occasion, not only was a high mass celebrated for the repose of his soul on August 8, but also the senior clergy of the diocese, with the archbishop presiding, assembled in Longford to elect a vicar capitular who was to govern the diocese until their new bishop was appointed. The clergy unanimously elected, as they had on the two previous occasions when their see had been widowed, Peter Dawson, the parish priest of Kiltoghert and vicar general of the late bishop. Indeed, Dawson, in the two previous elections of a *terna* for Ardagh, had been returned by the clergy as the *dignissimus,* but he had been passed over by Rome on both occasions as being unsuitable. Toward the close of the day's proceedings in Longford, six of the senior parish priests waited for the archbishop of Armagh in order to explain to him that on the two former occasions they had voted for Dawson but that, if he still had no chance in Rome, they would rather cast their votes for some other good priest. Several days later, on August 11, therefore, McGettigan wrote the rector of the Irish College in Rome to explain that it would be a very delicate matter for him, as a concerned party, to put such a question to the authorities in Rome, but, if Kirby saw no problem, he would appreciate his inquiring, and then writing him a simple yes or no in regard to Dawson's viability.[20] In a note made of his reply on this letter Kirby wrote, "He has no chance" (K).

When the clergy of Ardagh, therefore, met again in Longford, on September 6, to celebrate the customary memorial mass or "month's mind," for their deceased bishop and to select their *terna* to succeed him, Dawson's name was not among those commended. Of the thirty-four votes cast that day, Nicholas O'Flanagan, parish priest of Abbeylara, received thirteen, and Joseph Mullooly, prior of San Clemente, the Dominican house in Rome, received six votes, while James Reynolds, rector of the local diocesan seminary, and John Ivers, parish priest of Mohill, each received five votes.[21] The other five votes, which were not included in the commendation forwarded by the clergy to Propaganda, were distributed between three candidates. Richard Slevin, parish priest of Gortletteragh, and George Conroy, chaplain to Cullen and professor in the Dublin diocesan seminary at Clonliffe, each received two votes, while Patrick F. Moran, Cullen's half nephew and secretary, received one vote. When Cullen wrote to Kirby several days later, on September 9, he was obviously surprised because, after reporting the voting on the Ardagh *terna,* he noted, "Dr. Conroy had 2 and Dr. Moran 1!!" (C). Shortly after he learned of the voting, Cullen asked the bishop of Elphin, whose diocese

---

20. See also S.R.C., vol. 36, fol. 763 for an undated memorandum by Kirby.
21. A, vol 237, fols. 84–85.

bordered on that of Ardagh, discreetly to find out what he could about Nicholas O'Flanagan, the *dignissimus*. Though Cullen had known O'Flanagan more than twenty years before, when the latter was a student at the Irish College in Rome, he obviously wanted to find out how O'Flanagan had fared in the interim.

Gillooly finally was able to secure the desired information, and on September 23 he conveyed what he had learned about O'Flanagan (C).

> One of my priests, who had conversed on the subject of the Election with several of the Ardagh clergy, says: "They speak of him as learned, zealous & active; they say he stands high in the estimation of the Clergy & laity of their diocese—he is quite indifferent himself as to the decision in Rome and would rather remain as he is." An Ardagh P.P., advanced in years and of a *very high character,* writes to me regarding the *dignissimus:* "Mr. O'F. made *dignissimus* by a clique would be the least fitted for the mitre of all those mentioned. I am sorry to say he is neither respected nor trusted by the best of our priests; since it is found out that (in the lifetime of Dr. Higgins [bishop of Ardagh, 1829–53]) by false charges & calumnies against Dr. Dawson he brought our diocese into all its troubles. He thought that if the Doctor [Dawson] were put aside, he might become Coadjutor!"

"Of Fr. Mullooly," Gillooly added, referring to the second on the list, "he says: 'he was put forward to shut out strangers. From his standing in Rome no outsider could be preferred to him; but as he has not been in Ireland since his Ordination it may be feared that he might be led into mistakes if lending confidence to injudicious advisors.'"

Though the bishops of the province of Armagh had met on September 15, at Maynooth, to report on the commendation of the Raphoe clergy, they were not able to take advantage of the occasion to kill two birds with one stone by also reporting to Propaganda on the Ardagh *terna.* They could not do so because the procedure laid down in the Roman decree of 1829, and amended in 1861, for appointing Irish bishops made it mandatory that a ten-day interval elapse between the time the clergy met to commend a *terna* and the day the bishops convened to make their report. Since the meeting of the Ardagh clergy had taken place on September 6, therefore, the earliest the bishops could convene, technically, was September 16. Given the nature of the difficulties posed by the Ardagh *terna,* however, perhaps the bishops were just as pleased that the technicality in the procedure allowed them that much more time to consider the various imponderables involved. When they did finally meet, in Dundalk on October 20, more than a month after they had met in Maynooth on the Raphoe *terna,* their report was more interesting for the questions that it raised than for any that it purported to settle.[22] The seven bishops who assembled in Dundalk, though united in recog-

---

22. Ibid., fols. 101–2.

nizing the superior educational attainments of all of the four candidates commended by the Ardagh clergy, were also unanimous in finding that none of them was worthy of being promoted.

Of the *dignissimus,* O'Flanagan, they noted his cleverness, eloquence, and probity, but they did not recognize in him the zeal that was so necessary in a bishop, nor did he maintain that distance from relatives and from temporal affairs that every good ecclesiastic, and especially every bishop of the Church of God, ought to maintain. Of the *dignior,* Father Mullooly, the bishops pointed out that because he had not been in Ireland for thirty years, they had not the means, really, to form a judgment. They left it, therefore, to the sacred congregation to whom Mullooly was well known, observing only that a bishop in Ireland had need of that pastoral experience which they did not recognize in Mullooly. Father Ivers, moreover, could not be recommended both because he was too old and because he did not have the qualities required in a bishop. Father Reynolds also could not be recommended because, though a man of considerable gifts, he had so involved himself lately in politics and had acquired, thereby, such an unenviable notoriety that he ought to be excluded entirely from becoming a bishop. Having thus demolished the *terna,* the bishops concluded matter-of-factly, reporting without further comment that three other candidates—Slevin, Conroy, and Moran—had received five votes..

In what it said, and especially in what it left unsaid, this was a most interesting and astute performance on the part of the Armagh prelates. What they intended by rejecting the *terna,* of course, was to induce Propaganda to order a new *terna.* What caused them very grave concern, however, was the five votes cast for the other three candidates and, more particularly, the two votes cast for Conroy, who earlier in the year had figured so prominently in the election for Armagh. On that occasion Conroy had tied for third place on the *terna,* with five votes; in an attempt to exclude Conroy from consideration, the Armagh clergy had insisted on a second scrutiny of him and the other candidate who had tied for *dignus,* Francis Kelly, the bishop of Derry, who had received an overwhelming majority. After this reconsideration, Conroy was not included in the *terna* commended to Rome by the clergy. Cullen had complained bitterly that his chaplain and thirty-six-year-old protégé had been deprived of his place on the *terna* by this irregular procedure on the part of the Armagh clergy. Indeed, if two of the candidates on that *terna* had not been bishops, that is, McGettigan of Raphoe and Kelly of Derry, the *terna* would surely have been voided by Rome because of procedural irregularity.

In any case, if McGettigan had not been persuaded by his episcopal colleagues to accept his promotion and translation to Armagh, Conroy most certainly would have been chosen. In the case of Ardagh, therefore, the Armagh prelates were determined to follow the prescribed procedure to the letter in order to avoid giving the Roman authorities any excuse to impose Conroy on them. That is the reason that, when the Ardagh clergy forwarded their commendation, under the signature of McGettigan, who, as archbishop, had presided at their meeting, they not only included the two candidates who had tied for third place, but they also were careful to point out that immediately "after the first and *one and only* scrutiny (*Post primum et* unicus *scrutinium*)" the votes were counted.[23] Also in their report on the *terna*, the bishops repeated the same phrase, without the italics, to emphasize that the procedure had been duly observed.[24] Moreover, as has been noted already, though the bishops could have saved themselves considerable inconvenience by reporting on the Ardagh *terna* when they met on September 15 to report on the Raphoe *terna*, they did not do so because the required ten-day interval between commendation and report had not elapsed. The Armagh prelates, however, must have realized that the Ardagh clergy had made a very serious tactical error in forwarding their commendation without also noting that five votes had been received by three other candidates. The prelates had to decide, therefore, how to repair that omission. Because they understood that no mention whatsoever of the five votes easily might be taken amiss at Rome, especially since they had found all four of the candidates on the *terna* deficient in one way or another, the prelates decided only to mention them and by doing no more than that to emphasize that they were essentially incidental to the report. In this way, the Armagh prelates hoped not only to exclude Conroy once again but also to persuade Rome to order a new *terna*.

Some two weeks before the Armagh prelates reported on the Ardagh *terna* to Propaganda, Cullen decided that it was the appropriate moment to make his move on the five episcopal appointments then pending in the Irish Church. His letter to Barnabò of October 7 is quoted in full because it is at once an excellent summary of a very complicated set of circumstances and a good example of his masterfulness when matters of extraordinary moment were at stake.

> In Ireland three dioceses are actually vacant, and coadjutors must be nominated to two infirm bishops.
> The first diocese vacant is that of Raphoe, of which the bishop Monsignor McGettigan has been translated to Armagh. Communications are so rare between that diocese and Dublin that I do not know at all the clergy of that remote countryside. I have heard, however, that the ecclesiastics proposed to the Sacred Congregation are so well recommended that the choice is easy.
> The second diocese vacant is that of Clonfert of which the bishop was Monsignor Derry, who died soon after his return from Rome. The last two proposed in the *terna* had very few votes, and they did not have besides the qualities necessary to be promoted. The first on the *terna* is Father Derry

23. Ibid., fol. 101.
24. Ibid., fol. 102.

who is of a fit age, in good health and well informed. But there are some difficulties in regard to his appointment. It seems that he has been a little too much occupied in accumulating the things of this world, and is moreover the brother of the late bishop, who followed the archbishop of Tuam in everything. It is to be much feared if Father Derry is nominated, he will seek to support the authority of Monsignor MacHale, who has done much damage in Ireland, protecting Father Lavelle and the Fenians, and maintaining, as he has also done at the Council, doctrines hostile to the Holy See. Some of the bishops of the province of Tuam have proposed, in these circumstances, Father O'Rourke, professor of *belles lettres* in the college of Maynooth, as worthy of being chosen. I have reason to believe this priest is well informed and very pious, so that he could be promoted without any risk.

The third diocese vacant is that of Ardagh, of which the excellent and young bishop Monsignor McCabe died in Marseilles when returning from the Council. The last two priests nominated from the list forwarded to Rome are old and ill, and ought not to be chosen. The first on the list is Father Nicholas O'Flanagan, who more than twenty years ago was a pupil in the Irish College at Rome, and pursued his studies at the Roman College with great advantage. In college he was always very exemplary in his conduct and always enjoyed an excellent reputation and would easily be successful as a bishop. Several priests of the diocese have assured me, however, that he lacks energy, and that he has done little to promote the decorum of divine worship, which in the past because of the persecutions was much neglected in Ireland. The second proposed by the clergy is Father Mullooly of San Clemente of whom it is not for me to speak since he is well known in Rome.

In regard to the two coadjutors, in the diocese of Killala, Father Thomas MacHale was placed first on the list. He studied with advantage in the Irish College, and he is very well informed, but he is the nephew of the archbishop of Tuam, whose theologian he was at the Council, and like the uncle of a very dark and morose temperament, and I believe that his appointment would serve to maintain the system that the archbishop of Tuam has introduced in the handling of ecclesiastical affairs in Ireland. I do not know the other two on the *terna,* but the bishops of Galway and Elphin say that Father *Conway,* who is on the *terna,* is an excellent person.

As for the coadjutor of Achonry, the clergy has placed in first place on the *terna* a parish priest by the name of Terence O'Rorke. This priest was a professor in the Irish College at Paris, and he has the reputation of being a man of much talent. However there is reason to believe that he is a turbulent man. The rector of the College in Paris was very unhappy for this reason, and Monsignor Moran, the bishop of Dunedin in New Zealand, who had studied with him in Maynooth, has told me that O'Rorke is a man in whom it is not possible to place any faith, and that it would be a calamity for Ireland if he were made a bishop. He probably would be also a follower of Monsignor MacHale. I do not know the other priests who were placed on the *terna.* But the bishops of Elphin and Galway have told me they will recommend a

Passionist, a native of the diocese, and relative of the bishop, by the name of Father Pius Devine. This Father was for some time here in Dublin, and taught theology in the house of the order. He has written some works and has the reputation of being well informed. He is now in America making a visitation of the houses [of his order] in that Republic, but will return in a short time.[25]

The masterfulness of this letter, in an ascending order of importance, consists of its organization, its economy, its timing, and its arrangement of priorities. By distinguishing between vacant dioceses and those needing coadjutors, Cullen was able to organize his presentation around his priorities. He began with what was least crucial to him (Raphoe), proceeded to what was more personal (Ardagh), and concluded with what really mattered the most to him (Killala and Achonry). Cullen was also very much aware that the authorities at Propaganda were very busy men and that, like all bureaucrats, they were very appreciative of what would both lighten their load and help them make necessary decisions involving a minimum of risk—namely, memoranda that were both lucid and to the point. Cullen, therefore, wasted little time in his letter reviewing the intricacies of a very complicated set of interconnected circumstances, but, rather, cut to the heart of the matter, pointing out who should and, above all, who should not be promoted. Indeed, the authorities' appreciation of the economy of Cullen's letter was well illustrated by the fact that when the *Ponenza,* or presentation, was finally set into type, at the end of October, for the consideration of the cardinals of Propaganda, his letter served, in effect, as the conclusion to the *Ponenza.* When he wrote his letter on October 7, moreover, Cullen understood that the *Ponenza* would be considered during November, or early December, before the Christmas holidays, and that his letter would have a maximum effect, in terms of its timing, if it arrived in Rome in the middle of October. He also realized that the Armagh prelates would not meet until October 20 to present their report on the Ardagh *terna,* and, of the five appointments to be considered, he was not by the timing of his letter prejudging the one he, because of Conroy, was most personally interested in. Above all, however, what made his letter most effective was the way in which he ruthlessly ordered his priorities. Although he was, of course, very anxious to have Conroy chosen for Ardagh, he did not allow even that most desirable objective to obscure what he was most determined to achieve—the final destruction of MacHale's episcopal power base in the province of Tuam. Cullen was resolved, therefore, that whoever might be appointed in that province, he would not be an adherent of the archbishop of Tuam.

Not even Cullen, however, gifted as he was, was able to provide for all con-

25. Ibid., fols. 105–6.

tingencies. A week after he wrote his masterful letter to Propaganda, he wrote Kirby a hurried note about the appointment of Father Pius Devine to Achonry. "If the appointment," he advised Kirby on October 14, "of F. Pius can be delayed, it will be well to do so. Some ugly charges have been made against him by a person not knowing anything about his chance of promotion, and not hostile to him, indeed by a nun" (K). "The case may not turn out to be a valid one," Cullen concluded, "but it is well to stay proceedings." After completing his investigation of the charges made against Father Pius, Cullen wrote Barnabò explaining the situation. "Writing your Eminence some time ago," Cullen reminded Barnabò on October 31, "I said some things in praise of a Passionist, Father Pius Devine, who was proposed by the bishops of Galway and Elphin as worthy of being appointed coadjutor to the bishop of Achonry. Some time after I had written in that sense, a nun informed me that the said Father had acted or spoken with her in connection with confession in a way that required her denouncing him (la denunzia)."[26] "I believe," he further explained, "after having examined the matter that there was nothing very serious, but the same Father acknowledged that he had played the lad (fatto delle ragazzate [sic]) with the nun, and had acted imprudently and without reflection. I have admonished him never more to do such things especially when it would be a sacrament such as penance, and he has promised to attend to the instructions given him." "I mention these things to your Eminence," Cullen added, finally, "because they seem to me sufficient to prove that it would not be well to promote him to the episcopate, at least for the present. He is still young and will have time to give example of greater prudence and caution in the future before being released from the state of obedience in which he actually lives."

Several days before he wrote Barnabò, Cullen also had written both Gillooly and MacEvilly informing them of Devine's imprudence and advising them to write to Barnabò, withdrawing their recommendation of that priest. They did so on October 28 and 29, recommending at the same time that perhaps, faute de mieux, Matthew Finn, who had tied for second place on the Achonry terna with three votes, and about whom they had both been less than enthusiastic in their original reports, might be appointed after all.[27] In his letter of the 28th, Gillooly also suggested that if an extern were to be appointed, he would recommend Patrick Duggan, parish priest of Cummer, in the diocese of Tuam. When Barnabò received these letters, he realized that, because Finn had been declared by both MacHale and Durcan unfit for the office of coadjutor and because Gillooly and MacEvilly had been less than positive in their earlier reports, some other candidate would have to be nominated. He therefore asked Kirby to write to Cullen in that sense. "I have received a message," Cullen informed Gillooly on November 21,

26. Ibid., fol. 107.
27. Ibid., fols. 106–7.

"from Card. Barnabò requesting me to let your Lordship know that Father Devine will not be appointed to Achonry, and that the other persons proposed are also excluded. Hence his Eminence begs that you and Dr. MacEvilly and the others concerned would immediately propose a fit person to be appointed."[28] "It is well to do so," Cullen advised, "without delay, as Roman affairs may be more disturbed than they are at present." "I write also," he then explained, "to Dr. MacEvilly but to no one else. If you and he recommend it will be sufficient."

"I wrote immediately," Gillooly assured Cullen on November 23, "on receipt of your Eminence's letter, to Dr. MacEvilly, with a view to unite with him in recommending the same person—and if your Eminence does not object, I think I will in a few days be able to see Dr. Durcan and propose to him to join in our letter. It would be well to have the future Bishop recommended by the majority of the Bishops of the Province" (C). "Dr. McE. and I," he added interestingly, "had an understanding long ago, that we would recommend priests of this Province for the vacant Mitres of the Province."

> We also agreed, months ago, on the merits of two Tuam priests, namely Rev. Mr. O'Rourke of Maynooth & Rev. P. Duggan, P.P. near Tuam. The former we mentioned for Clonfert and I believe Dr. McE. named also with him the Rev. P. Duggan. I think myself that Fr. Duggan w^d better suit Achonry than Fr. O'Rourke. These two men are I believe the best of the Province for the two dioceses in question, and the two, outside the Election Lists, who will be received with least repugnance by the Clergy, and the Bishops concerned.

"I wish," he confessed in concluding, "the appointments were made and the new Bishops at their work. There is sad need of government in the three dioceses for which I am concerned in this Province." Cullen replied two days later. "If your Lordship and Dr. McEvilly," he assured Gillooly on November 25, "recommend R.P. Duggan, there will be no opposition to his appointment" (C). "You might add another name," he further advised Gillooly shrewdly, "so as to appear to leave some room for choice to the Propaganda. If you can get Dr. Durcan to agree with you so much the better—but it would create a difficulty were he to oppose."

MacEvilly, meanwhile, whom Cullen had also written, had replied the day before. "I deferred acknowledging your Eminence's kind letter," he explained on November 24, "until I first heard from Dr. Gillooly with whom I was anxious to act in concert. He requested of me to draw up a short document if I concurred with him as to the person he recommended & after signing it myself to forward it to Rome without delay. I did so this morning" (C). "The Priest he fixed upon," MacEvilly reported, "is the Rev. P. Duggan P.P. near Tuam. I know of no one whom I consider, everything considered, so fit as Fr. Duggan. He is a very learned, zealous Priest, very ready with pen & speech, yet very prudent. I believe he would

28. Gillooly Papers (G), Archives of the Diocese of Elphin, Sligo, Ireland.

be a very great acquisition to the Episcopal body in this country." "For years," MacEvilly assured Cullen further, "he has received very extraordinary treatment at the hands of Dr. MacHale without certainly any fault on his part, save that he did not think fit to pay court to Rev. Peter Conway, Lavelle & Co. While Dr. MacHale could say nothing against him, I am sure he would not vote for him." In the document, or report, drafted by MacEvilly and forwarded to Gillooly, he was very laudatory with regard to Duggan.[29] MacEvilly described him as a learned priest, whose way of life and character were sound, prudent in his actions, zealous for souls, and talented besides. In sending off the report, however, under both of their signatures, Gillooly took Cullen's advice to add another name for the consideration of Propaganda. He recommended, in a postscript, Francis MacCormack, a curate in the parish of Westport in the diocese of Tuam, praising him for both his character and ability but adding that perhaps he was not yet quite ripe enough for the episcopal office.

Though MacEvilly and Gillooly's joint recommendation of Duggan most likely arrived in Rome in early December, and Propaganda, therefore, had all the information it needed to make its own recommendation about the five episcopal appointments pending in Ireland to the pope for his authoritative approval, the fact that the papal government had been deprived finally of the remainder of its temporal power, when Rome was taken by the armies of the Kingdom of Italy on September 20, had materially disrupted the ordinary work of the cardinals of the Curia. The *Ponenza* for the presentation of the Irish appointments was not set in type finally until after Christmas, and the cardinals of Propaganda were not able to meet in a general congregation to discuss it until February 10, 1871. When they did meet, however, they recommended that Patrick Duggan be appointed as coadjutor to the bishop of Achonry, but they advised that before his promotion be made final both Cullen and MacHale should be consulted as to the appropriateness of his appointment.[30] In the case of the coadjutor to the bishop of Killala, the cardinals recommended that the appointment should be postponed until further information could be received about the fitness of the second on the list, Hugh Conway. For the vacancy to Raphoe, they recommended the appointment of James MacDevitt, the second on the list and the unanimous choice in the report of the Armagh prelates. In regard to the Clonfert vacancy, they recommended

29. Ibid., fols. 107–8. This letter is undated, but it was undoubtedly finally forwarded to Rome on November 26 or 27, 1870.
30. Ibid., fol. 88.

Hugh O'Rourke, the Maynooth professor, who had been suggested by Gillooly and MacEvilly at the prompting of Cullen. For Ardagh, the cardinals recommended George Conroy, who had received only two votes and was virtually ignored in the clergy's commendation of their *terna,* and in the bishop's report, but who was both a protégé and a favorite of Cullen. The recommendations of the cardinals were then submitted to the pope two days later, on February 12, when they were authoritatively approved by him in an audience with the secretary of Propaganda, Giovanni Simeoni.[31]

To all appearances, the recommendations of the cardinals of Propaganda had resulted in a clean sweep in the Irish Church for Cullen and his friends. Both Conroy and O'Rourke had been his personal nominees, and MacDevitt was certainly acceptable to him, even if he did not inspire enthusiasm. The postponement, moreover, of the appointments of the two coadjutors to Killala and Achonry, though somewhat irksome in terms of the delay, in the last analysis, actually had been referred to him for his considered opinion of the fitness of Conway and Duggan, and his endorsement would undoubtedly prove to be determinant. The real surprise of the *Ponenza,* however, and the one that must have proved most personally gratifying to Cullen, was the promotion of Conroy to Ardagh. Given the negative, though muted, position taken by the Ardagh clergy and the Armagh bishops, and the pronounced tendency in more recent years of the cardinals of Propaganda to place the greatest weight on the report of the bishops of the province in the making of Irish episcopal appointments, the promotion of Conroy calls for further comment. In drawing up the portion of the *Ponenza* called the *ristretto,* or synopsis of the case, which served as a brief for the cardinals, the secretary of Propaganda gave little indication of the disinterestedness and reserve that was usually exhibited by the secretary in such matters. His presentation was, in fact, an *ex parte* statement, and it undoubtedly had the approval of his superior, the cardinal prefect.

Toward the end of his presentation, after noting that the Armagh prelates had in their report rejected all four candidates on the *terna,* Simeoni admitted that perhaps a new *terna* might be necessary.[32] "At the end of the letter of the Bishops, however," he quickly added, "three other names are to be read, of which perhaps the Sacred Congregation will be able to avail itself for the election of which it is a question of." "Now," Simeoni then observed, referring to the Ardagh parish priest, Richard Slevin, who had received two votes, "though we don't have news of the

---

31. Ibid.
32. Ibid., fol. 85. How much this presentation, as well as a considerable number of others, owed to Simeoni's subordinate, Achilles Rinaldini, the *minutante* for British and Irish affairs at Propaganda, is very difficult to assess. Rinaldini probably drafted most of the *ristretti* concerning Ireland during this period, but certainly the responsibility for the final version was Simeoni's.

first of the three said ecclesiastics, the other two are well known in Propaganda by
having made their studies there, Conroy at the Urban College and Monsignor
Moran as a student of the Irish College. Both have left excellent records in every
respect, and the confidence that Cardinal Cullen has reposed in them fully confirms the judgement that was formed of both during their education."

> In regard to Conroy your Eminences will be pleased to recall the *Ponenza* of
> last year, in which the election of the archbishop of Armagh was dealt with,
> where not only the good qualities of Conroy will be found, but the sentiment
> of Cardinal Cullen, which would have suitably allowed him to be appointed
> primate of all Ireland, by promoting him to the see of Armagh. Now if it is
> recollected that Father George Conroy belongs to that province and is pro-
> vided with qualities so valuable to have him thought fit to hold the first place
> in the Irish episcopate, it would perhaps happen that your Eminences might
> wish to profit by him for the see of Ardagh, especially given the report of the
> bishops on the subjects commended by the clergy.

"As much could be said," Simeoni noted further, "in favor of Monsignor Moran,
but it is known in Propaganda that Cardinal Cullen, who is his uncle, has the
greatest affection for him, and that he would be very sorry to be deprived of him."
"Besides," he concluded, and most interestingly, "there is some thought that this
subject would be one day thought of for some much more important see than that
of Ardagh."

What was made very apparent in Simeoni's presentation is that the authorities at
Propaganda were determined to compliment Cullen by having Conroy appointed
to Ardagh. The reason they chose to do so, of course, was that Cullen had been
sorely disappointed the previous March when McGettigan had been appointed to
Armagh instead of Conroy. At that time, Barnabò had given Cullen to understand
that Conroy's appointment was virtually certain. The cardinals of Propaganda,
however, had not corresponded to the prediction of the cardinal prefect, and
Cullen was obliged to make a virtue of necessity. By his assurance to Cullen,
however, Barnabò had created a future obligation for himself in regard to Conroy.
For more than twenty years, Cullen had been looked upon as a protégé of Barnabò's, and, given the protocol of Roman ecclesiastical politics, the patron or
mentor was obliged to compensate his adherents for their inevitable disappointments. Barnabò's relationship to Cullen was well illustrated by a remark made by
Cullen in a letter to Conroy shortly after he had made his first great speech, on
May 19, in the Council criticizing the positions taken by Cardinals Schwarzenberg
and Rauscher. "Cardinal Barnabò," Cullen had observed to Conroy on May 21,
"told me to-day that whilst I was lecturing Schwarzenberg the other day, he was
near him, and that when I made a hard hit, he used to come round, take off his cap
and make a bow to his Eminence" (C). Cullen, then, understood that Roman
favor and time were on Conroy's side and that indeed, as Simeoni pointed out in

his *ristretto,* they were on Moran's as well. In all of his correspondence during this period, therefore, Cullen kept a very low profile in regard to Conroy, not mentioning him at all, in fact, after expressing his initial surprise in his report of the Ardagh voting to Kirby. He had also, it appears, prudently advised Conroy to do the same.[33] In the last analysis, therefore, the only way the Armagh prelates could have prevented Conroy's appointment would have been, if they had been able, to report favorably on one of the other candidates on the *terna.* Because they could not in good conscience do so, Conroy's appointment, once he received a vote, may be said to have been inevitable.

At their general congregation on February 10, the cardinals, besides making recommendations for the provisions to five Irish sees, had to examine another important matter. They had to consider what was to be done about the proposal made by the bishop of Galway the previous July to modify the procedure laid down in the Roman decree of 1829 for the appointment of Irish bishops. Mac-Evilly, it will be recalled, had recommended in his own name and that of a number of his episcopal colleagues that the procedure for the bishops of the province to report on the clergy's commendation of the *terna* be changed and that the bishops be allowed to report individually to the Propaganda rather than collectively. The proposed modification was not, in fact, entirely new; it had been suggested in 1861 by the bishop of Kerry, David Moriarty, when it was then a question of appointing a coadjutor to the bishop of Limerick.[34] At that time the cardinals of Propaganda had instructed the cardinal prefect to write to both Cullen and the then archbishop of Armagh, Joseph Dixon, for their opinions of the proposed change. Cullen and Dixon had both approved of the proposed modification but offered a number of suggestions to improve its efficiency. After further consideration, however, the cardinals decided against any change in the procedure, except to prescribe that a ten-day interval must be allowed to elapse between the meeting of the clergy to commend a *terna* and the bishops to report the names. Thus, the matter had stood for nearly ten years when MacEvilly again raised the question. When the cardinals met, therefore, on February 10, they decided to postpone any decision about modifying the procedure until they had more information on the matter.[35] They also resolved that a *voto,* or expert opinion, be prepared for their consideration by an appropriate consultor to the Propaganda.

Shortly after the pope approved the recommendations of the cardinals, on February 12, Barnabò began to make the necessary arrangements to implement the decisions. Writing to Cullen and MacHale about the provisional appointment of Duggan as coadjutor to the bishop of Achonry, Barnabò asked them their

33. K, Conroy to Kirby, March 21, 1871.

34. Emmet Larkin, *The Consolidation of the Roman Catholic Church in Ireland, 1860–1870* (Chapel Hill, 1987), pp. 203–6.

35. A, vol. 237, fol. 88.

opinions of the merits of the candidate and the appropriateness of his appointment. Their replies indicated that they both had some reservations about the
appointment.[36] The difficulty as far as Cullen was concerned was that Duggan
would not be acceptable to Durcan. MacHale, however, raised more serious questions about Duggan. Though he was, MacHale informed Barnabò on March 6, a
most commendable priest and nothing unworthy could be said about his life or
morals, he was in the habit of wandering too freely outside the limits of his parish,
and, when this defect was brought to his attention, he was unable to offer an
explanation for it.[37] Moreover, MacHale added, an uncle of Duggan's, who had
also served as the parish priest of Cummer, had been mentally ill for many years
before he died finally in a mental institution. Some sign of this infirmity, MacHale
pointed out, could be observed in Duggan, and, for that reason, the correction of
his tendency to wander should be diligently attended to, lest the illness, which was
now only latent, be given an opportunity to manifest itself more fully.

Barnabò then wrote Cullen, reporting what MacHale had said about there
being insanity in Duggan's immediate family, for when Cullen met MacEvilly in
Longford, on April 11, on the occasion of Conroy's consecration as bishop of
Ardagh, he asked him to put his views in writing in order that he might write
Barnabò explaining the situation. The visitation of a number of his outlying
parishes, however, caused some delay. Nevertheless, when MacEvilly wrote Cullen
on Low Sunday, April 16, he began by reminding Cullen that he (i.e., MacEvilly)
and Gillooly had recommended both Duggan and Francis MacCormack for Achonry the previous November. "Rev. Mr. Duggan's uncle," he added, coming immediately to the point, "who preceded him in the Parish of Cummer died in Dr. Lynch's
Asylum at Drumcondra. It must be to this circumstance allusion was made. If this
circumstance should weigh with your Eminence, there can be no doubt but the
other, Rev. F. MacCormack would be [a] most zealous, learned, holy Bishop" (C).
"He is," MacEvilly pointed out, "about 37 years of age, and has plenty of experience." "Father MacCormack is a Mayo man himself & knows it well," he then
assured Cullen, referring to the fact that the diocese of Achonry was located in
county Mayo. "Somehow or other he has not been in favor with Dr. MacHale. He
has always been too conscientious & high minded a Priest to join in every insane
cry against Bishops and Archbishops, & still higher—who may not chance to
please Dr. MacHale." MacEvilly then took the opportunity to remind Cullen of
their candidate, Hugh Conway, for the pending appointment to Killala. "I hear
Dr. Feeny," he reported, referring to the bishop of Killala, "is favorable to him. But
a certain clique in that Diocese, who are anxious for Dr. MacHale of Paris, would

36. Ibid., fol. 424, "Appendice alla Ponenza di Gennaio, 1871 sulla elezione dei Vescovi
Coadiutori per le Diocesi de Achonry e Killala, Agosto, 1871" (fols. 422–30).
37. Ibid., fol. 424.

leave nothing undone to blacken his reputation, which, I believe, to be beyond reproach." "He is," he further assured Cullen, "the very stamp of a man whom they dread, firm & prudent, who knows them well. That Diocese needs very much a zealous Bishop, who would give the example of labour to the Priest, and in this quality I know Dr. Thos. MacHale to be utterly deficient."

Soon after Barnabò wrote Cullen and MacHale about Achonry, he forwarded the briefs authorizing the consecration of the three new bishops provided by the pope for Raphoe, Ardagh, and Clonfert. When the briefs arrived in Ireland in late March, however, the bishop-elect of Clonfert began to express serious scruples because of the poor state of his health about accepting his provision. "Dr. O'Rourke," Cullen informed Kirby on April 18, "does not wish to go to Clonfert— as he is very nervous" (K). "Dr. Corrigan," he added, referring to a leading Catholic physician in Dublin, "thinks the change wd do him good. I have written to Card. Barnabò yesterday. Father O'Rourke got the opinion of other doctors stating that he w^d not be able to discharge the duties of the episcopacy." When MacEvilly wrote Kirby some three weeks later, however, he was more hopeful about O'Rourke accepting his provision. "I believe," MacEvilly explained on May 9, "he forwarded a strong statement as to the state of his health to the Holy See. He is, however, much improved, and prepared to proceed to his consecration, if the H. Father should so will it. He thought it right, however, to state to the Holy See how he felt as to health" (K). "He would be," MacEvilly further assured Kirby, "a Bishop of the *right stamp*, & of most *correct* ideas, both in regard to Education & all that the Holy See takes an interest in, without which I never like to see anyone made a Bishop in our country. For one Bishop entertaining wrong notions on these heads would be enough to neutralize the exertions of the rest."

MacEvilly then went on to explain to Kirby that when he and Gillooly had been in Dublin on the previous Sunday, May 7, to assist at the dedication of the new Vincentian Church of St. Peter's at Phibsboro, they had asked Cullen to write to Propaganda recommending MacCormack instead of Duggan as coadjutor for Achonry, and he had promised to do so. "We are in hopes," MacEvilly added, "that the Rev. Hugh Conway who we recommended will be appointed for Killala. It is reported that some of the Killala priests made some charges against him, but nothing could be more calumnious. There [are] three or four priests of that name in Killala and some of them not over commendable, but of Father Hugh Conway, P.P. Skreen, nothing can be said that is not deserving of commendation." "His parish," MacEvilly pointed out, "adjoins Sligo, and Dr. Gillooly knows him intimately and indeed so do I. It would [be] bad mischief if others were appointed; it would [be] construed in a very wrong sense; and would [be] great encouragement to some who already are the cause of dissension amongst us. It would be an unhappy day for our poor suffering Church if the *seeds* of such disunion were perpetuated."

In Gillooly and MacEvilly's conversation with Cullen in Dublin on May 7, the question also was raised apparently of what should be done if O'Rourke eventually declined his provision for Clonfert. In that event, they suggested to Cullen, Duggan should be appointed to Clonfert, and Cullen agreed to write Barnabò to that effect. Apparently, the point they made to Cullen was that the arrangement was more suitable because MacCormack was a Mayo man and Duggan a Galway man and because the diocese of Clonfert was entirely in the county of Galway, which would make the arrangement less repugnant to the clergy of both Clonfert and Achonry than the appointment of complete strangers. Whether Cullen did write about Duggan and MacCormack being appointed to Clonfert and Achonry respectively is difficult to determine because the letter he wrote to Barnabò on May 12 was not quoted in full in the *Ponenza*. He did, however, assure Barnabò in that letter that Gillooly and MacEvilly had declared the calumny on the good name of Conway unfounded and had asserted that he was very worthy of being promoted to Killala. "There were some other priests," Cullen explained to Barnabò, "of the same name, who have not conducted themselves well, and in speaking of Hugh Conway, it is probable that the defects of some others have been attributed to him."[38]

In any case, O'Rourke finally decided not to accept the dignity of a mitre, and he was reported by Cullen to Kirby on June 9 as being "now so excited that he thinks the ceremony of consecration would kill him" (K). In regard to promoting Duggan to Clonfert, Cullen explained to Kirby that his own vicar general and the parish priest of Kingstown, Edward McCabe, knew him well and said that he was a very good man. When MacEvilly also wrote to Kirby, two days later on June 11, he reviewed for him the whole situation regarding the three pending appointments, in the light of O'Rourke's refusal (K). In the course of his long letter, he referred to MacHale's charge that Duggan had exhibited indications of being somewhat odd in his behavior and pointed out that this perhaps was not to be wondered at because Duggan had "suffered much from Dr. MacHale in sending him in succession 5 or 6 Coadjutors [i.e., curates] ebriosos & perditis moribus [drunkards and abandoned characters] as wd set any man living mad." In his final summing up for Kirby, MacEvilly then reiterated the theme of the great need for episcopal unity in the Irish Church at that critical moment. "Nothing can be conceived," he assured Kirby, "more important now a days particularly for our poor Irish Church than the appointment of Bishops of whom one is morally sure. One Bishop of Government & Gallican tendencies wd. do a world of mischief to the entire Irish Church—as the Government & others wd. lay hold of such to thwart the rest in Educational and other National religious Questions."

When the news of O'Rourke's having declined the episcopal dignity became

---

38. Ibid., fol. 425.

more widely known, the rumors about the appointment to Clonfert began to become more prevalent. Indeed, three senior parish priests of that diocese, headed by Matthew Walsh, who had been returned as *dignus* on the *terna,* wrote the pope on July 1, explaining that their diocese had now been widowed for more than a year. They assured the pope that William Derry, the *dignissimus* on their *terna,* had received the great majority of the votes not merely because he was the late bishop's brother but rather because he was a good priest who had in good and bad times labored with great profit in the vineyard of the Lord for more than twenty-five years, and they begged the pope, now that O'Rourke had retired because of illness, to have their recommendation reviewed so that their vacant see might soon be provided for.[39] Apparently rumors continued to circulate about Clonfert, and finally, on July 25, the vicar capitular, Thomas Burke, who was responsible for the administration of the diocese during the long interregnum and who had been returned as *dignior* on the *terna,* decided that O'Rourke's refusal made it incumbent on him to write to Cullen. "I may take leave to assure your Eminence," Burke explained on July 25, "that the Priests of the Diocese were prepared to receive with hearty welcome any appointment of the Holy Father's. It was with a feeling akin to dismay they found that physical incapacity rendered the appointment unsuitable" (C).

"Believing then that the selection of Dr. O'Rorke [*sic*] has thrown over the names sent forward by the Priests on the occasion of the election," he then suggested, "I humbly take leave to commend to your Eminence, on behalf of the Priests of the Diocese, the name of an Ecclesiastic who, in the first place is fitted by his powers of intellect and fund of requirements, as well as by his untiring energy and zeal in the interests of Religion to take a seat on the Episcopal Bench; and who in the second place from his perfect Knowlege [*sic*] of the Irish language, would be specially suited to this Diocese in every part of which that language is spoken. If your Eminence will add to these qualities that he is well known to, and appreciated by, the Priests of the Diocese I think I have given solid reasons for presuming to interfere in this matter." "The Ecclesiastic to whom I refer," Burke said, finally coming to the point, after his long peroration, "is the very Rev. Ulick J. Bourke, the President of St. Jarlath's College in Tuam. His publications of an 'Irish Grammar' and 'Easy lessons in Irish' mark him out as a man of industry; and having no reason save the interests of Religion in the Diocese to influence me I beg to submit his name to your Eminence as one not unworthy to be recommended as a fitting successor to our late lamented Prelate."

Shortly after Cullen received this letter, he wrote MacEvilly advising him that he and Gillooly should write to Propaganda again in regard to Clonfert because their opponents were obviously becoming more active. He also asked MacEvilly

39. Ibid., fols. 428–29.

his opinion of Ulick Bourke. "I have written to Dr. Gillooly *confidentially*," MacEvilly assured Cullen in a letter marked "private" on August 1, "on the subject of your Eminence's letter. I suggested to him that each of us would write a separate letter to the H. See strongly urging the appointment of Father Duggan, saying also that one wrote with the concurrence of the other. I also suggested that in case the appointment of Father Duggan would not please that they would appoint Father Francis MacCormack of Westport. Before writing I will wait till I hear from Dr. Gillooly" (C). "The appointment of Father U. Burke [*sic*]," MacEvilly added, "would in my mind, be most disastrous. It is not considered that he has much sense and he is the most prominent representative & a very decided advocate of a system which if perpetuated would be a source of great evil to the Irish Church. He would be in fact, in every respect, Dr. MacHale reproduced. He is a very near relative of Dr. MacHale, and his appointment would be regarded as an approval at Rome of the course pursued by Dr. MacHale." "I am convinced," he then noted further, "from several vague rumours which I hear from time to time that there is something underhand going on. I heard the other day that Dr. Durcan is quite confident that he will get no coadjutor, that Dr. MacHale & the Primate had written to Rome to assure them he dont want one. I told the party that I did not believe a word of it so far as the Primate is concerned, but he persisted in his assertion. Killala and Achonry both sadly want some one to look after them, Killala in particular."

That same day, Gillooly wrote two long letters in French, one to the cardinal prefect and the other to the secretary of Propaganda, emphasizing the themes outlined by MacEvilly in his letter to Cullen. "The long delay at Propaganda, in appointing some bishops in this province of Tuam, forces me to remind you once again of the pressing needs of the three dioceses of which it is a question," Gillooly bluntly pointed out to Barnabò on August 1. "In the diocese of Clonfert, where the bishop has been dead for fifteen months, the total absence of nearly all government is sadly felt. In the dioceses of Achonry and of Killala the disorders are even greater; and in all three the difficulties for the future bishops grow day by day. The divisions and the intrigues are becoming more and more public: they are encouraged by the delays you take and by the uncertainty that is attributed to your decision."[40] "The priests that we have recommended, the bishop of Galway and I," Gillooly continued stiffly, "are by all reports the most worthy in the province. There is no longer a question of Father O'Rourke, professor at Maynooth, whose health has greatly failed since the time we recommended him. Fathers Duggan, Conway, and MacCormack whom we have lately recommended respectively for the dioceses of Clonfert, Killala and Achonry, are zealous, edifying, learned priests, devoted to the Holy See, and of one mind with the body of our bishops." "If our

---

40. Ibid., fol. 429.

venerable metropolitan, Monsignor MacHale," Gillooly asserted, "opposes their nomination, it is because they are *ultramontanes;* and that they would not join him in opposing our worthy Cardinal." "Two among them," he noted, referring to Duggan and MacCormack, "are his diocesans, but he would wish, it seems, to substitute two others for them, on whom he would be always able to count as *aides de camp.* To yield to his designs would be to perpetuate discord amongst us—and weaken also for a long time the authority of the Holy See." "I beg your Eminence then," Gillooly concluded, "to put an end to the evils that I have the honor of indicating to you and not to allow an opposition that, since the death of the bishop of Clonfert, is limited to our metropolitan alone, to be strengthened and perpetuated by the nomination of his adherents. You may be assured that the information that we have tendered *for* and *against* the priests mentioned in our letters is founded in the truth." Gillooly's letter to the secretary of Propaganda was in the same vein as that to the cardinal and was just as plain spoken and to the point.[41]

Gillooly then informed MacEvilly that he had written to Propaganda, and the latter immediately followed suit in a letter dated August 4.[42] "I also wrote at once in his name & my own stating that," MacEvilly assured Cullen on August 6, "'a rumour reached me to the effect that some Ecclesiastics meant to recommend to the H. See at the suggestion of a certain Prelate, for the vacant See of Clonfert, one or two Priests of whom it was notorious that they were infected with Fenianism or Liberalism, & one of whom was well known to [be] the party by whom a Paper, offensive to the H. See, termed the *Connaught Patriot*—now extinct—was conducted for years at Tuam.' (It is well known that it was Fr. U. B. that corrected the Patriot for Press for a number of years.) I then remarked upon the dreadful evil to religion which would result from the appointment of such persons to Episcopal sees" (C). "I did not mention," he then reported, "the name of the Prelate, at whose suggestion, certain Ecclesiastics were recommending objectionable Priests for the See of Clonfert, nor the Priests to whom rumour pointed as recommended. I chiefly referred to Fr. U. Burke [*sic*]." "If they appoint him," MacEvilly further explained, "they will surely have Dr. MacHale's policy perpetuated against us. By refering [*sic*] to the fact of such a rumour being in existence, I have sufficiently put the Roman authorities on their guard. I could not go further."

A month later, on September 5, the cardinals of Propaganda finally met in general congregation to consider the three appointments to be made in the province of Tuam. They decided, in effect, to recommend Duggan, MacCormack, and Conway for Clonfert, Achonry, and Killala, respectively. They also added the proviso in the latter two appointments that the two bishops should be consulted

41. Ibid., fols. 429–30.
42. Ibid., fol. 430.

before being provided with coadjutors by the pope and that Cullen also should be consulted in the matter. The pope then approved the cardinals' recommendations of September 10. In implementing these decisions, however, Barnabò not only wrote to Cullen, but he also decided to authorize MacEvilly to be the bearer of the pope's good tidings, and he enclosed in his letter to MacEvilly the letters to the two bishops informing them of the imminent assignment of their coadjutors. When Cullen received Barnabò's letter informing him of what had been done, he immediately wrote to MacEvilly that he thought the letters to the two bishops ought to be delivered personally by him. "I agree with your Eminence," MacEvilly replied on September 22, "it would be a great deal better, if the old Bishops were spoken to & the letters handed to them, *honoris specie* [for the sake of appearances]." MacEvilly then proposed that Gillooly, who knew the bishop of Achonry better than he, should visit Durcan and secure his authorization to write in his behalf to Rome that he was agreeable to accepting MacCormack as his coadjutor and that he would himself visit the bishop of Killala to receive his consent. The crucial thing, MacEvilly pointed out shrewdly, was to secure Durcan's authorization before he had time to consult with MacHale.

Cullen apparently wrote MacEvilly by return of post, advising him that he did not believe it would be wise to delegate his responsibility on the Achonry matter to Gillooly, especially as the cardinal prefect had sent both letters to MacEvilly. MacEvilly took Cullen's advice and visited both Durcan and Feeny the following week. On September 29, he finally reported to Cullen from Westport that his mission to both bishops had been successful (C). Though Durcan had been somewhat reluctant at first, MacEvilly explained, he had finally persuaded Durcan to allow him to write a letter to Barnabò in Durcan's name agreeing to accept MacCormack as his coadjutor, and Durcan had signed the letter and put his seal to it. Feeny promised to write Propaganda at once, but in the meantime he had authorized MacEvilly to intimate to Barnabò that Conway's appointment would be pleasing to him. "I saw most clearly," MacEvilly assured Cullen, "the wisdom of your Eminence's suggestion about visiting the old Bishops, as I fear Dr. Durcan would not understand the affair & would refer to Dr. MacHale, and Dr. Feeny would act rather slowly. Indeed, coadjutors are not sent to both places a day too soon." "I impressed on both Bishops," he added in a postscript, "the importance of secrecy until the matter is *finally* settled." Three weeks later, on November 21, the pope finally provided MacCormack and Conway as coadjutors with the right of succession to the bishops of Achonry and Killala.

The epilogue to this long and complicated story about the three episcopal appointments in the province of Tuam is provided by a short account of Mac-Hale's reaction when he received the briefs authorizing MacCormack's and Conway's consecration. "Dr. MacHale," MacEvilly informed Cullen on December 13, "has refused to consecrate Drs. Duggan & Conway. He told Dr. Duggan he would *never* cooperate in a violation of the Laws of the Irish Church" (C). "No doubt," MacEvilly observed somewhat sardonically, "it was the Pope violated them. If his nephew were appointed, we wd hear little about the violation of the Laws of the Irish Church or any other Church." "Dr. Duggan," he further reported, "found him [in] a rage, & his whole ire fell on the devoted head of Dr. MacCormack. He got the Briefs for Drs. MacCormack & Conway. But he did not condescend to inform Dr. MacCormack himself of the fact, but only informed him of it thro one of the Priests with whom Dr. MacCormack lives in Westport. Dr. MacCormack employed the same medium of communicn to request of him to send the Brief by post. He told Dr. Duggan & Dr. Conway he would not consecrate either them or Dr. MacCormack." "The account of his interview with Dr. Duggan," MacEvilly added, "is really fearful. He threatened to raise a storm. But, I suspect, he can only raise the wind. He promises Dr. MacCormack a warm reception in Achonry." "But," he concluded, "there as everywhere else his power is gone."

MacHale's power in ecclesiastical matters was indeed gone, but it had been on the wane since the middle of the 1850s, when it then had been broken for good by Cullen; the final combined assault during 1870–71 by his suffragans, Cullen, and Rome was merely its *coup de grâce.* MacHale, however, was right that the liquidation of his power had been the result of an extraordinary resort to the papal dispensing power. He was wrong, however, about there having been a violation of what he was fond of calling "the constitution," or Laws of the Irish Church, because that dispensing power was an integral part of the so-called constitution. What made the dispensing power subject to law, of course, was that it was only exercised on the basis of cause, and anyone who reviewed MacHale's relationship with Rome over the previous thirty years would understand that he had given Pius IX and his predecessor considerable reason to believe that they had sufficient cause to be disturbed about his conduct. Still, the extraordinary use of the papal dispensing power in regard to the procedure governing the appointments to Irish sees—in the cases of Clonfert, Achonry, and Killala—though certainly legitimate, was most unusual, and the fact that MacEvilly, Gillooly, and several of their colleagues attempted to have that dispensation incorporated as a permanent part of the procedure also indicated a certain amount of confusion on their part about the appropriate relationship of means to ends.

When the cardinals of Propaganda had met on September 5, they were obliged to consider again the proposal asking whether there should be a modification in the way the bishops reported on the commendation of the clergy in Ireland. At their February 10 congregation on Irish business, it will be recalled, they had postponed that decision and asked that an expert opinion, *voto,* be prepared by an appropriate consultant to Propaganda. In preparing the usual *ristretto,* which made up the first portion of the *Ponenza,* for the cardinals, the secretary of Propaganda explained that before literally executing the decision to secure a *voto,* it was believed expedient to write Cullen in regard to the proposed change. "Being obliged in fact," Simeoni added, "to invite one of the consultors of the Sacred Congregation to compile a *voto* on the subject, it was thought that his task would be facilitated by the reply received from Cardinal Cullen."[43] Accordingly, Barnabò wrote Cullen, and he responded on May 12. After reviewing the appointments pending in the province of Tuam, he offered his considered opinion on the proposal to modify the procedure. "It seems that in the small dioceses," he explained, "where there are fifteen or sixteen parish priests it is very difficult to find three priests worthy of the episcopate, and besides the voting parish priests never go outside the confines of their dioceses to find a worthy candidate. In the larger dioceses where the priests are more numerous, the same difficulty does not arise, and then as the bishops are obliged in every case to indicate the true state of things to the Holy See, it is not very easy to promote worthy persons."[44] "It seems to me, therefore," Cullen observed, "it is not expedient for the present to change anything, because if the Holy See exercises the power that it has, it will always be able to find, either in the proposed *terna,* or outside of it some priest worthy of being bishop." "In truth," Cullen concluded, "there is not great reason to complain of the choices made of bishops within the period since the introduction of the present system in 1829 until today."

Immediately after quoting the whole of the above in his *ristretto,* Simeoni noted that MacHale "had on July 9 also written in an analogous sense."[45] That prelate insisted in fact, Simeoni added, that the appointment of the bishop of Clonfert, and the delay occasioned in regard to it by "the letters written privately by some of his suffragans (the bishops of Elphin and Galway), revealed that grave disadvantages occurred when it was permitted to write particularly to the Holy See on the qualities of the priests proposed for the episcopacy." "Still," Simeoni pointed out, "it ought not to remain unobserved that other disadvantages, which were feared, particularly on the part of the same archbishop of Tuam (believed [to be] deferential towards his nephew, or about ecclesiastics of views similar to his own), gave occasion to the above expressed request of the bishops of Galway and of Elphin." "In any case," Simeoni concluded, "it seemed opportune to beg your Eminences to decide whether the special *Ponenza* prescribed in the general congregation of February 10 last ought to be proceeded with before writing to a consultor to meet the case, or whether to take rather the opinion of Cardinal Cullen, leaving things as they are found established in the Decree of 1829 for the election of Irish bishops." The cardinals decided, in fact, that for the present they would change nothing and allowed the whole question to drop. The pope approved their recom-

43. Ibid., fol. 423.
44. Ibid.
45. Ibid.

mendation on September 10, as well as those regarding the appointments in the province of Tuam.

The great surprise in all of this, of course, was not that the cardinals had decided to allow the whole matter to drop, for they had also come to essentially the same conclusion some ten years before when the question was first raised, but it was rather that Cullen had changed his mind over that same period. What the cardinals obviously realized was that the pope had dispensed with the procedure for cause, namely, the final containment of MacHale's ecclesiastical power and influence in the Irish Church in general and in the province of Tuam in particular. For twenty years, the Roman authorities had been attempting to break up Mac-Hale's episcopal power base in the Irish Church. Slowly but surely, with Cullen as their chief instrument, they had reduced that base, until only the province of Tuam remained. In the beginning, MacHale had had six suffragan bishops—Galway, Elphin, Clonfert, Achonry, Killala, and Kilmacduagh. In the 1850s Cullen had managed to cultivate two supporters, in Galway and Elphin, and in 1866 he had succeeded also in having the diocese of Kilmacduagh, upon the retirement of that bishop, put under the administration of the bishop of Galway. Still, in provincial matters, MacHale could generally muster the three other bishops to contain MacEvilly and Gillooly, and hence both were repugnant to any form of episcopal meeting in their province, especially to those concerning the appointment of bishops.

When, indeed, the incapacity of the bishops of Achonry and Killala was made apparent by their inability to attend the first Vatican Council and the bishop of Clonfert died unexpectedly at the end of June, the opportunity to eliminate Mac-Hale's ecclesiastical power and influence in his own province once and for all was too good an opportunity to be missed by his opponents. Once that had been achieved, however, and this was the real measure of Cullen's astuteness, the procedure for appointing Irish bishops could only work in favor of those who had the majority among the bishops in the province. Moreover, if there had been a lesson in the making of Irish episcopal appointments at Rome during the previous ten years, it was that the bishops' report had come to be the crucial element in that procedure. Now that his friends were in the majority in the province of Tuam, therefore, changing the system in the way suggested by MacEvilly and Gillooly would only work to the disadvantage of the majority because it would open up to the minority channels of communication and power that they would not ordinarily have access to under the established procedure. The proof positive of all this, ironically enough, was MacEvilly and Gillooly's success as a minority in liquidating the power base of the majority by reporting separately rather than collectively to Rome. Little wonder that Cullen in retrospect believed that the system had worked rather well, and no innovation was therefore necessary. Finally, if the cardinals of Propaganda and Cullen had any doubts about the wisdom of not changing the procedure in Irish episcopal appointments, the incredible complications over the previous eighteen months in regard to the three appointments in the province of Tuam certainly must have made them realize that the means employed from the procedural point of view could only be justified by the end achieved.

In the meantime, the coadjutor to the bishop of Killaloe in the province of Cashel, Nicholas Power, had died unexpectedly on March 20, 1871. Power had been appointed coadjutor to Michael Flannery in 1865 when it became obvious that the young and promising bishop of Killaloe would not recover from the nervous breakdown that had resulted in his voluntary retirement to the community of St. Sulpice in Paris. Because Flannery did not resign his see, however, it became necessary over his long life (he died in 1891) to appoint a series of coadjutors. Shortly after Power died, therefore, the archbishop of Cashel, Patrick Leahy, wrote Barnabò, on March 23, requesting that another coadjutor be appointed as soon as possible (L). Barnabò secured the necessary faculties from the pope to authorize Leahy to convoke the clergy of Killaloe in order to commend a *terna* to Propaganda and also to allow the archbishop to preside at the meeting, since Flannery was unable to be present.[46] On April 22, the cardinal prefect duly forwarded the necessary documents. When the clergy of the very large diocese of Killaloe met in the town of Killaloe on June 1, they cast fifty-five votes in favor of eight candidates.[47] The first on the list, Thomas MacRedmond, rector of the diocesan seminary near Ennis, received twenty-three votes, James Ryan, vicar general and parish priest of Nenagh, was second with fourteen votes, and Michael Dinan, vicar general and parish priest of Kilrush, and Father John F. Hogan, professor at the College of St. Sulpice in Paris, tied for third place with five votes each. Michael O'Hea, the bishop of Ross, and Michael Buglar, vicar general and parish priest of Birr, received three votes each, while Bartholomew Woodlock, rector of the Catholic University, and Michael Quinlivan, parish priest of Clondegan, had one vote each.

The curious thing about the commendation of the clergy, however, was that they returned only MacRedmond, Ryan, and Dinan, did not include Hogan, though he had tied for third place, and did not mention any of the other names. Even more strange was that when the bishops of the province of Cashel forwarded

46. Ibid., fol. 528, "Ristretto con Sommario sulla elezione di un Vescovo Coadiutore con futura successione a Mons. Michele Flannery Vescovo di Killaloe nella Provincia di Cashel in Irlanda, Settembre, 1871" (fols. 527–32).

47. Ibid., fol. 530.

their report, on June 19, after their meeting in Thurles, they reported on only the three names commended by the clergy, though the archbishop of Cashel had enclosed along with the report a list of all eight of the candidates and number of votes each had received.[48] The reason for Hogan's exclusion from the *terna* and the report of the Cashel bishops was not provided, nor was it even mentioned in the *ristretto* prepared by the secretary for the cardinals of Propaganda. The bishops, however, did note in their report that there had been only one scrutiny, as was prescribed in the decree of 1829 governing the procedure. By noting this they undoubtedly wanted it understood that they took the wording of the decree to mean that the clergy were obliged to return only three names and that the clergy were further privileged by the decree to discriminate between the candidates if there should be a tie for third place. By reviewing the qualifications of only the three names, the bishops were endorsing the clergy's interpretation of the decree. This was certainly a somewhat tortured interpretation of the decree, especially if viewed in light of either the imbroglio created by the elimination of Conroy, who also had tied for third place in a second scrutiny by the Armagh clergy the year before, or the more recent return of the candidates tied for third place on the *ternae* commended by the clergy of Killala, Raphoe, and Ardagh. Even more remarkable was that the secretary of Propaganda, in preparing the *ristretto* for the consideration of the cardinals, misread the enumeration of the eight candidates enclosed by the archbishop of Cashel along with the bishops' report and noted that there were "four other candidates among whom several votes were divided," when instead there were actually five other names.[49] If any of the cardinals, moreover, noticed the discrepancy in the *ristretto,* their remarks have not been recorded, and the likelihood is that in the rush of other business the lapse was simply overlooked.

The report of the bishops of the province was also somewhat curious in another way. In reviewing the qualities of all three candidates on the *terna* the bishops were very positive, but when they came to express their preference, they unanimously declared, all things considered, *omnibus pensatis,* in favor of James Ryan, the second on the list, without explaining the reason he was to be preferred to the other two, except to point out that he was the candidate most preferred by the actual bishop of Killaloe. The reason the first name on the list, Thomas MacRedmond, who had received twenty-three votes and who, by the bishops' own account, was a most distinguished and learned priest, though only thirty-six years of age, was excluded by the bishops was only made clear in a letter of Cullen's to Kirby shortly after the bishops had met. Barnabò, on receiving the commendation of the Killaloe clergy with only the three names and no account of the voting, had

48. Ibid., fol. 531.
49. Ibid., fol. 528.

written to Cullen requesting more information. Cullen wrote to Kirby on June 26, explaining the reason for MacRedmond's exclusion and asking Kirby to explain the situation to Barnabò (K). Some time later, on July 30, when Cullen was unable to procure more information, he formally wrote Barnabò. "In regard to the coadjutorship of Killaloe," he explained to Barnabò, "I have not been able to obtain further news other than that which I asked Monsignor Kirby to communicate to your Eminence."

> The first candidate, who had a great majority [correctly, plurality] of the votes of the clergy, is much praised for his personal qualities; but his family is connected to such a degree with Protestants, that it makes one fear here for his success. His mother, who is a widow, has married a Protestant soldier, or a clerk in the army, and two of his sisters have taken Protestants for husbands. His promotion in these circumstances does not appear expedient, and the archbishop of Cashel has told me that all the bishops of the province wish to exclude him. The second candidate is a man of about sixty-five years, and he has been a parish priest for a long time, but is still strong and in good health. A father of the company of St. Alphonsus, who knows him, has told me that he is a very studious man, and the archbishop of Cashel says that he is one of the best informed priests in Ireland. It seems also that he is a priest of edifying life, whence it appears that there is no reason to exclude him from the episcopacy. The archbishop of Cashel and the other bishops believe him very fit for the vacant coadjutorship. As for the third candidate, he had few votes, and the father cited above who knows him, says that he is not fit to govern a diocese.[50]

"The diocese of Killaloe," Cullen informed Barnabò in conclusion, "is very far from Dublin, and there is little communication between that clergy and ours, whereby the news I have been able to gather is very scanty." What was clear from Cullen's letter was that the bishops of the province of Cashel did not want to put their reasons for excluding MacRedmond in writing to Propaganda and preferred instead to allow Cullen to do what needed to be done. In any case, when the cardinals of Propaganda met on October 3, less than a month after they had met on the Tuam appointments, they recommended that Ryan be appointed coadjutor to the bishop of Killaloe, and on October 8 the pope authoritatively approved of the recommendation.[51]

At about the same time the previous March that the coadjutor to the bishop of Killaloe had died, the bishop of Ossory, Edward Walsh, who was over eighty years of age, suffered a stroke which left his mind in a very weakened state. In part, the reason for Walsh's affliction was that he had been having difficulties for some time with a number of his clergy, most particularly with Robert O'Keeffe, the parish priest of Callan, who was soon to become a *cause célèbre* in the Irish Church.

50. Ibid., fol. 532.
51. Ibid., fol. 529.

Nearly a month after Walsh's attack, Cullen noted briefly in a letter to Kirby that the bishop was not well. "Dr. Walsh of Kilkenny," he reported on April 18, "has got a softening of the brain and appears to have become childish. I will go down some day to see him" (K). Cullen was so busy with preparations for the pope's silver jubilee in Dublin and other diocesan business that he had little opportunity to follow up on his intention of visiting Walsh, but some two weeks later, Patrick Moran, his secretary, wrote Kirby, asking him to secure the necessary authority to do something about the situation in Ossory. "The Cardinal wrote to you some time ago," Moran reminded Kirby on May 31, "about Kilkenny [*sic*] diocese. The poor Bishop, who I believe is 82 years of age has had a deal to suffer from the doings in Callan. He is now totally unable to do business" (K). "There is," he then explained, "no authority now in the diocese to check the friends of disorder, and it is a great pity, for I believe there is not a better people in Ireland than the same good people."

> So get the authorities at once to give the Cardinal power to convene the clergy for electing a coadjutor or at least let him get power to interfere directly in Callan, to make such changes of the curates there as he may judge expedient, and to appoint *ad interim* [meanwhile] an administrator of that parish. I am sure if Father Nicholas Murphy was sent adm of that parish for a few months he would soon bring back all the people to union and peace.
> One of the delusions of the poor Bp. is that the Cardinal wants to bring away his new cathedral to Dublin. It is a great pity he is so ill, as at the present moment all his energies wd. be required to check the course of evil. No fewer than three law-suits are now pending in the public courts about the Callan business, and I fear that that is not the only source of law-suit that will soon be seen.

"Excuse the trouble that I give you," Moran begged in conclusion, "but pray them in Propaganda to allow no delay about doing something for Ossory. The people are so thoroughly good it is sad they sh be led astray. And the Cardinal is so busy I fear he may not have leisure to urge the matter as strongly as he would wish."

The Roman authorities did not respond apparently until Cullen wrote again at the end of July or early August to Barnabò, indicating that a coadjutor was necessary for Walsh. Barnabò then secured the necessary faculties from the pope for Cullen to convoke the Ossory clergy and wrote Cullen to that effect on August 19. Cullen then visited Walsh in Kilkenny, in the last week in August, to make the necessary arrangements. He reported to Barnabò on August 31 that not only had he seen the bishop, who was now in somewhat better health, but also Walsh was very pleased to be granted a coadjutor and the Ossory clergy would meet on September 19 to commend their *terna* to Rome.[52] On the appointed day, there-

---

52. S.R.C., vol. 36, fol. 965.

fore, the Ossory clergy assembled in their cathedral in Kilkenny, and, though the venerable bishop attended the meeting, the proceedings were actually presided over by Cullen.[53] Of the thirty-seven votes cast, Matthew Keefe, parish priest of Aghaboe, and Patrick Moran, Cullen's half nephew and secretary, were tied for first place with thirteen votes each, while Edward McDonald, vicar general and rector of the local diocesan seminary, received eight votes.[54] Daniel McCarthy, professor of sacred scripture and Hebrew at Maynooth, John Kelly, parish priest of Castlecomer, and Thomas Hennessy, parish priest of Inistioge, received one vote each. When Moran wrote Kirby some two weeks later, he noted that the clergy of Ossory had placed him in an anxious predicament. "What is strange," he observed, interestingly, on October 4, "I may say I never spoke a word to one of the P.P.'s of Ossory, nor had I any communication with them. The only exception was Dr. MacDonald the Vic., Gen. whom I occasionally met here. Hence they knew nothing about the person they were voting for. I hope you will put in a good word to get me out of the predicament" (K). Moran then concluded by pointing out that the bishops of the province of Dublin had met the previous week and that he trusted they had proven wiser than the priests of Ossory.

The bishops of the Dublin province, except for the bishop of Ossory, had met, in fact, on September 28, in Dublin.[55] Cullen had proposed to hold the meeting in Kilkenny in order that Walsh might attend, but the bishop had declined because of the state of his health, preferring to put his views on the *terna* in writing. At their meeting, the Dublin prelates reviewed the qualifications of the three candidates and reported that except for the bishop of Ossory they unanimously recommended Moran's appointment. They noted that he was forty-one years old, had been educated at the Irish and Urban colleges in Rome, and had taught Hebrew at the latter while serving as vice-rector of the former. For the previous six or seven years he had been Cullen's private secretary and had served at the same time as chaplain to the local prison, where he heard confessions and preached the word of God. He was also a distinguished Irish Church historian and knew Latin, Greek, Hebrew, French, German, and English. Curiously, they left out the fact that he was also fluent in Italian. In reviewing Keefe's qualifications, the bishops pointed out that though he was a good, learned, zealous, and accomplished priest, he was totally unacceptable to Walsh, who thought he was unfit to be his coadjutor. The reason that Walsh was so opposed to Keefe was that the priest had at one time been a devoted follower of the ultra-Nationalist and Tenant Right politician, Frederick Lucas, who had been an ardent advocate of the principle of "independent opposi-

---

53. A, vol. 237, fol. 541, "Ristretto con Sommario sulla scelta di un Coadiutore con carattere vescovile e diritto di successione al Vescovo di Ossory nella Provincia di Dublino, Novembre, 1871" (fols. 540–47).
54. Ibid., fol. 544.
55. Ibid., fols. 545–46.

tion" in Irish politics. Lucas had denounced Walsh for interdicting Keefe from participating in politics. Keefe had appealed his case to Rome, and, though he had lost his case there, Walsh had apparently neither forgiven nor forgotten the affront to his authority and dignity. He had transferred Keefe to another parish, and after a very long time finally promoted him to a small parish in the diocese. Given the sentiments of the bishop, therefore, the Dublin prelates explained that they did not dare suggest that Keefe be appointed his coadjutor. Finally, as far as the third name on the list, Edward McDonald, was concerned, the bishops reported that, though he was also a very distinguished priest, dean, and vicar general of the diocese, as well as rector of the diocesan seminary and the preferred candidate of the bishop, the clergy of the diocese were very jealous of him because of the many dignities and offices he held and because it was thought this was the result of his being the favorite of the bishop. In concluding, the bishops, therefore, recommended Moran again, everything considered, as the best choice. "The bishops," Cullen advised Barnabò in a letter describing the report of the prelates, written the next day, September 29, "think that it would be well to hurry the appointment of a coadjutor to put an end to any dissensions in the diocese. The bishop is over eighty years of age, and often loses his memory, whence he is unable to attend to business."[56] The cardinals of Propaganda met in general congregation on December 11 and recommended that Moran be appointed, and on December 17 the pope authoritatively approved the recommendation.[57] Kirby immediately telegraphed Cullen the good news. "I received the telegram," Cullen reported on December 21, "*affirmative et definitive.*; It came the other night at 12 o'clock, and I could not understand what it meant. However, I received your letter since, and I was glad to hear that Dr. Moran was appointed, but I am the loser by all these promotions. I have now lost Dr. Murray, Dr. Conroy, and Dr. Moran, all of whom were very faithful and useful" (K). Moran's reaction after he learned the news was less a sense of loss than of unworthiness. "I really do not know," he explained to Kirby on December 27, "what to write to you, but one thing I must say, I sincerely & heartily regret the Sac. Cong. & the Holy See have not selected for Ossory some one better suited than their present choice. I am really filled with fear when I look on my want of experience, and still more my want of zeal and every other virtue which should characterize a Bishop of God's Church" (K). By the time he had received his brief authorizing his consecration a month later, however, he was beginning to sound less introspective and more like his mentor and half uncle, the cardinal, in whose image and likeness he was very much made. "My view," he informed Kirby on January 26, "of the case is that I am, through the mercy of God, a soldier in the 'spiritual army' and when a soldier is told to occupy a post of

56. Ibid., fol. 547.
57. Ibid., fol. 543.

danger, no matter how unpleasant it may be it is his duty to obey and to encounter all the perils of that post as readily & as cheerfully as if he were allowed to remain quietly in the barracks" (K).

By December 1872, in a period of some fifteen months, the pope had provided for seven sees in a regular Irish hierarchy of twenty-seven bishops, or for more than a quarter of the whole body. No such renovation had taken place in the Irish Church in so short a period in modern times. In fact, by the end of 1872, all those Irish bishops who had been unable to attend the first Vatican Council because of age or illness had been provided with coadjutors or administrators, except the ailing bishop of Waterford and Lismore, Dominic O'Brien. In the late summer of 1872, however, O'Brien also decided to ask his metropolitan, Patrick Leahy, the archbishop of Cashel, to write to Propaganda to request that he be provided with a coadjutor with the right of succession to Waterford and Lismore. Leahy wrote to Propaganda, and the authorities referred the request, on September 22, to the pope.[58] He approved, and the rescript containing the necessary faculties was forwarded to Leahy on September 27, authorizing him to convene the clergy of Waterford and prescribing that he and O'Brien preside jointly at the meeting. The clergy duly assembled in their cathedral in Waterford on November 13, and they commended three names to Rome.[59] Of the thirty-four votes cast, Richard Fitzgerald, parish priest of Carrick-on-Suir, received fourteen, and John Power, parish priest of Clonmel, received ten, while James Murray, the bishop of Maitland in Australia, received seven votes. The other three votes were distributed among Charles Russell, the president of Maynooth, Pierce Power, professor in the local diocesan college, and Patrick Ryan, curate in St. Patrick's parish in Waterford City.

A week before the meeting of the clergy, O'Brien had written his old friend of some forty years' standing, Tobias Kirby, who was also a native of the diocese of Waterford, that though he was pleased to be relieved of the great burdens of the episcopacy, he did not want a stranger and his "anxious desire" was to have Fitzgerald as his coadjutor. "I would be particularly obliged," O'Brien had explained on November 6, "if you would use your influence in proper time and place, and in your own prudent way in carrying these my wishes into effect" (K). Cullen reported the results of the Waterford *terna* to Kirby the day after the meeting, and the next day, November 15, he reported that O'Brien had written him objecting to the fact that that bishop of Maitland had been introduced at the voting (K). Cullen also enclosed a letter from Timothy Dowley, parish priest of Rathcormack in the diocese of Waterford, which Kirby submitted to the Propa-

58. Ibid., vol. 239, fol. 128, "Ristretto con Sommario sulla nomina di un Coadiutore con futura successione al Vescovo di Waterford e Lismore in Irlanda, Gennaio, 1873" (fols. 127–38).
59. Ibid., fol. 133.

ganda authorities. "Our election for the coadjutor of this diocese," Dowley had informed Cullen on November 13, "has finished at this moment."[60] "The archbishop of Cashel and our bishop presided," he then added after naming the *terna*. "The latter was very weak and remained there hardly half the time. I am sorry to say that there was never such a manifestation of party spirit as took place in this diocese for three weeks before the election."

> There were seven or eight candidates, and the advocates of each sought with influence and impudence to obtain votes. The freedom of the election was destroyed by our poor bishop openly saying to the voters that we all ought to give our vote for Father Fitzgerald: and thus he obtained the majority [correctly, plurality]. I am sorry to say that Father Fitzgerald is a most excitable and impulsive man. He was for some years curate in the mensal parish of the bishop, who promoted him to the parish of Carrick. Having thus been in that dependent position for so long a time, many fear he would not have the authority or the courage to suggest or to apply the remedies to the present sad state of things; that he would leave matters in *statu quo*. Besides he has bad vision and not very good health.
>
> The second on the list is also very excitable and in delicate health, and rather old (65 years). Some members of his family have shown strong and indubitable signs of madness, and one of his sisters has been in a lunatic asylum in Waterford for more than twenty years.

"The only hope for our poor diocese," Dowley assured Cullen, "is to have Monsignor Murray appointed coadjutor without delay. If anything be said to the contrary at Rome, it does not merit any trust; since it is certain it will be done by interested persons."

> The nuns too in this place probably will involve themselves; and the influence that they have employed in appointments in the diocese is to be regretted. The good parish priests who have given their votes for Monsignor Murray have thus given proof of their concern for the restoration of religion, of sobriety, of peace, of charity, and of morality in the diocese. The document relative to the election has now been sent by post to Rome. I believe that the priests of strong party spirit will seek and have already sought to persuade the archbishop and the other bishops of the province, that Monsignor Murray because he is a stranger would not be well received. But in my humble view, in the present circumstances of the present case, Monsignor Murray would be the most fitted and the best accepted.

Several days later Cullen wrote more explicitly to Kirby about the appropriateness of Murray for the Waterford appointment. "If the Sacred Congregation thought of choosing Monsignor Murray," Cullen explained on November 21,

---

60. Ibid., fols. 136–37. The original of this letter is in the Cullen correspondence in the Irish College, Rome.

"some priests would believe it to be a benefit for the diocese. For some years the poor bishop of Waterford has not been able to do anything, and it is said that affairs there are in disorder; that drinking, playing cards etc. are common among the priests. Father Dowley and some other priests are very concerned to have a stranger" (K). Some two weeks later, Cullen decided to make his decisive move on behalf of Murray, who had been for many years his secretary before Murray's promotion to Maitland, by writing Kirby a long letter in Italian, which was obviously meant for the authorities in Propaganda. "The first," Cullen observed on December 3, referring to Fitzgerald, "is very much praised as an excellent priest, and worthy of every commendation. Some however say that he is disposed to leave things as they are, while the diocese really requires much reforming."

> For many years the old bishop has been very ill, and has not been able to do anything. Meanwhile it appears that the clergy have become very lax, and that now a strong hand would be necessary to restore discipline. It seems that the parish priests need to alter the way they conduct their temporal affairs. I was some years ago in two parishes, the priests of which lived far from their churches, and had great tracts of land in their possession, lands that they were obliged afterwards to leave to their families, although acquired with parochial dues. It will be necessary to put an end to this species of trade and nepotism, which gives great scandal to the people (K).

"I am told," Cullen added, "that Father Fitzgerald is sixty-three years of age, and that he is not robust. The second, Father Power is about sixty-six years. He has three brothers parish priests or curates and five or six others relatives. Some of these are very good." "There remains Monsignor Murray," Cullen then noted, "of whom I [shall] say nothing. I do not know how the parish priests were induced to nominate him, his not being connected with the diocese. But I do know the great promoter of the choice of this prelate was Father Timothy Dowley, an excellent priest, and brother of [the late] Father Philip Dowley, who rendered great service to religion by establishing here in Dublin the Congregation of the Mission of St. Vincent de Paul." "Father Dowley has written me repeatedly," Cullen concluded, "that the appointment of a stranger to the diocese to remedy the abuses that the native born priests do not appraise as they ought because they are accustomed to seeing them for such a long time."

"I scribbled out," Cullen explained to Kirby in his covering note to the above letter, "the preceeding lines in Italian. You can give the substance to the Cardinal, [but] if you do, it will be as well not to leave the paper" (K). "I think the Bishops of Cashel," he added, referring to the provincial meeting, "will meet tomorrow or today to recommend the candidate suited for the diocese. Dr. O'Brien is altogether for Dr. Fitzgerald, it is said Dr. Leahy would prefer Dr. Power, very probably some may be favourable to Dr. Murray—this is all conjecture—I hope God will direct them for the best."

The bishops of the province of Cashel did, in fact, meet the next day, December 4, at Thurles. The bishops' report on the three candidates was very long, full, and exhaustive.[61] They began by reviewing the qualifications of the candidates. They found Fitzgerald and Power good, learned, and experienced priests, who were worthy of the episcopate, and, significantly, they had nothing to say about the health of either. In regard to Murray's qualifications, they noted that there was nothing really to be said because he had several years before been promoted to the episcopacy by the Holy See. The bishops did proceed to observe, however, that they did not think there was sufficient reason to translate him from a distant and rising diocese in Australia to a coadjutorship in Ireland. Indeed, they added, it was clearly unwise to do so because Murray was not pleasing either to the bishop or to the great majority of the clergy of Waterford. Most significantly and interestingly, they then pointed out that there was certainly no need of a stranger to reform the diocese because it was very orderly, free of quarrels and factions among the priests, and flourishing religiously. The Cashel prelates then turned again to discuss the merits of the first two candidates on the *terna,* and, after long eulogies of both, they unanimously declared that they preferred Fitzgerald because he was the candidate most agreeable to the bishop and clergy of Waterford. In forwarding the report, the archbishop of Cashel enclosed separately, as he had in the Killaloe case, a list of all those who had received votes in the scrutiny and their numbers.

Shortly after the Cashel prelates' report reached Rome, Kirby wrote O'Brien, apparently to attempt to reconcile him to the appointment of Murray. O'Brien replied on December 16, reporting that he had received his consoling letter, but he did not want a stranger, nor did "the very good priests who voted for F. Power and F. Fitzgerald, all of whom would most cordially support my choice—Fr. Fitzgerald" (K). "As soon as you hear the good news," O'Brien added, "please to write and I shall keep it a profound secret." Kirby had also undoubtedly informed Cullen of the substance of the report of the Cashel prelates, for on December 23, Cullen forwarded him a letter from Maurice Mooney, the parish priest of Cahir in the diocese of Waterford and Lismore, emphasizing that the diocese needed reform and a stranger was therefore necessary. On the back of Mooney's letter, Cullen wrote in Italian,

> It will not be bad to give a summary of this letter to Propaganda. I believe Monsignor O'Brien has made every effort to have Father Fitzgerald chosen as his coadjutor. However, half the parish priests did not vote for him, as of 37 [correctly, 34] parish priests only 14 voted for him. I do not know what will be the view of Propaganda, but if it is believed it would be well to keep Monsignor Murray in Ireland, the occasion would be favourable. I believe he would be very favourably received by the people and clergy of Waterford. It seems

61. Ibid., fols. 134–36.

certain that things in that diocese are very perplexed because of the illness of
the bishop. Many think like the parish priest whose letter I enclose, that a
stranger would be necessary to reestablish order (K).

"Fathers Dowley, Crotty, and English," Cullen assured Kirby in conclusion, "all
three good, nay the best parish priests, and four others whom I do not know have
voted for Monsignor Murray. I mention these things because I believe that the case
merits consideration."

When the Waterford *Ponenza* was finally set in type early in the new year, it was
obvious that the Propaganda authorities had been very much influenced by the
point of view presented by Cullen and his friends. The *ristretto,* usually prepared
by the secretary of Propaganda, was even more explicitly pro-Cullen, if that were
possible, than the second *Ponenza* on the three appointments in the province of
Tuam. The crucial issue in the Waterford appointment, of course, was whether
there were serious disorders in the diocese that needed reform. The Cashel prelates had clearly stated that there was no real need for reform, while Cullen and his
friends had maintained exactly the opposite. What was most interesting in the
case set forth in the *ristretto* by the secretary of Propaganda was that he never
mentioned in his summary of the Cashel prelates' report that the prelates had
explicitly stated that there were no disorders, and the secretary then went on to
maintain that there were indeed very serious abuses in that diocese. After sum-
marizing Dowley's and Mooney's letters in his *ristretto,* Simeoni then asserted:

> To all this it must also be added on the part of Propaganda, that it knows
> that in Ireland very grave abuses truly exist as much among the secular clergy
> as the regular clergy, abuses to which it has many times called the attention of
> his Eminence the archbishop of Dublin, in order to find a way of correcting
> them (1). It is necessary, however, to recognize that the most efficacious remedy
> is to replace the old bishops brought up under the old system with Prelates
> formed in Rome. And in fact there are some at present who are giving effective
> action to the necessary reforms in the Churches entrusted to them, but even
> they are surprised on introducing in them [those Churches] the pieties and
> devotions in the precise ways that they saw practised in the capital of the Cath-
> olic world, and which in the same had hitherto been either unknown or posi-
> tively resisted. Now Monsignor Murray, a student of Propaganda, who was
> long at school with Cardinal Cullen, in the capacity of his secretary, is exactly
> one of those prelates that many would wish to see, in the Irish episcopate for
> the reasons mentioned.
>
> (1) Various memoranda have been passed on to the Cardinal *Ponente* [i.e.,
> the cardinal of Propaganda in charge of making the presentation or *Ponenza*
> to his fellow cardinals], which are of purpose kept in the Propaganda Secre-
> tariat and which are very often taken into account in promoting the necessary
> reforms.[62]

---

62. Ibid., fol. 130.

However, when the cardinals of Propaganda met on January 21, 1873, to consider the appointment to Waterford, they decided to postpone the decision and,
meanwhile, to write to the archbishop of Cashel that it had come to the attention
of the Holy See that not a little disorder existed in the diocese of Waterford and
that, before providing for that see, they desired to know from him if the first two
candidates on the *terna* were such that they would continue to tolerate such
disorders.[63] The Propaganda authorities wrote to Leahy immediately after the
pope approved the recommendation of the cardinals, on January 26, 1873, and,
when they received his reply, they set in type, in early April, an appendix to the
original *Ponenza*.[64] In the appendix, Simeoni reported that Leahy "had reas-
suringly replied that the first two candidates (Fathers Fitzgerald and Power) are
not such as to tolerate abuses in the diocese in which they had to exercise the
episcopal office. He thinks, however, that the second, that is Father Power, should
be preferred to the first, since he would not be subject to the exception produced
against Father Fitzgerald, namely, that he is too attached to the bishop of Waterford."[65] "The archbishop of Cashel," Simeoni explained, "adds that it now occurs
to him that when the *terna* was elected by the clergy, the bishop exercised a kind of
pressure in favor of the first of the three candidates proposed, that is, Fitzgerald,
and because of this he would prefer the second, that is, Father Power." "As for the
bishop of Maitland," Simeoni added, "who was placed last on the *terna,* and who
has already left for Australia, the archbishop of Cashel has indicated again that he
is adverse to his election because he is a stranger to the diocese of Waterford."

Apparently, however, Cullen and his friends did not concede lightly. Cullen
wrote Barnabò on January 2, 1873, to assure him again that Murray would be
welcomed by the clergy of Waterford,[66] and apparently he also advised Moran
that it was time to throw his weight into the balance. "Monsignor Moran, the
bishop of Ossory, however," Simeoni concluded in the appendix, after reporting
the reply of the archbishop of Cashel, "has recently expressed the view that he
preferred him [Murray] to the other two candidates, maintaining that he would be
of great benefit to the diocese of which it is a question, a diocese in which the
bishop of Ossory has a special interest, in that his diocese borders on that of
Waterford." When the cardinals finally met again, on April 28, they recommended
that the second on the list, John Power, be appointed coadjutor with the right of
succession to the bishop of Waterford and Lismore, and the pope authoritatively
approved their recommendation on May 4, 1873.[67] In breaking the news to his old

---

63. Ibid., fol. 131.
64. Ibid., fols. 485–86, "Appendice alla Ponenza di Gennaio, 1872 [correctly, 1873] sulla
nomina di un Coadiutore al Vescovo di Waterford e Lismore in Irlanda, Aprile, 1873."
65. Ibid., fol. 485.
66. S.R.C., vol. 36, fols. 1674–75.
67. A, vol. 239, fol. 486.

friend, the bishop of Waterford, Kirby first wrote, on May 16, to say that a coadjutor had been appointed and then wrote again, on May 20, to inform the bishop that it was Power. O'Brien, who was not well, replied through the good offices of the administrator of his mensal parish, Patrick Nolan, to thank him for his letters. "His Lordship," Nolan reported briefly on May 20, "thanks God that a stranger has not been appointed" (K). Indeed, O'Brien did not live to see his new coadjutor consecrated, for he died less than a month later, on June 22, 1873.

The Waterford appointment was both a very interesting and a very significant one—interesting for what it reveals about how the Roman Curia dealt with a very difficult and complex problem, and significant for what it tells about the long-term relationship between the Irish and Roman Churches. The Waterford appointment was very difficult for two reasons: first, Cullen had thrown his very considerable influence at home and at Rome to the side of the bishop of Maitland; second, the officials of Propaganda were obviously of like mind in endorsing the choice of the cardinal archbishop of Dublin. The main thrust of Cullen's and the Propaganda authorities' case was that the diocese of Waterford needed reform and the bishop of Maitland, as an extern, was the man able to do the necessary. Because the cardinals could hardly contradict their Dublin colleague, especially after being assured by their own bureaucratic apparatus that such a reform was necessary, they astutely decided not to question the main assumption but rather to determine whether the conclusions drawn from it necessarily followed. The real question, then, became, not whether there were disorders in the diocese of Waterford, but whether it was necessary to appoint a stranger to remedy those disorders. The cardinals, thereby, fastened on to the weak point in Cullen's case—he had not established really that either Fitzgerald or Power were unworthy of being appointed, especially as the Cashel prelates had testified in their report to the worthiness of both, though they had been obliged by the procedure involved to choose one above the other. The reason that the cardinals made such a distinction was that they were as much obliged to do what was right as to do what was expedient. They fully realized, of course, that to recommend the appointment of the bishop of Maitland would be to reflect adversely on the ecclesiastical character of those who had been returned ahead of him on the *terna,* and it was impossible in good conscience to lay such a stigma on two priests whose worthiness really had not been impugned. The cardinals, therefore, were obliged to postpone the appointment and require that the necessary assurances, of either Fitzgerald's or Power's ability to cope as a bishop with the alleged abuses, be secured. When the archbishop of Cashel then gave the required assurance, the appointment of the one or the other was inevitable.

The Waterford appointment, however, was not only very interesting, it was also very significant for the long-term relationship between the Irish and Roman Churches. When the eight episcopal appointments made in the Irish Church in the nearly three years between the late summer of 1870 and the late spring of 1873 are reviewed together, they would appear to reveal, if the Waterford case is excepted, that Cullen's influence at Rome was determinant and his power in the Irish Church virtually paramount. The appearance, however, actually belies the reality, and the Waterford case is really more representative of the rule than of the exception. For more than a decade before these eight appointments were made, Rome had been attempting to regularize the procedure in Irish episcopal appointments. In nearly every case of the eleven appointments that had been made in the decade of the sixties, either the first or the second name on the *terna* commended by the clergy had been appointed. But the really crucial factor in the final recommendation of the cardinals had come to be the report of the provincial bishops. Cullen, of course, as the pope's apostolic delegate in Ireland before 1866 and as a cardinal after 1866, also had considerable influence in the making of episcopal appointments, but his voice was not, in the sixties, the determinant one it had been in the fifties. The long-term effect of all this was that, by early 1870, the bishops had become a co-opting body as far as their membership was concerned.

The seeming departure from this *modus operandi* in the eight Irish episcopal appointments made between 1870 and 1873 was largely the result of the difficulties and complications of the three appointments in the province of Tuam. If, for the moment, these three appointments be excepted, however, the pattern that evolved in the sixties becomes self-evident. In the five appointments of Raphoe, Ardagh, Killaloe, Ossory, and Waterford only Ardagh proved to be an exception, but on further analysis it is actually the exception that proves the rule. In the other four appointments, the candidate chosen had been either the first or the second name on the *terna,* and in every case that candidate had been, in effect, the unanimous choice of the bishops of the province. Ardagh was the exception that proved the rule because the bishops of the province of Armagh, by not being able to endorse any of the candidates on the *terna,* had opened the door to Conroy's appointment. If any of the candidates on the Ardagh *terna* had proved acceptable to the Armagh prelates, it is hard to see how Conroy could have been appointed. The significance of the Waterford appointment, therefore, is that, being the last in an intense and long series, it both set the seal on the importance of the report of the provincial bishops, as reflected in this case finally by the judgment of their metropolitan, and defined the limits of Cullen's influence at Rome in regard to episcopal appointments.

The apparent exceptions to all of this, of course, were the appointments to Clonfert, Killala, and Achonry in the province of Tuam. What must be understood, however, is that these appointments were also part of an even more long-term policy on the part of Rome to liquidate the power and influence of the archbishop of Tuam in the Irish Church. For more than thirty years, MacHale had been a divisive force as far as the Irish bishops as a body was concerned. What also must be understood, therefore, is that the final breaking of MacHale's power and influence greatly enhanced the corporate will of the bishops as a body in the governing of the Irish Church. In the last analysis, moreover, what makes especially significant the fact that the Irish bishops continued to be a co-opting body into the decade of the seventies is that the three candidates that were eventually appointed to Clonfert, Killala, and Achonry were actually the nominees of Mac-Evilly and Gillooly and were, except through the recommendations of the bishops of Galway and Elphin, unknown to Cullen. In spite of appearances, therefore, any picture that includes either a ruthless and arbitrary cardinal archbishop of Dublin packing the episcopal body with his favorites and flunkies, or the Roman authorities exercising an irregular and capricious will in violation of the Constitution of the Irish Church simply will not stand up to a serious examination of the known facts.

Part II
Home Rule

Isaac Butt (courtesy of the National Gallery of Ireland)

III

The Constitutional Challenge
May 1870–August 1872

At the same time that the Irish bishops were successfully maintaining the gains they had made as a body by containing Cullen and regularizing their relationship with Rome, they were also struggling with a very serious and complicated political challenge to their power and influence. By early 1870, the bishops as a body had been giving continued and consistent support to the Irish-Liberal alliance in the British House of Commons for nearly two years. That alliance had been inaugurated in early 1868, when William Gladstone, the leader of the Liberal party, promised to do justice to Ireland according to Irish ideas by remedying her outstanding grievances. In the general election of 1868, the electorate gave Gladstone and his party the necessary mandate for his policy; his party gained 8 seats in Ireland and 25 in Britain, for an overall majority in the House of Commons of some 120. Upon assuming the premiership after the general election, Gladstone immediately proceeded to disestablish the Protestant Church of Ireland, and in early 1870 he introduced his long-awaited Irish land bill. The bill, however, proved to be generally disappointing in Ireland. The great difficulty was that in the two years since the inauguration of the Irish-Liberal alliance in 1868, public opinion in Ireland had gradually shifted to the left in regard to what was considered to be an acceptable solution to the land question. By 1870, in fact, the Irish claim of 1868 to a reasonable compensation for disturbance of outgoing tenants had escalated into a demand that would secure tenants fixity of tenure in their holdings subject only to the continued payment of rent. Faced with a property-conscious House of Commons, however, with an especially tender conscience about the rights of private property in land, Gladstone was forced to trim in regard to the demand for fixity of tenure if he ever hoped to see his measure become law.

The Irish bishops, who were nearly all in Rome in early 1870 when the measure was introduced, had privately advised Gladstone through the kind offices of

Archbishop Manning to incorporate fixity of tenure in his bill, as well as a considerable number of other amendments, in order to make it acceptable as a final solution to the vexatious Irish land question, but all to no avail. When Gladstone then insisted that, given the temper of the House of Commons, further concessions were impossible, the Irish bishops accepted the measure as a positive boon to the Irish tenant and continued to give their support as a body, whatever their individual misgivings, to the Irish-Liberal alliance. Their reasons for doing so, of course, were mixed. One of the reasons for their acquiescence was certainly that they sympathized with and appreciated Gladstone's considerable political difficulties with his own party. Another was that they were genuinely grateful for what he had already accomplished by his appointments in the Irish administration and in disestablishing the Protestant Church. Finally, they still had great hopes that the Irish-Liberal alliance in general, and Gladstone in particular, would finally resolve the grievance that interested them the most—the education question.

Their decision to continue to place their political trust in the Irish-Liberal alliance and the leadership of Gladstone, however, was not without some very considerable risk as far as their own political power and influence were concerned. The political effect of the recent shift in Irish public opinion in favor of a more radical solution to the land question, had been further complicated by the emergence at the same time of a demand for amnesty for all those who had been imprisoned in recent years for their part in the revolutionary conspiracy of the Irish Republican, or Fenian, Brotherhood to establish a republic in Ireland by force of arms. When the Amnesty Committee had failed to persuade Gladstone to release those who had been the leaders of the Fenian conspiracy, the Amnesty Association, which since had superseded the less Fenian-inspired Amnesty Committee, had begun to break up any and every meeting, including those of the recently founded Irish Tenant League, that would not declare amnesty as their first priority. The result of all this was that late in 1869 and early in 1870 there was an alarming increase in political violence and intimidation accompanied by a growing number of agrarian disorders and crimes. This turmoil was checked to some degree when the Irish bishops in Rome finally secured a formal decree from the pope, in early January, condemning the Fenian Brotherhood and Gladstone passed, in early March in the House of Commons, an effective coercion measure, which considerably increased the ability of the executive power in Ireland to deal with the accelerating violence.

The most disturbing feature of the Fenian-inspired disorders, however, was the basic threat they posed to the whole system of constitutional politics. The Fenians apparently hoped by their violence and intimidation at political and agrarian meetings and elections to subvert the constitutional process by demoralizing those who attempted to participate in it. Their most imaginative tactic, and, ironically, the one that ultimately proved their undoing, was their decision to run prominent

Fenian leaders who were still in prison as candidates in the parliamentary elections in county Tipperary. Because convicted felons could not legally take seats in Parliament, and because both the clergy and laity ultimately refused to be intimidated in the constituencies, this Fenian tactic was unsuccessful. But it did give a considerable number of the more politically conscious and thoughtful Fenians some serious cause for reflection. What they came to understand, eventually, was that they had a larger and harder core of followers in the constituencies than they had realized and that, by entering into the game of constitutional politics, they would not only help shift the Irish political structure measurably to the left, but they would also be in a better position to destroy what apparently was closest to the political hearts of their now openly declared and deadly enemies, the bishops and clergy—the Irish-Liberal alliance.

A good many of these crypto-Fenians and their new-found allies, the advanced Nationalists, instinctively realized that the Irish-Liberal alliance as inaugurated by Gladstone and subscribed to by the Irish bishops and their lay-politician satellites was subversive of the Irish political system articulated and established by Daniel O'Connell some fifty years before. If, indeed, Gladstone, the Irish bishops, and their political friends were allowed to have their way, the O'Connellite system of an effective Irish political consensus of leader, bishops, and party would be absorbed into the dominant British political system with Gladstone as leader, the Irish party as a mere tail of the Liberal party, and the Irish bishops as representatives of yet another voluntary association and vested interest. The charges of the crypto-Fenians and advanced Nationalists during this period, therefore, that the bishops did not understand the real interests, let alone the true needs, of the country merits some attention. Their further insinuation, however, that the bishops were willing to sell their national birthright for a mess of English educational pottage was a real misunderstanding of the motives of the bishops. In supporting the Irish-Liberal alliance the bishops were motivated by Gladstone's promise that he would remedy Irish grievances according to Irish rather than British ideas and that this, in effect, would provide the Irish people with equality under the law guaranteed by a *de facto* form of Home Rule.

What the bishops did not realize was that politically their view was both naive and dangerous, as well as being subversive in regard to the emergence of a viable Irish political system. Their views were naive in that they did not appreciate Gladstone's inability to deliver on his promise to legislate according to Irish ideas because of the political difficulties such legislation caused in his own party. This was made evident in the three measures he introduced to resolve the outstanding Irish grievances of the day—the established Protestant Church and the land and education questions. In framing the appropriate legislation to remedy these grievances, for example, Gladstone did not consult either the Irish bishops or the Irish parliamentary representatives who were not members of his government. He did, in effect, what British statesmen had been doing since the Act of Union; he gave them what he thought the political equation of parliamentary forces in the House of Commons would bear.[1] What neither the Irish bishops, nor Gladstone, apparently, understood was that his promise, if taken literally, was patently unconstitutional from the point of view of the British political system. If the Irish, for example, were to be governed strictly according to Irish ideas, the majority that passed such legislation in the House of Commons would be reduced to merely a ratifying rather than a sovereign body in regard to the expressed needs of a minority; this could result only in placing the majority in the ludicrous constitutional position of enjoying responsibility without power. Therefore, even if Gladstone had been able to resolve the practical difficulties of harmonizing in his own party the political differences over what might be an appropriate legislative measure for Ireland in a particular instance, he could not have fulfilled his promise, in the long run, without subverting the basic premise of the Victorian constitution of majority rule.

While the Irish bishops may be forgiven for being politically naive about the workings of the British political system—especially when it was obvious that Gladstone was not much wiser, in terms, at least, of his promises, if not his practice—they may not be so easily acquitted of the dangerous political consequences to their own considerable power and influence that were a result of their commitment to the Irish-Liberal alliance. By endorsing and sustaining the alliance, the Irish bishops greatly enhanced their own political power and influence. That increase, however, was gained at the expense of those other two essential elements in the Irish political system, the leader and the party, and if the bishops had not been forced eventually to forsake the alliance that system would have been virtually destroyed. The real problem in regard to the Irish political system was less that Gladstone became the acknowledged leader of both the British and the Irish in the alliance than that the Irish party became at once the tool of the Irish bishops and the tail of the Liberal party. It became a tool because the individual Irish members of Parliament were virtually dependent for their survival in the constituencies on the good will of the local bishop and the organizing power of his clergy, and a tail because after their election to Parliament they would become subject to a patronage system of rewards and punishments administered by the leader of the Liberal party. In such a scenario, bereft of leader and party, the Irish

1. On August 19, 1870, Gladstone wrote Chichester S. Fortescue, then chief secretary for Ireland, "It occurs to me that while information as to the views of the Roman Hierarchy on education, especially on higher education, cannot but be useful, yet in the present state of jealousy about them we cannot use too much caution as to any direct communication or proceeding which might be used. It seems to me that in the main we know what we ought to give them whether they will take it or not." Quoted in David Thornley, *Isaac Butt and Home Rule* (London, 1964), p. 147.

bishops would become the real power brokers in Irish politics, enjoying that most dangerous of all political commodities in a representative system, power without responsibility.

The reason that such a political scenario did not come to pass, of course, ironically had to do a great deal not only with the nature and strength of the British political system but also, and even more importantly, with the tenacity and determination of a handful of Irish lay politicians who never lost faith in the emergence of an Irish political system. Just as the exigencies, then, of the British constitutional system constrained Gladstone in his promise to govern Ireland according to Irish ideas, the emergence of a Home Rule movement in Ireland eventually undermined the commitment of the Irish bishops and their lay political supporters to the Irish-Liberal alliance. The undoing of that alliance, however, was to be no simple matter, but the process may be said to have formally begun when Isaac Butt, a prominent Irish nationalist politician and barrister, formed a committee at Bilton's Hotel in Dublin on May 19, 1870, to launch a movement for the restoration of an Irish Parliament.[2] The original committee consisted of some sixty-one members, twenty-eight of whom were prominent Irish Protestants, and the remainder of whom were a heterogeneous group of Nationalists, Liberals, and Fenians. The Protestants included a number of Fellows of Trinity College, several owners of influential newspapers, such as Major Laurence Knox of the *Irish Times,* and an assortment of landlords and prominent Dublin politicians. The committee held a number of organizing meetings in late May and June, and in July it published a list of 359 members, which included some 12 Catholic clergymen, the more important of whom were Richard B. O'Brien, the dean of Limerick, Patrick Lavelle, the parish priest of Cong in the diocese of Tuam, and Patrick Quaid, the parish priest of O'Callaghan's Mills in the diocese of Killaloe.

The crises that had precipitated the crystallization of this early movement for Home Rule were in the main two. For the Irish Protestants, the disestablishment of their church by Gladstone and his Nonconformist allies convinced them that their future would perhaps be more secure in an Irish Parliament, where even with a Catholic majority there could not be much less respect shown for their rights and privileges as a minority. For the Nationalists, the critical moment was the failure of Gladstone's land bill to provide a real solution to the land question in Ireland. Their dissatisfaction and disappointment was summed up well by the dean of

2. Ibid., pp. 92–93. See also Lawrence J. McCaffrey, *Irish Federalism in the 1870s: A Study in Conservative Nationalism* (Philadelphia, 1962), pp. 8–9.

Limerick, who wrote to Butt shortly after Gladstone had introduced his bill in the House of Commons, "I have been disappointed," O'Brien exclaimed on February 17, "by 'the Bill' and in it! The Bill is useless for any proximate good and too complicated to permit any certainty of remote benefit."[3] "Of course," he then noted, referring to the disestablishment of the Irish Church, "Mr. Gladstone has closed the line of Statesmen in whom I had any hope—a hope which ought not perhaps have been inspired by the legislation of last year which lost his class so little. English wisdom has failed to see the nature of the Crisis—and Irish warning has spoken in vain." "A new Bill," he then concluded sadly and prophetically, "is impossible in this generation; and the present bill is useless for the end it should have contemplated. Landlords and Statesmen have only one remaining chance of saving us from coming confusion, and that is to permit us to make our own laws. I cannot go on with a sham-battle—I am sure that many of my class share my opinions—these battles have lasted long enough." Several days later, A. M. Sullivan, the proprietor and editor of the influential Nationalist weekly, the *Nation,* wrote to William O'Neill Daunt, a long-time constitutional Nationalist and proponent of the Repeal of the Act of Union, suggesting a meeting with John Martin and a number of other prominent Repealers to launch a new political movement. Daunt then wrote P. J. Smyth, a former Young Irelander and Repealer, proposing that he and Sullivan should arrange a meeting with Butt and Major Knox of the *Irish Times.* The eventual result of all the various round robins was the earlier mentioned private meeting to begin the agitation, called for by Butt, to be held on May 19 at Bilton's Hotel.

The earliest Cullen received the news in Rome that there was a new political agitation in the offing was in late June. "We had," his secretary, George Conroy, reported on June 20, from Dublin, "a general Fenian demonstration on yesterday at the funeral of Mrs. Luby, mother of Luby the Fenian convict. It was precisely a repetition of the funeral of Carey some months ago. I suppose some 4,000 men walked in the procession. The green sashes were very common, and were generally bound up with orange rosettes" (C). "This was [by] the order of the Committee," Conroy explained, referring to the organizers of the demonstration, "and is a sign of the present policy advocated in every way by the party, viz: the fusion of Protestants and Catholics in a common body to agitate for Repeal of the Union. This is the scheme which Geo. H. Moore was engaged in promoting at the hour of his death; this is Lavelle's pet ideal; and Dean O'Brien has contributed not a little to encourage it by his letters. The *Irishman* promotes this policy by open and unblushing attacks on Rome, and on the influence of the Holy See in Ireland. The *Nation* also is quite eloquent on this new Union of Irishmen." "I think, however, that when we come to the 12th July," Conroy concluded, referring to the anniver-

---

3. Butt Papers (B), National Library of Ireland, Dublin.

sary of the battle of the Boyne, where the Protestant William III decisively defeated the Catholic James II, "there will be a breach in the party: the Orange blood will boil too fiercely to brook the neighbourhood of the viler Papist current." A week later, Conroy returned to the subject of the new agitation. "The Repeal, or Federal Parliament scheme," he reported to Cullen on June 26, "is being urged on by a body which will soon be in a position to do mischief although as yet is weak and without a seat [in Parliament]. The body counts as members Butt, Sir W. Wilde, Dean O'Brien, Pigott, A. M. Sullivan, Major Knox *et hoc genus omne* [and all of this class], and it is really growing" (C).

Conroy's alarm was undoubtedly prompted by the anticipated by-election soon to take place in Dublin because of the unseating of Sir Arthur Guinness, the Conservative candidate returned at the general election in 1868. The Home Rulers were expected to enter a candidate for Dublin just as they had recently entered one for the by-election in county Longford, which was the result of the recently elected member having been unseated because the Catholic clergy had engaged in bribery in the constituency. In that election Cullen had been appalled at the conduct of the clergy and had written the bishop of Ardagh, Neal McCabe, who was then in Rome attending the Council, protesting the conduct of his clergy. McCabe replied on April 19, assuring Cullen that he had just written to his vicar general and that there would be no recurrence of that unfortunate conduct on the part of his clergy in the upcoming by-election. In the election, which took place on May 16, G. F. N. Greville-Nugent, the brother of the unseated member, who was a Gladstonian Liberal, was opposed by Captain E. R. King-Harman, a scion of a very wealthy, Irish Protestant, Conservative family, who had declared himself a Home Ruler. The clergy worked very hard, if more cautiously and prudently, to return Greville-Nugent, but the Nationalist-Fenian-Conservative coalition proved more formidable than anticipated. Though the Home Rule coalition lost by 1,217 votes to 923, they succeeded in reducing the Liberal majority in the previous election by nearly 900 votes.[4] It was little wonder then that Conroy was worried about the approaching by-election in Dublin.

By the time that election took place on August 18, however, Cullen, who had just returned from Rome, was not in a very happy frame of mind. "We shall have," he informed Kirby on August 10, "an election next week in Dublin—there are two candidates, Mr. King-Harman, member of the Orange Lorton family, and Dr. Corrigan. The Fenians and Young Irelanders will support the first—I have written a letter to Corrigan explaining Catholic views on education—if he does not come out as a Catholic, I and the clergy will not support him" (K). "He wrote," Cullen explained, "in favour of the Queen's Colleges and mixed education. Unless he

4. Brian M. Walker, ed., *Parliamentary Election Results in Ireland, 1801–1922* (Dublin, 1978), p. 113.

retract, we cannot consistently support him." "You see," Cullen concluded sadly, "we are in a mess—all we can do is to keep aloof." Corrigan, who was a prominent Catholic physician and layman in Dublin, had long been a thorn in Cullen's side on the education question. He was representative of those among the Dublin Catholic upper middle class who had supported the educational policy of Cullen's predecessor as archbishop of Dublin, Daniel Murray. Members of this class, though not very numerous, were by virtue of their position and wealth both influential and independent. Corrigan had stood as a Liberal candidate for Dublin in the general election of 1868 and had come within nearly 200 votes in a poll of 11,000 of being elected. In that election he had satisfied Cullen in regard to educational principles by trimming a good deal to the expectant wind, but apparently he had reverted more recently to his former views. While Corrigan's reply to Cullen's letter was not entirely satisfactory, after some intense last-minute negotiations between him and Cullen's vicars general, a *modus vivendi* was worked out that allowed the Dublin clergy to give him their support. On election day, therefore, Corrigan defeated his Home Rule opponent, King-Harman, by 4,468 votes to 3,444.[5]

Whatever King-Harman's defeats in Longford and Dublin proved, they indicated at least that there was considerable voting power in the constituencies for the idea of Home Rule. Shortly after the Dublin election, therefore, the Home Government Association was founded at a meeting on September 1, 1870, at the Rotundo in Dublin, and offices were taken in the fashionable Grafton Street. In December, after a series of monthly meetings, an address was issued stating the basic aims of the association, with an appeal for support signed by the honorable secretaries—J. A. Galbraith, fellow of Trinity College, Dublin; George Ekins Browne, M.P. for county Mayo; and Laurence Waldron, former M.P. for county Tipperary and currently a commissioner of the Board of National Education.[6] Moreover, Galbraith was a Protestant clergyman, Browne had recently been elected in Mayo upon the death of George Henry Moore, who had been a long-time political protégé in that county of the archbishop of Tuam, and Waldron was a wealthy Catholic, who had in recent years fallen foul of Cullen on educational matters. The address of the association maintained that Ireland would not enjoy prosperity or peace without a domestic legislature, and it proposed, therefore, that a federal union be established with independent legislatures for England, Scotland, and Ireland, as well as that an Imperial Parliament be maintained for imperial business. "This is not the time," the authors of the address prudently added, "for offering the complete plan of such a federal union. That must come with the authority of a united Ireland. At present we invite the adhesion of all who

5. Ibid.
6. Thornley, p. 97.

are willing to cooperate in the general object of obtaining for Ireland a parliament of her own."[7] "When our association," the address promised, "becomes strong enough to recommend such a step, we propose to invite our countrymen to meet in a general conference finally to settle on the details of a plan such as Ireland may present for acceptance to an English parliament and ministers."

By the time the address had been issued, however, a number of the more prominent Home Rulers already had become very concerned about how few of the Catholic clergy had joined the association. About the middle of November, therefore, the corresponding secretary of the association, Captain John Dunne, wrote to O'Neill Daunt, whose Catholic credentials were impeccable, suggesting that, since only two bishops had signified their approval of the movement so far, he should contact those members of the hierarchy whom he personally knew to solicit their support for the movement. Daunt then wrote to both the archbishop of Cashel and the bishop of Ross. His original letter to the archbishop of Cashel does not appear to have survived, but in his reply of December 7, marked "private & confidential," Leahy assured Daunt, "I am with you for *home rule,* assenting & consenting to any thing in your esteemed Letter, except the vote of confidence in the existing Dublin Association."[8] "They have yet," he explained, "to win my confidence. All the antecedents of most of the prominent members would deter me from committing myself to their Association." "I cannot believe," he added somewhat ingenuously in conclusion, "that any Priest need be in fear of his Bishop for joining this Association. I will not believe it until proved beyond doubt." Daunt replied the next day, December 8, in a long letter also marked "private and confidential," in which he did not mince words. "I am," he informed Leahy, "very much rejoiced at your Grace's hearty concurrence in the National principles expressed in my letter, though indeed it is no more than I expected from you. I am also rejoiced at your incredulity respecting the restraint imposed in some quarters [said] to be exercised by bishops on the National action of their clergy."[9] "You have inevitably," Daunt added politely, "good means of knowing the facts; and that you are incredulous on the subject shows me that if the restraint in question exists it cannot be very generally experienced."

> Yet your Grace may rely on this, as undoubted; that one priest writing to me and sending his subscription stipulating that he should not be named, *not*

7. Ibid.

8. Daunt Papers (D), National Library of Ireland, Dublin, 8046 (7). See also Michael O'Hea, bishop of Ross, to Daunt, November 18, 1870, "My confidence in the amount of cooperation which may be expected from the discontented members of the disestablished C. is rather limited, and as a Catholic Bishop I should not like, unaccompanied and unsustained by my brother-prelates, to throw myself into the ranks of those who never manifested towards poor Ireland but slight and contempt" (D, 8047 [7]).

9. Leahy Papers (L), Archives of the archdiocese of Cashel, Thurles.

wishing to be made a martyr. Now, who could make a martyr of him unless his ecclesiastical superior? Again; two other priests subscribed, under similar conditions of privacy. A gentleman much interested in the Home Rule movement wrote to me that his brother, a *priest,* expressed to him his belief that til the Education question should be settled, the priests would not generally join the movement. Add to all this the patent fact that (some 20 or 30 exceptions) they have not heretofore joined it.

"I trust," he assured Leahy, "I am not a cold or indifferent catholic; I have during a long life anxiously watched Irish affairs; and if I dread and appreciate one Irish evil more than another, it is that Catholicity in Ireland should ever be divorced from Nationality—that the pastors of the Church should ever be, or be supposed to be, in any sort of league with the English government, involving the abandonment of the great and sacred cause of Self-Legislation for any minor object [i.e., education] whatever." "There is at the bottom of the Nation's heart," he further assured Leahy, "an irradicable distrust of the English government; and that distrust as a matter of course would attach to the clergy if they even *seemed* to traffic on such terms with our old, treacherous hereditary enemy."

I would respectfully ask your Grace to consider that although some of the promoters of the Dublin Association have had bad antecedents, their interests as well as ours are certainly bound up in the success of the movement. I look on their interest as a good guarantee of their sincerity. Butt, the hero of tenant-right is the founder of the movement. Major Knox's journal, the *Irish Times,* astonished me years ago by its spirited defense of Irish character against English attacks. Knox is one of our Committee; he has done vast service in nationalizing the Protestant mind by means of his paper. Rev. Mr. Galbraith lately declared at the Association that he deemed Protestant fear of Catholic hostility quite absurd; and that he would willingly confide the interests of the Irish Protestants to a College Green Parliament, even though wholly composed of Catholics!

"I confess," he added generously, "I would warmly grasp the hand thus extended to us by men who seem really disposed to forget all old quarrels." "And remember," he noted more prudently in conclusion, "a large Catholic *and clerical* accession to the movement *would necessarily neutralize any cause of distrust its present constitution might be supposed to give occasion for.*"

When Daunt received no reply to this letter, he wrote Leahy again, some two weeks later, to try to persuade him that the political future of Ireland was in the hands of the bishops and priests of Ireland. "I have never addressed your Grace," he assured Leahy on December 20, "with a deeper sense of the importance of the subject to which I wished to call your attention, or with a stronger anxiety for your concurrence, than I now take the liberty of doing" (L). "I should do you great injustice," Daunt explained, "if I thought you did not thoroughly know and deplore the mischief of the Union; which execrable measure eats like a cancer into all the sources of Irish prosperity. I have not the least doubt that the Catholic hierarchy, [and] priesthood of Ireland *have the fate of Home Rule in their hands.*" "How vast, then," he maintained, "is their responsibility! The Federal Association needs but a strong accession from their ranks to give it the force, elasticity, and popularity essential to success." "I would respectfully beg your Grace," Daunt then suggested, "to reflect that the existing Association, if well backed up by priests and People, affords our unfortunate country an opportunity of regaining self-government, which, if neglected, may not again occur."

> John Martin, who is the very soul of patriotic love for Ireland, has personally mixed with the leaders in Dublin at their meeting in Committee: and he writes me that their patriotic earnestness is undoubted. It is of course quite possible that the movement may include some untrustworthy individuals: such persons are always to be found in all large organizations; but the prominent men and the great majority of their followers are sound. There is nothing in the theory of Protestantism to make protestants bad Irishmen; that they have hitherto been bad Irishmen in general, is due to causes that are passing away. We have now got a large share of the protestant element—that very element whose hostility was declared by O'Connell to have been the cause of his failure. Shall the Protestant Repealers be enabled to complain that the hostility or at least the inaction, of the catholic element, is the cause of *their* failure in a struggle, the most vital of all possible struggles, for the welfare of Ireland? Can any Catholic Repealer whose fears, or doubts, or prejudices, keep him apart from the movement now inaugurated, point out the least chance of any other organization likely to recover Home Government, should the present attempt go to pieces?

"Home Rule," Daunt asserted finally, "can *Never* be achieved unless by the combined action of catholics and protestants. We have now the opportunity of effecting that combination, and if we neglect it we shall well deserve the popular malediction."

Apparently Leahy's reply was delayed because of the Christmas holidays. "After giving the subject of your last earnest Letter," Leahy assured Daunt on December 28, "further and, I think, mature attention—no—consideration, I cannot bring myself to join the Association for promoting *home rule*—And for two principle reasons."

> 1. I have no confidence whatever in the persons who have originated & who conduct the proceedings of the Association. Not that they are some of them Protestants, and fast Protestants. Not at all. I would work beside an honest Protestant for the regeneration of my country as soon as beside a Catholic. Nay, I would give my confidence to some of the Protestants of this Association much sooner than I would to some of their Catholic fellows.
>
> 2. I am convinced this Association will prove utterly abortive. Why I am so˙ so [*sic*] convinced it is unnecessary and would be [*sic*] long to state. But, such is my conviction.[10]

10. D, 8046 (7).

"On the subject of *Home-rule*," he assured Daunt in conclusion, "I will take an early opportunity to sound my Brother Bishops."

Besides being a very able attempt to persuade Leahy to join the Home Rule movement by a combination of the carrot and the stick, Daunt's letters were also classic statements of the constitutional Nationalist case in the nineteenth century. The central argument, of course, was that the people are sovereign. Derived from that proposition were the twin corollaries that the people are also absolute and inclusive. Divining the general will was the function of those who could intuit the "Nation's heart," and finding expression for that will was the work of those who could establish the necessary political institutions for its achievement. The people were not only absolute, however, they were also whole, and the Nation included all those who were prepared to work in its interest, irrespective of class or creed. The vision had been O'Connell's, and it had been carried into another generation, diminished by time and circumstance, by men such as the late John Blake Dillon, John Martin, and Daunt. The reason that Daunt's appeal to Leahy, however, and other appeals he was to make in the next few years to Leahy and to other bishops, fell on deaf ears, was not that they did not understand that he was right about the awful danger in even seeming to separate themselves from the people but rather that they were not yet quite sure who had better divined the "Nation's heart" at this political juncture, Daunt or they. Besides, the bishops were not completely free to make the choice. They had committed themselves in the general election of 1868 to the Irish-Liberal alliance, and both loyalty and honor forbade them from unilaterally breaking that contract as long as Gladstone manifested his undoubted goodwill in attempting to fulfill it.

In any event, that Daunt and his friends were right and the bishops wrong about the "Nation's heart," was slowly but surely made manifest in the next several years, in the place where the people did have the last word—the constituencies. Between early 1871 and the general election in early 1874, the Home Rulers contested eleven by-elections in Ireland, of which they won eight and lost three. Of the three elections they lost, two were, significantly enough, in Ulster constituencies and involved the complication of a Conservative candidate, while the third was in the very narrow borough of Mallow in county Cork, which they lost by only 13 votes in a total poll of 169, under rather unusual circumstances. The first election that the Home Rulers won took place in January 1871, shortly after the death of the senior member for county Meath, Matthew E. Corbally. The first in the field was George J. Plunkett, a younger brother of the Catholic earl of Fingall. Apparently the Meath clergy had met the month before, with their bishop, Thomas Nulty, presiding, and had endorsed Plunkett. Many of them, however, had second thoughts when John Martin soon declared that he would contest the seat on the Home Rule interest. On nomination day, January 2, 1871, neither Plunkett nor the parish priest who proposed him could secure a hearing in the courthouse in

Navan. The scene was described by C. O'Connell Murphy for James A. Dease, brother of the junior member for Queen's county, who apparently forwarded this letter to Cullen. "Well," Murphy informed Dease on January 2, "the nomination is over, and such a scene I never witnessed. The people have become completely brutalised. Father Dowling of Clonmellon [who] was not allowed to say a word addressed himself to the reporters, nor neither [*sic*] was Mr. Plunkett nor anyone favourable to Mr. Plunkett. The courthouse was packed with a mob you would imagine taken out of hell. So fearful were they I am afraid Martin will get in" (C). "The priests," Murphy maintained, "are not up to the mark. They are divided in every way and Mr. Plunkett's supporters are affording a luke warm support. I think Mr. Plunkett has been very badly treated." "There are no preparations and Hinds and the Fenians have the whole business in their hand," he further explained, referring to a local barrister, who had been an unsuccessful candidate in the recent general election. "Hinds is now taking vengeance for his defeat." "We had a meeting," Murphy then noted in a postscript, "after the Election [correctly, nomination], but did no good. A few priests were all divided." Though the Meath clergy did not apparently renege publicly on their endorsement of Plunkett, they certainly did not work very hard for him, for on election day, January 17, he was handily beaten by Martin, 1,140 votes to 684.[11]

On the day of the poll, Cullen's secretary, Patrick Moran, whose letters to Rome were always a faithful reflection of the cardinal's views, wrote Kirby to report what had happened in the Meath election. "Tell Father Maher," Moran suggested ironically, referring to Kirby's vice-rector, and a native of the diocese of Meath, "I congratulate him on his election in the Co. Meath. They rejected the brother of Lord Fingall, the best landlord and Catholic Nobleman in Ireland, to put in a Presbyterian" (K). "Mr Martin is however," Moran added, "himself a respectable man, but the party that returned him are the most rabid Fenians in the country. There was a regular but silent terrorism exercised & the burden of the Mob's cries was *down with the Priests*." "Dr. Nulty," he explained, referring to the bishop of Meath, "is very much blamed: he prevented the good Priests from using their just influence against the Fenian invasion, whilst some of his P.P.'s & C.C.'s canvassed [*sic*] for Martin." "The sad result of the election," Moran concluded, "will separate the clergy & people still more in that quarter." The *Freeman's Journal,* however, expressed another point of view about Martin's unexpected victory in Meath. "It can be accounted for," the journal pointed out on January 18, "in one way only. Mr. Martin is a sincere nationalist, an earnest repealer, and the Irish people have arrived at the conclusion that the policy of all English parties is to make such concessions only as may conduce to party power—to make none to the nation in deference to its will, and to stamp out the last vestiges of nationality."

11. Walker, p. 113.

"The Meath election," it added prophetically, "is a great fact. It may eventuate in nothing important, but even should it be so, it is still a great fact. It may, however prove to be the beginning of the end." And so it did.

Some three weeks later the bishop of Galway, John MacEvilly, reported to Cullen that the junior member for county Galway, Viscount Burke, a younger son of the marquis of Clanricarde, was about to give up his seat. "Lord Clancarty's third son, a Captain Trench," he explained on February 6, "is to stand on high tory, Orange principles. We have besides in the field two Liberals, a Captain Nolan, Ballinderry, of the Royal Artillery, and Mr. Mitchell Henry" (C). "Both the latter called on me," MacEvilly further explained, alluding to the fact that the archbishop of Tuam also exercised considerable ecclesiastical jurisdiction in the county Galway, "after having seen Dr. MacHale, who declined giving any positive promise till he would hear what I would do."

> This is the first time in his life he did such a thing as mind any Suffragan in such matters. However I see through it well. It is meant to throw the responsibility of a division on me. So, I told Mr. Mitchell Henry when he called on me yesterday that if Dr. MacHale would support him I would. Mr. Henry's address which he read for Dr. MacHale, & who, he tells me, approved of it, is very good. He is for Denomin Education, for supporting the Pope, and home rule, which latter is now becoming an Election War Cry. He tells me, Dr. MacHale promised him his support if I would. So, I at once declared I would, if Dr. MacHale did, as it would be awkward, however we may, as indeed we do, differ on several points, to have us in opposite camps on such an occasion. Mr. Henry is also supported by Lord Clanricarde. So, if Dr. MacHale dont back out of it, I don't see much difficulty in the way.

"Captain Nolan," MacEvilly pointed out, "has I hear engaged as his conducting agent Mr. Higgins of Tuam, Dr. MacHale's brother in law." "Against Captain Nolan," he then added, referring to some evictions in Connemara several years before, "there is one fearful objection. He had been guilty some years ago in the neighbourhood of Oughterard of the most cruel extermination. He says he is ready to repair it. But I suspect it is too late, & now impossible as the poor victims are some of them dead, others, out of the country."

Though Nolan was strongly supported by one of MacHale's most political priests in the county Galway, Peter Conway, the parish priest of Headford, his record as an evicting landlord was raised against him, and he was forced to retire. The third son of the earl of Clancarty, Captain William Trench, also decided not to contest the seat in the Conservative interest. "Captain Nolan," MacEvilly reported to Cullen on February 20, the day before the official polling, "very *prudently retires*. The exposure of his extermination is awful. Mr. Mitchell Henry goes in for the County without a Contest. Dr. MacHale was practically for Nolan. They found they would be dreadfully beaten" (C). "Rev. Peter Conway's scurrilous letters," MacEvilly noted further, "greatly scared Mr. Henry. Conway is really like a mad dog biting at every body." "If Conway come in here tomorrow," he then explained to Cullen, referring to the fact that the official polling would take place in the court house in Galway City, "as he threatens (a carriage has been ordered by him to go for him) I won't answer for the consequences as regards himself." "I have directed the Priests here," MacEvilly assured Cullen in concluding, "to keep aloof, if Conway be there, as it would be unpleasant, and no necessity now."

The next day, Conway was present in Galway at the courthouse when the high sheriff of the county declared Henry duly elected and, as MacEvilly feared, proceeded to create a scene. "Our Election," MacEvilly, obviously relieved, reported to Cullen on February 21, "is peaceably over. Mitchell Henry is our M.P. I have every hopes of him" (C). "A most disgraceful scene," MacEvilly added, "I hear occurred in court. In fact several County catholics came to me [to] complain. But of course I could do nothing, & so I refer it to your Eminence."

> Rev. Peter Conway came into court and [was] left alone with one or two others, laymen, in a jurors' box in the courthouse. In the presence of the whole crowded court, he had with him a basin full of water, washed his hands, and reenacted the whole scene in our Lord's Crucifixion, declaring he washed his hands &c &c out of the cursed County. He scattered the water on some under the box, who got into a terribly excited state. The Catholics were terribly scandalized at seeing a Priest doing such a thing, & the Protestants jeered and derided. Mr. Henry's speech, I hear was very excellent.

"All," he assured Cullen again, "has passed off quietly, thank God. Captain Nolan was patronized by Rev. P. Conway, & promised the patronage and support of Dr. MacHale. When it came to the point, Dr. MacHale would not venture to support the Exterminator, and so he retired." "I don't by any means," MacEvilly concluded, "expect any answer from your Eminence. But I wrote this as you might naturally feel no objection to get an authentic acc^t of how things went on here."

When MacEvilly wrote Kirby a week later on February 27, enclosing some £565 Peter's pence for the pope, he explained that they had just had a great electoral triumph in returning Mitchell Henry for the county and that Henry had promised to do his best for denominational education (K). Though he was a Protestant, MacEvilly pointed out that he was "a very liberal one" and that he had more confidence in Henry than in many a worthless Catholic. His opponent, Nolan, for example, was a Catholic, who had been supported by MacHale, but when his record as an exterminating landlord had been exposed he had had to withdraw. Besides, MacEvilly added finally, Henry had a brother who was a convert and a Jesuit to boot. This was a very clever performance on the part of MacEvilly, who had been placed in a very awkward position by the circumstances of the Galway election. In his correspondence with Cullen he chose to dwell at great length on MacHale's political insincerities and Conway's blasphemous extravagancies rather than on what was really at issue—the fact that he was supporting the return of a prominent Home Ruler. MacEvilly chose to represent Henry as a Liberal who was more interested in denominational education and defending the pope's temporal power than in advocating Home Rule, which he even implied was only a shibboleth in this case. Therefore, what MacEvilly was telling Cullen in his own oblique way was that really he had been forced to choose between the lesser of two evils, and that Henry, all things considered, was the less risky choice.

That Cullen was certainly not much pleased with the return of two successive Home Rulers in little more than a month's time may be inferred by a brief exchange he had, shortly after John Martin had been returned for county Meath, with the earl of Granard, a prominent Irish Catholic convert, on the subject of the timeliness of Repeal. Granard had just read a published letter of Gladstone's in which the prime minister had not been very sympathetic about the pope's recent loss of his temporal power, and he thought that a stronger line on the part of Irish Catholics toward English Liberals was now in order. "They seem determined," he explained to Cullen on January 26, "to throw us over for the Exeter Hall party, & that being so I think we should have to oppose them strenuously. For my own part, I look upon all this as the commencement of the rupture, which must come sooner or later . . . between the Catholic party & the English Liberals, who appear to me to aspire to being the infidel party of England" (C). "Nothing wd. embarrass them so much," he further assured Cullen, "as if the Repeal [cry] were to be taken up by our side, but then it is a dangerous weapon, though such a course might reunite all sections of the Catholic & liberal party here." Apparently Cullen was startled, perhaps even shocked, by a proposal to break up the Irish-Liberal alliance, which would have the result of throwing them all into the arms of the Home Rulers, and he wrote Granard immediately, cautioning him against such politically extravagant views. "I am much obliged to your Eminence," Granard replied, in his more usual and deferential tone, on January 29, "for your opinion, & shall regulate my conduct in accordance with it" (C). "I quite agree," he further assured Cullen, "in your estimate of the persons who are advocating the measure in question, & merely adverted to the matter, because I know, that the Govt. are very much afraid of the movement gaining ground."

During this period, however, Cullen not only was very hard on his political friends for their lack of faith in the Irish-Liberal alliance, but also apparently he was very annoyed still at the conduct of the bishop of Meath, Thomas Nulty, and his clergy in the recent by-election. So, when about a month after that election, on February 20, Nulty published a Lenten pastoral on the subject of the prevalence of secret societies and Ribbonmen in his diocese, Cullen, in effect, reported him to Rome for his ambivalence on the subject. "Monsignor Nulty," Cullen complained in Italian to Kirby on March 8, "has published a pastoral pamphlet about Ribbonmen, condemning them and defending them. This pastoral is much criticised and I fear will do harm. The County of Westmeath is in a disturbed state" (K).

Whenever Cullen wrote Kirby in Italian, of course, he meant that the letter should be read to the Roman authorities. To Cullen, the root of the ambivalence in the pastoral, which he had marked, was that, in condemning secret societies, Nulty had tempered his remarks with an equally strong condemnation of those social and economic conditions that had given rise to such unlawful combinations and which made their prevalence understandable even if they were illegal and morally reprehensible (C). Cullen was soon, however, to have even greater cause for complaint to Rome about Nulty and his clergy.

In the meantime, Irish politics had been further complicated for Cullen and the supporters of the Irish-Liberal alliance by the founding in February, in London, of the Catholic Union of Great Britain by a number of prominent English-Catholic laymen, led by the duke of Norfolk. "It has for its objects," the circular announcing the union's formation declared, "the restoration of the Holy Father to his legitimate rights as Sovereign of the Papal States, and the defence of all Catholic interests" (C). On March 18, the English Catholic weekly, the *Tablet,* provided a historical sketch of the circumstances that had led to founding the union, with a further description of its purposes and objects and a list of its officers and the members of its council (C). A short time later, apparently after consulting Cullen, the earl of Granard wrote to the editor of the *Tablet,* Herbert Vaughan, requesting more information about the British union, and Vaughan forwarded the relevant issue of the *Tablet.* "Will Your Eminence," Granard asked Cullen on April 20, "kindly look over it, & return it to me, with your opinion as to how far it may be adopted as a basis of our operations here" (C). "I wd. propose as a Council or Committee," he suggested, "Lds, Fingall, Gormanstown, Dunraven, Southwell,—Messrs. More O'Ferrall, Dease, Cogan, Sir D. Corrigan, Sir T. Esmonde, Major O'Reilly, O'Conor Don, myself & anyone else Your Eminence wd. advise." "I fear officials such as Ld. Castlerosse," he noted, referring to the eldest son of the earl of Kenmare, and vice-chamberlain of the Queen's household, "& the Judges would scarcely join?"

"I have been so occupied with other matters," Granard apologized to Cullen more than a month later, on May 23, "that I have been unable to do anything with reference to the proposed Irish Catholic Union" (C). "I now enclose a letter about [it] fr. Mr. Dease," he added, referring to the junior member of Parliament for Queen's county, "& wd. be glad to learn Your Eminence's final decision upon it, as well as upon the List for a Council or Committee which I sent to you some time ago. I also send the rules of the English Union which I obtained from Dr. Herbert Vaughan." "Our Bishop," he noted, referring to the bishop of Ardagh, George

Conroy, "thinks well of the movement. I suppose after hearing Yr. Eminence's views, my best plan will be in the first instance to write to Lord Fingall & the other persons in the list I furnished, and when we have enough consent to publish it in the papers? or hold a preliminary meeting in Dublin." Obviously, Cullen's reply was positive, for in early June, Granard wrote to those he had proposed to Cullen for the council to lend their names and support to the founding of an Irish Catholic union.

Though the earl of Fingall was the first to reply, his response was not very reassuring. "I am not in a position," he informed Granard somewhat brusquely on June 10, "to form an opinion on the proposed Catholic Union as I do not know in what the English one consists, what are its objects, and by what rules it is governed" (C). "In a political point of view," Fingall explained, "I do not think that our English brethren are good guides. Had our mode of proceeding been regulated by their advice or example Catholic Emancipation wd. not have been carried as it was; neither wd. the Church & Land questions have been settled as they have been." "I took no interest in the English 'Union,'" he further explained, referring to the fact that the English-Catholic aristocracy nearly all had become Conservative and Tory in their politics in recent years, while the Irish-Catholic aristocracy still had remained Whig and Liberal, "from my general idea as to the political status of our friends across channel and this will account for my ignorance on the subject." "If you will kindly let me know," he promised in conclusion, "where I can find the necessary information about the Irish one I will give it my best attention. Without knowing what it is I should not like to say I would join it & act on the Committee." In forwarding this letter to Cullen on June 10, Granard observed that Fingall's reply "was not what I should have expected fr. him" (C). Granard, who was not very quick politically, obviously had missed the point. What Fingall really was telling him was that he was not about to become involved in a political organization that might prove to be antagonistic to Gladstone and the Irish-Liberal alliance. Cullen, however, did not miss the point, for after Fingall's letter he allowed the subject of an Irish Catholic union to drop, and it was not taken up again for nearly a year.

In the meantime, the proponents of the Irish-Liberal alliance were about to suffer another defeat at the hands of the Home Rulers. At the end of May, the senior member for county Westmeath, William Pollard-Urquhart, died, and Cullen encouraged James A. Dease, brother of Edmund Dease, the junior member for Queen's county, to offer himself as a candidate. When Dease visited Westmeath in early June, however, he found that there were already two Home Rulers in the field, Nicholas Ennis, a local tenant farmer, and P. J. Smyth, a former Young Irelander and Repealer. On June 9, Dease wrote his good friend, William Monsell, senior member for county Limerick and recently appointed postmaster general in Gladstone's ministry, that he had not "a ghost of a chance," as the Fenian element had decided to run Smyth.[12] "My own P.P.," he then explained, "(a very steady, shrewd man) tells me he thinks the Priests will be '*afraid not* to go with the popular demand.'" Indeed, in order to avoid the turmoil of a contested election, the Westmeath clergy decided to interview the candidates and then express their preference, on the understanding that the disappointed candidates would retire. The clergy interviewed the candidates in Mullingar on June 13, and Dease reported the ordeal to Monsell the next day.

"I was put through my catechism," he explained, "by Dr. Nulty in the presence of some 40 'sacreds.'"[13] "I have reason to know," he then added, "that the bishop was personally strongly in my favour, as were the real sympathies of all the P.P.'s and several of the C.C.'s as well. 'Home Rule' was the sole difficulty. Great efforts were made to induce me to swallow that pledge and I have some curious letters (that I may show you some time or other) from priests and from others in the clerical influence, urging me to declare for 'Home rule' (with any kind of mental reservation I pleased) and preferring as a reason for so doing that 'the whole thing was a mere *cry of the moment* and would be *forgotten before the next* election.'" "Nothing could exceed the personal courtesy," he then assured Monsell, "I met with from the whole meeting—but the result was a declaration that they would support Smyth. One thing I am sure of—that Dr. Nulty and many of the priests— tho' they concur in this course, do so with bitter shame. The bishop told me privately in so many words that '*they were afraid to oppose the popular feeling that would be evoked*.'" Nulty then went on to explain, Dease noted, referring to the recent by-election in Meath, that "in those parishes where the priests worked hard (and very few they were, by the way) for George Plunkett, an antagonism has arisen between the [priests and people]."

Cullen, meanwhile, had also written his former secretary and now the new bishop of Ardagh, George Conroy, about the views of his clergy in that portion of Westmeath which was a part of his diocese. "I am so little acquainted as yet," Conroy, who had only been consecrated some three months before, replied on June 12, "with the Westmeath portion of this Diocese, that I can offer no opinion as to the state of public & clerical feeling in the matter of the election" (C). "I was very glad," he explained, "that neither Dease nor Ennis gave me any intimation of their intention to contest the County until they had issued their addresses. This relieves me of all responsibility in the matter. As far as I can learn their rival claims will vastly strengthen the position of Smyth." "Every day that I spend here," he assured Cullen in conclusion, interestingly, "brings home to me more and more the immense injury to religion that results from these elections in which the priests forget themselves through zeal for one or other candidate." When both Ennis and

---

12. Monsell Papers (M), National Library of Ireland, Dublin, 8317 (4).
13. Ibid, also quoted in Thornley, p. 118.

Dease prudently retired after being rejected by the Westmeath clergy, Smyth was returned unopposed, on June 17.

Cullen, however, was not so easily appeased, and, apparently, he wrote to Kirby suggesting that perhaps the Roman authorities should be made aware of the unfortunate political views of the bishop of Meath and his clergy, for Kirby prepared a long memorandum on the subject, which he submitted in early July to the Propaganda authorities. "In connection with the diocese of Meath," Kirby pointed out, "it might be observed that the trend of things there for some time past, in the view of many, [is] that the spirit of Fenianism is not a little propagated there."[14] "Among the [many] reasons that may be cited in confirmation of this," he explained, "for conciseness, [only] the following are mentioned."

> 1. Towards the end of December of last year there arose the question of choosing a member of Parliament. There were two candidates. One, Mr. Plunkett, brother of Lord Fingall, of one of the most ancient of Catholic noble families in Ireland, the other was a fellow *Martin,* who was put forward as a favorite of the Fenians. Well, the latter was chosen. The Bishop and priests did not oppose him. One of the vicars general [correctly, forane] of the Bishop voted publicly for Martin.
>
> 2. Some months later the Bishop published a pastoral letter that has been much criticized. He speaks in it against secret societies, but at the same time adopts a language which, it seems to others, is meant to diminish the effect [of it] against the Fenians.
>
> 3. Meanwhile the state of Meath became so disturbed that the Government established a Committee to inquire into the causes for it. Various persons were called to be examined, among them Monsignor Nulty. Of this, an authoritative person has written on April 28, "It appears that Monsignor Nulty has not cut a good figure before the Committee of inquiry. The Protestant members of Parliament say that he contradicted himself continually. He was put in a false position by his pastoral letter and as a consequence was forced to contradict himself by defending what he had said in defense of Ribbonism [in his pastoral]. I fear that our Fenians and Ribbonmen are connected with the French Republicans and the Italian Carbonari."
>
> 4. Lately, there has been another election of a member of Parliament in Meath. The Bishop meeting together with the clergy chose a fellow *Smyth.* On this choice, the praiseworthy person wrote on June 28, "The latest acts in Westmeath have done great harm. I am of the opinion that Monsignor Nulty, and his clergy are very responsible for it. They say here that *Smyth* who was elected to Parliament is a communist. It was he [i.e., his election] that induced some of the Irish to leave for France in October. Some say this Smyth is a religious man. In truth, all those witnesses have protested that he is religious. But in case of a revolution I do not wish to rely on it."

---

14. S.R.C., vol. 36, fols. 1210–11. This is an undated and unsigned memorandum in Kirby's handwriting.

"A pious lady now in Rome," Kirby concluded, "reported the day before yesterday she received a letter from a good priest named Molloy of that diocese of Meath, and he told her that Fenianism and unbelief have made pathetic progress in that diocese."

Barnabò submitted Kirby's somewhat naive memorandum to Bernard Smith, an Irish Benedictine long resident in Rome who had at one time been vice-rector of the Irish College under Kirby and who was no longer as friendly to the Cullen interest in Rome as he had once been, for his opinion. Smith, who often served as a consultor to Propaganda on Irish and American matters, prepared a short *voto,* or opinion, on the subject of the declaration of support for Smyth by the bishop and clergy of Meath raised in Kirby's memorandum. "The declaration made by the Bishop and Clergy of Meath," Smith reported, "cannot be charged with Fenianism. I do not commend the part taken by these ecclesiastics in a political matter, but to accuse them of Fenianism is a calumny."[15] "The declaration," he warned, "is very serious and may be the signal of a long agitation. In substance it comes down to the *Repeal* of the Union as regards an Irish Parliament. On the one side, England does not want to do justice to Catholics in Ireland, on the other side, the Irish believe—at least many of them—that the only remedy would be a domestic Parliament. They do not demand total Repeal of the Union as in the time of O'Connell. The Bishops of Ireland at that time were almost all in favor of *Repeal:* and also took part in the agitation that lasted for many years." "I hope," Smith advised Barnabò in conclusion, "that these few words will be enough to induce your Eminence to take time before writing to Monsignor Nulty about the declaration. A few days will make more known in regard to the matter; and if the candidate Smyth, for whom the declaration was made, is or not a Fenian."

After Smith's very shrewd *voto* on the subjects of Home Rule, Fenianism, and Repeal, Barnabò and the Propaganda authorities apparently did not pursue the matter any further. Cullen was still, however, very sore about the conduct of the Meath clergy and complained to Conroy about the part taken by the prior of the Carmelite house in Moate, at the late meeting of the Westmeath clergy in Mullingar, which was in the Westmeath portion of the Ardagh diocese. "I took occasion last week," Conroy assured Cullen on July 26, "to speak in private to Father MacDonnell the Carmelite prior of Moate, concerning his recommendation of Smyth for Westmeath. He spoke of him at the priests' meeting as a good Catholic & voted for him, and does not deny his admiration for the Home Rulers" (C). "I told Fr. MacDonnell that I would write to Y. E. to inquire," Conroy explained, referring to the Carmelite authorities in Dublin, "if these were the doctrines taught by the fathers at Aungier St & Dominick Street."

Cullen's various attempts to intimidate the clerical supporters of Home Rule

---

15. Ibid., fols. 1208–9. Undated but signed by Smith.

does not appear to have been very successful, and his temper could not have been improved by the news he was receiving from one of his priests, John Canon Farrell, whom he had sent to London to hold a watching brief for him on the progress being made in Parliament on Irish education. At the end of a long letter about educational matters written on July 26, Farrell reported that William Monsell, the postmaster general, had pointed out "that the Govemt was very uneasy about the Home rule Movement. He is anxious to know the probability as to its development—he thinks it will do great mischief & prevent concessions on the Education question" (C). Several days later, Farrell returned to the same theme at the end of another long letter to Cullen. "The Govemt.," he reported again on July 30, "appear very anxious about the Home-rule Movement. I told Mr. Monsell that we shall be driven into its ranks if our hopes on this Education question be baffled next Session." The government was so uneasy, of course, not only because it was concerned about the recent run of three by-elections in favor of the Home Rulers, but also because it was worried by the Dublin Corporation's declaration by a large majority, in early July, in favor of Home Rule, as well as the subsequent strong showing of the leader of the Home Rule movement, Isaac Butt, among the Catholic and Liberal electors in the recent by-election for county Monaghan.

Cullen, too, had been much embarrassed by both the vote in the Dublin Corporation and the emergence of Butt in the Monaghan election. In the corporation, Cullen's mouthpiece, Alderman Peter Paul MacSwiney, had failed in his attempt to table the declaration for six months, arguing that at the present time it would only result in the government's deferment of the education question. Cullen's embarrassment about Monaghan, though less public, was no less painful. He had become involved when H. Owen Lewis, a wealthy Catholic convert and a native of Monaghan, had written him about the vacancy. "I see by a letter," Lewis informed Cullen from London on June 26, "in the *Times* of this morning that Colonel Leslie M.P. for County Monaghan died yesterday" (C). "If possible," Lewis explained unabashedly, "I should wish to get in in his place, and if your Eminence would kindly write to the bishop of Clogher on my behalf, asking him to use his influence for me I think I should have a good chance." "If returned," he then promised, "I should give an independent support to the present Government, and try to obtain a religious system of Education for Ireland, which I believe to be the real panacea for its wants."

Apparently Cullen wrote to James Donnelly, the bishop of Clogher, on behalf of Lewis, for the latter announced his intention early in July to contest the seat as a Liberal and addressed the electors in favor of the secret ballot, denominational education, and the defence of the pope's temporal interest. At the same time, the Conservatives chose John Leslie, the son of the late member, to contest the seat in their interest, and it was widely suggested in the Nationalist press that Butt should offer himself as the Home Rule candidate. Butt had, in fact, made discreet inquiries through his son, Robert, about the possibilities of winning the seat. "After conferring with some gentlemen here," L. J. O'Neill reported to Robert from Monaghan town on July 2, "who know the relative strength of political parties in the county, I have come to the conclusion that it would be impossible to return Mr. Butt without a large accession to the catholic party" (B). "As I told you," O'Neill explained, "the catholics are in a minority of 4 or 500 on the registry. Then increase that minority by say another hundred who would be influenced by the landlords & you can calculate our disadvantage." "This is the opinion," he noted in concluding, "of more experienced men than I am. At the same time I do not wish you to suppose that I desire you to shape your course by my opinion." "I am afraid," O'Neill added in a postscript, "you could not reasonably hope to get from the orange ranks what would make us equal in numbers to the landlords forces— in this county all past experience proves it would be building on sand to trust in the orange party where Irish or catholic interests are at stake." Given this chilling analysis, Butt naturally was reluctant to offer himself as a candidate. This did not deter John Madden, however, who was a former Conservative and an Orangeman, and who was also a founding member of the Home Government Association and sat on its governing council, from addressing the electors on July 10 about Home Rule principles. Madden was endorsed immediately by not only a number of leading Home Rulers, including Sullivan, Martin, and Galbraith, but also by Father Thaddeus O'Malley, a Dublin priest, who was also a member of the Home Government Association council. O'Malley, who had had a most interesting clerical career, was at this time more than eighty years of age and had been suspended recently from his priestly functions for allegedly authoring the book, *Harmony in Religion,* which Cullen viewed as heretical because it challenged the infallible teaching authority of the pope.

In any case, Cullen was scandalized by O'Malley's endorsement and wrote the bishop of Clogher a letter, on July 15, about O'Malley, which he authorized Donnelly to publish if necessary. In thanking Cullen on Monday, July 17 for his letter, Donnelly assured him, "that no one here dreamed Father O'Malley represented in the matter, anybody but himself and perhaps his confrères of the Home Rule Association. There will now however be no need of making public use of Your Eminence's letter as Mr. Madden retired from the contest on Saturday last, and it was only in case of *necessity* Your Eminence authorized me to publish it" (C). In a postscript, Donnelly then charitably added, "I would humbly crave the exercise of *mercy* for poor crazy Father Thaddeus O'Malley. Ah, My dear Lord Cardinal perhaps contrition and a promise of amendment and of severance of the connection between himself & the Home Rule Junta might suffice for the present, especially as no actual harm has been done in the present case." Cullen's overreaction to O'Malley's conduct, of course, was still another indication of how upset he was really about the increasing power and influence of the Home Rule movement.

After Madden's withdrawal from the contest, however, worse followed. For rather than allow the election to go by default to either the Conservative Leslie or the Liberal Lewis, Butt allowed his name to be put in nomination at the last minute. The Catholic and Liberal interests in Monaghan then dropped Lewis and adopted Butt. In the ensuing election, which took place on July 22, Butt was defeated by Leslie, 2,538 votes to 1,451.[16] What the Monaghan election clearly proved, however, was that the Catholic electors in that county, at least, preferred Home Rule to the Gladstonian alliance as represented by Cullen's protégé, H. Owen Lewis. What it also proved, more significantly for the future of Home Rule, was that, now that Butt had indicated he was available as a parliamentary candidate, at the next vacancy in Ireland, where the majority of the electors were Catholic rather than Protestant, his return was inevitable.

In the meantime, the tide had begun to run so strongly in favor of Home Rule that the very shrewd and able political opportunist, and up until then a leading proponent of the Irish-Liberal alliance, James Francis Maguire, junior member for Cork City and proprietor of the leading daily paper in the south, the *Cork Examiner,* made a 180-degree turn in the middle of August and declared for Home Rule. The growing frustration and feeling of helplessness of the supporters of the Irish-Liberal alliance were well articulated by Cullen's secretary, Patrick Moran, in a letter written to Kirby, in Rome, toward the end of August. "The great political question now," he assured Kirby on August 25, "is *Home Rule,* but as usual this is only a mask for the real political views of the agitators" (K). Characterizing the adherents, Moran explained,

> Some have taken it up, in the hope to divide the people from the bishops and clergy and hence, the names of the most bitter Orangemen in Ireland will be found among the leaders of "Home Rule." Others have taken it up, merely to save Trinity-College, or they think by putting the people of Ireland on a false scent, that attention will not be given to the Trinity-College grievance: and hence some of the fellows in the cause of Fenianism, and hence all the Fenian newspapers and Fenian agents have adopted it as their cry. All the Tories have taken it up as a good party-cry against Mr. Gladstone; and in fine our trading agitators who are only seeking to feather their own nests and to obtain a seat in Parliament, have adopted the same popular cry preparing for the next election.

"All the young priests," he added, concluding his catalogue, "have also taken the matter up in some dioceses to the great annoyance of the peaceable parishioners." "Here in Dublin," Moran assured Kirby, "all our sensible people and all the clergy, knowing who the leaders are, stand aloof, and say: your present movement is a false one: we are not enemies of Repeal, but we will not follow such leaders: the time will come when that question [Repeal] may be fairly started." "But at the

16. Walker, p. 114.

same time," he concluded significantly, "no one wishes to attack the Home Rulers openly, thinking it better to let the bubble burst of its own accord."

When the senior member for Limerick City, F. W. Russell, died on August 30, five days after Moran wrote to Kirby, however, it soon became obvious that the Home Rule bubble was not about to burst. Butt, who was invited immediately, in early September, to stand for Limerick, by Philip Callan, member for the borough of Dundalk and a prominent Home Ruler, decided to contest the seat. Because of the state of his health, Butt refused to campaign in person and was represented in Limerick by his son Robert and a local committee of prominent Nationalists. The bishop of Limerick, George Butler, and William Monsell, the senior member for county Limerick, and a leading advocate of the Irish-Liberal alliance, attempted to field a Liberal candidate to oppose Butt, by enlisting the solicitor general of Ireland, Charles R. Barry, who was then without a seat. Barry, however, was too experienced an Irish politician not to realize that under the circumstances Butt was unbeatable. "No man," Barry assured Gladstone on September 6, "not putting 'Home Rule' forward as the strength of his programme would be listened to, and I fear it will be the same in every constituency."[17] Indeed, Barry was right, for Butt had taken the wind out of any opposition to him on the hustings, particularly any clerical opposition, by advocating in his election address a charter for the Catholic University, religious equality, and denominational education, as well as a measure of tenant right that would include fixity of tenure, fair rent, and free sale. After two more weeks of incredible enthusiasm and torchlight processions and speeches every evening, therefore, Butt was returned unopposed, on September 20, as the junior member for Limerick City.

The day after Butt's return, the senior member for county Limerick wrote to his good friend, James A. Dease, who had recently been disappointed in his candidacy for county Westmeath, to ask him what he thought of the current political situation. "I may premise," Dease replied to Monsell on September 29, "by saying that one circumstance—& one only—prevents me from having unmixed regret at the result of the Limerick Election. That circumstance is the proof it affords that when I decided on not going to the Poll in Westmeath I acted wisely."[18] "It must be pretty clear now," he explained, "that when the Fenians, with the Priests against them, put in Butt for Limerick, I had no chance in WMeath where the Priests & the Fenians were both opposed to me." "Now," he then added, "to answer your questions."

> You assume that "there is abroad among good men a desire, pretty sentimental & very vague to manage Irish affairs in Ireland."
> I must say I have met *very few such men*. I do not think the Home Rule

17. Quoted in Thornley, p. 122.
18. M, 8317 (4).

movement has made any way at all with the upper classes of any creed or Politics. A few Protestants embittered by the legislation on the Church—& a very few of the landlord class—who hate Mr. Gladstone for passing the Land Bill, have joined the movement chiefly to spite the present Ministry. A very short spell of *Tory rule* would set such men straight again.

With the middle class who are disposed to speak their real minds, I think distrust of the men who have got up the present agitation is so great that it quite outweighs the sentimental feeling the words Home Rule arouse. Such certainly was the feeling I observed amongst the respectable farmers & shop-keepers (& indeed among many of the *Priests* as well) at the time of the late Election here [Westmeath], tho' I am sure very many of these men would, if I had gone to the Poll, have been afraid to oppose Mr. P. J. Smyth in the face of the Fenian mob.

When however you descend a step lower I admit the cry has aroused a good deal of sympathy—but there is an entire absence of any definite idea of what is sought, beyond the one simple notion of "freeing ourselves from *Saxon thral-dom.*" Patriotism is a noble virtue, & Irishmen think they possess it in a high degree—but in truth Irish patriotism is less love of Ireland than it is hatred of England!

"Of the Priests," Dease pointed out, "I think the greater number of the men over thirty feel much as I have described the middle class as feeling. They intensely distrust the revolutionary spirit in which the present movement has originated, but at the same time they lack the moral courage which would enable them to take a course that they fear would be (for the moment at least) unpopular, & they dread losing that 'leadership' of the people which has made them so powerful for evil and for good—during the past forty years." "Of the Curates," he maintained, "many are acting, as they think, sincerely in favouring the Home Rule cry. The idea of Patriotism—especially in its more violent forms—is always attractive to young men & the Papers the Clergy exclusively read, pander incessantly to this feeling. But even they have no definite idea of what Home Rule means—beyond what I have attributed to the lower class of the population—hatred of England."

"Among those who call themselves Home Rulers," Dease further observed, "no three men you speak to agree in what they desire or hope for from the present agitation."

Most of them take shelter in the very plausible Federal idea because it saves them from the dilemma of choosing between Repeal—which means Revolu-tion—& maintaining the *status quo*—which entails unpopularity. But those who have aroused the agitation, those without whose impelling influence (backed as it has been, by the Fenian Spirit of the Masses) the mild quasi Fed-eralist would never have left the beaten track—those men have already gone far ahead of the policy embraced in the scheme of Federal Union.

Martin speaks of the army & navy of the Irish Nation! Smyth makes little concealment as to his Republican proclivities & the men who were the chief

supporters of both these gentlemen in Meath & in Westmeath, were notori-
ously the Fenian Leaders of their respective localities. Limerick I don't know
so well, but I see among Mr. Butt's chief supporters Mr. O'Sullivan of Kilmallock, if I mistake not—a lately liberated Fenian Convict! The truth is the
Home Rule movement in its present phase is nothing more or less than Fenianism under a thin, but very plausible, and cleverly constructed disguise.

The leaders mean *more* than they say—the "respectable" followers generally
mean *less*—while the "people," now as ever, cheer & follow those who talk
loudest & use the most violent language!

Were the movers of the Federal scheme reliable men—& were I not
convinced that the popularity of the Home Rule movement arises from hatred
to British Connexion & not from any honest desire to remove real grievances,
I own I should have been much disposed to have been a Federalist myself.

"The truth about Federalism," Dease then explained, "is this. The essence of a
Federal Union between any two Countries should be a desire to act in harmony.
Now this element is entirely wanting in the case of Great Britain & Ireland." "It
may read like an epigram," he confessed, "but I fear it is only the sober truth—
that—By the time Ireland is *fit* for Federal Union with England, she will, in all
probability, have ceased to desire it."

Dease's very able analysis of how far Home Rule had progressed in the collective minds of the various classes in Ireland by the early fall of 1871 certainly raises
some interesting questions. How accurate, for example, were his observations
about the impact of Home Rule across the Irish social spectrum? He was undoubtedly right about the limited impact of the agitation on the Irish "upper class"
because he was a member of that composite class and, therefore, had first-hand
experience of it. What may be said, however, of those classes, the middle and
lower, that he knew less well? His own recent experience in the Westmeath election had convinced him that the strong farmers and their cousinhood in the towns,
the substantial shopkeepers, that "respectable" class from whom the clergy were
largely recruited, were distrustful of the agitation. Though that is most likely true,
was the reason Dease gave for that distrust—that the farmers and shopkeepers did
not have much confidence in the leadership of the agitation—correct? This very
substantial Irish-Catholic middle class, which numbered perhaps three-quarters
of a million in a Catholic population in 1871 of some four million, had become,
since the famine, the crucial social and political class in Ireland. For more than
twenty years, then, this class had been moving economically from strength to
strength, and their attitude toward Home Rule had less to do, initially at least,
with their political sentiments than with their economic interests. While Dease
was therefore correct about the limited interest of this class in Home Rule, in 1871,
he was mistaken about the reason he assigned for it. The farmers' and shopkeepers' distrust of the leadership of the Home Rule movement, consisting as it
did of so many landlords and ascendancy types, provided this very economically

oriented middle class with a convenient ploy by which to politically excuse them-selves when confronted by their more patriotic countrymen. Dease was not, there-fore, unusual among his contemporaries; he was only more innocent, in finding a political cause for a political effect.

Finally, in his analysis of the Irish social pyramid, was Dease correct in asserting that the motivation of the lower classes in politics was less their love of Ireland than their hatred of England? The problem with such an assertion, of course, is that as a statement of cause it is essentially instinctive and not amenable, therefore, to any satisfactory historical measurement. It is, however, subject to some degree of historical analysis, which throws a great deal of light not only on the motives of people in Irish politics like Dease, who was a very fair representative of his class, but also, incidentally, on the reason that the Home Rule movement was feared by the bishops and a considerable number of their clergy as essentially a class move-ment in the guise of a national movement. Though Dease would undoubtedly have defended, on the basis of his empirical observations, his opinion that the political motivation of the Irish lower classes was rooted essentially in their hatred of England, it is interesting to note that this was also the long-held view of his very good friend, David Moriarty, the bishop of Kerry. In 1868, Moriarty had had occasion to write William Monsell a lengthy letter on the subject of disestablish-ing the Protestant Church in Ireland. "I do not fear revolution," Moriarty had confessed on March 2, "or rebellion or even sedition. I do not fear repeal of the Union!! But here we are in the midst of a people who have renounced their allegiance, and who know no patriotism except hatred for their rulers."[19] "I think this," he further asserted, "is a far deeper evil than rebellion itself." Irish Whigs, such as Moriarty, Dease, and Monsell had in the 1860s come to fear the "people" increasingly, in proportion to the increase of Fenianism in the affections of the lower classes. By late 1871, and this was the real lesson of Butt's election in Limerick, the Home Rulers and the Fenians obviously had become political allies in a combined constitutional agitation to modify the British connection. The real concern of these Whigs was that the Fenians, rooted as they were in the hatred of the "people" for the British connection, would swallow the Federalist Home Rulers whole and, with the constitutional side of the movement totally subverted, make their desperate bid for a republic and separation from England. In such a scenario, the only safe course for those such as Dease and his friends was to uphold the union at all costs.

The least satisfactory part of Dease's analysis, however, was his examination of the role of the clergy in regard to Home Rule. He began, unfortunately, by making a misleading distinction in differentiating between those priests who were over thirty years of age and those who were under. In a clerical body of, in 1871, about

---

19. J. H. Whyte, "Select Documents, XVIII," *Irish Historical Studies* 10, no. 38 (September, 1956): 198.

3,000 priests in Ireland, about 80 percent, or some 2,400, were probably over thirty years of age. Priests were not ordained in Ireland until their twenty-fourth year, curates did not usually succeed to a parish until they were in their midforties, and among the curates there was a pecking order in terms of seniors and juniors. Probably, what Dease really meant was to differentiate between those who acted like they were over and those who acted like they were under thirty, a much more subjective distinction, but perhaps more significant. In any case, Dease's original chronological distinction would imply that some 80 percent of the clerical body distrusted the revolutionary spirit of the Home Rule movement but lacked the moral courage to deal with it because the resulting unpopularity would cost them their political power and influence with the people. This moral cowardice was then compounded, according to Dease, by the sincere and natural, if misguided, political extravagances of those under thirty, who, like the lower classes, were mindlessly motivated by their hatred of England. On the face of it, this was simply a gross libel on the general character of the Irish clergy, and it certainly took its color from the way in which Dease was treated by the clergy in his bid for a parliamentary seat in Westmeath. If Dease is accepted as a fair representative of his class, however, this moral cowardice may be taken also as something more fundamental—a latent jealousy of the real political power and influence of the clergy, which the clergy now apparently were becoming more reluctant to invoke on behalf of Irish Whigs and Liberals, especially when they sensed that it would deeply divide the community. For it was this commitment of the clergy to upholding the unity of the community that gave legitimacy to their title as Irish Nationalists, and it was this title upon which their real political power and influence depended, not, as Dease and so many others of his class mistakenly perceived, the other way round.

In any case, by some three weeks after Butt's return to Parliament for Limerick City, the Home Rule movement had gained so much ground among the Irish in England that Archbishop Manning had to write Cullen to ask his advice in regard to it. "And now," Manning explained on October 11, "I wish for your Eminence's counsel on a grave matter, I mean the Home Rule movement" (C). "It is," he reported, "already active in London: & the 'Vindicator' is set up here to unite all Irish Catholics in England for its support."

> I will frankly open my mind to your Eminence about it. In the *personnel* I see somewhat to make me cautious & anxious.
>
> I see the danger that what begins in "Home Rule" may end in some wild excess. It may be that some already look beyond it.
>
> But so long as the programm of Imperial integrity is maintained, I am fully prepared for "Home Rule."
>
> If the program be violated, I should oppose that violation & not "Home Rule."
>
> I am strongly convinced that *political* questions ought to be Imperial.
>
> But that social, moral, religious, industrial questions (servantis servandis) [with the necessary reserves] ought to be local in the three Kingdoms (C).

"I shall be compelled to speak," he warned Cullen in conclusion, "and I wish to speak word for word as your Eminence does. Any discrepancy might be hurtful. Our agreement may perhaps have its good effect." "Any counsel," he finally assured Cullen, "your Eminence will give me shall be sub Sigillo S.R.T. [i.e., under the seal of the confessional]."

"In answer to your Grace's letter," Cullen replied on October 13, "I beg to state that I have determined to have nothing to do with the Home Rule movement for the present."[20] "The principal leaders in the movement here," he explained, "are professors of Trinity College who have never heretofore manifested any good feeling towards the people of Ireland and Orangemen who are still worse. Their object appears to be to put out the present ministry and get Disraeli into power when they will all give up the present agitation and declare against Home Rule. The other leaders are editors of half Fenian or anti-religious newspapers and some few wrongheaded or disappointed Catholics who are ready to engage in any new project whatever it may be." "Very few, perhaps ten or twelve priests," he assured Manning, "have taken part in this agitation, but I think all the bishops and the great mass of the clergy seem determined to keep aloof." "In the *Saunders* newspaper of this morning," Cullen further pointed out, "I find the enclosed notice which seems to indicate a union of the advocates of Home Rule with the International. If this statement have any foundation, it cannot but excite alarm in reference to Home Rule."

> The great mass of the people in Ireland are always ready to join any movement which is presented to them as something patriotic, but I think that Home Rule is still looked on with suspicion by them on account of its leaders. Ere yesterday I was at a town called Moate in Co. Westmeath and I am sure ten thousand persons came to meet me on my arrival and all went on their knees to get my blessing. They all knew that I had always condemned Fenianism and that I had given no sanction to Home Rule. The line of action I am determined to follow is to look on until we shall know more about the tendencies of the system and its leaders.

"I must add," Cullen finally noted, "that our newspapers make a great noise about this matter, but the movement is not as yet of any great power in the country." "I fear," he apologized in conclusion, "I have not been able to give your Grace as satisfactory an answer as I would wish but the fact is that I have not thought it necessary to do any more at present than to observe passing events." "Your Eminence's letter," Manning assured Cullen on the next day, October 14, "is all I need. I shall carefully follow the same course. Already I have been asked to allow the use of the Schools for Meetings. The obvious fear is the International. 'All rivers run into the Sea'" (C). "Your Eminence will render me," he suggested to Cullen in

---

20. Manning Papers (Ma), Westminster Diocesan Archives, London.

conclusion, "a valuable service if you will keep me informed of your decisions & acts in this matter."

What was most interesting about this important exchange between Manning and Cullen was that its real significance lay more perhaps in what was left unsaid than in what was said. On the face of the exchange, Manning had simply asked Cullen what he proposed to do about the emerging Home Rule movement in order that he might be able to adopt the same line. Cullen had replied that he proposed, in effect, to do nothing except watch and wait. Manning then assured Cullen he would do the same. There were, however, two very important assumptions in this exchange that were to prove to be very significant for the future development of both British and Irish politics. The first of these involved Manning's very deferential attitude toward Cullen. This attitude had a great deal more to it than the ordinary respect that might be expected from a subordinate for an ecclesiastical superior. Manning, who was himself a sublime connoisseur of power, was one of the few English Catholics in the nineteenth century who appreciated and worked with the realities of the Irish position in the British political system. He understood that the real political power of Catholics in the British system was actually a factor of the number of parliamentary seats they could control and that the Irish Catholics, therefore, were the basic factor in the British parliamentary power equation. What little political power and influence the English Catholics actually did possess—the Scottish Catholics had virtually none—was the result really of their privileged social and economic status rather than of their political position in English society. Manning never misunderstood this as long as he lived, and his deference to Cullen, therefore, was more than the traditional ritual respect for hierarchy and authority—it was also the salute of a political realist for the actual seat of power.

The second assumption in this exchange, which Manning articulated and in which Cullen acquiesced, was that the constitutional legitimacy of Home Rule as a political program was certain. In raising the question of Home Rule, Manning made its legitimacy clear by maintaining that he was prepared to adopt it in principle if Cullen approved. In his reply, Cullen chose to base his objection to the movement on the same grounds that had caused Manning to be cautious and anxious about it. Cullen argued that, indeed, the leadership of the movement was at once too Protestant and too Fenian rather than that there was anything intrinsically untoward about the principle of Home Rule itself. By then introducing the red herring of the alleged connection between the Home Rule movement and the First International, Cullen shrewdly raised the awful specter of the recent bloody experience of the Paris Commune and its suppression, and Manning astutely realized its value as far as guilt-by-association was concerned. The main point to be made here, however, is that, as much as Cullen feared and disliked the new movement, he was not able to denounce it publicly, and he was obliged, therefore, to learn to live with it as best he could.

Learning to live with the Home Rule movement, however, soon was going to prove to be even more difficult for Cullen and his friends than it had been in the past. Shortly after he had written Manning, Cullen had received a long letter from the bishop of Galway, John MacEvilly, about the second by-election within the year that was pending in county Galway. Rumors had, in fact, been circulating since the previous August that the senior member for the county, William Gregory, would soon be appointed governor of Ceylon, and therefore have to vacate his seat. By the time MacEvilly wrote to Cullen, on October 15, two Home Rule candidates were already in the field as well as a Conservative. The main difficulty for the bishops and clergy of the county was which of the Home Rule candidates, Hyacinth D'Arcy or Captain John Nolan, who had retired in the previous election when Mitchell Henry had been returned unopposed, should be adopted in order to prevent the Conservative, Captain William Trench, a younger son of the earl of Clancarty, from making this a three-cornered contest. A further difficulty was that the county Galway included the whole or part of five dioceses, since the archbishop of Tuam and the bishops of Galway, Kilmacduagh, Clonfert, and Elphin all shared some ecclesiastical jurisdiction in the county. Because the diocese of Kilmacduagh was now administered by the bishop of Galway, and Clonfert was at that moment vacant, however, only three bishops, MacHale, MacEvilly, and Gillooly really were concerned. Gillooly, who had the smallest jurisdiction of the three, however, proved to be the most aggressive among them in his effort to prevent a three-cornered contest, and this caused some serious misgivings on the part of his good friend and colleague, the bishop of Galway. "I received a letter from Dr. Gillooly," MacEvilly informed Cullen on October 15, in a letter marked "private," "enclosing a copy of a letter he meant to send our liberal & Catholic candidates Messrs. Nolan & D'Arcy, and stating that after reading the letter for your Eminence, you expressed a wish that he would send me a copy, as the course he pursued seemed the only means of preventing a contest &c." (C). "I have written Dr. Gillooly," he further explained, "on whom very little comparatively of the responsibility, having so few Parishes in the Co., must rest, agreeing on the necessity of adopting some effectual means of preventing a split in the liberal ranks, as otherwise a rank conservative & bigot, Lord Clancarty's son, would surely walk in, but differing altogether as to the means he intends adopting to secure union in the Liberal ranks." "I also expressed my conviction," he added, coming to the real purpose of his letter, "that your Eminence would adopt my views, if the real condition of things, both as regards the disposition of the Candidates, &, what is more important still of their respective supporters was explained to your Eminence."

> They would never hear of deciding by *lot* as Dr. Gillooly suggests. If the principle of casting lots were once admitted every political schemer would sow divisions in the hope of have [*sic*] the lots turn out in his favor. We might have Peter Gill and O'Donovan Rossa quietly returned to Parliament by lot. The proposition which seems to me the only reasonable one, and to which no one could reasonably object, would be to have the parties compare votes, show their support, & have persons appointed on both sides to see them carried out *bona fide* & then let the weaker make way for the stronger. This was the course we successfully adopted at our late borough Election, when we returned Lord St. Lawrence. The plan of casting lots was never thought of, nor would Lord St. Lawrence ever consent, nor ought he.

"Even as regards the plan which I suggest," MacEvilly added, "there is a difficulty arising out of the following circumstances."

> On our return last August from the Maynooth meeting, Dr. Gillooly called me over to Dr. MacHale at Mullingar, and said, "as regards this coming Election, we must all go together," [and] to this I expressed my assent. This certainly would mean nothing else than that as Dr. MacHale had already declared for Nolan, we would do the same. This Dr. MacHale more than once told the Tuam priests of Galway Co., and when I was asked by them afterwards if it were so, I declared it to be a fact.
>
> I had no objection in the world to this because I felt and do feel that the chief responsibility would rest on Dr. MacHale, who promised Nolan without reference to any one else (I never meant to go to the length he would go in the management of the Election for the reason, apart from any other higher ones, that he & his would expose the Member to be turned out on petition). But if I were to go against Dr. MacHale, or even act a neutral part, the blame of allowing Lord Clancarty's son to be our M.P. would be sought to be fastened on me. Dr. MacHale, I am convinced, would prefer to the success of a dozen Elections to place us in a wrong position, & injure our ["spiritual" crossed out] influence over our own people.

"The course now proposed by Dr. Gillooly," MacEvilly pointed out, "after what occurred at Mullingar would give him an open at us, altho' Dr. Gillooly, no doubt, means what is best."

"I have not yet spoken," he then assured Cullen, "to either the clergy of Galway or Kilmacduagh on the subject. The Kilmacduagh [clergy] particularly occupy a very important part of the County. I prefer waiting a little as the time for the Election is yet distant, and I am most anxious to give Dr. MacHale no open at us, and I know apart from other things, he will never pardon the part taken in Mr. Mitchell Henry's Election, & the exposure to which himself & Peter Conway were subjected." "For beyond all doubt," MacEvilly explained again, "he prom-

ised Henry & Nolan his support, & if the contest went on, both would have
exposed him, if he did not support them, and to get out of the difficulty, he got
Nolan to withdraw, with a promise of future support. I would not venture to state
these things to your Eminence only that I know them to be *undoubtedly true*." "I
fear I have taken too great a liberty," MacEvilly apologized in conclusion, "in
writing this long letter. But as there are few things I desire more, than to carry out
your Eminence's wishes, which I know to be always for Country and religion, I
think it right to give my reasons in the case . . . being laid before you." "It is very
possible," MacEvilly added in a postscript, "some other liberal worth returning
may start. For as regards either Nolan or D'Arcy, they are hardly worth troubling
one self about them, only that Trench is in question."

In the event, MacEvilly had his way, D'Arcy retired and Nolan was the candidate behind whom the bishops and clergy threw their very considerable political
weight. Nolan, who had been forced to retire from the previous contest because of
the charges leveled against him as an evicting landlord, had agreed to make
amends by proposing to accept arbitration in restoring those tenants who felt they
had a claim, thereby agreeing to the principle of tenant right. The landlords of
county Galway, Liberal and Conservative, Catholic as well as Protestant, therefore
looked upon Nolan as a renegade to their class and combined against him in favor
of Trench. "Our County election," MacEvilly reported to Cullen on December 31,
"will be a terrible fight. Some liberal Landlords, or rather most of them have
united with the bigotted Clancartys to put out Gladstone & put down the Priests"
(C). "Dr. MacHale," he explained again, "made a great mistake in the beginning
in selecting Nolan without consulting any one: I felt myself as placed between two
evils, and I selected what I conceived to be the lesser. If my priests & myself folded
our arms and let Trench in, the whole would be laid at our doors & by estranging
a great number of our best people wd. damage our spiritual influence." "In any
case," he assured Cullen, "I would sacrifice my own feelings a hundred times
sooner than let Trench in, as far as I could prevent it."

In early January, Gregory was officially appointed governor of Ceylon, and the
election for his seat was scheduled for early February 1872. "The complete success
of the Priests' Candidate," MacEvilly assured Cullen on January 23, "is now
ascertained to be beyond question" (C). "It is said," he reported, alluding to an
effort to upset the election of Nolan on the grounds of clerical intimidation, "Cap.
Trench will trust to the issue of a Petition. I have warned the Priests of Galway &
Kilmacduagh against giving any grounds for it." "The defeat of the Priests,"
MacEvilly pointed out, "would, in my opinion, be very injurious to the Education
question, as the Government might then think they might not care for the influence of the Priests. Moreover, the Clancarty family are such detestable bigots and
persecutors of everything Catholic, that the return of one of them, however personally liberal (and that is yet to be seen) would be a great humiliation." "Lord

Clanricarde's hatred of the present Government," he further noted, referring to the leading Liberal and Whig landlord in county Galway, "who did not like him among them, is the cause of the Landlord Coalition. But I suspect his power is gone forever, and it is no loss to religion, that the host of Garibaldi should lose his political influence." "Some people," MacEvilly then reported in a postscript, "have been laying great stress on Trench's liberal professions. But what else would he say now, & who cares for his liberal professions if he join as he would be sure to do against Gladstone & the Liberal party?" "Nolan," he added, offering Cullen some further consolation, "is not by any means, all one would like. But in present circumstances he is a *minus malum* [lesser evil]. I really think Henry & St. Lawrence will work well for the Catholic cause."

On polling day, some two weeks later, on February 7, Nolan won by an enormous majority over Trench with 2,823 votes to only 658.[21] "Our success in the County," MacEvilly reported to Cullen that same day, "is most triumphant. The question was not voting for Nolan or Trench, but the Priests, of whose influence, even Catholic Landlords especially in Galway were so jealous, & the Protestant Peers whom the smaller Landlord fry followed" (C). "I hope," he added vauntingly, "they have received a salutary lesson. They speak of petition, but so far as Galway & Kilmacduagh are concerned, there is no ground whatever." "I was rather uneasy," he confessed, "lest by any mishap the Priests wd. not succeed, as I feared a defeat would tell on the spiritual interests of our excitable people. The return of a member of the Clancarty family by a Catholic constituency would be looked on as a proof that the Priests & people were disunited." The moral of the county Galway election, however, was different from that which MacEvilly drew from it for Cullen. What that "salutary lesson" proved was what the elections in the counties of Mayo, Cork, and Queen's had all proved in the general election of 1868, that it was the end of landlord power in those constituencies forever. The other moral to be drawn from the "lesson" was that the apparent power of the clergy was less a function of their influence with the people qua voters, than it was of their good sense in accepting what the people qua voters wanted. In brief, the landlords' refusal to defer had resulted in their political destruction, and the clergy were not so foolish, even in the interests of the Irish-Liberal alliance, as to follow their example. The moral and the lesson could not have been lost on Cullen, who had now watched the lesser of two evils triumph in two successive by-elections in county Galway, in the persons of Mitchell Henry and Nolan. Indeed, he well might have wondered whether even a Fenian might not be justified in the near future on the principle of the lesser of two evils.

By the time that Cullen had received the news of this "triumphant" success in county Galway, however, he had also learned of the dreadful defeat suffered by

21. Walker, p. 114.

the supporters of the Irish-Liberal alliance in a by-election in county Kerry.[22] In December, the junior member for the county, Viscount Castlerosse, the son of the earl of Kenmare, succeeded to the House of Lords on the death of his father. On December 30, 1871, James A. Dease, the disappointed candidate in Westmeath, who was also a cousin of Kenmare's, wrote Cullen to solicit his support for Kerry. "You will probably have seen," Dease explained, "that I have been invited to stand for Kerry, & the invitation has come from such influential quarters that I am much tempted to accept it. I go this day to Lord Kenmare's house at Killarney" (C). "I am aware," he noted, "of the friendly wishes your Eminence has been so good as to express in my regard on a like occasion elsewhere, & this makes me hope I may have the benefit of your your [sic] wishes, & perhaps your good word on the present occasion." "I have just had," he added encouragingly, referring to the bishop of Kerry, "a letter from Dr. Moriarty who has *volunteered* me his active support. The only probable opposition will be from the same party that kept me out of Westmeath, but I have no fears that the Bishop of Kerry will be less bold now than he has ever been in his opposition to the revolutionary spirit, & I trust the clergy of Kerry will be really bold & really wise."

Two days later, Moriarty also wrote to Cullen, asking him to support Dease in the by-election against the Home Rule candidate, R. P. Blennerhassett. "We are endeavouring," Moriarty explained on January 1, 1872, "to secure the return of James A. Dease for the County. I think he would be a valuable member on the Education question. It occurred to me that if your Eminence was of the same opinion, you might express it either publicly or privately and thus give a helping hand" (C). "We fear," he added, "that Isaac Butt and Galbraith will raise the County against us." "I was very happy," Cullen replied on January 5, "to learn that you were determined to support Mr. Dease as a candidate for the representation of Kerry. He is a good practical Catholic, well acquainted with the wants of Ireland and likely to render good services to the country if he be returned to Parliament."[23] "Mr. Dease labours under one disadvantage:" Cullen explained, "he is most conscientious and will not promise to perform things which he believes to be unpractical whilst we meet with other candidates who never hesitate to promise whatever may please their constituents, though they may not have any chance of ever fulfilling their promises." "I wish Mr. Dease," Cullen assured Moriarty in conclusion, "every success and I am sure your Lordship will confer a great blessing on the country by promoting his return." "I wrote some days ago," he added in a postscript, "to Mr. Dease at Lord Kenmare's residence in Killarney."

"I am greatly obliged," Dease informed Cullen on January 5, "by your kind

22. Brendán Ó Cathaoir, "The Kerry 'Home Rule' By-Election, 1872," *Journal of the Kerry Archaelogical and Historical Society* 3 (1970): 154–70, esp. 165.

23. M, 3819 (4).

letter. Dr. Moriarty, & I am happy to say all his P.P.s but one or at most two, are on my side & the gentry are nearly unanimous as against the so called Home Rule cry" (C). "We shall however have a very severe contest," he added, apologizing for his inability to accept Cullen's invitation to a public meeting on the education question in Dublin, "& my time is so entirely occupied in canvassing this very large & *scattered* constituency that I greatly fear it will not be in my power to absent myself for the three days that would be required for my attendance on the meeting on the 17th." When he wrote to Cullen again, after a week of canvassing, in which he had to be protected by the police from hostile crowds and suffered two broken ribs at a riot caused by his presence in Castle Island, Dease was a good deal less optimistic about his electoral prospects.[24] In a letter dated on Saturday, and probably written on January 13, Dease complained to the cardinal that the attitude of the bishops and their clergy in the by-election then going on in county Galway was very embarrassing. "The position of the clergy in Galway," he explained to Cullen in a long letter marked "confidential," "is doing me immense injury here. Here the Conservatives have been most loyally working in concert with the Liberal & Catholic party including the Bishop & the majority of the Priests to support law & order in my person against the so called 'Home Rule' but really Fenian candidate."

> Lord Ventry, the Tory county leader, has shewn within the last few days a disposition to back out of my support & his *doing so* would make my return *hopeless* in the face of the frightful intimidation brought to bear against me.
>
> I have seen Ld. V[entry]. & had a long interview with him. He seemed impressed with the notion (however acquired) that there was foul play on our side, because the Bishops in Galway took a different line from Dr. Moriarty here, & he evidently seemed to think that the Bps. of Elphin & Galway were acting as they have done *at your Eminence's instigation.* I assured him of the misapprehension of the whole facts of the case that he was under. I also, of my individual conviction, [added] that your Eminence's views on the question of "Home Rule" as at present advocated (apart altogether from the complicated issues that have been joined in Galway) were in entire accord with mine, and in so far, with his own.
>
> I pressed on him that the position of the Bishops in Galway had been taken up *before* he promised me his support & that as *I* had not broken our virtual agreement in any way, he was bound to me in honour.
>
> Eventually this reasoning prevailed & I am not to lose his support, but I cannot help seeing that even now it would be of very great service if [I] were in a position to *assure* him that your Eminence is *averse to the* present Home Rule agitation.
>
> This might be done without in any way expressing disapproval of any other Ecclesiastic, in Galway or elsewhere. In truth the *position* in Galway is curi-

---

24. Ó Cathaoir, p. 156.

ously complicated, from Nolan's extreme views (be they real or sham) on the land question, as well as by the anti-Catholic aroma that is exhaled by the very name of Trench.

I mention all these matters to your Eminence in confidence, & leave the issue to your discretion (C).

"My position here," Dease assured Cullen in conclusion, "is extremely difficult from the mixed character of the support I receive. I have to be more than usually cautious in all my expressions of opinion for fear of running counter to some ones susceptibilities. I find the Education question *very difficult* to deal with, so many of my friends being strongly anti-Denominational." "May I ask," Dease then added in postscript, "your special prayers for a hope [of] deliverance from my present difficult & *dangerous* position?"

In the meantime, Moriarty had written the bishop of Galway, apparently explaining that he had received a letter from Cullen endorsing Dease and asking him for a similar letter to show that the Irish bishops were really of one mind about politics. MacEvilly did not reply until January 19, when he explained that the preparations for the bishop of Clonfert's consecration the previous Sunday and election business since had prevented him from acknowledging Moriarty's letter.[25] "We have so much hard work on hand," he further explained, "to keep out a Tory of the deepest dye, Lord Clancarty's dutiful son (qualis pater, talis filius [like father, like son]) that nothing can induce me to write a word or do an act politically that has no reference to the Galway Election in which we must not be beaten." Shortly before he had written to MacEvilly, Moriarty had also dropped a personal note to his old friend the bishop of Cork, William Delany, concerning a mutual friend, in the course of which he mentioned his current electoral difficulties. In his reply, Delany commiserated with Moriarty about his political troubles, but, in assuring Moriarty that they would speedily pass, Delany was something less than his usual oblique and slightly ironic self. "The object of the present agitation," Delany, who was deemed by the advanced Nationalists to be a Whig of Whigs, pointed out interestingly and surprisingly, on January 10, "differs from Fenianism, it is not criminal in the eyes of Religion as to its object or means."[26] "What a pity," he lamented, reverting to his more usual style, "it was not started sooner. It would have excluded the other [Fenianism] & would probably be over just now. I fear people will come to disregard any expression of Irish feeling or opinion when men find multitudes take up a subject with fiery ardour & drop it after so brief a space of time." "I was," he confessed, "a repealer myself long ago on the score of sentiment, but with extremely small hope of seeing its accomplishment. Yet I would not wonder now if we obtained something, such as a national

25. M, 8319 (3).
26. Ibid.

grand jury for Irish affairs. Mr. Gladstone seemed to me to intimate obscurely such a thing in his Glasgow speech." "As far I can understand the rational portion of the present Nationalists," Delany finally noted in concluding, "they don't contemplate much more. We need not have or fear serious impiety."

When Moriarty received Delany's letter he must have been somewhat embarrassed because several days before he had written a scathing public indictment of the Home Rule movement, which had just appeared in the *Tralee Chronicle.*[27] "The agitation for what is called Home Rule," Moriarty had warned the electors of Kerry, "is in the present circumstances of the country, one of the most mischievous movements to which you have ever been urged or excited." Moriarty then maintained that those who formed "the motive power" of the agitation were their enemies. "Amongst them," he noted, alluding to the abortive Fenian rising in Kerry in 1867, "are those who, a few years ago, sought to plunge you into rebellion, which ended in shame before it had time to end in slaughter." "They are now acting under cover," he charged, "under the disguise of a constitutional agitation . . . if you give them their way, you will have household suffrage; and then manhood suffrage; and then your labourers and servant boys, and the journeymen of your towns will chose [*sic*] your representatives and become your masters, and then." Moriarty, however, not only had just as difficult a time persuading the electors to his point of view as he had had convincing his episcopal colleagues to offer him some aid and comfort, but also he had great difficulties convincing his clergy that they should present a united front on behalf of Dease. Though Moriarty was supported formally by the weightier portion of his clergy, the diocesan dignitaries and senior parish priests, a considerable number preferred to remain neutral in the contest and several openly defied him. John Bourke, the parish priest of Murher and Knockanure, for example, wrote Canon M. J. McDonnell, the parish priest of Listowel and a prominent member of Dease's electoral committee, on January 6, explaining that he could not allow his name to be put on the committee because he "could not go against the people here, who are all the other way," and his curate, Daniel Harrington, also refused his name.[28] McDonnell forwarded Bourke's letter to Moriarty on January 7, apprising him that there were perhaps worse things than neutrality and reporting another unnamed priest as declaring, "if the D-l from Hell were to publish Blennerhassett's address we would adopt him."[29] The day before, Blennerhassett had been adopted, with six priests in attendance, by the North Kerry Farmers' Club, and Michael O'Sullivan, the parish priest of Aghavallon, near Ballylongford, was reported as saying that the person who opposed Blennerhassett on religious grounds was

27. Ó Cathaoir, p. 158.
28. Quoted in Thornley, p. 129.
29. M, 8319 (3).

either a humbug, a bigot, or the parasite of some hostile landlord.[30] Troubles were not coming in single numbers for the bishop of Kerry, however, in this election. "The Rev. Mr. Roche, P.P. of Lixnaw," Moriarty reported to Monsell on Monday, January 15, "who was a tower of strength on Dease's Committee, died suddenly in his Church on Saturday. This morning's post brings me a letter written by him a few hours before his death saying he fears Dease's voters will not come to the poll through dread of the Fenian mobs."[31]

When three of Moriarty's clergy, however, attended a political meeting on Sunday, January 21, in favor of Blennerhassett, without receiving the necessary approval of the local parish priest, Moriarty decided to take action to prevent such occurrences. "In order to lessen, as far as possible," Moriarty explained in a circular letter to his clergy on January 22, "the appearance of division among the clergy at the coming election, we hereby command that no priest shall interfere by canvassing, speeching, attending meetings, or other public action, in another's parish, unless with the leave or invitation of the Parish Priest. We except of course the recording of your votes" (C). "Although we cannot anticipate disobedience," he added, "to a command calculated to preserve brotherly harmony and mutual respect, yet that due canonical warning may be given, we hereby inform you that violation of it will be punished by ecclesiastical censures."

When Blennerhassett then asked Moriarty for special leave for a parish priest to propose his name at the nomination of candidates on February 6, in Tralee, Moriarty not only refused but also, in order to make his meaning clear, issued a second injunction to his clergy, on February 2, specifically forbidding them to appear on the hustings in Tralee (C). The day before the nominations, however, the parish priest of Ardfert, Denis O'Donoghue, appealed against Moriarty's injunctions to the archbishop of Cashel, Patrick Leahy, in his capacity as metropolitan of the province. "I declare," O'Donoghue maintained in his appeal to Leahy on February 5, referring to the first of Moriarty's injunctions, "this mandate to‘be bad and invalid in form and substance, to be *ultra vires Episcopi* [beyond the lawful powers of a bishop], and to be a partisan device to secure by an abuse of the Episcopal office the election of a certain candidate at the coming election, whom the Bishop has chosen to support as an Elector of this County" (L). Of the second injunction, of February 2, O'Donoghue maintained that as it was printed and unsigned, it had no validity. "I intend by this appeal," O'Donoghue then pointed out in conclusion, "to suspend from all and every effect both the mandate under the Bishop's own hand, and the document in printed form, until judgement according to the canons be had and obtained from the proper ecclesiastical court." As soon as Leahy received this appeal, he wrote by return of post

30. Ó Cathaoir, p. 156, quoting *Cork Herald,* January 6, 1872.
31. M, 8318 (14).

to O'Donoghue, on February 6, that he declined to receive it and, moreover, gave no reasons for his refusal (L). He also wrote Moriarty that same day explaining what he had done.

Having lodged his appeal, O'Donoghue then appeared on the hustings in Tralee on February 6 and, in the course of nominating Blennerhassett, had some very hard things to say about his clerical colleagues and bishop, referring to the "Muckross House Caucus, the Tammany Ring of Kerry Electioneering."[32] Muckross Abbey was, of course, the ancestral home of the Herbert family, who were large landlords in and around Killarney and who for some twenty years had agreed to divide the representation of county Kerry with the earls of Kenmare. The "Muckross House Caucus," therefore, was a veiled reference to the Herbert and Kenmare families as well as to Moriarty, who all resided in Killarney and, presumably, allegedly did their political caucusing at Muckross Abbey. Several days later, when the poll was finally declared on February 9, Blennerhassett roundly defeated Dease by 2,237 votes to 1,358, and the clergy and bishop of Kerry were greatly humbled and much annoyed.[33] On February 10, therefore, Moriarty wrote to both Leahy and Cullen, asking their advice on how to proceed against O'Donoghue (L). In his letter to Cullen, Moriarty enclosed copies of all of the relevant documents, including O'Donoghue's appeal to Leahy, noting that O'Donoghue had intimated in a letter to the *Freeman's Journal* on February 7, that he had sent the appeal to Rome. "Should I inflict a temporary suspension," Moriarty pointed out, "he will of course appeal from it. Am I to consider such an appeal suspensive?" (C). "It seems to me," he added, "that I should as the gravamen, if it existed, would have been endured by him, before the appeal could be decided. On the other hand he ought to have obliged, and priests and people expect prompt punishment." "I would be thankful," he concluded, "for a line to-morrow."

Apparently Cullen advised Moriarty to cite O'Donoghue to appear before him and suspend him on the spot if he refused to make a due submission and reparation. On February 2, therefore, Moriarty wrote O'Donoghue, summoning him to appear before him on February 16, "to answer for your public disobedience to your Bishop, for your public and slanderous abuse of certain individuals, and holding up your Bishop to the contempt of the people of your parish, and for abusive language, which is alledged you addressed Rev Mr. Higgins, P.P., Lixnaw" (C). "If you do not comply," Moriarty warned, "with this summons I shall proceed against you without further warning as contumacious." O'Donoghue wrote to Moriarty the next day, enclosing a copy of his appeal to Leahy, maintaining that no action could be taken by Moriarty against him until his appeal had

32. Kieran O'Shea, "David Moriarty (1814–77): III, Politics," *Journal of the Kerry Archaeological and Historical Society* 5 (1972): 101.
33. Walker, p. 114.

been considered by the appropriate ecclesiastical court. Moriarty, however, was not to be put off and wrote to O'Donoghue again on February 14, repeating his citation. "Again I warn you," he declared, "that you shall be proceeded against as contumacious if you do not appear at the time and place appointed."

Upon receiving Moriarty's second citation, O'Donoghue appealed his case to Cullen, enclosing copies of Moriarty's citations and explaining that Leahy had declined to entertain his appeal. O'Donoghue explained, on February 15,

> I therefore being fully persuaded that my Bishop, influenced as he is at present by acute chagrin arising from the defeat of the candidate, whose partisan he notoriously had been, is not in a judicial frame of mind to judge soberly and impartially the acts of one who contributed to bring about that defeat, do hereby, in intent and effect, as far as the Canons direct and require, for my just vindication and due protection from partisan vengeance, lay this my Canonical appeal before your Eminence, as the Delegate Apostolic of the Holy See in Ireland, and if your Jurisdiction does not apply to such cases, I intend by this appeal to invoke the judgement of the Supreme Court of the Apostolic See, upon all matters at issue between me and my Bishop, Dr. Moriarty (C).

If O'Donoghue intended by his appeal to Cullen to provide ground for ignoring Moriarty's summons, he obviously had some prudent second thoughts, for he appeared as directed at the palace in Killarney at twelve o'clock noon on February 16, though not in a very submissive mood. "The unpleasant business," Moriarty reported to Cullen on February 16, "ended well to-day. Rev. Mr. O'Donoghue appeared before me as insolent and as defiant as ever. I had to suspend him usque recipiscentiur et reparapionem scandali [until he retracted and repaired the scandals]" (C). "After some hours," he added, "the grace of God touched him, he asked pardon on bended knees, and signed an act of submission &c. &c. I absolved him immediately." "I am most grateful," Moriarty added in a postscript, "for your Eminence's kind advice."

O'Donoghue's account of his submission, however, was somewhat less dramatic. "I beg to thank you very sincerely," he assured Cullen on February 17, "for the kindly paternal advice you have given me, and I am glad to have to announce to you that I have acted on it by anticipation in every particular on yesterday" (C). "I answered the citation," he further explained, "which I never had an intention of disregarding, and tho' at first held out on the strength of my appeal against the force & effect of the Bp's mandates, pleaded ousted jurisdiction &c., after some reflexion and consultation with brother priests, I did just what your Eminence has recommended, viz. made ample apology to my worthy Bishop, who at once on my signing an expression of my regret &c. most charitably relieved me from all difficulties." "Those election affairs," O'Donoghue noted prudently in conclusion, "are really not worth all the trouble we or some of us give ourselves about them, and certainly not worth running the risk of scandalizing the faithful or

imperilling the interests of Holy Church, which, I hope, I have dearly at heart."
Moriarty, however, had the last word. In writing Cullen that same day to explain
that he and the bishop of Cloyne would leave on February 26 to make their
visitation of the Irish College of Paris on behalf of the bishops as a body, he noted
that O'Donoghue was "a religious and virtuous priest, but headstrong and ill-
tempered" (C).

The virtually simultaneous by-elections in the counties of Galway and Kerry
certainly provide some interesting food for thought about the course of Irish
politics in this period. By way of comparison, the landlords suffered crushing
defeats in both counties, and, by way of contrast, the role of the bishops and their
clergy in each allows for some fruitful speculation about the sources of ecclesiastical power and influence in Irish politics. The basic lesson of both by-elections was not that the Catholic tenant farmers were now the determinant factor in
politics in the counties outside of Ulster (that had been virtually the case since the
Act of Union in 1800) but rather that the tenants had now demonstrated that they
had developed not only a political mind of their own but also a political will to
make that mind effective. Since 1800, the landlords generally had been able, either
through the deference accorded them by their tenants or by sheer intimidation, or
a combination of the two, to command their tenants' votes. The countervailing
force in Irish politics, essentially, had been the Catholic clergy, who were able on
occasion, when the issue could be presented as a conscientious principle involving
religion or patriotism—as in Catholic Emancipation or Repeal—to persuade the
tenants to defy their landlords. Once the tenants developed a political mind and
will that made their conscience in such matters their own, however, the political
power and influence of both the landlords and the clergy came to depend really on
the extent to which they were ready to defer to the tenants' views.

In the Galway and Kerry by-elections, the landlords' refusal to defer to their
tenants' views resulted in the absolute destruction of the landlords' political power
and influence in Galway and a very serious limitation of it in Kerry. The Catholic
landlords in both Galway and Kerry sided with their class, and, though they were
not a very large group in either county, by alienating themselves from their tenants
they facilitated the rapid radicalization and democratization of Irish politics that
was soon to occur. As far as the clergy were concerned, Galway and Kerry provided interesting object lessons for the future. By deferring to the tenants in
Galway, the clergy were able to continue to enjoy harmony and unity with their
people and at the same time enjoy the illusion that they were still the political
guides and mentors of their people. The outcome in Kerry, on the other hand,
made it clear that the clergy's failure to defer to the tenants' views would result in
the clergy being ignored in politics, and, thus, this outcome was fraught with
serious implications for the future if the clergy persisted in their obstinance. The
whole matter was, in fact, put very plainly by the bishop of Down and Connor,

Patrick Dorrian, when writing to Kirby about a great mission, soon to take place in Belfast, that would involve sixteen Redemptorists. "I am glad," he informed Kirby on February 20, "the Kerry Election and the suspension of Father O'Donoghue have been arranged. If Dr. Moriarty wished his priests not to interfere, he should, I think, not have interfered himself" (K). "It is bad," he maintained, "to drive the people away from the Priests. We have had too much of that."

The political estrangement caused by the conduct of the bishop of Kerry and the weightier part of his clergy in the recent by-election, however, was soon to be eclipsed by the excitement created by the effort to unseat Nolan by petition on the ground of clerical intimidation. The trial, which took place in Galway City and was presided over by William Keogh, judge of the court of common pleas, began in early April and was not concluded until the last week in May. "As I presume," MacEvilly explained to Cullen on April 4, "your Eminence may feel some interest in our Petition here, I have been waiting for the last two or three days to catch up something definite to communicate" (C).

> Serjeant Armstrong, [the queen's counsel presenting the case for the petitioners] has preferred a very terrible indictment against the Clergy. If a tithe of it was proved it would be very bad indeed. A great deal of it I know to be utterly untrue, so far as Galway & Kilmacduagh are concerned. Some very slight allusion to myself (and he hardly made any allusion to me, while he came out dreadfully on Dr. MacHale) I am in a position to disprove from Documentary Evidence. Charges were made in the opening speech or rather Indictment against some Priests of Kilmacduagh, which I know, &, they will prove, to be utterly false. There were charges of threats to refuse sacraments, of which the parties accused, even in an Election excitement, are utterly incapable.

"I have attended Court," MacEvilly pointed out, "all through. I must say, I never felt so humbled in my life (Indeed, I would have given anything to be out of court this day) when I heard charges of a very damaging kind *proved* against Fr. Conway, P.P., of Headford and a Father Loftus, C.C. of Dunmore in the Diocese of Tuam." "Conway," he added sadly, "is a shocking man. Indeed, so long as Dr. MacHale lives, he will be a source of bitter humiliation to all who are in his neighbourhood."

> The evidence given this day (so far as I can judge from past experience) will, I fear, greatly endanger Nolan's seat, principally owing to Conway's & Loftus' *barbarous* uncontrolled conduct.
> Serjeant Armstrong has very artfully endeavoured to make it appear that *all* the Bishops are but Dr. MacHale's *Satellites.* So far as I am concerned a most

unfounded charge, but a charge calculated to tell on the Judge. This, of course, I shall refute, with as much regard to edification as possible, but still, he has made the impression altho' most unfounded. Drs. MacHale & Duggan together with myself are cited.

"I respectfully invited," MacEvilly finally explained, "Dr. MacHale to stop with me during his stay. He declined, saying he hoped to return home on the day his attendance at Court would be required."

Cullen then wrote to MacEvilly asking him what he thought the result of the petition would be. "The opinion here," MacEvilly replied on April 7, "is that Nolan will be unseated, and that Trench will not get the seat."

The gross conduct of Fr. P. Conway alone, which I believe to be proved & not to be refuted would unseat Nolan. I . . . observed the Judge take particular notice of one thing alledged against Conway. On polling day after one of his Parishioners (a tenant of a Mr. Burke, whom he is [correctly, has] always denounced) voted, he is alleged to have said, "go home now and tell your Master & Mistress to keep within doors & not venture out." This was recorded on the spot on the polling books. He is really mad, but, still, he can manage Dr. MacHale as he pleases and has the Tuam priests in terror. He receives scant courtesy from every other quarter. His Headford speech, in which he ostentatiously sneers at the Education Question is said to have been submitted to Dr. MacHale before it was sent to press. A most respectable gentleman assured me this is the case, but, no doubt, it will be denied.

"I think Trench," MacEvilly noted, returning to Cullen's question, "won't be seated. The admission made by Lady Burke will, it is thought prove fatal to him. Her family, [her] Father, Lord Westmeath, a most shocking old man, her husband and brother in Law, are at the bottom of all this, wish to expose the clergy."

"My duty will be," he assured Cullen, "to dissociate myself from anything unworthy of the Clergy, to show my abhorrence of any unproper and unclerical conduct, if such can be established. It would be very disastrous if the conduct of some few Priests in this vast County would not be disavowed by authority." "This and this alone," he added, "I propose to myself in my examination."

"Somehow, I would not regret to see Trench seated in the event of Nolan's defeat. I have the greatest fear that under Dr. MacHale's patronage and encouragement some *wild* candidate may start. Indeed, it is whispered that Butt will vacate Limerick for Nolan & start for Galway, carrying out his Mazzinian threat that his people will be returned in spite of the Clergy. It would be a desperate business with Dr. MacHale at his back. However we must await events. If Dr. Duggan joins me (and I am sure he will) and that we can get a popular Catholic candidate I am sure we would defeat him."

"For my part," he vowed, "after this ordeal, come what will I will never again have anything to say to Dr. MacHale's candidate." "None of the Bishops," he pointed out in conclusion, "have been yet examined. I shall from time to time inform your Eminence of how matters progress, when any thing new arises."

Two days later MacEvilly wrote to Cullen again. "Dr. MacHale," he reported on April 9, "was in the witness box today. He was asked for some Papers which he gave in. He was not examined by the Trench Counsel who cited him and he this afternoon returned to Tuam" (C). "I hardly think," MacEvilly then explained, "the Trench people will call the Bishops on the direct [examination]. It is not their game. We must be called by Nolan's people to remove the bad impressions made. I have the assurance of MacDonagh and McDermott, Nolan's Counsel, that Dr. MacHale will be called first. He was the first to bring on the war, and he must be the first to fight the battle."

> I need not say, I and Dr. Duggan entered the contest exclusively to keep out the son of the greatest bigot in Europe, the greatest enemy of Catholicity, and also not allow the Priests [to] be trampled upon, to prevent inroads of Communism [and] Internationalism, which would result from destroying the influence of the Clergy. And whatever may be said, as to the modus of maintaining the influence of the Clergy (and in some cases, which should not be imputed to the body of the Clergy) it was, I fear very censurable, the influence of the Clergy with the people was clearly proved by the immense majority at the Poll.

"Some of our Catholic Gentry," MacEvilly added by way of concluding, "are acting very basely, particularly the Joyce's. They are married to English women who have no respect but for English Clergy, & unfortunately rule their husbands."

Cullen, meanwhile, who had been reading the extensive reports of the trial in the *Freeman's Journal,* was scandalized by the accounts given of the clergy's conduct in the recent election. "If you see the Freeman," he had informed Kirby on April 7, "you will be greatly annoyed by the scenes it describes in connection with the late Co. Galway election. The *sacerdoti* appear to have been most violent, and to have made the altars the place for personal abuse and political discussions" (K). "Dr. MacHale," Cullen observed fastening on once again to his favorite scapegoat, "poor man is answerable for a good deal of this, as he put forward a candidate who divided the rich Catholics from the poor." "Dr. Gillooly and Dr. MacEvilly," Cullen explained, somewhat equivocally, "were opposed to him, but they could do nothing. If they opposed him, they would have created a 3rd party." "An immensity of scandal," he concluded sadly, "will be given by the revelations at the trial, and Judge Keogh will turn all very probably against the clergy."

The trial continued for several weeks more, until the defense finally got its opportunity to rebut the charges made by the petitioners, and the three bishops were called by Nolan's counsel to give evidence. "Dr. MacHale," MacEvilly reported to Cullen on April 27, "was examined first on yesterday for the defense. I see it is very accurately given in the Freeman. It was sought to make it appear, that the Bishops conspired with Dr. MacHale and in quite a subordinate way. It was hoped too that an expression of adverse feeling might be elicited from him towards the Bishops of the Co. and *vice versa*" (C). "However, I thought it right and becoming," MacEvilly maintained, "whatever my feelings & opinions might be, to be as respectful in my expressions regarding him as possible. I see the Freeman reports my evidence very badly, reporting certain sentences as utterly unmeaning." "Dr. Duggan," he added, referring to the recently appointed bishop of Clonfert, "gave very excellent evidence this morning. The other evidence given was very favorable to Nolan, so that it is impossible to say what may be the result."

In replying to this letter Cullen complimented MacEvilly on his evidence, and, in thanking the cardinal several days later, on May 2, MacEvilly also reported that he had just been asked to give an explanation, required by Judge Keogh, of the decrees of the Council of Trent (C). "I took the opportunity," MacEvilly further explained, referring to the national synod that had taken place at Thurles in 1850, "of bringing before him the decrees of Thurles on the subject of denunciations, which are carried to a terrible extent in a part of Tuam, particularly Headford, and no redress. In fact some Priests seem not to know anything of such a statute at all, nor of the decree of 1854." "I am convinced," he then added, "great good to religion will come of having the salutary provisions of the Irish Church known to the public, so that if there be abuses, it is not the fault of the Church." "Some of our gentry here," MacEvilly further noted, "are acting a most extraordinary part, actually coming into Court and detailing every chance conversation which may be unguardedly carried on in their presence. It will, however, have the effect of making the Priests keep their own place, a thing much needed in some districts."

In writing to the bishop of Elphin two days later, on May 4, about his proposal to arrange a visitation by the bishops of the national seminary at Maynooth, Cullen expressed surprise that he had not been called to give evidence as had the other bishops (G). "The Galway Petitioners," Gillooly replied the following day, "have treated me with great contempt, for which I feel truly grateful to them. The episcopal bench of our Province was well represented & defended there without me, as your Eminence must have seen by the newspaper reports. Our Elphin priests of the C. Galway took only a very mild interest in the Election and had no quarreling with the Landlords" (C). "I fear the Election," Gillooly concluded astutely, "and still more the Petition, has opened a wide branch in Galway between the Clergy & Cath. Gentry." Before the end of the week, however, all of the witnesses had been called and all of the evidence presented, and the counsel of the petitioner and the defense began their summations. "The great case," MacEvilly finally reported to Cullen on Saturday, May 11, "has closed this day, so far as witnesses are concerned. Counsel on both sides will I am told, occupy next week in their addresses, and the Judge it is reported, will finally decide on Monday & Tuesday week. No one can possibly tell the result" (C).

"I look forward," MacEvilly then confessed, "to the consequences of the Peti-

tion with a good deal of uneasiness. All would be right only for the perversity of
Dr. MacHale, who will take council with no one. I even believe, if he knew the
mind of others he would adopt the opposite course to that which they contemplated." Referring ironically to a celebrated Galway landlord, MacEvilly further
reported, "Staunton of Clydagh, Fr. Conway's friend was shown up terribly in the
rebutting case last evening."

"He is a kind man to his Tenants, but, it seems, fearfully despotic. His letters,
read in Court, addressed to his Tenants were the most menacing I ever heard. I am
quite sure he never meant in reality to carry out what he threatened, but still it was
very awkward to have such letters read. In fact, it seems to have been the settled
impression of the Landlords, that if they told their tenants [to] vote for Mazzini or
Garibaldi, they should in gratitude do so, without any regard for their own
feelings."

"Whatever may be the result of the Petition," MacEvilly pointed out, "one good
will result. It will unite the Masses of the people with the Priests. Indeed, it was
nearly a question of choosing between the people & [a] few unreliable Landlords.
It will also make the Priests more cautious in the future." "The chief saddening
feature in the whole case," he concluded, referring to the landlords, "was the
exposure of the meanness of men, who heretofore held a respectable position, &
indeed, some of them were very mean."

Because the summations for each side took a good deal longer than was anticipated, however, the final judgment was delayed for another week. "The Petition,"
MacEvilly informed Cullen on Tuesday, May 21, "is now about closed. Murphy,
Keogh's son in law, finished his harangue this day, and Keogh is to give his
judgement on Friday next" (C). "Murphy," MacEvilly charged, "is a scurrilous
ranter."

> He spoke for more than four days. His manifest object was to abuse Priests
> and Bishops. He did not speak at all to evidence. He seemed to have no regard
> at all to what was utterly disproved. He repeated the same charges which
> Armstrong alleged in his opening indictment without caring whether they
> were proved or not. In fact, I heard him repeat three or four charges against
> myself, for which not a particle of evidence was adduced to prove, and which
> were utterly disproved in evidence. But I suppose the Judge in his charge will
> carefully distinguish between what was proved in evidence and merely asserted
> without evidence.

"The general opinion here," he reported, "is that Nolan will be unseated. If he be
saddled with the costs, it will be utterly ruinous to him. The costs are enormous.
The Trench party think the question of seating Trench will be referred by Keogh
to the Court of Common Pleas, where the result will be undoubted."

"The conduct," MacEvilly then pointed out, "of some of the Galway men &
ladies is utterly disgraceful. They crow[d]ed the Court, while Armstrong &

Murphy were attacking the Priests, & deserted it while MacDonnell was ably defending them. I fear the worse possible results the moment the Petition is over. The Landlords seem to be absolutely rabid. I feel greatly for the poor tenants." "The clergy on the whole," he further assured Cullen, "have come out of it well, with two or three exceptions, which after all, in a large County, would hardly be wondered at. Conway & Loftus made a very sorry exhibition. I attended the whole time save Ascension Thursday & this day." "I understand," he added, "Dr. MacHale is for having one of Nolan's brothers returned in case of a vacancy. I question very much the propriety of such a course, inasmuch as I don't believe one of them worthy." "I would however have less objection to that than to a nominee of a certain party from the Home Rule Association," he noted, referring to Isaac Butt. "But really as regards even the former I would be very slow in affording any active cooperation." "I shall at once," MacEvilly assured Cullen in conclusion, "apprise your Eminence of the result."

Keogh's judgment, however, was delayed, and was not finally delivered until Monday, May 27. When MacEvilly wrote to Cullen late that evening, he was apparently still in a state of shock. "It was nearly 8 o.c.," he explained, "when Keogh finished the most awful tirade I ever heard of or read against the Clergy. Murphy was a lamb compared to him. He unseated Nolan with *all* costs, and reserved Trench's case for the Court of Common Pleas" (C). "Anything so outrageous," MacEvilly then explained again, "I never heard of. He did not mind the evidence at all. His attacks on religion, Education &c. it was most painful to listen to. However, I heard him out." "He was very hard," MacEvilly then added, "on me, so far as the Election went. But he was very unjust towards Dr. Duggan, and he referred to the Abp. of Tuam only incidentally in connexion with Fr. Conway. He was very complimentary to Dr. Gillooly." "Only for him [Gillooly]," MacEvilly pointed out to Cullen, revealing how badly he had been stung by Keogh's judgment, "at the meeting of Mullingar I would have been very slow to take up Capt. Nolan. However, the keeping out of Trench, the son of Lord Clancarty, to whom Keogh was very complimentary, was the chief thing that influenced me." "Keogh's praises of Oliver Cromwell," MacEvilly noted in conclusion, "were most disgusting. He denounced denominational Educ & praised the Queen's Colleges to the stars. I never heard so much infidelity uttered in the whole course of my life."

Perhaps no one in Ireland had a more unenviable reputation than William Keogh at the time of the Galway petition case, and his judgment in that case set the seal forever in the Irish popular mind on his perfidy and baseness. Twenty years before he had been looked upon by many as worthy of succeeding the great Daniel O'Connell. He had been elected in 1847 to the borough of Athlone and was returned again for that borough in the general election of 1852, after pledging himself to support the principle of an independent Irish party in the House of

Commons. When he then took office as solicitor general for Ireland in Lord Aberdeen's coalition ministry of 1852–55, he was denounced by his former colleagues as having betrayed his and their political principles in the grossest manner and was held from that time on in execration by every shade of Nationalist opinion in Ireland. No one had, in fact, been more responsible for his being held up to public obloquy than the archbishop of Tuam and his clergy, and, as a native of Galway, Keogh had been more than ordinarily stung by their political and personal abuse. He was, therefore, in his judgment in the Galway case, in large part paying off old scores for political scars acquired over the years.

The judgment, which took nearly nine hours to deliver, and the paraphrase of it in the *Freeman's Journal,* which took up eight full columns, was everything the bishop of Galway described it as to Cullen, and more.[34] It was less a judicial decision than a denunciation that alternated between a diatribe and a harangue. Keogh began by fulsomely and effusively complimenting the legal counsel on both sides. He then proceeded to preface his judgment with a long "glance at the historical, geographical, and moral position" of the county Galway, which took up more than an hour and was largely an exercise in reminisce, nostalgia, and self-praise. Coming finally to his judgment, Keogh pointed out that the case of the petitioners really turned on whether "treating" could be attributed to Captain Nolan and/or "undue influence" was used by the Catholic clergy in securing that candidate's election. Treating, he maintained, had not been proved by the petitioners, and accordingly he acquitted the sitting member of that charge. "Now, dealing with the great constitutional question that the election was not free," Keogh explained, "but was controlled from first to last by the hierarchy and clergy of the Roman Catholic Church, I ask what is undue influence?"

> The 17th and 18th Vic., C. 102, sec. 5 says—"Every person who shall, directly or indirectly, by himself or by any other person on his behalf, make use of or threaten any force, violence, or other restraint, or inflict, or threaten infliction of any injury, damage, or loss, or in any other way shall practise intimidation upon or against any persons in order to induce or compel such person to vote or to refrain from voting, or on account of such person having voted at any election, or who shall, by abduction, duress, or any fraudulent device, or contrivance, impede, prevent, or otherwise interfere with, the free exercise of the franchise of any voter, either to give, or to refrain from giving his vote to any candidate, shall be deemed to have committed the offense of undue influence." Then, by a clause in another act, the seat of the member in whose interest such influence had been used is voided, and if it is proved . . . to have been exercised by himself or his agent, the member is incapacitated from again seeking the suffrages of the constituency during the then existing Parliament. That is the definition and the consequence of undue influence, and it is impos-

---

34. *Freeman's Journal,* May 28, 1872.

sible for any vocabulary in the English language to add one single word to the fulness of the definition of the statute I have quoted.

"The only other section to which I will refer," Keogh added, "is the 44th clause of the 31 and 32 Vic., cap. 125, which provides that if any candidate employs as his agent or canvasses any person, and knowing that such person has been within seven years reported guilty of any corrupt practices, by a Committee of the House of Commons or other competent tribunal, the election of such candidate shall be void."

Keogh then spent the greater part of the early afternoon arguing that the bishops and clergy of county Galway were guilty of what the law defined as undue influence and its penalties, and he was insultingly personal in his remarks. He described Patrick Lavelle, the celebrated parish priest of Cong, for example, as "a priest who goes to that altar, who does not perform but desecrates that tremendous Mystery which was celebrated upon Calvary," and "the patron of an accused assassin, who denounces unchristian wrath against harmless men." "On the whole of the evidence," Keogh said then in summary, before adjourning for a quarter of an hour, "he should proclaim that never had there been a more astounding attempt at ecclesiastical tyranny in the whole history of priestly interference in public affairs than was presented in this case." Keogh's temper was not, however, much improved by the brief adjournment because in the late afternoon and early evening he became even more provocative and personal in his remarks than he had been earlier. "The Rev. Mr. Cannon," Keogh maintained, referring to a curate in the parish of Tynagh in the diocese of Clonfert, "had spoken slightingly of the bones of Oliver Cromwell. He (his lordship) hoped he was a loyal man, and that he believed implicitly that no form of government that ever existed more tends to secure the public liberties than the mixed constitution under which we live. But if he were to place his hand on distinguished greatness of character, on a personage of the noblest and most eminent men of history, he should unhesitatingly say the greatest sovereign that ever ruled in England was Oliver Cromwell." "What was the use," Keogh asked, referring again to Father Cannon, "of going down to the grave, ghoul or vampire-like, to drag up the bodies, to rake up the ashes of the dead?"

Perhaps no part of his judgment offended Irish sensibilities more than this eulogy of the English political system, legitimized, as it were, by his reference to Cromwell, whose career of slaughter and sacrilege in Ireland was an indelible and terrible fact in the Irish-Catholic mind. In his continued and epic arraignment of the conduct of the clergy, moreover, Keogh depicted them as men who were capable of the most heinous crimes. His catalogue extended from representing them as men who were willing to break even the seal of the confessional in the interests of preserving their political power and influence, to being perjurers and bullies. In referring to a Father Cowan, for example, who was presumably, P. Coen, a curate in the parish of Upper Ballynakill in the diocese of Clonfert, Keogh denounced him for not contradicting those witnesses who had accused him of threatening to subvert the secret ballot, then under consideration in Parliament, by means of the confessional. "The Ballot Bill was not yet the law of the land, Parliament was still sitting," Keogh maintained, extending Coen's alleged crime to the whole of the Irish clergy, "and the Ministry and Legislature should know that the Catholic clergy, represented by the Rev. Mr. Cowan, meant to use the confessional for purposes of election intimidation in case the Ballot becomes the law of the land." Turning to another celebrated political priest in Tuam diocese, Peter Loftus, a curate in the parish of Dunmore, Keogh charged that he "contradicted every witness who testified against him, among these being two deputy lieutenants, three magistrates, and an officer in the army. In his opinion the evidence of this man was neither more nor less than deliberate perjury. This wretch—who could never have climbed a father's knee or embraced a mother's neck— . . . this dreadful priest—had endeavoured to vamp up his debauched evidence." In discussing the conduct of James Staunton, the administrator of the parish of Kilcornan in the diocese of Kilmacduagh, who had been accused of denouncing one of his parishioners from the altar, Keogh declared that "the spectacle he exhibited in giving evidence was so disgusting that the people in the court screened their faces when he was making such an exhibition of himself."

"What had brought the people to this condition?" Keogh then asked after his long arraignment of the clergy, referring to those who had supported Nolan, "To what was this state of things attributable?" "The evidence established in his mind," he maintained, "a determination on the part of the Archbishop, his suffragan bishops and almost the entire parish priests and curates of the county, to strain every point, to work every engine, to use every influence to gain their object, an object which he solemnly believed to have been, whether so intended or not, the overthrow of all free will and civil liberty in this electoral portion of the country." "He had been told," Keogh admitted, "that the people would have done what they did if left to themselves. Kerry had been pointed [out] to him. He answered—The question was not what or might have been done. The question for his consideration was whether such undue influence had been used by Captain Nolan, either by himself, or his agents, as to void the election?" "He was satisfied," Keogh finally concluded, "that both at Common Law and under the Statute Law the election of Captain Nolan should be declared void."

In his closing remarks, Keogh explained that he would report to the speaker of the House of Commons not only that there had been "an organised system of intimidation," but that "the Archbishop of Tuam, the Bishop of Clonfert, and all the clergy whose cases he had mentioned, had been guilty of an organised attempt to defeat the free franchise, and that Nolan by himself and his brother Sebastian, as his agent in company with all these episcopal and clerical personages, had been so guilty." "He would guard the franchise," he further explained, "for the next seven years, and see that these persons could not take hand, act, or part in again conducting an election for a representative for Galway for that period," in order that those approximately 2,800 electors who voted for Nolan, and "who were the mindless, brainless, coward instruments in the hands of ecclesiastical despots," might not be soon imposed on again. "A most painful part of the case remained—it was . . . the direction as to costs," Keogh finally noted. "He should decide that the expenses of the petition were to be borne by Captain Nolan, those of his antagonist as well as his own." The *Freeman's Journal,* the next day, May 28, in publishing the judgment, called for a national subscription to defray the enormous costs imposed upon Nolan and led the way with a subscription of fifty pounds to the "vindication fund."

"I sent you the Freeman," Cullen informed Kirby on May 28. "It contains a ferocious speech of Judge Keogh against the priests and bishops of the Co. Galway. They were rather violent, and I hope the lesson will do good—but the Judge cannot be defended" (K). "Keogh," he then added, "is to denounce Dr. McHale, Dr. Duggan and Dr. McEvilly to Parliament. Dr. McEv. engaged in the business against his will, but sooner than have a fight with Dr. McHale he followed him. Dr. Gillooly kept out of the scrape." "If the priests," he concluded, "wd. observe the synod of Thurles and the regulations of 1854 about altar denunciations, they would [avoid] a great deal of scandal, and they could exercise the same power or more." "I sent you yesterday," Cullen reported to Kirby again, on May 30, "Keogh's judgement in the Galway case. It is most outrageous, a phillipic not a judgement" (K). "It places me," he explained, "in a very awkward position. The priests certainly behaved very badly in the County Galway and profaned the altars by the violent personal denunciations. On the other side the people are most indignant at the Judge's violence, and I think some of our trading politicians will turn this feeling to account, and get up a declaration of sympathy with the Patriarch of the West and his clergy, and approve all their violence and total disregard of the statutes of Thurles and the decrees of the Bishops in 1854 which were confirmed by the Pope." "If I join with the sympathisers," Cullen pointed out, "I will seem to approve the bad conduct of the priests—if I keep aloof they will make me responsible for Keogh's abominable attack on the Catholic Church. In this way there is great danger of dissensions." "I will hold a meeting," he further explained, "of some of the more prudent of our clergy tomorrow to see *quid agendum.*"

Cullen wrote to Kirby again on the following day, May 31, obviously before he had the opportunity to meet with his clergy to decide what was to be done about Keogh's judgment. "The Galway business," he noted sadly, "will injure the Cath. clergy very much. Dr. McHale has the merit of having brought on the contest. His friends will now endeavour to make a hero of him, tho he deserves nothing but blame" (K). "Keogh acted," he concluded sharply, "like a madman." Indeed, this appeared to be the consensus among all those who were concerned. "You will hear in a day or two," W. G. Todd, for example, reported to Kirby on May 31, from St. Mary's Orphanage in London, "of Judge Keogh's judgement in Galway. There can be little doubt that the priests went too far, and I fear that their conduct will be used as an excuse for not making concessions on the Education Question" (K). "But whatever their shortcomings may have been," Todd assured Kirby, "Keogh is a scoundral, & deserves execration for his attack on Arcbp. MacHale & the Bishops. He gains a momentary popularity with the Protestants, but even the *Times* is obliged to admit that his judgement is too *sensational*." Two days later, on June 2, the administrator of the bishop's parish in Waterford City, Patrick Nolan, also wrote to Kirby in reference to Keogh (K). "We are all disgusted," he reported, "with Judge Keogh's judgement. It is considered not to be a judgement but an attack on the Bishops and Priests of Ireland for which he was seeking an opportunity for many years, and an attempt to gain the favor of the 'Shoneen Catholics' of Galway amongst whom he intends to reside when he resigns the Judgeship."

> The faithful are most excited against him. A very steady and religious man said to a priest in Waterford a few days ago "I wish I were a Priest for one half hour and to have Judge Keogh in my power. I would '*read over him*'* and turn him into a goat and leave him so all his life."
>
> (*that is the prayers of the Church) thus the people express it.

Several days later, shortly after Cullen consulted with his clergy about how to deal with Keogh's philippic, the Dublin clergy published an address on the subject.

Some 250 of the Dublin clergy, secular and regular, assembled in St. Kevin's Chapel at the procathedral in Marlboro St. on June 6 to append their names to an address entitled "To The Catholics of The Diocese of Dublin." The address, which was read for the assembled clergy by Laurence Canon Forde, one of Cullen's two vicars general, was a very cautious and measured document. The address opened with a sad commentary on how much damage had been done by Keogh's judgment to that basic respect for the law which is fundamental to orderliness of civil society. The address then disclaimed all intention of entering into the merits of the case or of contemplating itself as an instrument of judicial review. "But whilst we disclaim all intention of reviewing the conclusion to which the Judge has arrived, we must enter our most solemn protest against the outrage on all propriety implied in the most unbecoming language which the reports of the public journals put into his mouth. And whilst we protest against these reported words, we, with unfeigned indignation, repudiate the calumnious misrepresentation, by which it is attempted to be established that the priesthood of Ireland is prepared to prostitute the most sacred institution of religion to the unworthy purposes of low political intrigue."[35]

35. Ibid., June 7, 1872.

The address then proceeded to a spirited defense of the character of the Irish clergy, maintaining that instead of their being, as Keogh had claimed, conspirators against the liberties of the people, the Catholic priesthood had been the true defenders of real Irish freedom, even in the worst of times. The address then turned from Keogh's efforts to revile the Irish priesthood to his gratuitous eulogies of all that was most repugnant to Irish-Catholic sensibilities—including, among other things, his good friend, the novelist Charles Lever, "who made it his study to paint Irish priests as ideals of buffoonery and ignorance," and the Galway Queen's College, which had been anathematized by the Church as a godless institution, "a centre of light and heat, under whose benign influence this land of ours is to become a blooming garden." "One might well imagine," the address continued, "that these outrages on the feelings of a Catholic country would have satisfied the most unbounded appetite for insult. But the compound is yet sufficiently bitter."

> There stands in the record of Irish woes a name which at once expresses all that is hateful, odious and cruel—Cromwell—the regicide Cromwell, on whose head rests the blood of a monarch, through whom the royal line has come down to our present Queen—must be taken up as a demi-god by the judge who sits behind her Majesty's commission; the man who made the streets and churches of our towns flow with torrents of innocent blood; the man who depopulated the land, so that over twenty or thirty miles of country scarcely a trace of human life could be found; the man who transported, in thousands, the children of our race to do the work of slaves upon the Island of Barbadoes; the man who made this Kingdom almost a desert, so that for the want of human inhabitants the savage wolf must supply the deficiency—this man, regicide, hypocrite, and exterminator, must be held up in a public court as an object for the admiration of our people.

"But, although this judgement," the address then maintained, "has, for the moment, wrought mischief, good, great good will come forth from it. It has aroused already the indignation of the whole Kingdom against the insult offered to the national pride and to the religious convictions of the people; and when the great battle of Irish education is to be fought, our countrymen will then remember that one of their own flesh and blood and religion, through the withering curse of a hostile university [Trinity College], was prepared to act a part from which, we firmly believe, the honest instincts of a Protestant-born man would make him shrink." "We must not conclude," the address finally pointed out, coming full circle, "without putting on record our firm conviction that the courts of justice in Ireland will not retain the respect or command the confidence of our people if men capable of thus insulting all they hold venerable and holy are allowed to preside on their benches."

"I sent you," Cullen reported to Kirby on June 12, "the *address* of the Dublin clergy about Keogh. All the people are furious with him. However on yesterday he succeeded in giving the seat for Galway to Captn Trench son of Lord Clancarty a great bigot" (K). "All this," he assured Kirby, "will do great mischief—it makes the people look with suspicion on all law and its administrators. Keogh was joined by Morris another Catholic judge, said to be a Freemason, and Lawson a pretended liberal Protestant. The Chief Justice Monahan fought against them in vain. Keogh's proceedings will do a great deal to destroy all respect for law in the country." On June 16, Cullen reported to Kirby that Keogh had now recommended to Parliament that MacHale, Duggan, MacEvilly and some thirty Galway priests should be prosecuted for their activities in the Galway election, and on June 21 P. J. Tynan, Cullen's new secretary, who had only just arrived in Ireland from Rome, informed Kirby that "Judge Keogh is being burned in effigy everywhere throughout Ireland. There is a very strong feeling against him, and great numbers of the poorer classes seem to think that it would be very little crime to shoot him" (K). On June 28, moreover, Cullen wrote Kirby one of his carefully constructed letters in Italian, designed to be read for the authorities of Propaganda, at the end of which he reviewed the whole of the Keogh affair. In reporting that the Peter's pence collection for the pope in the diocese was over two thousand pounds and would be some four hundred pounds more than the previous year, Cullen assured Kirby that it was all attributable to the reaction against Keogh. In fact, Cullen reported, by way of example, the chief baron of the Court of Exchequer, David R. Pigot, had subscribed to the Peter's pence in his parish church for the first time since the collection had been initiated in 1860.

Indeed, the excitement with regard to Keogh in clerical circles did not begin to die down until the beginning of August, when Cullen wrote Kirby another carefully constructed letter in Italian. "He has recommended," Cullen advised Kirby, referring to Keogh, on August 2, "to the government to institute a prosecution against the archbishop of Tuam, the bishop of Galway, and the bishop of Clonfert for having adopted unlawful means in order to procure the election of a certain Nolan, a Catholic to be a member of Parliament, and to exclude a Protestant—it seems that some priests will [also] be prosecuted, but it will all probably end in smoke" (K). "However, it appears certain," Cullen pointed out, "that some priests conducted themselves very badly, making use of the altar to inveigh against the Protestant and those that supported him." "The Catholic," he concluded, "had about 2,800 votes—the Protestant about 600—the judge however excluded the Catholic and declared the Protestant elected (*membro*) under the pretext that the priests had used violence." This was a very astute performance on the part of Cullen. He was concerned about preparing the Roman authorities first for the eventuality that some of the bishops and clergy would be prosecuted in the Galway case, and, second, by admitting that some of the clergy were culpable, for the worst that might happen. At the same time, by reducing the whole complicated situation to a disagreement between a Protestant and a Catholic and emphasizing that the Catholic had received nearly five times as many votes as the Protestant, Cullen, at one and the same time, pointed out that the bad conduct of the clergy, though certainly real, was not actually the decisive factor in the election and that awarding the seat to a Protestant in the face of such a majority for the Catholic on such a pretext was, therefore, patently unjust.

About this time, apparently, Cullen also warned MacEvilly about the prudence of covering the Roman flank with as much reasoned information as possible, for two days after Cullen had written to Kirby, MacEvilly wrote the rector of the Irish College a long letter about the Galway affair. "I hope," he began on August 4, while enclosing £324 Peter's pence for the pope, "you are all well in Rome and particularly at the cherished St. Agatha" (K). "Indeed," he added sadly, "I fear we have fallen on evil times. Everywhere is the church suffering. A terrible spirit has gone abroad. It is no longer Heresy so called. It is utter materialism. The utter denial of God himself and of everything spiritual. It will require the utmost vigilance to stem this torrent even in our favored Church of Ireland."

> We of the County Galway have been lately brought very prominently before the World, by a Galway man, born in this very town, the famous Judge Keogh. The Election he was appointed to adjudicate on, was strictly speaking a religious one. It was in reality a question whether Priests were to exercise their influence for good over their people, and direct them in the exercise of their civil rights, & save them from following false guides or be relegated to their sacristies as nobodies in Society. A greater evil could not befal religion and society in Ireland than the latter alternative. Put the Priest aside, and God help the people. No one would contemplate the result without a shudder. Fenianism, Carbonarism, Communism, & every wicked *ism* would soon be in the ascendant with our impulsive warm-hearted people. It was this the priests sought to prevent, and hence the cry against them. Moreover they could not bear to have a son of Lord Clancarty whose family are noted for their hatred of Catholicity in every part of the Kingdom, as the representative of the *Catholic County of Galway*.

"I freely admit," MacEvilly confessed, "some two or three went to unwarrantable lengths, for which they should be punished, and none would more gladly join in reprobating such disreputable conduct than the clergy themselves. But Judge Keogh attacked all, never minded evidence, lauded every act of cruelty on the part of Landlords, and censured every act done by Ecclesiastics."

> However he over did it. An immense amount of good has come of it. It has had a wonderful effect in uniting people and Priests,—a union which for some time was seriously threatened. It will also have the effect of preventing any excess in future on the part of any clergyman at Elections. Our Catholic Gentry, as a body, are a very bad lot. No man on Earth requires so much a *Catholic* Education. To hear some of these men talk of the Holy Father, & his temporal Power &c. would actually shock you. The leaven of Protestantism has adhered to them.

"I hope," he concluded, "this infamous outrageous Judgement of Keogh will have the effect of bringing some of them back to a sense of duty."

The last word on the Keogh judgment, however, is, perhaps, best left to James

A. Dease, who in writing to William Monsell had some very perceptive things to say about its impact on Irish politics. "I quite share your feeling," he assured Monsell on August 25, "with regard to that most unfortunate Keogh affair. It has thrown us back twenty years—or at any rate has disclosed the powerful fact that the antagonistic feelings between Creeds & classes are as strong & as bitter as they were twenty years ago."[36] "The action of the Grand Juries," he maintained, "shewed this most clearly—all the Protestants, as a matter of course joining in congratulating the Judge—while equally of course (or *nearly* so) the Catholics took the other side."

> *Our* difficulty was this. That we fully coincided in Keogh's opinion that the *unseating* of *Nolan* was *just,* as also was his reprobation of the violence of the clergy during the Election—& of the conduct of several of them while under examination during the trial of the Petition. In this country the spirit of partisanship is so strong on all sides that there is little room for men who try—& wish—to be impartial—& many of the higher class of Catholics are looked on as *deserting their own side* because they cannot honestly refuse to admit any justification for the greater part of Keogh's judgement.
>
> The tone & manner & some of the language of that judgement were entirely inexcusable, & have tended to weaken most deplorably the respect for the Bench & the growing belief in the impartiality of the Judges.

"You say that you fear," Dease then observed, "some think that 'a rupture has been made between the clergy & the upper class of Catholics whose sympathy with them in their troubles is cold,' & that 'Gov*t* believe Fenianism has disposed of clerical influence . . . therefore abandons the clergy—their power being gone.'"

> I do not think the upper classes of Catholics open to the imputation of "wanting sympathy with the clergy." As I have already said we cannot *approve* of Father Loftus & his *modus* of conducting an Election—but we certainly disapprove of Keogh's gratuitous insults, & have *very generally* said so boldly, out of Galway (where party bitterness of course still prevails). I know of no Catholic of position who has spoken otherwise than *against* Keogh. Moreover we well know that there are *Ecclesiastics* in high places who feel exactly as *we* feel in this matter, as an analysis of the list of subscribers to the Nolan Defense fund shews clearly enough.

"As to the 'power of the clergy being gone,'" Dease then noted, turning to the second of Monsell's propositions, "I believe it to be true in this sense (as was shewn in Kerry) that when the clergy are *against* the National spirit (which I consider synonymous now with the *Fenian* spirit) they are nearly powerless—that is, that one *patriot* Priest (like Father O'Donoghue of Ardfert) will have more power for evil than twenty steady prudent men who oppose him will have for good." "This being the case," Dease shrewdly prophesied, "you will find that there will be *very*

---

36. M, 8317 (4).

few Priests found at the next General Election to *oppose* the extreme party. They will pretend to *lead*—in truth being *driven*." "All this," he admitted, "is deplorable enough to Irish Catholics who have really at heart the interests of Catholic Ireland—but I fear we are utterly powerless at present to avert the evils we see so plainly." "I have entirely renounced," he concluded sadly, "the hope of taking any active part in politics. My only chance of a seat in Parliament would be to become a *Sham Home Ruler*—but 'the game is not worth the candle!'"

Meanwhile, in the midst of the Galway petition trial and its aftermath, the Home Rule cause in the constituencies continued to make headway. In early April 1872, the sitting member for the borough of Wexford, Richard J. Devereux, a wealthy Catholic and a Gladstonian Liberal, resigned his seat. The borough was then contested by two candidates, both of whom who had declared for Home Rule, and William Archer Redmond was easily returned on April 20 with 321 votes to his opponent's 51.[37] Because Redmond was a very popular local Catholic landlord and a sincere Home Ruler, very little political stir appears to have been created by the election; his return went unnoticed in all the various clerical correspondences. Still, the election of another Home Rule member only made it all the more obvious that it was becoming more difficult, if not impossible, to be returned for an Irish-Catholic constituency without declaring for Home Rule. When a Home Rule candidate, John George MacCarthy, was defeated only some six weeks later, on June 7, in the very small borough of Mallow in county Cork, by William F. Munster, an English Catholic standing as a Liberal, however, the appearance belied the reality, for Mallow was really the exception that proved the rule. The seat had been vacated in May by the appointment of George Waters as chairman of the quarter sessions of county Waterford, and MacCarthy, the son of a Cork merchant, and a solicitor and land agent who had written an able pamphlet in favor of Home Rule, immediately offered himself as a candidate. He was endorsed by the council of the Home Government Association, and was supported locally by his namesake, John McCarthy, the influential parish priest of Mallow, and his curate Patrick Ahern. Butt soon learned from his close friend D. A. Nagle, the owner and editor of the *Cork Herald,* that MacCarthy was very unpopular with the Fenians and advanced Nationalists in Cork. The lengths to which the Fenian-inspired opponents of MacCarthy were willing to go was soon revealed in a letter from Nagle to Butt. "I cannot bear fully til morning," Nagle explained on May 19, "so as to write you. Suffice it to say that a demonstration in favour of MacC. being expected today, a contingent went down from Cork to break it up. The *demonstrators* got afraid & the candidate avoided the town" (B). "So much," Nagle concluded contemptuously, "for the candidate of the people's choice. Shall write you by morning post."

---

37. Walker, p. 114.

Nagle was as good as his word, for the next day he wrote Butt a long and interesting letter marked "strictly confidential," about both the situation in Mallow and its implications for the Nationalist movement. "My informant from Mallow," he reported on May 20, "tells me that McC. has no support but that of the P.P. who has got promises for him. Were the P.P. out of the way he wd be non est [still born]" (B).

> The fact [is] he is personally detested as a politician because he was always considered in his capacity as President of the [Catholic] Young Men's Soc. to have been a repressive foe to anything like National spirit among its members. Besides there is a great deal of nepotism in his selection, and also it is believed he is the mere residuary legatee of Waters. As some confirmation of this view, I may say, I have every reason for believing that a vacancy wd have been made for my cousin Colonel Hickie long since had he given a pledge he wd go for Gladstone, through *thick & thin*. This he never wd do.

"I am careless," Nagle further explained, in the sense of being disinterested, "about this election. I have no objection to McC. except that politically speaking I dont trust him, & hence it is, the paper [*Cork Herald*] has been silent in his regard."

"I can make no forecast," Nagle added, "abt the election. The popular resentment is very great against him, & I am certain it will increase. I am told Martin & Maguire have gone down for him. Martin is an honest man, but I think he is too simple & too *unsophisticated* for this business. Maguire on the principle of 'scratch me & I will scratch you' is bound to support the man, who is the Atlas sustaining his testimonial affair. I dont believe M. believes in his protege, still gratitude compels him to stand to him." "It is plain," Nagle pointed out, "the Association have acted prematurely. I agree with you in thinking it must be re-organised. There is too much haste in its action in this business, & I honestly tell you if you establish that whatever may be a man's anti-national tendencies & anti-national sympathies, all can be condoned & cancelled, provided he writes or pirates a pamphlet, to support the views of the Association, and that in this case the Association will give him a clean bill of political health, so sure as this is the case, the body will & ought to lose the political support of the lower strata." "You know well," he reminded Butt, "it is on those you must rely. The upper classes & the upper class of the middle class are corrupted & imbecile & it is my theory that [it] is from the lowest stratum working up, that Ireland's regeneration will be achieved. You know well but for this leaven in society you wd not now be M.P. for Limerick. In some way or the other, the Association must retrieve itself." "This letter," Nagle then concluded, "is solely for yourself & I shall be glad if it enables you to form some idea of the case. I believe his [MacCarthy's] candidature for Mallow would be only equalled by that of Dean O'Brien (if it could take place) for Lim'k City."

By this time, however, Butt had received a letter from Patrick Ahern, one of the two curates in the parish of Mallow, which confirmed the fact that, whatever opposition there was to MacCarthy, he would have the support of the local clergy. "I have heard to-day with surprise," Ahern explained on May 19, "that you had been informed that I publickly denounced Mr. MacCarthy, the present candidate for the representation of the borough" (B). "Allow me to say," he added, "that I always had been an admirer of his and am now one of his ardent supporters." "The lies and calumnies now circulated about him," Ahern assured Butt in conclusion, "have caused me to fling myself with more vigor into the contest." Though Butt did persuade the council of the Home Government Association to rescind its endorsement of MacCarthy, a significant number of individual members, such as Galbraith, Sullivan, and Martin, did go down to Mallow to campaign on his behalf. The opposition of Nagle and the advanced Nationalists, however, was apparently just enough to secure MacCarthy's defeat on June 7, as he lost to Munster by 78 votes to 91.[38] The defeat of the Home Rule candidate by a Liberal could hardly have provided much aid and comfort to those who opposed the Home Rule movement, such as Cullen, if they really understood what had happened because the Liberal victory in Mallow was, ironically enough, purely a Fenian inspiration.

In the approximately two years that had elapsed between the founding of the Home Government Association in May 1870 and the by-election in Mallow in June 1872, the Home Rule movement had made very considerable progress in the constituencies. With each succeeding by-election, it had become increasingly obvious that the Irish-Liberal alliance was in serious trouble and that, if the trend toward Home Rule should continue, the Liberal party outside of Ulster eventually would be decimated at the next general election. What the by-elections also had made clear was that the mainstay of that alliance in Ireland, the Irish bishops and their clergy, not only had been unable to stem the Home Rule tide, but also a good many of them prudently and astutely had begun to swim with the tide in the constituencies. Though the Irish bishops and their clergy had enthusiastically taken up the Irish-Liberal alliance at the general election of 1868, by early 1870 their enthusiasm for that alliance, especially in regard to the second point in the Gladstonian program, land reform, had cooled considerably. Even in their disappointment, however, the alternative offered by Home Rule did not immediately win their allegiance. In 1872, for example, in a body of some twenty-seven bish-

38. Ibid.

ops and three coadjutors, only one bishop, the redoubtable archbishop of Tuam, had declared for Home Rule. The other twenty-nine bishops, whatever approval some of them might have given individually to Home Rule candidates in the constituencies, had refused as a body to endorse the Home Rule movement as a movement. The bishops refused to endorse the movement because either they agreed with Cullen that it was at once too Protestant and too Fenian in its leadership or they deferred to his view, even if they did not completely agree with it, in the interest of the unity of their body and in the hope of what yet might be received from the Irish-Liberal alliance on the education question.

Indeed, the apparent unanimity of the bishops as a body on the question of Home Rule marked an interesting divergence of opinion in the body. Among the thirty bishops present in 1872, there were three main points of view, with several variations of each.[39] There were, apparently, about a dozen bishops who supported Cullen's view that the leadership of the movement was both suspect and dangerous and should not be endorsed. There were about a half dozen bishops who thought, given the doubtful circumstances, that prudence and caution dictated a wait-and-see policy. The remaining dozen bishops, who were more Nationalist in their sympathies, were both more favorable to the movement and less suspicious of its leadership but were nevertheless prepared to defer to their colleagues in the interest of preserving the unity of the body. The reason these latter twelve bishops were able to defer was that it had been decided that a distinction could be made between Home Rule as a principle and Home Rule as a movement. There was not a bishop in the Irish Church in 1872, in fact, with Moriarty as the possible exception, who was prepared to condemn Home Rule in principle. If it was not condemned in principle, therefore, each individual bishop could decide in terms of the circumstances in his own spiritual jurisdiction whether he could endorse the candidate who advocated Home Rule without extending that approval to the Home Rule movement and its leadership in general. In this way the bishops could continue to enjoy the best of all political worlds. At one and the same time they could continue to maintain their political power and influence with people in their constituencies by supporting Home Rule candidates if necessary, and, by not individually endorsing the Home Rule movement on the national level, could continue to maintain the unity of their body, looking forward to the expected fruits of the Irish-Liberal alliance on the education question.

---

39. The bishops who would have supported Cullen's point of view were McGettigan, Conroy, Walshe, Lynch, Walsh, Delany, Moriarty, Ryan, MacEvilly, and Gillooly. Those who would have preferred to wait on circumstances were Leahy (Dromore), Kelly, McDevitt, Furlong, Butler, and O'Brien. Those who were more Nationalist in their sympathies were Leahy (Cashel), Nulty, Dorrian, Donnelly, Conaty, Keane, O'Hea, Duggan, Durcan, MacCormack, Feeny, and Conway. Finally, there was MacHale, who was always a host in himself.

IV

The Catholic Response
March 1872–January 1874

Before the Galway election petition trial had gotten under way and the by-elections in Wexford and Mallow had taken place, the earl of Granard, who had attempted the previous year to launch a Catholic union of Ireland in imitation of the one founded in Britain, wrote to Cullen that he and his diocesan, the bishop of Ardagh, George Conroy, had concluded that it was perhaps now time to take some positive political action at the national level in order to counteract the considerable gains that were being made by the Home Rule movement in the country at large. "I mentioned some time ago," Granard explained on March 15, "to Dr. Conroy, that I thought it would be necessary to take some steps to counteract the growing influence of the Home Rule Association, as I feared, that if this were not done, some of our best men might be unseated at a General Election, & replaced by adventurers, and I suggested as my opinion, that the easiest mode to do this would be to revise the old Repeal platform, and that I thought the National Association might be used for the purpose. He requested me to mention my views to your Eminence, and I accordingly do so" (C). "It appears to me," Granard further suggested, "that before the General Election a settled plan of action ought to be determined upon." "Of course," he concluded, "I merely mention this as my private opinion."

Cullen, however, who had just written to Gladstone at the end of February about having something done on the Irish education question and had received a reply that at least he construed to be encouraging, was not about to rock the political boat by endangering the Irish-Liberal alliance. So, apparently, as he had in the case of the Catholic union the previous year, he allowed the matter to drop. When several months later, at the end of June, Granard wrote a public letter to the press criticizing Keogh's judgment, Granard was taken to task by one of his colleagues in the House of Lords. His colleague had pointed out that as one of her majesty's lords lieutenant under the present government, Granard was not free to criticize her administration, and he should, therefore, offer his resignation. Asking Cullen for advice on June 29, Granard explained, "I have received no communication from the Govt. upon the subject, neither do I think that I exceeded official Etiquette in writing the letter I did, however they are only too glad to attack me if they can" (C). Cullen advised him to ignore the criticism but to be more prudent in the future in his public letter writing. "I know," Granard replied on July 3, "that my great fault is acting upon impulse, when my feelings are roused, but I shall endeavour to be more prudent for the future" (C). "I need hardly say," Granard then concluded, "that I shall resign my Lieutenancy sooner than modify or retract my comment on Judge Keogh's aspersions on the Clergy." Two weeks later Granard was compelled to write Cullen again. "After mature consideration," he informed the cardinal on July 20, "I have sent in my resignation of the Ltcy. of Longford to the Queen, praying H.M. to accept it, & on Monday I shall make a short statement to the House, saying, that having gone through the papers delivered to the House in the Galway judgement, that I am still unable conscientiously to modify or retract a single expression in my letter & that not wishing to cause embarrassment to Govt. & without any *pressure* from *them,* I had sent in my resignation" (C). "I hope your Eminence," he added deferentially, "will consider the determination I have arrived at, as an honourable one, & that it will meet with your approval." "The Ministers," he noted further, "have been very kind in the matter, & regret my resignation, though they approve of my conduct in resigning." "The business &c." he concluded sadly, referring to the numerous petitions forwarded from Ireland to Parliament calling for Keogh's removal from the bench, "have produced quite a feeling in favor of Keogh in both Houses & it is quite useless to say anything against the renegade."

Cullen was not very pleased with the government for accepting Granard's resignation because Granard was considered to be his own mouthpiece in the House of Lords. He expressed his displeasure, for example, by writing to Kirby on August 2, noting that Granard, in effect, had been dismissed by the government and complaining that the government was doing a great deal of mischief by supporting the abuse of Catholics (K). Therefore, when Granard forwarded him, a short time later, a copy of a constitution for a Catholic union of Ireland drawn up by the bishop of Elphin, which ran to some eleven handscript pages in foolscap, Cullen was more amenable to such a proposal than he had been the previous year. "Lord Granard," Cullen informed Gillooly on August 29, "has shown me your Lordship's project for a Catholic Union" (G). "Something of the kind," he admitted, "appears necessary but I think it should be limited to the general interests of the Church for the present." Sometime during the next week, in order to redress matters and not be taken for granted, Cullen decided to sanction the launching of a Catholic union and to ask Granard to become its president. Apparently, Granard then circularized once again a number of prominent Catholic laymen and bishops inviting them to an organizational meeting on September 17, in Dublin. "I have got notice," Gillooly assured Cullen on September 6, "of the proposed meeting of the 17th and propose D.V. [*Deus Voluntas*—God willing] to attend it" (C). "I think," Gillooly maintained, "the organization of the Union shd. be made parochial & Diocesan from the very beginning, and that its objects shd. be known to embrace all our Catholic wants & interests; whilst at the same time it shd. be stated & clearly understood, that it wd. be the duty of the Councils or Committees to fix the time & order, in which these objects shd. be severally taken up by the Union." "Without the parochial & diocesan organisation," he warned, "the Union in reality wd. be nothing more than a few meetings in Dublin, which will be of little or no help toward the united action of the Catholics of Ireland. I believe it is the local organisations alone that will make the Union felt & feared by our opponents."

Two days after the organizational meeting, Cullen wrote to Kirby to report the proceedings. "We are trying," he explained on September 19, "to get up a Catholic Union. We have induced Lord Granard to become president, and a good many of our high Catholics have agreed to become members. I hope it will be able to do some good" (K). "Drs. Moran and Conroy," he added, "were here ere yesterday to assist at a preliminary meeting of the Union. Lord Granard and about thirty of the gentlemen (including the two Bishops) dined with me." "All *here*," Cullen concluded most significantly, "appear well disposed, but I apprehend that some of the Bishops will not encourage us." Between those, like Gillooly, who wanted to make the union a political organization with teeth and those who were prepared only to do nothing, Cullen and those who thought like him were bound to encounter difficulties in mobilizing the bishops as a body in the interests of the Catholic union. The fact that the only two bishops at the preliminary meeting were, in effect, Cullen's protégés, though invitations had undoubtedly been sent to nearly all the bishops, was yet another ill omen.

Moreover, Cullen was uneasy at this time for reasons other than those having to do with the launching of the Catholic union. For nearly a year he had been involved in difficulties with Robert O'Keeffe, the parish priest of Callan in the diocese of Ossory, whom he had suspended in November 1871 for contumacious behavior toward his own bishop and diocesan authorities.[1] The previous May, Cullen had asked for and received the requisite power from Rome to hear and act in the case. O'Keeffe had then, in February 1872, sued Cullen for ten thousand pounds damages, in a civil action for libel, and the trial was expected to take place before the end of the year. In a letter to Kirby at the end of August, therefore, Cullen suggested that a short visit to Rome to fortify himself spiritually for the

---

1. Peadar MacSuibhne, *Paul Cullen and His Contemporaries* (Naas, 1977), 5:44–45.

expected ordeal might be in order. "To-day early in the morning," he reported to Kirby on August 29, "the thought took possession of my mind that it would be a good thing for me to pay a visit in Rome towards the end of September. Father O'Keeffe cannot bring on the trial until the middle or end of November so I could spend a fortnight in Rome, paying homage to the Pope, inquire about Father O'Keeffe's case and be back in time to be put in the dock" (C). "What," he asked, "do you think of this project?" "I must wait," he further explained, "for the meeting of the Bishops on the Maynooth Board on the 24th September and I could be in Rome for the Angel Guardians quid vobis videtur [how does it appear to you]—I have not spoken to any of my advisers about the matter—will you let me know whether it would be proper for me to go or not." "I would be glad," he added, "to see the Pope, and Cardinal Barnabò and the other Cardinals and yourself. I shall be examined at my trial and it would give me great confidence to hear viva voce what the Pope thinks." "Write me a line," he advised Kirby in conclusion, "but do not let anyone know what I have written."

Kirby replied that Cullen would be most welcome in Rome, so Cullen left Dublin on September 26, arriving in Rome for the feast of the Angel Guardians on October 2. He spent four weeks in Rome; about the middle of his stay, he received a letter from Granard that reported the progress of the union. "We have done nothing about the Union," Granard explained on October 11, from Castle Forbes in Longford, "since Your Eminence's departure, except to send out Circulars, to which favourable answers have been received and the work is progressing steadily" (C). "I sent one of our Circulars to Dr. Herbert Vaughan, the new Bishop," he noted, referring to the recently appointed bishop of Salford in England, "who has written in today's Tablet a most favourable & useful article. I sent the same to the Freeman in which also a very good article appears. I thought the time had arrived for ventilating the objects of the Union, & I hope this view may be approved by Your Eminence." "If Your Eminence," he assured Cullen in conclusion, "could obtain the Holy Father's blessing for the Union, it wd. be a great thing for us."

Cullen's stay in Rome of nearly a month, meanwhile, had produced an interesting reaction from the British government, which did nothing to ease the growing tension in regard to the faltering Irish-Liberal alliance. H. Clarke Jervoise, who had replaced Odo Russell as the unofficial British agent to the Holy See shortly after the close of the first Vatican Council, wrote to the Earl Granville who was the foreign secretary, shortly after Cullen left Rome, to report a conversation that he had just initiated with Cardinal Antonelli, the papal secretary of state. "Having heard from a quarter generally well informed," Jervoise explained to Granville on November 6, "that Cardinal Cullen while in Rome had been desirous to obtain from the Pope some indication of moral support of the bishops & clergy whose proceedings in the Galway election were reported in the House of Commons by Justice Keogh,* I took an opportunity of mentioning the rumor to Cardinal

Antonelli, & of enquiring at the same time whether on some previous occasion H.H. had not ordered the Irish priests to abstain from interfering in elections."

His Eminence assured me with some energy that such a report could not be true inasmuch as it was an established rule with the Pope not to interfere in matters solely connected with the domestic policy of foreign countries, and how could it be expected that H.H. should attempt to control the free exercise of his vote by any citizen. Some years ago he continued Sir H. Bulwer had endeavoured to obtain from the Pope a promise that his authority should be used to influence the Irish clergy but his request had never been entertained. In the case of the Fenians, the Pope had condemned them [solely] as members of a secret society.

I said that H.E. must not misunderstand me. That the right of every priest to record his vote in favor of the candidate most acceptable to him could not be contested, but that in the Galway election after a lengthy examination of the case it had been proved that the clergy had exercised undue influence over their congregations & had coerced them by threats of spiritual & temporal injuries to vote or to abstain from voting, in accordance with the instruction received from the said clergy.

Cardinal Antonelli expressed his disbelief that the Irish clergy had so acted & said that were it true (for I had amongst other things mentioned that persons in the County of Galway who had refused to obey the orders of the priests at the last election were now denied the offices of the Church & that there was reason to fear that the confessional would be used against others) they would certainly be severely punished by their ecclesiastical superiors.

*That the Pope had replied that any interference on his part anywhere in political matters was in his present position very undesirable & that moreover the instructions he had already given for the guidance of the Irish priesthood forbidding political agitations on their part would prevent his now sanctioning proceedings which contravene those instructions.[2]

"Immediately after this conversation," Jervoise further reported to Granville, "I read in the French, Italian, and English newspapers a repetition of the supposed purport of Cardinal Cullen's journey to Rome as alluded to above, and yesterday I again drew Cardinal Antonelli's attention to the subject, pointing out that he would see from the extract I placed before him how nearly the story as I had heard it in the first instance had been repeated abroad with certain additions." "I also again stated," Jervoise assured Granville, "what I had said on the previous occasion that neither when I was in England this summer nor since my return to Rome had I received any instructions from H.M. Gov to bring the subject forward, & that I was induced to do so now solely on account of rumour with regard to Cardinal Cullen's wishes & the Pope's reported refusal & with respect to the truth of which I should be glad to have some information."

2. Foreign Office Papers (F.O.), Public Record Office, London, 170/191.

Cardinal Antonelli replied that though he had seen Cardinal Cullen on different occasions last month H.E. had never mentioned the subject of the Galway election to him; that he had recounted to him the history of his dispute with the Rev Mr. O'Keeffe, that neither had the Pope during the Cardinal's visit nor since his departure last week ever spoken of the Galway priests, but that as I had drawn his attention to the matter he would if I would leave with him the newspaper extract I had brought with me ask H.H. whether the subject had been raised by Cardinal Cullen. In accepting H.E.'s offer I again begged he would understand that I had no authority for having broached with him the subject of the proceedings of the Irish clergy in connection with the Galway election.

"Having observed on the first occasion of speaking with H.E. on the matter," Jervoise continued,

that he appeared entirely ignorant of the circumstances as well as incredulous that the priests should have so misconducted themselves, I took with me to the Vatican yesterday a short summary, which I read, of passages bearing especially to the proceedings of the priests taken from Mr. Justice Keogh's report to the speaker of the House of Commons dated from Dublin, the 11th of June as well as from his judgement delivered on the 27th of May last, selecting the evidence given which bearing on the conduct of the Rev Mr. Lynskey as will be found at page 21, the testimony of Mr. Forde & that referring to Lord Delvin at page 23, the threats of the Rev Messers. Greene & Coen at pages 26 & 28, Lord Gough's evidence at page 30, and Mr. Carter's page 35, and Mr. Burke's at page 37 where "he swears that the Rev Mr. Conway in the chapel at Headford said the landlords should be hung by the heels & not by the head, he said this at mass, he said this after the communion, he said this with his vestments on, he said this with the chalice on the altar," and in conclusion I added the evidence with regard to the Rev Mr. Considine at page 38, who Constable Healy swears said "that any renegade Catholic who would not vote for Captain Nolan would be a disgrace to his God, his religion, and his country, & that he would go to Hell."

"Cardinal Antonelli," Jervoise assured Granville in concluding this long despatch, "seemed much struck by the perusal of the passages I had quoted, particularly so when I informed him that they were but a small portion of the evidence of the same character sworn to by the witnesses at a trial which had been continued from the 1st of April from day to day until the 27th of May last."

Two days later, on November 8, Jervoise reported to Granville that Antonelli had just informed him that morning that he (Antonelli) had spoken to the pope on the subject of the Galway election, and the pope had stated that Cullen had not mentioned the matter to him, though Cullen had spoken about the O'Keeffe case.[3] "The cardinal secretary of state," Jervoise noted further, "added that he had also named to the Pope the accusations laid to the charge of certain of the Roman

3. Ibid.

Catholic bishops and clergy of having exercised undue influence and intimidation at the aforesaid election as I had described them at our last interview, the particulars of which, he said had not been previously brought to his Holiness's knowledge." "His Eminence likewise told me," Jervoise added, "that it was his intention to make enquiry of the Propaganda with a view to ascertain how far the circumstances were known there." "From all that I have been able to learn," Jervoise explained to Granville in conclusion, "I am disposed to believe that if this matter has at all been reported at the Vatican it has been done in a most imperfect and casual manner." In spite of Jervoise's repeated disclaimers that he had received no formal instructions from his government to raise the issue of the Galway election and the untoward political conduct of the Irish clergy, he had, in effect, managed to call the subject to the attention of both the cardinal secretary of state and the pope. He had also revealed to Antonelli and the pope the fact that they had not been kept properly informed about the matter by either the Propaganda authorities or by Cullen on his recent visit. Granville, moreover, could maintain that he had not initiated the subject, so he had not obligated himself or his government to the pope and his administration; yet he had, at the same time, the undoubted pleasure of giving Cullen a diplomatic tit-for-tat for Cullen's part in promoting an Irish Catholic union and for having named Lord Granard as its president. In all, though it was a very able performance on the part of Granville, it could not have improved Cullen's temper or disposition regarding the sincerity or the good will of those on the other side of the Irish-Liberal alliance.

Some three weeks after Cullen's return from Rome and this exchange between the British government and the Roman authorities, the Catholic Union of Ireland was finally and formally launched, on November 26 at a meeting in St. Kevin's Chapel in the procathedral in Dublin. Of the some one hundred notables who attended the meeting, there were besides Cullen and Granard, three bishops, six members of Parliament, forty-five clergymen, and some forty laymen.[4] Five other bishops and four M.P.'s tendered their regrets to the secretary at not being able to attend.[5] As president, Granard took the chair and opened the proceedings with an

---

4. *Freeman's Journal,* November 27, 1872. The bishops present were Furlong (Ferns), Lynch (coadjutor to Kildare and Leighlin), and James Murray (Maitland, Australia). The M.P.'s present were O'Reilly (Longford), Cogan (Kildare), Redmond (Wexford, Bor.), D'Arcy (Wexford, Co.), and Smyth (Westmeath).

5. Ibid. The bishops who tendered regrets were O'Hea (Ross), Moran (Ossory), Conaty (Kilmore), Gillooly (Elphin), and MacEvilly (Galway). The M.P.'s were Dease (Queen's), Sherlock (King's), Synan (Limerick), and Heron (Tipperary).

explanation of the objectives of the union and the reasons they should be sup-ported by the Catholics of Ireland. "Through this association," Granard main-tained, "the voice of Catholic Ireland, in unison with the defenders of Catholicity and the rights of the Holy See in every part of the world, will protest against the spoliation of the Vicar of Christ, the persecution of the religious orders, and the attempts to undermine the authority of the parent and the Church in the education of Catholic children (applause)."[6] "Being essentially Catholic and non-political," he added significantly, "the mission of the Union is to proclaim the sovereignty of Catholic interests as paramount to every other consideration, and thus to afford a common platform to men of diverse political opinions to unite in furthering the objects I have alluded to as the primary ones of the Association; and I am glad to be able to state that this aim has been to a great degree arrived at already by the enrollment of members representing different shades of politics (hear, hear, and applause)."

What Granard was alluding to, of course, was the presence of P. J. Smyth, who had been elected recently as a Home Ruler for county Westmeath and had been designated to move the third resolution of the six to be presented at and passed by the meeting. The first resolution, moved by Viscount Southwell and seconded by Sir John Bradstreet, proposed the names of some thirty laymen who were to constitute the council of the union for the coming year. The second resolution, which called for the restoration of the temporal power of the pope, was moved by Matthew P. D'Arcy, M.P. for county Wexford and seconded by Edward Maguire. When Smyth moved the third resolution, in support of the Catholic bishop of Ermeland, who had resisted the efforts of Bismarck to encroach on the rights of the Church in Germany, he took occasion to say that he was "greatly honoured in being asked to take part in a meeting such as that, with the objects of which he profoundly sympathised."[7] "He belonged," he confessed, "to that school of pol-itics whose founder was O'Connell, which recognized the necessity of a union of Irishmen, without distinction of creed, for the attainment of common objects of national utility. If, however, the especial interests of any particular section of Irishmen are menaced, it is the right and the duty of that section, be they Protes-tants, Presbyterians, or Catholics, to unite for their defence." "So doing," Smyth maintained, "they only prove their sincerity as religionists; and he held that the better the Protestant, the better the Presbyterian, the better the Catholic, the better will be the Irishman." Smyth's motion was seconded by George Errington, a young, ambitious politician from county Longford.

The final three resolutions presented to the meeting were concerned with the persecution of Catholics in the Swiss canton of Geneva, the preparation of ad-

6. Ibid.
7. Ibid.

dresses to the pope and to those who defended the German and Swiss Catholics, and the penal laws passed against religious orders in Italy and Germany. They were all proposed and seconded by either members of Parliament or representative laymen. The only cleric who addressed the meeting, in fact, was Cullen, who closed the proceedings with a relatively short exhortation to support the union. He was careful to emphasize, as had Granard, that the union was non-political, and he had not a word to say explicitly about the education question. "I trust that the Union," he explained, "will be carried on in the strictest principles of religion, and of Justice and Charity (applause), so that all members may unite in asserting the rights of the Catholic Church, and persevere until those rights have been properly acknowledged (hear, hear). We should be prudent and cautious, and we should continually have recourse to prayer."[8] Cullen reported, then, that his recent trip to Rome had made him even more aware that the pope and his people, in spite of all the efforts of the Italian government, were still one and that this example of unity between pastors and people was the great lesson of the Catholic Church to the modern world. Cullen's concept of ecumenism, therefore, had little to do with Smyth's, and it certainly did not include Irish Protestants and Presbyterians. In an apology to Cullen for his absence from the meeting, occasioned by a confusion in his calendar, written the following day, the bishop of Ardagh commented on Smyth's attendance. "I dont know well," Conroy confessed, "what to say about the prominence given to the M.P. for Westmeath. I fear that it will repel many Catholics of position from the Union" (C).

The same day that Conroy wrote to Cullen, November 27, the council of the Catholic union held its first meeting and decided that all the Irish Catholic bishops, peers, privy councillors, and members of Parliament were to be *ex officio* members of the council.[9] It was also announced that nine members of Parliament, including Smyth, had signified their intentions of acting on the council.[10] The only other business done that day was the election of Bartholomew Teeling, who had served in the ill-fated Irish papal brigade in the early 1860s, as paid secretary of the union. The council met again the following week, on December 5, and settled the important questions of what the dues were to be and the classes of membership available.[11] Full members of the union were to subscribe one pound per year and associate members were to pay one shilling. The council also took the unique step for an Irish voluntary association at this time of approving the applications of the many ladies who had requested membership. The council apparently did not choose to set up a regular schedule of meetings, but decided

8. Ibid.
9. Ibid., November 29, 1872.
10. Ibid. The M.P.'s who so signified were those who attended the inaugural meeting and those who tendered their regrets for being unable to attend.
11. Ibid., December 7, 1872.

instead to hold its next meeting early in the new year, on January 8. At the end of December, therefore, P. J. Smyth wrote to Granard, explaining that he thought that the meetings of the union should be held more regularly.

"My suggestion was," Smyth noted on December 28, reporting a conversation that had taken place a few days earlier with several other members of the union, "that public meetings of the Union should be held regularly once a month, and Council meetings, regularly, on stated days, once a week" (C). "The effect of the public meetings," he further maintained, "would be to keep the Association before the public, and present to the country—what at present it does not possess—a Catholic platform."

> Catholics in every class feel deeply the present position of the Church, and look to a body like the Union to afford them opportunities of proclaiming their sentiments. If such opportunities are not afforded, if the Union acts only through its Council, these persons argue that they are not wanted, and so the body loses in popularity. So trained have we in Ireland been to the agency of public meetings, that I believe it to be impossible for any Association to become a power (and the Catholic Union, I think, should aim at that) which does not constantly keep itself before the public eye, and work and act in public.

"The advisability," Smyth then suggested, "of holding Ward or Parish meetings in Dublin and elsewhere, under the auspices of the local clergy, may be a matter also deserving the consideration of the Council." "If the ideas I venture to submit," he concluded, politely acknowledging where real power lay, "should meet with your Lordship's approval and that of His Eminence, I believe their adoption would tend to strengthen and consolidate the Union, and be attended with public benefit." Granard forwarded this letter to Cullen on December 31 and observed that there was a good deal to be said for Smyth's remarks, but he thought quarterly public meetings would serve the union better than would monthly ones.

At this stage, however, Cullen had no intention of turning the union into an effective grass-roots political organization. His main concern was how to keep Gladstone and his colleagues up to the mark in regard to Irish educational needs, especially as Gladstone was expected to introduce his Irish University bill shortly after Parliament convened in early February. Cullen was faced, therefore, with the delicate task of how to put considerable pressure on Gladstone without jeopardizing the Irish-Liberal alliance upon which a satisfactory educational measure depended. Cullen hoped to achieve this by mobilizing Irish-Catholic lay opinion in the Catholic union, which, as an elitist organization, was not yet the electoral threat that practicing politicians such as Smyth wanted it to be. This was why both Cullen and Granard had emphasized at the inaugural meeting that the union was nonpolitical, even as they insisted that Catholic rights, of which the most immediate was educational equality, be attended to. During December, therefore, Cullen and Granard drew up an address to be approved at the next meeting of the union's council, which would then be presented to Gladstone. "I return the education Address," Granard explained to Cullen on December 28, "I have cut out the last paragraph, which I believe will bring it into harmony with Y Eminence's views, perhaps therefore unless you have any other corrections to make to it, you w^d kindly send it to Mr. Teeling, who will copy it, & submit it to the Council" (C).

The council apparently approved of the address at their meeting on January 8, but it was not forwarded to Gladstone for nearly two weeks because Cullen wanted to take advantage of a general meeting of the Irish bishops, on January 21 and 22, to forward a like address from the body. "I enclose to Your Eminence," Granard reported to Cullen on January 24, "Mr. Gladstone's reply to my letter transmitting to him our declaration upon Education with inclosures, viz. the declarations of the Hierarchy & the Laity" (C). "I have forwarded to him," Granard added interestingly, "a copy of the Rules of the Union, & by this post write to Mr. Teeling to send him a complete list of the Council." "I think," he suggested "we had better now send our declaration to the Papers. I think it however as well not to publish Mr. Gladstone's letter." The final text of the declaration of the council of the Catholic Union of Ireland read:

> It is generally looked on as certain that Parliament will, in the coming session, be called on to consider the necessity of making important changes in the conditions of University Education in Ireland.
>
> This subject being one of vital import to the spiritual and temporal interests of Irish Catholics, we think it is the duty of the Catholic Union of Ireland to declare once again the principles on which the coming legislation should be based, if it be intended to meet the just and reasonable requirements of Catholics.
>
> These principles have been affirmed again and again in authoritative declarations of the Catholic Hierarchy, and in the resolutions adopted at the meeting of Archbishops and Bishops of Ireland, held at Maynooth, in August, 1869.
>
> Only two years ago they were endorsed by the signatures of the largest body of educated Catholic laymen which have ever been attached to any public document in Ireland.
>
> The two documents referred to are appended. The principles embodied in them are unchanged and unchangeable.
>
> On behalf of the Council, President GRANARD, of the Catholic Union of Ireland.[12]

What was most significant about this document was that when the bishops met on January 21 and 22 they decided not to publish any new resolutions on the education question but, instead, to indicate, by having the council of the union refer to their resolutions of August 1869, that their educational grievances were at least as longstanding as the Irish-Liberal alliance. Cullen's strategy for the Catholic union

12. Ibid., January 28, 1873.

apparently had succeeded very well. He had formally advised Gladstone of what both the bishops and a representative body of the Irish laity expected in the way of an acceptable solution to the Irish University question, and at the same time had attempted to convey through the rules and the membership list of the union that the organization of the laity posed no threat to the Irish-Liberal alliance because the union had no pretensions as a political organization.

Indeed, a number of the bishops who initially had been hostile to the union because they viewed it as essentially a political association changed their minds and decided to patronize it. "Dr. Moriarty," Conroy reported to Cullen on December 31, referring to the bishop of Kerry, "did not approve of the Catholic Union on the ground that since the abrogation of the penal laws there is no reason why Catholics should constitute themselves as a class apart from others, as if their interests were different from those of other citizens" (C). "But," Conroy assured Cullen, "he has given up this view, and will patronize the Union." The case of the bishop of Meath was even more interesting because he was, aside from MacHale, perhaps the most advanced Nationalist among the bishops. Nulty, whose diocese included the largest parts of Meath and Westmeath, apparently had come to distrust, along with a significant number of his priests, the junior member for Westmeath. "I am informed," Conroy reported to Cullen on January 4, "that P. J. Smyth has lost favour with some of his most ardent clerical supporters in W. Meath because he has taken such a leading part in 'Cardinal Cullen's Union'" (C). "This is very remarkable if true," Conroy noted. A week later Nulty wrote to Granard to explain that after some initial hesitation he was now prepared to join the union. "I had a letter," Granard reported to Cullen on January 13, "from the Bishop of Meath authorising me to have him elected a Member. He said that he had hesitated up to this, fearing, that the Union might be turned into a political association, but that of course as long as it remained what it professed to be, that he approved of the objects, his only fear being that designing persons might get on the Council to use it for their own purposes" (C). What is interesting about the attitudes of the bishops of Kerry and Meath is that they represented the extremes in the Irish political spectrum. Moriarty was as devoted a supporter of Gladstone and the Irish-Liberal alliance as could be found among the bishops, while Nulty was an advanced Nationalist and an ardent Tenant Righter. Both were suspicious of the union for their own reasons: the former because he thought it subversive of the Irish-Liberal alliance, and the latter because he viewed it as designed to destroy the movement for Home Rule. They were both wrong, for Cullen was ultimately playing his own hand—in an effort to secure a satisfactory settlement of the University question from Gladstone and his colleagues.

In the meantime, while Cullen was attempting to mobilize public opinion on the education question under the nonpolitical auspices of the Catholic union, he continued to take some very hard political knocks in regard to by-elections and the Irish-Liberal alliance, at the hands of the advocates of Home Rule. In early November, the Irish attorney general, Richard Dowse, was promoted to the bench as a baron of the Court of Exchequer in Ireland, which required him to vacate his seat in Parliament for the borough of Londonderry. He was succeeded as attorney general by Christopher Palles, the solicitor general and one of the most distinguished members at the Irish bar, who was also asked by the government to contest Dowse's vacated seat in Derry.[13] However, Palles had the double misfortune of being both a Roman Catholic and a strong supporter of Cullen's views on denominational education. Because the numbers of Protestant and Catholic voters in Derry, which usually translated directly into Conservative and Liberal, were approximately equal, political contests were usually decided by the number of Presbyterians who voted Liberal. Many of the Presbyterians who were inclined to do so, however, were not only the enemies of denominational education but also very much opposed to the ultramontane views that allegedly attached to any friend of Cardinal Cullen. Thus, when the Liberals of Derry, Presbyterian and Catholic, asked a native son, Dr. Evory Kennedy, a prominent Dublin obstetrician, to contest the seat in their interest, the government asked him to withdraw in favor of Palles; and, much to the chagrin of the Presbyterians, he did so.

At the same time, the Conservatives were having similar difficulties in deciding upon a candidate: the local organization selected Bartholomew McCorkell, a Derry merchant, while the Conservative central office nominated a London solicitor, Charles E. Lewis, who was much resented by the local men as a "carpetbagger." The electoral situation was then further complicated by the announcement that Joseph F. Biggar, president of the Belfast Home Rule Association, would also contest the seat. Because the Conservatives were evenly divided between McCorkell and Lewis and neither of these showed any indication of retiring, the question became whether Biggar could secure enough of the Catholic vote to allow one of the Conservatives to be returned. How the Catholic vote in Derry would be cast, of course, depended to a very large degree on whom the Catholic bishop of Derry, Francis Kelly, and his clergy were prepared to support. Though Kelly and his clergy were in favor of Palles, the campaign mounted by Biggar and his supporters against Palles, whom they vehemently denounced for the role he would soon have to play as attorney general in prosecuting the Galway bishops and priests for their part in the Galway election, prevented the Derry clergy from taking up Palles's cause with their usual enthusiasm. Cullen had written the bishop of Derry on behalf of Palles, and Kelly replied on November 16, reporting that there were still four candidates in the field. "Now should one of the Conservatives," he explained, "withdraw, & this is expected—Mr. Palles will certainly be defeated. Should both go to the poll, the A. General, in my opinion, will have a

13. V. T. H. Delany, *Christopher Palles* (Dublin, 1960), p. 66.

good chance" (C). "The home rulers," he further complained, "are most obsti-
nate. The Priests have made every effort to secure unanimity but I regret to say
without success."

Meanwhile, Biggar and his friends were unmerciful in their denunciations of
Palles in the press and on the platform. One of the chief offenders in the denunciation of Palles was the Belfast *Daily Examiner,* a Catholic paper reputed to be under
the patronage, if not the control, of the Catholic bishop of Down and Connor,
Patrick Dorrian. Cullen was so upset by the abuse of Palles in the *Examiner* that he
wrote Dorrian asking him to exert his influence to interfere. "I have no more
right," Dorrian had replied on November 11, "to interfere with the *Examiner* than
your Eminence has to control the *Nation* or Dr. Delany the *Cork Examiner*" (C).
"I am very wrongly charged," Dorrian complained, "with everything wrong or
foolish that may appear in it, whereas I have *never controlled a single line in it* and
could not without a stretch of authority which would be arbitrary, and thus do
great harm. As long as it is an *open question* [i.e., Home Rule] it would not be safe
to act with too high a hand." "I have the greatest respect for Mr. Palles," he further
assured Cullen, "but there is a very angry feeling against him for coming in to
break up the party after Mr. Biggar had got 500 votes promised. At least I have
heard this."

> And, as feeling runs high, there is now no lack of argument on both sides.
> But into that I wont enter.
>
> I only know that the party who have invited Mr. Palles are our worst ene-
> mies. Still I should be glad to see him on the Bench. But I have no power to
> interfere further than I have done to disapprove of the tone and phrases ap-
> plied to him personally.
>
> I need not trouble your Eminence more. This division is sad but it is the
> work of Presbyterian Liberals: and the Catholics seem tired of longer playing
> Second Fiddle to them.

"I am no great advocate of Mr. Biggar," Dorrian concluded firmly, "but that is a
question for the Electors—and it would be tyranny on my part to attempt further
interference than by expressing my opinion which I have already done."

Cullen then wrote to Kelly to say that Dorrian had disavowed any control over
the *Examiner,* and when Kelly wrote Cullen again, he explained that he had just
received a visit from Palles and had also conveyed Cullen's disclaimer on behalf of
Dorrian to his priests. "I am happy to say," he reported with reference to Palles, on
November 18, "he is in excellent spirits—is quite satisfied with his canvass. The
Catholics, with few exceptions, have promised to vote for him. But the issue is
very uncertain as one of the Conservatives may retire at the last hour" (C). "The
paper to which your Eminence referred," Kelly noted, "has done much mischief
on our people. I have stated to the priests that Dr. Dorrian had declared that he
had no control over the paper. They will endeavour quietly to contradict the

rumours that have been circulated here regarding the Bishop [i.e., Dorrian was in favor of Biggar]." The fact was, however, that Dorrian was the real owner of the *Daily Examiner,* and one of his curates in his mensal parish of St. Patrick's in Belfast, Michael Henry Cahill, was the actual editor of the paper and its nominal proprietor. Dorrian had apparently invested heavily in the *Examiner,* and when the paper was finally sold in 1877 because of financial difficulties, the loss to Dorrian was estimated at not less than £6,000.[14]

In any case, the denunciations of Palles by Biggar and his supporters did not abate. On November 21, for example, two days before the poll was declared, A. M. Sullivan, the owner and editor of the *Nation* and an ardent and prominent Home Ruler, who addressed the Derry electors on behalf of Biggar, made a most savage attack on Palles, denouncing him as "the liveried servant of the Castle, who went there with religion on his lips and perfidy in his heart," and whose "name would go down in history as the greatest Judas that ever sold his country and his God."[15] In spite of all the rhetoric and the sectarian nature of the contest, the election passed relatively quietly for an Irish election, and it was the first in Ireland to be conducted secretly, under the terms of the recently passed Ballot Act. The evening before the election, however, Kelly's intimation that the Conservative candidates would reach an accommodation was borne out. A meeting of the Derry Conservative electors was held, and a vote was taken by the supporters of McCorkell and Lewis; Lewis received a majority, and McCorkell then withdrew from the contest. When the poll was declared the next day, November 23, the Conservative, Lewis, won with an overall majority of 83 in a poll of more than 1,300.[16] Lewis had, received 696 votes, while Palles had received 522. Biggar had polled only 89 votes, and McCorkell received the votes of two unrepentant local die-hards. Lewis would have won the election, therefore, even if Biggar had withdrawn and the Catholic vote was not divided. The real cause of Palles's defeat was the defection of a considerable number of Presbyterian Liberals who perceived Palles to be both an ultramontane Catholic and a supporter of the denominational educational views of Cardinal Cullen. The bitterness of the election, however, and the lengths to which the Home Rulers were willing to go in denouncing their opponents—not even the episcopal character of the bishop of Derry was spared by A. M. Sullivan and his friends—were very disturbing to Cullen, who must have realized, in the light of Dorrian's letter to him, that the issue of Home Rule was acquiring a divisive potential among even the bishops as a body.

14. Ambrose Macaulay, *Patrick Dorrian, Bishop of Down and Connor, 1865–85* (Dublin, 1987), pp. 202–15. See also Thomas Macknight, *Ulster As It Is* (London, 1896), 2:269.
15. Delany, p. 71.
16. Brian M. Walker, ed., *Parliamentary Election Results in Ireland, 1801–1922* (Dublin, 1978), p. 114.

The inability of the bishops and their clergy to contain the Home Rule tide became even more pronounced some two weeks after the Derry election in another by-election in Cork City. The occasion was the death, on November 1, of John Francis Maguire, the junior member for Cork City and the proprietor of the *Cork Examiner*. Three candidates declared immediately that they would contest the vacant seat; two of these were avowed Home Rulers and the other was a Liberal.[17] The Liberal was J. C. Mathew, a nephew of the celebrated Capuchin temperance crusader of the 1840s, Father Theobald Mathew. The two Home Rulers were John Daly, the mayor of Cork, and Joseph P. Ronayne, a distinguished civil engineer and proprietor of the Cork-Macroom railroad. Daly was the less radical of the two and enjoyed the confidence of the Cork Liberal middle class, while Ronayne was an advanced Nationalist who had the support of both the local Fenians and the advanced Nationalists in the city. Given that more than a thousand electors in Cork were Protestants and voted Conservative, and that they had nominated a candidate, J. E. Pim, who would certainly realize their voting potential, a split among the Catholics and the various shades of Liberals and Home Rulers could only result in the return of Pim. Accordingly, both Mathew and Daly withdrew from the contest, and the Catholic clergy, facing a straight fight with a Conservative, finally endorsed Ronayne in spite of his separatist propensities and Fenian support. In the wake of the clerical endorsement, the senior member for Cork City, N. D. Murphy, who had until this time been a staunch supporter of the Gladstonian alliance, not only endorsed Ronayne but also, with an eye to the next general election, declared for Home Rule. Ronayne then declared himself in favor of the principle of denominational education. In the election, the results of which were declared on December 10, Ronayne handily won over Pim with 1,883 votes to his opponent's 1,110.[18]

The combined lesson of the Derry and Cork elections was not that the Irish-Liberal alliance was in great jeopardy but rather that the very survival of Gladstone's government was now in question. The defection of the Presbyterian Liberals in Derry was, in fact, a portent for the English and Scots Nonconformists of what was to come in regard to Gladstone's legislation for higher education for Roman Catholics, which he hoped to introduce at the next session of Parliament in February 1873. Whichever way Gladstone modified his measure, he was bound to alienate either the Nonconformists, who virtually made up the backbone of his party and who detested, even more than the system itself, being asked to endow denominational education, or the Catholics, who in the name of equality were demanding both the system and the endowment and who felt, moreover, that Gladstone's failure to meet their educational needs over the previous three years

17. David Thornley, *Isaac Butt and Home Rule* (London, 1964), p. 136.
18. Walker, p. 114.

had, by impairing their political credibility, delivered them into the hands of their bitterest political enemies, the proponents of Home Rule. When and if push finally did come to shove as far as the survival of his ministry was concerned, however, there was little doubt that Gladstone would prefer to be wrecked on the rocks of Catholic disappointment than to be drowned in the whirlpool of the Nonconformist conscience.

In the event, the crisis could not be long delayed, for Gladstone had begun to prepare his measure of higher education for Roman Catholics by the middle of November 1872, and he held his first cabinet on November 22, to discuss the heads of his proposed bill with his colleagues.[19] Early in December Cullen wrote to Manning, asking him whether he had any information with regard to the government's intentions. "The Government are keeping their counsel so well," Manning replied on December 8, "that I have no knowledge of their intentions as to the Irish higher Education. But from observation of the signs of the times I am not without hope that they will propose a scheme not impossible of acceptance to Catholics" (C). "One only point," he added, "is I think certain, namely that both sides of the House will unite in refusing direct endowment to our colleges. To ask for endowment was five years ago hopeless & dangerous; to ask for it now would be still more so." "I remember," Manning noted, referring to the negotiations that had taken place between the Irish bishops and the Conservative government in 1868, "that your Eminence would have accepted a Charter without endowment. And I hope that the next scheme proposed may not be lost by demanding endowment. The House would, I believe, consent to found & endow a system in which we should have equal rights: but it would give us nothing as Catholics." "If we demand the integrity of Catholic education," he advised Cullen "and treat the endowment question as the Irish Bishops treated the Establish[ed] Church Fund, I believe we shall gain even endowments in the end." "Pray forgive," he concluded more cautiously, "my writing thus. I do so because I wish to know what to answer if I am ever asked."

If Cullen replied to Manning's probe, the letter apparently has not survived. When Manning learned something more about Gladstone's intentions, it appears that he wrote to Cullen again, for the latter discussed the matter on December 18 with Woodlock. "Since I saw your Eminence to-day," Woodlock explained, "I have been thinking over the scheme mentioned by Dr. Manning. Of course, I cannot speak with great certainty, not having the precise terms before me" (C).

19. John Morley, *The Life of William Ewart Gladstone* (London, 1906), 2:45.

"But I understood that it is proposed:" he recapitulated, "to create a central Gov Board like the London Univ, which shall have power to appoint courses of studies & examiners, and to confer Degrees on all comers, including students from the Catholic Colleges & Schools, while Trinity College & the Queen's Colleges shall be left with their present revenues &c." "If this be the scheme," Woodlock maintained, "I think it would be a most dangerous, or rather ruinous one for the interests of Religion in Ireland. I believe its potential effect in a very few years would be: that nearly all the Catholic laity aspiring to Higher Education would go to one of the Godless Colleges." Cullen apparently grew more uneasy about Gladstone's intentions after his conversation with Woodlock, and he decided to ask the archbishop of Cashel's advice about whether the Irish bishops should make their views on what would be acceptable to them known before Gladstone introduced his bill in the House of Commons in February. "It deserves consideration," Leahy pointed out politely to Cullen on December 31, "whether it would be advisable *just now* to address our flocks moreover on *the general question of Education*" (C). "Our sentiments," he added, referring to the educational views of the bishops, "are unmistakable. Were we to come out *now* with such an Address, without doubt the Secularists would raise a howl against us that forsooth we wanted to forestall the deliberations of Parliament & to intimidate the Government into the adoption of our views." "Any expression of the collective opinions of the Bishops, any line of action to be adopted, with reference to the general question of Education," he advised Cullen sensibly, "would come much more fitly after the opening of Parliament & the statement by the Government of their plan of University Education." Cullen took Leahy's advice and confined himself to airing his views on the education question in the person of Lord Granard through the medium of the Catholic union.

As the momentous day upon which Gladstone was to introduce his bill approached, Manning wrote to Cullen to alert him that English public opinion might be about to take an ugly turn. "I would ask your Eminence," Manning advised on Wednesday, January 28, 1873, "to look at the Times of Monday last, and yesterday. You will see the mean acts with which they are trying to get up two things, first a howl at the opening of Parliament to be turned on the Irish education question: and next a public sympathy with the German penal laws against the Catholic Church" (C). "I hope the Papers in Ireland will be as outspoken as its Bishops," he added, referring to the recent joint pastoral of the Irish bishops, which condemned Bismarck's *Kulturkampf* against the Church in Germany. "We are here," he explained, "only your skirmishers thrown out in irregular order. We have no daily paper. Our Catholic papers are only weekly; and are read only by a few out of the Church. They do not reach public opinion with promptness or breadth; & therefore the enemy has the public mind to himself." "I wish some Irish Papers," he suggested pugnaciously, "would for the next six months *attack the Times by name.* We will back it up here. I shall have opportunities, which the Times will certainly attack: & then I can make them publish a reply." "The sooner we attack them," he advised Cullen in conclusion, "the better. They will go on creating an adverse feeling which will grow strong in time."

On the evening of February 13, Gladstone finally introduced his long-awaited bill to an expectant House of Commons in a magnificent three-hour effort.[20] The complexity of his proposed measure was matched only by its ingenuity. He proposed to establish a new central or national university in Dublin that was to be a teaching, examining, and degree-granting body. Accordingly, the two existing universities—Dublin and Queen's—were to be suppressed, and Trinity College, the only constituent college of Dublin University, was to become an affiliated college of the new university. Of the three constituent colleges of the Queen's University—Belfast, Cork, and Galway—Galway was to be suppressed, and Belfast and Cork, like Trinity, were to become affiliated colleges of the new university. The Catholic University College and Magee College, a Presbyterian institution, also were to be affiliated with the new university. The new university was to be provided with an income of £45,000, of which £12,000 was to come out of the £50,000 endowment of Trinity College and the remaining £33,000 was to be provided by the consolidated fund, the church fund, and student fees.[21] The Belfast and Cork colleges were to continue to be subsidized by the state out of the consolidated fund, but the Catholic University and Magee College were to be left as they had been, without state support. There were to be no religious tests for teachers or students in the new university, and all instruction was to be strictly secular; necessary religious instruction, however, was to be provided by the affiliated colleges without state support. Trinity College, which was essentially a Church of Ireland institution, was to be secularized, and its prizes, honors, and emoluments were to be made available to everyone without distinction as to creed. The theological faculty of Trinity College was to be severed from that institution and transferred with the necessary funding to a representative body of the now disestablished Church of Ireland.

The government of the new university was to be vested in a chancellor and vice-chancellor, and a council of twenty-eight ordinary members was to be named in the bill. The council were to be nominees in part of the lord lieutenant and in part

20. *Hansard's Parliamentary Debates,* 3d series, 214:378–426.

21. The consolidated fund had been established by William Pitt in the 1780s. All taxes that did not have to be renewed annually by Parliament were paid into that fund. Charges on the fund, therefore, became a permanent charge on the revenue of the state and did not have to be voted annually by Parliament. The church fund had been established at the disestablishment and disendowment of the Church of Ireland in 1869 from the surplus property of that church, and over the following fifty years various good works, including intermediate and university education, were provided for out of that fund.

of the heads of the various affiliated colleges. For the first ten years, vacancies were to be filled alternately by appointment by the crown and co-option by the council. Ten years after the council's establishment, four of the twenty-eight ordinary members were to retire annually, and their places were to be filled respectively by the crown, the council, the professors, and the senate. The affiliated colleges were to be allowed to elect, in addition to the twenty-eight ordinary members, one or two council members, depending on the number of students in the particular affiliated college. The new university was also to have the power to affiliate other institutions as constituent colleges, and all of these affiliated colleges were to be allowed to form their own governments. Finally, in order to allay the fears of Roman Catholics about the dangers of the secular and mixed nature of the new university, Gladstone introduced two safeguards, which later were derided by their critics as "gagging clauses." In the first, he provided that the teaching of history, theology, and mental and moral philosophy all were to be excluded from the curriculum of the new university, though they might, of course, be provided by the affiliated colleges. In the second clause, Gladstone provided that a teacher or other person of authority in the new university might be suspended from or deprived of his office if he were held to have willfully given offence, in speaking or writing, to the religious convictions of any member of the university.

Apparently, all those who heard Gladstone's presentation were very favorably impressed. On leaving the visitors' gallery of the House of Commons that evening, Manning met the celebrated editor of the London *Times,* J. T. Delane, who was apparently as enthusiastic about the measure as the archbishop and remarked that this was "a bill made to pass."[22] "Last night," Manning reported to Cullen the next morning, February 14, "I heard Mr. Gladstone's statement: but it will be in your Eminence's hands before this letter can reach Dublin, so that I do not attempt to describe it" (C). "The chief good," he explained, "I see in it for the Catholic Church is 1) the complete freedom of its own Collegiate education. 2) the freedom to multiply & affiliate Colleges to the University hereafter. 3) the power to obtain degrees without residence. 4) the exclusion of mental philosophy and modern History. 5) the freedom to found Halls in Dublin for students not fit for the Catholic University."

> Your Eminence will see two things.
> 1. That grants of public money to Catholic Colleges was treated as 'ex concesso' impossible.
> 2. That Trinity College retains its income ceasing to be denominational and by becoming open to all.
> Now I do not venture to make any comment upon the plan. Your Eminence will better know what to say to Government.

---

22. Morley, 2:47.

The only side of the question I can judge of is the English, & Political side
and on this I would venture to say that I think it would be our best prudence to
make as much noise as will lead our enemies to believe that we do not like it,
but to hold fast by the plan. My reasons are:

1. That it is certain we shall never get anything better. The opposition if in
Office would not give us anything better: & they are going to oppose even
this.

2. That it is certain we may & I think should get something much worse.

Government has fixed the maximum of concession & of consideration
towards us, the best of them being judges. Their supporters will perhaps refuse even this.

The opposition will never rise to the maximum.

The two parties therefore would unite against anything more favourable to
the Catholic Church.

"If we do not hold fast to this," Manning then emphasized to Cullen, "as Government offers it I fear we shall be in danger of some scheme which it will be
impossible for us to accept." "It seems to me inevitable," he then concluded, "that
the Catholic education in Ireland will prevail over everything hereafter as the Faith
of Ireland has prevailed hitherto. All it needs is freedom, & that this Bill offers to
us."

"I wrote yesterday," Manning informed Gladstone briefly, in a letter marked
"*confidential*," written on February 15, "both to Cardinal Cullen and the Rector
of the Catholic University, urging them to accept the Bill."[23] "I am fully prepared,"
he assured Gladstone, "for objections, and am aware not only that I am more
easily satisfied than they are, but am more easily satisfied than, perhaps, I should
be if I were in Ireland." However, Cullen, who had been laid low by an attack of
influenza at the end of January and was still recuperating in the county Meath
when he read Gladstone's speech and received Manning's letter, apparently was
very disappointed with the proposed measure. Indeed, the clergy in Ireland were
generally disappointed. As John Canon Farrell, the parish priest of St. Catherine's
in Dublin and one of Cullen's trusted confidants in educational matters, explained
on February 20, to Edmund Dease, the junior member for Queen's county, who
had just asked about his reaction to Gladstone's bill, "We are all at sea about the
University Bill, it involves so many considerations that it requires serious deliberation before we adopt a fixed course of policy."[24] "Dr. Woodlock," he reported,
referring to the rector of the Catholic University, "went down to Meath on Saturday [February 15] to consult the Cardinal. His Eminence would then give no
opinion. He said he must take time to consider the measure in all its bearings & to
consult with the Bishops & others who are interested. I believe he is to be home

23. Shane Leslie, "Irish Pages from the Postbags of Manning, Cullen, and Gladstone," *The
Dublin Review* 165 (1919): 185.

24. M, 8319 (9).

today & as the matter is pressing, some action will be at once taken, possibly the Bishops will be again summoned to consider the important question." "The bill, as you say," Farrell admitted, "affords us certain important advantages provided we can avail ourselves of them." "Financially," he added as a *caveat,* "we are shamefully treated[,] left to our own very limited resources, whilst our opponents have an enormous endowment." "Thus heavily weighted," he concluded sadly, "we must be beaten in the race."

The day before, in fact, Cullen had written to Kirby, confiding his own disappointment. "Gladstone's bill on university education," he reported on February 19, "is calculated to disappoint everybody—it gives Trinity College £50,000 [*sic*] per an. with all the present buildings etc. making it a mixed College. It gives £50,000 [*sic*] more to a new mixed university to which Catholics will have access for degrees. To the Catholic University he gives nothing except the privilege of sending its students to the new university for examination" (K). "Altogether," Cullen maintained grimly, "the bill would appear to be worthy of another Bismarck." "Dr. Manning," Cullen added, most interestingly, "disapproves of it but he thinks we ought to accept the little it gives us." "Probably," he concluded, "we must hold a meeting of the Bishops." The following day, February 20, after having consulted with the archbishop of Cashel, Cullen circularized the bishops asking them to meet in Dublin on February 27 to consider Gladstone's bill. In the next several days Cullen's views on the bill began to harden, but he was still undecided about the course of action he would take. "You have probably seen," Cullen surmised, in a letter to Kirby on February 23, "Gladstone's bill on University education. It has disappointed and displeased all Catholics. I fear it will be as difficult to get any good out of it, as to gather grapes from thistles" (K). "However," he further explained, "it is pretty sure to pass as Whigs and Tories will unite in carrying any measure hostile to Catholic interests. All the Archbishops (even Dr. McHale) and nearly all the Bishops (except some sick ones) will meet on Thursday next 27th inst. to see what is to be done. It is hard however to see what course ought to be adopted." "Dublin," he added sadly, "will suffer a great deal if a monster Queen's College with £50,000 per an. and all Protestant teachers be established in it." "Gladstone," Cullen then concluded very bitterly, "will scarcely yield an inch to us. He must be very anti-Catholic or rather fond of his place which he might lose were he to do anything for Catholics."

What Cullen was most concerned about, of course, was that, even if the bishops rejected Gladstone's measure, Gladstone would still be able to force it on them because of his large majority in the House of Commons. Indeed, this had been the basic underlying political assumption in Manning's letter to him of February 14, and when Cullen received that letter, he forwarded it to Lord Granard for his opinion. "I return His Grace's Letter," Granard replied on February 17. "There is a great deal in it, it appears to me, worthy of careful consideration, in view of the fanaticism & hostility of the Dissenters & so called Liberals of England, but it is hard, that Trinity Coll: retains its revenues whilst no question of restitution is entertained for us" (C). "The Archbishop's views coincide very much with those of our friend Dr. Conroy, who dined with [me] last night," he further informed Cullen, referring to the bishop of Ardagh. Several days later, Granard wrote to Cullen again, explaining that he had just seen the lord lieutenant, Earl Spencer, and they had discussed the education bill at some length. "I dined on Thursday," Granard reported on Saturday, February 22, "with Lord Spencer, and he spoke to me a good deal about the Education Bill respecting which he seems very conscious."

> I told him that we could not but consider the Bill as very inadequate that it left us on a par without endowment with the Magee College, that it reaffirmed the principle of Godless Colleges, and it could not be said to concede that educational equality for which we had contended. His Excellency then said that allowances should be made for the difficulties of Gov^t, that the question of endowment was impossible, as they could not carry it, and he said, that Catholic students w^d obtain advantages by the scholarships &c that w^d be open to them, and also by being represented fully in the New Council. I replied, that I was quite aware of the good intentions of himself & other Members of the Gov^t, as far as we were concerned, but that if Catholics of the stamp of Morris, Corrigan, Waldron & Kane were to be placed on the Council, such representation w^d not give us confidence in the scheme.
>
> He said Gov^t w^d be most desirous of meeting our wishes as far as possible, & asked me "Do you think any of your Bishops w^d accept a seat on the Council?" I said, I could not answer that question, but that I thought that the Bishops w^d be inclined to give every fair consideration to any proposal emanating from the Gov^t, as far as their principles w^d allow them. He said Mr. Gladstone is most anxious to receive any suggestions about the Bill, and requested me to let him know anything of the kind, that I might hear (C).

"On the whole," Granard then observed shrewdly, "it appears to me, that the Gov^t are exceedingly nervous about the fate of their Bill, although my London letters inform me that they consider themselves safe, it also appears to me, that they are anxious to meet the views of your Lordships', as far as they can, and to deprecate strongly anything like a rupture between the Catholic party and themselves." "I shall of course," Granard assured Cullen in conclusion, "be very happy after His Excellency's intimation to place before him any suggestion Your Eminence w^d wish to offer should you prefer doing it in that way to writing directly to him."

In the next few days, however, Spencer's anxiety increased to such a degree that he invited Cullen to meet with him shortly before the bishops were to convene. "The Lord Lieutenant," Cullen reported to Kirby on March 2, "sent for me a couple of days before our meeting to see if he could gain me to his views. I gave him my mind most fully, and told him that we could never accept such a system of Godless education as was proposed, and that we would oppose it with all our might. He said the government would take care to appoint good Catholics in the Council (the governing body) and two good professors" (K). "I told him," Cullen explained, "I did not expect any such thing—we got the same promises in reference to the Queen's Colleges yet one of the first professors appointed was Vericour a French infidel, and one of the last made by Lord Spencer himself was an immoral poet by name Armstrong who finishes a poem against the confessional with these words 'Now, may good Christ rid us of all priests.' I had the book of poetry in my pocket and I showed the poem to his Excellency." "I had a very long interview with him," Cullen assured Kirby, "and I am sure I gave such a dose of truth as he never got before since he came to Ireland. He will look on me as an audacious fanatic for speaking so freely."

Shortly after his interview with Lord Spencer, Cullen broke the news to Manning of his determination to oppose Gladstone's bill. "I cannot see," he maintained, "how we can in any way co-operate in carrying out the proposed measure, or remain silent whilst others undertake to promote."[25]

> In the first place, mixed education, or education without religion, is directly sanctioned by the establishment of a Queen's College in Dublin, to be called Trinity College. This institution will have the immense buildings of the present Trinity College, with its libraries and museums, all of which, or nearly all are public property, and, besides, £50,000 per annum. Secondly the new University will be a mixed teaching body endowed with immense revenues, which will serve to attract Catholic students. Mr. Gladstone, in his speech, says that any of the present professors of Trinity College, who cannot be provided for in the new mixed college, may be appointed to chairs in the new university. In this way an ascendency for Protestant teaching will be secured for the future.

"Moreover, it is reported," Cullen added in conclusion, "that Mr. Gladstone intends giving professorships to distinguished Germans and Frenchmen who will bring Hegelism and infidelity with them, as Mr. Vericour, a nephew of Guizot, did to the Cork College." "I thank your Eminence," Manning replied the next day, February 26, "for the valuable letter received this morning" (C). "Since I wrote on the Gov Bill," he then explained, beating his retreat, "I have been afraid that I might have seemed to be in favour of it. I am in favour of one point in it; which is vital to us & threatened by dangers on every side." "Judging from the Papers here," Manning then observed, "if it were thought that the Catholic Bishops were not opposed to the Bill, an anti-Catholic noise would be got up." "I cannot but repeat," he advised Cullen once again, "that I think it most expedient to raise a loud opposition on the endowment injustice, but very inexpedient to make endowment a condition to accepting any part of the Bill. A noise about it will be a healthy & safe diversion, & a cheap victory to the enemy here." "I write this with submission," he assured Cullen in conclusion, "& more as a Politician or a Watch at the masthead than anything else."

---

25. Leslie, p. 186.

The next day, February 27, the bishops met at the presbytery of the procathedral in Dublin. Twenty-two bishops, in a national hierarchy of some thirty, were present at the deliberations. They decided to draw up a set of resolutions condemning those features in the bill that they could not accept and to send a petition to Parliament embodying the protest made in their resolutions. As the resolutions and the petition had yet to be drawn up and approved, they decided to meet again the following day. "I write one line," Cullen reported to Manning at the end of the first day's proceedings, "to say that our bishops met to-day and will meet again to-morrow. All are sadly disappointed with Mr. Gladstone's Bill, and speak against it much more strongly than I did in my letters to your Grace. The Bishop of Limerick was the only one who attempted to defend the Bill. In the end we agreed to send a Petition to Parliament against everything in the Bill that sanctions mixed education."[26] At the end of the next day's proceedings, Cullen forwarded the bishops' resolutions to Manning.

RESOLUTIONS OF THE ARCHBISHOPS AND BISHOPS OF IRELAND,
ASSEMBLED FOR THE CONSIDERATION OF THE
PROPOSED IRISH UNIVERSITY BILL

1. That, viewing with alarm the widespread ruin caused by godless systems of education, and adhering to the declarations of the Holy See, we reiterate our condemnation of mixed education as fraught with danger to that Divine faith which is to be prized above all earthly things; for "without faith it is impossible to please God" (Heb xi 6), and "what doth it profit a man if he gain the whole world and suffer the loss of his own soul?" (Mat xvi 26)

2. That, whilst we sincerely desire for the Catholic youth of Ireland a full participation in the advantages of University Education, and in the honours, prizes and degrees intended for the encouragement of learning, we are constrained by a sense of the duty we owe to our flocks to declare that the plàn of University Education now before Parliament, as being framed on the principle of mixed and purely secular education, is such as Catholic youth cannot avail themselves of without danger to their faith and morals.

3. That, the distinguished proposer of this Bill, proclaiming, as he does, in his opening speech that the condition of Roman Catholics in Ireland in regard to University Education is "miserably bad"—"scandalously bad," and professing to redress this admitted grievance, brings forward a measure singularly inconsistent with his professions, because instead of redressing, it perpetuates that grievance upholding two out of three of the Queen's Colleges, and planting in the metropolis two other great teaching institutions the same in principle with the Queen's Colleges.

4. That, putting out of view the few Catholics who may avail themselves of mixed education, the new bill, without its being avowed, in point of fact gives to Protestant Episcopalians, to Presbyterians, and to the new sect of Secu-

26. Ibid., p. 187.

larists, the immense endowments for university education in this country—to Trinity College some 50,000£ or more, with splendid buildings, Library and Museum—to the new University 50,000£, to the Cork College, 10,000£, to the Belfast College 10,000£, while to the Catholic University is given *nothing;* and, furthermore, the Catholic people of Ireland, the great majority of the nation, and the poorest part of it, are left to provide themselves with endowments for their colleges out of their own resources.

5. That, this injustice is aggravated by another circumstance. The measure provides that the degrees and prizes of the new University shall be open to Catholics; but, it provides for Catholics no endowed Intermediate Schools, no endowment for their one college, no well-stocked library, museum, or other collegiate requisites, no professorial staff, none of the means for coping on fair and equal terms with their Protestant or other competitors; and, then, Catholics, thus overweighted, are told that they are free to contend in the race for university prizes and distinctions.

6. That, as the legal owners of the Catholic University, and at the same time acting on behalf of the Catholic people of Ireland, for whose advantage and by whose generosity it has been established, in the exercise of that right of ownership, we will not consent to the affiliation of the Catholic University to the new University unless the proposed scheme be largely modified; and we have the same objection to the affiliation of other Catholic colleges in Ireland.

7. That we invite the Catholic clergy and laity of Ireland to use all constitutional means to oppose the passing of the bill in its present form, and to call on their Parliamentary representatives to give it the most energetic opposition.

8. That now more than ever it behoves the Catholics of Ireland to contribute to the support of the Catholic University, the one only institution of the kind in the country where Catholic youth can receive university education based upon religion.

9. That we address to the Imperial Parliament petitions embodying these resolutions, and praying for the amendment of the Bill.[27]

"The Resolutions of the Bishops," Manning informed Cullen the next day, March 1, "are admirable. They affirm all our principles: & take the chief blots in the bill with great force" (C). "The refusal to affiliate our Colleges," he assured Cullen, "is unanswerable. And the whole is as strong as a rejection without an absolute break. This is what I most desired and believe that it will make the Government try to modify, and will make the adversaries believe that they have worsted us." "Last night," he warned Cullen, "the Opposition believed that the Irish Members would vote against the bill, & that with them they might defeat the Government." "Immediately," he added, referring to the Conservatives, "they shut up and would not talk of Endowment. They could not give it if they would: & they would not if they could. I will believe them when they will try a division on it: not before." "Would it not be possible," he suggested, "to demand an Examining University distinct from Dublin, so making two Centres in two distinct places in

27. *Freeman's Journal,* March 1, 1873.

Ireland? This would meet the 'mixed' objection: but it would leave unredressed the gross inequality of endowments &c: for which I see no remedy." "The tyrannous liberalism of this country," Manning noted rather unhelpfully in conclusion, "can be cured by nothing short of a public disaster, which may God avert." What Manning was attempting to avert by this very timely letter, of course, was an attempt by the Irish bishops to advise the Irish members to vote against the second reading of the Bill, thereby breaking up the Irish-Liberal alliance, with the likelihood of bringing down the government as well.

On receiving this cautionary letter the next day, March 2, Cullen wrote Kirby a long letter in which he reported all the events of the previous week. "Dr. Manning," Cullen noted, most significantly, at the end of his letter, "wrote to me highly approving of our resolutions, but he clings still a little to Gladstone" (C). Cullen apparently had decided that as far as the Irish bishops were concerned the Irish-Liberal alliance was now a serious political liability and that Gladstone must be opposed by the Irish members of Parliament on the second reading of the bill, even if it should result in the fall of the ministry and the succession of Disraeli and a Conservative government. Several days later, in another letter to Kirby, he made his intentions very clear. "I fear," he reported on March 5, "Mr. Gladstone will play the part of Bismark in regard to education. His bill is an injury and insult. However he will make every effort to pass it" (K). "The Daily Post a Liverpool paper," he alerted Kirby, "announces ere yesterday, that Dr. Manning has undertaken to plead Gladstone's case in Rome, and to get the Pope to compel the Irish Bishops to withdraw their resolutions." "I suppose," Cullen added, "there is not a grain of truth in this report, but it shows how anxious the government is to pass the bill."

> Probably indeed they will carry it, but as long as all the clergy here oppose it, it can do no great harm. Were we to adopt it infidelity would soon be spread through the land, and the foundations of all faith shaken.
>
> Some of our Catholics are for the bill, because they fear the loss of their places if Gladstone should be defeated—if the ministry go out Lord O'Hagan loses £4,000 per an. and Mr. Monsell loses his office in the ministry, and his salary whatever it is. However the Catholics who lose are very few, and in any case the faith of the people cannot be sacrificed to their interests.
>
> Lord O'Hagan has come from London to agitate in favour of the bill. He asked me to write to our M.P.s to get them to vote in favour of the second reading. I refused saying I would not get into a fine scrape in order to get Mr. Gladstone out of the mess into which he has willfully thrown himself.

"I suppose," he noted sadly in conclusion, "the government will carry its point by brute force."

In an attempt to avert that sad calamity, however, Cullen wrote a pastoral letter to his clergy the next day, March 6, which was to be read in all the Dublin churches the following Sunday, March 9. In the course of announcing a novena in preparation for the national festival honoring St. Patrick, Cullen introduced the subject of Gladstone's proposed bill. "The Catholic Bishops, except some few who were prevented by sickness from attending their late meeting," Cullen explained to his clergy, "have fully expressed their views on this measure, and respectfully but earnestly petitioned Parliament either to reject it or radically to change it. You, Reverend Brethren, are acquainted with the proceedings of the Bishops, and I hope you and your flock will use all your influence to secure the attainment of a Catholic system of education, which is necessary for the preservation of our religion, and, without which great disadvantages will continue to press down the Catholic majority of the country, whilst honours and emoluments will be given with an unsparing hand to a small Protestant and presbyterian minority."[28] "Get up petitions to Parliament," he advised, "against this Godless education; call on your representatives to oppose it; and as a general election is approaching, take timely means for the selection of members who will promote your just claims for the religious education of Catholic children."

The debate on the second reading of the bill had begun March 3, and though the cabinet was holding firm in regard to the bill, Gladstone's party in the House of Commons was less solid. Gladstone had no doubt about the cause of the crisis, as he explained to the queen on March 8.

> Strange to say, it is the opposition of the Roman catholic bishops that brings about the present difficulty; and this although they have not declared an opposition to the bill outright, but have wound up their list of objections with a resolution to present petitions praying for its amendment. Still their attitude of what may be called growling hostility has had these important results. Firstly, it has deadened that general willingness of the liberal party, which the measure itself had created, to look favourably on a plan such as they might hope would obtain acquiescence, and bring about contentment. Secondly, the great majority of the bishops are even more hostile than the resolutions, which were apparently somewhat softened as the price of unanimity; and all *these* bishops, working upon liberal Irish members through their political interest in their seats, have proceeded so far that from twenty to twenty-five may go against the bill, and as many may stay away.

"When to these," Gladstone pointed out glumly, "are added the small knot of discontented liberals and mere fanatics which so large a party commonly contains, the government majority, now taken at only 85, disappears." When Gladstone read Cullen's pastoral on the following Monday, March 10, he could not have taken much comfort in the fact that he had been a true prophet in his letter to the queen.

The day before, in fact, Cullen had finally closed his net by writing a long letter

---

28. Patrick Francis Moran, ed., *The Pastoral Letters and Other Writings of Cardinal Cullen* (Dublin, 1882) 3:501.

to Cardinal Barnabò. Reporting to Kirby the next day, March 10, Cullen explained that he had told Barnabò that if he found any difficulty with the statements, Kirby would be happy to provide the necessary gloss. Cullen then proceeded in masterful fashion to lay out Kirby's brief.

> I think Gladstone's bill is as bad as it could be made. It would establish a grand Queen's College in Dublin instead of Trinity College. In this last institution they teach Protestantism. In the new College the professors and the superiors would continue Protestant, but the teaching would be tinged with infidelity.
>
> The new University would be founded on the principle of excluding religion.
>
> Besides the Queen's Colleges of Cork and Belfast would be maintained, and probably also that of Galway. What is worse Mr. Gladstone promises us a system of intermediate schools on the Godless plan, so that the growing up youths would be therein prepared for a total loss of faith in their University course.
>
> Some of the Catholics who occupy high places praise the bill, and think it a mad thing to expose them to the danger of losing some thousands per annum which they now receive from government. In my humble opinion it is more important to attend to the works of our Saviour Quid prodest homini [what does it profit a man (that he gain the whole of the world and lose his soul)].
>
> I dare say those Catholics will try to do something in Rome. They will say everything good of themselves and recommend the bill most strenuously. I suppose they will not succeed, but it is well to put Propaganda on their guard.
>
> Dr. Manning leans very much towards Gladstone's policy, and he thinks if we were to let the bill pass, we might turn it to a good account. I am quite of [a] different way of thinking, and all the Catholics with the few exceptions just mentioned are of the same way of thinking. At all events watch the proceedings and let us know what is to be done (K).

"Perhaps," he concluded more hopefully, "the bill may not pass."

Indeed, over the previous week, Cullen had been doing everything possible to ensure that the bill would not pass. He had sent the rector of the Catholic University, Bartholomew Woodlock, to London to hold a watching brief for him at the commencement of the second reading of the bill on Monday, March 3. In the course of the week, Woodlock was in constant communication with Cullen, sometimes writing two and three times a day. Though Cullen had certainly decided by the second evening of the debate on the second reading, Thursday, March 6, that the bill should be opposed, this was not the opinion of a number of the Irish M.P.'s. or, even, of all the Irish bishops. On the afternoon of the evening that the debate was to begin, the bishop of Limerick, George Butler, telegraphed Woodlock from Dublin. "Our resolutions," he explained on March 3, "do not require opposition to the second reading but suppose the bill to go into Committee with the view of effecting modifications. This is the Cardinal's opinion. Tell it to the Catholic members" (C). "I telegraphed to you from Dublin," Butler explained in a letter written, apparently, that same evening, "after a conversation with the Cardinal, that the petition & resolutions of the Bishops did not suggest opposition to the 2d reading of the Bill; but rather invited a consideration of the bill in Committee with the view of effecting such modifications as would make it acceptable" (W). "I wanted the Cardinal to write to Major O'Reilly in this sense;" Butler reported, referring to the senior member for county Longford, who was generally considered to be Cullen's spokesman among the Irish members on educational matters, "but he declined, saying that Major O'Reilly & our other friends in Parliament could not fail to see this themselves, and he would therefore prefer to leave them to their own discretion."

> It seems to me that refusing to let the bill go into Committee, where alone the modifications suggested by the Bishops can be proposed, would be rather opposing than sanctioning the resolutions; and I hope that you will be able to make the Irish members take this view. As the bill is not absolutely bad, but, by the admission of all, has much good in it, the opposition to it should be not absolute, but qualified & conditional. To vote against the second reading would be a declaration that no changes or modifications would make it acceptable. Let it therefore go into Committee, and if the necessary changes cannot be obtained, let all our friends oppose the third reading.

"Let us not," Butler concluded with a final plea, "exhibit the appearance of factious opposition to a measure which however unsatisfactory to us, was, no doubt, meant well & kindly by its framer."

Cullen, however, decided not to leave Major O'Reilly and their other friends to their own discretion in deciding how to vote on the second reading. "I am a bad judge of Parliamentary tactics," Cullen confessed to O'Reilly somewhat artfully on March 4, "but as far as I can understand matters, I w^d vote against the second reading of the Bill or not vote at all" (C). "The bill," he emphasized, "is so bad, so unjust, & so utterly opposed to Catholic interests that I w^d not give it the smallest encouragement." "But as I said before," he concluded, even more ingenuously, "I am a bad judge of Parliamentary proceedings, & I thus w^d not attempt to lay down a rule for anyone except myself." That same day, apparently after receiving Butler's letter, which he forwarded to Cullen, Woodlock informed the cardinal that he hesitated to advise the Irish M.P.'s on how to vote (C).

The next day, March 5, Woodlock reported in a series of letters that the Irish M.P.'s had not much confidence in each other, but they had agreed finally to send a deputation to Gladstone to inform him that they would oppose the bill on the second reading unless it was to be satisfactorily amended (C). The deputation met with Gladstone on March 6, and the next day Woodlock reported that their interview was unsatisfactory since Gladstone refused to pledge himself to their required amendments (C). That same day, the senior member for county Limerick, William Monsell, who was postmaster general, also wrote Cullen. In a long and confidential letter, Monsell, who, if the ministry survived the present crisis, probably would soon enjoy cabinet rank, attempted to persuade Cullen of the dangers of turning the Liberal government out of office. "I am so deeply grieved at the present aspect of affairs," he explained on March 7, "that I cannot help writing to your Eminence" (C). "If the University bill is thrown out, Fawcett's bill will be passed—the Tories will come in—the alliance between Catholics & the liberals will be dissolved—this last result will follow from the Catholics voting against the second reading—it would not follow from their opposing clauses in the bill in committee—in the present aspect of the world it would be dangerous for us to have both the great parties in the State our enemies." Monsell's warning referred specifically to the proposal made perennially by Henry Fawcett, Radical member for Brighton, to undo the denominational character of Trinity College by opening its faculty and government and all its honors, privileges, and emoluments to every creed, including Catholics—a proposal that Cullen and the Irish bishops had long viewed with horror because they viewed it as yet another insidious attempt to foist mixed education on Catholics. "I have been in the House of Commons," Monsell then confessed, "for $\frac{1}{4}$ of a century & never felt in such low spirits as to public affairs as I now do. The separation between the Catholics & liberals in 1851 was made by an attack by the liberals on the Catholics. In this case the liberal party will feel that we have thrown them over when they were trying to serve us." "On this," Monsell then concluded, referring to the second reading, "we should vote with the government, & I need not point out to your Eminence the great difference to our future prospects that would be made by the government being defeated notwithstanding our support instead of their being defeated by us."

"I regret very much," Cullen replied to Monsell on March 11, "that the Irish University bill has brought the Ministry in to so many difficulties & involves their friends in so many troubles" (C). "If Mr. Gladstone," Cullen pointed out, going immediately to the heart of the matter, "had consulted the feelings of the Irish Catholics more than he did things might not have turned out so badly. But unfortunately he appears to have thought he c^d gain over all the bigots of England to his side by telling them as he did that he had not consulted those who were most interested in the question at issue."

> I rec^d several letters asking me to recommend the Catholic Members to vote for the 2nd reading of the bill. My answer was that I c^d not venture to dictate any course to those gentlemen, but that were I called to vote I w^d go directly against the bill. Indeed I cannot see how I c^d do otherwise. The bill certainly implies a recommendation of mixed education or of education without religion; it implies that Catholic education has no claim to endowment or protection from the State, whilst it assumes that the non-religious system sh^d be patronized & endowed. It is clearly also insinuated in the bill that it is the public opinion of England that sh^d decide what sort of education is to be given to Irish Catholics, whilst those Catholics themselves are not to be consulted or even heard upon a

question as important to the salvation of souls & the future existence of religion in this country. These considerations make me be firm in not giving any approbation whatever to the bill. However I suppose it is useless to manifest those sentiments at present, as it is probable that the fate of the bill itself will be decided tonight, before this line can reach London. However I state my views because I think they are the views of the great body of the Irish Catholics. It may be that we shall have to suffer a great deal from the want of higher education, but it is better to suffer losses in temporal affairs than to run the risk of bringing ruin by bad education even upon one soul.

"In conclusion," Cullen maintained, "I must repeat again that the present question is surrounded by many difficulties, from which I see no way of escaping, especially as Mr. Gladstone has manifested so much readiness to remove from the bill those few clauses from which Catholics could hope any little advantages."

In the meantime, especially after the failure of their deputation to make any impression on Gladstone, a large number of the Irish M.P.'s had come to the same conclusion as Cullen. "Mr. E. Dease & myself," O'Reilly reported to Cullen on Monday, March 10, referring to the junior member for Queen's county, "have discussed with Dr. Woodlock for a couple of hours the course to be pursued by us as to the bill & Dr. Woodlock has stated to us your Eminence's views" (C). "I need hardly say," he assured Cullen, "that with the bishops' strictures on the bill we fully agree." "But the practical question remains," he then explained, "as to the course to be taken on the second reading. Dr. Woodlock has clearly expressed to us your Eminence's opinion that the principles of the bill are such as we cannot allow and our course is to vote against it & ensure its rejection."

We have had considerable opportunities by conference with other members Catholic & otherwise of ascertaining the probable course of events, & we believe that we most probably can by taking the course advised ensure the rejection of the bill. The further results will be that we the Catholics will be free to claim & agitate for our rights & may hope to obtain them from a future government. The present gov (we have just been told by an M.P. who conversed on the subject with Mr. Gladstone last night) will resign. The M.P. said that Mr. Gladstone said if the bill was in globo rejected by the Catholics— he would resign.

"Mr. Fawcett's bill," O'Reilly further explained, "will of course be passed as there will then be no opposition to it except that of the Catholics." "Under these circumstances," O'Reilly then added, "& wishing, as not only we but many other Catholic members do, to be guided by your Eminence's advice in a case of such grave responsibility, I write at the request & with the concurrence of the others to ask are we right in understanding (as we do from Dr. Woodlock) that it is your opinion that we should vote against & procure the rejection of the bill." "As in order to procure as much unanimity as possible," O'Reilly explained in conclusion, "amongst the Catholic members in the approaching division which may take place on any day after today, it is necessary to decide our course at once, may I beg your Eminence will favour me with an answer tomorrow."

Cullen obviously gave O'Reilly the assurances that he needed, for when the division took place in the early morning of March 12, the bill was rejected. "This morning," a jubilant Cullen reported to Kirby, "the division took place in Parliament on the University bill. At two o'clock after midnight 284 voted for Godless education and 287 voted against by a majority of *three*. See what a close fight, and what a number 284 was against us—here in Dublin we say three Hail Marys after every mass against the persecutors of the Church" (K). "A good poor man came to me today," Cullen noted, "and said in a most triumphant manner, Oh it was our three Hail Marys that secured the majority of three. I suppose he was quite right, and I trust the consecration of the country to the Sacred Heart of Jesus contributed very much to our success. However we are not safe as yet—the enemy will return again to the assault, and we must be preparing to meet him." "Dr. Manning," he then explained, "was rather in favour of the government bill because he thought we could not defeat it. However the Bishops' resolutions produced a wonderful effect. Forty Irish M.P.'s who always followed Mr. Gladstone, on this occasion went against him and thus left him in a minority." "The only two Catholics, who voted for Gladstone," Cullen noted further, "were Sir Dominic Corrigan, M.P. for Dublin, for whom I voted at the last election, and Sir Rowland Blennerhassett, M.P. for Galway, a disciple of Dr. Dollinger. I hope at the next election we shall be able to pay off Sir Dominic. I am sure Dr. MacEvilly will settle accounts with Sir R. Blennerhassett." "The danger now," he pointed out, "is that Mr. Fawcett will bring in a bill for infidel education, but it is better that we should have to fight with an open infidel that [sic] with wolves in sheep's clothing. Mr. Gladstone's bill pretended to be favourable to Catholics but was all hostile—we asked for fish and they gave us a serpent." "Nothing," Cullen said finally, unrepentantly and characteristically, "could be worse than Mr. Gladstone's bill."

Cullen's analysis of the Irish vote, though somewhat incomplete, was accurate enough. Of the 64 among the 103 Irish members who generally voted with the Liberals, 37 voted against the government, 11 voted for, and 16 were absent.[29] Of the 37 who voted against, 26 were Catholics and 11 were Protestants; of the 11 who voted for, 4 were Catholics and 7 Protestants; and of the 16 absentees, 6 were Catholics and 10 Protestants. In addition to Corrigan and Blennerhassett, the two other Catholics who voted with the government were William Monsell, who as

29. *Hansard's Parliamentary Debates*, 214:1863-68.

postmaster general and a member of the ministry was by honor bound to vote for the government, and George Gavin, the senior member for Limerick City, who seemed simply to have voted his conscience. None of the four who voted with the government, however, found it worthwhile to contest their seats at the ensuing general election. On the Conservative side, of the 39 Irish members, 30 voted against the government, only 1 for, and 8 were absent. In sum then, of the 103 Irish members, 67 voted against, 12 for, and 24 were absent. Some 8 English and Scotch Liberals, moreover, also voted against the government. While the combination was just sufficient to defeat the ministry, there was little doubt that it was the Irish vote, influenced by the Irish bishops, that had been the decisive factor. No one, in fact, was more conscious or delighted about the demonstration of their own power and influence than were the Irish bishops.

"We have indeed reason," a very self-satisfied archbishop of Cashel, Patrick Leahy, wrote to Cullen on March 13, "to congratulate ourselves on the rejection of the University Bill, and to say from our inmost soul *Deo gratias* [thanks be to God]" (C). "What could augur better," he asked, drawing the moral from the story, "for the cause than the unanimity of the Bishops? And that of the Irish Catholic M.P.'s with a few exceptions was unexampled. Oh si sic semper [if only it were always so]. The result shows that, say what our enemies will, the Bishops are a power, and a great power." "I feel," he added more magnanimously, "for poor Gladstone. Whoever was against us, I believe he was for us. But, he was surrounded by a bad set." "It is a pity," Leahy lamented, "he did not stick to principle to the end. Even a great mind like his, & naturally a just one, was turned aside from the path of rectitude by what he considered the exigencies of party." "His fall," Leahy concluded, "is great and sudden. And, the worst is he can scarce retrieve himself to the end of his life."

"That the question of Catholic Education," the bishop of Ardagh, George Conroy, exulted in a letter to Cullen two days later on March 15, "should have been raised in one week to be *the* great imperial question of the session is surely in itself a great victory for the good cause" (C). "Once we get a hearing," he maintained, "we are sure of success. But that this question should be forced on John Bull's attention as able to upset a powerful ministry because it did *not go far enough* to redress admitted grievances, is a still greater triumph, and a pledge of future advantage." "St. Patrick," he added, "has certainly signalised his moment this year by a tremendous onslaught on the *serpents*." "I have received," he noted more seriously, referring to the junior member for county Longford, "an explanation from George Greville of his absence at the voting. It is plausible and, probably, quite accurate. But it will not go down with the people." "If we," he assured Cullen aggressively, "could now keep the MPs well in hand, we could gain all we required." Conroy's last proposition, however, assumed that there was a purpose and a will among the bishops as a body to maintain the kind of control over the

Irish members that would result in their doing what the bishops required. Though certainly a number of the bishops, including Cullen and Conroy, would have subscribed to such a proposition, it is doubtful whether the bishops as a body would have. On reflection, the bishops as a body must have realized that they were not all in agreement about what they required or about the means to secure whatever they did require politically. Though they may all have agreed about the necessity for denominational education or even fixity of tenure for the Irish tenant, they did not agree on the vital question of Home Rule, and as the recent case of the bishop of Limerick emphasized, they did not agree even about the tactics by which to pursue what they required in educational matters. Indeed, in that crisis, the bishop of Limerick had gone so far as to write a number of the Irish members, asking them to vote for the second reading of the University bill. This was what undoubtedly prompted O'Reilly's letter to Cullen on the eve of the vote asking him for an explicit endorsement in writing, rather than the oral assurance that he had been given by Woodlock, that the second reading should be opposed.

The inability of the bishops as a body to mobilize the Irish members in the interests of what the bishops required became especially pronounced when Henry Fawcett, the Radical M.P. for Brighton, soon after the defeat of Gladstone's bill, brought in his measure for access to Trinity College for all denominations. Ironically enough, it was Conroy who outlined the dilemma to Cullen. "After having escaped the Scylla of Gladstone's Bill," Conroy pointed out, "we seem to be drifting into the Charybdis of Fawcett's scheme" (C). "I fear," he confided, "that our Irish Members are not as united as they ought to be. I know on the best authority that a certain Bishop wrote to some of them to urge the necessity of voting for the second reading of the rejected bill of Gladstone. This being known to the Members, it is not to be wondered at if they try to vote as best they conceive likely to promote their own interests and themselves." "The voting on Fawcett's Bill will be a fresh difficulty, as most of the Catholic members voted for the abolition of tests in the English Universities," Conroy noted in conclusion, referring to the recent legislation that had opened up Oxford and Cambridge Universities to all creeds.

The danger of the developing situation was certainly not lost on Conroy's colleague, the bishop of Elphin. "I fear there is a new & formidable danger threatening us," Gillooly explained to Cullen on March 21, "in Mr. Fawcett's Bill, and that after having vanquished, we may be surprised & defeated, by, those Infidel Liberals of the House of Commons."

> If the Ministers do not actively oppose Fawcett's Bill and force their party to oppose it, it will pass by a large majority. The Liberals will support it more ardently than ever in order to retrieve their late defeat and to lessen our chances of a favourable University scheme in the future—whilst the Conservatives will vote for it in order to save the privileges & endowments of Trinity College

from further State encroachments. It appears to me very probable that a Coalition of this kind will be formed, and I think it also probable that great
pressure from our friends in the House will be needed, to induce Gladstone to
give a steadfast opposition to the measure (C).

"The important question then is," he maintained, "how is such pressure to be
exercised?"

I see no successful means except an intimation from our members, that if he
does not oppose & prevent the passing of Fawcett's Bill, they will vote against
him on every Party Division. I suppose your Eminence has already taken some
steps to provide against the danger I refer to. I think we should all take combined action on the matter, and call on our Parliam representatives to adopt
the course I suggest or some other that may be considered more prudent &
effectual. Surely there is no time to be lost, and if the Bishops, and thro them
the MPs, do not act in concert, we are doomed to suffer a disastrous defeat.

"It is all important," he urged in conclusion, "that Gladstone sh receive early
notice of the intended opposition of our Members."

The most interesting thing about Gillooly's letter was that, though his prediction about what was likely to happen could not be faulted, the measures he
proposed to prevent such a likelihood were so politically unreal as to be actually
perverse, and to no one more so, perhaps, than to Cullen. To understand this, it is
necessary to appreciate that the reason that Gladstone found himself in the situation he did, and that his party was breaking in his hand, was not simply that he had
been defeated on the Irish University bill. That had been the occasion but not the
cause for the disintegration of his ministry. The cause was that, over the previous
two years, various sections of the Liberal party had degenerated into special
interest groups; this was especially true of Gladstone's Nonconformist supporters. He was plagued by those who wanted their own way, *coûte que coûte,* about
their various educational, temperance, and disestablishment demands. He was, in
effect, undone by the factions, of whom the Irish were only one among the many,
which made up the coalition that was the Liberal majority. Gillooly, in this context, therefore, not only emerges as a particularly good example of the general
problem faced by Gladstone, but also he provides an excellent illustration of how
perverse a factious insistence on one's own special interest, especially if viewed as a
matter of principle, can be for party politics. By recommending that the Irish
members, with the sanction and approval of the Irish bishops, give an indiscrimi-
nate opposition to every measure undertaken by Gladstone unless he agreed to
oppose Fawcett's bill, Gillooly was advocating, in effect, nothing less than the
principle of "independent opposition," which to Cullen was the political anathema of anathemas. For more than twenty years, Cullen had done his best to
relegate that proposition to the nether regions of Irish politics, so to have it now
proposed as the practical political solution to securing the bishops' educational

requirements by one of his most loyal supporters in the episcopal body must have appeared to him as a supreme irony.

To make matters worse, from an Irish point of view (and one of the reasons that Gillooly was so upset) though the bishops had defeated the government and succeeded in bringing on a ministerial crisis, in less than a week Gladstone re-sumed office as prime minister. When the cabinet had met on the afternoon of March 12, following the adverse vote in the House of Commons that morning, the general feeling among the ministers was that they would prefer to resign rather than to advise the queen to dissolve Parliament and call a general election. The next day the cabinet did decide to resign, and Gladstone accordingly tendered his resignation to the queen later that day. The queen then sent for Disraeli, who, after protracted discussions over the next several days, decided he could not undertake the responsibility of assuming office. On March 16, therefore, Gladstone saw the queen again and agreed to resume his duties as her prime minister. He then settled matters with his cabinet, on March 18, and two days later, on March 20, he made his explanations to the House of Commons.[30] Why Gladstone chose to resign rather than to dissolve Parliament is an interesting and important question. He was, of course, honor bound to resign in light of what he had said he would do if defeated on the Irish University bill. Apparently he did not choose dissolution because he perceived, probably correctly, that he would not thereby improve the position of his party in the House of Commons. The Irish University bill certainly was not an issue that he wanted to go to the country on, and though the fac-tiousness of the Liberal majority had given him considerable cause for concern in recent years, his party in the recent division on the University bill had behaved remarkably well. Of the some 309 British Liberals, 272 voted for the government, 8 voted against the government, and 29 (about 9 percent) were absent. Of the 246 British Conservatives, all of those present voted against the government, and 34 (14 percent) were absent. Of the 64 Irish Liberals, as has been noted, only 11 voted with the government, 37 voted against, and 16 (25 percent) were absent. Of the 39 Irish Conservatives, 1 voted with the government, 30 voted against, and 8 (20 per-cent) were absent. The point, of course, is that Gladstone could not have attrib-uted his defeat to the factiousness of his Nonconformist supporters, the great majority of whom were in their places for the division, and he had no cause, therefore, to dissolve as far as they were concerned. He could have dissolved Parliament, of course, in order to teach a salutary political lesson to those Irish Liberals who voted against the government, but it was likely that they not only would have been able, with episcopal backing, to retain their seats, but also that they would all also have declared for Home Rule. For this reason Disraeli refused to take office. He understood that Gladstone's working majority disintegrated as

30. Ibid., cols. 1924–29.

the Irish-Liberal alliance broke up, and, given the general factiousness of his Nonconformist supporters, he was destined to toil in chains for as long as he retained office. Disraeli also realized shrewdly that the longer Gladstone remained in office, the more terrible the day of political retribution would be for Liberals when the general election finally was held.

"We are now menaced," a more chastened Cullen reported to Kirby on March 27, "with Fawcett's bill. He leaves Trinity College in regard to teaching and revenues as it is at present, but opens it to pagans, Turks, Jews, and Catholics" (K). "The plan," he assured Kirby, "will not do us so much harm as Gladstone's scheme." "Fawcett's bill," he reported again a week later on April 4, "was brought in last night. It leaves Trinity College with the same revenues and professors, but abolishes all the oaths which fellows and superiors were obliged to take" (K). "They were obliged," he explained, "to renounce popery, and to swear to the 39 articles. For the past Trinity was Protestant, it will now become infidel." Several days later Cullen returned to the theme of Protestantism and infidelity in another letter to Kirby. "It appears evident," he maintained on April 8, "that the devil is let loose, and he is showing himself even here."

> A short time ago in a hotel in Belfast a large company sat down to dinner among whom was a professor of the Queen's College. This gentleman spoke a great deal against religion, and he spoke very blasphemously. At length a Catholic interrupted him and called him to an account for insulting our Lord. The professor replied, What, Sir, do you pretend to compel me in the nineteenth century to believe the farce of Calvary. Another professor in Dublin University denied the resurrection of the body, and when St. Paul was objected to him, he said St. Paul was a pantheist.

"How fast," Cullen concluded grimly, "Protestantism is going into infidelity—but Protestants or infidels equally hate Catholicity."

In the meantime, Isaac Butt, the head of what Cullen believed to be the chief repository of Protestants and infidels, the Home Rule movement, had been doing his best to soften the heterodox image held by so many of the bishops and clergy of the movement. When Judge Keogh, for example, had delivered his celebrated judgment in the Galway election petition trial the previous May, Butt had taken the lead among the small band of Irish members in the House of Commons who impugned the conduct of Keogh and demanded his censure. When the government finally decided to proceed to the prosecution of the bishop of Clonfert, Patrick Duggan, and some twenty Galway priests for undue influence and intimidation, Butt accepted the brief for the defense. The first of the scheduled trials, that of Patrick Loftus, a curate in the parish of Dunmore in the diocese of Tuam, began on Monday, February 10, 1873, in Dublin in the Court of Queen's Bench, with the chief justice, James Whiteside, presiding.[31] After three days, the case

---

31. *Freeman's Journal*, February 11, 1873.

finally went to the jury, who could not agree on a verdict even after deliberating for some four hours and were duly discharged by Whiteside. The second trial, that of Bartholomew Quinn, a curate in the parish of Craughwell in the diocese of Kilmacduagh, took place on Thursday, February 13, and lasted only two days, after which the jury, who deliberated for some three and a half hours, disagreed and was, again, discharged.[32] Finally, on Saturday, February 15, the trial of the bishop of Clonfert got under way before a crowded court amidst very great excitement. Duggan was escorted to court by the bishops of Galway and Limerick and Sir John Gray, M.P. for Kilkenny City and editor and proprietor of the *Freeman's Journal*. He was charged with having invoked, in a sermon at Ballinasloe, an anathema on the heads of all those who would not vote for Nolan for county Galway.[33] The trial continued for four days, during which Butt made a great forensic display, especially in the cross-examination of the prosecution's witnesses. On February 19, the day the case was to go to the jury, Cullen wrote to Kirby, reporting the situation. "The government," he explained, "is prosecuting here in Dublin about 20 priests from Galway and Dr. Duggan for undue influence at a late election. Two priests have got off, the jury having disagreed" (K). "Dr. Duggan is on to-day," he added, "and I hope he will be acquitted. The charges against him are merely ridiculous." Amidst scenes of the wildest enthusiasm, Duggan was acquitted that afternoon by a jury that had deliberated for only twenty minutes, and the attorney general, Christopher Palles, informed the chief justice that the government had decided, for the present, not to pursue the other scheduled cases.[34]

In his conduct of the defense, Butt was at his very best as a barrister, and not only did he win, naturally, the gratitude of the bishop of Clonfert, but also he made a very considerable impression on the bishop of Galway, John MacEvilly, who up until the trial had been one of his more persistent, though private, critics among the bishops. When Cullen had occasion the day after the trial to circularize the bishops, informing them that he had convened a meeting of the body for February 27 to discuss Gladstone's proposed University bill, MacEvilly replied that he most certainly would be there on the appointed day and also he had taken a most interesting initiative in regard to Butt. "It would," MacEvilly maintained on February 21, "be of great importance to have an analysis of the Bill" (C). "Having met Mr. Butt," he further explained, "more than once during the few days I was at Dr. Duggan's trial, I spoke of the importance of having an analysis of the bill and an exposition of its tendencies. He said he would give it, and I requested Dr. Woodlock to see him." "It occured to me," MacEvilly confessed somewhat lamely, "that, possibly, a Protestant is not the man to enlighten us, but

---

32. Ibid., February 17, 1873.
33. Ibid.
34. Ibid., February 20, 1873.

as Mr. Butt seems to be the ablest man we have, and as it would be of great moment for the Bishops to have a clear view of the position, it would seem a secondary matter what the man's religion is, if the best qualified to give an opinion." "Moreover," MacEvilly concluded, even more lamely, "it might be of importance for us to hear the legal opinion of such a lawyer." Accordingly, Butt drew up a memorandum marked "confidential" of some sixty-five hundred words and twenty printed pages for the consideration of the bishops (C). In his analysis, he was critical of those features of the bill that most concerned the bishops—mixed education, no real episcopal control, and no endowment for the Catholic University. In concluding his presentation, however, Butt attempted, in appropriate judicial fashion, to weigh the pros and cons evenhandedly.

> If the effect would be to weaken or subvert the institution [the Catholic University], the country would be deprived of the great advantages which must result from the existence of a great educational institution which ought to be the centre of Catholic intelligence and thought. A University essentially secular in its spirit and teaching would be left without any organized element of pure Catholicity to control or modify, or counteract its influence upon Irish society.
> On the other hand, it may be worthy of consideration whether the bill does not establish principles which may hereafter be more fully carried out. If the Catholic College be chartered and affiliated, the time may not be distant when wiser and more liberal sentiments may govern Irish affairs, and when justice would be done to Catholics by an endowment at least as liberal as that which is left to Trinity College. It might, perhaps, be possible to obtain modifications in the bill, which might prevent any irreparable mischief, or throw any difficulties hereafter in the way of a perfect and equitable arrangement.

"In this imperfect sketch," Butt concluded diffidently, "it has been difficult clearly to state even the details of the bill, impossible to trace the remote consequences which may result from the working out of those details."

Obviously, this was not one of Butt's better political performances. In effect, he appeared to be recommending, however cautiously, that the bill be allowed to pass its second reading and that its defects then be amended in committee. His recommendation, therefore, could not have gone down well with either Cullen or the great majority of the bishops, who were determined to oppose the bill altogether, come what may. Shortly after Butt had submitted his memorandum, Woodlock wrote, on March 1, to thank him for his analysis and enclosed an honorarium for his professional services (B). Butt, though he certainly could have used the money, generously refused to accept the honorarium. If it had been Butt's intention simply to please the bishops, he obviously misjudged the situation. There is some circumstantial evidence, however, that Butt was offering the bishops his conscientious and professional opinion of the bill rather than taking the opportunity to score political points. The moment of truth for Butt, of course, was his own vote on the second reading. He abstained, and his decision was all the more pointed because, of the sixteen professed Home Rule members, including Butt, thirteen voted against the bill, and one other, John Martin, abstained as a matter of principle.[35]

It is likely, therefore, that Butt's abstention was a conscientious one, and, although it speaks well for his integrity as a public man, it probably did little to endear him to Cullen or to most of the bishops who shared the cardinal's views on politics. Cullen's distrust of Butt, however, perhaps went deeper than his merely being a Protestant or his not being amenable to the episcopal lead on the education question. Some five years before, Cullen had received an interesting letter from a close clerical friend and confidant of Butt's, Father James Rice, the administrator of the bishop of Cloyne's mensal parish of Queenstown. "I believe your Eminence," Rice informed Cullen on August 14, 1867, "is aware that the spiritual as well as temporal affairs of our illustrious countryman, I. Butt are in a sad state. I have lately had several letters from Mr. Butt and two from his wife, and husband and wife believe that a visit from me is most desirable" (C). "I shall therefore," he explained, "leave here on next Monday for Dublin; and, as my absence from this parish must be as short as possible, I write to beg your Eminence would grant me all the faculties necessary for the reception of Mr. Butt into the Catholic Church and to administer to him the sacrament of Penance." "If I should have occasion," Rice assured Cullen in conclusion, "to exercise the first of these powers, your Eminence shall in due course hear again from your most obedient humble servant in Christ." Rice, however, did not have occasion, for Butt continued to be a member of the Church of Ireland until his death some twelve years later in May 1878.

At the time Rice wrote this letter to Cullen, Butt had just acquired a national reputation through his celebrated defense at the State Trials of those Fenians who had been arrested in the fall of 1865 and later. In addition to his national reputation, however, Butt had acquired over the years an unenviable moral reputation concerning his extramarital activities, drinking, and bad debts, which were common knowledge among the political cognoscenti. When Butt launched the Home Rule movement in May of 1870, therefore, he was well known to Cullen as an unconverted Protestant, a Fenian fellow traveler, and a man whose personal life and conduct certainly left a great deal to be desired. In spite of the recent wreck of the Irish-Liberal alliance and the increased attractiveness of the Home Rule platform to Cullen and a great many of the bishops, Butt was not the man they were willing to endorse as the leader of the Irish people. When the bishops and clergy did not indicate any intention of adopting the Home Rule program in the months immediately after the demise of the Irish-Liberal alliance, the leadership of the Home Rule movement was as annoyed as it was perplexed. William O'Neill

---

35. Martin refused to vote on any issue except Home Rule. The other absentee was McCarthy Downing, M.P. for county Cork, whose absence was not explained.

Daunt, the secretary of the Home Government Association, apparently wrote to John George MacCarthy, the late unsuccessful Home Rule candidate for the borough of Mallow, complaining that the clergy were still dragging their feet in regard to the movement. MacCarthy was both pointed and pithy in his reply of April 4. "Why don't the priests join?" he asked. "Because the Bishops don't begin. And why don't the Bishops? Because they are always cautious, and because they don't trust B, and because they think the Fenians dominate you, and that the Internationalists are allied to you."[36]

Because of the movement's disappointment in the clergy and the imminence of a general election for which it was obviously badly prepared, the Home Rule movement underwent a serious crisis in the late spring and early summer of 1873. The lack of organizational enthusiasm in the country and strong leadership at the center became readily and sadly apparent in the two by-elections that took place in succession in June and July in the counties of Roscommon and Waterford. The Home Rule Association did not enter a candidate in either case, and the result was the return unopposed of two Liberals who were, at best, ambiguous about Home Rule.[37] The impending general election made it evident to many Home Rulers that some preparations must be made to organize the constituencies, and to the more conscientious among them, it became obvious that the association was not up to the task. Some then began to demand that a national conference be called to discuss the best means for implementing the Home Rule program. The chorus for such a conference began to grow, and, finally, in the middle of September, the bishop of Cloyne, William Keane, and his clergy publicly announced their support for the Home Rule Association and called for a national conference "without distinction of creed or class—for the purpose of placing, by constitutional means, on a broad and definite basis, the nation's demand for the restoration of its plundered rights."[38]

Finally, in early October, a requisition was issued under the names of Daunt, King-Harman, Philip Callan, and William Shaw on the authority of the Home Rule Association calling for "the right of domestic legislation" and requesting signatures for the organization of a national conference.[39] Two bishops, John MacHale of Tuam, and Michael O'Hea of Ross, had already agreed to sign the requisition. The Home Rule leadership then undertook to write those bishops with whom they thought they had any influence, in order to secure their signatures as well.[40] Of the ten bishops who were approached, however, only one,

36. Quoted in Thornley, p. 155.
37. Walker, p. 114.
38. Thornley, p. 157.
39. A. M. Sullivan, *New Ireland* (London, n.d., 16th ed.), p. 382.
40. The bishops written to were Duggan (Clonfert), Dorrian (Down and Connor), Donnelly (Clogher), McGettigan (Armagh), MacEvilly (Galway), Conroy (Ardagh), Butler (Limerick), Conaty (Kilmore), and Nulty (Meath).

the previously committed bishop of Cloyne, agreed to sign the requisition. Though the signatures of three bishops in a body then numbering thirty-two was not exactly a resounding vote of confidence in Home Rule, the requisition was also signed by twenty-six members of Parliament and, even more importantly, by some twenty-four thousand local worthies. "The people," Cullen noted briefly in a letter to Kirby on October 28, "are getting up a great agitation about home rule. I fear it will not do any good. Dr. McHale and Dr. Keane have declared in favor of it" (K).

The national conference was convened in Dublin at the Rotundo on November 18, and it lasted for four days.[41] Some eight hundred participants were present at the daily meetings, and the list in the *Freeman's Journal's* account of the first day's proceedings included some four hundred names. Among them were twenty-five members of Parliament and about thirty Catholic clergymen.[42] The purposes of the conference were essentially two—to define the end, Home Rule, and to set up the effective means, the Home Rule League, to the achievement of that end. This was to be done by proposing and passing two sets or series of resolutions dealing respectively with the end and means. The first series included eight resolutions that attempted to define what its proponents meant by Home Rule.

1. That, as the basis of the proceedings of this Conference, we declare our conviction that it is essentially necessary to the peace and prosperity of Ireland that the right of domestic legislation on all Irish affairs should be restored to our country.

2. That, solemnly reasserting the inalienable right of the Irish people to self-government we declare that the time, in our opinion, has come when a combined and energetic effort should be made to obtain the restoration of that right.

3. That, in accordance with the ancient and constitutional rights of the Irish Nation, we claim the privilege of managing our own affairs by a Parliament assembled in Ireland and composed of the Sovereign, the Lords, and the Commons of Ireland.

4. That, in claiming these rights and privileges for our country, we adopt the principle of a Federal arrangement, which would secure to the Irish Parliament the right of legislating for and regulating all matters relating to the internal affairs of Ireland, while leaving to the Imperial Parliament the power of dealing with all questions affecting the Imperial Crown and Government, legislation regarding the colonies and other dependencies of the Crown, the relations of the Empire with foreign states, and all matters appertaining to the defence and stability of the Empire at large, as well as the power of granting and providing supplies necessary for Imperial purposes.

41. *Freeman's Journal,* November 19–22, 1873. See also *Nation,* November 22, 1873.

42. The members of Parliament who attended were Butt, Bryan, Browne, Blennerhassett, Brady, Callan, Downing, D'Arcy, Dease, Digby, Delahunty, French, Gray, Henry, Martin, Murphy, O'Reilly, D. M. O'Conor, O'Conor Don, O'Brien, Redmond, Ronayne, Synan, Smyth, and Shaw. For this list see Thornley, p. 160, n. 87. Thornley also states that some fifty Catholic priests and ten Protestant clergymen attended.

5. That, such an arrangement does not involve any change in the existing constitution of the Imperial Parliament or any interference with the prerogatives of the Crown or disturbance of the principles of the constitution.

6. That, to secure to the Irish people the advantages of constitutional government, it is essential that there should be in Ireland an administration for Irish affairs, controlled according to constitutional principles, by the Irish Parliament, and conducted by ministers constitutionally responsible to that Parliament.

7. That, in the opinion of this Conference, a Federal arrangement based on these principles would consolidate the strength and maintain the integrity of the Empire, and add to the dignity and power of the Imperial Crown.

8. That, while we believe that in an Irish Parliament the rights and liberties of all classes of our countrymen would find their best and surest protection, we are willing that these should be incorporated in the Federal Constitution articles supplying the amplest guarantees that no change shall be made by that Parliament in the present settlement of property in Ireland, and that no legislation shall be adopted to establish any religious ascendency in Ireland, or to subject any person to disabilities on account of his religious opinions.

The conference was formally opened with William Shaw, M.P. for the borough of Bandon and a prominent Protestant Cork businessman and banker, being moved to the chair, and the appointment of John O. Blunden, Philip Callan, W. J. O'Neill Daunt, E. R. King-Harman, and Alfred Webb, as honorable secretaries. The chairman opened the proceedings with a short address. "One part of our business this day," he assured those present, "will be to show the men outside that are looking on us that we mean what we say (hear, hear)—that we are honest and earnest in this movement (hear, hear)—that we do not wish in any shape to put it as if it were against property, against order, against religion (hear, hear). Quite the opposite (hear, hear)." "I believe," he further assured his auditors, "that there are no people in the world who have a truer and more earnest love for order, for rank, for property, for morality, and above all, for religion, than the Irish people (applause); and if we attempted in any way to disturb these foundations of social order, I am certain the Irish people would not adopt us and follow our lead (hear, hear)." Then, after expressing his confidence in the success of the movement, the chairman called on Butt to introduce the first series of resolutions, of which Butt was apparently the author, and to move the first resolution. Butt began by pointing out that the resolutions, which also had been approved by the conference committee, would be moved and seconded individually and each was subject to amendment and discussion. When they had all been considered, it would be open to anyone who thought they were not a sufficient declaration of the principle of Home Rule to move any additional resolution that would supply the deficiency. Butt then began a long and eloquent nationalist version of the approximately six-hundred-year history of parliamentary institutions in Ireland, which had climaxed in the late eighteenth century with Irish legislative independence. Under its own parliament, Butt maintained, Ireland had become prosperous and self-sufficient, and it had remained so until the Act of Union, "carried by a system of force, and fraud, and corruption, for which no parallel is to be found in the history of a free nation (applause)," was passed in 1801. All of Ireland's ills since then, according to Butt, could be attributed to that perfidious Act, and the task before them as patriotic Irishmen was simply to undo it. O'Connell had tried with his movement for Repeal, but when that had failed he had been converted to Federalism. Butt then explained his proposed Federal constitution and concluded his presentation by moving the first of the resolutions, which was seconded and passed unanimously. The conference then proceeded to the second and third resolutions, which were also passed unanimously.

In the discussion on the third resolution, Kenelm Digby, the senior member for Queen's county, questioned the appropriateness of calling for a restoration of the Irish House of Lords in a democratic age, and he called on Butt to justify such a political anachronism. Butt replied that he would defend it on the basis of historical precedent, claiming that Ireland was entitled to the restoration of all of those ancient rights that made up her constitutional inheritance. In raising the question, Digby had unwittingly opened up a constitutional can of worms, and Butt undoubtedly had seen the danger. An amendment was immediately proposed by D. A. Nagle, editor of the *Cork Herald,* who was accounted a Fenian sympathizer, that the resolution end with the words "manage our own affairs by a Parliament assembled in Ireland." This proposition was seconded by Nagle's good friend, C. G. Doran, who was secretary of the supreme council of the Irish Republican, or Fenian, Brotherhood. The point of the amendment, of course, was that by eliminating the words, "and composed of the Sovereign, the Lords, and the Commons of Ireland," they implicitly would allow also for the Fenian alternative of a democratic republic. This Fenian gambit brought A. M. Sullivan, the owner and editor of the *Nation* and long an opponent of physical force as a means in politics, to his feet to oppose the amendment. "Are we, or are we not," he asked, "to claim our ancient constitution, consisting of a House of Peers? or are we to consider ourselves, what Thomas Davis has declared we are not—a sandbank thrown up by the waves of yesterday, and not an ancient nation claiming its historic rights (loud cheers)?" "Now, if we were a new community," he added more pointedly, "starting with a clean page to open—if we were a new territory like the United States of America, having to shape our own constitution and organization, I, for one, would sympathise with Mr. Nagle. I am not a believer in the abstract theory of hereditary wisdom, when we have surrounding us proofs of hereditary folly (cheers)." "The English nation," Sullivan then warned, alluding to republican principles, "would greatly desire to see us led away by many of these attractive philosophical and political theories (cheers). The very men who would use against us the excuse that we were going in for destroying the aristocratic feature of the British Imperial Constitution are the very men who would be delighted to hear us say we would not have our ancient constitution in the shape in which it roused the admiration and fealty of Grattan and the Volunteers of 1782 (hear, hear)." Sullivan then concluded by calling on the conference to demand the restoration of their national legislature as it formerly existed. Those in attendance at the conference sided undoubtedly and overwhelmingly with Butt's and Sullivan's views, and Nagle and Doran had the good sense to withdraw their amendment in the interests of harmony and unity. The resolution was then passed unanimously, and the first day's proceedings were brought to a close.

All of the next day's proceedings, November 19, were taken up by the discussion of the fourth resolution, which outlined the federal arrangement of the proposed Home Rule constitution. The discussion turned on the difference between those who thought that the fourth resolution, and by implication the resolutions preceding it, went too far and those who thought that the fourth resolution did not go far enough. The former view was expressed by those—such as The O'Conor Don, the junior member for county Roscommon, and Myles O'Reilly, the senior member for county Longford—who maintained, in effect, that, though they supported Home Rule, they did not believe it was yet time for its implementation and the specifics of the resolution were, therefore, actually detrimental to the general end in view— Home Rule. The latter view was held by those—such as Sir John Gray, the member for the borough of Kilkenny, and P. J. Smyth, the junior member for county Westmeath—who, though they had been life-long Repealers and remained Repealers, were willing to accept Federalism as obtainable and as a first step in the right direction. To those who thought like The O'Conor Don, Butt pointed out that the second resolution, which affirmed that it was now time for achieving Home Rule, precluded any reconsideration of the measure's opportuneness and those who could not accept the second resolution, therefore, had no business at the conference. As to those who declared themselves still Repealers at heart, Butt welcomed them to the vineyard without asking them to sacrifice their ideal, pointing out at the same time that the Federal scheme not only was more likely than Repeal to be achieved at that moment, but also it gave them more than Repeal could because it assured them of a continued and considerable representation in the Parliament at Westminster and, thereby, of an effective voice in colonial and imperial affairs, as well as control over their domestic affairs. Finally, at the end of the long day's discussion, the fourth resolution was passed with only one dissentient voice.

The greater part of the third day's proceedings, November 20, was taken up with the last four resolutions. The fifth, sixth, and seventh resolutions were passed unanimously, but the eighth and last, was objected to by John Canon McDermott, the parish priest of Cloonacool in the diocese of Achonry, as a "most degrading proposition." The canon was not given the opportunity to explain what he meant, however, since the floor was taken by C. G. Doran, who, it will be recalled, had on the first day seconded the Fenian-inspired amendment to the third resolution regarding the restoration of the Irish House of Lords. Doran explained that it gave him great pleasure to introduce his resolution on the question of "independent parliamentary action."

That, this Conference cannot separate without calling on the Irish constitu-encies at the next general election to return men earnestly and truly devoted to the great cause which this Conference has been called on [to] promote, and who in any emergency that may arise, will be ready to take counsel with a great National Conference to be called in such a manner as to represent the opinions and feelings of the Irish nation, and that with a view to rendering members of Parliament and their constituents more in accord on all questions affecting the welfare of the country, it is recommended by this Conference that at the close of each session of Parliament the representatives should render to their constituents an account of their stewardship.

The resolution was seconded by John O'Connor Power, who, like the mover of the resolution, was a Fenian and a member of the supreme council of the Broth-erhood. In a long and able speech, the twenty-seven-year-old Power explained that the great problem of parliamentary independence was the difficulty of keep-ing parliamentary representatives from being corrupted by English influence. The best way of preventing this, he claimed, was not to make them pledge themselves to independent opposition but to make them more responsible to their constitu-ents. "Ireland has been powerless," Power maintained, "because she has not been able to watch her representatives, and the English Minister has taken care to corrupt them, so that the genius of Ireland has been prostituted to maintenance of its [England's] dignity (cheers)." "If this is to continue," he warned in conclusion, issuing a veiled Fenian threat, "there is no hope for Ireland except in measures which he would deplore the necessity of resorting to. He stood there to support them now, and he would stand there again, if that movement should fail, and would be prepared to take part in any action which the national voice of his country may determine (loud cheers)." On the conclusion of Power's remarks, the chairman informed the conference that an amendment to the above resolution had been handed in, but he thought it wiser to defer it to the following day. There being loud demands that the amendment should be read, the chairman, nev-ertheless, agreed to read it. "That, to render the Irish vote effective, we recom-mend that the Irish members shall, after the general election, form themselves into a permanent committee for the public discussion of every ministerial or other proposal which may affect the interests of Ireland; that no individual represen-tative shall introduce any bill or give notice of any notion of importance unless his proceeding shall be sanctioned and supported by such committee; and finally that the Irish members shall always vote in a body, or abstain from voting, in all party divisions, as the majority may direct." The conference was then adjourned to the following day.

When the conference reconvened the next morning, November 21, the chairman explained that, upon reflection, he believed he had acted too hastily the day before in foreclosing the discussion on the eighth resolution and that, as soon as the resolution and amendment were once again properly before the chair, he would ask that Canon McDermott be heard by the conference. The amendment then was formally moved by P. Cahill, of the Queen's County Independent Club, whose rambling and ambivalent speech did little to help his point of view. Such was not the case, however, with the person who seconded the amendment, Joseph G. Biggar, who the year before had vigorously contested the borough of Londonderry and lost. Biggar began by explaining that the introduction of this resolution and amendment signaled, he believed, that "the most important part of the business of the Conference had been reached. They had hitherto been enumerating abstract principles which were perfectly true, and they had got rid of personal difficulties, which might afterwards create embarrassments, and now came to the practical working of the Conference—namely to find out the best mode of getting Home Rule for Ireland (cheers)." "He regretted," Biggar explained, "that some of the members of Parliament, with their knowledge and experience, had not brought forward these propositions (hear, hear). He considered the amendment preferable to the resolution." "The only objection he had to it," he maintained, most interestingly, "was that it did not go far enough, and that there should have been a clause introduced calling upon candidates for parliamentary honours to give written pledges. He was aware that many men in whose judgement and honesty he had the utmost confidence thought otherwise, but he believed it would be more convenient and desirable that there should be clear and explicit written pledges, which would prevent any misunderstanding (hear, hear)."

"The amendment he considered quite reasonable in all its parts. It recommended organised action on the part of the Home Rule members, and if there was that organisation they could carry whatever they pleased in the British House of Commons. It also recommended voting and abstaining from voting on party divisions. What did they care about Whig or Tory; or whether Gladstone or Disraeli was in power if they could get accomplished the object they have in view for the benefit of the country."

"One great objection," Biggar admitted, "raised at the Conference was that the land and the education questions were not to be brought before them. These things had been kept very fairly in the background." "Their one great object," he asserted finally, "was to gain Home Rule for Ireland, and the only way to get Home Rule from the English Parliament was for the Irish Home Rule members to keep compactly and honestly together."

Immediately after Biggar had concluded his very able, even prophetic, remarks, the chairman called on Canon McDermott to speak to the eighth resolution. McDermott explained that not only did he find the guarantees offered to Protestants for their property and their religion in that resolution degrading and self-accusing, but also they would not meet the object for which they were framed because it would not bring that section of the community, "the kid-gloved gentry," into the Home Rule camp. Butt, in reply, admitted to the authorship of the resolution and confessed that he had initially shared the Canon's misgivings about it. He would never have assented to that resolution, he further explained, had he not found a similar provision in the American Constitution that was far more stringently against any act of the legislature adverse to religious liberty and the rights of property. He did not believe, therefore, that what Washington, Henry, and Jefferson had assented to could be held to humiliate the conference. When McDermott then concluded his remarks, the conference turned in earnest to a discussion of the resolution and amendment on the mode of parliamentary action before the chair.

The most remarkable thing about the discussion was that not one participant spoke for the amendment. The real distinction in the discussion was between those who only spoke in favor of the resolution, and the great majority, who spoke against the amendment. Butt was the only speaker perceptive enough to realize that the resolution had not been done real justice in the discussion, though his own analysis of both the resolution and the crucial distinction to be made between it and the amendment as modes of political action was rather feeble. The fundamental difference between the resolution and the amendment, of course, was that it raised the question of to whom a member of Parliament was really responsible—to the electors in the constituencies represented in a national conference or to a majority of the member's parliamentary colleagues. The difference was more practical than theoretical. The advocates of both the resolution and the amendment were agreed in theory; the will of the people was ultimately sovereign. The real question was whether the conference or the party was the most practical means for making the people's will effective. Time would tell that the party was a more practical means, but the reluctance of the electors at the grassroots to abandon populist politics has reverberated in Ireland even to the present day.

In 1873, however, the great majority at the conference were still opposed to any pledge that would bind members of Parliament to act on the views of the majority of their colleagues. Butt expressed the general feeling best when he pointed out that the amendment asked him "to suspend his conviction and his judgement into the hands of a number of men who were not yet elected, of whom he knew nothing (hear, hear)—who might be some of them Knaves—(hear, hear)—he hoped they would not, but he had no security." "If they asked him," Butt then asserted, "to leave it in the hands of the twenty-five men who had proved their fidelity by coming there, he would not agree to leave his conscience in their hands. An occasion might arise in which he might be obliged to dissent from them. It would only be in an extreme case that he would set himself against them, but a case may arise in which it would be his duty to dissent from them." "He believed," Butt further asserted, "that he would betray his own principles, his dignity, his personal honour, and personal honesty, if he now gave a pledge that he would submit his future conduct to the judgement of any tribunal on earth except his own conscience, and that higher tribunal, his responsibility to God (cheer)." These were noble words, but they had the effect of delaying the emergence of a disciplined, purposeful, Irish party in the House of Commons for nearly a decade. Butt then concluded his remarks on the amendment by asking Cahill to withdraw it. Cahill did so, and the chairman finally put forward the resolution, which passed unanimously.

The conference adjourned for lunch, and in the afternoon the second series of resolutions, designed to supply the effective means for the realization of Home Rule, were put forward and passed unanimously. They included some fifteen resolutions, the first and most important of which read: "That, in order to carry these objects into practical effect, an association be now formed, to be called 'The Irish Home Rule League,' of which the essential and fundamental principles shall be those declared in the resolutions adopted at this Conference, and of which the object, and only object, shall be to obtain for Ireland, by peaceable and constitutional means, the self-government contained in these resolutions." The succeeding resolutions were concerned mainly with providing for the rules, by-laws, and the funding of the league. A committee of sixteen was appointed to draw up the rules and by-laws, the annual dues were fixed at one pound for full members, and provision was made to enroll the mass of the people. In addition, a special fund was inaugurated that was vested in fifteen trustees, headed by the archbishop of Tuam. The proceedings were then brought to a close by votes of thanks to the honorary secretaries and the chairman. In moving the adjournment of the conference, Butt confessed that he had been somewhat anxious at its opening. "He felt it was a solemn step—that confusion, dissension, or distraction would have lowered the cause and retarded its success, while regularity, moderation, and order in their proceedings would immeasurably advance it. They had passed through four days that formed a crisis in the destiny of Ireland (hear, hear), and never were four days more gloriously passed by a nation and people on their trial (hear, hear). The moderation and wisdom displayed had answered the expectations of their friends, and disappointed bitterly the malignant prophesies of their foes (applause)." "He believed God," Butt concluded, "watched over their proceedings and gave them His blessing, and he felt confident that the efforts originated in the National Conference now closed would achieve for them the liberty of their native land (loud applause)."

Butt was certainly quite right in emphasizing that the great achievement at the conference was its harmony and unity. This was all the more remarkable because the conference represented in a most comprehensive way the whole spectrum of

Irish Nationalist politics. Three main groups in attendance at the conference may be distinguished: Fenians, advanced Nationalists, and moderates. No harmony and unity could have emerged, of course, if the Fenians had not decided to take up in earnest the game of constitutional politics. This Fenian change of heart was the result of the disastrous Fenian rising in February 1867, followed, at the end of the year, by a mad attempt to rescue a Fenian prisoner at Clerkenwell prison in London in which twelve innocent people were killed.[43] The Brotherhood was reorganized and its structure made more representative. Instead of the autocratic rule of a head center, a supreme council was established that consisted of one representative from each of the four Irish provinces, and one each from Scotland, north England, and south England. These seven representative members were empowered to co-opt four honorary members, to make up the full complement of eleven members. In March of 1873, the supreme council, as the governing body, called a representative meeting of the Brotherhood to amend its constitution. The amended constitution opened the way for Fenian cooperation with the constitutional Nationalists, and the result was the attendance at the national conference in November of four members of the supreme council, Charles G. Doran, John O'Connor Power, John Walsh, and John Barry, along with a good many rank-and-file Fenians. Among these Fenians, two types may be discerned. One is the so-called opportunists, such as Power and Barry, who were willing to totally commit themselves to the constitutional process, even if it involved their becoming candidates for parliamentary honors, and the other was the ultras, such as Doran, who were more reserved about their commitment and looked upon the recent constitutional innovation as essentially experimental and certainly provisional.

The second main grouping at the conference was the advanced Nationalists. Like the Fenians, two types of advanced Nationalists emerged at the conference, and the passage of time would make this distinction even more clear. For the sake of classification they may be designated as popular and parliamentary Nationalists, and they were best represented at the conference by those who backed the resolution and those who backed the amendment to insure that the Irish members of Parliament live up to their Home Rule professions. The proponents of the resolution, it will be recalled, recommended conference as the best means to insure this result, while those who supported the amendment advocated a pledge-bound Irish parliamentary party as the means for keeping Irish members up to the mark. The Fenians at the conference had, of course, supported the resolution (indeed they had proposed and seconded it), as well as the popular Nationalist position, which they thought would, theoretically at least, keep real political power in the constituencies where their own power and influence over the people

43. T. W. Moody and Leon O'Broin, "Select Documents: XXXII, The I.R.B. Supreme Council, 1868–78," *Irish Historical Studies* 19, no. 75 (March 1975): 286–332.

were greatest, rather than concentrated in an independent Irish party out of reach
at Westminster. The real gain of the advanced Nationalists, popular and parliamentary, at the conference, was that as a group they had absorbed the Fenians and
won unequivocal recognition of their end, Home Rule. The great irony, of course,
was that the essentially more conservative means of a pledge-bound, independent
Irish parliamentary party, which eventually would emerge as the foundation of the
modern Irish political system, was looked upon by the consensus at the conference
as a radical alternative to the popular Nationalist proposal of conference.

Indeed, it is hard to see how the consensus articulated by Butt could have been
achieved without the common denominator provided by the popular Nationalist
resolution. The moderate Nationalists, the third main grouping at the conference,
never could have been brought to acquiesce in the amendment. Constituting
such a heterogeneous group, consisting of Irish Whigs (such as The O'Conor
Don), Catholic and Protestant Liberals (such as Myles O'Reilly and Mitchell
Henry), and ambitious political opportunists (such as Sir John Gray), the moderates were only agreed with one another in endorsing Butt's denunciation of the
amendment as an infringement on conscience that could never be abided and,
with the popular Nationalists, in accepting the resolution as a gesture, albeit more
pious than sincere on their part, to the concept of popular sovereignty. Hammer-
ing out this consensus among the Fenians, advanced Nationalists, and moderates
was Butt's great personal achievement at the conference, and it won for him the
opportunity to become the leader of the Irish people at home and abroad. His
authority at the conference was made manifest not simply by his demonstrated
intellectual superiority and eloquence but also by his ability to articulate the
consensus at the critical moment, and at no time was this ability more evident than
in his remarks on the celebrated resolution and amendment. In effect, then, the
real achievement of the conference was that it offered the Irish people both a
program and a leader, and the great question now became whether the Irish
people would have them or not.

Though some might accept the Home Rule program and the leadership of Butt,
it was apparent almost immediately that Cullen would not. Two days after the
conference closed, he informed Kirby that he thought the conference did not bode
well for the future. "We had," he reported on November 23, "a great home rule
meeting here—I do not know what it will effect. But my opinion is that if we had a
little parliament here, half Protestant or more than half, and perhaps less than half
Catholic, the M.P.s in order to give themselves something to do, would begin to
make laws for priests & bishops and to fetter the action of the church" (K). "At the

home rule meeting," he explained, "some of the speakers were Protestants and Presbyterians. There were also some Catholic priests, but no one from Dublin." These remarks, of course, were intended to reassure the Roman authorities that Cullen did not approve of the new agitation, nor had anyone within his ecclesiastical jurisdiction given it any aid or comfort. Indeed, the alarm had already been sounded in an interesting and oblique way in Rome by Sir Augustus Paget, the English ambassador to the Kingdom of Italy. "I beg leave," Paget officially informed the Earl Granville, the foreign secretary, on October 23, "to call to your Lordship's attention to the paragraph which I have the honor to inclose together with a translation from the *Osservatore Romano,* the official or semi-official organ of the Vatican in which while refuting the charge of want of patriotism on the part of the Catholic clergy, their conduct during the late war [Franco-Prussian] is alluded, to, and the efforts they are now making in Ireland to establish Home Rule are held up to admiration."[44] "In bringing this paragraph under your Lordship's notice," Paget suggested, "it occurs to me that Her Majesty's Government may possibly take into their consideration whether it is desireable or expedient to continue even unofficial diplomatic communications with a power, which through its agents, is openly and avowedly advocating and promoting schemes for dismemberment of the British Empire."

Shortly after his return to Rome from an extended holiday at home, H. Clarke Jervoise, the unofficial British agent to the Vatican, wrote Granville a long despatch that obviously was inspired by Paget's complaint about the endorsement of Home Rule by the pope's official press organ. Jervoise reported that upon his return to Rome he had had an interesting conversation with Baron Antoine de Cetto, the Bavarian chargé d'affaires accredited to the Vatican. "Baron de Cetto, as your Lordship knows," Jervoise explained on October 31, "has Irish blood in his veins. His mother having been a Miss Beresford, he was born and entirely educated in England and retains the warmest interest in the welfare of the land of his birth; he is moreover a sincere Roman Catholic devoted to and enjoying the confidence of the Holy See, but having had considerable experience for many years past from his official communications with the Vatican is fully alive to the motives activating those by whom its policy is directed."

> Baron de Cetto went on to tell me that a few days before we met the possibility of the Pope going to Malta had been brought to his notice by a prelate who is perhaps more than anybody else in His Holiness's confidence and through whom it is sometimes possible to communicate indirectly with the Pontiff, when the usual channels are not available.
> The opportunity thus presenting itself, he had expressed to this prelate some doubts as to whether it was quite certain that the Pope would find that Malta

44. F.O., 45/220.

would be accessible to him, for, said he, the conduct of the Irish Bishops is not such as to encourage the friendly dispositions that England has hitherto manifested towards the Papacy—or to promote the conviction that in reality the complete liberty enjoyed by the Roman Catholic religion in Her Majesty's dominions, a liberty greater it has been often asserted than that granted to it in any Catholic country, is as fully appreciated by His Holiness as it should be, the Home Rule movement as he [de Cetto] asserted signalizing neither more nor less than treason. It was surprising, he thought, that such a movement should be countenanced by the Bishops who must be supposed to be acting under superior orders from Rome.[45]

"From some remarks dropped by this person," Jervoise observed, most likely referring to Monsignor Edward Henry Howard, an Englishman who, the year before (1872), significantly, had been made the coadjutor to the cardinal bishop of Frascati, Felippo Maria Guidi, who had fallen foul of the pope at the first Vatican Council, "Baron de Cetto drew the conclusion that the Irish Bishops are not easily controlled. The prelate went on to say that he was not aware what was meant by Home Rule, but that he would inquire respecting it at the Propaganda."

A few days later he called on Baron de Cetto to inform him that he had been unable to obtain information on the subject at the Propaganda and invited him to write a Memorandum upon it, which [invitation] was declined [by de Cetto]. He [the prelate] said there existed no means at Rome of getting at the truth, and that there was no Catholic here who would enlighten the Pope on such a question.

He then enquired whether it was likely that I should have instructions to bring it to the notice of the cardinal secretary of state, and was told that it was impossible to answer the question, as there had been no communications between Baron de Cetto and myself thereupon,—that the remarks offered had been spontaneously made and with a view of conveying a warning as to a great danger into which the Papacy was probably being drawn unawares.

"These conversations," Jervoise then pointed out to Granville, referring to the talks between the Baron and the prelate, "having been renewed since I returned, I have called Baron de Cetto's attention to the article on Home Rule in the *Osservatore Romano* of the 17th instant, which was transmitted to the Foreign Office with Sir A. Paget's despatch N 318 of the 23rd instant and to the resolutions adopted by the Irish Bishops at Dublin on the 15th and 16th instant, and he has I know submitted them to the prelate in question." "I have no doubt whatever therefore," he further assured Granville, "that ere now the Pope and Cardinal Antonelli are acquainted with their substance."

"It was suggested to Baron de Cetto," Jervoise also explained, "that the Pope would be unwilling to interfere with the Irish Bishops unless he were invited to do so, as he is careful not to meddle in the home policy of other countries at a time

45. Ibid., 43/123.

when he is so generally accused of doing so. He had discountenanced the Fenian movement and might be persuaded to use his influence on the present occasion if good reasons were given him for doing so." "It was even possible," Jervoise reported, "it was hinted, that a promise should be given before-hand that a copy would be confidentially placed in my hands of the reply returned by the Bishops to explanations they might be called upon to give."

> I have thanked Baron de Cetto for the information he has given me and for the interest he has shewn in this question. I have told him that it must un-doubtedly occupy the serious attention of Her Majesty's Government, and that speaking from my own personal impressions I felt that the countenance given to the Home Rule movement by the Irish Catholic hierarchy must render my position here nugatory if not impossible unless it were checked. It was a mock-ery I said to ask us to believe that the Pope could not control the Bishops if he was determined to do so, or that no influence could be exercised over what everywhere outside the Vatican is accepted as its official mouthpiece.

"From what I have stated above," Jervoise then observed, "your Lordship will perhaps be disposed to think that a good opportunity is offered for me to bring the matter to the attention of the cardinal secretary of state and that I might have done so at once." "I am however," he suggested, "of opinion that the ground is not sufficiently prepared. I believe the Vatican to be extremely ill-informed on all matters of foreign politics, and I very much doubt if it has anything approaching a correct notion of what takes place in Ireland. It should be enlightened through some less impassioned, more impartial channel than the Irish hierarchy." "The admission," Jervoise pointed out shrewdly, "that such is not to be found in Rome from a Catholic quarter is valuable."

"Your Lordship will recollect," he reminded Granville, "that last year I brought the subject of the Galway election before Cardinal Antonelli, stating that I had done so without instructions from the Foreign Office, and in a similar way I spoke to his Eminence on the tone of the *Osservatore Romano* towards Great Britain, and I respectfully beg to remind your Lordship how unsatisfactory and evasive were the replies I received on both occasions." "Every diplomat," he maintained, "who has had dealings with the Roman Curia has had similar experiences,— delay, evasions, prevarications and disregard to advice given or appeals for sup-port asked for." "Circumstances are now changed," Jervoise noted, referring to the growing feeling of diplomatic isolation at the Vatican and especially the import of the recent reception of Victor Emmanuel at the Courts of Berlin and Vienna, "and perhaps a clear indication expressed in moderate terms that the time for trifling is past, accompanied by assurances of a desire to remain on good terms with the Papacy might not be ineffectual." "The questions of Home Rule and education," he warned Granville, "have been artfully interwoven. It will be said that education and religion are inseparable, and much care will be necessary to separate the connection of the first with the other two." "A clear exposition," Jervoise advised in conclusion, "of the merit of the case and the views of Her Majesty's Government is then I venture to suggest desirable and might be beneficially offered at this moment."

What Jervoise was suggesting, of course, was that the British government should demand that the Roman authorities condemn the Home Rule movement so as to prevent the Irish bishops and clergy from participating in it and, failing that, to withdraw their unofficial mission, of which he was the representative, to the Vatican. Before Granville could respond to this very radical suggestion, however, the crisis already had been precipitated by the three bishops who signed the requisition for a national conference to promote Home Rule and by the attendance of a significant number of the clergy at the conference. Shortly after the conference, apparently, Granville instructed Jervoise to see Antonelli informally and to protest the episcopal and clerical involvement. At their interview, Jervoise reported MacHale (Tuam), Keane (Cloyne), and Butler (Limerick) to Antonelli as the offending bishops. He obviously mistook Butler, who had not signed the requisition, for O'Hea (Ross) who had. After his interview, Jervoise telegraphed Granville on November 28, in cypher: "Private. Cardinal Antonelli asks whether the opinions of Irish Bishops respecting Home Rule have been published. I told him the three had publicly declared in favor of the movement.

"It would be very useful if I could be furnished with the letters of the Bishops on the subject."[46] Antonelli must also have written to the cardinal prefect of Propaganda requesting information on the subject, for Barnabò wrote to Cullen asking him for his views about the truth of the complaints made by the British government in regard to the bishops and clergy. Barnabò, however, was under the impression that the complaints had been made by Paget rather than by Jervoise. Cullen replied in a long and masterful letter written on December 12, which he summed up succinctly for Kirby that same day.[47] "Card. Barnabò," he reported, "wrote to me that Sir A. Paget had complained about Dr. McHale, Dr. Butler, and Dr. Keane. Poor Dr. Keane is dying—Dr. Butler supported the University Bill against all the other Bishops and is not opposed to the government. Dr. MacHale cares very little about Home Rule, but he is fond of opposition. That is my answer" (K). "I added," Cullen noted further, "A. Paget had made a speech at Turin praising the violence and usurpations of Italy—*quo jure* [by what right] will he apply a different rule to us?" "A Capuchin and a Carmelite," he concluded, referring to the Dublin clergy, "have joined Home Rule. No other priest in this diocese has joined."

The following day, December 13, the bishop of Ardagh, who had just arrived in

46. Ibid., 170/203.
47. S.R.C., vol. 36, fols. 1421–22, Cullen to Barnabò.

Rome on diocesan business, wrote to Cullen, reporting the latest news. "Card. Barnabò told me," Conroy explained, "that the English minister here, Sir A. Paget has made a formal complaint to Cardinal Antonelli of the conduct of Mgri MacHale, Butler and Keane in the matter of Home Rule. He [Paget] insinuated that it was the Propaganda which had encouraged these Prelates to take the position they have lately taken. Some think that the complaint is a mere ruse to give some excuse to the Government for its shameful abandonment of Irish Catholic interests here."[48] "Card. Barnabò says," Conroy further reported, "that the English minister is 'un vasallo' [a vassal, i.e., a low fellow] and 'un bastardo'." "They appear however," Conroy added interestingly, "to be somewhat frightened in Propaganda by the attitude lately assumed by the English Government towards Ireland." Several days later, after an interview with the pope, Conroy wrote to Cullen again. "He said," Conroy reported of the pope on December 17, "that the English Government had conveyed to him their apprehensions of the '*mene*' [lead] which the Irish bishops were engaged in, in the matter of Home Rule, but they had expressly excepted your Eminence from all blame" (C). "His Holiness," Conroy noted, "had a very correct idea of what Home Rule is, and he laughed when I said that 'it was well to have one Catholic country, at least, where the Bishops could frighten a Government, whereas in every other country the Government was frightening the Bishops.'"

By the time Cullen received this reassuring news from Conroy about the pope, his letter of December 12 to Barnabò had been received in Rome. Conroy apparently did not have the opportunity to speak to Barnabò again until the middle of January because the cardinal prefect had been very ill. "Your Eminence's letter about the Home Rule question," Conroy finally reported to Cullen on January 23, 1874, "has been pronounced by Card. Barnabò to be '*bellissima*' [very fine]. He told me that he sent it on 'to the *Secretaria de Stato per norma di quella genta là* [Secretary of State for the information of those people there]" (C). In the meantime, Jervoise, who had been waiting for a reply from Antonelli, decided to press matters a little. "Thinking that sufficient time had elapsed," he informed Granville on December 31, "for information to have reached the Vatican from Dublin with reference to some observations I made some time ago on the connection of the Roman Catholic hierarchy and clergy in Ireland with the Home Rule movement, I sought an opportunity last week of again broaching the subject to Cardinal Antonelli."[49] "His Eminence," Jervoise reported, "was good enough to read to me extracts from a letter written in Italian by a Roman Catholic as he informed me, who I suspect was Cardinal Cullen."

48. This was a reference to the British government's supposed inaction to the threats made allegedly by the Italian government to confiscate part of the property owned by the Irish College in Rome.
49. F.O., 43/123.

Archbishop MacHale was therein described as being in constant opposition
to his colleagues and scarcely to be considered as a reasonable being. I may say
here that *fool* and *madman* are terms I have heard applied to his Grace on
various occasions by members of the Papal Court.

The Bishop of Cloyne, the writer said was too ill to attend to business, and
his vicar general had made an unwarrented use of his name. I pointed out
however, that the vicar general's letter had been most distinct in asserting that
the resolutions of the deanery of Dunmore [correctly, Donoughmore] were
sanctioned and approved by Bishop Keane.

The Bishop of Limerick, whom I had named on a previous occasion as
having declared himself an advocate for Home Rule did not appear on enquiry
to have done so. I said that his name had been mentioned to me in conversation with a friend since I returned to Rome this autumn. I was glad, I said, to
learn I had been misinformed, and begged to express my sincere regret that
that prelate's name had been coupled with those of Drs. MacHale and Keane
on the topic under discussion.

"Cardinal Antonelli's correspondent," Jervoise added, "distinctly expressed his
own disapprobation of the movement which he asserted instead of being service-
able to Catholic interests would far more likely be detrimental to them." "The
leader of the movement," Jervoise noted further, still paraphrasing Cullen, and
referring to Butt, "besides being a Protestant was described as an 'homme exalté'
[hot-headed man]. An Irish parliament instituted under such influences as now
patronized it would be disposed to take up Roman Catholic questions in a spirit
quite foreign to that of Roman Catholics themselves."

"Following up the conversation," Jervoise continued, "Cardinal Antonelli repeated, as he had done before, that the Holy See could not for a moment be
suspected of encouraging or looking with favor upon such a movement."

It was contrary to its principles to countenance political agitation against
established order, and it was not necessary to have the assurances contained in
Lord Hartington's speech [the chief secretary for Ireland] before the House of
Commons on the 2nd of May, 1872 (which I had read to his Eminence), to
satisfy him that the present cry and Fenianism were closely allied. His own
experience of what occured here in 1848 when the Pope conceded a "Conseil
d'Etat pour les Finances" [Council of State for Finances] convinced him that
were a Parliament granted to the Irish their wants would not rest there, and
would be such as could not be yielded.

"Such being the sentiments of the Holy See, his Eminence continued," Jervoise
then noted, as Antonelli vigorously proceeded to point out that the Holy See had
some grievances of its own about the support of established order to lay before the
British government, "he could not but express his astonishment at the assertion
contained in Earl Russell's letter to Sir G. Bowyer, viz, that the autonomy of
Ireland is asserted at Rome. The accusation was untrue, and he would not let the

opportunity pass by without referring to it, and to a speech of the English minister [Paget] at the Cavour banquet at Turin."

> Both these incidents he said created a most painful impression amongst Catholics in Ireland. That a public meeting should be called under the presidency of a British statesman for the purpose of expressing his sympathy with the persecution in Germany of their Church and co-religionists was not calculated to inspire them with conciliatory feelings, and he could not but forsee would be resented by them.
>
> I replied that without pretending to know the precise grounds on which Earl Russell based his statement I could only suppose that they originated, and very naturally so, from a perusal of the declarations made by or on behalf of two members of the Irish hierarchy together with the memorials of several deaneries (naming Tuam, Dunmore [*sic*], Ballinrobe and Millstreet) to which were attached the signatures of many of the R.C. Clergy. Some of these memorials, moreover, I added, as his Eminence would recollect I had pointed out already had been endorsed with the approval of the clerical press in Rome.

"To the passing allusion," Jervoise then explained, "to Sir A. Paget's speech I made no remark." "I have used," he finally assured Granville, referring to the line he had taken with Antonelli, "the same language in other parts where I thought it advisable to do so and I must now express my firm conviction that Home Rule is not being encouraged at the Vatican, nor do I doubt, though I have not been told so, that such of the clergy as have advocated it in their ecclesiastical capacity have been warmly reproved."

When Jervoise later had his annual, formal audience with the pope in early January 1874, the influence of Antonelli was readily apparent in the pope's remarks. "England," Jervoise reported on January 14, paraphrasing the pope, "he looked on as the happiest in her lot of all countries at the present day, a passive observer of the stormy scenes acting around her but which touched her not."[50] "'That old Lord Russell, however,'" Jervoise added, quoting the pope, "he said, 'is about to do an impolitic thing in expressing his sympathy with the persecutors of the Church in Germany. He and Mr. Disraeli are no friends of the Pope. Lord Russell is very old, and his present proceedings are not those of a statesman, and will afflict and vex (*sturberanno*) his Catholic countrymen.'" "I here observed," Jervoise added, "that his Lordship had alluded to disaffection in Ireland, and I supposed that he referred to articles that had been published by the Catholic press in Rome and to the proceedings of some of the clergy in the country. The advocates of Home Rule, I said, were not all loyal, many of them were known to have Fenian sympathies." "The Pope replied," he explained, "that he was aware this was

50. Ibid., 43/124.

so, & that he had condemned Fenianism, but that with one or two exceptions the Irish Bishops were all loyal. As for the Archbishop of Tuam he was a 'uomo florido' [overwrought man], a 'testa turbido' [troubled head] who never got on with Cardinal Cullen." At this point, the pope realized that he had gone too far in criticizing a bishop, especially to a layman and a Protestant, and he abruptly changed the subject by beginning a discussion of the consistory to be held on the following Friday.

At the end of 1873, on the eve of the general election that was to take place in January 1874, it was obvious that Cullen not only retained the complete confidence of the pope and the Roman authorities, but also he had held his ground remarkably well in the episcopal body in regard to the Home Rule movement. In spite of the disruption of the Irish-Liberal alliance which had followed on the defeat of Gladstone's University bill in early March 1873, and the eventual demise of all hope for educational reform, only two bishops, besides the previously committed archbishop of Tuam, broke ranks to sign the requisition in October calling for a national conference on Home Rule in Dublin. Both the bishop of Cloyne and his close friend and neighbor, the bishop of Ross, had long held very advanced-Nationalist political views, and the only reasons they had refrained for so long from endorsing the Home Rule movement were their very great respect for Cullen and their reluctance to impair the unity of the body. Still, three bishops in a body of about thirty was not exactly a resounding vote of confidence in either the Home Rule movement or its leadership. Why did not more bishops, especially those who were more Nationalist in their sympathies, endorse the requisition for a national conference? Though a number of them might have been so inclined, they also, in fact, must have realized that to divide the body on the eve of a general election would serve no useful purpose and might even do great harm. If there was to be a moment of truth for the body of bishops on the issue of the Home Rule movement, better it be after, rather than before, the general election.

V

The General Election
January–March 1874

On January 24, 1874, Gladstone announced that the queen had agreed to dissolve Parliament and that a general election would be held immediately. After Gladstone's resumption of office the previous March, following his defeat on the Irish University bill, his ministry had continued to lose ground in both the House of Commons and the country, and by the early summer it had become obvious that if the ministry was to survive it would have to be reconstructed. The occasion for its reorganization took place at the end of July, when a very serious administrative scandal at the post office forced the resignations of the three ministers who were responsible. The chief Irish casualty was the postmaster general, William Monsell, who was replaced by the distinguished Scottish chemist and M.P. for the University of Edinburgh, Lyon Playfair. Gladstone assumed the duties of the chancellor of the Exchequer, Robert Lowe, who had resigned the Exchequer to assume the home office, and Gladstone asked John Bright, the radical member for Birmingham, to enter the cabinet as chancellor for the duchy of Lancaster. Though Gladstone also promoted a number of other very able men, such as Playfair, to junior ministries, the government was not able to gain any momentum. Morale in the cabinet and the country did not improve during the autumn since all the by-elections except one continued to go against the government. Finally, when yet another by-election was lost in early January, and shortly after, the Liberal majority at Newcastle-on-Tyne was seriously reduced in a by-election there, (though the Liberals managed to hold the seat), Gladstone decided not to meet Parliament in February.

The news of the dissolution came as a complete surprise to many and to none more so than the Irish. "What an exciting piece of news," the bishop of Elphin exclaimed in a letter to Cullen on January 25, "Mr. Gladstone supplied to us yesterday!" (C). "It has set many a man in motion today," Gillooly observed, "and amongst those whom it affects in Ireland, there are few whom it more behooves to prepare for the coming contest than our own body. If the result of the Elections will show that the Clergy have lost their influence over the Electors and have been supplanted by the Landlords or the Mob, the consequences, social & legislative, will be most detrimental to the interests of religion." "I think therefore," he maintained, "we should at once gird our loins for the fight and organise our strength. If we take prompt & prudent action in our several dioceses, I confidently expect that the Election returns will prove beyond question that clerical influence has been strengthened and made supreme by the Ballot." "The all important point," he further advised, "for the Clergy will be the selection of suitable Candidates, and prompt, organised opposition to the candidature of rowdies & traitors." "I am anxious," he added, referring to the coadjutor to the bishop of Achonry, "to learn the whereabouts of Dr. McCormack in order to write to him and, if possible to get him home at once. In his absence it will be hard to manage several of his young priests, who are hotheaded patriots and not disposed to act in Concert with the rest of the County." "The late disappointed Candidate for the Mitre," he warned, referring to Terence O'Rorke, the archdeacon, and parish priest of Ballysodare, "will, I fear, take advantage of the Election Contest to give annoyance to Elphin." "I expect to meet & confer with Dr. Conway some day this week. It would be useless to consult Dr. Durcan," he then concluded, referring to the coadjutor to the bishop of Killala and the bishop of Achonry.

Cullen had, in fact, written to Gillooly that same day asking whether Gillooly preferred that the next monthly meeting of the council of the Catholic union take place on February 10 or February 23. "The approach of the Elections," Gillooly explained, "oblige me to alter some of my diocesan arrangements and in consequence it will make little or no difference to me whether the C.U. Council meeting take place on the 10th or 23d" (C). "The earlier day," he suggested, "might be more advisable as the Council might then send a Circular to each of the Bishops reminding them of the Parliamentary Action we lately resolved to take in support of Cat[c] Education and requesting them to require an explicit statement & promise from *their* Candidates on this subject of Education." "Our two members for Roscom[n]," he assured Cullen, "O'Conor Don & French, will be returned, I am sure, without a Contest." "I am taking steps," he added, "to prevent a contest in this [Sligo] County." "To select & support good Candidates and eliminate bad ones is our great work—and indeed in many cases it will be no easy one. May God guide & sustain us," Gillooly then concluded, after recommending the proscription of the junior member for Dublin City, Sir Dominic Corrigan, who was one of the four Catholics who voted for Gladstone's University bill.

Gillooly also wrote to Bartholomew Woodlock, the rector of the Catholic University, that same day, January 27, urging him to draw up a form of the pledge he had suggested to Cullen and to distribute it to all of the bishops in order that they might present it to parliamentary candidates as a condition for endorsement (C).

Woodlock declined to act on the first part of Gillooly's suggestion, however, probably because he suspected, and rightly so, that it would be viewed by any number of the bishops as a piece of pure effrontery on his part. "I do not see," Woodlock explained to Cullen on the evening of January 27, enclosing Gillooly's letter, "how I could supply the form of pledge mentioned by Dr. Gillooly. But I am writing to the Bishops" (C). By this time, however, Cullen had already found a more effectual and appropriate way of acting on Gillooly's suggestion. When Cullen learned of the dissolution, he had immediately written to Lord Granard, the president of the Catholic union, to alert him to the crisis. "I sincerely trust," Granard had replied on January 25, "we may be able to return some 60 or 70 Members pledged to Catholic Interests. If we do, Education will not be long unsettled" (C). "Would Your Eminence," he suggested, "approve of the Union issuing an address to the Constituencies on Education & other Catholic grievances?"

Cullen did approve, and two days later, on January 27, the address was issued to their "CATHOLIC FELLOW-COUNTRYMEN," signed on behalf of the council by the secretary of the Catholic union, Bartholomew Teeling (C). "At this unexpected crisis," the address read, "the Catholic Union of Ireland feels that it is called upon to address a few words of advice to the Catholic Electors of the Country."

> Earnestly desirous, as its members are, for the welfare of our common country, and having no hostility to any legitimate movement that contemplates its prosperity, the Catholic Union at the same time wishes to declare that it has no concern with, and does not presume to suggest, much less to dictate, a course of conduct in matters of politics, properly so called. But as the occasion is one when vast Catholic interests are at issue, the Union calls upon the Catholics of Ireland to be faithful to the Catholic traditions of the past and to the duty that now devolves upon them.
>
> It cannot be silent whilst an impious usurpation continues at Rome, and whilst, in violation of indisputable rights, and of the principles of all constitutions, the lawful Sovereign of the Eternal City is doomed to a cruel captivity in the precincts of his own palace. The Catholic Electors should demand of the Candidate who seeks their suffrages that he shall by word and by act make protest against this iniquity, and urge that Government which asks for his support to use its best efforts to remove it. The cause of free Catholic Education, untrammelled by State restrictions as to the time and mode of Catholic teaching, has yet to be brought to a satisfactory result. The state of University Education as regards Catholics is "scandalously bad," and the effort of the last Parliament to remedy it was perfectly inadequate so far as the Catholics of Ireland were concerned. The manifestation of a great Catholic interest in this sacred cause, by the return of Members pledged to advocate a measure that will satisfy Catholic claims and Catholic consciences, and in whose honour reliance for the fulfillment of their pledges can be placed, will have a powerful effect in hastening the accomplishment of the object we have all so warmly at heart (C).

"Irish Catholicity," the address concluded, "is on its trial just now, and has a splendid opportunity of testifying to its constancy in the Faith, to its unbroken attachment to the successor of St. Peter, and to its undiminished desire for Religious Education. It can now give proof that the infidelity and indifferentism of the Continent has got no footing on Irish soil, and that come what may, nothing has availed to weaken the loyalty of the Irish People to the Faith of their Fathers and to the Chair of St. Peter."

The significance of the above address was really twofold. It was significant first, and most obviously, because it required all candidates for parliamentary honors to pledge themselves to two things before they received the endorsement of the bishops and their clergy in the constituencies. They must support the temporal power of the pope and they must accept the views on education set forth by the bishops as a body. It was significant second because it left Home Rule, in effect, as an open question, and Catholics and their bishops were free, therefore, to support any candidate's political views. The result was that those lay politicians who had a propensity for Catholic-Whig-Liberal politics, as exemplified by Cullen, all declared, with a few hardy exceptions, for Home Rule, while those politicians who were ardent Home Rulers and advanced Nationalists, best represented by Mac-Hale, all declared for the pope and denominational education. The real question in the election, therefore, became less the sincerity of the Home Rulers who had declared for the pope and denominational education, and more the honesty of that large number of candidates who had adopted Home Rule so capriciously.

Cullen was soon very much aware of the problem posed by Home Rule in the general election. Writing to Kirby about the effects of Gladstone's surprise dissolution, he also discussed the patent insincerity of some of those who had taken up the cry of Home Rule to get into Parliament. "We are here in the turmoil of a general election," he reported on January 29, "Gladstone has dissolved the Parliament so unexpectedly that there has been no time for preparation. I fear therefore that the Catholics will not benefit much by the election" (K). "The home rule question," he explained, "has also divided very much the minds of the people. Some who care very little for us or our religion will be elected on the ground of being home rulers and great patriots. Several Protestants and even orangemen have taken up this cry merely to get into Parliament." "Altogether our prospects are not good," he observed sadly, "to darken them still more many priests appear to think of nothing but home rule, and they are ready to support any one however objectionable he may be, provided he adopts that cry." "However," he concluded more hopefully, "God may draw some good out of this chaos."

In 1874, 64 Irish constituencies returned 103 members to Parliament, of which 64 represented county, 37 borough, and 2 university seats. Of these 103 seats, the 32 Irish counties and Dublin University returned 2 members each, while 25 of the 31 boroughs returned 1 member, and 6 returned 2. In early 1874, the Catholic vote was decisive, at least in theory, in 40 constituencies comprising 66 seats. However, given the exigencies of Irish politics at this time, not to mention its vagaries, practice did not always conform to theory. Still, if the bishops and clergy could mobilize the Catholic vote successfully in the constituencies, collectively they had the potential to return some two-thirds of the Irish representation of 103 members. The bishops and their clergy, it will be recalled, had in the general election of 1868 become highly politicized—individually in the constituencies and collectively in the country—in the interest of the Gladstonian Irish-Liberal alliance. By 1874, with the Irish-Liberal alliance in ruins, the issue that gave them their energy and focus was the education question. Every candidate who was a candidate for parliamentary honors in constituencies where the bishops and clergy had any influence was obliged to pledge himself to the line laid down by the bishops on that question. The effectiveness of the educational pledge became evident through the proscription of all members who had not voted appropriately on Gladstone's University bill. In that fateful division, it will be recalled, of the sixty-two Irish Liberal and Home Rule members, thirty-seven voted against the second reading of the bill, eleven voted for, and fourteen abstained. Of the eleven who voted for, all, except Lord St. Lawrence in Galway City, either decided not to run again or ran again and were defeated. Of the fourteen who abstained, eight either did not run again or ran and were defeated, and six survived into the next Parliament. Presumably, those six, with the possible exception of Butt, whose political position was too strong to be significantly affected, were required to give a satisfactory explanation for their absence. Thus, the bishops and clergy were able not only to impose their educational pledge but also to demonstrate by their proscription of some nineteen members of Parliament that the violation of the pledge would be fraught with the direst of political consequences.

Whatever may be said about the success of the bishops as a body in laying down the law on the education question, their decision to leave the Home Rule question open had resulted in a very awkward political situation for the majority of them, who, like Cullen, had been and still were opposed to the movement. As soon as the general election was announced, virtually all of the candidates in constituencies with decisive Catholic votes declared for Home Rule. Therefore, those bishops who had opposed the movement found themselves in the uncomfortable position of having to remain neutral in the contest; find suitable candidates on very short notice, who would probably be defeated; or support those who were now pledged to Home Rule, many of whom were incumbents and the bishops' political protégés. Most of the bishops, who thought like Cullen, took the latter course, but their expediency in doing so was testimony neither to their own consistency nor to the political integrity of their lay protégés. Though this early debasement of the political coinage was to have some serious consequences in the future, it did little in the short run to impair either the energy or the determination of the bishops and their clergy in the constituencies to return the candidates of their choice in the general election.

The key episcopal figure, as evidenced in his early correspondence with Gillooly and Granard, was Cullen. Besides trying to provide for general electoral needs through the Catholic union, Cullen also was active in about a dozen constituencies. The amount and intensity of his activity was certainly greater than he had shown at any previous general election. He was involved not only in perhaps a half-dozen constituencies in his own diocese and province but also in some five constituencies outside his own ecclesiastical jurisdiction. The incidence of his success in these constituencies, moreover, provides an interesting comment on the upper limits of the electoral influence of the most powerful man in the Irish Church. The constituencies in which Cullen interfered that were outside his own spiritual jurisdiction were county Longford, the boroughs of Athlone and Galway, and the counties Louth and Meath. Because the period of the general election was so brief, from the dissolution on January 24 to the last election in Ireland on February 17, Cullen was involved almost simultaneously in all of them, and therefore no linear or narrative presentation can do justice to the pressure or complexity of these events.

The political situation that gave Cullen the greatest cause for immediate concern was the parliamentary representation in the diocese of Ardagh. There were three seats at stake, two in county Longford and one in the borough of Athlone. The difficulty was that the bishop of Ardagh, George Conroy, was absent in Rome. The senior member for the county, Major Myles O'Reilly, who had for many years served as the bishops' spokesman on educational questions in the House of Commons and who had just declared for Home Rule, was not in any danger. The junior member for the county, however, G. F. N. Greville-Nugent, the second son of the politically influential Baron Greville of Clonyn (who had represented the county for some seventeen years before he had been raised to the peerage) had become less pleasing to Catholics because he and his brother, the senior member for Westmeath, had absented themselves from the voting on the University bill. Apparently, therefore, Cullen encouraged the candidacy of George Errington, a native of Longford who had lately acquired some prominence in the founding of the Catholic union and who was one of its honorary secretaries. The question of Errington's replacing Greville was one of the reasons that Cullen wrote to Granard immediately after he received the news of the dissolution. "I received a telegram from Mr. Errington," Granard reported to Cullen on January 25, "asking me whether I thought he should telegraph to the Bishop. I replied that there could be no objection to doing so, but that I was ignorant of his [Conroy's] views." "Yesterday," he explained, "I wrote to Dr. Conroy, telling him that I would neither pledge myself nor express any opinion, until I knew his views, that I was persuaded that united action on the part of every Catholic w^d be required & that I hoped he w^d return as soon as he could." "Both Mr. Lewis," Granard noted, referring to the lately unsuccessful candidate for county Monaghan who was a protégé of Cullen's, "and Mr. Errington are as Your Eminence says excellent men, and even if it may be considered judicious or possible to fight the battle with Mr. Greville Nugent, there will be vacancies elsewhere, in Leitrim for instance, as I fear Mr. Edward Maguire will scarcely be induced to stand."

Cullen had also written to the vicar general of the diocese of Ardagh and the parish priest of Abbeylara, Nicholas O'Flanagan, on the news of the dissolution, and O'Flanagan had replied on January 25. "I had the honour of receiving your Eminence's favour this morning," he explained, "for which I feel most deeply obliged. We have indeed been taken by surprise by the unexpected dissolution of Parliament, but it is very satisfactory to know that we cannot be at a loss for good and worthy Catholic gentlemen to represent us. I have every reason to hope that our priests will be unanimous and that our faithful people will as usual follow our advice. The spirit of persecution now so rife against the Church will be an additional incentive to union" (C). "I shall take an early opportunity," he assured Cullen, "of seeing all the priests of the County, and sounding them as to their views on the approaching election, bearing always in mind the names on which your Eminence has been kind enough to suggest. Our great drawback in Longford has always been a dearth of suitable candidates. But now with such men to choose from, I think Catholic interests need not suffer." "I will lose no time," he concluded, "in communicating with Dr. Conroy on the subject."

"I have seen both candidates," Granard informed Cullen two days later, on Tuesday, January 27, clearly referring to O'Reilly and Errington, "& several of the leading Priests of the C°. The Vicar General has convened a meeting for Thursday to deliberate, this is to be followed by a meeting to which the laity are to be invited at which the candidates will be selected on Monday" (C). In the meantime Conroy wrote Cullen a most interesting letter from Florence, interesting especially in light of all the telegrams that must have passed between him and his vicar general and Granard. "The news of the dissolution of Parliament," Conroy informed Cullen on January 29, "came on me in the midst of my delightful journey like a cloud on a summer's day" (C). "My first impulse," he confessed, "was to return at once. But on reflection I thought that this step would be of little use until I should have heard what was likely to be done." "If I were to move from this place homewards," he explained, "it would not be possible for me to receive any telegrams, and as the time allowed was so short it was absolutely necessary I should know what was happening. Besides, I had already given my views to the Vicar General, and knew that he was willing and able to carry them into effect." "I have telegraphed to the meeting today," he then reported, referring to the meeting of the clergy held on January 29, "that if possible the present or late members should be retained on condition of their adopting a pledge for Catholic education and 'popular views!' It would only lead to another Longford scandal if they should say a word against the present craze for Home Rule." "I have just now heard," he reported further, referring to the meeting of the clergy that had adopted O'Reilly and Errington, "that the priests have agreed to their programme for Monday's meeting." "I am glad," Conroy then added, "to know that Y. Em. has befriended Ennis for Athlone."

The discrepancy between what Conroy, before he left for Rome, had arranged with his vicar general about the representation for Longford and what Cullen finally succeeded in achieving is obvious. Errington was Cullen's preferred candidate from the beginning, and this accounts for the diffidence in both O'Flanagan's and Granard's letters of January 25 to Cullen, in which they felt it was necessary for Errington to be cleared by Conroy before he was adopted to replace Greville, the sitting member. Shortly before the joint meeting on February 2, which selected O'Reilly and Errington, Greville retired. He must have realized that without the support of the clergy he had no chance, and the fact that Greville refused to declare for Home Rule made it easier to replace him with Errington, who had so declared because, as Conroy had indicated in his letter to Cullen, one of Conroy's conditions was that the candidate pledge himself to "popular views." In any case, Cullen must have been much relieved at Greville's retirement, which allowed him to avoid any direct confrontation with his protégé, the bishop of Ardagh, over the representation in Longford. On February 10, therefore, O'Reilly and Errington were returned unopposed for the county. Such was not to be the case, however, in the borough of Athlone, in reference to which Conroy had thanked Cullen for befriending the sitting member, John James Ennis. Ennis was the eldest son of Sir John J. Ennis, a very wealthy Dublin merchant-banker who owned considerable property in Athlone and had represented the borough from 1857 to 1865, when he was then defeated mainly by the efforts of the bishops of Elphin and Ardagh, both of whom held ecclesiastical jurisdiction in the town. His son regained the seat in the general election of 1868, and in the interim had apparently won the confidence of Conroy, who had been appointed to Ardagh, it will be recalled, in early 1871.

Athlone, which had the reputation of being one of the most corrupt boroughs in Ireland, was usually besieged at election time by a large number of candidates. The great surprise of the contest, however, was the candidacy of Edward Sheil, who was only twenty-three years old. He was the son of General Sir Justin Sheil and a nephew of the late celebrated Irish politician, Richard Lalor Sheil. Edward Sheil had been educated at Newman's Oratory School in Birmingham and at Oxford, and, though most people did not realize it, he was Cullen's candidate. The situations in the borough and in the election were graphically described for Cullen by Gillooly the day after the polling took place. "All my Election troubles," Gillooly reported on February 6, "are now over, thank God. In Sligo Co. we put in our two old members without a contest and that course was approved of, I may say unanimously, by the Clergy of the three dioceses concerned. In Roscommon Co. our two young Catholic Members, O'Conor Don & French, were also re-elected without a contest. In both places a good deal of vigilance & management was required to prevent a contest now easily forced on Constituencies under the Ballot Act" (C). "Yesterday," he added, "was the polling day here in Athlone between Ennis and your *protegé* Mr. Sheil, who by the way is a very nice intelligent young fellow."

> Ennis & his father had been for years notoriously engaged, directly & thro Agents in corrupting the Electors by *loans* of money, which after young E's election were to be instantly converted into gifts. Over a hundred Electors were universally believed to be bound in this way to support him and many others were held in subjection as his tenants for Town Plots, of which he owns a good number on the Leinster side of the Town. For over 20 years this horrible machinery of corruption has been systematically employed by him and for no election so extensively as for the present. The Town was utterly demoralised by it.

"I was happy to have," Gillooly admitted, "a young honest clean handed Catholic in the person of Mr. Sheil to oppose this rotten Ennis clique—and accordingly he was taken up by our priests & people on the Connaught side [of the Shannon River]."

"On Wednesday," Gillooly then explained, referring to February 4, "in compliance with a requisition of Electors I presided at a Public Meeting, and urged the people to support Sheil and put down the corrupt practices that had so long disgraced the Borough." "The Clergy on the Ardagh side of the Shannon," he assured Cullen, "were all through of one mind with ours and took part in our Meeting—but owing to Telegrams received from Dr. Conroy, in which he declared himself favorable to Ennis, they gave no active opposition to that gentleman." "In my address," he further reported, and Cullen must have winced, "I expressed my Conviction that if Dr. Conroy was at home and knew of the criminal demoralising agencies employed for Ennis, that his views & wishes w^d be found perfectly in accordance with mine." "His Telegrams," Gillooly added, "created much surprise & dissatisfaction amongst honest people in both dioceses. I did what I could, and I hope successfully to remove those unfavorable impressions. I hope he will do the needful himself in this matter on his return. We sh^d remove, if possible, even the suspicion of approving or seconding bribery." "The result of yesterday's Election," he pointed out finally, "was, thank God, a triumph for the honest section of the Electors." "Sheil got 162 Catholic votes. Ennis had only 151 supporters, amongst whom were believed 40 & 50 Protestants. Of the Voting Papers put into the Ballot Box the Sheriff disallowed 33—of which 22 were for Sheil—and in this way the number of allowed votes was made 140 for each Candidate. Mr. Sheil's conducting agent has no doubt but the Sheriff decided illegally against Sheil in sixteen cases—and that he must be declared the elected Member." "Even in the event," Gillooly assured Cullen in concluding, "of another Election or of an Election Petition Sheil is, I think & hope, sure to be successful."

As things turned out, Gillooly proved to be a true prophet, for on a petition to amend the poll decided the following April, Sheil was declared elected by 153 votes to 148 for Ennis.[1] In the meantime, Cullen could not have looked forward with much pleasure to Conroy's return to Ireland. Indeed, when Conroy returned, he was apparently very annoyed at what had happened in Athlone, for Gillooly felt constrained to write Cullen about the situation. "I am privately informed from Athlone," Gillooly explained in a passage dated May 16 and marked "private & confidential," "that Dr. Conroy has severely reprimanded & proposes removing from Athlone, the Curate who was there during the late Election—for the course he adopted with reference to Mr. Ennis's Candidature—a course which I lately explained to your Eminence and which was in my judgement, both upright & prudent" (C). "Dr. Conroy," Gillooly pointed out, "ought to feel grateful to this young priest, and to me also for having saved him from the public censure which his Telegrams were so much calculated to bring upon him." "I shd regret deeply," he added, "for Dr. C's own sake as well as in the religious interests of our people on both sides of the Shannon, that the corruption so systematically & shamelessly practiced for Ennis, shd appear to be approved & upheld by his bishop—and such wd surely be the conclusion every one would draw from the punishment of the Rev. Mr. O'Flynn." "Your Eminence," Gillooly concluded, squarely placing the responsibility, "may be able to prevent this evil." It does not appear from the evidence available that Cullen interfered any further, and this is circumstantially confirmed by the fact that the young curate, Michael Flynn, was removed by Conroy to the parish of Kiltoghert, constituted by the town of Carrick-on-Shannon. In fairness to Conroy, and perhaps to Cullen, it must be also pointed out that Kiltoghert was one of the better parishes in the diocese of Ardagh and that, if Conroy had been so inclined, he certainly could have found a more remote and less attractive curacy for Flynn.

At the same time that Cullen was attempting to promote the interests of Errington and Sheil in Longford and Athlone, he also was actively pursuing the interests of at least three other candidates outside his own ecclesiastical jurisdiction. The three candidates were Frank Hugh O'Donnell in the borough of Galway, Chichester S. Fortescue, the former senior member for county Louth in the late Parliament, and Peter Paul MacSwiney, the former lord mayor of Dublin for county Meath. Not only were all these political candidacies interesting in themselves, but they also were significant for what they revealed about the limits of Cullen's

---

1. Brian M. Walker, ed., *Parliamentary Election Results in Ireland, 1801-1922* (Dublin, 1978), p. 115.

influence and, by extension, the influence of his brother bishops in political matters. One of the more interesting candidates and candidacies on the basis of this criteria was that of O'Donnell in Galway. At first glance, O'Donnell's credentials were hardly those that would recommend him to Cullen. He was an impecunious, if clever, young journalist of twenty-six, who was a native of Galway City and a graduate of the Queen's College there. While learning his trade at London's *Morning Post,* O'Donnell made the acquaintance and won the confidence of Archbishop Manning, through his very able and partisan attacks on Bismarck and his *Kulturkampf* in Germany. Apparently, Manning had introduced him to Woodlock in London in early 1873 and had recommended him to Cullen as a bright young Catholic worthy of being patronized. When Gladstone announced his dissolution, therefore, O'Donnell immediately telegraphed Woodlock that he was prepared to offer himself to any Irish constituency that might stand in need of his services. "I wrote to-day," Woodlock informed Cullen on January 27, enclosing O'Donnell's telegram, "to Dr. MacEvilly [Galway], Dr. Ryan of Killaloe, and Dr. Power of Waterford, who is at present in Clonmel, about Mr. O'Donnell" (C).

None of the bishops approached by Woodlock and Cullen, however, were able to adopt O'Donnell as a candidate either because of prior commitments or because of existing political exigencies. "I was most anxious," the bishop of Galway assured Cullen on January 30, "and so are all of the Priests (who are acting as one) for Mr. F. O'Donnell. But we find it utterly impossible to carry him thro this time as we had no preparation, and his own relatives here are not favorable to him" (C). "But he would be," MacEvilly admitted, "invaluable in Parliament on the Education Question. The one about I for my part feel chiefly concerned." "If I had the power," he assured Cullen again, "I would be most anxious to see him Member for Galway, as no other could so well expose the Queen's University. But he is not a Prophet in his own country." In the course of this letter, MacEvilly also attempted to explain what had happened in the borough to make O'Donnell's endorsement by him and his clergy impossible. The sitting members for the borough were Sir Rowland Blennerhassett and Viscount St. Lawrence, the eldest son of the earl of Howth. Blennerhassett, it will be recalled, was one of the four Catholics who had voted for the second reading of Gladstone's University bill, and, as a consequence, MacEvilly and his clergy were determined to exclude him from the representation of the borough. St. Lawrence, who had voted against the second reading, was acceptable to the clergy because he was a supporter of denominational education. He was also willing to meet the requirements of the popular party in the borough by making a vague declaration in favor of Home Rule.

Unfortunately, however, the former member for the borough, George Morris, who had run afoul of MacEvilly and his clergy in the general election of 1868 because of his Conservative voting propensities in the House of Commons and his refusal to give an explicit pledge to support Gladstone and the Liberal alliance, had decided to contest the borough and had declared in favor of Home Rule. Morris also labored under the political burden of having to explain the recent conduct of his brother, Michael Morris, who as one of the judges in the Court of Queens' Bench, had not proven very friendly to Cullen's interests in the celebrated lawsuit taken against him by Robert O'Keeffe, the parish priest of Callan. "Thinking that George Morris," MacEvilly explained to Cullen in his letter of January 27, "would carry out the feelings and principles of his Brother, the Judge, the clergy, upon whom the matter [i.e., the election] had come quite unexpectedly, were anxiously looking about for some person of position & character to replace the Dollingerite Blennerhassett who voted for the 2^d reading of the University bill & to oppose George Morris, who had been for some time canvassing hard & had made full preparations for a struggle" (C). "In fact," he confessed, "we never heeded it, as we knew the people would sustain us, if we got a proper man, and we made no doubt, there were plenty to be had when time would come round, which was thought to be remote. When the time came, there was not one to be had whom we could carry through (and we would not risk a defeat with one whom the people would not join in adopting)." "George Morris," MacEvilly then reported, "came forward yesterday, and declared in favor of religious Education &c., the defence of the Pope, and being asked about O'Keeffe's case & the conduct of his brother the Judge, he then solemnly declared, that the only time in his life he had a difference with his brother was about the favor shown by the latter to O'Keeffe."

> That as a Catholic he detested O'Keeffe's conduct, and that as a proof of his sincerity he pledged himself if Bouverie's motion [to set up a parliamentary committee to inquire into the case] came on, he would vote against him. The people who attended the meeting, many of them with the view of thwarting him, came off perfectly satisfied. Many of them who were all thru opposed to the Morrises and had a horror of Judge Morris for the part he had taken in favor of O'Keeffe & his supposed opposition to your Eminence, begged of me not to interfere. Seeing we had no better man with whom we could succeed, I thought it better to advise the clergy—as they could not help it—to a course of abstention as regards George Morris.

"Lord St. Lawrence," MacEvilly noted in concluding, "whom all are anxious to return, has not made his appearance, and great fears are entertained that Blennerhassett, or Francis Nolan, a very headless young Barrister, brother of Capt. Nolan, may get in."

MacEvilly was telling Cullen, of course, that Morris could not be beaten, that if O'Donnell contested the seat, his votes would take away from those of St. Lawrence, and that the final result, if Blennerhassett or Nolan persisted, would be the victory of one of the latter. Explaining all of this to Cullen again two days later, February 1, MacEvilly reported, "Lord St. Lawrence who is here, and promised me this day to oppose O'Keeffe—he had he says already promised the same to the Marquis of Kildare—will likely be returned" (C). "Mr. F. O'Donnell's friends," MacEvilly added, "are going to the Poll, or at least will have him nominated. I think their view is, should they withdraw him before the poll is taken, to get promises from Lord St. Lawrence in his favor at the next Election." "Lord St. Lawrence," he further explained, "told me today it is likely owing to his father's state of health, he may not continue very long M.P. for Galway. It would be a great triumph for the cause of Catholic Education, if we could return O'Donnell, which I think not very unlikely may happen before long." "The only question," he reassured Cullen finally, "I feel any deep interest in is the Education Question w^h is the question of questions."

In spite of the clergy's efforts to dissuade him from going to the poll, O'Donnell insisted on a contest, and on election day, February 4, he was defeated, polling only 409 votes to Morris's 761 and St. Lawrence's 604.[2] On that same day, however, St. Lawrence's father died, making a by-election necessary, and O'Donnell immediately declared his candidacy. The local Catholic gentry then decided not to let the by-election go by default and entered a candidate of their own, a scion of one of the more notable Galway families, Pierce Joyce. "O'Donnell is now canvassing," MacEvilly reported to Cullen on February 11, "& the Priests have to almost a man joined in supporting him. I regard his return as morally certain, tho' wonderful efforts are made by Protestants, Queen's College people, & worse than all, aristocratic Catholics, who feel humbled that one from the ranks of the people should represent Galway" (C). "O'Donnell," he further explained to Cullen, "had no chance whatever on the late occasion, owing to influences & considerations unsuited to him & hence the Priests dissuaded him from going to the Poll." "I myself, as cautiously as I could," MacEvilly confided, alluding to Judge Keogh's insistence that he not interfere in election matters for seven years, "made terms with Lord St. Lawrence, to give O'Donnell *all* his influence at the Election, which Lord St. Lawrence, even if his father lived, told me he was determined to bring on, & I told this to O'Donnell & his friends. Still, they should go on, & be beaten." "But if O'Donnell and his friends," MacEvilly then added, "took our advice, he would now have a walkover. However, although I am silenced by Keogh I make no doubt O'Donnell will succeed, or rather the Catholic University *versus* the Queen's Colleges, altho, I must regard it as a very dangerous game to send so young & penniless a man to Parliament."

As MacEvilly predicted, O'Donnell won the by-election handily. On election day, March 20, he received 579 votes to Joyce's 358.[3] The triumph, however, was not without some further misgivings on the part of both MacEvilly and his clergy.

2. Ibid., p. 117.
3. Ibid., p. 120.

"Our triumph here," MacEvilly reported to Cullen on March 24, "was certainly a great triumph for the Clergy & Catholic Education."

> In fact, O'Donnell was altogether lost sight of in the whole affair. Every Prot-estant without exception was arrayed against us. They & the Queen's college people gave Joyce a start of nearly 200 votes. Then Lord Clanricarde who has a large tenantry in the neighbourhood did his very best [against us], tho' Lord Howth promised me he would not interfere. They called in votes from the most distant quarters, the gentry to a man opposed us. Some, because they did not wish to see one not belonging to the upper ten thousand represent them. Others, because they wished to have *Religion* banished from the County at large [and to prevent it from] getting a footing in the borough, & their idea is that the clergy should retire to the Sacristy & strive to say their prayers (C).

"Glad the clergy would be," MacEvilly assured Cullen, "to so promise if they could. But if they did it would be worse for the Landlords, religion & society in this country."

"I hope O'Donnell," MacEvilly further explained, "may not disappoint us, tho' the clergy are not satisfied on the subject. Had the conduct of himself & his backers, all healthy strong young men, been known, the clergy would have re-tired." "The V.G.," he reported, referring to Peter Dooly, the parish priest of St. Nicholas, "found them on a Friday, eating *meat & fish* at the Hotel, and the servants & all connected with the Hotel scandalised by them. I told the clergy they must let it pass. But they felt indignant that men who were returned on high Catholic principles, should act so unprincipled a part." "They [were] going to have Illuminations, fire works &c.," MacEvilly added, "but I told them if they were unnecessarily to interfere with the season of Lent, I would be obliged to denounce them. So they gave up the illuminations. I told Mr. O'Donnell yesterday that his great forte was the Education Question, the only one the clergy felt a deep interest in—& that if he did not make that question his *Specialty,* it would be all over with him. I make no doubt he will, and no one else can do godless Education more harm." "What I stated above," MacEvilly confided in conclusion, "is meant for your *Eminence only,* as it is right you should know the real state of things." Hardly was the election over, however, when Joyce entered a petition on the grounds of clerical intimidation, which eventuated in O'Donnell's unseating and the necessity of another by-election. This, however, anticipates the story of the aftermath of the general election.

In the meantime, Cullen fared no better in his two other efforts to provide protégés outside his ecclesiastical jurisdiction with parliamentary seats. His most signal failure, certainly, was in county Louth, where in an effort to have the former senior member, Chichester S. Fortescue, reelected, he provided the outstanding example of the real limits of episcopal power and influence that came into conflict with the determined views of the people and clergy. Fortescue had represented the county for twenty-seven years as a Liberal, and had had a most distinguished political career. In the late ministry he had served in the cabinet as chief secretary for Ireland, and in late 1870 he had been promoted to the presidency of the board of trade. He was, therefore, the most prominent supporter and representative of the Liberal party in Ireland, and for that very reason the Home Rulers were determined to defeat both him and his junior colleague, Matthew O'Reilly Dease. The Home Rule League, therefore, chose Philip Callan, the former member for the borough of Dundalk in county Louth, and A. M. Sullivan, the editor and publisher of the nationalist weekly, the *Nation,* to contest the county. Callan, who was the leading Home Ruler in the county, decided not only to contest the county but also to stand again for the borough of Dundalk. He had launched his campaign for the county in the central parishes of Louth on Sunday, January 25. The next day, at a meeting of the Louth Independent Club in Dundalk, he and A. M. Sullivan were nominated as the candidates for the county by Patrick McCullough, the parish priest of Darver, with four other parish priests and four curates, as well as a large body of laity in attendance.4 At a meeting the following day, Tuesday, January 27, in Drogheda, the chief town in southern Louth, the clergy of the deanery of Drogheda, presided over by the archdeacon of Armagh, Anthony Gossan, vicar general and parish priest of St. Peter's, Drogheda, the following resolution was adopted. "That we the clergy pledge ourselves to support no candidate at the coming election for the county who will not adopt the programme laid down by the County Louth Independent Club, *i.e.* Home Rule, denominational education, the extension of the Ulster tenant-right to the rest of Ireland, and the release of the political prisoners; and also to aid in securing the independence of the Holy Father."5

When Cullen read the resolution, he undoubtedly understood that if the clergy persisted in their pledge it would mean the exclusion of Fortescue, and he wrote the archbishop of Armagh, Daniel McGettigan, within whose ecclesiastical jurisdiction the county Louth fell. "My best wishes," McGettigan assured Cullen on January 30, from Armagh, "are for Mr. Fortescue's return, for he is the best and greatest man sent from Ireland. I think he is sure of success. The Papers are misleading the public" (C). "The influential Priests," he maintained surprisingly (especially surprising after the Drogheda resolution), "are for him, and the sound portion of the people also are warm supporters. It is very probable that Mr. Callan will not be returned for Dundalk. The move in putting him forward for Louth & Dundalk is made with the view of having a place for Mr. Butt if rejected for Limerick. The poor man [Callan] is burning the candle at both ends, if he have

4. *Freeman's Journal,* January 27, 1874. For a more complete report see ibid., January 29, 1874.
5. Ibid., January 28, 1874.

a candle to burn." "In the meeting held at Dundalk," McGettigan reported, "there was not a half a dozen of voters. It was a miserable miscarriage. If four go to the Poll, the only fear is that a Conservative may go in. As yet there is none named, but they are surely looking for an open. In any case I have every reason to believe that Mr. Fortescue will win. If I can do anything to secure this happy result, I will consider it a duty to cooperate." "I intend going to Dundalk on Monday [February 2]," he concluded, "and remaining there until the excitement is over."

In the meantime, the late postmaster general, William Monsell, who in December had been recommended by Gladstone for a peerage as Baron Emly of Tervoe, also interested himself on behalf of his former colleague. Emly wrote Patrick J. Keenan, a commissioner of Irish education, who was a native of Louth and well connected there, in Fortescue's favor. "The Primate *will* write," Keenan promised Emly on February 2, referring to a letter McGettigan was to write for public consumption, "and this day too. *THE letter* of course Mr. F. should get it posted on every gate & wall in the county."[6] "I had a long letter," Keenan further reported, "from his Grace to-day. He arrives to-day in Dundalk as I suggested to do duty as sentinel and watch pending the contest. He says that even in Dundalk Callan is sure to be defeated, a certain forerunner of defeat in the county. Fiat [Let it be done], he adds, and a second time, Fiat." "From Mr. F. himself," Keenan explained, "I had a gloomy note this morning. He said that everything would depend on the *known* & active exertion of the Primate." "The Cardinal & Dr. Manning," he confided, "have been writing to Dr. McGettigan strongly in Mr. F.'s interest. But the less known of this support, it would appear, the better." "Ten to one on Fortescue and the same on Russell [Callan's Liberal opponent in Dundalk] may be fairly laid," Keenan then assured Emly.

McGettigan had initiated his public letter in support of Fortescue somewhat circuitously by writing, of all people, Archdeacon Gossan to elicit a letter from him in order that he could reply. "No one," McGettigan maintained in his letter to Gossan on February 4, "can look with a careless eye on the coming contest for the County of Louth."[7] "There are four candidates," he pointed out, "and only two places. The late members seek re-election; two freshmen are in the field to displace them. There are many parts of Ireland which have been worse represented in Parliament than Louth. One of her late representatives have served Louth for upwards of twenty-six years with a fidelity, ability, and success without a parallel in this country. During that long period he made many promises and gave many pledges and never broke one of them." "My dear Archdeacon," McGettigan then added, "I know you are grateful, and the same is true of most of our priests and people. They and you have unbounded confidence in Mr. Fortescue. Depend on

6. M, 8317 (14).
7. *Freeman's Journal*, February 6, 1874.

the man with a good heart, a clear head, and a love of fair play. The man is sure to advance. Progress is the law he loves and must obey." "There is a passage in Mr. Fortescue's address," he noted, "on a subject that is dear to our hearts, namely, the Education Question. He says: —'I am still convinced, as I have long been, that Irish Questions, such as the vital Question of Education, ought to be dealt with in accordance with the circumstances and feelings of Ireland.' No one knows better than Mr. Fortescue the circumstances and feeling of this country; he promises his powerful aid to carry measures that will meet them; and he is sure to fulfill his word." "Will you kindly," he advised Gossan in conclusion, saving his worst for last, "take the earliest opportunity to meet the good priests of your district, and in concert with them and the faithful people of Louth devise a way of averting this painful contest?"

By the time McGettigan's eulogy of Fortescue appeared in the *Freeman's Journal* on February 6, the election in Dundalk had taken place (the day before), and Callan had defeated Charles Russell, the Liberal candidate by 257 votes to 225, in spite of the facts that Dundalk was the archbishop's mensal parish and the archbishop had persuaded the four priests in that parish to canvass on behalf of Russell.[8] To make matters worse, that same day, February 5, the Home Rule candidate, Dr. William H. O'Leary, with clerical support had defeated by 284 votes to 274, the Liberal, Benjamin Whitworth, a very popular and prominent local Protestant manufacturer, in Drogheda, the other electoral borough in county Louth.[9] It should be pointed out, however, that Whitworth had given his political opponents in the borough a deadly advantage when he had voted for the second reading of Gladstone's University bill the year before. Having thus lost the two borough seats within his ecclesiastical jurisdiction, McGettigan, in order to prevent a complete rout, called his clergy together in Dundalk on February 9 and exhorted them to support Fortescue for the county. "It would appear," the special correspondent of the *Freeman's Journal* politely reported from Dundalk on that same day, "that, after considerable conversation, the clergy came to the decision to adhere to the resolutions passed at Drogheda some few weeks since—that only candidates in favour of Home Rule were worthy of their support."[10] "This decision," the special correspondent added, "it is anticipated, will be very prejudicial to Mr. Fortescue's prospects of success, as he cannot give any pledge in favour of the Home Rule programme." Fortescue had quickly and correctly read the political signs, and, a few days before the poll was to take place, he wrote to Gladstone explaining that he expected to be defeated and asking that, in view of his past services and those he might yet be able to render, he be raised to the peerage.

8. Walker, p. 116.
9. Ibid.
10. *Freeman's Journal*, February 10, 1874.

Gladstone replied on February 11 that he considered Fortescue's claim for a peerage to be "indisputable."[11] On polling day, February 12, Fortescue and Dease were not just defeated; they were routed, as Sullivan and Callan received 1,250 and 1,202 votes, respectively, to their 608 and 205.[12]

The political humiliation of McGettigan and, by extension, of Manning and Cullen was very considerable. Rejection by the Catholic voters of Louth was one thing, but repudiation by your own clergy, almost to a man, was quite another. This political revolt of the Louth clergy against their own bishop was a very rare phenomenon in the Irish Church. In fact, there had been no other revolt of such proportions since O'Connell had first brought the priests into politics in the 1820s, and the reasons for the revolt were both complicated and peculiar to the archdiocese of Armagh. First, though perhaps not foremost, the reasons had to do with the character and personality of McGettigan, who was a good and gentle man without a mean or vindictive bone in his body. In fact, he found it very difficult to take decided and effective action against anybody or for anything, especially if it did not involve a religious principle. His clergy, therefore, realizing that in the last analysis there was no real price to be paid for thwarting him in political matters, did not fear him. In any case, even if McGettigan had been inclined to take sanctions, the scale of the revolt among his clergy would have precluded them, and that magnitude raises the question of the historical and cultural dimensions of the phenomenon. The archdiocese of Armagh by 1874 had been divided for more than a hundred years between the northerners, clergy who resided in the county Armagh and parts of the counties of Tyrone and Derry, and the southerners, who resided in county Louth. In effect, the northerners were Ulstermen and the southerners Leinstermen, with all the cultural overtones that those designations imply. This factionalism of the northerners and southerners had resulted in the appointment of archbishops to Armagh who were generally strangers to the diocese in order to keep the peace between the factions. In 1869, when McGettigan was chosen *dignissimus* on the Armagh *terna*, he was the choice of the northern clergy, who voted solidly for him though he was a Donegal man and not a native of the diocese. He was, therefore, as far as the southerners were concerned, not only the choice of the northerners but also a stranger. Indeed, McGettigan was very conscious that he was a northerner, and it is most significant that, though Dundalk was one of McGettigan's mensal parishes, he chose to reside instead in his other mensal parish, the town of Armagh, where he obviously felt much more at home.

Besides McGettigan's amiable deficiencies as a politician, lay and ecclesiastical, and the long-term historical and cultural differences that gave rise to his problems

11. John Morley, *The Life of William Ewart Gladstone* (London, 1906), 2:100.
12. Walker, p. 118.

with the Louth clergy, the very interesting problem of contrasting political styles between northerners and southerners further complicated matters. At this time the Louth clergy had acquired a reputation for political aggressiveness, which was rooted in a political consciousness that had originated in the heady agitation for Catholic Emancipation in the 1820s. The northern clergy and their bishops, on the other hand, were in 1874 only just acquiring the political consciousness which their southern brethren had developed some fifty years before under the tutelage of Daniel O'Connell. Among the eighteen members returned by the nine Ulster counties in the general election of 1868, for example, all eighteen were Conservatives. Of the eleven members returned by the ten Ulster boroughs, seven were Conservatives and four were Liberals; in ensuing by-elections the Liberals were reduced to two. When Parliament was dissolved in 1874, therefore, there were only two Liberals in a total Ulster representation of twenty-nine. All of the Ulster members, moreover, whether Liberal or Conservative, were Protestants. In the shadow of this enduring overwhelmingly Protestant and Conservative preponderance, the northern clergy had learned to keep a very low political profile, showing their faces only rarely and usually in support of a Protestant Liberal. Fear of precipitating violence through aggressive political behavior, especially in the days before the Ballot Act of 1872, when voting was open and the voters were very vulnerable to social and physical coercion, was the governing factor in the political behavior of the northern clergy. McGettigan, of course, was a product of this political ambience, having been the bishop of Raphoe, a diocese that included nearly all of county Donegal, for fourteen years before his translation to Armagh in 1870. Fortescue, who represented much of the best in the Irish Liberal Protestant tradition, therefore, was very pleasing in 1874 to those who, like McGettigan, found the political aggressiveness of the Louth clergy foreign and even dangerous in the light of their own political experience. Still, what must be emphasized is that the Louth electoral experience and the 1874 breakdown in the relationship between the clergy and their bishop were aberrational in Ireland, and they were the results of a very special set of circumstances, unique to the archdiocese of Armagh. What was most significant about the Louth elections, however, was that they portended for the future that the clergy would go with their people, in spite of the injunctions of their bishop. In the next decade in Ireland, the clergy and their bishops would take up the same position in regard to the injunctions of the pope in political and agrarian matters.

If the triumph of the Home Rulers in Louth dealt a sore blow to Cullen and McGettigan, the rebuff of Cullen's candidate by the bishop and clergy of county Meath, must have been even more painful to Cullen. In comparison to Louth, Meath had been the most consistently radical constituency in political and agrarian matters since the days of Catholic Emancipation. For some fifty years, the Meath bishops and their clergy had been in the vanguard of movements to create an independent Irish party in the House of Commons and to achieve fixity of tenure at a fair rent for the tenant-farming class. Thus, when Cullen's long-time, politically conservative factotum in local Dublin politics, Alderman Peter Paul MacSwiney, offered himself with Cullen's approval as a candidate for county Meath, the bishop and his clergy faced the challenge of deciding how to reject MacSwiney without further offending Cullen. As had been usual in Meath for more than twenty years and increasingly common in most other constituencies since 1852, the clergy of county Meath met in Navan on February 3, under the presidency of their bishop, Thomas Nulty, to interview each of the candidates for county honors. After the interviews, the clergy reviewed the relative merits and qualifications of the candidates and unanimously announced to the public whom they would support in the approaching election. The process was usually a consensual one, but if there was a marked difference of opinion, a vote was taken and the opinion of the majority was binding on the minority, hence the unanimous public declaration. The day after the meeting of the Meath clergy, on February 3, the *Freeman's Journal* reported: "The clergy of this county assembled in Navan today were, after a most patient and protracted inquiry, unanimously of the opinion that Mr. John Martin and Mr. Nicholas Ennis, of Claremont would be regarded by the vast majority of the electors as the most suitable and eligible men that would offer themselves to represent them in Parliament. Many members of the clergy, in deference to the manifest wishes of the electors, have abandoned their own personal opinion, and heartily agreed to accept the choice of the people."

The bishop of Meath, writing to Cullen the day after this meeting, provided a most interesting gloss on the report of the *Freeman's Journal*. Cullen obviously had not only written to Nulty on behalf of MacSwiney, but he also had complained of the absence of the former junior member for Meath, John Martin, at the vote on the second reading of Gladstone's University bill. Martin, it will be recalled, refused on principle to vote on any issue in the House of Commons except that of Home Rule. The fact that Edward McEvoy, the senior member for Meath, who had represented the county for nearly twenty years, had decided to retire because he could not in good conscience subscribe to the Home Rule pledge required by the clergy and electorate made it even more difficult to reject Mac-Swiney on the grounds of there being no room. In any case, the bishop of Meath and his clergy demonstrated considerable political finesse in dealing with this very delicate matter. "I held a meeting of the Clergy of the Co. here on yesterday," Nulty informed Cullen from Navan on February 4, "They *unanimously* refused to accept Martin except on the *distinct pledge* that [he] w^d on *all occasions* support by his *vote* as well as by his voice the Cause of Catholic Education. After hearing the statement, he made—and certainly it had at least the *appearance* of sincerity and earnestness stamped on it—and taking the Education pledge they all *unanimously* voted to support him. *One* Priest hesitated for a time but he afterwards gave in his adhesion also" (C). "The other; Nicholas Ennis, is James Cullen's friend," Nulty further observed, referring to the second candidate endorsed by the clergy, and then to Cullen's uncle, who resided in Meath. "Certainly it was James that *first* suggested him. He too was elected *unanimously*." "He is," Nulty noted ironically, referring again to Ennis, "a *little* radical; but is an excellent Catholic, and is moreover a brother to a most respected P.P. of ours who died lately." "Naper of Loughcrew, Hinds the solicitor," Nulty added, referring to the Conservative candidate and a local Home Ruler, "and lastly Alderman McSweeny addressed the Meeting. All their addresses were satisfactory and even Naper *went* in substantially for Cath. Education." "The priests shewed the greatest respect for McSweeny but they w^d not be induced to adopt him chiefly because of his unpopularity with the *small* shopkeepers in the different towns whose [interests] McSweeny's Establishment has injured," he assured Cullen (the alderman owned one of the largest mercantile establishments in Dublin). Nulty then closed his very able letter by turning to the discussion of a case he and one of his parish priests were involved with in Rome. As things turned out, both Ennis and Martin were returned as Home Rulers on election day, February 7, with 1,716 and 1,709 votes, respectively, while the Conservative candidate, James L. Naper, a substantial Meath landlord, received 992 votes.[13]

It is clear that outside his own ecclesiastical jurisdiction Cullen was not remarkably successful in securing the return of his political protégés for parliamentary seats. Of his five candidates, only Errington for Longford had been returned without any difficulty, and Sheil of Athlone had had to wait to take his seat until April, when a recount of the ballots finally resolved the tie in his favor. Fortescue had been badly beaten in Louth, MacSwiney never made it to the hustings in Meath, and O'Donnell, as shall be seen, was eventually unseated in Galway. Within his own immediate ecclesiastical jurisdiction, however, Cullen fared somewhat better.

There were six parliamentary seats within the large archdiocese of Dublin, but two of those seats, in county Dublin, were outside the reach of Catholic or clerical influence. The Conservatives had, in fact, controlled the county Dublin seats for more than twenty years, and in 1874 their Protestant majority in the county of about a thousand votes precluded Catholic representation. In the city, however, the two former members were Liberals. The first, Jonathan Pim, was a Quaker merchant who had been supported by Cullen at the general election of 1868, and

13. Ibid.

the second was Sir Dominic Corrigan, a prominent Catholic physician, who, it will be recalled, had defeated a Home Rule candidate in August 1870, when the Conservative, Sir Arthur Guinness, had been unseated for bribery at the general election. Corrigan had been supported by Cullen and his clergy in 1870, but not without considerable misgivings and negotiations in regard to his views on education. By 1874, both Pim and Corrigan were no longer acceptable to Cullen because they had the year before voted for Gladstone's University bill. Cullen and his clergy were able to force Corrigan's retirement, and the Dublin Liberal organization chose Maurice Brooks, the current Liberal, Protestant lord mayor of Dublin, who had declared for Home Rule, denominational education, and amnesty. Pim refused to retire, declaring his candidacy even though the Liberal organization refused to nominate him as its second candidate and intimated that Liberals should vote only, or plump, for Brooks.[14] A second Home Rule candidate, Edward Fox, then announced that he would contest the seat.

Cullen was determined to return Brooks, defeat Pim, and exclude Fox, even if it assured the return of a Conservative. He therefore privately advised his clergy to vote only for Brooks and, implicitly, to counsel the voters in the same course. Cullen's real electoral strategy is evidenced by a brief reply to a letter of his own from the guardian of the Franciscan house at Merchant's Quay in Dublin. "Being engaged," Father James P. Hanrahan apologized on polling day, February 6, "on a short mission in the parish of Ferns, Co. Wexford, since the 20th of last January, it is only last evening on my return home, I received your Eminence's letters" (C). "Understanding, however, that it is the wish of your Eminence," he assured Cullen, "to secure, as far as possible, the Lord Mayor's election all our Brethren who have votes shall plump for Mr. Brooks." Cullen's strategy was very successful, for, when the poll was declared that day, the Conservative candidate, Sir Arthur Guinness, was returned at the head of the poll with 5,213 votes, Brooks took the second seat with 4,838, and Pim and the other Home Ruler, Fox, received only 1,937 and 515 votes respectively.[15]

The final two parliamentary seats within Cullen's immediate ecclesiastical jurisdiction were those for the county Wicklow. The former members, both of whom declared their candidacy, were W. W. F. Dick, a local Conservative landlord of some 5,000 acres, and W. H. W. Fitzwilliam, a Liberal and the second son of the Earl Fitzwilliam. The earl, who owned some 90,000 acres, was the largest landlord in the county. Fitzwilliam's election agent, Frederick Ponsonby, wrote to Richard Galvin, the politically influential parish priest of Rathdrum, on January 27, asking him for his valuable support (C). Galvin replied to Ponsonby the next day and laid down in his letter the terms that would be required for his support. "I

---

14. *Freeman's Journal,* January 31, 1874.
15. Walker, p. 116.

hope Mr. Fitzwilliam," Galvin explained on January 28, "will come out at once with a good liberal *Irish* programme on this the first great trial of the Ballot act, and that he will declare himself an advocate of the improvement of the Land Act so as to guard the Tenant against capricious eviction and exorbitant rents without encroaching on the just rights of the Landlord."

> The Tenant Class now all-powerful, without distinction of creed, unanimously insist everywhere on this point.
>
> Any shortcoming in this business on the part of Mr. Fitzwilliam will be decidedly fatal to him.
>
> To insure the catholic vote he will have to declare himself an advocate of the freedom of Conscience and of the rights of the catholic people of this Country to a Catholic education for their children and to a full participation in all of the advantages which are conferred by charter and by grant on their protestant fellow Countrymen.
>
> If he does not come up fairly to these two points my influence with the people or my support would be utterly unavailing.

"Two gentlemen," he reported, "of substance standing and position in the County have offered themselves *on these terms.*" "I will do what I can," he assured Ponsonby in conclusion, "to have *only one* of them put forward should Mr. Fitzwilliam *thus far* agree to the Programme adopted at our side of the county."

The two gentlemen referred to by Galvin were apparently D. Mahony, a local landlord of some 5,700 acres, who offered himself on purely Liberal principles, and W. R. O'Byrne, another local landlord, who owned some 2,500 acres, and an advocate of Home Rule. The most curious thing about Galvin's letter to Ponsonby, in the light of what was to come, was that it made no mention of Home Rule. In any case, Galvin forwarded a copy of this correspondence to Cullen. The Wicklow Farmers' Club and Tenants' Defence Association, which acted as the local Home Rule organization in this election, meanwhile, called for a meeting of its members in Wicklow town on Monday, February 2. At the meeting, the Farmers' Club nominated O'Byrne and Charles Archer, the secretary of the club, as the Home Rule candidates.[16] In the meantime, James Redmond, the parish priest of Arklow and the archdeacon of Glendalough, had called for a meeting of the Wicklow clergy for Tuesday, February 3, the day after the Farmers' Club meeting, in Rathdrum. Cullen apparently had advised the archdeacon that Fitzwilliam and O'Byrne should be adopted at the clerical meeting, and Redmond, who could not attend the meeting because he was ill, telegraphed Cullen's preferences. Before he learned what had happened at the clerical meeting, Redmond reported to Cullen that the Home Rulers were insisting on both of their candidates to the exclusion of Fitzwilliam. "The curse of division," the archdeacon wrote to Cullen from Arklow

---

16. *Freeman's Journal,* February 3, 1874.

on February 3, "is upon us. There was great excitement last night. Shouting for Archer the Amnesty Chairman & O'Byrne, the Home Rulers, & groans for Fitzwilliam whose Family supported civil & religious liberty in this County to my own Knowledge these Forty years in opposition to the Orangemen & never coalesced with one of them, the liberal party bringing them in by their dissensions" (C). "I fear we will never do any good," Redmond added sadly. "I will declare here to the Electors that I will vote for O'Byrne & Fitzwilliam & let each Elector vote according to his judgement & conscience." "The Enniscorthy men," he further reported, referring to the electors for county Wexford, "say they will vote for whom they please, in spite of Priest or Bishop. The Home Rule movement is producing the fruit I expected from it."

The same day, February 3, matters were further complicated when John Howard Parnell also announced his candidacy. Parnell was really running at the behest of his brother, Charles Stewart Parnell, who would have been the candidate himself except that he had been appointed high sheriff for county Wicklow for the year and was precluded by that office from standing for Parliament. John Howard's very able election address was written by his brother. It included declarations for Home Rule, which was the new name for Repeal, fixity of tenure, denominational education, and amnesty.[17] At the clerical meeting in Rathdrum also on the same day, the clergy decided, in spite of Cullen's advice, to support O'Byrne and Parnell, and on February 4, Archer retired from the contest.[18] "Amidst the wretched divisions of the Liberal party," Redmond reported dolefully to Cullen, "I strongly apprehend Orange Dick will slip in. I find a deep & widespread repugnance to Fitzwilliam & why I cannot tell unless that he has not raised the Cuckoo Cry of Home Rule" (C). "I promised to support," he then reassured Cullen, "O'Byrne & Fitzwilliam & now Parnell is taken up & I am urged to reject Fitzwilliam, but I will not break my word for any set of men. The Electors are to meet me tomorrow at 11 o'clock & I am determined to tell them that I will support O'Byrne & Fitzwilliam & will let them follow my example or please themselves."

After the decision made at the clerical meeting in Rathdrum, Galvin and his colleagues campaigned vigorously on behalf of Parnell, and on Friday morning, February 6, the day before the polling was to take place, Galvin wrote Cullen a hurried note in which he attempted to explain why he and his fellow priests had adopted Parnell. "The leading Clergy," he reported, "from this side of the County, several from the Fitzw^m strongholds, have sent in their adhesion to O'Byrne & *Parnell,* the most independent of the lot, everything to the contrary notwithstanding" (C). "We cannot," Galvin maintained, "stultify ourselves with our people. The R.C. voters are 2 to 1, and are certain to carry the day, no doubt of it had

17. Ibid.
18. Ibid., February 6, 1874. See Archer's letter of February 4, 1874.

there been no pressure to the contrary from Headquarters." The headquarters Galvin was alluding to, of course, was Cullen's residence in Dublin, which also housed the vicariate that administered the diocese. He was, therefore, telling Cullen that his decision to support Fitzwilliam was a mistake and that Parnell could have been carried if the advice from Dublin had not divided the Wicklow clergy. In any case, when the poll was declared the next day, February 7, the premonitions of both Redmond and Galvin were verified. O'Byrne who had the advantage of being the Home Rule candidate, and who was apparently the recipient of the second vote of the Fitzwilliam tenants and supporters, headed the poll with 1,511 votes.[19] The Conservative candidate, Dick, secured the second seat with 1,141 votes, and Fitzwilliam and Parnell spoiled each other's chances with 927 and 553 votes, respectively. Dick was returned, of course, because the Protestants in Wicklow, of which there were many, voted only for him, declining to cast their second votes. The lesson of the Wicklow election must have been sobering for Cullen; it revealed that not even he could command the complete political obedience of his clergy if they really felt that such a view would jeopardize their influence on the people.

Just as it was in the areas outside his ecclesiastical jurisdiction, then, Cullen's electoral influence within his immediate jurisdiction was limited. In Dublin City for example, he had been able to keep Pim out but had had to accept Brooks, the Home Ruler, because it was no longer possible to return a mere Liberal. This became most clear in county Wicklow, where Cullen was unable to secure the return of Fitzwilliam, the declared Liberal, in the face of the determination of a large part of the electorate for a Home Ruler, and the result there, as it had been in Dublin, was the return of a Conservative for one of the seats. Nevertheless, because the elections extended over some two and a half weeks and the polling in the various constituencies was staggered, a number of successes were mixed in with Cullen's disappointments, especially in those areas where he had some influence with his suffragan bishops. Shortly after the dissolution, Cullen had written his suffragan, the bishop of Kildare and Leighlin, about the candidates whose return he was most interested in securing, namely, W. H. F. Cogan, the Catholic and Liberal incumbent for county Kildare, and the protégé he had supported two years before for the by-election in county Monaghan, Henry Owen Lewis. "I am justly very anxious for Mr. Cogan's return," James Walshe assured Cullen in his reply on February 1, "I think the clergy generally at least know that. However I have written today a circular to one *parish* priest, in the County Kildare." "We have had Thank God a quiet Election here," he added, "Mr. Lewis was returned without opposition." "There is a small section," Walshe explained, referring to Orange Conservatives and radical Home Rulers, "of *both* trite parties here *always*

19. Walker, p. 119.

anxious for a *contest*. A Conservative gentleman of some property resident here & very popular was persuaded to become a candidate for the Borough. I happen to be well acquainted with him; I remonstrated with him and asked him to retire which he did and left us a calm return." "No new Conservatives appeared," he concluded, "and I do believe that the upper section of the Conservative party did not advise a contest in the Borough." What was interesting about Lewis's return for Carlow borough was that even he, with all his episcopal patronage, was obliged to declare for Home Rule. What Walshe was referring to by the upper section, as distinguished from the Orange section, of the Conservative party was that two Conservatives were about to be returned unopposed for the county Carlow, and they were not interested in precipitating an election in the county by challenging the Catholics in the borough.

In any case, Cullen not only had his protégé returned for the borough of Carlow, but also he had the satisfaction of seeing Cogan finally returned on February 12, for county Kildare. In spite of his episcopal support, however, Cogan did not have an easy passage. A landlord of some 4,000 acres, Cogan had been returned unopposed in 1868 in company with Lord Otho Fitzgerald, the third son of the duke of Leinster. The duke owned some 73,000 acres in Kildare. Both Cogan and Fitzgerald were avowed Liberals and refused to declare for Home Rule. On the Sunday, February 1, that the bishop of Kildare and Leighlin was writing to Cullen, the parish priest of Kildare, John Nolan, was holding a large meeting, attended by many people of influence, after mass, on his chapel grounds, to forward the candidacy of Charles H. Meldon, a thirty-three-year-old barrister from Dublin and the son of a substantial Catholic landlord in Galway, who had adopted Home Rule and the popular program. After chairing the meeting, in a long speech introducing Meldon, Nolan explained that he was saving himself for the formal selection of candidates that was to take place the following day in Newbridge. Nolan then ominously concluded his remarks by noting that at the Newbridge meeting he felt it would be his duty "to knock off [*sic*] at least two or three inches of dust off Mr. Cogan (cheers)."[20]

At Newbridge the following day, February 2, Nolan was as good as his word. Upon taking the chair, he was received with great enthusiasm, and he opened the meeting with a lengthy denunciation of the former member. "He asked those present," the *Freeman's* reporter informed his readers, "if they were satisfied with their present members (loud cries of 'No, no')? If they were, he wished them luck of their bargain, but he would not have them (cheers)."[21] "As Catholics, they would ask him," Nolan continued, turning to Cogan, "was he in favour of the

20. *Freeman's Journal,* February 2, 1874.
21. Ibid., February 3, 1874.

Catholic member for the county (loud cries of 'no, no,' and 'yes, yes,' from some on the platform). If they were, he was not (cheers)."

> He then complained that Mr. Cogan had joined the ranks of the aristocracy; that he walked out of the house when the Coercion Bill was introduced; that he had not vindicated the priests from the vile slanders heaped upon them by Judge Keogh, whom the speaker described amid groans as Cromwell the Second; that he would not come forward when the Leinster Leases were being discussed; and that he had been misrepresenting the finest county in Ireland for twenty-two years. He then stated there was a candidate to come before them who would worthily represent them and the cause of Home Rule—Mr. Charles Meldon, barrister-at-law, whom he (the chairman) well knew who was a Catholic, and who was prepared to advocate the national programme as defined at the Dublin Conference, and also Religious Education, Fixity of Tenure, and the release of the political prisoners.

"This announcement," the *Freeman's* reporter explained, "was received with great cheering, and Mr. Cogan was loudly groaned."

Cogan then came forward and attempted to address the meeting. "I wish for a hearing," he explained, "Will I get it? (Loud cries of 'no, no,' and 'yes,' from some on the platform)." "Will you hear Mr. Cogan?" the chairman asked, and was greeted with cries of "No, no." After further uproar, the chairman finally secured Cogan a hearing by asking that he be listened to in his public capacity. Cogan no sooner addressed a few words to the meeting than the shouts and noise became so great that he could not be heard, and he addressed the remainder of his remarks to the reporters present. While he was thus explaining himself, he was again interrupted, by Patrick Ryan, a curate in the parish of Naas, who asked him, "Are you prepared to support Home Rule, as defined by the Dublin Conference?"

> Mr. Cogan—I am prepared to discuss it.
> Rev. Mr. Ryan—It is too late to discuss that now.
> Mr. Cogan—I require to be heard before I can give an explicit answer.
> A Voice—This is not the time for a qualified answer.
> Another Voice—Sever yourself from the Whig party and become a leader of the people; support Home Rule, and we will forget the past.
> Rev. Mr. Ryan—Answer yes or no. Will you vote for Home Rule?
> Mr. Cogan—If you allow me to proceed, I will explain my views on the question.
> Rev. Mr. Ryan—Say yes or no.
> Mr. Cogan—Allow me—
> Rev. Mr. Ryan (addressing the meeting)—Mr. Cogan refuses to answer the question (groans).
> Mr. Cogan—Is this fair? (Cries of 'yes, yes.') I refuse to pledge myself to any programme without explaining my views on the whole matter (groans, during which Mr. Cogan retired, and shortly afterwards left the platform).

Several Home Rule candidates then addressed the meeting, among whom were Charles Meldon, who had been Nolan's nominee from the outset, and Captain H. F. Morgan, an English Protestant, after which a resolution was passed pledging those present to support Meldon as the Home Rule candidate. In the intervening ten days before the election, Lord Otho and Cogan canvassed assiduously but avoided public meetings. Fathers Nolan and Ryan appeared to be the exceptions, as far as Cogan was concerned, since the clergy around Monastereven, for example, were reported to be for him.[22] Lord Otho, moreover, suffered from the fatal disability of having voted for Gladstone's University bill the previous year. On election day, therefore, Meldon topped the poll with 1,296 votes, Cogan was returned as the second member with 964 votes, and Lord Otho and Captain Morgan received 772 and 226 votes, respectively.[23] In this election, Cogan was distinguished by the fact that he was one of the very few Catholic Liberals (only three in fact) outside of Ulster to be returned.

Another of Cullen's suffragans, the bishop of Ossory, Patrick F. Moran, also wrote to Cullen shortly after the dissolution, explaining that their good mutual friend, Sir John Gray, the owner and editor of the *Freeman's Journal,* might be in great danger in the borough of Kilkenny. "I am told that some people are asking Michael Sullivan to stand for the city against Sir John Gray," Moran informed Cullen on January 26, referring to the popular former member, who served for Kilkenny City from 1847 to 1865. "If he does so, Sir John Gray will have a bad chance of being returned" (C). "The friends of the Smithwicks," he explained further, referring to an influential local Catholic brewing family, "who are very numerous in the town have little sympathy with Sir John, on account of his dealings with the National Bank, of which the Smithwicks are the great patrons here; & also on account of the way the Freeman has treated Mr. Bryan [the junior member for county Kilkenny] in its Parliamentary Reports." "There is no stir as yet about the county," Moran further reported, "as our Members & aspirants are all away, but it is expected that there will be half-a-dozen candidates in the field. If a good man can be got to stand together with Mr. Bryan they will probably be returned without opposition." "A good man," of course, was Moran's euphemism for a Catholic. The senior member for county Kilkenny was L. G. F. Agar Ellis, heir presumptive to some 50,000 acres, (35,000 of which were in county Kilkenny), a Liberal, and a Protestant, who had sat for the county for some seventeen years. A Catholic candidate was found in Patrick L. Martin, a forty-three-year-old Dublin barrister whose connections to Kilkenny appear to have been mainly through marriage. Both Bryan and Martin declared for Home Rule, but they were joined on the hustings by another Home Ruler and prominent local Tenant

22. Ibid., February 5, 1874.
23. Walker, p. 117.

Righter, E. P. Mulhallen Marum. "Mr. Martin," Moran reported to Cullen on Saturday, January 31, "stands a very good chance of being returned. We have the nominations for the County on Tuesday. There were four candidates till this evening, when Mr. Marum resigned. Now Bryan and Martin represent the Catholic vote, & Ellis represents the Protestant vote. I think the two Catholics will be returned by an overwhelming majority" (C). "In the city," he further reported, "the Protestants are doing all they can to get out Mr. Michael Sullivan to stand on conservative principles. Even Disraeli has written to him asking him to stand. I hope however that Sir John will escape a contest."

"Sir John Gray," Moran reported two days later, on February 2, "has been returned to-day without opposition. Great efforts were made to incite a contest against him" (C). "Lord Ormonde & the Marchioness," he explained, "went over in person to old Mr. Sullivan to ask him to stand for the city in opposition to Sir John Gray. However now all is settled without a contest." "We have every hope," Moran then added, referring to the county election, "that the two Catholics will be returned. The only difficulty is that they are not working in unison. I have done everything I could to link them together. Mr. Martin is not half so good a canvasser as his wife. She with her sister is driving out most actively asking everyone to vote for Martin. Her father, however, Mr. Cahill, is very unpopular, & will be the chief obstacle to Martin's return." Moran left little to chance, however, and on that same day he issued an address in support of Martin. He maintained that in the present crisis it was "most important that our Catholic people should have as their representatives in Parliament men able and willing to defend our religious as well as our national interest."[24] "Your address, like that of Mr. Bryan," he assured Martin, alluding as gently as he could to Home Rule, "is most Catholic, and sets forth, in no uncertain terms, the popular principles of this county."

Several days later, Moran was still concerned about Martin's return, and he wrote to Cullen about the difficulties involved. "The contest here," he assured Cullen on February 5, the day before the polling, "will be a very warm one. All the Conservatives have taken up Ellis & are using all the influence of the landlords & agents to put out Martin. Even Bryan is trying to get his friends to plump for himself & not to give a vote to Martin. Still I have great hopes that Martin will be returned."

> Though the County is small in extent it has 5,200 voters. Meath though so large has only 3,100 [correctly, 4,000] voters. The proportion of our Conservatives is small as they count only one thousand voters, but they are all compact & every one of them will vote. We have 4,200 Catholic voters, but several of them will not come to the poll, & several of them are afraid to vote against the Landlords.

24. *Freeman's Journal,* February 3, 1874.

It is only on such occasions that the ultra-Protestants show their real spirit against us. It is amazing to find what a compact party they are when they attack the Catholics. They fight among themselves about everything else but they will agree when they assail us.

"I will send your Eminence a telegram," he assured Cullen in conclusion, "announcing the result of our poll, if I sh^d happen to hear it tomorrow evening although this is almost impossible."

Moran was not able to forward the results of the election until the day after the polling, and, when he did, he apparently did not realize that his figures were still only partial. "We have had," he informed Cullen on February 7, "the declaration of the poll. Bryan & Martin have been returned by a large majority. Ellis only got 464 votes, notwithstanding all the unfair influence which the landlords brought to bear in his favor" (C). "Mr. Kavanagh," Moran explained, referring to an extensive local landlord who had just been elected unopposed for county Carlow, and who had been born without limbs, "without legs or arms, went to Ballysaggett & with his agent Colonel Ball, & five or six other high people surveyed the voters as they came in to record their vote." "In Gowran," he further noted, referring to Agar-Ellis's family seat and agent, "Brassington got himself appointed the person to receive the votes. A sub-agent was the person appointed to receive the votes in Pilltown." "The people however," Moran observed with obvious satisfaction, "were true to their colours. It is a great & well deserved disappointment for Agar-Ellis, the more so as he has been boasting these days past that he would be a thousand at the head of the poll above all other candidates." When all the votes were finally counted, however, it was Bryan who headed the poll with 2,603 votes, while Martin received 2,139, and Agar-Ellis received only 1,151.[25]

A short time after the elections in Kilkenny, Moran wrote to Kirby, explaining what he thought was the meaning of the results there, in particular, and in Ireland generally. "In this County," he assured Kirby on February 11, "we have turned out a Liberal of the Lord Russell stamp & we have returned to Parliament in his stead a worthy Catholic gentleman, Mr. Martin. The Protestant bigots are terribly annoyed as all the landlords had done their utmost for this false Liberal, but the people proved themselves true & gave a most triumphant majority in favour of our Catholic representatives" (K). "We will have," he then prophesied somewhat optimistically, "in the new Parliament at least seventy M.P.'s who are independent men & pledged to uphold our Catholic principles. I expect they will be able to effect a great deal, as the English Tories & Liberals will be both so balanced that our 70 votes can turn the tide of victory whatever way they please." "However," he added more prudently, "*homo proponit* [Man proposes], it is only God that can give effect to these proposals." "The *ballot* has been the greatest blessing to our

25. Walker, p. 117.

voters. Everything went on with the greatest order & regularity. There was no rioting or disorder. Everyone voted quietly just as he liked & no one knew anything about it. One of the real old style of electioneering canvassers, seeing everything go on so smoothly without any fight or spree at all, cried out from the steps of the Court House, 'well, boys! God be with the times when we would be after throwing the Orangemen over the balustrades here.'" "We have been told here," Moran noted in a less humorous vein in conclusion, "that some English agent in Rome has been complaining of the Irish Clergy as if we were all going in for 'Home Rule.' It is no wonder that we shd. when such English agents so constantly misrepresent our Country & our clergy, & when the British legislators in London refuse to grant us Catholic Education & to redress our grievances."

Finally, there is the question of Cullen's electoral influence with the last of his suffragans, Thomas Furlong, the bishop of Ferns. The diocese of Ferns included three parliamentary constituencies, the boroughs of New Ross and Wexford and the county Wexford, for a total of four seats. The real excitement in this election was in the contest for the county, as three Home Rulers and a Conservative entered the lists. Among the two incumbents, John Talbot Power and M. P. D'Arcy, both of whom had been returned unopposed in 1868, D'Arcy decided to retire. Power, who was the son of Sir James Power, a wealthy distiller and a substantial Catholic landlord in Wexford, declared himself a candidate again and in favor of Home Rule. Sir George Bowyer, an English Catholic convert, who had represented the borough of Dundalk for sixteen years before he had been defeated in 1868 and who had been searching for a seat with great assiduity ever since, also took the field. Bowyer had been defeated in Dundalk for his obvious Conservative propensities, so when Butt launched the Home Rule movement, Bowyer became an early convert. In the intervening period, Bowyer had been in correspondence with both Cullen, who had favored his return for Dundalk in 1868, and Butt about securing a seat in Parliament. There is no direct evidence that Cullen was instrumental in persuading the bishop of Ferns to adopt Bowyer, but Furlong and the Ferns clergy did endorse both Bowyer and Chevalier Keyes O'Clery, a papal knight, who had earned that distinction as papal zouave in the defense of the gate at Porta Pia when Rome was taken on September 20, 1870, by the troops of the Kingdom of Italy, as their candidates for county Wexford. Finally, a Conservative, R. W. H. Dare, also declared himself a candidate, obviously in the hope that the split among the Home Rulers would allow him to slip in.

Archdeacon Redmond, whose parish of Arklow bordered on the county Wexford, when writing to Cullen on February 3 about election matters in Wicklow, also, it will be recalled, had some hard things to say about the kind of fruit the Home Rule movement was producing in the county Wexford. Cullen, who had long experienced the archdeacon's impulsiveness and rash behavior, wrote to him the next day, cautioning him to leave well enough alone. "As there are so many

Catholics," Cullen warned in a postscript to his letter of February 4, "up for the C⁰ Wexford, it is better for us to let the Catholic people and the Catholic bishop & priests of that gt County manage for themselves" (C). The archdeacon, however, who had taken a violent dislike to Chevalier O'Clery, could not be contained, and on Sunday, February 15, two days before the election, he wrote to Cullen again. "I have just returned from addressing a large number of Electors in the chapel yard at Johnstown in favor of 'Power & Bowyer,'" he unabashedly informed Cullen, referring to a small village some four miles from Arklow on the Wicklow-Wexford county border, "& if other Divisions be addressed in the same strain those gentlemen shall have little difficulty in finding their way into Parliament" (C). "But," he complained, referring to the local Wexford priests who were conforming to the consensus of their body to support Bowyer and O'Clery, "one Parish Priest, & one curate from one Parish & one from another, have sown dragon's teeth of division & no one can tell the issue." The archdeacon, who appears to have had less political sense, even, than common sense, however, had seriously misread the political signs. Bowyer and O'Clery were easily returned on February 17, with 3,407 and 2,784 votes, respectively, while Power and Dare received only 1,332 and 1,224 votes.[26] Though Cullen apparently had not interceded directly for Bowyer with Furlong, his warning Redmond not to interfere was undoubtedly true to his sentiments regarding Bowyer's effort to secure a seat in Parliament.

What emerges clearly from this examination of the some dozen constituencies in which Cullen attempted to exert his influence in the general election of 1874 is a sense of how limited Cullen's influence actually was. If indeed the most influential man in the Irish Church had such limited influence, what may be said of the role of his episcopal colleagues and their clergy in the other twenty-eight constituencies outside of Ulster in which the Catholic vote was decisive, or even in those Ulster constituencies where the Catholic vote was becoming an important consideration? A survey of all of these constituencies is, of course, impossible here, but a number are representative of the nature and extent of episcopal and clerical influence. As it was for Cullen, the chief factor that limited episcopal and clerical influence in the constituencies was the issue of Home Rule. In the vast majority of constituencies outside of Ulster, the candidates were obliged to declare for Home Rule if they hoped to be elected. They were so obliged, of course, because the voters would not accept less, and, as was clearly demonstrated in the case of county Louth and the archbishop of Armagh, if pressured, the clergy would invariably side with the people even against their own bishop.

26. Ibid., p. 119.

Indeed, in the one case in which the clergy did go with their bishop against the people, the result was a standing object lesson on the dangers of thwarting the people's sense of what was politically necessary. The occasion for this stern lesson was the contest in the county Limerick. The struggle had actually begun about a month before the dissolution of Parliament, when William Monsell, the senior member for the county and Gladstone's former postmaster general, was raised to the peerage as Baron Emly of Tervoe. The first candidate to take the field was John J. Kelly, the son of a middling Limerick landlord whose father's holdings of some 7,000 acres extended into the neighboring counties of Clare and Galway. Shortly after Kelly announced his candidature, John Ellard, a Limerick solicitor, wrote to Butt, characterizing both Kelly and his father. "The County of Limerick," Ellard, who was also Butt's election agent, informed him on December 23, "is at last free to choose for itself, but the Whig party still cling to the hope of holding it, even under the cover of Home Rule."

> Young Kelly, John J. Kelly, has already stepped into the field, his father repre-
> sented our City as a Repealer [1844–47] and I believe was honest when all was
> corrupt at Concilliation [*sic*] Hall, & seeing the humbug he resigned. He has
> since become a perfect oddity. The son, the Candidate, is a nephew of Lord
> Fermoy's, he is completely in the leading strings of Wm Roche, the Crown Sol^r
> & c. of Harcourt Street, an ardent Whig & anti Nationalist, and thro him I
> believe he is the nominee of the Gormanstown party. He [Kelly] has a right to
> have plenty of money but is very close. His father is spoken of by the Members
> of the C^o Farmers' Club as one of the worst Landlords in Ireland, that he
> Exterminated a lot of his tenants, and if you heard M^l Ryan & O'Sullivan of
> Kilmallock denounce the idea of his son being a repre. of the C^o you would
> think he has little chance. I hope we will get a good man (B).

"Why not Waldron," Ellard suggested, referring to a prominent member of the Home Rule League who was also a former member for county Tipperary, "or some leading man of the League, or if we had a good tenant Farmer he would carry the day." "The C^o Club," he explained, referring to the Limerick and Clare Farmers' Club, "will meet on Saturday next. I will go there. I wish I knew your views as I could get them carried out."

Apparently, Butt replied by return of post, for Ellard wrote to him again on Thursday, December 25, saying that he had received his letter that morning. "Kelly," he reported, "is going actively to work today for the County. I was sent a retainer for him last evening. I will not of course accept it and have intimated so" (B). "Blackall," Ellard explained, referring to another Limerick solicitor, "is acting today as Kelly's conducting agent and all the little Whigs and satellites of Monsell here have been off to several places about Limerick to secure the services of the bailiffs on the Estates for Kelly." "Is Kelly a Member of the League," Ellard asked, "& was he a Member of the Home Gov^t Association? Did he attend the Con-ference or sign the requisition?" "The opinion here," he added, "is that he is a mere nominee of Monsell's & the Bishop and that he has been allowed to come out for Home Rule, which he makes a secondary question to Education in his address." "I will suggest Lord R. Montagu," he assured Butt, referring to the Conservative member for Maidstone, who was a recent convert to Catholicism and an even more recent convert to Home Rule, "quietly to the Club, but my own opinion is you should be Elected taking care however you should not resign [Limerick City] until your Election was secure." "Let me know," he then requested of Butt again, "about Kelly's membership of the League, as I want the information for the Club Meeting on Saturday."

Meanwhile, Butt had written to W. H. O'Sullivan, a large tenant farmer and hotel proprietor from Kilmallock who was an influential member of the Limerick and Clare Farmers' Club, asking O'Sullivan if he thought of offering himself as a candidate and also what he thought of the idea of his (Butt's) resigning Limerick City and running for the county. "You may rest satisfied," O'Sullivan assured Butt the next day, December 24, "no one has a chance in this County unless he is A one on the Home Rule Ticket. Mock H. Rulers like Major O'Reilly S[ir] P. O'Brien and a host of others who I could name have no chance whatever in this County" (B). "Regarding J. Kelly whose address has appeared," he explained, "he has no chance whatever. His Father is the most *extensive Exterminator* in our County. Will you take *particular care that the H.R. League* have nothing to do with him as it would ruin our Cause with many Farmers throughout the Province of Munster." "As to your kind remarks about myself," O'Sullivan then observed, "I am as anxious as anyone to serve the Cause of my Country and I flatter myself there are not more than five men in the Country would poll more than I would in the County as there is not a Parish in it but I am as well known as in Kilmallock and scarcely a Town Land in which I would not have volunteers but the fact is I could not at present afford a Contest and a Contest there would be to a certaintity [*sic*] if *I was put forward*." "As to your being returned if put forward," he assured Butt, "there would not be the *least doubt* whatever *about it* but would it not be a mistake to abandon the City on the eve of an expected General Election and leave it perhaps drop again into the hands of the same faction who had it for over twenty years." "If anything should occur to you," O'Sullivan then added in a postscript, "before Saturday (Club Meeting day) you might drop me a line or wire."

When the Farmers' Club met on Saturday, December 27, in Limerick, a motion to nominate O'Sullivan was deferred to a more representative meeting of the whole county scheduled for the following Thursday, New Year's Day. That meeting, held in the Theatre Royal in Limerick, which was attended by the members of the Farmers' Club and delegates from the different parishes of the county, proved to be a very stormy one.[27] After the chair was taken by Joseph Gubbins, the vice-

---

27. *Freeman's Journal,* January 2, 1874.

chairman of the Farmers' Club, the honorable secretary of the meeting, James Starkie, read a letter in which "the writer alluded to an eviction which had been carried out by Mr. Kelly's father, though the family was the seventh generation in possession." Starkie then thought it only right to read a letter from Kelly to Thomas Fitzgerald, the parish priest of Fedamore near Bruff, in which Kelly stated that "if ever he became possessed of the Ballybrickin property he would do his best to right the wrongs which had been committed (hear, hear, and applause)." A motion was then made to define the kind of representative needed, the spirit of which would have excluded Kelly, for it called for in part "a thoroughgoing, well tried and sincere nationalist (great applause); and that we further believe the time has come when the county of Limerick should be represented by a member of that party whose politics alone can give expression to the feelings and aspirations of the people." After the motion was seconded, Timothy Shanahan, the parish priest of Ballingarry, asked to be heard before the resolution was put to the meeting. Shanahan agreed that any candidate endorsed by the meeting should be a sincere advocate of Home Rule, "and if any man came forward whom they did not believe, let them kick him from them as a serpent (applause)." "But if they believed a man to be sincere," Shanahan continued, "let them adopt him. There was a man at present before the county who went in for education—to educate their children as they thought fit. If they were now true to their ancestors, it was their duty to aid the Catholic Church. This man promised to get them this."

When Shanahan explained that he was the son of a tenant farmer and he also knew of bitter acts of extermination, he was interrupted by a voice calling "at Ballybrickin (tremendous cheering)." Shanahan protested that he was not there to support the man who was guilty of such acts, and he was again interrupted.

A Voice—Are you rewarded?
Rev. Mr. Shanahan said that was a most unwarrantable attack.
A Voice—We want O'Sullivan, and nobody else (tremendous applause).
At this stage of the proceedings a terrific row occured in the pit, sticks were drawn, and for a time it appeared the people would have to quit the theatre and dissolve the meeting. A "free fight" was going on at one end, sticks being freely used.
The Chairman begged the meeting to observe order. Was it going to go to the Press that the Nationalists of Limerick were not able to conduct themselves? (Loud cries of "no!" "We'll have O'Sullivan, and nobody else!")
Rev. Mr. Shanahan disclaimed the idea that he wanted to force Kelly on them. Let them support O'Sullivan if they thought he was the proper man (applause). Kelly had joined the Home Rule League.
A Voice—How long? (Great interruption, and tremendous cheers for O'Sullivan.)
Rev. Mr. Shanahan—If you believe in Kelly vote for him.
A Voice—We don't believe in him, then (laughter and applause).

Rev. Mr. Shanahan—One honest word more.

A Voice—Let it be honest then.

Rev. Mr. Shanahan. It will be from the bottom of my heart.

A Voice—Did not his father make a bullock walks of his property and evict honest farmers?

Rev. Mr. Shanahan—I am not here to defend such acts.

A Voice—Oh! we have heard plenty of you.

After some further remarks, the resolution was finally put forth and passed unanimously amidst great applause. Shanahan then came forward again and, amidst groans and hisses, nominated Kelly, who was duly seconded. Michael Ryan, a popular and influential tenant farmer from Bruree, then nominated O'Sullivan and almost the entire assembly rose, amidst cheers and the waving of hats, to approve his choice. After O'Sullivan's name was seconded, the chairman put the names to the meeting and declared that O'Sullivan had been unanimously selected. O'Sullivan then thanked the meeting, and, significantly, the proceedings were closed by John Daly, reputed to be the head of the local Fenians, who assured those present that "the Nationalists of Limerick and the Farmers' Club would be in thorough accord during the approaching contest."

Meanwhile, in an obvious effort to head off a confrontation between the advanced Nationalists and the Fenians, as represented by O'Sullivan on the one hand and the Whig-Liberals on the other, the dean of Limerick and the parish priest of Newcastle West, Richard B. O'Brien, wrote to Butt to see if he could work out a compromise. "Tell me *confidentially*," he asked Butt in an undated letter, probably written on December 28, "do *you* think of the County Limerick?—if you do, likely we shall have no contest" (B). "Also tell me," he added, suggesting the names of a number of modest Catholic landlords in the county who might serve as compromise candidates, "if E. W. O'Brien came out on popular principles would *he* not be a great accession. He is sternly true and finely educated. H. Considine of Dherk is another who would help the cause powerfully. Long since, he has declared for H.R." "I think," he further suggested, "we should sweep everything if it were clearly understood by them that unless one of them or Stephen de Vere came out *you* would come out." "Give this ten minutes thought," O'Brien advised in conclusion, "and write to me tomorrow." By the time this letter reached Dublin, Butt had already left for England, and his son Robert forwarded the letter, after having opened it and discussed its contents with A. M. Sullivan. "It rather confirms us," Robert explained to his father on Tuesday, December 30, "as far as it goes in thinking you are just as well away" (B). "I don't see," he explained, referring to the meeting scheduled for the Theatre Royal in Limerick, "that you need to do anything until after the meeting on Thursday. You have I suppose decided right (whatever your decision was) about writing to the Farmers' Club." "Thinking over it myself," Robert further observed, "I don't see why you should interfere or be brought into it at all. If they get into difficulties let them ask you to stand and yet I am afraid your doing so would only leave a worse mess in the City." Apparently, Butt was of the same mind as his son, for though both sides appealed to him for his endorsement, and though he was privately in favor of O'Sullivan, he did not interfere in what was soon to become a very bitter and violent contest.

While Dean O'Brien was writing to Butt, Kelly was writing to the archbishop of Cashel for his support. Leahy, however, declined to commit himself until a fairly constituted meeting of the electors of the county was declared. After the meeting at the Theatre Royal, therefore, Kelly wrote to the archbishop again asking him for his support. "On yesterday," Kelly explained on January 2, "a meeting of what purported to be representatives of the electors of Co. Limerick (though as far as I can learn very few bona fide electors attended) was held here at which Mr. O'Sullivan and I were proposed. The feeling of the meeting was in Mr. O'Sullivan's favour as was to be expected and his candidature I believe was put forward before the County" (L). "I need not say," Kelly added, "that having in my canvass up to this received so much encouragement from almost everyone upon whom I called, and having also the support of Most Rev^d Dr. Butler, of Dean O'Brien, and so many of the Clergymen of the County, I consider it my duty to persevere to the end in the contest for the representation of my native County. Having so determined I think it only right to lay my case before your Grace and ask for a favourable verdict." "I have the pleasure of sending you," he further noted, "a copy of the Limerick Chronicle of this morning, containing a letter written by my brother in defense of my father's conduct in his property in the County." Leahy replied to Kelly two days later. "The unfortunate dissensions," he explained on January 4, "which have broken out in the popular party, the Catholic party, in the County of Limerick, and which threaten to become worse, are enough to make me as a Bishop pause before committing myself to any kind of interference whatever in so unfortunate a state of things" (L). "Then, as to the meeting held on New Year's day by the Farmers' Club," Leahy maintained, "I am not sufficiently acquainted with the manner of convening it or its constitution, as the conduct of its proceedings to know in what light I should view it—whether as fairly representing the Liberal opinion of the County, or if only a section of it." "I should be uncandid," he confessed, "did I not add that according to reports which I look upon as trustworthy, the bulk of the People & Clergy in the County Limerick portion of the Diocese of Emly are whether rightly or wrongly, opposed and strongly opposed to your Candidature." "Under all the circumstances," Leahy concluded, "the only course I can at present approve to myself is that of non-interference."

When Dean O'Brien read the reports of the meeting in the Theatre Royal in Limerick, he wrote to Butt again. "Is there no way," he asked desperately in an undated letter, probably written on Friday, January 2, "of avoiding the impending break between the Clergy of this Diocese and Home Rule and I fear between them and you?" "Can you not," he then begged of Butt, "get O'Sullivan withdrawn. Kelly takes our programme and more; he promises to Compensate any his father wronged if he ever be able. What more can we demand?" "And then," he added, "are we to set all the reasonable men in England laughing at us? Try and do something." In part the reason that the Dean was so upset was that the supporters of O'Sullivan had scheduled a meeting in his parish on Sunday, January 4, to make it clear that, in spite of his clerical endorsement, Kelly had no popular support. "The Dean of Limerick," the *Freeman's Journal* correspondent reported on January 5, "on Sunday, at first and last Masses, made a solemn declaration that a meeting to be held in Newcastle that day (Sunday) was to be held against his (the Dean's) will and judgement."[28] "He, moreover, declared," the correspondent added, "that his judgement was—and he declared it before the altar—that this meeting had a tendency to put back Ireland for twenty years; that it tended to separate the priests and people, and led to make an Italy and Germany of Ireland; and that the chances of Home Rule were jeopardised by such meetings to a degree that made workers for Ireland shudder." The meeting in Newcastle West that afternoon was well attended by representatives from the surrounding districts and was orderly and quiet. The only priest there was a young curate from the bishop's mensal parish of St. Michael's in Limerick City, Edward O'Dwyer, who was opposed to O'Sullivan's candidature but refused the invitation to explain his views from the platform.

The following day, Monday, January 5, a large number of Kelly's supporters, clerical and lay, met at Cruise's Hotel in Limerick, to further the cause of their candidate.[29] The parish priest of Ballybrickin, in the diocese of Cashel and Emly, Thomas Meagher, explained at great length the details of the alleged evictions attributed to Kelly's father. "There were but three persons," Meagher explained, "in all evicted, and these evictions took place in the year 1850 for non-payment of rent. Those three persons who were evicted were middlemen, and held the lands at a very low rent, whilst they received a very high rent from the undertenants (hear, hear)." Kelly then addressed the meeting and referred to the slanders that had been circulated in respect to his father, which had now been completely refuted. Finally, Kelly's brother Thomas concluded the meeting by attempting to explain why his brother had been so late in declaring for Home Rule. The reason "was that he had ever been an ardent and sincere Repealer (cheers), and it was only recently he had become convinced that Home Rule was most desirable for the people of the country than simple Repeal." "It was simply a slander on his brother's honour," Thomas maintained, "to think that he would adopt political views

28. Ibid., January 6, 1874.
29. Ibid.

merely to suit the exigencies of the time." The meeting was concluded with a unanimous resolution that Kelly should immediately undertake a canvass of the entire county.

The bishop and clergy of Limerick, however, unfortunately were not satisfied to leave well enough alone. The bishop of Limerick, George Butler, called for a meeting of his clergy in Limerick on Friday, January 9, at which, it was announced in the press, the Limerick clergy would declare themselves for Kelly.[30] After their meeting, presided over by Butler, some 80 priests, with only 4 dissentients, of a body that numbered about 115, issued an address under the signatures of the bishop, the dean, and the archdeacon of Limerick, "To the Catholic Electors of the Diocese."[31] The address was certainly not among the Irish clergy's best efforts in the nineteenth century, but it is quoted in full because it is an interesting attempt at self-justification, and it is, therefore, a significant example of how the bulk of the Limerick clergy thought about themselves and their role vis à vis their people.

DEAR FRIENDS—We have assembled together to address you at a crisis of great importance, the results of which no human being can clearly foresee. We feel bound to take this course by our love for our county, our love for you, and by very grave evils which now threaten Ireland, should unwise counsels at the present moment prevail among the people. In offering you our advice we desire to disclaim all intentions of dictating to you.

We have no power, nor have we the slightest disposition to dictate, but have a right to tell you honestly what we think and what we advise, and you would blame us yourselves, as our consciences would blame us, if at a time like the present we withheld our views and our advice from our faithful people. Remember that your priests who address you are sprung for the most part from the great farming class of the county; more are your kith and kin, your own blood and household, your brothers, and near and dear relatives and friends. Add to this, to seek your happiness is our duty by the supreme law which has given us charge of your immortal interests, and which makes us one family in Christ as we are one family in nature.

We add, you can never have different interests, and by God's help we shall never have divided counsels. We owe to you our affectionate and disinterested advice, and we this day pronounce it. What are the questions which engage all hearts and minds at this moment, and what, therefore, are the principles which should govern us at this coming county election?

The hearts of priests and people are set upon domestic government, popularly called Home Rule; upon the education of the people according to the people's faith; upon a fixity of tenure in the land at a fair rent; and an amnesty to the political prisoners. For the efficient advocacy of all these questions your representative should be a man of education, intelligence, position, and ability. One of any other description would only provoke the Parliament to mock and

30. Ibid., January 9, 1874.
31. Ibid., January 10, 1874.

repulse us, to say that we are unfit to manage our own affairs, and that we know not what we want.

There are two gentlemen seeking the representation upon the Liberal interest—Mr. J. J. Kelly and Mr. W. H. O'Sullivan; and we feel no hesitation in saying that only the former of these gentlemen answers to the description of the representative whom you require. Mr. Kelly has come into the field without any invitation from any of us, or, as far as we know from anyone else. He comes before the county on his own responsibility, and puts before you the political principles which he declares to be his honest convictions, and on which he declares himself prepared to act, whether in or out of Parliament. He pledges himself to work for Home Rule as explained at the National Conference in Dublin. He pledges himself to advocate Denominational Education and the improvement of the Land Act to the extent of fixity of tenure, at fair rents; and amnesty to the political prisoners. In a word, his political creed on all the leading questions that interest you is exactly identical with your own. He is, moreover, an educated, intelligent, able man, sprung from an old Catholic stock of Limerick, having a large stake in our county and city, and without stain of any kind upon his personal character, as far as we can discover.

The single thing alleged against Mr. Kelly is that his father is an exterminator. If this be true—and it now appears that the charges of extermination made against Mr. James Kelly are in several instances unfounded, while in most of the cases alleged they are really exaggerated—but if it be true that to any extent Mr. James Kelly has been an exterminator, it is not the priests of Limerick who will be found to excuse or palliate his conduct. We have no sympathy with exterminators. We condemn them as heartily as you can do yourselves, and our voices shall ever be raised against a system of legalised wrong which has been the blight and bane of Ireland. But is it fair to visit upon Mr. J. J. Kelly the sins of his father? Has he had hand, act, or part in these sins? Did he approve of them, or could he have hindered them, or did he ever profit by them a single shilling—or would he, if he became the owner of the estate, commit like sins himself. To each of these questions Mr. J. J. Kelly had emphatically answered No! We believe his answer to be honest and true, and we have, therefore, no hesitation in saying to you that, in present circumstances, when, to our regret, no more eligible candidate has come before us you cannot do better than give him your support.

We believe that you will be safe in confiding to him the great interests which are at stake, and that he will honourably and manfully guard and advance them to the best of his power.

Of the other candidate (Mr. O'Sullivan), we desire to speak with due respect, but we feel constrained to declare to you our conviction that his return, as a member for the county, would be a Crushing Disaster to the Liberal cause, while to the cause of Home Rule it would simply be a death-blow.

The Home Rulers have been charged with seeking "separation" under the pretence of seeking Home Rule. Mr. O'Sullivan's return would tend most powerfully to establish this charge of our opponents. We have been charged with seeking "confiscation," under the pretence of an equitable settlement of the land question. Would not Mr. O'Sullivan's return be, in the eyes of the Three Kingdoms, a strong justification of such an impeachment?

We do not say that Mr. O'Sullivan is a Separatist or a Revolutionist, but everyone understands that Mr. O'Sullivan represents extreme views, and, whatever may be his private opinions, his position as our representative would be fatal to our national expectations.

We have only to look at the manner in which his claims have been put forward and all the circumstances of his candidature, to be convinced of the judgment which all observant men in England and elsewhere must form of his opinions.

We need not add that the judgment formed in England of the class into whose hands public affairs would fall if we obtained Home Rule is one of our prominent and serious difficulties. Englishmen say that our Irish Parliament would be an assembly of uneducated, violent, reckless men, unfit to govern, and all rational legislation would become an impossibility. Would not the return of Mr. O'Sullivan contribute powerfully—and we mean him no disrespect—to prove their ill-founded prophecies?

We have felt bound to say so much through our love for our country, for you, and to fulfil our duty as your pastors. Our interests are your interests. Our cause is your cause. Our success your success. Our failure your failure. We are one. We give you our solemn judgment of your duty to God and your country, and we leave the issue in your own hands.

Thank God the ballot now protects you all from the violence and injustice of the landlord and the mob, and that you are free to follow without fear the dictates of your own conscience.

The most significant aspect of this address was that it was an overt, if largely unconscious, appeal by a clerical elite to a class. It was, not an address to the people, but an appeal to "Catholic Electors," who were, in effect, the "farming class of the county," from whom the clergy were very conscious they had sprung. Not only were the members of this class the blood of their blood and the bone of their bone, but also they were tenant farmers of more than thirty acres, who essentially constituted the 6,300 electors of county Limerick. Members of this class, and the clerical elite who were their sons and brothers, moreover, perceived themselves as the bone and sinew of the nation, and perhaps as the nation proper. The clergy's appeal to the Catholic electorate to stand by, as kin should in times of crisis, the interests of their class, which was the clergy's own class of origin, testifies to the rising political conscience of the farming class in the 1870s. The supreme irony in this clerical appeal *cum* address, is of course, their decision to choose, not one of their own, but rather the son of a substantial Catholic landlord to represent them. Their inability to come to terms with O'Sullivan, however, was not the result merely of their social snobbishness and Whig propensities, which were pathetically betrayed in their fear of English ridicule for being still only one step removed from a kilt and a club, but it was also a very real awareness that O'Sullivan represented the menace of Fenianism and all the social implications inherent in that radical political movement. Hence the Limerick clergy's grateful acknowledgement, in their conclusion, of the secret ballot, which would protect the voter not so much, as they maintained, from the landlords, whose political power was now marginal, as from the mob informed by the Fenian veto of violence.

On the day of the clergy's meeting in Limerick, and before he could have read their address, Edward J. Synan, the junior member for county Limerick, also wrote to Butt begging him to offer himself as the compromise candidate. "The state of affairs in the County," Synan reported, on January 9, "is most melancholy and a most disastrous contest is being carried on and the effect in my opinion will be most fatal to Home Rule here on whichever side the victory may be" (B). "The parties who accepted a candidate," he explained, "without consulting with the people regret what they have done, I believe, and are willing to accept a candidate that may be acceptable to both sections of Home Rulers. The advanced section of Home Rulers having proposed Mr. O'Sullivan, I believe, as a protest against dictation may be induced by you and the council of the League to withdraw him in your favour." "If matters are allowed to proceed as at present," Synan warned, echoing the dean of Limerick, "all moderate men and all ecclesiastics tell me they will despair of any good from Home Rule." "If you unite both sections of Home Rulers," he assured Butt in conclusion, "by taking a bold course now, before a month you will have every Ecclesiastic & every leading Elector in this County members of the League. The solution rests with you and I pray for one that will serve the Cause."

"You, of course, have seen the address of the Bishop & Clergy to the Electors," Synan wrote to Butt the next day, "Whether the expression of their 'regret at not having a better man than Kelly to fight with' leaves any, or rather was intended to leave any 'door of escape' may be doubtful; but that I have been informed it was so intended" (B). "You were & are wrong," he assured Butt in regard to the Limerick clergy, "that they would not have you. In fact they know that at present or at any time they could win with no other." "The only difficulty," Synan admitted, "is how to deal with O'Sullivan, and of that you are the best judge. If O'Sullivan is as sincere a nationalist as he gets credit for he could not object to make way for a man who could unite all sections of the party. Whether the League would carry a resolution to that effect you must decide. It is hardly possible O'Sullivan could refuse to comply." "As to Kelly," he further assured Butt, "he would be abandoned by the Priests at a moments notice. In fact he is a mere Puppet and you must regard him as nothing more." "The occasion seems to me," he added, "one of a most important & critical character. The Contest here has assumed two aspects, one of division between Home Rulers, the other of a fight of class ag^st class, and both are equally fatal to the Cause." "Now is the time," he urged Butt in conclusion, "for you & the League to act if you have the power."

That same day, January 10, Butt's election agent in Limerick, John Ellard, wrote to him explaining that matters had now gone too far for any compromise solution. "You will not be again asked," he maintained, "to interfere in our Election and you should not do so. We can win in a canter without you, the Bishop's Manifesto notwithstanding, which is considered a fine Whig Manifesto. What active support have either the Priests or Bishop of Limerick given to Home Rule? None, but have [and] are doing all they can to damn it in the interest of the Whigs" (B). "The Priests of Limerick," Ellard assured Butt, "are not & were not at the meeting all for Kelly, and the Cashel Priests are in our favor. The feeling against the Dean is very great. The Farmers' Club people today were very indignant about the Bishop's letter & I met several of the Farmers who are not members and they all said no Bishop or Priest will induce the people of their districts to support Kelly." "As to a reconciliation between the parties by withdrawing their Candidates," Ellard reported, "that is out of the question. The Farmers' Club and Nationalists will never think of it. I hinted it & it was scouted & O'Sullivan I believe would not withdraw for any man. The feeling is to defeat Monsell & his Whig agents, the Bishop, Dean and Priests who must do as they [i.e., the Whigs] tell them." "The Farmers' Club people arranged privately today," Ellard noted, "to raise a fund to defray every election expense if necessary. I never saw greater firmness & determination at an Election before." "I may tell you," Ellard warned, "that the Bishop is already arranging his Candidates for the City." "Your friend the Dean," he added in conclusion, "is in the Conclave."

"The Manifesto of the Bishop and Priests," Ellard assured Butt again two days later, on January 12, "will have no effect against us, quite the reverse" (B). "The P.P. of Bruree," he reported, "read it half thro' on yesterday from the Altar, & then said he did not interfere in politics they all knew & that any one who wished to read the letter would find it in the Newspapers. His Curate, a Whig, at a subsequent Mass said he would not delay the Congregation, as he knew many of them wanted to attend the Kilmallock Meeting [for O'Sullivan]." "The Curate of Bulgaden Parish," Ellard further noted, "read the document. It would not be listened to, and several stood up in the Chapel & protested against it, and he had to cease as a great commotion was getting up. I did not hear of any other places yet, where it was read." "Five Priests," he added, "made a very vigorous resistance agt. the Bishop, Dean & Co. to the adoption of their address. I believe Father Cleary [correctly, O'Cleary] was one of them. The poor Dean is looked on as a regular deceiver. He can never again appear here in public."

On January 13, when Butt, in Dublin, received this letter from Ellard, he wrote to his good friend and colleague Mitchell Henry, the senior member for county Galway, to reassure him about the situation in county Limerick. "I wish," Butt explained, "I had prevented such a contest by going down at once and offering myself for the county. But the contest will not do the harm I at first feared" (B). "It has drawn," he pointed out shrewdly, "as you have seen from the Bishop and clergy the strongest declaration in favor of Home Rule." "Dean O'Brien," Butt added, "has led them into a great mistake in their address in sneering at O'Sullivan personally and branding his canvass as Fenian. I believe he will be elected by a large majority. The clerical party will try and get both to retire to invite me. Their address has I think made this impossible." "O'Sullivan," he assured Henry, "would be very far from disgracing us. A grand example of his class in manner and appearance, far better than many we have and thoroughly honest and true man." The outstanding features of the Limerick contest's progression from the publication of the Limerick clergy's address on January 10 to the announcement of a general election on January 24 were its increasing bitterness and violence. Rival mobs all over the county clashed frequently.[32] On January 16, for example, in the town of Abbeyfeale on the Kerry-Limerick border, O'Sullivan and a group of supporters were attacked with sticks and knives, and three of his party were stabbed.[33] The violence did not abate when the Limerick contest was swallowed up in the general election; if anything it became more intense with the local factions around Herbertstown, known as the three- and four-year-olds, taking sides.[34] The violence finally culminated in the murder by a blast from a musket of one of O'Sullivan's supporters at the door of the man's shop. The unfortunate man had quarreled with a number of Kelly's partisans earlier in the day.[35] The announcement of the general election, meanwhile, had changed the terms in the county election, for there were now three candidates, O'Sullivan, Kelly, and the former junior member, E. J. Synan, contesting two seats. The Farmers' Club met again on February 1, in Limerick, and a motion to back Synan was amended by one of O'Sullivan's chief supporters, Michael Ryan, to the effect that the club should take no action in the matter, leaving the choice between Kelly and Synan to the voters.[36] The amendment was carried by a vote of 28 to 17. The club was recommending, in effect, that the voters give their first votes to O'Sullivan, but it left their second votes to the voters' discretion. Shortly before the Farmers' Club had met, Cullen had written to Kirby about the sad situation in Limerick and the scandal that had ensued. "In Limerick," he had explained on January 29, "a great split has taken place between priests and people. It is a very scandalous affair. I think some of the priests went too far in encouraging every foolish pretention of the mob—now the priests wish to stop progress and the people abuse them

32. Ibid., January 14, 16, and 21, 1874.
33. Ibid., January 17, 1874.
34. Ibid., February 11, 1874.
35. Ibid., February 6, 1874.
36. Ibid., February 2, 1874.

atrociously and threaten them" (K). When the polling finally did take place on February 10, O'Sullivan and Synan were returned with 3,521 and 2,856 votes, respectively, while Kelly ran a poor third with only 995 votes.[37]

In the meantime, the bishop of Limerick's good friend and neighbor, the bishop of Kerry, had fared somewhat better than his colleague in the electoral trials. In early 1874, Moriarty was still both an unrepentant Gladstonian Liberal and an inveterate enemy of Home Rule. He had, however, learned his lesson in the 1872 by-election, when the Home Rule candidate, R. P. Blennerhassett, had been returned in spite of him and his senior clergy. Though he kept a very low political profile in the general election, he did have the satisfaction of seeing two Gladstonian Liberals returned for the three parliamentary seats within his spiritual jurisdiction. The diocese of Kerry included nearly all of county Kerry and the borough of Tralee. On the announcement of the dissolution, both Blennerhassett and the senior member for the county, H. A. Herbert, declared their candidacies. Herbert, who, like the bishop of Kerry, was a confirmed Liberal in his politics, refused to declare for Home Rule. The Herberts, in fact, who owned some 50,000 acres in the county, had long been a power in Kerry politics and since 1847 had shared the representation of the county with the nominees of the earl of Kenmare, until Blennerhassett had upset the Kenmare interest in 1872. Though there were early rumors that the North Kerry Farmers' Club would nominate a second Home Ruler to oppose Herbert, apparently they were unable to find a candidate, and Herbert and Blennerhassett were quietly returned unopposed on February 2.[38]

In the borough of Tralee, however, the Home Rulers decided not to remain passive. They were determined to turn out their former member, The O'Donoghue, who for more than ten years had been patronized by Moriarty and the local clergy and who, in recent years, had become an anathema to all shades of Nationalist opinion. O'Donoghue's entry into politics nearly twenty years before, as a member for the prestigious county Tipperary, had excited great hopes. He had been looked upon as the likely successor to his near relative, the great Daniel O'Connell. Over the years he had slowly but surely drifted to the right in the Irish political spectrum, until, by 1874, he and Moriarty were essentially of one mind about Irish politics. O'Donoghue had opposed Blennerhassett in 1872, and a majority of his constituents actually had called on that occasion for his resignation. His passage, therefore, in the contest for Tralee was not likely to be an easy one. At first, however, the Home Rulers had some difficulty finding an appropriate candidate to oppose O'Donoghue. They eventually persuaded John Daly, the former mayor of Cork, to contest the seat, and he arrived in Tralee on Sunday, February 1, to address a large meeting that evening. The correspondent of the

37. Walker, p. 117.
38. Ibid., p. 119.

Freeman's Journal reported that Daly had declared O'Donoghue's "defection filled every Irish heart with sorrow. He traced his career, comparing now, when he walked surrounded with police amongst his own people, to when he was the popular idol, and declared voting for him would be stabbing Ireland in the heart."[39] Meanwhile, The O'Donoghue's namesake and parish priest of Ardfert, Denis O'Donoghue, who had caused a scene at the by-election in 1872 when, contrary to Moriarty's written injunction, he had nominated Blennerhassett at the hustings, had taken the precaution on this occasion of writing the parish priest of Tralee and dean of the diocese, John Mawe, to request his permission to be allowed to speak at the nomination meeting on Monday, February 2, in Tralee. Mawe refused, and Father O'Donoghue then wrote a bitter letter to the press denouncing his namesake. The election, which took place on February 4, proved to be a very close contest, with O'Donoghue polling 143 to Daly's 140 votes, and O'Donoghue thus was returned as the Liberal member for Tralee.[40]

Shortly after the election, apparently, Father O'Donoghue visited Dublin and called on Cullen. In their interview, O'Donoghue complained about Moriarty's recent diocesan regulations in regard to marriage dispensations and also accused his bishop of harassing him for his political opinions when he was only exercising his legitimate rights as a citizen. Cullen must then have written to Moriarty about O'Donoghue's complaints, for Moriarty replied on March 1, explaining why he had introduced the new diocesan regulations and turning then to the charge of harassment. "As to his second grievance," Moriarty further explained, "he was refused permission by the Dean to make in Tralee one of those election speeches by which he disgraced us all two years ago. He then vented his rage against The O'Donoghue in a violent and most offensive letter" (C). "I thought some reparation," he added, "was due, and I wrote to The O'Donoghue expressing my regret that a priest should have published such a document, and that the Rev. Mr. O'D. could be eloquent only in abuse and not in his pulpit." "For notwithstanding very considerable ability," Moriarty noted, "and great power in political speeches, he is the worst preacher in the Diocese." "Two years ago," he then reminded Cullen, "he got my name hooted by a mob at the very door of his Church, and after giving him a full pardon he blackguarded me in the newspapers. I never rebuked him, but merely kept my distance with him." "He is a man of correct priestly life," Moriarty concluded somewhat helplessly, "attentive always to his parish, and has no fault except this political lunacy which shows itself in most outrageous violence. I must let the fit pass." In the last analysis, in spite of the difficulties caused by Father O'Donoghue, Moriarty must have been pleased to be able to leave well enough alone in Kerry, for in the whole of the Irish representation outside of Ulster, only

39. *Freeman's Journal,* February 2, 1874.
40. Walker, p. 119.

four Gladstonian Liberals had been returned, and Herbert and The O'Donoghue were two of them.[41]

If the bishops and clergy of Limerick and Kerry had had difficulties, in recent years, containing the Fenians and advanced Nationalists in the parliamentary constituencies within their spiritual jurisdictions, the situation for the bishops and clergy in the county Tipperary had been even more complicated and more difficult. The complication had to do with the fact that three bishops exercised spiritual jurisdiction in Tipperary, namely, the archbishop of Cashel and the bishops of Killaloe and of Waterford and Lismore. The problem of coordinating their efforts in making nominations, and then in electing their candidates, provided a real challenge to their organizational and political skills. The difficulty posed for the bishops and clergy in Tipperary was that the Fenians and their sympathizers were not only very numerous, but also they were very aggressive, especially in the southern half of the county. Since the days of O'Connell, the clergy had been perhaps the most important element in Tipperary politics, but in late 1869 the Fenians and their friends, it will be recalled, decided at a by-election to challenge that ascendancy by nominating Jeremiah O'Donovan Rossa, who was then serving a life sentence for his Fenian activities. To the great surprise and mortification of the Tipperary clergy, Rossa defeated their candidate, Denis Caulfield Heron, a Gladstonian Liberal, by the narrow margin of a hundred votes. Rossa was then declared disqualified because he was a convicted felon, and when a new election writ was issued in early 1870, the Fenians and their friends proceeded to nominate Charles Kickham, another convicted Fenian, who had just been released from prison because of the precarious state of his health, after serving some four years of a fourteen-year sentence. In the ensuing election, Heron defeated Kickham by the margin of only four votes, and the result was looked upon by many of a less radical political persuasion as a moral victory for the Fenians and their sympathizers. What the Fenians, in alliance with the advanced Nationalists since the late Home Rule conference in Dublin in November, would do at the pending election in Tipperary, therefore, was a very worrisome question for the bishops and clergy concerned.

Of the two former members, Colonel Charles W. White and Heron, the latter decided not to offer himself as a candidate, while the former declared both his candidacy and his endorsement of Home Rule. A second candidate was soon in

41. The others were W. H. F. Cogan for Kildare, and Alexander Swanston, son of the duke of Devonshire's land agent in County Cork, for the borough of Bandon in County Cork.

the field in the person of W. F. O. O'Callaghan, the twenty-two-year-old, second son of Viscount Lismore. The viscount, in fact, owned some 35,000 acres in Tipperary. O'Callaghan, in his election address, also declared for Home Rule, as had White, and for the rest of the popular program as well. The Fenians and advanced Nationalists were naturally not pleased with White's and O'Callaghan's candidacies, but apparently they were having some difficulty mobilizing for the challenge, for the correspondent of the *Freeman's Journal* reported from Thurles on January 28 that the holding of the customary county meeting of the electors to choose their candidates was in some doubt because there was a great division among them on the issue of Home Rule.[42] The next evening, the *Freeman's* correspondent reported that the town of Thurles was placarded with posters asking the electors not to pledge their votes because an effort was being made to find sincere Nationalists and Home Rulers, who were not "eleventh hour converts," to contest the county.[43] On the following evening, February 1, a well-attended meeting of delegates representing the Nationalist party in Tipperary was held at Boyton's Hotel in Thurles.[44] The meeting, at which, apparently, there were no clergy, was constituted by advanced Nationalists and Fenian sympathizers. They unanimously adopted John Mitchell, the former Young Irelander, who had been convicted of treason felony in 1848 and transported to Australia. He eventually escaped to the United States, and in recent years he had been living in exile in Paris. It was then proposed that his running mate should be Charles Kickham, who had been defeated by Heron in early 1870, but the chairman of the meeting read a letter from Kickham in which he declined the nomination. The meeting was therefore obliged to choose between Peter Gill, the proprietor of the *Tipperary Advocate,* a Fenian sympathizer, and George Roe, a local Protestant landlord of some 5,000 acres, whose claim to political fame was that he had posted security for the costs of the Tipperary election petition consequent on Heron's defeat of Kickham in 1870. Gill refused to make way for Roe but assured those at the meeting that he would be willing to abide "by the wishes of the people." After considerable discussion, the chairman confessed that he could not decide who the candidate should be, and, in an interesting salute to the concept of popular sovereignty, he appealed to those outside the hotel, who had been waiting to hold a public meeting, which would endorse the nominees of the delegates' meeting, to help make the decision. The public meeting was accordingly addressed by the chairman and candidates, and the delegates apparently having taken the sense of the meeting, reconvened and adopted Mitchell and Roe as their candidates. Gill refused to abide by the decision of "the people," however, and the *Freeman's*

---

42. *Freeman's Journal,* January 29, 1874.
43. Ibid., January 30, 1874.
44. Ibid., February 2, 1874.

correspondent reported that the situation had been further complicated by Richard Butler's announcement that he would contest the county as a Liberal.

Several days later, on February 5, the clergy of that portion of the diocese of Killaloe which comprised north Tipperary met in the town of Killaloe, with their bishop James Ryan in the chair, and endorsed White and O'Callaghan as their candidates for the county.[45] Two days later, on February 7, the clergy of the dioceses of Cashel and Emly, and Waterford and Lismore, which comprised the rest of the county, met in Thurles with the archbishop of Cashel in the chair.[46] After interviewing White, O'Callaghan, and Butler, the clerical meeting unanimously resolved to support White and O'Callaghan.[47] The issue, therefore, was clearly joined between those candidates backed by the united body of bishops and clergy in Tipperary and the candidates supported by the advanced Nationalists and their Fenian supporters. The great irony, of course, was that the clerical candidates went to the poll as Home Rulers, and their opponents went as independent Nationalists. On election day, February 11, the Home Rulers White and O'Callaghan, headed the poll with 3,023 and 2,755 votes, respectively, while the independent Nationalists, Mitchell and Roe, received 1,788 and 705 votes, respectively.[48] The other two candidates, Gill and Butler, received 635 and 281 votes, respectively.

The lesson of the Tipperary election, of course, was that the advanced Nationalist-Fenian alliance was finding more favor among the voters and that the electorate was, in fact, being radicalized by the running of symbolic candidates. In a normal contest, the clergy and their constitutional lay allies could muster a vote of about 3,500 on behalf of a presentable candidate, and the advanced Nationalists and their friends could muster about 1,000 votes. In the three successive elections in the county since 1869, the independent Nationalists had polled some 1,100, 1,650, and 1,800 votes, with a corresponding reduction in the vote of the clergy and their friends. When the Tipperary election was over, however, the archbishop of Cashel not only was relieved, but also he was grateful for small mercies. "Our Electors in this County," Leahy informed Cullen several days later on February 17, "have passed off most satisfactorily, I thank God. Everything very quiet and the result what Bishops & Clergy wished for" (C). "If Mitchell had been returned here," he then explained, "we could not hold up our heads—and I wonder he was not returned. There never was a greater apathy & want of organization than there was on the side of White & O'Callaghan, whilst there was both energy & organisation on the part of the Mitchellites." "But for the Priests," Leahy assured Cullen, "Mitchell would have been returned."

45. Ibid., February 6, 1874.
46. Ibid., February 9, 1874.
47. Ibid., February 10, 1874.
48. Walker, p. 119.

Earlier in this letter, Leahy had reported to Cullen that the election in the borough of Clonmel, which was the chief town in southern Tipperary, had resulted in a great victory for their side. "The triumph in Clonmel was a most signal one," he explained, referring to the recently appointed bishop of Waterford and Lismore, who before his promotion had been the parish priest of Clonmel, "and for it we are indebted to the prudence & firmness of the Bishop, Dr. Power. It was providential that he was yet in Clonmel to direct his people in the emergency." "Bagwell," Leahy maintained, referring to the former Liberal member for the borough, who had voted for Gladstone's University bill, "began his political life as a Tory, and he ended as he began, a Tory." Leahy was alluding to the fact that Bagwell had been elected as a Conservative for Clonmel in the general election of 1832 and had lost the seat to a Repealer in the general election of 1835. He finally regained the seat in the general election of 1857 running as a Liberal, and he held it until 1874 on that interest. In 1874, he compounded his difficulties by refusing to declare for Home Rule and was thus a persona non grata both with the Nationalists, for his political views, and with the clergy, for his educational opinions. At a public meeting held in Clonmel on January 29 to select a candidate for the borough, at which Bagwell was present, resolutions in favor of Home Rule were unanimously adopted. "Mr. Bagwell," the local correspondent of the *Freeman's Journal* reported, "explained that he opposed Home Rule because it meant the disintegration of the British Empire. He was in favour of Amnesty and opposed to Denominational Education, believing the National System [of primary education] to be the most perfect that could by possibility be devised. He declined to contest the borough on the conditions submitted."[49]

Two Home Rule candidates were then proposed by their friends at the meeting. One was William L. Hackett, a local barrister, and the other was Arthur Moore, the very wealthy son of the late member for county Tipperary, who held some 10,000 acres in the county. The meeting then proceeded to select Hackett as their candidate. The local Nationalists, however, were not satisfied with Hackett, who appeared to them to be a Liberal in the guise of a Home Ruler, and they appealed to the bishop of Waterford and Lismore to conduct a test secret ballot of the electors, to choose between Hackett and Moore. Power consented, and on Sunday evening, February 1, a meeting of the electors of the borough was held with the bishop presiding. In his opening remarks, the bishop endorsed Moore so strongly that Hackett declared that he preferred to forgo the present ballot rather than cause a split in the Home Rule ranks and allow a Conservative to slip in. Power then praised Hackett for his "noble" declaration, but Hackett's friends insisted that they proceed with the proposed ballot, and the bishop agreed that that would be the proper course. These remarkable proceedings were described shortly there-

49. *Freeman's Journal,* January 30, 1874.

after in a letter from a Clonmel elector to the editor of the *Freeman's Journal,* and that letter is well worth quoting from for the interesting insight it gives into the imaginative way local politics were conducted.

> The list of electors was called over by Alderman Crean, J.P., and as each came to the table he got two cards, on each of which was the name of a candidate, and he deposited in a ballot-box the card on which the candidate of his choice was printed. Two Liberal electors in the room, one of them a relative of Mr. Hackett, did not vote through some inadvertance, and the votes of two Protestant gentlemen were rejected because one of them had been on a deputation to Mr. Bagwell to invite him to reconsider his intention of retiring from the borough. When the votes were counted there were for Moore 92 and for Hackett 88, so that the former was selected by a majority of *four*! Mr. Hackett then declared he would do all in his power to secure the return of Mr. Moore, and that he did so with great ability all the friends of the young member [Moore] freely admit.[50]

As indicated in the above letter, Moore was returned as the member for Clonmel. The expected Conservative candidate did not materialize, though Bagwell eventually decided to go to the poll. He was, however, handily beaten by Moore on February 6, with 220 votes to 149.[51] Little wonder, therefore, that the archbishop of Cashel had been well pleased with the election results within his jurisdiction. The three Home Rulers returned for Tipperary were all substantial landlords who had not the least connection with the advanced Nationalist-Fenian alliance.

Of course, no account of the clerical and, more especially, episcopal influence in any Irish general election would be either representative or complete without a consideration of the role of the archbishop of Tuam, who was esteemed by his friends and denounced by his enemies as the premier clerical politician of his day. In 1868, MacHale had effectively sounded the death knell for landlord influence in county Mayo, and the work he had begun there, as has already been seen, was then effectively extended to county Galway, in two successive by-elections in 1870 and 1872. Ironically enough, the seal to his work had been set by the Ballot Act, passed in late spring of 1872 by the British Parliament. It is, therefore, interesting to examine the nature and extent of MacHale's political power and influence in what had long been considered his electoral stronghold, the counties of Galway and Mayo, in the general election of 1874, especially in the light of the demise of landlord power and influence in those counties. In Galway, it will be recalled, the two sitting members at the time of the dissolution of Parliament were Mitchell Henry, an avowed Home Ruler, and Captain William Trench, the Conservative, who had been declared elected in the place of Captain John Nolan, by the court of

50. Ibid., February 14, 1874. The letter is dated February 12, 1874.
51. Walker, p. 115.

common pleas on the recommendation of Judge Keogh. Trench, of course, realized he had no chance of being returned, and he accordingly retired. Mitchell Henry and Nolan were then adopted by MacHale and his clergy as the Home Rule candidates for the county. The bishop of Galway, however, was very much put out at not being consulted in the matter, and he reported to Cullen that he had been approached by one of the more prominent and substantial Catholic landlords in the county about the possibility of filling Trench's vacated seat. "Mr. Redington of Kilcornan," MacEvilly explained on January 30, "a most excellent young man, has some idea of coming forward to contest the County with [i.e., against] Nolan, who is universally *disliked*."

> I think the *hatred* of Keogh, & the necessity of giving a *full* answer to him will cause the people to rally round Nolan. It is *Keogh* & *Keogh* alone that returns him (and sure all the Landlords admit Keogh has ruined them) but if another election after this occurred in a month, Nolan would not get a 100 votes.
>
> I have told Mr. Redington who has consulted me, if he was not morally sure of success I would not advise him to incur the risk & expense of a contest. Altho very orthodox on the Education Question, he is not up to the mark on the restitution of the temporal Power (C).

"All I could do for him," MacEvilly observed, most interestingly, in conclusion, "would be of a *negative* character, as Dr. MacHale will be for Nolan, and it would not do to have Bishop against Bishop in public."

Two days later MacEvilly wrote to Cullen again. "I don't know," he confessed on February 1, "what may happen in the County Galway. Mr. Mitchell Henry will certainly be returned" (C). "He *seems* to forget," MacEvilly complained, "what Galway *Diocese* did for him in the first instance as he is going round the county to help them elsewhere, but never gives us any helping hand here. Some people here are not so much in love with him as they were. They think he has kept aloof from here to please Dr. MacHale, who would like to see Galway borough affairs in confusion." "It is hard to say," he added, "who the second member may be. Trench has retired. If a good man stood against Nolan, who is universally disliked, he might succeed." MacEvilly's wish was certainly the father to the thought if not the deed, for another candidate did take up the running. Hyacinth D'Arcy, a substantial Catholic landlord of some 10,000 acres, who had declared his candidacy in the by-election in 1871 but had withdrawn, announced he would contest the seat. "The issue of our County Election," MacEvilly reported on February 11, "is not yet ascertained. The votes are being counted, & probably before I seal this, I will be in a position to inform you. It is however regarded as certain that Henry & Nolan are the Members" (C). "D'Arcy," he explained, "who called on me & to whom I gave neither advice nor opinion, it is thought will be in a hopeless minority." "The Priests of Galway & Kilmacduagh," MacEvilly then noted, referring to his own ecclesiastical jurisdiction, "took no part whatever. But, the people were determined to be influenced *by Keogh.*" "We cannot afford to go against them," he further maintained, "unless in cases of Secret Societies or in matters against faith or morals. All the candidates were for Denominational Education & so far as I am concerned they may go for anything else they please of an indifferent character. All too are strongly outspoken about the Pope." "I have just heard," MacEvilly added in a postscript, "that Nolan is at the head of the Poll. Henry second, & D'Arcy is out. Keogh gave Nolan that place. No power on Earth could influence them [the electors] not to give Keogh and Co. a salutary lesson." The actual voting, in fact, resulted in Nolan receiving 2,348 votes, while Henry received 2,270, and D'Arcy only 1,080.[52]

In the meantime, the election for county Mayo had already taken place. Lord Bingham, the Conservative senior member, decided not to stand for re-election, and the real question became who would stand as the second Home Rule candidate with the former junior member, George Ekins Browne. It was rumored early that the second candidate would be John O'Connor Power, who had distinguished himself the previous November at the Home Rule conference with his populist resolution for keeping Irish members of Parliament up to the Nationalist mark.[53] Power was not only a protégé of MacHale's who had taught in the archbishop's diocesan seminary of St. Jarlath's, but also he was the representative from Connaught on the supreme council that governed the Fenian Brotherhood. As it happened, the customary meeting of the bishops and clergy of the county, at which they would make their recommendations for candidates to the electors, was convened on February 4, in the town of Castlebar. "A conference of the clergy of the diocese," the special correspondent of the *Freeman's Journal* telegraphed his editor that same day, "presided over by Archbishop MacHale was held to-day to select a candidate in the Home Rule interest. After a short deliberation they elected Mr. George Browne, and requested Mr. Thomas Tighe, of Ballinrobe, to come forward as his colleague."[54] A week after the clerical meeting, MacEvilly was finally able to explain to Cullen why O'Connor Power was not chosen, and Tighe was asked to stand as the second candidate. "Things took a dreadful turn in Mayo," MacEvilly reported on February 11. "Dr. MacHale & the Priests were *hooted* because they did not support a Mr. O'Connor Power, a *student* of St. Jarlath & the recognized head of the Fenians in this country. The following extract from a Mayo Priest will tell all."

"Please observe that the Archbp. came from Tuam accompanied by his
cousin Rev. U. Burke to promote the candidature of madman Power, the Fenian.
But thanks to the stand made by Dr. Conway [coadjutor to the bishop of

52. Ibid., p. 117.
53. *Freeman's Journal,* January 30, 1874.
54. Ibid., February 5, 1874.

Killala], & all the Priests of the County here, he was obliged to set *him aside*.
He could not conceal his humiliation by his embarrassed manner, nervous &
choking voice. The roughs & all the Phalanx of Fenians paraded the town
round & round with banners, fife & drum, shouting and hurraing [*sic*] for
Power. Father Lavelle was mobbed & hooted. Priests & Bishops denounced as
Traitors. Threats used that the Supplies [i.e., clerical dues] would be withdrawn. The mob passed backwards & forwards before the Presbytery where
the Abp was [i.e., after the clerical meeting], hooting & shouting & groaning,
and so on Thursday morning, the day appointed for the adjourned meeting
[i.e., the meeting of the electors to endorse the clergy's recommendations], he
fled to Tuam amidst the reproaches and hootings of the mob. Grand times,
grand result of Fenian Lectures, & the coming down of our St. Jarlath pupils
who daily associate with the young Candidates for the Priesthood &c."

"They absolutely cheered," a scandalized MacEvilly added, "for Bismark." "The
writer of the above," he assured Cullen in conclusion, "is a most truthful man, a
P.P. near Westport."

In any case, Tighe, who was a young Catholic landlord of modest estate and
moderate talents, accepted the nomination by the clerical meeting and issued an
address to the electors of the the county the following day.[55] Power made the best
of a very awkward situation by announcing the same day that, in "deference to the
wishes of his Grace the archbishop of Tuam and the Bishops and Clergy assembled yesterday," he would not seek election for the county.[56] Browne and
Tighe therefore were returned unopposed on February 6, but they both were
unseated on a petition because of a violation of election procedures, and a writ
was issued accordingly for a new election. The contest, however, did not take
place until the end of May, and in the meantime it became evident not only that
Power would contest the election but also that the Mayo clergy were divided
about the merits of his doing so. MacHale, who had come to the clerical meeting
on February 4 in Castlebar ready to endorse Power, obviously was embarrassed
that the majority of clergy there disagreed with him. The measure of that disagreement may be seen in the fact that MacHale's political protégé of some fifteen
years, Patrick Lavelle, the parish priest of Cong, opposed his choice of Power.
Lavelle's reasons for opposing Power, however, appeared to be less political than
social, for he wrote to Butt on March 12, in regard to Power's antecedents. "You
may have often heard the question put," Lavelle explained, "'Who is this Mr.
O'Connor Power'?—I often did but I never could get an answer" (B). "I am
however now in a position," he added, "to tell you he is the bastard son of a police-
man named Fleming from Co. Cavan, and a house painter by trade, who has
managed to live on his wits and the gullibility of others and myself for years—!!!"

55. Ibid., February 6, 1874.
56. Ibid.

Realizing that he had not written "private" on this potentially libelous letter, Lavelle prudently wrote again to Butt the next day. "Please regard my note of yesterday," he begged on March 13, "as *Private* for the present" (B).

About a month later, MacEvilly wrote to Cullen about the apparent contretemps between MacHale and Lavelle. "From 'the Tuam News,' Dr. MacHale's Paper," he reported on April 17, "it appears Fr. Lavelle & the Archbishop have a little difference of opinion connected with the late Mayo Election" (C). "The *corrected* report of the Archbishop's speech," MacEvilly explained, referring to the gathering on February 4, at Castlebar, "at the meeting of the Mayo Clergy was *altogether* different from what he spoke, as I am informed by one of the Clergy present." What apparently happened is that MacHale's difference of opinion with the clergy at the Castlebar meeting over Power's merits had not been resolved in the interim. When Power officially declared his candidacy in early May, for the by-election that was to take place at the end of the month, MacHale was placed in an awkward position. If he convened the customary meeting of the Mayo clergy to recommend candidates to the electorate, his views on Power likely would be voted down, as they had been at Castlebar the previous February. Therefore, apparently, he decided not to hold a meeting, leaving those priests who might be inclined, as he was, to favor Power free to do so. The coadjutors to the bishops of Killala and Achonry, however, were not of the same mind, and they urged their clergy in county Mayo to support Browne and Tighe rather than Power. Several days before the election was to take place, MacEvilly wrote to Cullen again. "The Mayo [contest]," he reported on May 25, "is a bad business. O'C. P. is a Fenian & swore in as Fenians some *alumni* of the College [St. Jarlath's] he was in, among them the Brother of a P.P. in the Diocese of T[uam]. It would be most humiliating if he were returned" (C). "Drs. Conway & MacCormack," MacEvilly assured Cullen, referring to the coadjutors to the bishops of Killala and Achonry, respectively, "are dead against him. I hope they will succeed." They did not succeed, however, and MacHale had the satisfaction of seeing Power returned as a member for Mayo. The results of the very close poll on May 29 were 1,330 votes for Browne, 1,319 for Power, and 1,279 for Tighe.[57] This was certainly a most signal and significant victory for those who advocated the advanced Nationalist-Fenian alliance in the interest of Home Rule. The victory, however, was a very costly one for MacHale because it placed him in the position, for the first time in his long political life, of being opposed by a very significant number of his clergy.

Finally, in this survey of the general election of 1874, there remains only the task of characterizing the influence of the bishops and clergy in Ulster. Since the Act of Union in 1801, in fact, the northern bishops and clergy had kept a very low profile in politics. Their attitude for more than seventy years was summed up aptly at the

---

57. Walker, p. 120.

end of 1873 in a reply from the bishop of Down and Connor, Patrick Dorrian, to a letter from Butt requesting Dorrian's support for the new Home Rule League to be launched at the national conference in November. "My adhesion in any public way," Dorrian explained in a letter marked "private" on October 8 from Belfast, "would, I believe, irritate rather than sooth the opponents of Home Rule in this part" (B). "What is most desirable," he advised, "would be to conciliate and weld together the different classes and to try and make the movement far more *protestant* especially in the north. These faction or party fights through the country for 'Home Rule' and 'no Home Rule' are a source of much mischief. And, it is, I think, essential to show that if 'Home Rule' were obtained, Protestants and Catholics would cease these broils and live in peace. For without this a Home Government would be impossible." "I need not suggest anything," Dorrian added, "that could promote this national and brotherly spirit, but I think Catholics would sometimes do well to forebear even when in the right, and that they ought to be taught to do so." "I have been unable to write sooner," he apologized in conclusion, "but all I can say is, make progress with the Orange and protestant party and the Catholics will see then how to assist."

The great irony in Dorrian's advice, of course, was that, if Butt took it too far, he could only succeed in further alienating the southern bishops who thought that the Home Rule movement was already much too Protestant and Orange. Dorrian, who was the most aggressively Nationalist Catholic bishop to appear in the Protestant heartland of Ulster in modern times, undoubtedly was looking forward, in this letter to Butt, to the next general election, in which perhaps an alliance between Catholics and Presbyterians might shake the Conservative and Protestant Church of Ireland ascendancy in Ulster politics. Indeed, immediately before the general election of 1874, that ascendancy never appeared greater. In the general election of 1868, for example, all of the 18 members returned by the 9 counties that comprised the province of Ulster were Conservatives.[58] Of the 11 members returned by 10 Ulster boroughs in 1868, 7 were Conservatives and 4 were Liberals, and those 4 were reduced to 2 in ensuing by-elections. In 1868, moreover, only 1 of the county seats and 6 of the borough seats were contested. At the dissolution in 1874, therefore, of the 29 Ulster members, 27 were Conservatives, 2 were Liberals, and none was a Catholic. In the general election of 1874, however, the Liberals gained 5 seats in Ulster and the Home Rulers, 2. After the election, the Liberals held 7 seats, 4 in the counties and 3 in the boroughs, and the Home Rulers held 2 county seats, for an overall gain against the Conservatives of 7 seats. The real measure of the Liberal resurgence in Ulster in 1874, however, was less the number of seats they won and lost than it was the number of seats they

58. Ibid., pp. 107–11.

contested. Of the 18 county seats, they contested 9, and of the 11 borough seats, they contested 8.

To a very large degree, this Liberal revival can be attributed to the alliance of Presbyterians and Catholics in those constituencies where together they made up a majority. In the borough of Belfast, for example, the former Liberal member, Thomas McClure, a prominent Presbyterian, was supported by the local "Catholic Association."[59] An even better example of Catholic and Presbyterian cooperation took place in county Donegal, where a determined effort was made to unseat the former Conservative members. The Catholics and Presbyterians selected Evory Kennedy and his brother Tristam Kennedy. The former was a prominent Dublin obstetrician who had been the original choice of the Presbyterians for the by-election in Derry City in November 1872 and who had retired, on that occasion, in deference to the Liberal attorney general for Ireland, Christopher Palles. His brother Tristram had sat for county Louth from 1852 to 1857 and again from 1865 to 1868. The Kennedys began their campaign for county Donegal in Letterkenny on January 30, with a large meeting that included a very considerable number of local Presbyterian worthies and clergy. The meeting was addressed, most significantly, by Patrick Daly, the administrator of the bishop of Raphoe's mensal parish in that town.[60] The significance, of course, was that Daly would not have been able to appear without the approval of his bishop. Several days later, on February 4, in the town of Donegal, a similar meeting was held, and the parish priest of Killybegs and vicar forane of the diocese, James Stephens, was reported by the *Freeman's Journal* correspondent to have been present along with his curate, Thomas Slevin.[61] The combined Catholic and Presbyterian effort, however, was not quite enough to offset Conservative voting strength. The two Conservatives, the Marquis of Hamilton and Thomas Conolly, were returned with 2,102 and 1,866 votes, respectively.[62] Tristram Kennedy, however, lost only by 40 votes, polling 1,826, and Evory received 1,757 votes. In general, the Liberals did equally well in the other Ulster seats they contested, and, with better organization and a heightened political consciousness, the Catholic and Presbyterian alliance could expect to do even better in the future.

The great surprise of the general election in Ulster, however, was the victory of the two Catholic Home Rulers in county Cavan. The former members for the

59. *Freeman's Journal*, February 2, 1874. McClure, however, lost his seat in this election, apparently because the electorate in the constituency had been expanded by some 4,000 voters since 1868, which was approximately the number of votes by which he lost (see Walker, p. 115).

60. *Freeman's Journal*, January 31, 1874.

61. Ibid., February 6, 1874.

62. Walker, p. 116.

county were Hugh Annesley, brother of the Earl Annesley, a large landlord in county Cavan, a Conservative, and E. J. Saunderson, a Liberal with very conservative political views, who owned some 12,000 acres in Cavan. "The electors of this fine Catholic county," the correspondent of the *Freeman's Journal* telegraphed his editor on Saturday, January 24 from Cavan, "are determined to be no longer represented by their present members. The Cavan Farmers' Club has girt up its loins for the struggle, and are to hold a public meeting at the Farnham Arm's Hotel for the purpose of selecting a candidate."[63] "The Bailieborough Home Rule Association are also on the alert, and have passed a resolution," he explained, "asking the electors not to promise their support to any candidate, however generous their promises, but to reserve their support for a genuine Home Ruler." On the following Monday, January 26, at the Globe Hotel in Cavan, a meeting of "twenty gentlemen connected with the Home Rule movement" was held to select two Home Rule candidates for the county.[64] The meeting proceeded to nominate unanimously Joseph G. Biggar, the Belfast provision merchant who had in November 1872 contested Derry City against Christopher Palles in the Home Ruler interest, and Charles J. Fay, a native of the county who had become a very successful solicitor practicing in Dublin. The *Freeman's* correspondent also noted that Biggar came very highly recommended by Patrick Dorrian, the bishop of Down and Connor.

In order not to allow the initiative for the selection of candidates for the county to slip entirely out of his and his clergy's hands, however, the bishop of Kilmore, Nicholas Conaty, issued a circular letter to his parish priests the next day under the signature of the senior curate in his mensal parish in the town of Cavan, Peter Galligan.[65] "I am directed respectively and urgently," Galligan explained, "to request that you, your curates, and the Electors of your parish will attend a Meeting to be held in CAVAN, on FRIDAY NEXT, 30th Instant, at TWELVE O'Clock, to SELECT CANDIDATES to represent the County in Parliament, in the interests of HOME RULE, DENOMINATIONAL EDUCATION, FIXITY OF TENURE, and whatever other popular measures may be agreed to by the Meeting." "To promote harmony amongst the Electors," Galligan advised in conclusion, "it is most important that each parish should be fully represented at the proposed Meeting." The purpose of the bishop's circular, of course, was to prevent a caucus of some "twenty gentlemen" from ignoring the clergy or the electors in the nomination process. The proposed meeting, therefore, was held on Friday, January 30, and the *Freeman's* correspondent telegraphed his account of the proceedings that same day.[66] "A meeting of the clergy of this county," he reported, "was held to-day in the Kilmore Seminary for the purpose of selecting

63. *Freeman's Journal,* January 26, 1874.
64. Ibid., January 29, 1874.
65. Ibid., January 28, 1874.
66. Ibid., January 31, 1874.

Candidates to represent them. There was a crowded and most enthusiastic assemblage, and the entire proceedings were characterised by the greatest unanimity and good feeling." "The chair was occupied," he explained, "by the most Rev. Dr. Conaty, Bishop of Kilmore. The chairman mentioned Mr. Biggar of Belfast; Mr. Kennedy of Cowan; and Dr. Devon of London, as the gentlemen whose names would be put before the meeting." "Preliminary resolutions," the correspondent further explained, "similar to those already adopted in Dundalk having been passed, Mr. Biggar and Mr. Charles Fay of Dublin and Cavan were unanimously chosen as the most desirable candidates."

Obviously, Conaty had made his point in assembling a representative meeting of the county, and he wisely and prudently accepted what was undoubtedly the popular choice. On nomination day, February 3, Conaty, in company with one of his vicars general and one of his vicars forane, signed Biggar's and Fay's nomination papers.[67] For the next two weeks, Biggar and Fay assiduously canvassed the county in company with the local clergy, and on polling day, February 16, they were rewarded with the fruits of their labors. Annesley, the Conservative candidate, decided not to seek reelection, but the Liberal candidate of conservative propensities, E. J. Saunderson, went to the poll. Fay and Biggar received 3,229 and 3,079 votes, respectively, while Saunderson polled 2,310 votes. The return of Biggar and Fay was auspicious because it signaled the beginning of the end of Conservative ascendancy in all those constituencies, and they constituted at least half of those in Ulster where there was a Catholic majority. Taken in conjunction with the Liberal revival in Ulster, the emergence of the Home Rulers did not augur well for the future of Conservative political power in Ireland. The election of Biggar was also a most significant event because, in the next several years, he would prove himself to be the most imaginative and daring man in Irish politics. In Parliament he would soon introduce the obstructive tactics that in time would capture the political imagination of the Irish people and lead, in the end, to the creation of an effective Irish Parliamentary party in the House of Commons. More interesting and important for the short-term course of Irish politics was Biggar's daring join the Fenian Brotherhood shortly after his election and his success in having himself co-opted to the eleven-man supreme council of that organization, where he innovatively and imaginatively attempted with considerable success to persuade that body to continue to support the constitutional initiative they had recently taken in Irish politics.

Though the Conservatives lost eight seats in the general election in Ireland, and nearly all of them in Ulster, they gained some eighty seats in England and Scotland, for an overall majority of about fifty in the House of Commons. The result was that the sixty nominal Home Rulers, even if they could form an effective Irish

67. Ibid., February 4, 1874.

party in the House, had no real political leverage. Two days after Disraeli assumed office, Cullen wrote to Barnabò, reporting the results of the election but drawing a rather unrealistic moral from it. "It is a matter also for observation," Cullen explained on February 22, "that there were in Ireland fifteen members of Parliament, of whom five were Catholic, the other ten Protestants elected by Catholics who voted in favor of Gladstone's bill, which was designed (*destinata*) to found a university without religion in Ireland—that every one of these members have lost their seats in the last election." "The number of Catholics," Cullen further pointed out, "that have been just elected rise to fifty one in Ireland, so that it may be hoped that the government will not be able to do anything in the way of establishing an anti-Catholic system of education." "In the last Parliament," he noted by way of conclusion, "there were thirty seven Catholic members from Ireland, and one from England. Now, there is not even one from England or Scotland, but if those from Ireland remain united, it will be difficult to introduce the Bismarkian system in this Kingdom." In a letter to Kirby two days later, however, Cullen was somewhat more realistic about the results of the recent elections. "You have long ere now," he noted on February 24, "heard of the change of ministry. I dare say the change will do good to Catholics on the continent but here we do not see what will occur" (K). "The Tories generally," he explained, "put all power in the hands of Orangemen when they come into office. If they do so now, of course, we shall have trouble in Ireland." "If they treat the Catholics in a spirit of fairness," he added, "the Catholics, I think, will give them great assistance. Everything depends on the turn that Disraeli will give to his policy. It is supposed that the Tories will be friendly to the Pope. God grant it, but I recollect that not very long ago, one of them, a minister of state, said that the Pope's states were a plague spot on the surface of Europe." "I think there are," Cullen concluded, a good deal more diffidently than he had to Barnabò, "fifty one or two Catholic M.P.'s in Ireland—there are also about 25 liberal Protestants who will go with the Catholics. If all these can keep together they may keep our enemies from attempting anything against Catholics at home or abroad. But God alone knows what is to come or what is best."

Cullen's analysis of the results of the general election in his letters to Barnabò and Kirby was most revealing. In writing to Barnabò, he had chosen to dwell on Catholic power by pointing out that not only had every one of the fifteen M.P.'s who had voted for Gladstone's University bill the previous year lost their seats, but also Catholics had increased their numbers in Parliament from 37 to 51, and, if they remained united, it was very unlikely that the present government would be able to imitate Bismarck in his persecution of German Catholics. What Cullen was telling Barnabò, in effect, was that Catholics in the United Kingdom were now on the defensive and the best that they could do was to prevent the worst. In his letter to Kirby, who knew a great deal more about the intricacies of British and Irish politics than Barnabò, however, Cullen unerringly had put his finger on the heart of the matter by noting that all would now depend on what Disraeli decided to do, and given his, and especially his party's, sectarian antecedents, there was not much hope in them for Catholics, either at home or abroad.

The most revealing thing about Cullen's analysis of the general election for his Roman correspondents, however, is less what he chose to say than what he chose not to say. He did not say a word, for example, about the most significant aspect of the election from an Irish point of view, the return of some sixty members pledged to Home Rule. He dwelt instead on the Catholic and even the Liberal character of those elected. The reason that Cullen did not mention Home Rule, and, indeed, it does not appear that he ever mentioned it again in his correspondence with Rome, was that from his point of view, at least, Home Rule was an unmitigated disaster. It was so not because some sixty Home Rulers were returned but rather because Home Rule had captured the political imagination of the people. Cullen realized as well as anyone that a great many of those elected were something less than sincere in their new-found political professions, but he also understood that those who had elected them were deadly earnest about Home Rule. Popular politics, therefore, was once again going to prove to be a divisive force among Irish Catholics, and Cullen's concern was not only about how he was going to keep the Catholic body united but also about how he was going to keep their political differences from dividing the clergy and impairing the unity of the bishops as a body, which he had done so much to foster over the previous twenty-five years. Before the political consequences of the general election of 1874 can be considered at any length, however, it is first necessary to discuss the theme that the bishops as a body had come to claim as peculiarly their own—the education question.

Part III
The Education Question

Catholic University of Ireland.

DIOCESAN COLLECTIONS FOR 1873.

PROVINCE OF ARMAGH.

		£	s.	d.	£	s.	d.
Diocese of Armagh	...	507	16	5			
„ Derry	...	299	13	5			
„ Clogher	...	359	3	3			
„ Raphoe	...	238	9	8			
„ Down and Connor		316	19	10			
Do. for Burses		90	0	0			
„ Ardagh and Clon- macnoise	...	234	13	8			
„ Kilmore	...	260	0	0			
„ Meath, including £7 7s. 7d. from preceding year,		24	5	11			
„ Dromore	...	145	0	0—	2276	2	2

PROVINCE OF DUBLIN.

		£	s.	d.	£	s.	d.
Diocese of Dublin	...	1,894	11	4			
„ Kildare and Leighlin		442	16	6			
Do. for Burse		14	6	8			
„ Ossory	...	340	0	0			
„ Ferns	...	472	14	3—	3164	8	9

PROVINCE OF CASHEL.

		£	s.	d.	£	s.	d.
Diocese of Cashel and Emly		440	14	2			
„ Cork		360	19	3			
„ Killaloe	...	574	11	3			
„ Kerry	...	242	4	5			
„ Limerick	...	627	4	9			
„ Waterford & Lismore		603	6	8			
„ Cloyne	...	336	13	3			
„ Ross	...	83	0	0			
„ Kilfenora	...	64	4	0—	3332	17	9

PROVINCE OF TUAM.

		£	s.	d.	£	s.	d.
Diocese of Clonfert	...	191	0	0			
„ Achonry	...	36	1	0			
„ Elphin	...	278	14	0			
Do. for Burses		69	13	6			
„ Kilmacduagh	...	58	19	0			
„ Galway	...	88	7	10			
„ Killala	...	114	11	7—	837	6	11

	£	s.	d.
Total Diocesan Collections	9,610	15	7
Special Donations	190	3	0
	£9,800	18	7

BARTH. WOODLOCK, *Rector.*
THOS. SCRATTON, *Acting Bursar.*

CATHOLIC UNIVERSITY, *3rd Nov.*, 1874.

Catholic University balance sheet showing diocesan collections for 1873

VI

The Difficulties
August 1869–November 1872

In the decade of the 1860s, the Irish bishops as a body had come to be virtually as one about the education question. By 1870 they also were determined that Irish education on all levels—primary, intermediate, and university—would be denominational and absolutely under their control as a body. They had, in fact, by 1870 won their twenty-five-year struggle with the Board of National Education, which administered the primary system, for the *de facto* control of that system outside of Ulster. They also had managed by 1870 to set up an intermediate system, which, though it still left a great deal to be desired, was at least adequate to the educational needs of Catholics and was completely under their control and denominational. The achievement of the bishops on the university level during the 1860s, however, was not nearly as impressive as it had been on the primary and secondary levels. By 1870, the Catholic University, which the bishops had founded in 1854, was still seriously hampered financially because of its inadequate income and hampered academically because of its lack of a charter of incorporation from the state, which would allow it to grant degrees to its students. By virtue of the recently inaugurated Irish-Liberal alliance, however, the Irish bishops were confident that the prime minister, William Gladstone, who had promised to legislate on the University question according to Irish ideas, would soon fulfill their needs for both a charter and an endowment.

Indeed, on August 18, 1869, some three weeks after the Protestant Church in Ireland had been finally disestablished by law, the Irish bishops had assembled in Maynooth and had issued a series of resolutions that outlined their position on the grievances Gladstone had promised to address through his legislative program for Ireland—the education and land questions. The resolutions, which had been drafted by Bartholomew Woodlock, the rector of the Catholic University, and Patrick F. Moran, Cullen's secretary and half nephew, were ten in number:

I. They reiterate their condemnation of the mixed system of Education, whether Primary, Intermediate or University, as grievously and intrinsically dangerous to the faith and morals of Catholic youth; they declare that to Catholics only, and under the supreme control of the Church in all things appertaining to faith and morals, can the teaching of Catholics be safely entrusted. Fully relying on the love which the Catholics of Ireland have ever cherished for their ancient Faith, and on the filial obedience they have uniformly manifested towards their pastors, the Bishops call upon the clergy and the laity of their respective flocks to oppose by every constitutional means the extension or perpetuation of the mixed system, whether by the creation of new institutions, by the maintenance of old ones, or by changing Trinity College, Dublin, into a mixed College.

II. At the same time they recognize the right, as well as the duty, of Catholic parents to procure as far as possible for their children the advantages of a good secular education. Justice demands that Catholic youth should enjoy endowments and all other privileges on terms of perfect equality with the youth of other persuasions; without which equality in the matter of education religious equality cannot be said to have any real existence.

III. The Bishops, without any wish to interfere with the rights of persons of a different denomination, demand for Catholics Catholic education, which alone is consonant to their religious principles.

IV. The assembled Prelates, learning with pleasure that it is the intention of her Majesty's present advisers to legislate for Ireland in accordance with the wishes of its people,—and of this they have given good earnest—trust that the distinguished Statesman now at the head of the Government will, with the aid of his able colleagues, give to Irish Catholics a complete system of secular education based upon religion; for it alone can be in keeping with the feelings and requirements of the vast majority of the nation.

V. As regards higher education, since the Protestants of this county have had a Protestant University for three hundred years, and have it still, the Catholic people of Ireland clearly have a right to a Catholic University.

VI. But should her Majesty's Government be unwilling to increase the number of Universities in this country, the Bishops declare that religious equality cannot be realized unless the Degrees, Endowments, and other privileges enjoyed by their fellow-subjects of a different religion, be placed within the reach of Catholics in the fullest sense of equality. The injustice of denying to them a participation in those advantages, except at the cost of principle and conscience, is aggravated by the consideration, that, whilst they contribute their share to the public funds for the support of Educational Institutions from which conscience warns them away, they have moreover to tax themselves for the education of their children in their own Colleges and University.

VII. Should it please her Majesty's Government, therefore, to remove the many grievances to which Catholics are subjected by existing University arrangements, and to establish one National University in this kingdom for examining Candidates and conferring Degrees, the Catholic people of Ireland are entitled in justice to demand that in such a University, or annexed to it,

(a) They shall have a distinct College, conducted upon purely Catholic principles, and at the same time fully participating in the privileges enjoyed by other Colleges of whatsoever denomination or character—

(b) That the University honours and emoluments be accessible to Catholics equally with their Protestant fellow-subjects—

(c) That the Examinations and all other details of University arrangement be free from every influence hostile to the religious sentiments of Catholics, and that with this view the Catholic element be adequately represented upon the Senate, or other supreme University body, by persons enjoying the confidence of the Catholic bishops, priests, and people of Ireland.

VIII. The Bishops also declare, that the Catholics of Ireland are justly entitled to their due proportion of the public funds hitherto set apart for Education in the Royal and other Endowed Schools.

IX. The Bishops furthermore declare, that a settlement of the University question, to be complete and, at the same time, in accordance with the wishes of the Catholic people of Ireland, must include the re-arrangement of the Queen's Colleges on the Denominational principle.

X. Finally, the Bishops of Ireland, deeply sympathising with the sufferings of their faithful flocks, believe that the settlement of the land question is essential to the peace and welfare of the United Kingdom. They recognize the rights and the duties of landlords. They claim, in the same spirit, the rights as they recognize the duties of tenants. They believe that the comparative destitution, the chronic discontent, and the depressing discouragement of the people of Ireland, are, at this period of her history, to be attributed more to the want of a settlement of this question on fair and equitable principles than to any other cause. Therefore, in the interest of all classes, they earnestly hope that the responsible advisors of the Crown will take this most important subject into immediate consideration, and propose to Parliament such measures as may restore confidence, stimulate industry, increase national wealth, and lead to general union, contentment, and happiness (W).

The resolutions, which were unanimously adopted by the bishops, made it very obvious that the prelates thought Gladstone should give priority to the education question rather than to the land question in his legislative agenda for Ireland. It must be admitted that the resolutions were very artfully constructed according to the ends the bishops had in view. The grievances concerning primary and intermediate education were relatively deemphasized by the greater specificity with which the University grievance was treated. The first three resolutions dealt with the education question in general, under the rubrics of a condemnation of the mixed system, a right to an equal share of support as far as public funds were concerned, and the right of Catholics to a religious education. The fourth resolution, significantly, welcomed the professed intention of Gladstone and his colleagues "to legislate for Ireland in accordance with the wishes of its people," which presumably would result in the implementation of the principles described in the first three resolutions. The grievance concerning university education was treated in the next three resolutions. The fifth maintained that Catholics had the same right to a university as Protestants, and the sixth declared that religious equality could not be achieved unless a charter and an endowment were also forthcoming. The seventh resolution, however, was key because it detailed what would be a satisfactory solution as far as the Catholic body was concerned. In the eighth resolution, the bishops referred to the increasing burden of having to support an intermediate system without state aid and expressed their desire to have a proportional share of the public and endowed funds allocated to Irish intermediate education. The ninth resolution, of course, dealt with the educational bête noir of the bishops, the Queen's Colleges, which were to them the exemplar of everything that was wrong with university education in Ireland. The tenth and final resolution on the land question was remarkable only for its vagueness about its good intentions.

The bishops were so restrained in dealing with the primary and intermediate aspects of the education question because the royal commission, better known as the Powis commission, which had been appointed to inquire into and report on Irish primary education, was still sitting and taking evidence, and the bishops did not want to appear to prejudge the findings of the commission or to prejudice its final report. When the names of the fourteen commissioners to be appointed to the royal commission were being mooted in the fall of 1867, the Irish bishops had taken great care that none either of their own body or of the second order of clergy would accept such an appointment. The bishops as a body in general, and Cullen in particular, were very concerned that no difference of opinion should emerge in the clerical body on the education question, and they therefore advised the bishop of Kerry, David Moriarty, who was inclined to accept a place on the commission, that such was not the view of the body.[1] When the seven Catholic commissioners, all laymen, were finally appointed, in early 1868, however, Cullen was not much pleased with those who were chosen to sit with the seven Protestant commissioners. For various reasons, four of the Catholic commissioners—the earl of Dunraven, a convert and a good friend of the bishop of Kerry; Michael Morris, a justice of the Court of Queen's Bench and a Conservative in politics; Sir Robert Kane, president of the Queen's College, Cork; and Laurence Waldron, former member of Parliament for Tipperary and a member of the Board of National Education—were not pleasing to either Cullen or to the bishops as a body. The other three Catholic commissioners, James A. Dease, a small landlord and aspiring politician of Whig propensities; S. N. Stokes, an inspector of schools; and W. K. Sullivan, professor of chemistry in the Catholic University, while more accept-

---

1. Emmet Larkin, *The Consolidation of the Roman Catholic Church in Ireland, 1860–1870* (Chapel Hill, 1987), p. 501

able, were not of much social or political weight in terms of their public positions or abilities (although Sullivan was quite able).

Though Cullen was determined that no bishop or priest would sit on the commission, he made every effort to see that those Catholics, clerical and lay, who might give evidence before the commission were orthodox on the education question. "I hope your Lordship," he wrote the bishop of Elphin on April 2, 1868, "will assist in bringing the Catholic claims before the Royal Commission on education" (G). "Dr. Dorrian," he reported of the bishop of Down and Connor, "will explain the injustice inflicted on Catholics in the North. I dare say the model school of Sligo would afford ground for serious charges against the Board, and for throwing away the public money." "If some Catholic Bishops and priests," he warned, "do not make out a case, Protestants will raise a shout of triumph." "If your Lordship," Cullen finally suggested, "could get a priest to give evidence about any attempts at proselytism made in Ballina or elsewhere in the West, a great good would be effected." Several days later Cullen wrote Gillooly again to urge him on in the good work. "It will be very useful," he suggested on April 8, "for the cause that your Lordship should attend and give evidence before the Commission on primary education. It will be well to have the general principles inculcated in the evidence as a useful impression will be thus made" (G). "I suppose it will be well to get Kavanagh to go to Ballina and pick up evidence there," he then added, referring to the professor of elementary mathematics at the Catholic University and the chief lay apologist on the subject of Catholic education in Ireland. "He is acquainted with the Bishop & clergy."

Cullen, who in such situations was usually anxious to testify first in order to set forth the case he expected others to follow, assured Gillooly on July 1 that there was no real hurry about his giving evidence and that the commissioners would be pleased to hear him whenever he felt ready (G). "The Commission," Cullen reported to Kirby the following week, on July 7, "on National education is sitting here in Dublin. I am to be examined Tuesday 14th instant—Pray that I may be able to bear witness to the truth" (K). "I will do all I can," he further assured Kirby, "to damage mixed education—and to show the necessity of religious training. The people here are greatly dissatisfied with the Commissioners as in appointing Assistant Commissioners they selected no Irishmen—they determined to appoint only Scotch and English—seven are Protestants, three Catholics: one of the last is Mr. Renouf who was brought over to the Catholic University by Dr. Newman. He was after made Inspector of Catholic schools in England." "Lately he published a very wicked dissertation proving that Honorius was a real heretic and condemned as such," Cullen reported, referring to the seventh-century pope. "He is now sent to enlighten us all in Ireland." The evening before he was scheduled to testify, however, Cullen was laid low by a near-fatal attack of cholera, and he did not make his presentation until the following year, in late February 1869.

In the interim, though Gillooly did not give evidence, a number of bishops, clergy, and laity did.[2] The bishops of Down and Connor (Dorrian) and Cloyne (Keane) both appeared before the commission in Dublin as witnesses, while the archbishop of Armagh (Kieran) and the bishop of Kerry (Moriarty) submitted their views in writing. Besides the bishops, two priests—Laurence Forde, Cullen's vicar general, and John M'Menamin, the parish priest of Stranorlar, in the diocese of Raphoe—and two brothers—J. A. Grace, a Christian Brother and a director of their schools in Dublin, and P. Townshend, a Presentation Brother and superior of their community in Cork—also appeared as witnesses. The Catholic laymen who gave evidence included Stephen de Vere, former member of Parliament for county Limerick; James Duffy, the Dublin publisher; Myles O'Reilly, the senior member of Parliament for county Longford; and James Kavanagh, professor of elementary mathematics at the Catholic University. When Cullen was finally able to bear witness, his three-day-long testimony on February 22–24 was certainly an impressive and comprehensive tour-de-force, amounting in its reprinted form to some 100,000 words, or nearly three hundred pages.[3]

Cullen's presentation may be divided into three parts. In the first he insisted that education that was not religious was not really education at all, and he quoted scripture, Protestant divines, English philosophers and statesmen (including John Locke, Lord John Russell, and Sir Robert Peel), as well as such foreign luminaries as George Washington and Napoleon I to prove his point.[4] In the second part of his presentation, he denounced mixed education between Catholics and Protestants and declared in favor of a complete system of denominational education.[5] He described a considerable number of educational systems in the Old World and in the New, quoting copiously from the Roman Catholic authorities who were involved with those systems, who not surprisingly professed themselves in favor of denominational education. In the third and most substantial portion of his presentation, Cullen undertook to examine the national system of primary education as it then existed in Ireland and to explain why it was unsatisfactory as far as Catholics were concerned.[6] In effect, Cullen argued, the system was objectionable

2. Royal Commission of Inquiry Into Primary Education (Ireland), vol. 3: Minutes of Evidence Taken before the Commissioners, from March 12 to October 30, 1868, (C-6II), H.C. 1870, 28, pt. 3; vol. 4: Minutes of Evidence Taken before the Commissioners, from November 24, 1868 to May 29, 1869 (C6-III), H.C. 1870, 28, pt. 3.

3. Ibid., 4:1177–1203, 1219–66. Cullen's evidence has been reprinted in Patrick Francis Moran, ed., The Pastoral Letters and Other Writings of Cardinal Cullen (Dublin, 1882), 2:517–802.

4. Royal Commission, 4:1177–79.

5. Ibid., 1179–1203.

6. Ibid., 1219–66.

because it was based on the principle of mixed education and, moreover, since the system had been established by Lord Stanley in 1831, insult had been added to injury because the rules by which the system was administered had been modified to such an extent by its governing national board, to the great prejudice of Catholics, that the system had now become objectionable in practice as well as in principle. He then proceeded to discuss particular objectionable modifications, under some seven headings: that the books introduced for religious instruction by the board had been compiled and written exclusively by Protestants; that the non-vested schools (i.e., those vested in managers or patrons rather than in the board) could exclude all religious instruction if they were so inclined; that the schools of the Christian Brothers and various orders of nuns were discriminated against; that the board had attempted to make the schools the property of the board rather than of their managers or patrons; that the board had given their inspectors the right to appoint monitors in the schools and some 2,000 of these assistant teachers had been appointed without the concurrence of the managers or patrons; that the rights of the pastors of the people in regard to religious instruction in the schools, which had been explicitly recognized in the original rules, had now been virtually eliminated; and that the rights of the parents had been encroached upon by successive modifications of the rules regarding their consent for religious instruction. The sad cumulative effect of all of these modifications, Cullen maintained, was that they encouraged the proseltyzing of Catholics by Protestants and that this had certainly been the intention of one of the founders and chief proponents of the system, Richard Whately, the Protestant archbishop of Dublin. The only satisfactory solution, therefore, Cullen pointed out, to the settlement of Catholic grievances in principle and practice in regard to primary education in Ireland, was to create a system of purely denominational education.

Cullen then proceeded to analyze closely the national system, attempting to prove that the adoption of a purely denominational system was not only structurally feasible and better suited educationally to the needs of those it purported to serve but also that such a system would be more efficient and less costly to the community in the long run. The figures that Cullen adduced to prove the first of his points made it clear that the national system was already, for all practical purposes, denominational.[7] He pointed out that of the 6,382 national schools in Ireland, there were 2,365 schools (37 percent of all schools), which educated 360,000 Catholic and no Protestant children. There were also 2,649 schools (42 percent of all schools) educating 330,000 Catholic and 24,800 Protestant children, and only 132 schools (2 percent) educating 13,000 Catholic and 14,000 Protestant children. There were, moreover, 197 schools (3 percent) educating 19,800 Protestant and no Catholic children, and there were 1,039 schools (16 percent), mainly in

7. Ibid., 1225.

Ulster, with 115,000 Protestant and 29,000 Catholic children. From Cullen's point of view, therefore, of the 732,000 Catholic children in attendance at national schools, the 42,000 being educated with Protestants were his greatest concern. Because these students constituted only about 6 percent of all the Catholic children attending the national schools, one might think Cullen and his episcopal colleagues could have accepted it, but it was precisely because the figure was only 6 percent that they thought the system should be declared denominational and the dangerous anomaly of having even one Catholic so educated be resolved to everyone's satisfaction.

Turning from the feasibility of transforming the national system into a denominational one, to the educational deficiencies of the system, Cullen concentrated his attack on the books supplied by the board.[8] He not only found the books objectionable because they were compiled and written exclusively by Protestants, but he also complained that their scriptural extracts were misleading with regard to Catholic teaching. He also argued that they were prejudiced and derogatory toward the Irish people, contained serious errors of fact, and were too difficult, not to say often irrelevant, for those whom they were intended to educate. As examples of the prejudiced and misleading nature of the books, Cullen quoted from a historical portion of the "Fourth Book" provided by the board: "The people of these islands have one and the same language (all, at least who are educated); one and the same Queen—the same laws; and though they differ in their religious worships, they serve all the same God, and call themselves by the name of Christ."[9] "This passage," Cullen complained, "intimates that no one who speaks Irish is educated." The chairman of the commission, the earl of Powis, who was a Welshman, then observed, "Or Welsh?"[10] "Or Welsh, or Scotch," Cullen rejoined, "I believe there are a great many well educated men in Ireland, plenty in Wales—more again in Scotland, who speak the respective languages of their own countries. I do not think the children ought to be taught such things." "The passage adds," Cullen further pointed out, noting the West-British emphasis of the quotation, "that England and Ireland have 'the same laws.' That is not correct. There are a great many laws in Ireland which are not adopted in England—and many laws in England which we have not in Ireland." "The last words tend," he added for good measure, "to make children believe that all the inhabitants of these islands profess in substance the same religion, whilst in reality there are essential differences between the doctrines of Catholics and Protestants."

Finally, noting the inefficiency and costliness of the national system, Cullen compared that system to the schools of the Christian Brothers and to those conducted by the various orders of nuns.[11] "The Christian Brothers," Cullen ex-

8. Ibid., 1227–28.
9. Ibid., 1228.
10. Ibid.
11. Ibid., 1230–31.

plained, "are closely connected with the question of primary education in Ireland. They were founded in the beginning of this century, about the year 1807. Since then they have extended themselves very much. They were connected with the National Board at its commencement; but afterwards, when they would not be allowed to carry on their own system they separated from it." "At present," he pointed out, "they have sixty distinct establishments in Ireland and 225 schools, and something between 25,000 and 30,000 children on their rolls. A very large amount of money had been expended in building the schools—the Brothers calculate it at about £154,000." "Their schools," Cullen added, "are conducted in a most admirable manner, and most economically for the country. Indeed the State contributes nothing whatsoever to the support of their schools."

In offering the commissioners some basis for comparison in regard to efficiency and costs, Cullen took as an example a national school in one of his city parishes in Dublin, Westland Row, which had been taken over from the board by the Christian Brothers some four years before.[12] For the last five years that the school was governed by the board, from 1859–63, the average daily attendance was 293 children, the salaries of the teachers averaged out at £201 per year, and the average cost per student per year was 32 shillings. The three-year average of the same school's daily attendance when governed by the Christian Brothers, from 1865 to 1867, was 548, the salaries of the teachers were £200 per annum, and the cost per student per year was 7 shillings. In other words, the Christian Brothers, Cullen maintained, educated nearly twice as many students per year at between one-fifth and one-quarter of the cost spent by the national board. Cullen also insisted that the efficiency of the Christian Brothers was second only to the academic proficiency of their students. The schools run by the nuns, Cullen then explained, constituted "a very important feature in the statistics of the National Board."[13] "There are about 140 or more convent schools," he reported, "with 72,000 children on the rolls, or an average of 516 for each school. The number in [average daily] attendance is 31,017, or 221 per school. The whole of the subsidy which the nuns now get for themselves amounts to about £12,000, which at the proportion of £20 for every 100 children, is 4 s. per head." "I think if the merits of the nuns were taken into consideration," Cullen pointed out, referring to the fact that the lay teachers in the system were remunerated at the rate of about 20 shillings per head per annum, "they ought to be put at least on as good a footing as any other teachers— and certainly they would contribute very much, if their numbers were increased, to spread education through the country, and to make the National Board more popular and more useful to the great mass of the people."

In the course of his analysis of the deficiencies of the national system, Cullen singled out for particular criticism the model, or training, schools that had been

12. Ibid., 1231–32.
13. Ibid., 1232–33.

set up in Dublin and in many of the chief towns in Ireland.[14] The model schools were designed to provide an opportunity for the formal training of national school teachers, the vast majority of whom had little or no such training. Cullen objected to the model schools because their 7,500 students, teacher trainees, and supervisory teachers, or professors, were all religiously eclectic. "These training schools," Cullen maintained, "are a sort of mixed boarding-schools, for Protestants, Catholics, and Presbyterians. Young men of every religion live together in the same houses, and are trained up together. They are left with very little religious teaching, and I think very little care is taken to make them practice any religion." "I heard on one occasion," he reported, "that if one of the young men in some of these establishments would attempt to say his prayers, he would be laughed at or hooted by others." "Young teachers," he concluded, "cannot be well trained in such establishments." Cullen then went on to quote Myles O'Reilly, the senior member for county Longford, who, in discussing the model schools in the House of Commons, had said on May 15, 1866 that such "a system could not be satisfactory—not to mention particular scandals to which it had given rise—he would state its effect in respect to Fenianism. He did not say these training schools were hot-beds of Fenianism; but many of those superficially-educated young men were connected with Fenianism, while several of the informers as to the movements of the conspirators had been teachers who had been carefully trained in the model schools." "In the central training school," O'Reilly then asserted, referring to the school in Marlboro' Street in Dublin, "there was actually established a lodge of female Fenians." Finally, Cullen indicted the training schools' deficiencies in curriculum and the amount of time they allowed for the completion of a course of study. He pointed out that there was no history, particularly no Irish history, in the curriculum and that four months was not a sufficient period of time in which to train a teacher. He also complained about the inordinate cost of the model and training schools, especially of the agricultural schools, which were a large component of the system. The central training school in Dublin had cost about £113,000 plus repairs since the inception of the system in 1848; the district model schools throughout the country had cost some £154,000 and £12,000 in repairs; and the agricultural schools, which except for the one at Glasnevin in Dublin were educationally useless, had cost over £82,000. The total cost over the previous twenty years had amounted to some £383,000, while the annual cost of supporting the whole establishment was about £51,000, which amounted to the extraordinary charge on the public purse of nearly £6, or 120 shillings, per child per annum.

After completing this portion of his evidence, Cullen was subjected to a close cross-examination by the commissioners. The chairman, Lord Powis, began by asking, "Does your Eminence think it would be possible or desirable at the present

14. Ibid., 1225–27.

moment to revert to Lord Stanley's original plan?"[15] In his reply, Cullen put forth the argument that he would make for the rest of the day—the argument that the Irish bishops as a body would stand by for the rest of the century. "I think the plan," Cullen maintained unequivocally, "was founded on the mixed principle with certain safeguards. Now the system has failed to such an extent in conciliating the people that I think it would be quite useless to return to Lord Stanley's original project."

> But I think the system as it stands could be reformed in such a way, without very much difficulty, as to render it satisfactory to the country. If you allow me I will sketch out what suggests itself to me. The schools should be declared denominational. The difficulties that arise then are to be taken into account. If the population be divided as to religion in a town or district, and if the numbers be sufficient for the purpose, let there be two schools—one school for Catholics, another for Protestants, and if there be Presbyterians, a third for them. Let the three religious denominations teach their own doctrines and their own opinions quite freely in their schools, and let them be dependent on the National Board only in financial and literary matters.[16]

"I would not let the Board," he concluded firmly, "interfere in anything except in matters connected with finances and letters."

Several days later, when Cullen wrote to Kirby, reporting the results of his examination, he obviously was very pleased by both the way his presentation was received and its likely effect. "During the last week," he reported on February 28, "I was examined for three successive days by a Royal Commission on the state of primary education in Ireland. I said all that I could against mixed education, and to demonstrate its evils I presented a copy in Latin and English of a letter of the Holy Father to the Archbishop of Fribourg in 1864. It appears to me that the business will result in much good" (K). "All the Protestant Royal Commissioners," Cullen further explained, "showed me every courtesy." "The only one who was a little insolent," he added, apparently referring to the president of Queen's College, Cork, Sir Robert Kane, "was a Catholic, who is a declared Freemason—but nothing can be expected from that breed." During the more than a year that the royal commission had been collecting evidence, and in spite of Cullen's original distrust of the majority of those who had been appointed commissioners and assistant commissioners, Cullen obviously had come to hope that the report of the commission would be more favorable than he had expected. Consequently, when it came time to draw up the resolutions for the general meeting of the bishops in August 1869, Cullen and his episcopal colleagues preferred to dwell at length on university rather than primary education.

15. Ibid., 1233.
16. Ibid.

There was another reason, however, for the bishops' emphasis on the University question in the resolutions published after their August meeting, and especially for their insistence on giving it priority over even the land question. The Catholic University was once again in serious difficulties with regard to both its finances and students. A similar crisis in the early sixties had been resolved to some degree by the appointment of Bartholomew Woodlock as rector, on the resignation of John Henry Newman. After the initial burst of energy as a result of the new leadership and a renewed commitment on the part of the bishops as a body to provide the necessary funds, however, the University did not continue to prosper. Between 1862 and 1868, in fact, the University limped along financially, with its income just barely meeting its annual expenses of some £8,000 per year.[17] Over that same period, however, the number of students declined from an all-time high of 196 to 161.[18] In 1862 there had been 80 students enrolled in the faculty of arts and 116 in medicine. By 1868 the numbers of students in the arts and medical faculties were 64 and 97. When the Catholic University failed to gain any legislative relief in the form of either a charter or an endowment, after protracted negotiations in the spring of 1868 between the Irish bishops and Disraeli's Conservative ministry, its position with regard to both funds and students rapidly began to deteriorate. In the five years between 1868 and 1873, for example, the annual collections for the University, which were usually made by the Irish bishops on the third Sunday in November, declined from £6,800 to £4,100.[19] By the end of 1873, moreover, the University was some £4,000 in debt, and the situation would have been much worse if the annual collections had not been supplemented between 1868 and 1873 with some £4,600 collected in Australia and New Zealand. After 1868, moreover, not only did the student body begin to decline even more rapidly than in the previous period, but also the number of faculty began to shrink. The number of students declined from 161 in 1868 to 97 in 1873, which included only 14 in the faculty of arts (W). In order to retrench in terms of expenses, the faculty members who retired or resigned were not replaced, and, though this had the salutary financial effect of reducing the largest item in the University budget from £5,000 to £4,000 for salaries, it also had the unfortunate affect of impairing the morale and vitality of both the faculty and the student body.[20]

Decreasing annual collections, numbers of students, especially in the arts fac-

17. C, 45/4. See October 1862 for unsigned memorandum about notes of collections, dividends, and payments. See also "Diocesan Collections for 1862" (November 10, 1863) and for 1863 (November, 1864).

18. Woodlock Papers (W), Dublin Diocesan Archives. Undated memorandum in Woodlock's hand for number of students 1868–72.

19. C, 45/5. See "Diocesan Collections for 1867" (October 29, 1868), "1868" (November 9, 1969), "1872" (November 2, 1873).

20. See Irish Catholic Directory (I.C.D.), 1868–73.

ulty, and numbers of faculty, however, were only the outward and visible signs of the decline of the Catholic University. The real reason for the decline of the University lay much deeper. The chief difficulty was that the University did not have a charter from the state, which would allow it to grant degrees and thereby to give its students the legal educational status so necessary to their future professional attainments and careers. The reason for Parliament's refusal to grant the Catholic University a charter, therefore, is crucial. The reason was that the Irish bishops would not allow the Catholic laity a part in governing the University. Woodlock had realized the nature of the impasse early on, and, during the early 1860s, he had worked very hard to secure some representation for the laity in the University's governance but without success. The story of this curious and interesting episode has already been told, but what needs to be emphasized here is that without a charter the Catholic University was doomed, and whether the ministry of the day could be persuaded to grant one, in light of the bishops' adamant refusal to allow the laity to share in the governing of the University, was to become the crucial question between 1869 and 1873.

During this period, the responsibility for both keeping the University afloat and attempting to persuade Gladstone and his colleagues to give it a new lease on life by legislating a University bill that would give it a charter and an endowment, fell mainly to Woodlock. Toward the end of 1869, with all the bishops scheduled to depart for the first Vatican Council in late November, Woodlock was very concerned that the bishops of the Catholic University board, which consisted of the four archbishops and two suffragan bishops from each province, should meet to settle the necessary business of the University before they left for Rome. Writing to Cullen on October 14, asking him for permission to summon the University board on October 20, Woodlock outlined his proposed agenda:

> The chief business for your Lordships is:
>
> I. To arrange about the Clonliffe land.
> II. ———about petitions to Parliament.
> III. To arrange about the Collection in November.
> IV. to give your directions about such questions as may arise in your absence in Rome.
>
> There are some other matters of detail (C).

The University board was not able to meet until October 27, and when they did only four of the twelve bishops, including Cullen, were in attendance.

In regard to the lands at Clonliffe West in North Dublin, it should be explained that, in May 1862, the bishops had taken a thousand-year lease on some thirty-four acres, at an annual rent of about £10 per acre, as the site on which they proposed to build the Catholic University. Because of the ensuing legal difficulties, they had not been able to build, and the annual rent of £344, on top of the recent legal costs, had become a serious liability over the years. In order to remedy the situation, Woodlock proposed to sublease the land to several subtenants for periods of twenty-one to thirty-one years, at the same rent that the bishops had to pay. The bishops present at the University board meeting decided to authorize Cullen and Woodlock to make the necessary arrangements and requested that Cullen and the archbishop of Cashel, as the lessees of the Clonliffe lands, execute the required leases. The second item on the agenda was apparently the result of a concern expressed by Woodlock to get up a number of petitions throughout the country in order to persuade Gladstone to introduce a University bill in the next session of Parliament, which was scheduled to open in early February. Because the great majority of the bishops were about to leave for Rome and thus would not be able to personally encourage the proposed petitions in their respective dioceses, and because a number of prominent laymen were just then engaged in promoting a Catholic lay declaration in favor of the University and equality of education, the bishops of the board decided, apparently, to take no action in the matter.

The item on the agenda that was of most concern to Woodlock, of course, was the one regarding the annual collection scheduled for the third Sunday in November. He well understood that the absence of so many bishops from the board meeting did not augur well for the collection. Indeed, as the appointed Sunday approached, and Cullen had not yet authorized the collection in his diocese—especially since Dublin was the mainstay of the collection, contributing usually one-fifth of the total sum collected in Ireland—Woodlock became somewhat apprehensive. He therefore wrote Cullen's secretary, Patrick Moran, asking him to remind the cardinal to authorize the collection. "I fear," he confessed to Moran on November 11, explaining the cause of his apprehension, "several of the dioceses will be in default this year. Dr. Power of Killaloe & Dr. Donnelly of Clogher tell me they can have no collection—however the latter has given me a donation of £250 as a consolation" (C). "A Limerick priest told Dean O'Loughlin today," he further reported, referring to a dean of residence in the University, "that there will be none in their diocese. In Ferns it is postponed until March. Waterford & Meath had none last year, and I do not know whether they or Armagh will have any this time." "All these defalcations," he added, "make it more & more necessary that Dublin should do its duty, as it always does." "They also seem to me," he noted finally, "to make more clear the necessity of urging on the Govt. to do something this year: i.e. during the next Session of Parliament."

Cullen did, of course, authorize the collection before he left for the Council, but when Woodlock wrote again on December 26 to Moran, who had accompanied the cardinal to Rome, he was still in a very apprehensive mood. "I fear," he explained, "nothing will be done next session about our University. If you could help on the question in any way, I wish you would as you may, perhaps, meet in Rome some persons who would have influence in doing so: ex. gr. Dr. Manning, Lord Acton (who is orthodox on this point), or others who may visit Rome during the Spring. It is very unfair to the young men here & throughout Ireland to have years allowed to follow years without any settlement. It is now more than four years & a half, since Mr. Gladstone & the then Home Secretary, Sir George Grey, admitted the existence of the grievance, & promised on the part of the Govt to redress it" (C). "I am sorry to say," Woodlock added, "that our numbers both here and in the Medical School are very much diminished this year—indeed the only wonder to me is: how we have any students at all. However if our numbers are small, I am happy to say that the Professors report there is an excellent spirit of study among them."

> The Collections too have not, I fear, been made in more than 6 or 8 dioceses: *Dublin,* where the results seem even better than last year—*Kildare; Dromore; Ossory;* & a few parishes in *Kerry*. Providentially, I have received £2,000 from Melbourne from Father Hickie, collected by him in New Zealand, Tasmania & Australia: God's Providence having thus sent us help from our Antipodes at the moment it was needed for: '*Domini est terra plentitude ejus*' [The Lord is the master of the earth and its fullness]—I mention all this to your, my dear Mg-re, in order to show you, that, although I believe there is not reason to despair of the work, still it is most necessary to urge it forward as much as possible.

"The Declaration of the Laity is," he further reported, "I understand, going on very favorably—they have got the signatures, I am told, of every Catholic of position in the Country; and it will now very soon be sent round generally, with a printed list of all who have given their names, asking others, who are sure to follow, to give theirs also." "I wish you would," Woodlock suggested, "give me your opinion & the opinion of wise persons with you, as to the expediency of trying to get up another stronger one from the middle classes. I fear such a movement might seem in opposition to the one now on foot. On the other hand, this inconvenience might be guarded against by embodying the present declaration in the new one, or expressing approval of it."

Within the week, Woodlock also wrote from Blarney near Cork City, where he was spending the New Year's holiday with his sister, to Cullen, to wish the cardinal many happy returns of the day. "There is little or nothing new," he explained on January 1, "respecting the Education question since your Eminence left Ireland" (C). "Dr. Dunne told me," he reported, referring to the professor of logic and metaphysics at the Catholic University, and a secretary to the royal commission on primary education, "about ten days ago, that when writing to your Eminence, I might mention to you that the deliberations of the Primary School Commission are going on favorably. For the week or so before X-mas the Commissioners were engaged in preparing their Report. I believe it will be quite in favor of denominational Education, and against the Model Schools in their present form. It will, probably, be laid before Parliament before Easter." "I fear," Woodlock added more glumly, "nothing will be done next Session about our Univy question, although time & opportunity will be found, if common report be true for legislating on Education in England & Scotland. I hope no step may be taken in that legislation, which may be a bad precedent against us."

"Our Prof. Sullivan," he further reported, referring to the professor of chemistry at the Catholic University,

> told me before X-mas, that the lay declaration on Education had now received the signatures of between 80 and 100, including nearly all the Catholics distinguished in any special way by position in Ireland—that now, without further delay, the document and also the names will be printed and sent to all the other Catholic Magistrates, land-owners, professional men, &c., who, it is expected, will be sure to follow those who have already signed. I do not think it is the intention of the promoters to publish the declaration until some favorable opportunity arises, or the question is mooted in Parliament.

"A few days ago I had a message from Mr. More O'Ferrall," Woodlock noted, referring to one of the chief promoters of the lay declaration, "to the effect that he would be glad to hear from me at the *Poste Restante, Nice:* accordingly I have written to him, & among other things I have consulted him about the expediency of our getting up a second declaration among the middle-classes, distinctly against mixed Education & in favor of Cath. Univy Education. Your Eminence is aware, that the declaration which is now going the rounds, is not expressly in favor of any system, but merely demand equality for Catholic Education with other systems." "If not too troublesome," Woodlock finally asked, coming to his point, "I wish your Eminence would give me your advice as to the desirability of getting up a second declaration. My reason for being unwilling to do so is: lest it should seem or be represented as in opposition to the first, which, otherwise, is, I think, likely to have great weight."

Woodlock, who was obviously very worried about the state of the University in regard to both funds and students, evidently realized that something had to be done, and quickly, to bring the subject of University education to the attention of Gladstone and his colleagues if the matter was to receive any attention in the upcoming session. Hence his rather desperate suggestions to Moran about enlisting Gladstone's good friends, Archbishop Manning and Lord Acton, in the good cause, and his additional suggestions to both Moran and Cullen about the expediency of mobilizing public opinion in Ireland by a more direct and widely based middle-class declaration on the subject of university education. Shortly after he had written to Cullen, Woodlock wrote to his old friend William Monsell, the senior member for county Limerick and undersecretary for colonial affairs in Gladstone's government, to express his concern about the urgency of treating the University question. Thanking Woodlock for his letter on January 7, 1870, Monsell was, however, not very reassuring. "I doubt much," he explained, "urgent as I agree with you in thinking it, that the Education (Ireland) question will turn up this year" (W). "How can it," he asked, referring to the land question, "when tenant right stops the way—yet I have my doubts as to whether a really good education system, intermediate as well as university, would not do more good than even a poor land bill." "However," he added philosophically, "we are the creatures of circumstances & must only try to mold them as best we can."

Though apparently neither Cullen nor Moran commented on his suggestion to mobilize Irish public opinion with a second declaration, Woodlock doggedly persevered. Forwarding a copy of the first lay declaration to Kirby, who was in Rome, on January 13, Woodlock noted that John Bright, the radical member for Birmingham and president of the board of trade in Gladstone's cabinet, had just made a very clever speech to his constituents in which he maintained that now that the Protestant Church in Ireland had been disestablished, though there still might be Irish grievances, there was no such thing as a Catholic grievance. After brooding over Bright's speech for two weeks, Woodlock finally, on January 26, wrote him a very long letter in which he insisted that there was certainly a Catholic grievance in regard to university education. He pointed out that the Catholic University had neither an endowment nor a charter. Not only did Catholics have to tax themselves to the extent of some £8,000 per year while Trinity College was endowed with some 200,000 acres yielding an annual income of £60,000, but also the Catholic University had neither legal recognition as a corporation nor the power to grant degrees, while Trinity College had enjoyed those privileges for the last three hundred years. Woodlock obviously intended his letter, which was full of rhetorical flourish, to draw Bright into a correspondence that might be published and, thus, to acquire the notice in the press he thought so desirable. Bright, however, was too experienced a politician to be so enticed, and he replied through his secretary that he would not forget the points referred to by Woodlock.[21]

The day before he wrote Bright, Woodlock had written to Moran, confessing that he feared "nothing will be done next Session about our business; unless perhaps, towards the end of the Session in June or July, when if our friends manage their work well, I think they will be able to make the Govt declare its policy & promise to settle the matter during the autumn or next winter" (K). "This, you may remember," he reminded Moran, "was what was done before the Supplemen-

21. K, Woodlock to Kirby, February 4, 1870.

tal Charter in 1864. Mr. Bruce, now Home Secretary, came over in August to arrange the details & the 4 Archbishops had their interview with the Govt in London at the end of November. I hope the next negotiation will be more successful." "Here in the Univy," Woodlock then reported, "everything is pretty much *in statu quo*. The number of students very small: the diocesan collections coming in very slowly: we have not as yet received £2,000 since November. And I fear very many of the dioceses will send nothing. I wish you had an opportunity of urging the matter on their Lordships and also on H. E. Card. Barnabò." "Again," he suggested delicately, in conclusion, "might it not be well to say something about the admission of some laymen to a share in the government of the University? You will see if an occasion offer."

In the next week, Woodlock was given even greater cause for concern as far as the future of the Catholic University was concerned. "Lest your Eminence should not have seen," he informed Cullen in a very long letter on March 3, "the Declaration of the Trinity College people in favor of mixed education, i.e. of converting their Institution with a fourth Queen's College. I enclose a copy."

> I also enclose a form of declaration which I intend to send to Mr. Gladstone in opposition to it. I have got over 150 signatures to mine. As yet I have not decided as to the best mode of publishing it, as not to interfere with the Lay Declaration in favor of Educational Equality, which, as your Eminence knows has already got about 500 names attached to it, & probably will have twice that number. I thought it desirable that as the Fellows of Trinity Coll. spoke from their experience in the work of teaching, Catholic teachers should also declare their experience. Before this letter reaches Rome, your Eminence will have seen that Fawcett [radical member of Parliament for Brighton], the unceasing advocate of this scheme for opening Trinity Coll., has given notice in the House of Commons, that on the 29th of this month he will move a resolution approving of the declaration that Gov^t ought to bring in without delay a Bill to give effect to that declaration (C).

"I think then," he warned Cullen, "that the whole question will be before parliament sooner than we expected."

"Your Eminence is aware," he reminded Cullen, "that Gov^t promised (in the Queen's Speech) to bring in a bill this Session to abolish the Tests [religious] in the Univ^{ies} & Colleges of Oxford & Cambridge; i.e. to convert them into mixed Univ^{ies} & Colleges. I fear lest Fawcett, or some one who agrees with him, should get a clause inserted into that Bill extending it to Trinity College."

> I have written to the O'Conor Don [member of Parliament for county Roscommon] to put him on his guard against a surprise in this way. I have also asked him, to let me know should he think there would be any use in my going to London. I have suggested to him, whether it might not be well to have a meeting of the Irish M.P.s to consult together as to the best mode of defeating Fawcett & the Trinity Coll. folk, and of getting the Gov^t to give us fair play in this Univ^y business. Your Eminence will have seen, that Lord Howard, Lord

Petre & one or two other English Catholics have formed themselves into a sort of Committee to watch the English Education Bill [primary].

"Might it not be well," he suggested, "if the O'Conor Don and a few other good Catholics did the same with respect to the Univ^y question?"

"Now while in Rome," Woodlock further suggested, "would your Eminence think it well of bringing again before the Holy See the question of the admission of the laity to some connection with the government of the Univ^y?" "I fear," Woodlock candidly confessed, "that the mass of the people, in Dublin, as well as elsewhere, take no interest in our Institution. This is true, I fear, even of a large number of the Priests."

> One would think that even apart from Degrees a great many young men ought to find it very useful to attend D. Dunne's excellent Lectures on Logic, or Ethics; or Mr. Stewart's Lectures on Greek, or F^r Penny's on Mathematics—such excellent instructions they have an opportunity of getting at their very door, and at little or no cost; and still with the exception of the Marist students, 15 or 16 of whom attend D. Dunne, and a few other who attend one or two other courses of lectures, we have scarcely more than a dozen *bona fide* students attending the schools here in Stephen's Green. The financial position of the Univ^y is also, I think, due in great measure to this want of interest on the part of the Catholic body. And again, the want of funds by hindering us from developing the Institution, hinders us from attracting students to our halls.

"And still," he then asked, coming full circle, "are not those financial difficulties due in a great measure to the want of interest on the part of the laity & even of many Priests?"

"Referring to the question of finance," Woodlock observed, "I think it well to mention to your Eminence, in order to your bringing it before the Prelates, and if necessary before the S.C., or Holy Father, that as yet only *eight* dioceses have made any returns for the Univ^y Collection for the current year: these dioceses are: Armagh, Dublin, Ardagh, Clogher, Dromore, Elphin, Kildare & Leighlin, and Ossory. I believe the Collection has been made or is about to be made in Cashel, Ferns, & Cloyne—but of the other dioceses I know nothing, and the amount received up to this time is not much over £2,000—; while, as your Eminence knows, the salaries alone, for which the Bishops are responsible, amount to about £4,000 a year." "The proceeds of the Australian & N. Zealand collections, £2,000," he further reported, "—which I received lately from Fr. Hickie, have come most opportunely; but it would at this moment be of the greatest moment in opposing the Trinity Coll. movement, for our University to be able to show vitality & to develop itself [torn] otherwise our enemies are but too well inclined to say: we are dying out."

"I hope your Eminence will pardon me for troubling you with all this," Woodlock further explained, "but it has been brought forcibly to my mind lately, both by the important phase on which the Univ^y question has just entered through the moves of Trinity Coll. and Mr. Fawcett, and also through some remarks made at a recent meeting our medical Professors & I had to consider the best way of increasing & developing our School of Medicine, where there are less than 90 students, while there are, I believe, 200 or more in the medical School of Trinity College." "If I may take the liberty," Woodlock added, "of offering a suggestion, I think there is every reason to fear that the mixed system will be set up in Trin. Coll. with all the weight of that old Institution, and with no corresponding advantage for Cath. Education, unless the Bishops take some decided step for interesting the laity generally in the work, and for urging on the Liberal M.P.[s] to *press* upon the Gov^t the claims of Catholics;—and one of the most powerful means for convincing our friends & enemies of our sincerity would be by some new & general effort to get in funds for the consolidation & extension of the University." "I fear I have wearied your Eminence," Woodlock finally apologized, "by this long & disagreeable letter: but I hope you will pardon me. I am extremely anxious about this business at the present conjuncture, which seems to me a most critical one."

In the meantime, Woodlock had also written to William Monsell, undersecretary for colonial affairs, asking him, apparently, what he thought had best be done in the crisis precipitated by the Trinity College declaration. "I think the time has come," Monsell replied on March 3, referring to the Catholic lay declaration, "for issuing our Manifesto. It ought to produce a good effect" (W). "I do not think," he further advised, "we ought to propose any plan but simply refuse to accept the proposal of Trinity College. Then when the time comes we can put forward the Catholic Univ^y plan." "I am," he confessed in conclusion, "for the first time in my life in low spirits about Ireland." Sometime shortly after he wrote to Cullen and received Monsell's despondent letter, Woodlock became even more alarmed by the prospects of Fawcett's motion, which was scheduled for March 29. He finally decided to beg Moran to alert the bishops in Rome to the approaching crisis, in order that they might take appropriate action. "I lost no time," Moran assured Woodlock on March 22, "in representing your views, stated in your last letter, to the Irish Bishops here, of course with permission of His Eminence" (W). "They entered very warmly into the matter," he reported, "and a meeting of all was held here on yesterday evening at 4 o'clock. *Inter caesteros* [among the rest] Dr. MacHale was present. They resolved to send each of the Catholic M.P's their views regarding the Fawcett movement. A short Resolution will be added to the Episcopal Resolution of last August and all will be transmitted to its destiny, but I doubt if it will reach the M.P.'s till after the 1st of April." "The B'ps," Moran further explained, "adjourned their sitting till tomorrow (Wednesday) evening when the new Resolution will be brought up by the Abp. of Cashel & hence even if no change be deemed necessary cannot be sent off until Thursday or Friday."

Meanwhile, Woodlock had written The O'Conor Don, asking him if he thought that he should come to London in the crisis. "I do not think," the Don replied on March 26, "you could accomplish any practical result by giving yourself the trouble of coming over here just now" (W). "I am told," he reported, "the gov. intend to oppose Fawcetts motion on the ground that this whole university question should be dealt with at once & that it cannot be dealt with this year." "I do not think," he further explained, "that you could do much therefore just now & it is better in the eyes of English liberals who protest the very appearance of a priest not to alarm them by your coming over on Fawcetts motion for this I think would rather tend to giving support to that motion." "I fear our cause in this university question," he added even more pessimistically, "has not a very pleasant prospect. The feeling against denominationalism is every day gaining strength, & it was a great misfortune that four or five years ago when overtures were made to the bishops by the then liberal government that something practical was not done." "We shall now," he assured Woodlock in conclusion, "have very uphill work & I am not very sanguine of success." When Fawcett's motion was postponed to Friday, April 1, Woodlock wrote The O'Conor Don again about coming to London and about attempting to extract a promise from the government as to when they proposed to deal with the University question. "I am still of the opinion," the Don replied on March 29, "expressed in my last letter that your coming over now would not accomplish any good & might do harm" (W). "I intend," he assured Woodlock, "if I get the chance to speak on Friday & so will some others I think. It seems to me however that it would not be desireable to press the government to express any opinion on this question just now. It is rather the object of *Fawcett* to force them to such an expression & I don't think we should aid him at all. He is anxious that if the government intend to do anything in the direction of our view that intention should be made known now as to get up agitation against it between this & next year & it would be very foolish on our part to aid this." "Besides," the Don concluded, advising Woodlock, in effect, to make a virtue of necessity, "I know the gov. will give no pledge or promise at all or will express no opinion, either in private or public. This is the resolution they have come to & it would be useless to try & change it."

On Friday, April 1, Fawcett moved an amendment to the motion that the House go into committee to discuss supply, which in effect approved in principle the opening up of Trinity College to all religious denominations. In a long and eloquent reply, Gladstone protested that no important measure on university education should be preempted by a private member's motion, rather than allowing the government, which was pledged to the solution of the question, to deal with it comprehensively in its own way and in its own good time. "With regard to the future," Gladstone explained in concluding his remarks, "our intention is not to lose a moment, when the state of Public Business and the time of Parliament permits, in proceeding to deal with the question of higher education in Ireland. We shall endeavour to deal with it in the same spirit in which we have endeavoured to deal with the questions of the Church and the land in that country. That is, to give fair and full effect to the great public principles—with all the consideration we can allow to interests and feelings on every side."[22] To emphasize the importance he gave to the question, Gladstone had made the rejection of Fawcett's motion a matter of a vote of confidence in the government. When the opposition then proposed to adjourn, Gladstone refused, pointing out that adjourning would mean that the question would have to be discussed again, and, since the government did not propose to deal with it that session, the government could not give the question any more time because of the pressure of public business. When the opposition insisted on the motion to adjourn, the government was sustained by a vote of 232 to 96, with a good many Conservatives voting with the government on the principle of supporting ministerial prerogative on so important a question. Fawcett's motion, therefore, was shelved for another year.

Some ten days after the adjournment of Fawcett's motion on April 1, Cullen, accompanied by Moran, arrived in Dublin. He had returned to Ireland because he was very concerned about the unsettled state of the country in the aftermath of the Roman condemnation of Fenianism and Gladstone's refusal to grant amnesty to any more of the Fenian prisoners. While in Dublin for some three weeks, Cullen also discussed the crisis precipitated by the Trinity College declaration and Fawcett's motion. Apparently he was able to convince Woodlock that in the long-term interests of the Irish-Liberal alliance, any forward move on the education question, while the land bill was still pending in Parliament, would not be prudent. Woodlock then suggested to Cullen that, when he returned to Rome, perhaps he could persuade Gladstone's good friend, Archbishop Manning, to write to the prime minister in the interests of opening negotiations on the University question. Before leaving Dublin on May 1, Cullen had asked Woodlock to pay close attention to the education question and to keep him au courant while in Rome. Woodlock wrote to Cullen on May 5, therefore, apprising him of the latest developments and reminding him to speak to Manning about writing to Gladstone, but his letter appears to have gone astray. When Woodlock received no reply, he wrote to both Moran and Patrick Leahy, the archbishop of Cashel, to alert them to the fact that in Belfast the Presbyterians had formed an Education League to work with the English League to promote secular education.

In his letter to Leahy, written on May 17, Woodlock pointed out also that some effort needed to be made not to urge their own claims on the government (C). The best approach would be to form an Irish Education League, but (presumably in the interests of the Irish-Liberal alliance) this, perhaps, was not expedient at the moment. Instead, Woodlock suggested that the bishops promote two concurrent declarations—one from the priests declaring in favor of the first of the resolutions

22. *Hansard's Parliamentary Debates,* 3d series, 200:1132.

published by the bishops in August 1869, and the other from the registered voters among the Catholic middle classes. Woodlock also explained to Leahy that he had written to Cullen on the subject of the declarations, and he asked the archbishop, if he and the cardinal thought it prudent, to recommend his suggested course of action to the other bishops. When Woodlock later learned from Moran that Cullen had not received Woodlock's letter of May 5, he wrote the cardinal a long letter recapitulating all that had happened. "Your Eminence may remember," he reminded Cullen on June 2, "that I took the liberty of suggesting to you to ask the Abp. of Westminster to write to Mr. Gladstone about our University-business. I have several reasons for suggesting just now the course that I have mentioned."

> The onward movement of Trinity College, first by approving of Mr. Fawcett's motion, & still more lately, by establishing 40 Exhibitions [prizes] of £25 — each, chiefly intended for Catholics (as would appear from the terms of their foundation,) seems to necessitate some movement on our part also,—and without any unnecessary delay—otherwise we may be too late.
>
> Again: The Land Bill is now out of the House of Commons: Mr. G. is pledged to deal with the Irish University question, as soon as the former question is settled. In all human probability, then, the details of the arrangement will have to be settled during the coming Autumn—perhaps within the next 2 or 3 months. Perhaps, as Mr. Bruce was sent over in 1864, some such person will, within the next few weeks, be sent by Mr. G. to make inquiries here on the spot, and, it might be, even to come to some preliminary arrangements. The terms we shall get will depend, in a great measure, on the preparation we shall have made in the meantime.
>
> Again: The Report of the Irish Primary School Commission has just been laid before Parliament. It would seem desirable that our claims should be urged upon Mr. G. without delay; and by whom more effectually than by His Grace [Manning], whom he respects so much.
>
> In fine: The English Universities' Tests Bill, which is now before Parliament, gives a good excuse for urging our views. It also creates a new, and as it seems to me, *very great and imminent* danger. For the M.P.s for Trinity College intend it is said to move that its provisions be established for their University. If this motion be carried, it will be equivalent to the adoption of Mr. Fawcett's for changing Trinity College into a mixed College, or fourth Queen's College. And still The O'Conor Don writes, that he much fears, the proposal will be adopted by the house of Commons. He says that nearly all our Cath. M.P.s voted for the Bill; (he thinks most imprudently;) and he does not see how they can refuse to extend to Trinity Coll., wh. seeks it, what they are forcing on Oxford & Cambridge. I hope Mr. G. will resist the motion (C).

"For all these reasons," Woodlock noted, "it seems to me, that a letter from the Abp. to Mr. G. at this moment would be of the greatest service."

"I would respectfully suggest," Woodlock further explained, turning from the method to the substance of his proposed gambit, "that the point to be urged on Mr. G. is one, wh. was lately well expressed by Mr. Lowe: viz. that to exclude all

Religion is, in fact, to introduce a new Religion or Deism. This new form of Religion is (to say the least) as much opposed to Catholicity as is Protestantism itself: therefore, if Mr. G. wishes to give us Educational Equality, it will not be sufficient to change the existing Protestant system into a secular or Deistical system: he must give Catholics a Catholic College or University." "This is the only way," Woodlock insisted, "he can meet the wishes of the Catholics of Ireland, who are essentially a Catholic people, i.e. in favor of religious education. If secularists are to have endowments and Colleges without Religion, Catholics have a right to endowments for a Cath. College, i.e. for a College with Religion such as they deserve." "If Parliament will not give an endowment to a Cath. College," he further maintained, "I see no alternative, but that the Prot. & Godless Colleges, including Trinity Coll., should be disendowed. We should thus have Equality in Disendowment, if they will not give us Equality in Endowment."

"Besides begging your Eminence to ask Dr. Manning to write to Mr. G.," Woodlock added, "may I hope that you will favor me with your advice on the scheme wh. I suggested to the Abp. of Cashel, and also, through Dr. Moran, to your Eminence."

> I mean; two concurrent Declarations, one from the priests, another from the Cath. middle classes, on Education in all its branches. Looking at the words of the Maynooth Resolutions of August last in wh. your Lordships *call* on the Clergy & Laity to use every constitutional means to advance Cath. Education, I was thinking I might address a circular to the Clergy, asking them to sign & get signed two Declarations such as I have mentioned. But Dr. Derry [the bishop of Clonfert],—who, I am sorry to say, is very poorly since his return— & Canon McCabe [Cullen's vicar general] were of opinion that I ought to have a more formal sanction before taking so important a step—in fact, its success must depend on the Clergy's taking it up *warmly;* & their interest must be awakened chiefly by the respective Bishops.

"I would, therefore," Woodlock suggested, "respectfully beg your Eminence, & Dr. Leahy, to urge the Bishops each one to write to the Administrator who now represents him in the diocese, and to impress on the Priests the necessity of co-operating in this movement; which, if successful will have the advantage among others of freeing their poor people from the annual Collection for the Univ^y." "If your Eminence & the Abp would think well of sending me the forms of Declaration," he added, "I could get them printed here & sent throughout Ireland. I would suggest, as I said in my letter to Dr. Leahy, that the Lay Declaration should not go below the class of registered Parliamentary Electors—and by being divided by parishes & Counties, it would have immense weight both with our Irish M.P.s & with the Gov^t." "I now leave the matter," Woodlock finally concluded his long letter, "in the hands of your Eminence, confident that what you will direct, will be for the best."

"I am desired by his Eminence," Moran replied on June 10, "to say that Dr.

Manning will write to Mr. Gladstone as you desired" (W). "As regards the petition of the Clergy," he added, "the Abp of Cashel as well as his Eminence is of the opinion that it is better to wait till the Bishops return to Ireland, as they are not entirely sure that in the absence of their Lordships the matter would be taken up very warmly by the clergy. It seems also rather late in the season for a petition now to produce any effect this Session, and hence they deem it more prudent to defer the general lay petition also till they return." "So much," Moran further explained, obviously attempting to reassure the disappointed Woodlock, "for my official communication. Now in my unofficial capacity allow me to say that I think the Bps will take up the whole question of higher education with real earnest when they return to Ireland, and that not only for laity but also for the Clergy." "If there were no other result," he observed, "from the present Council it alone would be a sufficient blessing to open the eyes of everyone that has eyes to see as to the absolute necessity of raising the standard of our schools and checking the Protestant or Rationalistic spirit which has monopolised instruction in so many countries and as a consequence has completely destroyed the solid Catholic teaching of former times."

Contrary to Moran's expectations, however, the bishops did not take up the whole question of higher education when they returned to Ireland at the end of July and early August. Indeed, circumstances conspired to prevent the bishops from dealing with the urgent question of Catholic University education for more than a year after their return from Rome. Most of the bishops had been absent from their dioceses for more than eights months, and upon their return they faced considerable arrears in regard to the annual visitation of the parishes in their dioceses, which usually were conducted during July and August. The fall of Rome in September, to the troops of the Kingdom of Italy, and the subsequent virtual incarceration of Pius IX in the Vatican palace, moreover, caused great and continued concern in Ireland throughout the fall and winter of 1870–71. The most pressing and immediate problem for the bishops on their return, however, was the need to do something about Maynooth, their national seminary. That college had been, along with the Protestant Church of Ireland, disestablished by act of Parliament the previous year. Under the terms of the act, the bishops had to assume responsibility for the college on January 1, 1871. Shortly after the bill had received the royal assent, in late July 1869, the bishops had met in Maynooth and set up an episcopal commission to arrange for the transfer of responsibility from the state to their body. The commission consisted of the four archbishops, the bishops of Cork, Clonfert, and Meath, and the coadjutor to Kildare and Leighlin. The charge given the commission by the body of the bishops was to inquire "into the actual state of the College discipline; to examine the rule and Statutes with a view to reporting on the improvement that may be made in the same; to inquire also which changes may be made in the curriculum of studies, & and what economic changes may be made in the College funds."[23]

Shortly after their return to Ireland from the Council, the bishops convened again at Maynooth on August 16, 1870, to make arrangements for their assumption of responsibility for the college at the new year, but they were unable to conduct any business because only six trustees were present and a quorum of seven was necessary. They were obliged, therefore, to adjourn their meeting to the following October. In writing to Kirby on August 16, Cullen had explained that the number of students in the college would now have to be reduced because of the diminished income but that there was a great advantage in the new arrangement: "the College will be free" (K). Shortly before the October meeting of the bishops, the bishop of Elphin, who apparently had replaced the recently deceased bishop of Clonfert as a member of the episcopal commission, wrote to Cullen suggesting that a more efficient procedure was necessary if anything was to be accomplished at their meeting. "As I may not have time," Gillooly informed Cullen on Wednesday, October 12, "to speak to your Eminence on Monday before our Meeting, I take the liberty of submitting now for your consideration an order of proceeding which I think w^d economise time and enable us to get through the large amount of very heavy and important business fixed for Monday & Tuesday" (C).

"The deliberation of those days," he explained, "will to a great extent determine the resolutions of Wednesday, which will exercise no small influence on the future of our Irish Church."

> The course I w^d suggest is—
> 1° To refer the subjects of our inquiry to four heads—viz: Discipline, Studies, Finance, & Health
> 2° To select on Monday morning two members of the Commission to make inquiry during that day into each of those departments—with the assistance of the College officers. The 8 Commissioners w^d be thus simultaneously engaged.
> 3° The Commissioners to meet together on Tuesday to receive reports & recommendations from the Sub-Commissions—and to adopt definite resolutions on each of the four heads.
> 4. A report for the Board of Wedn^y to be then prepared by the two Commis^{rs} and submitted to the Body [of Commissioners] on Tuesday Even^{ng} or Wedn^y morning to be finally approved and signed by the Commission.

"Without some arrangement like this," he advised in conclusion, "I fear the result of our meetings will not be satisfactory." In his reply the next day, Cullen was a

---

23. C, C. W. Russell to Cullen, February 17, 1871.

good deal less enthusiastic about what might be achieved at the meeting. "I fear," he warned Gillooly on October 13, "we shall be able to do little in Maynooth as there appears to be a wish on the part of some to leave things as they have been in the past, merely diminishing the number of students who shall be maintained at the expense of the College. The Committee will not be able to do anything or to get any information" (G). "In my opinion," he advised, "the best way to settle matters would be to depute two or three visitors who would live in the College for a month or two and report accordingly, having seen everything with their own eyes." "We must do something at our meeting," Cullen added, "for the Pope. All the Bishops ought to write in protesting the infamous proceedings of the Italian Government. The Pope is now a prisoner."

What Cullen was alluding to at the end of his letter, of course, was that the remainder of the pope's temporal power, the city of Rome and its environs, had fallen on September 20 to the armies of the Kingdom of Italy. The indignation in Ireland at the usurpation of the pope's temporal power was only exceeded by the concern for his personal safety. "We are all very much obliged for your letters," Moran informed Kirby on October 11, the week before the bishops were sched-uled to meet, "but all the general encouragement you give to get up an agitation is of no use unless you supply the *facts* to enable persons here to defend the good cause" (K). "The Bps. all meet," he then reported, "on Tuesday & Wednesday next. Send me a telegram if there be anything new or important on these days." "They will adopt," he added, referring to the bishops, "an address to the Pope, & one to the people of Ireland. Meetings will be held in every Parish & a deputation will be app^d to wait on Mr. Gladstone." The day after the bishops' meeting closed, Cullen wrote to Kirby, reporting that all the bishops were present except those who were sick or infirm and that they had adopted a letter to the pope and an address to the Irish people as well as endorsing the organization of a series of meetings all over the country.[24] "Dr. MacHale," Cullen observed, "was very tame at our meeting. He made no objection to the letter to the Pope or to the address."

In the meantime, Cullen had been in close contact with Archbishop Manning for more than a month about Roman affairs. "I have received," he reported to Manning on September 12, a week before the fall of Rome, "very bad news from Rome to-day and from a source not likely to be much mistaken. Those in author-ity are in great alarm about the safety of Rome itself and they fear that it will be immediately occupied by the Italians."[25] "Would it be possible," Cullen asked, "to get two or three ships sent to Civita Vechia [*sic*]? The vessel now there is too large to approach the harbour; a small vessel in the port would be of great advantage." "If the powers could be induced," he further suggested to Manning, "to declare

24. C, October 21, 1870.
25. Peadar MacSuibhne, *Paul Cullen and His Contemporaries* (Naas, 1877), 5:145.

Rome Neutral ground and to menace any power that would interfere with it the city might be saved. Belgium is protected in this way. Why could not something be done for the centre of Christianity?" "Perhaps your Grace," he added, "would have the kindness to speak to Mr. Gladstone on the matter." Manning was not able to reply for some ten days, and by that time Rome had fallen to the Italians. "I have not neglected your Eminence's suggestion," Manning replied on September 22, in a letter marked "private," "on the subject of Rome: but events have out run everything. There is however one thing that may still be done namely to urge our government to represent to the Italians that the Roman question affects all Europe & must be treated by a Congress"(C). "This would stop the Italians," he maintained, "from making bad worse, & would gain time." "If the Lord Lt. knew this wd be the views of your Eminence & the Bishops," Manning suggested, referring to the Earl Spencer, the Irish viceroy, "he would make it known here, with good effect. It would also be of much advantage if by meetings or speeches, or Journals, the sense of Ireland would be unmistakably declared. The gov^t. would then see that the Roman question is a question also." "Your Eminence will be glad to know," Manning further reported, writing on a separate sheet of paper marked "to be burnt," "that Mr. Gladstone, at my request, had ordered the Defence frigate to Civita Vecchia with instructions to protect the *personal safety,* & and liberty of the Holy Father. The Defence is already there: and the rumours of our ships being there have been in the papers, but this fact is distinct from them: and it will be safer that we do not let it become known as to affect upon Italy. France & Prussia might hinder our aim."

"The affairs of Rome," Cullen wrote in another letter to Manning, on November 19, "appear to be assuming a very alarming aspect. It is reported Mr. Gladstone had given a new impulse to the Pope's enemies by an article in the *Edinburgh Review,* and by withdrawing the frigate from Civita Vecchia. I hope these statements though reported have no foundation."

> We shall have a meeting of the people of Dublin on the 30th of November which I trust will be attended by all our respectable Catholics and a great mass of people. If it be true that Mr. Gladstone is author of the article referred to, would it not be well to get some of the speakers to speak strongly against him? However, I would not promote anything of the kind unless the charge of authorship be true and unless some good would come of it. Would your Grace direct us in the matter.
>
> At our meeting it is proposed to adopt an address to the Pope. It was also proposed to send a memorial to Mr. Gladstone but if he have openly declared himself hostile to his Holiness I suppose it would be useless to address him.[26]

"Very important meetings," Cullen then reported, "have been held in favor of the

---

26. Ibid., 154–55.

Pope in Wexford, Kilkenny, Cork and Belfast and I suppose all the other towns will follow their example." "The article in the Edinburgh Review," Manning replied on November 22, "was written, I believe, by young Mr. Gladstone, under his Father's eye. At least so I hear"(C). "Gladstone is, I fear," he added sadly, "responsible, and I greatly lament it. As this is not public, it would hardly be right to charge it on him. But without naming him, the article has no claim to be spared." "The Defence," he further explained, "was not moved from Civita Vecchia by the change of policy. It could not enter the harbour. But it is ready at Naples for any moment." "I think," he suggested ambivalently, in conclusion, "a deputation to Mr. Gladstone by Irish members would be useful. But I am afraid of his committing himself against us."

Of all the meetings held in sympathy with the pope, the Dublin meeting, which was convened by a requisition to Cullen of some 40,000 signatures, was the most impressive. On December 2, Cullen wrote to Kirby, giving him a detailed account of the whole proceedings.

> On Wednesday 30th Nov. the Church Marlboro St. was crowded at 12 o'c^k, and I opened the proceedings by a long discourse. Lord Granard came next, then the M.P. for Dublin Sir Dominic Corrigan, then Lord Southwell, Sir John Esmonde, John O'Hagan, Q.C., Serjeant Sherlock, M.P., Mr. Cogan, M.P., Jas. Arthur Dease, Sir James Power, More O'Ferrall followed in succession. The speeches were all good and F. [Father] Burke gave a long harangue. We adopted a letter to the Pope, an address to the people of Ireland and a letter to Gladstone. I sent you the Freeman of the 17th Decr with these documents and the speeches which occupy 17 full columns of that paper in small type. (K)

"We have also appointed," Cullen then reported, "a committee to carry out the objects of the meeting of which Lord Granard and the other speakers will be members. You see we have acted in accordance with your suggestions. I hope some good may come of our proceedings."

> The crowds were great all day at the meeting, and every respectable man in Dublin appeared at it—except the judges and Government officials who always keep back, tho' they were all raised to their present position by the influence of Catholics.
>
> I got a letter from an influential person in London who writes Mr. Gladstone is greatly put about by our meetings. The speeches were all so strong in favor of the Pope, that Gladstone must pay some attention to them.
>
> I hope you get the reports of the other meetings which I sent. They were all good, but of course in Dublin we say our own was the best.

"Write to us," Cullen added in conclusion, "and give us news—I inserted everything in my speech I had heard from you, and I think the people were glad to learn facts."

Kirby wrote not only to Cullen but also to Granard, to impress upon Granard and his committee that something more than protest meetings was necessary in the present awful crisis. Kirby was, however, preaching to the converted, for in his reply on January 1, 1871, Granard maintained that "if the Holy Father has no rights how can anyone else pretend to possess them. But I hope that the force of Catholic opinion may eventually influence their Govts., & I hope with you, that something more than meetings will be brought to bear upon the Govts" (K). "Here," Granard added, "our task is easy. If Gladstone goes with Victor Emmanuel and his brigands we must embarrass and oppose him in every way, & the Irish vote is not an element to be despised in the H. of Commons." A few days later, Manning wrote to Cullen, also raising the possibility of the Irish Catholic members taking action on behalf of the pope. "My purpose in writing," he explained to Cullen on January 3, "is to ask whether it be not possible for the Catholic members of both Houses to agree upon a line of action towards both Gov^t & opposition: telling both that any policy against Rome would compel a united opposition to whatsoever party may be in power. If only we were united in some such sense it might neutralize the action of England" (C). "If your Eminence," Manning suggested, "will kindly give me your judgement, I shall be happy to do what I can on this side of the water." "I hope Lord Hartington," he concluded, referring to the recently appointed chief secretary for Ireland, who had replaced Chichester S. Fortescue, "will be fair as secretary for Ireland."

Cullen approved Manning's suggestion, for as he explained to Kirby some three weeks later, on January 23, "We are to get the members of both Houses to write in threatening opposition to the Government, if the Ministers do or propose anything favorable to Victor Emmanuel" (K). "Lord Granard," he reported, "is very active and well disposed in those matters. I wish all our old Catholics were like him." "But the bigots in England," Cullen then added, "are now very furious, and they abuse Mr. Gladstone as too favorable to the Pope, whilst in reality he is hostile." When Manning was finally able to convene a meeting of the Irish Catholic members, in London, shortly after the opening of Parliament, however, he was obliged to explain to Cullen that they were something less than enthusiastic about coming to the defense of the pope. "Today," he reported on February 23, "twelve or fourteen of the Irish members met here, & discussed whether it was expedient for Major O'Reilly to raise discussion tomorrow on the subject of Rome" (C). "After full consideration," he informed Cullen, "we were unanimous in thinking that it would be inexpedient to raise any discussion in our Anti Catholic country and Parliament *until France has had opportunity to declare itself*." "We here already got the *maximum* of our Government in the letter to Mr. Dease," he further explained, referring to a letter replying to the junior member for Queen's county in regard to the Government's position on the occupation of Rome by the Italians. "Mr. Gladstone adhered to this on Tuesday night," he added, referring to the prime minister's remarks in the House. "He will never say more. He may easily be tempted or driven to say less. And that would undo all that he has now been constrained to say." "I confess," Manning maintained, "I am very strongly of this conviction. I hope that your Eminence will not see reason to disapprove of this conclusion; to which the more I think of it, the more strongly I feel obliged to come." "It will be," he concluded, "much satisfaction to know that your Eminence does not disapprove of it."

On reflection Cullen must have realized that the Irish members as a body were not enthusiastic about defending the temporal power of the pope in the House of Commons. The twelve or fourteen members who met at Manning's residence in London were probably the maximum number in the body of some sixty that could be counted on to speak up for the pope, but that even they would be willing to risk bringing down Gladstone's government on the issue was very doubtful, as indeed their meeting proved. They chose instead to set the impossible condition that France speak out first, when that country was literally prostrated after its recent defeat by the Germans in the Franco-Prussian war. Furthermore, Cullen must have realized also that any action taken by the greater part of the Irish members against the government must result, if successful, in the destruction of the Irish-Liberal alliance and in a general election, which if fought on the issue of the pope's temporal power could only prove to be a disaster to Irish and Catholic interests in both Britain and Ireland. All this, moreover, would have to be done in the name of a political principle, "independent opposition," which Cullen loathed, and which only just had been made, once again, a practical politics by the emergence of the Home Rule movement. Finally, if these were not quite enough, to assail the government in the interest of the pope's temporal power would also mean, and this undoubtedly had the greatest weight with Cullen and the bishops, the end of any hope for a satisfactory settlement of the education question on all its various levels in Ireland for Cullen's generation.

In the meantime, the bishop of Elphin had been attempting to keep the educational issue alive in spite of all the other concerns. Shortly after Cullen's impressive meeting in Dublin, on November 30, on behalf of the pope, Gillooly wrote to Cullen on December 2 to congratulate him for his efforts. "Now for the meeting on the Education Question," Gillooly added encouragingly, "which will I hope be equally worthy of our truly Catholic Metropolis" (C). "There is no time to be lost," he explained, "in making an impression on our Infidel statesmen—they are already, I suppose, concocting their Educat. Scheme." Gillooly was mistaken, however, for the government had decided that the English and Scottish education question should have priority over the politically divisive Irish education question. Moran, writing to Kirby shortly after he and Cullen had dined with the Lord Lieutenant, attempted to explain the situation. "The Government," he reported on February 17, "has determined to shelve the Education question if possible, as they fear to incur the displeasure of some of their English & Scottish supporters" (K). "However," he added, "our Catholic M.P.'s are determined to urge it on."

"Mr. Heron," he noted, referring to the junior member for Tipperary, "has one scheme drawn up and printed, & several leading men met at More O'Ferrall's to arrange a regular plan of University Education. Among them were Judge O'Brien, The O'Conor Don, Professor Sullivan, Major O'Reilly & Dr. Woodlock." "I am in great hopes," Moran concluded, "that something good will result from this union of our M.P.'s & that they may force the Gov't to put down Trinity College & the Queen's Colleges."

Heron had, in fact, submitted the draft of his bill to Woodlock the previous November, and Woodlock, who was not very pleased with it, wrote to the archbishop of Cashel to complain about the defects of his member's bill.[27] Woodlock had promised Leahy that he would forward Heron's proposed bill and his comments thereon, but he apparently was prevented from doing so by the pressure of business until the third week in January 1871. "I have looked over Mr. Heron's Paper," Leahy reported on January 22, "will send him a few notes tomorrow, which he will no doubt show you" (W). "There is," he further observed, "the technical accuracy & finish of the Lawyer about the details. It is far from unobjectionable in principle, especially as regards the constitution of the Catholic University or College. There it falls short of the requirements of the Bishops as made known more than once." "Your own objection to the proposal," Leahy agreed, referring to the fact that according to Heron's bill the University would not be endowed by a capital sum, but rather by an annual vote of Parliament, "to endow out of the Consolidated Fund is unanswerable. So is that other objection—that he leaves the immense property enjoyed by Trin. College untouched." "I greatly doubt the prudence," Leahy advised, "of allowing Mr. H. to bring forward his measure even on his own single responsibility. Being a man of some mark, he would be quoted as an argument/objection against our higher demands. We could never recede from the high ground we have taken & descend to such low ground as his. *Cui bono* [for whose advantage], then, his proposal, unless it be to create an argument & a difficulty in our way?" "From all I hear & see," he further reported, "the Government will do nothing for us this time [in Parliament]. Anything, therefore, he could propose would go for nothing, or worse." "Should not the Cardinal," Leahy then suggested in conclusion, "be consulted as to whether Mr. H. would proceed or not?"

In spite of Woodlock and Leahy's demurrers, however, Heron appears to have been determined to proceed on his own responsibility. "Mr. Heron," Leahy reported to Woodlock on February 13, "is persevering with his Motion. He is expecting to get the approval of some of us. He won't get mine" (W). "Something," he advised, "ought to be done, I should like to know what the Cardinal

27. See W, Leahy to Woodlock, November 22, 1870.

thinks. What does the Primate think? I ask the question on the assumption that you are free to answer it." Cullen had, in fact, already endorsed the effort to force the government to take the action mentioned in Moran's letter to Kirby on February 17. That effort was taken by those who had met at the home of Richard More O'Ferrall, and who believed it was more expedient to have the University bill brought in as a government measure than as a private member's bill because without the ministry's support a private member's bill would have no chance of succeeding. Heron, however, continued to be a difficult man to dissuade, and he wrote again to both Woodlock and Leahy, suggesting that his proposed bill might be modified to meet their approval. Both replied, independently of each other, that his bill could not be repaired and should be withdrawn.[28] The day after Leahy had written to Woodlock informing Woodlock of what he had done, Leahy wrote again. "I send you a letter," he told Woodlock on March 8, "I've had from Mr. Heron today. I forgot mentioning in my last to you that I had informed him there was another scheme of a University on the *tapis* [carpet] which appeared to be much more acceptable than his—one which it was not intended that any member should propose in his place in the House—that is in the first instance—but which, it was hoped, the Government might adopt as its own" (W). "He does not seem to be," Leahy assured Woodlock in conclusion, "in the least nettled for the falling through of his own Scheme."

"I had a long conversation yesterday evening," the bishop of Elphin reported to Woodlock the next day, on March 9, "on the University question with The O'Conor Don & his brother" (W). "The latter," Gillooly noted, referring to Denis M. O'Conor, the junior member for county Sligo, "leaves today for London. The Don must remain at home for another day. He will see you on his way thro Dublin. I expect he will do his utmost to forward our interests." "He does not think," he further informed Woodlock, "the Ministry will consent to propose a measure or any other scheme in the present Session. And he is rightly of opinion that it w^d be not only useless but prejudicial to us, to put forward our scheme ag^s the wish of the Gov^{nt}, merely as a private Bill." "But after a good deal of discussion," Gillooly added, "I led him to agree, that, even with the prospect & certainty of failure, we sh^d urge the Gov^{nt} to bring forward the question during the present Session. We must shew earnestness & anxiety about it, and a persistent determination to obtain our right—else the question will be shelved even in the next Session and the Catholic Body, will be represented as being indifferent about it." "He say[s] very truly," Gillooly explained, "that he & the other Catholic Members will have no chance of success in their efforts with the Gov^{nt} unless Public Opinion in Ireland comes to their aid. It is therefore necessary to obtain a strong pronouncement

28. See ibid., March 7, 1871.

from the municipality [i.e., the Dublin Corporation] and other representative bodies." "See to this at once," Gillooly advised, in conclusion, "without waiting for your Conference with him."

Apparently Woodlock was able to convince Sir John Gray, the proprietor of the *Freeman's Journal,* to give the University question some attention in his paper and also to take up the question in the Dublin Corporation. "I am happy to find our University prospects are looking brighter," Gillooly congratulated Woodlock on March 15. "The Freeman's Leader on Monday was very good—watch him and keep him to his work" (W). "I fear our Town Council here," he explained, referring to Sligo, "will not move in the Univ^y Question except against us—the majority of the members are Conservatives. I will sound them." "The Agitation now," he then advised, "should now be earnest & influential—and every movement should be widely published, and of course brought to the knowledge of the Gov^{nt}." "Could you not get the Sullivans," he asked, referring to the brothers A.M. and T.D. of the *Nation,* "to sustain our views in their papers?" In the next several weeks, the agitation began to pick up momentum, and Cullen wrote to Gillooly, suggesting that it might be opportune to convene a meeting of the Irish M.P.'s, in Dublin during the Easter recess, to arrange for the discussion of the Irish education question when Parliament reconvened. "I have written to & rec^d an answer," Gillooly reported to Cullen on April 3, "from the O'Conor Don on the subject of the proposed Confer^n in Dublin. He thinks it w^d be very difficult to get the MPs, who are in Ireland, to meet on any fixed day, as they are busily engaged and have different days fixed for returning to London" (C). "He thinks the discussion in the House," Gillooly then explained, "might be as well and even better prepared & provided for in London. However, if your Eminence wishes the Conference to be held on the 17th, he will arrange to attend. He is entirely in favor of an early Discussion, and will be prepared to take the lead himself in it, if no one else be selected."

"Major O'Reilly would, he thinks," Gillooly added, referring to the senior member for Longford, "be the best person to make a motion on the Primary Education Question. Should the Dublin Meeting be held he w^d consider Major O'R's attendance at it, most desirable. It is clear that the prospect of a conference in Dublin is very distasteful to him—and if to him, it will be still more so, I dare say, to others." "Perhaps then," he advised, "it w^d be better [to] give up the idea, and employ some other means of securing unity of opinion & action in London. Your Eminence might manage to see most of them on their way through to London and some clergymen might be asked to go over to London to urge our Catholic representatives to action." "I wish you would," he further suggested, "confide that mission to Dr. Moran. I fear the Rector's appeals would have but little novelty or efficacy with those gentlemen." Cullen apparently followed Gillooly's advice to forgo the meeting in Dublin, for Gillooly wrote to him again some three weeks later, explaining that he had worked out a *modus vivendi* with The O'Conor Don on the subject. "I had a long conversation on Wedn^y," he reported on Friday, April 21, "with The O'Conor Don regarding the best mode of introducing & conducting the discussion in the House of Commons on the Education Question and we agreed on a course which will I hope meet with your Eminence's approbation. I will not explain it here as the O'Conor Don promised me he would call to see your Eminence and ascertain your opinion of it" (C). "I write now," he explained, "to suggest to your Eminence the prudence of entrusting the lead & and guidance of the coming discussion to the Don—and preventing Sir J. Gray from constituting himself the Leader." "That may be done," he further suggested, "by a word from your Eminence, requesting Sir John to lend his powerful *Cooperation* to the O'Conor Don, and informing him that the latter has undertaken to introduce the Discussion and take all the necessary preliminary steps for that purpose." "A very favorable opportunity for renewing our complaints & demands," Gillooly pointed out, referring to the recently appointed chief secretary for Ireland, "on the Primary Educ^n Question will arise on the voting of the Educ^n Estimates for Ireland, when the Marquis of Hartington will, according to promise, refer specially to our Nat^l System, and any member will then have a right to state his objections to the system, without having given previous notice of a resolution or discussion on the subject. O'Conor Don would wish that Major O'Reilly would lead on that occasion, and I venture to suggest to your Eminence the advantage of asking him or getting Dr. Conroy to ask him to do so." "The late discussion in the Corporation," Gillooly observed in conclusion, "will be of great service. Sir John did his work there most efficiently, but it wd never do to place him or to let him place himself at the head of the MPs. They seem, as far as I can judge, to dislike & distrust him not a little."

The discussion in Parliament proved to be unsatisfactory because it elicited no response from the government as to how or when they would deal with the urgent question of Irish education, and Cullen approved the project of sending a representative deputation to Gladstone to press for a declaration on the part of the ministry. The deputation was to represent the spectrum of Irish public opinion on the question and was to include M.P.'s, municipal worthies, and influential laity and clergy. Woodlock accompanied the deputation to London, and Cullen also had despatched another of his clergy, John Canon Farrell, the parish priest of St. Catherine's in Dublin, who was very well known to a large number of Irish M.P.s and had served before as the cardinal's intermediary with them on the education question. Cullen also had written to Richard More O'Ferrall, who was in London arranging the details of the deputation to the prime minister, advising him on July 14 that under no circumstances should the Irish-Liberal alliance be placed in jeopardy by any loose talk on the part of a member of the deputation. "I trust," O'Ferrall replied on Saturday, July 15, "the deputation may be successful. We could not avoid taking some steps, but I agree with your Eminence that it may work good, or evil. We have many wily enemies and some false friends" (C). "I trust we may be able," he explained, "to ascertain beforehand what question Mr. Gladstone will ask (if any). Both parties are interested in keeping the peace. Deputations are often hard to manage. One troublesome man may do irreparable mischief, and if one speaks twenty may follow." "The principle effect the deputation will produce," he assured Cullen, "is to prove that the whole country takes an interest in University education." "I am glad to hear," he then concluded, "that Canon Farrell arrives on Monday." Several days later, Sir John Gray wrote to Cullen, reporting Gladstone's reaction to the proposed deputation. "Mr. Gladstone wanted me," he explained on July 18 from the House of Commons, "to 'arrange' to have the Education deputation put off. I need hardly tell you that my reply was decisive—that I *could not* if I would and *would not* if I could" (C). "I have mentioned the whole matter," Gray added, "to Canon Farrell who is here and he quite approves of the *details* of the answer I gave." "In fact," Gray further pointed out, referring to Gladstone, "I told him cordially that no I[ris]h member *dare* venture to make such a suggestion."

On the Friday, July 21, before the Monday the deputation was to meet with Gladstone, Woodlock wrote to Cullen from London. "As yet," he reported, "I have no special news to give your Eminence respecting our Deputation. Canon Farrell has given you a full account of our interview with Dr. Manning.[29] His Grace seems to expect some good results from the Deputation. So do our other friends here, but they all seem to agree that its usefulness must depend on the number of M.P.s, who will accompany it; and on its confining itself to one point, viz., to urge Mr. Gladstone to settle the question next Session & give us a pledge to that effect" (C). "Major O'Reilly, whom I saw today," Woodlock noted, "says: that we shall have the greatest difficulty in getting even this promise. A member of the Cabinet, to whom he was speaking lately, while admitting our great forebearance in not urging the question this year, said: that to bring it forward at any time will be a death-blow to the Gov^t. The Major replied very properly, that the difficulty of settling it will not be diminishing but increasing by delay." "As to the number of M.P.s, who will attend," he observed, referring to the senior member for county Limerick and undersecretary for the colonies, "Mr. Monsell says: that if we have 50, no Minister can refuse our demands, & even the House of Commons, must respect such a demonstration." "Please God," he added hopefully, "we shall have between 30 & 40; perhaps over the latter number. I shall let your Eminence know the exact number by telegram: I will call them *M*.s. I shall call Mr. Gladstone the chief buyer."

"I have just telegraphed," Woodlock reported on Monday, July 24, "to your

---

29. C, Farrell to Cullen, July 21, 1871.

Eminence a report of the Deputation, which took place at 3½ Ocl. Our friends, the Ld Mayor, Messrs M. O'Ferrall Cogan, Dease &c. seem very well satisfied with the results. There were 33 or 35 M.P.s present; a large number. I believe about 20 Municipal Towns were represented. The Lord Mayor handed in the Declaration of Cath. Electors, signed by over 22,500 persons. He was the only person, who spoke at any length. Some of the corporators from other towns also said a few words; but nothing inconvenient was said" (C). "Gladstone repeated," Woodlock explained, "his declaration, that he considered the position of Higher Education a grievance, and should be dealt with as such, on the principles which had guided them in dealing with the Prot. Church. His former declarations referred chiefly to this portion of the Education question." "Intermediate & Primary," Woodlock added, still paraphrasing Gladstone, "must be dealt with on other principles of policy [tho'] he did not deny, there might be shortcomings in them too: the time of Parliament is very much occupied; he could not say, when he would be able to take up the question—but admitting its importance, & being anxious to redress the grievance, he would deal with it as soon as he can." "Your Eminence sees, then," Woodlock concluded, "that he has given us no pledge as to the time when he will settle the question: but the deputation was a very important demonstration, and cannot, in my humble judgement, fail to be productive of good."

Canon Farrell also wrote Cullen an account of the deputation, but he was somewhat more pessimistic about the future. "Dr. Woodlock has told your Eminence of the Deputation," he explained on July 26, "It has given general satisfaction to our friends here. Mr. Monsell pronounces it an *unqualified* success. He says it was well managed, as nothing occurred to mar its effect, although it required some diplomatic skill to restrain the impulsive patriotism of some provincial Town Commissioners" (C). "When I objected that Gladstone had given no pledge to deal with the question next Session," Farrell reported, "Monsell observed that even though he [Gladstone] had his Bills ready & in his pocket, he would not have told us so. The fact is, said he, the opposition we have to contend against is so great that our only chance of carrying a satisfactory measure is by a 'Coup' & taking them unawares. If Gladstone fixed a time, we would have had the Education League & the Northern Presbyterians up in arms & a furious agitation would have been carried on during the winter." "Although 35 Irish Members attended the Deputation," Farrell further observed revealingly, "at least ten others might have been pressed into service."

> Tipperary was wholly unrepresented save by Bagwell [Clonmel] who attended under pressure, & openly avowed to me that he is quite opposed to our views— Blennerhassett [Galway City] did not attend but Mr. Monsell tells me that he is sound & quite with us—Sir Col^n O'Loughlin [Clare], the two Greville's [Longford and Meath] & McEvoy [Meath] were absent. Surely these might have

been brought up by a little pressure. It was only in the 11th hour that I could succeed in converting O'Reilly Dease [Louth] & then only by flattering his vanity, but on the whole we have reason to rejoice at the large attendance.

"Mr. Monsell," Farrell then reported, "is uneasy & anxious about Fawcett's Motion on next Tuesday. Many of our Irish Members have already left Town & he says that if we do not make a good fight, the Governt will be disheartened & may allow the Measure to pass." "He is very anxious," the Canon suggested obliquely, "that O'Conor Don should come over & take a leading part in the debate. Our Members appear not to be agreed as to the policy which ought to be pursued—some think it would be better not to vote, but to speak against the Motion, in the sense that the Protestants may open Trinity College if they please but that it will not satisfy us nor induce us to avail ourselves of the doubtful privileges they offer." "Tis a pity," he added, "that the O'Conor Don, Major O'Reilly, Mr. Dease & other recognized leaders on the Education question will be absent. Mr. Monsell suggests that your Eminence might possibly induce the former to come over as Madame O'Conor is now so much better." That same day Woodlock also wrote to Cullen endorsing what Farrell had suggested. "I shall only repeat," Woodlock explained, "what he said: that I think it *most important* that O'Conor Don should be here on Tuesday next to speak against the 2nd reading of Fawcett's Trinity College Bill" (C). "At the same time," he added, "I hope he & our other friends in the House of Commons will insist on the Govt setting aside the Bill in some way or another; for Mr. Gladstone has just admitted, that we have a grievance & surely he will not allow Mr. Fawcett to offer us a stone instead of the bread to which we have a right." "I am very anxious to get away from London," Woodlock then confessed, "but on the other hand it may be well that I should stay here till after Fawcett's Motion comes on." "Will your Eminence," he begged in conclusion, "tell me what to do? And also what course it is best for me to advise the M.P.s?"

Apparently Cullen advised both Woodlock and Farrell to remain in London for the debate on Fawcett's motion, for Farrell wrote to Cullen again the Sunday before the motion was to be discussed. "With regard to Fawcett's motion," he reported on July 30, "we found great want of concord among the Irish members as to how it should be dealt with" (C). "Some thought they could not consistently vote against it," he explained, referring to the fact that many of the Irish members had recently voted to open Oxford and Cambridge Universities to all denominations, "—others that they should not vote, but should speak against it in the sense mentioned in my last letter, which is, that Fawcett's measure will not satisfy our requirements—all were in doubt as to whether the Governt would support or oppose it." "Under the circumstances," the canon further explained, "I went to Mr. Monsell & he assured me that it should be defeated in some way or other, but he feared they could not command a majority if it came to a division, as so many of the Irish members had left London, hence the only way to defeat it, is to talk it out—the discussion will commence at about ½ past 12 on Wednesday, & must close at 6 o Clk."

> I then went down to the House with Mr. Monsell & I was fortunate in Meeting in the Lobby nearly all the Irish Members who are at present in London— we had a long discussion. They appear to be all agreed & united on the policy of talking against time—they fear we shall be defeated if it comes to a vote.
>
> Sir Rowland Blennerhassett [Galway City], Sir Don^c Corrigan [Dublin City], Maguire [Cork City], Synan [Limerick], Sir John Gray [Kilkenny City], McCarthy Downing [Cork], & Pim [Dublin City] have promised to make long speeches. Pim told me he would speak against the measure as injurious to Protestant Interests—they have no doubt that they will succeed in obstructing it for the present. They think it would be a great misfortune, if the Bill passed, as the House would then be committed to its policy & Gladstone would find it all the more difficult to pass a measure that would be satisfactory to us.

"The few members who remain," Farrell assured Cullen finally, "are able & apparently very earnest."

On the Saturday after the debate, Woodlock wrote to Cullen from Blarney in county Cork, where he had gone to spend a few days with his sister. "Before leaving London on Thursday," Woodlock explained on August 5, "I sent your Eminence a copy of the 'Times,' which contained a very full report of the proceedings in the House of Commons on the preceeding day. It also contained a leading article on the same subject, which was very bad, especially as showing what we may expect from the so-called 'Liberal' party in England" (C). "The other papers of Thursday," he observed, "of which I saw two or three, also contained very bad articles, in which Mr. Gladstone was denounced for not accepting at once Mr. Fawcett's proposal, declaring that he would give us nothing but mixed Education in Ireland." "I saw Dr. Manning on Wednesday evening," Woodlock noted, "after the Debate was over. He advises us to continue our agitation during the autumn & winter." "Does your Eminence think," he asked, "there would be any use in urging this course on the Bishops, and in my going for this purpose to Maynooth on the 17th of this month? I have heard your Lordships will have a meeting there on that day. Perhaps, it will be only a meeting of the Commission on the College itself, and in that case my going there would be of no use." "But it seems to me most important," he insisted, "that we should follow up by agitation anything that the Deputation & the Debate on Fawcett's Bill have done in London."

"I am sorry to tell your Eminence," Woodlock further informed Cullen, "that the feeling in the House of Commons was very bad, and if a division had taken place, I fear Mr. Gladstone and our friends would have been beaten, perhaps two to one in their effort to postpone the decision." "Mr. Monsell," he then further reported, "whom I saw before I left London on Thursday, was very well pleased with Gladstone's speech and the result of the Debate; but he spoke very despondingly of the tone of public journals. He seemed to think that if Mr. Gladstone brings forward the question, he will be beaten, and have to resign; and he asked, whether such a line of conduct would not give him great claims on the support of Ireland?" "I wish it would free him from that clique of *doctrinaires*," Woodlock confessed, referring to the leaders of the radical wing of the Liberal Party, "such as Lowe, Stansfield and Fawcett, to which he is now so closely united. I think we shall never get anything good from him in the way of Education till he gets rid of that set of men." "I am to send Dr. Manning," he added "a copy of More O'Ferrall's scheme for the University. The archbishop will show it or explain its provisions to Gladstone, with a view to his having it before him when considering the question & the mode of settling it." "But so great will be the opposition he is sure to meet with," Woodlock maintained in conclusion, "I think he will defer the question again, and perhaps for years, unless we show our determination here in Ireland to give trouble, if they do not grant us a Cath. system of Education."

Cullen apparently explained to Woodlock that the meeting of the bishops at Maynooth on August 17 would be entirely taken up with the business of attempting to reform that college, and there would be no time therefore for a serious consideration of the question of education, so it would be better left to the next regular meeting of the bishops, scheduled for the third week in October. Some three weeks before that meeting, Gillooly wrote to Cullen to sound him on a conference of the bishops and the Irish members of Parliament. "What would your Eminence think," he asked on September 27, "of holding a Conference, at the time of our next Meeting in Dublin—17th prox—with some of our leading MPs & others—with a view to organize Meetings &c on the Education Question and to lay down the programme, by which all such meetings shall be guided?" (C). "There w^d not be time," he explained, between this and the 17th to prepare for a public meeting—but time enough for a Conference, which would appear almost necessary if we are to engage the laity in a general movement in support of Religious Educ^n." "A working Committee," he suggested, "of first class men should also be found in Dublin with cooperating members in each of our dioceses." "If your Eminence approve of this view," Gillooly advised in conclusion, "I beg you will have it worked out as soon as possible by Dr. Woodlock—*aided and directed* by two or three able, practical men."

Cullen, who generally preferred that laymen have as little to do with the education question as possible, undoubtedly vetoed this suggestion, for when the bishops met in Dublin from October 17 to the twentieth, they virtually kept the management of the whole question in their own hands. At the close of their meeting, the bishops adopted a series of resolutions on the education question and issued a joint pastoral to the clergy and laity of some 11,000 words in thirty printed pages on the dangers of mixed education.[30] The resolutions were twelve in number:

30. Moran, 3:375–406.

1. We hereby declare our unalterable conviction that Catholic education is indispensably necessary for the preservation of the faith and morals of our Catholic people.

2. In union with the Holy see and the Bishops of the Catholic world, we again renew our often-repeated condemnation of mixed education as intrinsically and grievously dangerous to faith and morals, and tending to perpetuate disunion, insubordination, and disaffection in this country.

3. Recent events known to all, and especially the acts of secret societies and of revolutionary organizations, have strengthened our convictions, and furnished conclusive evidence that godless education is subversive not only of religion and morality, but also of domestic peace, of the rights of property, and of all social order.

4. As religious equality, which, according to the constitution of this country, is our inalienable right, is incomplete without educational freedom and equality, we demand as a right that in all the approaching legislation on the subject of education, the principle of educational equality shall be acted on.

5. We repudiate the pretensions of those who, holding different religious principles from ours, seek to violate the civil rights of our Catholic people, by forcing upon us a system of education repugnant to our religious conviction, and destructive alike of our temporal and eternal interests.

6. In the present effort to force godless education on this country, we recognize another phase of persecution for conscience's sake. Hence, following the example of our fathers, who sacrificed all earthly interests and life itself, rather than imperil their faith, we shall never cease to oppose to the utmost of our power the Model Schools, the Queen's Colleges, and Trinity College, and all similar institutions dangerous to the faith and morals of Catholics.

7. We call on all members of Parliament as representatives of the feelings and interests of their constituents, to sustain the principles embodied in these resolutions in Parliament and elsewhere, and to oppose any political party that will attempt to force upon this country any godless scheme of education, or refuse to redress our admitted education grievances.

8. In future elections of members of Parliament and other representatives, we pledge ourselves to oppose the return of any candidate who will not uphold the principle of denominational education for our Catholic people.

9. Knowing the zealous attachment of our people to the Catholic faith, we invite them to hold meetings and sign petitions in their respective parishes, under the guidance of their clergy, making known their determination to accept no system of education except in conformity with the principles here announced.

10. We request His Eminence Cardinal Cullen, Archbishop of Dublin, to take immediate steps towards the establishment of a Central Training School of Catholic Teachers, and we pledge ourselves to assist His Eminence by our subscriptions and by our best influence in our respective dioceses.

11. Contemplating with deep concern the melancholy wreck in other countries of all order, moral and social, mainly caused by the wide diffusion of literature immoral and hostile to religion and society, we, the divinely-constituted guardians of the spiritual interests of our people—solicitous, more-

over, for their temporal welfare, and following the example of the Father of the Faithful, emphatically warn our flocks to abstain from the perusal of all publications, in whatever form, in which the maxims of our holy religion and its ministers are misrepresented and assailed, and principles inculcated subversive of social order and Christian morality.

12. These resolutions will be read on the first convenient Sunday, at one of the Public Masses in each of the Churches and Chapels in this kingdom.[31]

The bishops were even more explicit in their joint pastoral than they had been in their ninth resolution about how Catholic public opinion in Ireland with regard to the education question should be stirred up. "In conclusion," the bishops advised their clergy and laity, "we direct the clergy of our respective dioceses to read this address or a portion of it to their flocks on two successive Sundays in the month of November next. We further request, dearly beloved brethren, that on one of those two Sundays you will hold, where practicable, a parochial meeting in each parish; or at least that you will sign a declaration embodying your views on this subject; and that you will on or before the 1st of December next, forward to the Prime Minister the declaration, with your signatures, and the resolutions of your public meeting."[32] In early November, in order to provide a lead and direction, Cullen arranged to sign a requisition to convene a large public meeting in Dublin at the end of November.[33] Writing to Kirby on November 10, Cullen explained that he was pleased that the recent joint-pastoral of the bishops had gained his approval (K). "I think," he added, "it has done a great deal of good among Catholics, but it has set the Protestant newspapers quite furious. They cannot find words sufficiently strong to denounce us." "We expect," he then reported, "to have a grand meeting on education towards the end of the month. Lord Granard and other high people have promised to speak. God grant we may succeed well."

Because of the difficulties in finding a convenient date that would suit all who were invited, the meeting had to be postponed until December 12, and when the Prince of Wales then fell dangerously ill from an attack of typhoid fever and his life was thought to be in danger, the meeting was postponed again until January 17. In the meantime, Cullen had received the disquieting news, from the bishop of Ardagh, that some of the bishops were not as enthusiastic about holding meetings in their dioceses as they might have been. Conroy explained to Cullen that he had just met the bishops of Limerick, Down and Connor, and Kilmore, while responding to the invitation of the latter to inspect the progress of his new seminary at Cullies in Cavan. "None of the bishops," Conroy reported on November 18, "whom I have met will have a meeting on the Education Question. They appear to think that the Dublin one is to do for all." "Dr. Butler," he added, referring to the

31. Ibid., 407–8.
32. Ibid., 405.
33. C, see memorandum in Cullen's hand, dated November 2, 1871.

bishop of Limerick, "said that in his diocese it is very hard to rouse the people on the question of education. He is infatuated in his admiration of the National system, and quoted the evidence of his nuns who say that they could not have a better system." A short time later, Conroy had additional painful news for Cullen, about the attitude of some of the clergy. "The Meath priests," he reported on December 11, "at least the younger portion of them, refuse to address petitions on the Education question to Mr. Gladstone. They contend that his act would be an admission that his Government is acceptable to the Irish people" (C).

Indeed, most of the Irish bishops and clergy believed, apparently, that the Dublin meeting alone would suffice, for, with the exception of about a half dozen of Cullen's more loyal supporters in the body, the rest chose to leave well enough alone. As usual, it was the indefatigable bishop of Elphin who was in the vanguard of the effort to promote the agitation. "I take the liberty," he informed Cullen on December 13, "of enclosing a Copy of Resolutions drafted for our Ed^l Meetings, which I have fixed in our principle towns for the 7th Jan^y, and in the other Parishes for the 14th" (C). "I am strongly inclined to think myself," he then suggested, "that to overcome & to help Gladstone to overcome the fearful opposition that is organized ag^t us—we must speak out not only firmly but threateningly—at the same time that we should avoid giving countenance or promise of any kind to the present Home Rule association." At the end of the month, the bishop of Galway also wrote Cullen to assure him that he too had just made his best effort. "We had," MacEvilly reported on December 31, "a truly imposing meeting here today on the Education Question. It was all but a monster meeting. Not a Catholic of any note in the vicinity but was present" (C). Two weeks later, Cullen's suffragan, the bishop of Ferns, wrote to Kirby, describing their recent meeting in Wexford. "It was," Furlong assured Kirby on January 14, "a complete success, though some of our Catholic gentry were absent in France & England" (K). "We feel a little vain," he added revealingly, "that it was the first County meeting held in Ireland. I also sent a memorial to Mr. Gladstone signed by upwards of 8,000 of the inhabitants of Wexford."

In the meantime, the anxieties and the cares of the previous ten years had taken their toll of the rector of the Catholic University. Toward the end of November 1871, Woodlock had suffered a nervous breakdown, and he was advised by his physician and brother-in-law, Sir Dominic Corrigan, to give up all work and take an extended vacation. Though Woodlock agreed to visit with his sister in Blarney, near Cork City, to recoup his shattered nerves, he still continued his efforts to sustain, in part at least, his voluminous correspondence. "Your Eminence has, without doubt," he alerted Cullen on December 31, after wishing him a happy new year, "seen the article in the 'Daily Telegraph,' which would seem to indicate a likelihood of the Education question being deferred" (C). "I hope," he added anxiously, "there is no danger of further delay. I fear that the youth of the country, especially as regards higher Education, is slipping away from us every day more & more; and each delay makes it more difficult to keep them away from Trinity Coll., and the Queen's Colleges." "Has your Eminence," Woodlock asked, "heard anything about the intention of the Gov^t?" "I would take the liberty," he advised, referring to the Dublin meeting scheduled for January 17, "to suggest that one of the points to be urged at the approaching meeting is: to protest against further delay." "The Meeting in Cork," Woodlock further explained, "is not to be held till after the one in Dublin. It has been arranged here, that the meeting should be *exclusively* a lay one. The Requisition is to be addressed to the Mayor, who is a Catholic—the Bishop will take no part; neither will any priest speak." "I think, this is a mistake;" he maintained, "but there was a preliminary meeting at Dr. Delany's [the bishop of Cork] where all was settled." "Thank God," he then assured Cullen, "I think I am improving; although sometimes, especially as it seems to me on alternate days, I feel very weak. However, when the sun is shining, I try to take a walk in my sister's garden for a quarter of an hour." "I was able," he finally added in a postscript, "to say only one Mass on X-mas Day, and not since, until this morning."

When Cullen received this letter the next day, he asked Moran to reply to it in his name. "Our Education Meeting," Moran assured Woodlock on January 1, 1872, "is fixed for the 17th inst. and I trust it will be a great success. The article in the Telegraph cast a little cold water on the ardour of our Educationalists, but I believe it referred only to the general question of Education & not to the Univ.^{y} question with which the Gov.^{t} volens nolens [willing or not willing] will have to deal for blind Fawcett is determined to force them to a division on that question."[34] "The Cardinal desires me," he then added, "to thank you for your letter. He is just starting for the C^o Meath for a few days. He bids me to say that nothing is known as to the intention of the Gov.^{t}"

A week later, Woodlock wrote Moran a letter marked "private," and asked him to show it to the cardinal. "The Gov^t plan, I am told," he informed Moran on January 7, "comprises two things:"

> 1st they will *not* bring forward the Univ^y question this year—nay more, they will not allow it to be brought forward.
> 2^{ndly} they will bring forward a *large measure* of Grand Jury Reform. There

---

34. The reference to Fawcett being blind was that he had lost his sight as a young man in a hunting accident.

will be very extensive powers given to the new Reformed Grand Jury to deal with local matters; railways, public buildings &c.

All this would be very well, but then it would be easy to authorize such a body to levy a School-rate, and thus transfer to it the control of the Schools. The clergy would then have to deal with an irresponsible local Board. And, I need not say, what a pretty state things would be in very soon.

It would be proposed to transfer at once to the new Grand Jury, or to a Committee of it, the position of patron and manager of the model schools.

This scheme, it is said, would have much to recommend it. It will be a concession to Irish demands in the way of self-government—it will get rid of the troublesome school-rate question—and it will leave the Priests to settle their claims with the laity—and in particular with the educated lay Catholics!!

"I suppose," Woodlock conjectured, "The next step would be to put the Queen's Colleges and the Cath. University under this new local Board." "This has not been given to me," he added, "as part of the plan. But I remember, that Corrigan in his famous pamphlet on University Education (in 1865) suggested, that the Queen's Colleges should be reformed by being placed under some such local management." "What do you think," he then asked, referring to the chief secretary, who had just made a speech that was very hostile to any increase of clerical influence in Irish education, "of Lord Hartington's speech? Is it any wonder, people should be discontented, when such a man is virtually the chief governor of the country. He has, certainly, succeeded in insulting every body." "Of course," Woodlock noted in conclusion, "you will not mention my name in connection with all these rumours. But I hope means may be taken to secure no further delay."

"Thanks for letter this morning," Moran replied the next day, January 8, "I fear the Gov^t is bent on mischief, and all this because they wish to put themselves into the hands of a few Catholics who are liberal of their Catholicity" (W). "We have lost some of our Education speakers [for the Dublin meeting]," he then reported, "Sir John Esmonde being away in France, and the Lord Mayor Campbell & Dr. Cruice &c. So there has been a little trouble in rearranging our lists. However, they are once more almost complete." "What about the letters of your friends on Irish Education?" Moran then asked, referring to a collection of essays about to be published as *Intermediate Education in Ireland*. "Just when they wd be useful & purchased preparing for the Meetings, they cannot be got out. The Cardinal is very much annoyed at it." The volume on intermediate education, which had been produced by a committee of four, was, in fact, already in press.[35] "At length," Woodlock explained to Moran on January 11, "the book on 'Intermediate Educa-

---

35. The committee consisted of Sullivan, William Woodlock, John O'Hagan, and David B. Dunne. See W, Dunne to Woodlock, January 12, 13, 15, and 18, 1872 for the details of its production.

tion,' is complete, and I expect the Cardinal will have some copies of it tomorrow night" (C). "I have had a letter," Woodlock informed Moran earlier in this letter, "from the O'Conor Don in which he expressed a fear that Govt will accept Fawcett's Bill, saying that they do not consider it a settlement of the question, and that they will bring in a supplementary measure at some future time, that is: *ad Kal. Graecas* [to an indeterminate future]. This would be ruinous; better a thousand times leave things as they are, than offer this new bait to catch unwary Cath. youths, and worldly Cath parents." "Thank God," he then assured Moran, "I continue to improve, although for the last couple of days I feel unaccountably weak at times." "I hope to be able to return to Dublin on Monday or Tuesday," he added, referring to January 15 and 16, the days immediately preceding the Dublin meeting. The following day, January 12, however, Woodlock reported to Cullen that he would have to postpone his return to Dublin. "After writing to Dr. Moran yesterday," Woodlock explained, "and saying to him, that I hope to return to Dublin on Monday, I received a note from Sir Dominic, advising me not to come home yet—and adding, that when we arrange about my return, I had better be ready to go South—say to Rome—for that as to resuming my duties in this climate during our harsh Spring months I must not think of it" (C). "I have deemed it my duty," Woodlock added obediently, "to mention this to your Eminence. Of course, in this as well as, I hope, always and in everything else, I shall be in your hands." Cullen apparently advised Woodlock to follow his doctor's orders, for Woodlock did not travel up to Dublin for the meeting on January 17 but remained at Blarney until the end of January.

The Dublin meeting, which had been convened by a requisition to Cullen containing some 30,000 signatures, was from all accounts a very great success.[36] As usual Cullen had prepared carefully for the meeting, which took place in the procathedral on Marlboro' Street and continued for more than six hours. In an opening statement of more than 10,000 words, which took up nearly seven columns of close type in the *Freeman's Journal* and nearly one and one-half hours to deliver, Cullen laid down the ground rules for the other speakers who would move and second the some dozen resolutions that previously had been drafted for the meeting. Cullen began by reminding his audience that they were assembled in the house of God and that they should avoid in their proceedings "everything tending to violate charity, or infringe in any way on the Divine law." "Indeed," he added, "we should eschew every matter not closely connected with the object of our meeting, convened for the sacred purpose of asserting the right of Catholics to get Catholic education for their children." Some of their open enemies or pretended friends, Cullen pointed out, insisted that "the discussion of the education

36. *Freeman's Journal*, January 18, 1872. See also Moran, 3:418–51 for Cullen's address in a slightly edited form.

question should be put off for the present, under the pretence that our adversaries are now very much excited, and that it would be well for us to do nothing until their feeling shall subside." "Are we to wait," he then asked rhetorically, "until our opponents, with whose educational rights we never interfere, shall think fit to allow our claims to be examined? Are we to allow the Votaries of an unsectarian education, whose professed object is to disturb the belief of Catholic children, and to rob the people of Ireland of their faith—the true source of all the glories of our country, and of any power we possess—shall we allow such men to determine in what way our children shall be brought up?"

"However," Cullen then maintained, "we are not left alone in our struggle for religious education. With us we have the sympathy of Catholics of the world, who are fighting the same battle as we ourselves, and cheer us on by their example. We have with us the blessing of the successor of St. Peter, who has repeatedly approved of the justice of our cause, and we have the sanction of Christ Himself for the safety of the lambs of whose fold we are labouring." "But omitting all this," he further argued, "I believe that the most influential and distinguished members, lay and clerical, of the Anglican body, are with us, and that the principal liberal and enlightened Protestants of the empire wish us success." "We may also expect," Cullen added, coming to the point, "that Mr. Gladstone, and such Ministers as act with him, will be anxious to fulfil the promises which they made years ago, and will endeavour by introducing a satisfactory educational system for Ireland, to complete the work of pacification which they commenced by disestablishing the Irish Church and carrying the Land Act—two measures of great importance, well calculated gradually to promote the public welfare of the country."

Cullen then denied that the Catholic Church was the enemy of learning and knowledge, as was so often asserted, arguing instead that the enemies of religion were the ones who actually subverted learning and knowledge, under the guise of promoting the liberal arts and sciences. These wolves in sheeps' clothing were, in fact, involved in a three-pronged attack. "In order," Cullen charged, "to give a greater impulse to study, by securing protection for it, some insist that the full control of public instruction should be given to the government of each country, to be carried on by ministers of state or public boards; others attach so much importance to the development of intellectual faculties that they call for compulsory and gratuitous education, in order to give a great degree of culture to all classes; and others, in fine, demand an unsectarian education, pretending that God should be banished from the school, and children brought up without being subjected to any religious influences." Cullen then refuted these errors in detail for the rest of his address. The first, state control of education, he argued, was essentially a usurpation of the rights of both the parents and the Church. The second, compulsory and gratuitous education, Cullen denounced because it had been advocated by Martin Luther in Germany, Jules Simon in France, and T. H.

Huxley in England, all notorious enemies of true religion, and free education he denounced because it was not fair to tax all to supply gratuitously those who have the means of paying for an education themselves. "Besides," Cullen added, "as compulsion renders education odious, so giving it gratuitously will in some cases lessen the value attached to it, and in other cases it will have the effect of filling the country with half-educated young men, too high for menial employment, and aspiring to respectable professions and offices without being properly qualified to fill them—a class of persons not only useless but dangerous to society."

For the third error, unsectarian or mixed education, Cullen had saved his worst and longest harangue. The worst feature of the mixed system, he explained, was that, in the name of all, it prevented religion from being taught to any. Such a system could only promote indifference. "We feel," Cullen argued, "that children having learned dangerous and lax principles in school, act on them in their after lives, they will probably abandon altogether the true faith, or fall into apathy and indifferentism to all religion, and thus sacrifice their immortal souls." A mixed system, moreover, admitted non-Catholic students, Protestant teachers, and non-religious books, all of which would reinforce the tendency to indifferentism, if not to absolute loss of faith. Cullen then gave examples of the effect of such a system on the Irish in the United States, adducing much of the same evidence he had presented some three years before to the Powis commission, and he maintained that the great experiment conducted in that country had been pronounced a failure as far as religion was concerned, on the evidence of both Catholics and Protestants. Why then did Catholic bishops and priests, Cullen asked, agree to receive so pernicious a system when it was first introduced in Ireland in 1831? They did so because, he explained, they received it only as an experiment, and even its warmest supporters tolerated it only until they could see what results it produced. But why then did the Catholic bishops and clergy, Cullen asked again, still continue their connection with so pernicious a system? Because, he replied, in the greater part of Ireland, the system was in fact, not mixed, but denominational, and it was therefore tolerated for the good that was in it rather than for the principle on which it was based. Cullen then concluded his very long and able address by denouncing the Queen's Colleges and Trinity College in Dublin for being anti-Catholic and dangerous to the souls of the faithful.

The first of the twelve resolutions was then introduced and moved by the earl of Granard, president of the Catholic union, and seconded by Sergeant David Sherlock, the junior member for King's county, both of whom, as did all of those who followed, strongly endorsed Cullen's lead. The twelfth and final resolution conveniently proposed embodying the resolutions in an address to the prime minister, which read:

> Sir—We the Roman Catholic people of the diocese of Dublin, in public meeting assembled, having considered the disabilities and disadvantages under which we labour in the matter of education, deem it our duty to call your

attention to those grievances and to request that you will devise measures for bringing about their speedy redress.

It is our conscientious [*sic*] conviction that, in order to be fruitful of good, education must be based upon religion, and that it is the duty of Catholic parents to give to their children an education in accordance with the principles of their religion.

Hence, whenever the state interferes with Catholic parents in the discharge of this solemn duty, by granting privileges to education systems from a participation in which Catholics are conscientiously debarred, it violates their constitutional rights, it inflicts civil disabilities for religious opinions, and it refuses to Catholics a footing of equality with their Protestant fellow-citizens.

We further declare that the distribution of public aid for secular instruction, in order to be just, ought to be free from the odious taint of exclusiveness on the score of religious profession, dependent solely on the capability of educational institutions to produce results satisfactory to society. The Catholics of Ireland desire to be judged by no other standard. Hence we regard as sophistical and misleading the outcry which has been lately raised against the allocation of State aid for secular results when these happen to be associated with religious methods of instruction, and we believe that this outcry has been adopted for the purpose of masking hostility to all religious influences.

While Trinity College has been endowed with 200,000 acres, and has had conferred upon it other public advantages and emoluments, and while the Queen's Colleges and Queen's University enjoy an income from the State of about 29,000£ a year, the Catholics of Ireland, who conscientiously object to those institutions on religious grounds, receive no aid whatever in the matter of higher education, and hence are not, in this respect, on an equality with their Protestant fellow countrymen. This hardship becomes aggravated by the fact that owing to the confiscations and penal laws of past time, the Catholics are, of all sections of the population, the least able to support educational establishments out of their own resources.

Moreover, we consider it a serious grievance that the existing model schools and training establishments of the National Board, as well as the Queen's Colleges, should continue to be maintained at the public expense, not only because they embody those principles of mixed education which our religion condemns, but also because they have established and involve an extravagant waste of the public money.

There are very many National schools, spread over a large part of Ireland, which are frequented wholly, or almost exclusively, by Catholics, and yet by a fiction of the National Board are treated as mixed schools. In other National schools, which are placed under Protestant managers and teachers, the Catholic scholars are exposed to the danger of receiving impressions and imbibing doctrines contrary to their faith. We call for such changes in the rules of the National Board as will allow the practice of Catholic exercises of piety and Catholic teaching in those schools which are practically Catholic; and we demand that, if in any particular circumstances the existence of mixed schools cannot be avoided, measures shall be adopted to protect Catholic children from the dangers of proselytism.

We further ask that the funds which, having been originally derived from public sources, are devoted to promote Protestant education in the Royal and other endowed schools in Ireland, shall be made available for the intermediate education of the whole nation, by admitting students in Catholic schools and colleges to their fair share in those endowments.

We beg to remind you that Catholics are at present virtually deprived of the advantages of a higher education. Hence, we call upon the Government to take at once into serious consideration the wishes of the Catholic laity of Ireland, expressed in a declaration addressed to you, and laid before the House of Commons on the 30th March, 1870, and to establish in this country a university system of which Catholics can conscientiously avail themselves.

We also beg to remind you that we do not question the right of Protestants to claim for themselves any system of education which they deem desirable. But, at the same time, we protest against their endeavours to dictate for the Catholcs [sic] of Ireland a system of education which we conscientiously reject. And, further, we emphatically insist that upon the question of the education of Catholic youth, our conviction ought to be regarded, and not the views and opinions of men who differ so widely from us on all matters connected with religion and education, and do not understand or appreciate our feelings and convictions.

In this matter of education, we beg solemnly to assure you of our union with the bishops of our church, and to repudiate indignantly the allegations, so lightly made by a hostile press, that in the matter of education the Catholic laity of Ireland do not share the sentiments of their clergy.

In conclusion, we beg to express the hope that the enlightened wisdom which has already guided you in the redress of two capital and inveterate grievances of our country will also guide you to the removal of the disabilities and inequalities of which we complain in the matter of education.

And we are encouraged in this hope by the recollection that on more than one occasion you have eloquently and emphatically spoken of those disabilities and inequalities, and declared yourself and your colleagues in the Government pledged to accomplish their removal.

The address was duly forwarded to the prime minister under the signatures of Cullen and the secretaries of the meeting, but apparently Gladstone did no more than merely acknowledge it.

Several days after the Dublin meeting, the archbishop of Cashel wrote Cullen both to congratulate him and to explain why he had not yet convened a meeting for county Tipperary. "It must, if anything can," Leahy assured Cullen about his meeting on January 20, "move the Government to action" (C). "Why are we not stirring here?" he asked. "Well," he explained, "some of our leading Catholics in the County Tipperary are outside this Diocese." "The sentiments of some of these," Leahy confessed, "& of some within the Diocese, I could not be sure of. For these and other reasons the success of a Diocesan Meeting would be doubtful. So would that of a County Meeting. It is at all times, very difficult to get up a good

Diocesan or county Meeting here. We have not many Catholics of distinction, nor could we just now reckon on a fair muster of those we have." "On the whole," Leahy maintained, "I consider it better to get up Meetings in Towns which would be all successful and would help to spread and to elicit a sound public opinion on the question of Education."

> Accordingly I have arranged the holding of meetings in Thurles, Cashel, Tipperary, Fethard, Templemore, besides that Petitions have been signed in, I believe, every Parish of the Diocese. I have also written privately to the Vicar General in Clonmel (Dr. Power: Diocese of Waterford) suggesting the adoption of a similar course in the Co. Tipperary part of the Diocese of Waterford. He writes to me saying meetings will be held in Clonmel, Cahir, Carrick-on-Suir, and Clogheen, and that petitions will be forwarded from the rural parishes. When these meetings shall have been held, and petitions so forwarded, some little shall have been done to help in the good cause.

"The course which the Education question has taken," Leahy assured Cullen, "though apparently adverse to us—the howl of Protestant bigotry raised against us on all sides—has like the persecution of the Holy Father, done great good by uniting Catholics more closely and strengthening Catholic sentiments." "The Education question," he insisted, in concluding, "is now truly a Catholic question no one can be indifferent about it but one who cares nothing about his religion."

Shortly after his return to Dublin, en route to Rome, Woodlock decided, undoubtedly with Cullen's consent, to write to Gladstone's eldest son, William Henry, to elicit some kind of a response about his father's intentions regarding the Irish education question. "Some friends of mine," Woodlock explained to young Gladstone on January 29, "have lately published a small work on intermediate Educ^n in Ireland, of wh. I beg to send you a copy. One has I believe been sent to the Premier also; but as in the hurry of business he may not have time to attend to it, I take the liberty to ask you to glance over the book" (W). "I hope," Woodlock then added, "the Presbyterians, Independents, & Baptists' of London and its vicinity are not to be the guides in the settlement of our admitted grievances. You are aware that in this country those gentlemens' co-religionists do not number altogether one-tenth of the population and in three of our four provinces they are not, I believe, one in a hundred." "Still," Woodlock complained in concluding, "they pretend to dictate to us how we are to bring up R. C. youth." A week later young Gladstone finally replied. "I should have thanked you," he apologized briefly on February 6, "ere now for the volume you have kindly sent me. I suppose when Scotch Education is finished your turn will come—but the shoals and quicksands of the English and Scotch bills are not pleasant auguries for dealing with the question in Ireland" (W).

On Saturday, February 10, Woodlock, in company with his brother William and his brother's wife, finally set out for Rome. He arrived in London the following evening and wrote to Cullen the next day. "This morning," he reported on February 12, "I saw Sir John Gray. He fears we are 'sold'; to use his own expression as regards to Education. The only thing he thinks possible, *if it be possible,* will be: to get Fawcett's Scheme modified, or rather changed, in Committee before the 3rd Reading of the Bill. I take the liberty to recommend this especially to your Eminence's consideration" (C). "It is to be read a second time," he then alerted Cullen, "on Wednesday, 20th March, I think." "I ought to try and be in London," he suggested, "before then, although Sir Dominic advises me to defer my return till late in April." "I shall go on tomorrow, please God," Woodlock then explained, "to Paris, where I shall stay for 2 or 3 days; and then go on through Florence to Rome." "The amendments to Fawcett's Bill," he added in a postscript, "which I suggest, would be: to found a second College, Catholic in reality, if not in name, in the University of Dublin." Woodlock had not been able to see Manning on his way through London because the archbishop had been in the country nursing a cold. He was unable, therefore, to provide Cullen with any more information about Gladstone's intentions. The day after he received Woodlock's letter, however, Cullen decided to write to Manning.

"I fear," he confessed on February 14, "we shall have great trouble with the education question. All our Catholic rich and poor are determined to have Catholic education. Some government officials and adherants of state education, who are very few in number, are to be excepted."[37] "On the other hand," Cullen pointed out, taking the same line Woodlock had taken with Gladstone's son, "the Presbyterians are crying out that religion should be excluded from school[s], but they form only a very small party in the greater part of Ireland. In Dublin and the twelve counties of Leinster there are only 11,961 Presbyterians to 1,141,406 Catholics. In Munster only 3,891 Presbyterians to 1,302,475 Catholic, and in Connaught only 3,184 Presbyterians to 803,532 Catholics." "Yet this handful of Presbyterians," he complained, "pretends to impose the views upon Catholics and Lord Hartington and others connected with the government appear to encourage their pretensions." "We do not know," Cullen explained, coming to his point, "what Mr. Gladstone will do with Trinity College and the endowed schools." "Mr. Fawcett's motion," he then warned, "if carried, will only add to the three Queen's Colleges already existing, a fourth mixed college more wealthy and more mischievous than it predecessors." "If Mr. Gladstone," he concluded grimly, "does not oppose that motion, he will only increase the power of the Fenians and the Home Rule party in Ireland."

The following day, February 15, Cullen wrote Manning again to explain that he had forgotten to ask his advice about whether he thought a public Thanksgiving

---

37. MacSuibhne, 5:177–78.

should be held in their churches for the recent recovery of the Prince of Wales.[38] Cullen pointed out that he was reluctant to do so because, when the prince visited Ireland the previous August, he had made a speech at a Freemason's lodge, where he was installed as protector of the body, in defense of the craft and condemnatory of the discipline of the Catholic Church. Cullen explained that good practical Catholics had been much offended by the prince's speech and that if he now said anything in favor of the prince it would look as if he had abandoned his opposition to freemasonry. In his reply on February 16, Manning chose to reply to the second rather than to the first of Cullen's letters, noting that he felt "the difference is great between Dublin and London, and the unhappy Freemason folly raises a distinct and local difficulty" (C). In effect, Manning had ignored Cullen's probe into what he thought Gladstone's intentions were regarding Irish education and, more particularly, the line he would take on Fawcett's now perennial motion. In the meantime, Cullen had received another disquieting note from the bishop of Ardagh. "Dr. Gillooly," Conroy had reported on February 14, "is very angry with Mr. Gladstone for his neglect of the Education question" (C). "He is anxious," Conroy alerted Cullen, "to have a meeting of all the Bishops to take action in the matter: but I think we have not as yet sufficient information as to Mr. Gladstone's intention."

Cullen undoubtedly was perplexed about how to proceed. From Manning's evasive reply, he certainly must have understood that the archbishop had no reliable information to give and that Gladstone was intent on keeping his thoughts to himself on the question of Irish education. On the other hand, the more zealous of the bishops concerned about the question, like Gillooly, were growing restless, while perhaps even more, like the bishops of Limerick and Meath, for their own reasons, were not anxious to press Gladstone. The bishop of Ardagh, therefore, had posed the problem nicely for Cullen—it was not prudent or safe to press Gladstone without knowing what he really intended to do. After some reflection, therefore, Cullen decided to write personally to the prime minister. "I take the liberty," Cullen explained on February 25, "of forwarding to you by the post some late small publications connected with education, viz."

> 1st a little book entitled *Intermediate Education in Ireland* which gives a brief account of the endowed and model schools in this country and shows from authentic sources how unfairly Catholics have been dealt with in reference to such institutions. 2ndly a list of Catholics of this diocese who called on me to convene a public meeting of the diocese for the purpose of urging on government the necessity of granting to the Catholics of this country a system of education Catholic in all its branches, primary, intermediate and university.

38. Ibid., 178–79.

The three thousand names published in this list have been selected as representing the most respectable and influential Catholic families in this diocese from over thirty thousand names signed to the original requisition. 3rdly a report of the meeting of the Catholics of this diocese which was convened in compliance with the above-mentioned requisition. 4thly a copy of a speech delivered at the public meeting on education of the diocese of Ardagh and Clonmacnoise by the Right Rev. Dr. Conroy, Catholic bishop.[39]

"I do not expect" Cullen further explained, "that you will find leisure to read these publications or that you will approve of all they contain, but I am confident that if, in the immensity of business pressing on you, one moment can be spared to glance over them, they will convince you that the Catholic laity and clergy are all of one mind on the necessity of Catholic education for Catholic children and that they are quite determined to persevere in asking and receiving this boon for themselves without interfering with the claims and wishes of others."

It cannot be denied that the Catholics of Ireland have suffered in the past and are still suffering serious grievances in reference to education. They now expect that these wrongs will be repaired and through your powerful influence some compensation will be made for past injustice by establishing a system of public instruction of which Catholics rich and poor may avail themselves for their children without exposing their faith or morals to danger. It is the firm and general persuasion of the Catholics of Ireland that this security from danger cannot be obtained and that a proper religious culture cannot be given in schools practically managed in the mixed principle or in schools in which it is prohibited to teach the doctrines and practices of the Catholic Church to which the immense majority of the people belongs.

As to university education, I shall merely say that if you read the preface to the report of the Dublin meeting, you will find some resolutions most offensive to Catholics lately published by an Orange lodge which holds its meetings in Trinity College. It is easy to see that Catholics will not consider it a boon to get free admission to a place from which such declarations emanate. Besides it is known to everyone that many Catholics have lost their faith in that college and become dignitaries in the Protestant church whilst others have not merely lost their faith but have become enemies of the Christian religion. This is not to be wondered at, for it is known that professors in the university have assailed the eternity of punishment in the other world, the inspiration of parts of the Scripture and the redemption of mankind by the sufferings of Christ.

"I shall add no more," Cullen finally observed, "but conclude by begging of you to attribute this intrusion to the great desire which I entertain of seeing a good system of education introduced into Ireland under which the Catholics could be fully instructed in the doctrines and practices of their religion and at the same time trained to be good and faithful subjects of the State and to hate those revolting principles now so prevalent which are strongly condemned by the Catholic Church."

---

39. Ibid., 180–81.

In his reply to this very able statement of Catholic claims, Gladstone was especially ambiguous and convoluted. "I have the honour to acknowledge," he noted on February 28, "your Eminence's letter of the 25th and the words which accompany it and which relate to the question of education in Ireland in its several branches."[40] "Your Eminence may be assured," Gladstone added, "that I shall endeavor to make myself master of them and of all such information as may be accessible before Parliament if invited by her Majesty's Government to take any steps upon points of a nature to require investigation." "Her Majesty's Government," he explained, "have found it necessary to deal with this subject so intimately affecting the three kingdoms . . . . by part; the Endowed Schools Act of 1869 and the English Act of 1870 will they hope be followed by a Scotch Act of 1872, each of them intended to combine as far as circumstances permit a certain consistency of general principles with a due regard to any peculiar features which each case may present. We have at the same time taken important steps in 1871 in respect to the ancient universities of England." "Sensible that the difficulties," he assured Cullen in conclusion, "which have been encountered at every step are not likely to be diminished when we approach the practical solution of any question connected with the state and wants of education in Ireland, we shall do all that in us lies to avoid augmenting those difficulties whether by prejudice, by timidity, or by partial views and we shall endeavor to take for our guides the principles of equity towards Ireland."

Beyond being a statement of his good intentions, Gladstone's reply, which was certainly worthy of the oracle of Delphi, left Cullen really no better informed than he had been. "I understand," Cullen explained to Manning some two days later, on March 10, "that Mr. Fawcett will in a few days bring in a motion to open Trinity College, Dublin, to Catholics leaving the teaching body and the governing body just as they are. This would be to constitute a fourth Queen's College in Ireland, and to give a new impulse to mixed education. I hope if your Grace meet any M.P.s you will encourage them to vote against Mr. Fawcett."[41] "I wrote to Mr. Gladstone," Cullen further explained, "on this matter. His answer is not very clear, but he seems to say that in any government measure on education the claims of the majority of the Irish nation will not be overlooked." "I have not," Cullen added interestingly, "given any publicity to his letter in order that the bigoted party may not be calling Mr. Gladstone to account for his words." In order, however, to calm the fears of those who might be apprehensive about Gladstone's refusal to commit himself regarding either the extent or the time of his proposed reform of Irish education, Cullen let it be known privately that he had received a satisfactory reply on the question from the prime minister. The gloss that Cullen

40. Ibid., 181–82.
41. Ibid., 182–83.

apparently had put on Gladstone's letter, and which had been explicit in young Gladstone's letter to Woodlock in early February, was that as soon as the prime minister completed his British educational agenda, with the Scottish Education Act of 1872, he would turn his attention to the question of Irish education. This would mean that legislation on the Irish question was certain to be introduced in the 1873 session of Parliament. "I am delighted," the earl of Granard responded to Cullen's good news on March 15, "to hear that Mr. Gladstone has sent so favourable a reply. I have communicated the good news to the Bᵖ of Ferns who was here today" (C). "If they will give us," Granard added, "a really good measure on Education the delay of this Session will not matter much, but they are not so strong, as they were, and if they went out, our interests wᵈ be seriously affected."

By this time, however, Woodlock had finally made his way to Rome via Paris and Florence, and about a week after his arrival, on March 11, Woodlock wrote to Cullen. After explaining that he, his brother, and his sister-in-law had just been presented to the pope by Monsignor Kirby and recounting the latest Roman news, Woodlock finally came to the real purpose of his letter. "As I saw the Holy Father today only *in transition* in the presence of many others," he reported, "I had no opportunity of speaking to him, or he to me about the University. Still I think it most desirable he should know something about the state of things—and I have been thinking of asking for a special audience, such as I had nine years ago, in order to speak to him" (C). "I was unwilling," he confessed, "to act on my own judgement; I have consulted Dr. Kirby and he has advised me to write to your Eminence. It occurs to me, that it would be of the greatest service to the Cath. University & to the whole question of Cath. Education, if His Holiness would write to the Bishops of Ireland, praising them for all they have done for Education in particular and for founding & maintaining the University; but urging them strongly not to relax their efforts; but to support the Univy as the centre of Cath. teaching, and in addition to their own Colleges, Seminaries &c." "Your Eminence is aware," he explained, "that little by little the Bishops are dropping off in the annual Collections—up to this time Dean O'Loughlin tells me, only about £2,500 have come in for last November['s] Collection, over £1,000 of that sum being from the diocese of Dublin." "Some of the Bishops," he admitted, "are building Seminaries, others Cathedrals &c—and neither they in many instances, nor the Clergy or people see the necessity of keeping up the University. A word from the Holy Father would have great power in encouraging us all; and now when we may hope to be coming near the end of the long fight, it is, I think, absolutely necessary; certainly [it] would be most useful." "Will your Eminence," he begged, "kindly tell me what to do? I do not see how we can keep up the University without some such letter." "I fear," he noted in conclusion, "our business will certainly be deferred this year. Mr. Fawcett's Bill is fixed for Wednesday, the 20th."

"I have received your letter," Cullen replied on March 21, "some days ago. I have deferred answering it until we should hear the fate of Fawcett's motion" (W). "It came on last night," he reported, "but had the same fate as last year. I sent you the Freeman of this morning in which you will see the whole debate. Mr. Gladstone does not appear to have done anything or said anything favorable to us. However, the Irish M.Ps. Synan, O'Connor [*sic*] Don, Butt, Smyth, kept up the talking until 6 o'clock when the matter was dropped." "I wrote to the principle members," he then explained, "some days ago calling on them to make a decided display against Fawcett. I hope the question will be shelved for this year." "About getting the Pope to write to the Bishops," Cullen then added, "it can do no harm. However, you should inform him that in some dioceses the collection has been always made, and in some others *never* since 1854 the time of the opening of the University. So far from assisting, some dioceses made strong efforts to injure the cause. If all could be got to unite the University would get on."

Woodlock apparently had anticipated Cullen's approval of his proposal to secure the pope's support of the Catholic University. "I had the happiness," he reported on March 27, upon receiving Cullen's letter, "of an Audience of the Holy Father on the evening of St. Patrick's Day" (C). "Mgr Simeoni," he explained, referring to the secretary of Propaganda, "took me with him. His Holiness was, as usual, most gracious and kind, asked for your Eminence, entered into the University-question fully with me." "He said," Woodlock then added, "he would get the Propaganda to write to the Bishops about the Univ^y. He said, that the present seemed a favorable time for our Bishops to obtain concessions in favor of Cath. Education; for the English Gov^t knows their [the bishops'] influence on the one hand, & on the other, is now beginning to open its eyes to the necessity of opposing the spread of revolutionary & unreligious principles by means of Education." "Before going to the Holy Father I had at the request of Mgr. Simeoni & of Can[oni]co Rinaldini given the former a memorandum on the Univy of which I enclose a copy," Woodlock further explained, referring to a short memorandum in Italian, dated March 14. "I shall supplement it in any way your Eminence suggests, the first time I go to Propaganda. They are quite alive there to the fact of Dr. MacHale's opposition: and they also know the efforts made by your Eminence and other Prelates for its maintenance. Rinaldini asked me to put the facts in writing, as I have endeavoured to do in the enclosed memorandum; and he would know how to write '*con buon inchiosto*' [with good ink]." "I shall call there immediately," he then assured Cullen, referring to the Propaganda, "after the holidays; and I hope to see the letter to the Bishops, or the draft of it, before I leave Rome."

"As for the debate in Parliament on Fawcett's Bill," Woodlock noted, "my brother got me the 'Times' of Thursday, which contains a much fuller report than the 'Freeman,' wh. your Eminence had the goodness to send me, & for which I beg to thank you." "It does not seem certain from that report," he pointed out very delicately, "that the debate will not be renewed after Easter; it is optional with Fawcett to do so." "Would there be no means," he asked, "of getting an arrangement made by our friends with Mr. Gladstone somewhat in accordance with his speech; so that while a portion of Fawcett's scheme would be accepted, amendments would be added, recognising our Catholic University College?" "I should wish to be in London about April 20th," Woodlock then observed anxiously, "and to press upon our M.P.'s the plan alluded to above, if possible; for I think it very unfortunate that the question should be postponed for another year: the youth of the country & their friends are getting impatient & are gradually slipping away from our hands." "So I think it would be very well," he insisted again in concluding, "if we could get Gladstone to amend Fawcett's Bill in such a way as to give us a College for Higher Education in some way with proper security for the teaching and for the conduct of our young men." "After finishing this letter yesterday, I met Rinaldini out walking," Woodlock added in postscript, referring again to the under-secretary for British and Irish affairs at the Propaganda, "he told me, that at the 'Congresso' in the morning it had been arranged to write to your Eminence before writing the Bishops generally. Later I happened to meet Mgr Simeoni at the Seminario Romano: I showed him your letter, & he told me to see Card. Barnabò, which I shall do, please God, as soon as possible." "The 'Osservatore,'" he reported, "announces, that on Tuesday last Fawcett's Bill was read a second time, despite the protest of the Cath. Members. Perhaps so much the better; as something must now be done: we shall see whether Gladstone will stand by his own declarations." "Might it not all be well," Woodlock suggested again in conclusion, "for me to be in London when the Bill goes into Committee after Easter?"

Cullen's misreading of the *Freeman's Journal* report of the debate on Fawcett's bill was a most interesting and significant slip, and Woodlock's attribution of that slip to the brevity of the *Freeman's* account was a respectful and diplomatic strategy on his part. He knew better, however, because apparently no one but Cullen had misunderstood either what had happened or who was responsible for it. The same day that Cullen had written to Woodlock, for example, the archbishop of Cashel also had written to Woodlock about the debate in Parliament. "You will have seen by the Papers," Leahy reported on March 21, "ere this reaches Rome how upon Fawcett's motion respecting Trinity College Gladstone played us false, speaking against the motion & for us, but voting first in part—in whole, indeed, on the second reading, whilst signifying that he & the Government would be against that part of the measure which relates to the constitution and government of Trinity College & University" (W). "I really see no alternative for us," Leahy concluded grimly, "but to break altogether with Gladstone & his Government." The real question is how could Cullen who seldom ever was to be found looking at the world through rose-colored glasses, have so misread the debate on Fawcett's motion? The answer, of course, lies not only in his misreading of the account of that debate but also in the much too favorable gloss he had put on

Gladstone's recent letter to him in his account of that letter to both Manning and Granard. He was desperately intent on trying to preserve the Irish-Liberal alliance, not only in the hope of what it might eventually secure for Irish education, but also in the fear of the radical political alternative to that alliance, Home Rule.

Cullen's real problem, however, as the archbishop of Cashel's letter to Woodlock indicated, was not so much how to preserve the Irish-Liberal alliance as how to maintain the unity of the bishops as a body on which that alliance depended, in the face of Gladstone's apparent ambivalence about Fawcett's motion. If Cullen had any doubts about the nature of the difficulty, he was certainly disabused of them by a letter he received from the bishop of Elphin shortly after the debate. "I feel very uneasy," Gillooly confessed on March 24, "about the present state of the Education question in Parliament, and I fear difficulties & dangers will thicken speedily around us, if we are slow or neglectful in resisting the anticatholic movement led by Mr. Fawcett" (C). "I think," he suggested, "we should meet and take combined action of some kind without delay." "Even the passing of the Tests Removal Clauses of Fawcett's Bill," Gillooly warned, referring to those clauses that abolished all religious requirements in Trinity College, "would be a grave evil for us. Every available means sh^d. be at once employed to prevent the second reading of his bill during the present Session."

> I would infer from paragraphs I read in the Newspapers that Gladstone may manage if he wish, to prevent it from coming on again for consideration. The Irish Cath. Members shd. firmly call on him to use his right in that way. And it occurs to me, that a line from your Eminence to the leading Members would get them to act unitedly & immediately in the matter—or that you might send some one over to London to secure such action more effectually. A present delay of only a few days may prove most detrimental. If the discussion of the Question in Parliament is postponed to next Session, we will be better able to prepare our defenses.

"I think that in any case," he urged Cullen again, "an early meeting of the Bishops or even of the Maynooth Committee, would be most desirable." "I cannot help feeling," Gillooly added somewhat de trop, "that the faith of our people was never in such danger as it is at present, and the Educat^l persecution is one that it [*sic*] belongs almost exclusively to the Pastors of the Church to confront & overcome." "Our priests & our people," he assured Cullen, "will follow our guidance as they have ever done—but guidance they want and expect. May our good God guide us all and keep us of one mind & one heart. Our great want is unity of action, and it is to your Eminence we shall be indebted for that necessary condition of success." "Could there be a meeting," he suggested in conclusion, "of M.P.'s managed in Dublin during the Easter Holidays? I suppose most of them will come home this week."

There appears to be no record of Cullen's reply, but even if he did reply in writing to this rather alarmist letter from Gillooly, the bishops nevertheless did not meet as a body until their regular meeting in late June at Maynooth, and by that time the crisis over Fawcett's bill had passed. The reason Cullen did not act on Gillooly's suggestion, of course, was that he was opposed to extraordinary general meetings unless he was morally certain that the bishops would not be divided on the issue that they had been convened to consider. Thus he avoided at all costs any meeting that was likely to result in a serious difference of opinion. Cullen must have realized that because the bishops would be united as a body in opposing Fawcett's bill, the question of how to make their collective will effective in this opposition would be inevitably raised. Thus, their discussion would have turned on whether to continue to give Gladstone and the Irish-Liberal alliance their support, and on that issue the bishops were not likely to be united. Because Cullen was very decided in his opinion to support that alliance, he was not about to authorize a general meeting of the body at which they might decide to reverse the policy and thereby, both ruin the Catholics' long-term educational prospects and open the political door to the Home Rulers in Ireland. Finally Cullen must have realized that even if Gladstone and his government could be persuaded to oppose Fawcett's bill at the behest of the bishops as a body, it was likely that he and his ministry would be defeated, which would certainly extinguish Irish educational hopes for that generation.

While Cullen was attempting to prevent the Irish-Liberal alliance from being broken up, Woodlock was receiving very gloomy accounts of the education debate in both the Catholic University and in Parliament from David B. Dunne, professor of logic and metaphysics at the University. "I hear nothing," Dunne reported despondingly on Easter Monday, April 1, mentioning his colleague, the professor of chemistry, "about the Education Question now; nor does Sullivan" (W). "Monsell's scheme," he added, "is now the name by which the transfer to Ireland of the London University system is known. He is reported to have taken this up (abandoning his former ideas) as most feasible, and most likely to meet the views of the bishops."

Some two weeks later, Dunne reported again to Woodlock. "This morning's Paper," he explained on April 17, "brings us news of the Ministerial decision on Fawcett's Bill. The Government will propose to the House on the 23rd Inst, to divide the Bill. They will accept the part relating to the abolition of tests; they will give every assistance to pass this part. They will propose to drop the rest" (W). "There is no use," he added stoically, "in idly lamenting what looks like a piece of thorough-faced treachery. We must face the fact that next October we shall have to contend with a fourth Queen's College, wealthier and stronger in every way, than all the rest put together." "What will the Bps do," Dunne maintained, "is the question that naturally arises to every one's mind." "The number of students is very low," he then reported, referring to the arts faculty, in which there "I reckoned last Friday with Sullivan only 4. I am told others are worse off. These are things that cannot be kept private—they get out among the public. They get talked about among our foes and sneaking friends."

A week later, Thomas Scratton, professor of grammar, and bursar at the University, in reply to a letter from Woodlock, confirmed Dunne's gloomy reports. "The fact is," Scratton reported on April 24, "we are in a very depressed condition. It is useless to conceal the fact that there are hardly any students to be taught in Arts" (W). "The Professors, with the exception of K.," he added, referring to the professor of elementary mathematics, James Kavanagh, "who has never yet turned up since the vacation, have been regular at their posts, but have found few or none to teach. We could not be lower without sinking altogether." "I am glad to tell you," he observed somewhat more encouragingly, "that in spite of our rickety condition the country has been liberal. No less than £4,600 has been paid from collection since the beginning of the Session: this includes of course the Australian Bill of [£]1,600." "Nevertheless," he noted, "we are even now indebted to the Bank more than £700 which will swell to more than £1,700 before the end of next week." "Nothing has yet been done," Scratton then explained, "about Fawcett's measure and the day is not yet fixed for the debate." "Meanwhile Heron," he further reported, referring to the junior member for Tipperary, "is trying by means of amendments to secure something for us, but I fear he has not the smallest hope of success." "Last night," he added even more gloomily, "[there] appeared in the Telegraph an ominous article proposing to disestablish and disendow all university education whatever which while it would be death to us would practically maintain Trin. Coll. much as it is for some time to come and perhaps for generations."

Meanwhile, Woodlock had left Rome about the middle of April, and, on his way to Aix-la-Chapelle for the baths, he had stopped at Lake Como, in northern Italy, where he spent some ten days. He wrote Cullen from Bellagio, on April 19, that though he had hoped to be in London in time for the committee stage of Fawcett's bill, that had proved impossible because Sir Dominic Corrigan had ordered him to Aix-la-Chapelle for two weeks (C). "I have written to Sir Dominic," Woodlock reported, "asking his further directions about the baths &c, and at the same time saying I am anxious to see him. As I feel, thank God, much improved, I hope he will not require me to stay in Aix-la-Chapelle as long as he first mentioned. I shall apprize your Eminence, as soon as he thinks it safe for me to return to London." "If I were once there," he explained, "I think I might be of some little use in trying to watch Fawcett's movements. I see by the 'Times' of last Tuesday, that on that evening he was to ask the Gov^t, whether they would by Friday (this day) let the house know what amendments they intend to propose to his Bill." "Now will be the time, therefore," Woodlock maintained, "to try to make changes which will render it such as the Bishops can accept, by giving us Cath. Education." "If this cannot be done in the House of Commons," he suggested, "what would your Eminence think of our trying to effect it *in the House of Lords?*" "If you approve of this suggestion," he added, "Lord Granard, and I think Lord Denbigh, Lord Gainsborough and other Peers whom your Eminence knows, would I am sure, help to give effect to your wishes. When in London, I could wait on them individually, and explain the details to them." "If we succeeded in getting some good changes introduced," he assured Cullen in concluding, "we should in all probability, at the very least, make Fawcett give up his scheme for this year."

A week after he arrived in Aix-la-Chapelle, Woodlock again wrote to Cullen, on May 6, explaining that the doctor there wished him to stay for another fort-night (C). He also enclosed a letter he had just received from The O'Conor Don. "I think it well," he explained to Cullen, "you should see what he says about Glad-stone's having pledged himself against endowing any Catholic Colleges;—es-pecially after the remark in your last letter, that he (Mr. G.) intended and prom-ised to settle the Education-question next year." "In my reply to the O'Conor Don," Woodlock reported, "I tell him that I do not think the Bishops will have anything to do with a scheme which would leave Catholics to shift for themselves, while leaving Trinity College or the Queen's Colleges in possession of their rich endowment. I added, that of course, I had no authority to speak for the Bishops, but that I thought they would formally condemn any attempt to force upon us (what is called) the London University System, while leaving their endowments to the existing four Colleges." "I said," Woodlock added, "that I thought it might be well, Mr. Gladstone should know this, if he (The O'Conor Don) found a favorable opportunity of letting him know it quietly."

Shortly after Woodlock wrote to Cullen, he received yet another very pessi-mistic letter from Dunne about the state of the education question. "It seems to be generally admitted," Dunne reported on May 8, from Dublin, "that the Educa-tion Question is in a very critical position; and here in the C.U. I think some, at least, regard it as next thing to doomed." "I hear from some quarters," he added, "that Gladstone is favorable to 'indirect' endowment, *if* it can be accomplished." "But indirect endowment may mean Mr. Keenan's plan," Dunne explained, men-tioning the recently appointed resident commissioner to the National Board of Education, who was an Irishman, a Catholic, and an advocate of the London University model for Ireland, "or, as it is now (to make it more acceptable, I presume) called 'Mr. Monsell's scheme'?" "Can anything," Dunne asked, "be more fatal to the cause of education? or to religion and religious influences?" "You cannot wonder," he pointed out, "that men should under such circumstances lose heart, and despair of seeing any good effected through their exertions." "Sul-livan," he further explained, "to whom I shewed your note is not disposed to take upon himself any communication with any persons. He is not inclined to view favourably the position in which we find ourselves, or the tissue of events by which we have drifted there." "He looks upon it thus," Dunne frankly informed Woodlock, "that you are too much influenced by Corrigan and men of the same way of thinking. They do not desire an institution of Catholic University teaching whether as a University or a College. In the next place they are aware of the difficulty which the Government would have to establish such an institution; and they prefer to maintain the Government at the cost of what they look upon not as a sacrifice but as a gain." "Persons who think," Dunne maintained, "that genuine higher education is of more importance than Mr. Gladstone's Premiership—and especially when combined with Catholic influences manifesting themselves in the training of Students—will not agree with the views of those gentlemen. They will prefer to wait on, rather than acquiesce in a miserable and degrading arrangement."

That same day, James Kavanagh, professor of elementary mathematics in the Catholic University, also wrote to Woodlock with a generally pessimistic view about the future. "As to the public aspect of our case," Kavanagh explained on May 6, "I believe Gladstone to be thoroughly sound, but I fear that his scheme will be a low & limping type, that which will afford us the least amount of relief, while offending fewest of his followers" (W). "I have now, within a few weeks," he then reported, "been amongst the Bishops and Clergy of the four Provinces and there is no hearty interest, no enthusiasm, no knowledge of the subject abroad. Look at the few meetings, and the *time* they were held. Where was the *lay* element—where the laity who were able to handle the question, or to expound it, from a lay stand-point, to families?" "What are we to think," he then exclaimed, "of 33 Bishops, 3,300 Priests, and 4,141,433, Catholics, whose Petitions from 1,080 Parishes number 195, and where signatures are less than double the number of Catholics in the Protestant town of Belfast!!!" "Let them serve their time," Kavanagh concluded contemptuously, referring to the fact that the 195 petitions in favor of Irish Catholic education contained only 110,394 signatures total, compared to the 716 petitions in favor of women's rights containing 312,466 signatures, "to the promoters of Women's Rights if they would succeed."

By the time Woodlock finally arrived in London at the end of May, apparently restored to health, the crisis over Fawcett's bill had been resolved by its author, who withdrew it in the face of the amendments because they would have changed its character. "Last night," Woodlock, who had arrived the day before from Belgium, reported to Cullen on May 30, "I had a long conversation with the O'Conor Don & Major O'Reilly. I have seen O'Conor Don again to-day, and also Dr. Manning. They all think, that as I am here I ought to make it a point to see some of those persons, who are likely to have influence with Gladstone, when settling his scheme for Higher Education for Ireland, as he has promised to do during the next few months" (C). "The Archbishop thinks," Woodlock added, referring to Manning, "I would do well to try & see even Mr. Gladstone himself, as well as his son, Mr. Bruce, Lord Acton, & Mr. Monsell. I shall endeavor to call on them within the next few days, but I have not wished to do so

without writing to your Eminence, that I might have the benefit of your guidance." "I can say to them," he explained, "that, happening to pass through on
my way home from the Continent, I have thought it well to call on them, as I
found them very kind on former occasions."

Though apparently Woodlock was unable to see Gladstone, he was reassured
by those he did visit that it was the prime minister's intention to introduce his
Irish University bill finally in the next session of Parliament, which was scheduled to open in February 1873. On returning to Dublin, Woodlock undoubtedly
told Cullen the good news, for both of them settled down to a period of watchful waiting, as Woodlock attempted to carry on the affairs of the faltering
University as best he could. In the last week of August, however, while taking the
waters at Spa in Belgium, Woodlock became alarmed by the rumors that were
circulating in London about Gladstone's intentions in regard to the University.
"I was sorry to see it hinted lately," he informed Cullen on August 27, "in a
leading London newspaper that our University question will, perhaps, be deferred again next Session" (C). "May I hope," he asked, "that your Eminence will
use your influence with Lord Spencer & the Lord Chancellor to prevent this
new delay?"

> Indeed, I will ask you to urge on both these noblemen the necessity of settling
> this question, and to explain to them the points, which must be secured, in
> order that the Bishops may be able to accept the offer of the Gov^t: I would
> especially single out; (a) the recognition & endowment of our Cath. Univer-
> sity College; (b) its independence of State control; and (c) the equality of
> Catholics with others in the common University. In a private conversation with
> Lord O'Hagan or the Lord Lieutenant your Eminence would be able to say
> many things which might help considerably to a favourable settlement.

"Your Eminence may not be aware," Woodlock explained, "that, in all probability *even now* Mr. Gladstone is beginning to form his plans; they will be
matured in September, so as to be submitted to the Cabinet in October or
November for their final decision before they are brought before Parliament."
"Dr. Manning, whom I saw in London," he assured Cullen, "has kindly promised to take some occasion to let Mr. Gladstone know our views & to urge them
upon him." "With respect to the meeting of the Bishops on the 24th September,"
Woodlock warned, "I fear more harm than good to the cause might follow from
your Lordships' addressing the Gov^t or publicly declaring your claims." "But,"
Woodlock added, turning to his greatest concern, "would your Eminence think
well of urging on the Prelates the necessity of making the University Collection
generally next November?" "You know," he further noted, "how many dioceses
failed to do so last year. It would be better to 'wind up' the Institution than for
the Bishops to abandon it one by one. But I trust neither is necessary; and that
your Eminence's long struggle for Catholic Education will, through God's bless-

ing, be now ere long crowned with success." "I had thought," Woodlock finally concluded, "that before now the Propaganda would have written on the subject. Your Eminence is aware, I mentioned the matter to the Holy Father: he referred it to the Sacred Congregation, and Cardinal Barnabò said, he would write to your Eminence." At the meeting of the prelates in Maynooth on September 24, the bishops of the Catholic University board did not formally convene, thereby resolving the problem of having to issue any statement about the University question. Whether Cullen urged the University collection on the bishops who were present, and who did meet formally for the Maynooth board, is not clear, but in any case the November collection was a dismal failure, bringing in only about £4,000, approximately half the sum necessary each year to keep the University financially solvent. Given this very difficult financial situation, it becomes clear why the bishops' expectations of Gladstone's bill, and the expectations of Cullen and Woodlock in particular, were so great, and also why their disappointment in its shortcomings was even greater. They had hoped that Gladstone's bill would provide not only a charter but also an endowment generous enough to relieve them of the increasing annual burden of having to collect a sufficient sum to keep the University going. After their rejection of Gladstone's bill, therefore, the real question for the bishops was how they would be able to continue to keep the Catholic University viable as an institution of higher learning in the face of the evident discontent of both the clergy and laity, and, even more important, in the face of the faltering will of their own body.

VII

The Achievement
August 1869–March 1874

In the nearly three years between the issuing of the report of the royal commission on primary education in Ireland, in May 1870, and Gladstone's introduction of his University bill in February 1873, the Irish bishops certainly were greatly frustrated by the amount of time they invested in the education question. All was not loss, however, because during that time the bishops did succeed, finally, in reforming Maynooth College, their national seminary, as well as in managing to maintain some hold on primary education, despite their archenemy, the Board of National Education, which administered the system. The issue of reforming Maynooth was as important for the bishops as it was complicated. The college was important because it provided virtually the entire Irish mission with priests. When Maynooth was disestablished by act of Parliament in July 1869, there were some 625 clerical students in training at the college, and the number of priests ordained each year, about 90, was approximately equal to the number of Irish priests that died annually. The complications that arose in the effort to reform the college were the result of the many and varied interests of those involved in such a reform, as well as the natural tendency in well-established institutions, with a long tradition of their own, to resist change. In October 1870, it will be recalled, the bishop of Elphin, in writing to Cullen, attempted to outline the dimensions of the problem, namely, "Discipline, Studies, Finance & Health." Cullen replied, in effect, that all of Gillooly's good intentions regarding the various dimensions would prove useless unless the disposition of those who were to be reformed could be improved. It must be admitted, however, despite Cullen's pessimism, that Gillooly had at least defined the problem, even if he had not devised the means for its solution.

Of those dimensions defined by Gillooly, certainly the most immediate and critical in 1869 was finance. Since 1845, the College had received an annual parliamentary grant of £26,360 to support and maintain some 21 faculty and 520 students.[1] Of that sum, the faculty received £6,000 in salaries, and the students were provided for with the remaining £20,360. The maintenance of each of the 520 students was calculated at £28 per year, or £14,560. In addition, 250 of the senior, or divinity, students, that is, those who had advanced to theology, each received a stipend of £20 per year, or £5,000. Finally, the 20 graduate students, or Dunboyne scholars, received a stipend of £40 per year, accounting for the remaining £800. The Dunboyne scholars, moreover, received an additional stipend of £25 per year each from a private endowment, which made their total stipend £65 per year. Besides the 500 students and 20 Dunboyne scholars supported by public funds, there were an additional 25 maintained by private endowment. In addition to these 545 students on burses, public and private at Maynooth, there were also some 75 students enrolled who met their own expenses.[2] In all, then, there were over 600 students receiving an ecclesiastical education in Maynooth when it was disestablished in 1869.

In compensation for the loss of the annual grant of £26,360, the state awarded the trustees of Maynooth the capital sum of £369,040, calculated at fourteen years' purchase of the annual grant.[3] This sum, if invested at the prevailing $3\frac{1}{2}$ percent rate of interest, would yield some £13,000, or about half of the annual grant. This meant, of course, that the number of free places in Maynooth would have to be drastically reduced. The reduction would have to be, in fact, much greater than half because the faculty had, under the new arrangement, secured a life interest in their salaries and pensions, which meant that for the immediate future, at least, the annual £6,000 for their salaries would consume nearly half of the reduced income of £13,000 per year.[4] Furthermore, the vested interests of those students, who were being supported on the public endowment when the college was disestablished, would also remain a charge on the £13,000 until they finished their course of studies. When the trustees met in August 1869, shortly after the college had been disestablished, therefore, the first thing they did was to require all students entering the college after that date to pay full pension of £28 per year.

This moratorium on free places was further augmented by reductions in expenditures for the faculty, staff, and dietary in the college. When the prefect of the Dunboyne establishment died in 1871, for example, both his office and the establishment were abolished, effecting a savings of some £300 for the prefect's salary and of at least £1,860 for the cost of the establishment. Moreover, when the vice-

1. John Healy, *Maynooth College, Its Centenary History, 1795–1895* (Dublin, 1895), pp. 414–15.
2. See ibid., p. 440, for cutting of sixteen free stipends of £20/year in 1862–63 and in the following years.
3. Ibid., p. 481.
4. Ibid., p. 479.

president resigned in 1872, the professor of sacred scripture and Hebrew was asked to assume that office and salary, while continuing to teach sacred scripture and Hebrew, thus saving the college his professor's salary of some £265. Finally, after a lean and straight period of some four years, the trustees in June 1873 formally reestablished some 167 free places, while raising the pension from £28 to £30 per annum, which amounted to a charge of £5,000 on their endowed income of £13,000.[5] In addition, there also remained some 25 free places available on private foundations, for a total of 192 free places, compared to the 545 before 1870.[6] The most important and significant fact to emerge from all of this, however, was that the abolition, in effect, of some 330 free places between 1870 and 1873 does not appear to have affected the student population of Maynooth very much. Indeed, except perhaps for a brief contraction during this early period, the total number of students in the College over the next twenty-five years remained at something over 600. By 1880, the trustees had increased the total number of free places on the public endowment to 200, and by 1895, the centenary year of the college, to 300.[7] By 1895, moreover, the trustees had increased the number of free places on the private endowment from 25 in 1870 to 69. The real significance of all these figures, of course, was that they were a proof positive that in the last third of the nineteenth century there was no shortage in Ireland of either vocations for the priesthood or parents and relatives prepared to pay for them.

While the bishops were thus effecting financial reform in Maynooth, they were also attempting to deal with the other dimensions of the problem of reform. Their approach to discipline, studies, and health, however, in spite of the best efforts of the bishop of Elphin, was something less than systematic. One reason for the ad hoc nature of the bishops' approach was that a significant number of them had either a deep antipathy for the institution itself, or they had come to have serious misgivings about its effectiveness in training young men for the priesthood. The antipathy, not to say hostility, was perhaps best represented by Cullen, who had long disliked Maynooth primarily because it was a government subsidized institution, which meant not only that it was a standing and ironic reminder of the bishops' lack of complete authority in an education establishment that was closest to their hearts, but also that it was comparatively much better off financially than the rest of the ecclesiastical educational establishments. Cullen particularly disliked what he thought to be the incipient Gallican tendencies of Maynooth and the relative independence of the faculty, who, though Maynooth was within his spiritual jurisdiction, were not really subject to his control. In order to lessen his own dependence on Maynooth for priests, for example, Cullen had founded his

5. Ibid., pp. 729–30, Appendix XIII.
6. Ibid., pp. 726–28, Appendix XII.
7. Ibid., p. 730.

own seminary of the Holy Cross at Clonliffe in Dublin in 1863. By 1870, there were some 70 students being trained in Clonliffe, and to Cullen's great satisfaction, it was able to supply most of the Dublin archdiocese's needs for priests. This was the reason that Cullen was so pleased when Maynooth was finally disestablished, remarking to Kirby that though the College would be poorer, it would now be "free," which was his euphemism for greater episcopal control.[8]

The misgivings about Maynooth, as distinguished from antipathy, among some of the bishops, were perhaps best represented by the very gifted, if somewhat unpredictable, bishop of Kerry. Writing to Cullen shortly after Maynooth was disestablished in July 1869, Moriarty, who had been educated in Maynooth, offered his views about reforming the course of studies in the college. In 1870, the formal course of study for the priesthood consisted of about eight years, depending at which level the candidate entered in view of his previous preparation. The first four years were equally divided between "humanity" and philosophy. The two years of humanity consisted of elementary and advanced Latin and Greek, and the two years of philosophy were divided between mental and natural, or more precisely, between logic, metaphysics, and ethics and physics, mathematics, and the other sciences. The second four years were devoted to the study of theology, dogmatic and moral, taught in combination by a different professor each year. "I think," Moriarty explained to Cullen on June 9, 1869, "we could make retrenchments in Maynooth more beneficial than prejudicial to the efficiency of the College" (C). "By dividing the Dogma and Moral," he suggested, "and combining Natural Philosophy with the other Junior classes we could share three or four professors or apply them to things which are much neglected." "Nobody teaches these young men," Moriarty pointed out, "how or what to preach." "Half of the servants of the College," he added, "might be dismissed with advantage, and a quarter at least of the mutton might be suppressed." "The whole system," he concluded, "might become more absolute, and better calculated to foster humility and obedience."

Though Cullen realized that he and a number of the other bishops felt as did Moriarty, he also understood that the great majority of the bishops had been educated at Maynooth, and many had been superiors and professors in the college before being promoted to the episcopacy, and, unlike Moriarty, a good many of them would be loathe to very drastically reform their alma mater. When this reluctance of many of the bishops is construed in light of the faculty's feeling that

---

8. K, August 16, 1870. Cullen's attitude was undoubtedly strongly reinforced by the views about Maynooth taken by the Propaganda authorities at this time. Beginning in early 1869 there had been some strong criticism from Rome about the alleged faulty nature of the seminary training at Maynooth, and this certainly facilitated the efforts of the advocates of reform of that college among the bishops. This will be treated more fully in the first chapter of my next volume (1874–1878).

any necessary change should be initiated from the bottom up rather than from the top down, Cullen's cautious approach to reforming Maynooth was most understandable. The reform was further complicated by the fact that the bishops as a body were a democratic institution, so that, for example, the bishop of Ross, with only eleven parishes in West Cork, had as large a voice in the body, one vote, as did the cardinal archbishop of Dublin. The actual reform of Maynooth, moreover, was undertaken not by the old board of trustees, which consisted of the four archbishops, seven of their suffragan bishops, and six laymen, but by the bishops as a body, in two general meetings held in August 1869 and October 1870. All of the lay trustees, except Lord Ffrench, had voluntarily resigned after the legislation concerning Maynooth was passed in July 1869, and in their places five bishops had been appointed, increasing the episcopal representation to sixteen, or more than half the whole number of bishops.[9] A meeting of the newly constituted Maynooth board after 1870, if all attended, therefore, was almost tantamount to a meeting of the body, and accompanied by all the problems of inertia consequent on such an enlargement.[10]

Though the foregoing may account for the slow pace at which the reform of Maynooth proceeded, it does not account for what the bishops eventually were able to accomplish. Responsibility for the college, it will be recalled, had been assumed by the new board of trustees on January 1, 1871, and early in March the episcopal commission that had been appointed to arrange the transfer of responsibility in August 1869 met to make further recommendations. "They seem resolved," Moran reported to Kirby on March 7, "to divide the whole body of students into four divisions entirely distinct" (K). "This is a step in the right direction," he added dryly, "if it can be carried out." When the new board of trustees met for the first time on June 20, 1871, they appointed a committee of six bishops—Cork, Meath, Clogher, Elphin, Ardagh, and the coadjutor to Kildare and Leighlin—to implement the recommendations of the episcopal commission of the four archbishops and their four suffragans. The committee was "requested to have the resolutions adopted at our present meeting and draft of Statutes printed and forwarded to each of the bishops of Ireland" in order that they might be discussed and approved at a general meeting of the bishops the following August. The committee of six bishops also was asked to meet with the bursar of the college "regarding the dietary of the College, arrangements for servants, the material changes which they may consider necessary for the approved subdivision

9. Healy, p. 485.

10. In January 1875, the board of trustees resolved that it was desirable to increase the number of trustees from seventeen to thirty, which would have, in effect, included the body of bishops, and the trustees delegated three of their number to attempt to secure the necessary parliamentary legislation. The effort to secure such legislation, however, proved fruitless. See Healy, p. 494.

of the College and other financial affairs."[11] The trustees, at this meeting, also took the extraordinary step of recommending a loan of some £92,000 to the earl of Granard, secured on the mortgage of his estate, which amounted to a quarter of the whole Maynooth endowment.

At this board meeting, the senior dean in the college, who had been ill for several years, James O'Kane, signified to the trustees that he would like to retire. For some time, Cullen and a number of his colleagues had, in fact, been concerned about the way in which the deans, or superiors, had been appointed in Maynooth. There were actually four deans, a senior and three juniors, responsible for the piety and discipline of some 600 students. In more recent years, when a dean, usually the senior dean, retired, he was replaced by the senior junior dean, and the other deans then moved up a place. The resulting vacant place of the third junior dean was usually filled by appointing one of the more promising senior students of the Dunboyne establishment, who was generally about twenty-six years of age at the time of his appointment and without, of course, any real academic or pastoral experience. Cullen and his colleagues thought this was too young an age to assume so serious a responsibility. After O'Kane intimated his desire to retire, therefore, Cullen decided to ask the professor of sacred scripture and Hebrew, Daniel McCarthy, who had been a professor in the college for more than twenty-five years, to assume the vacant office of senior dean. "I feel bound," McCarthy explained to Cullen on June 24, "even in gratitude to refer to the proposals made to me by the good Bishop of Elphin, chiefly at your Eminence's suggestion. I never desired any change in my position, and I can have no wish to assume the duties of senior dean. Yet if your Eminence and the other Trustees deem it expedient that I should take a share in the government of the College, where two of the old and trusted members of the administration are obliged to retire for a time, it seems to me that I should not, when thus called upon, shrink from the responsibility" (C). "I may do some little good," he added, "by giving the Trustees time for considering the merits of candidates for the office. I only ask that if appointed as dean I may be entrusted with the care of the junior students."

Shortly before the general meeting in August, to which the board's resolution of June 20 would be referred, the bishop of Elphin, who had been entrusted with the revision of the statutes governing the college, wrote to Cullen, attempting as usual to expedite matters. "I don't know," Gillooly explained on August 3, "whether it was arranged at our last Meeting at Maynooth that the Committee should meet & confer together on the 16th Inst. in order to prepare for the work of the General Meeting the next day" (C). "If such an arrangement has not yet been made I would request it thro' Dr. Lee to the several members of the Committee," he suggested, referring to the secretary of the board of trustees. "It will take us several hours to

11. "Minutes of the Board of Trustees of Maynooth College," June 22, 1871.

inspect the works which we ordered to be executed during the Vacation, and to prepare a report thereon for the Trustees. Then there will be a Draft of Statutes to be reconsidered, and the *Regula Pietatis* [Rule of Piety], which is being prepared by Dʳ Conroy." "This preparatory Meeting," he advised Cullen again in conclusion, "is of extreme importance, so I again beg your Eminence to provide for it."

At their general meeting on August 17, the bishops approved the resolutions adopted the previous June. They also approved the appointment of McCarthy as senior dean, who would also continue as professor of sacred scripture and Hebrew.[12] "All our Bishops," Moran reported to Kirby on August 27, "met last week in Maynooth and adopted some good resolutions on the new endowments of the College. It will now be divided into four distinct divisions. The kitchen had also been entirely modified. Instead of the heavy meat of former times, the continental system will be in great part introduced" (K). "*Resto vedero* [It remains to be seen]," he further observed, "whether the regulations will be carried out." To see that their regulations were carried out, the bishops had also approved at their August meeting the appointment of a visiting committee, consisting of the four archbishops and the bishops of Limerick, Meath, Elphin, and the coadjutor of Kildare and Leighlin.[13] The suffragan bishops on this committee were chosen by ballot for the year 1871–72, and they were instructed to meet in the college on October 14, some three days before the scheduled meeting of the trustees on October 17 in Dublin. At the October meeting, the report of the visiting committee was read and approved, and the rules for students were also read, discussed, amended, and adopted. The resolutions submitted to the meeting by the visiting committee relative to discipline and studies were also adopted and ordered to be printed, and the meeting was adjourned to the following June.

In early May 1872, when the bishop of Elphin still had received no notice that the visiting committee would be convened, he wrote to Cullen asking him what was to be done before the June meeting about the visitation of the college. "Regarding the visitation of Maynooth," Cullen replied to Gillooly on May 24, "I have got a letter from Dr. McCarthy in which he says a visitation would be most desirable" (G). "At our meeting," he explained, referring to the board meeting the previous October, "I got no authority to convoke the visitors and I suppose they would not be satisfied that I would assume that power. However if you think well to call the visitors together I will attend the meeting if possible or if I cannot I will assist in carrying out your regulations." "I think one dean," Cullen added, "can scarcely manage the highest class which consists of about 200 students, but the visitors cannot apply a remedy to that evil." "If the visitors meet," he advised Gillooly, "they should do so without delay as the examinations etc. will soon

12. Ibid., August 18, 1871.
13. Ibid.

commence and the Board will meet on St. John's Day [June 24]. I think there is another meeting of the visitors immediately before the Board." Indeed, as Cullen had intimated to Gillooly, the new senior dean of Maynooth had written Cullen some three weeks before. "I heard that the episcopal visitors," McCarthy had explained on April 15, "are about coming to the College. If so, I would say—*this day* rather than tomorrow" (C). "Our inspection of the first and most important division," he reported, "is quite inadequate. We leave two hundred students, at the end of their course, practically in charge of one dean, who cannot watch over them." "I do not like," he confessed, "to interfere, nor would I suggest a visitation. But if we are to have one, may it be *quamprimum* [immediately]."

"Every successive report," Gillooly assured Cullen on May 5, the day he received Cullen's letter of May 4, "I receive from Maynooth convinces me more strongly of the necessity of holding an extraordinary Visitation of the College with the least possible delay" (C). "I foresaw this necessity from the beginning," he added unblushingly, "and attempted to provide for it by getting a Secretary appointed to the Visitors who w^d be charged with the summoning of Meetings &c; but I was allowed to be overruled by the abp of Tuam; and no other provision was made for the due action of the Visitors." "Under present circumstances," Gillooly pointed out, "it is only your Eminence that can get the Visitors or as many of them as will form a quorum, to agree to meet at Maynooth. It would be folly & presumption of me to interfere in the matter, unless commissioned by your Eminence to do so in your name—and in that case it w^d seem to me necessary to be able to announce, that your Eminence would attend our meeting. There is scarcely any thing, connected with the religious interests of our Irish Church, that demands or deserves more immediate & unstinted attention, than the reorganisation of our Nat^l Seminary—and without the action & guidance of our head no effectual reform will be effected." "There must be," he warned Cullen in conclusion "a display as well as an exercise of united action on our part to restrain those who are working against us—and to give Courage to those who respect our authority."

"As the meeting of the Board," Cullen replied the next day, May 6, "is soon near, and as there is a previous meeting of the visitors to be held as a preparation for the general meeting, I daresay some of the Bishops will think it unnecessary to hold a visitation just now" (G). "However," Cullen added, "if your Lordship thinks that any good can be done by meeting this month I will be happy to attend if possible, and you may say so to the other visitors, or make any other use of my name." "But as I said," he explained again, "the visitation ordered to be held must take place about the 20th of June and then one visitation would be scarcely a month distant from the other." Gillooly did not reply to this letter for several days, but when he did, he decided to take another tack, which threw a good deal of inadvertent light on the problems involved in reforming Maynooth. "On reflexion," he informed Cullen on May 9, "I think with your Eminence that as the fixed meeting is so near at hand and as the Bishops are now so urgently engaged in home duties, it is on the whole more advisable not to attempt bringing them together within the present month" (C). "In the absence of the visitation," he then explained, referring to the president of Maynooth, "it occured to me that some other check on the College officials might be devised—and I am venturing to apply one—in the shape of a confidential communication to Dr. Russell."

> I am writing to him this day about the ordination of our students, and in a P.S. I inform him of the reports that have been sent from the College to several of the Bps—of the anxiety of the latter regarding the alleged covert opposition of some of the superiors—and of the desire conveyed to myself by Bishops, that a Visitation of the College sh^ld be held without waiting for the fixed term in June. I feel some hope that this friendly warning will have a good effect, and I think it is the best remedy that can be applied at present. It will make all concerned feel the necessity of preparing for a strict scrutiny at the end of the [academic] year, and it will prepare them for a more strict & constant supervision in the future.

"One of our first resolutions," Gillooly advised in conclusion, "at [our] next meeting should provide for the regular, controlling action of the *Visiting Committee*—the very thing that Dr. Russell managed to prevent, thro' the Abps of Cashel & Tuam, at our last Genl Meeting."

"I had a letter," Gillooly reassured Cullen a week later, on May 16, "a few days ago from Dr. Russell, from which I infer, that my friendly notification about the College affairs made the desired impression and is likely to restrain the oppositionists" (C). "Dr. Lee," Gillooly again reported to Cullen, a month later, on June 7, referring to the secretary of the Maynooth board, "has sent me notice of our next meeting of Trustees, fixed for the 25th Inst. I have written to him, requesting he would give notice also to the members of the Visiting Committee to meet on the 22d & following days" (C). "I think," he further observed, "the two notices should always be sent together. If the Visitors meet at Maynooth on Saturday [June 22], a preliminary meeting in Dublin, of which I was thinking, would not be required. A few of us could meet privately before the official proceedings would be commenced." Two days later, however, Gillooly was obliged to write Cullen again, complaining of the machinations of those artful men in Maynooth. "I have just received a letter," he reported again on June 9, referring to the president of Maynooth, "from Dr. Russell with reference to my students—in which he informs me in a Postscript, that the Visiting Prelates are to meet at St. Patrick's [i.e., Maynooth College] on the *24th*—the eve of the meeting of the Trustees" (C). "If this be so," Gillooly declared, "the Visitation will be a mere sham—and I for one will take no part whatever in it." "The three preceeding days," he maintained, "or such portion of them as the ordinations will leave available will be absolutely necessary for the work to be done—a work as difficult as it is important." "It is for your Eminence," he insisted, "to fix the time, and to defeat the artifices of the diplomatic gentlemen we have to deal with in that Institution."

Apparently Gillooly not only achieved an earlier meeting of the visiting committee, but also he had his own way at the June 25 meeting of the board of trustees.[14] At that meeting, the visiting committee was elected by ballot for the ensuing year and all the same members were reelected. Moreover, it was resolved that all ordinary meetings of the committee would be convoked by the secretary to the trustees two days before the meeting of the board, but extraordinary meetings of the committee could be convened by the secretary of the committee, Gillooly, on the requisition of the archbishops. Also, concerned to both reform and retrench the curriculum, the trustees adopted a number of changes in the course of studies constituted by the theology and philosophy years. At this board meeting also, the vice-president of the college, Robert French Whitehead, having served in that office for twenty-seven years, and in the college for forty-three, submitted his resignation to the trustees. Finally, the draft of the statutes for the colleges, prepared by Gillooly, was read, amended, and approved by the trustees, subject to verbal corrections by Gillooly in consultation with the president of the college.

"I send your Eminence," Gillooly informed Cullen some five weeks later, on August 2, "by this Post a Copy of the corrected Statutes for Maynooth which came to me two or three weeks ago from the printer. There are some typographical errors, but very few, considering the number of verbal corrections to be made" (C). "I hope your Eminence," Gillooly suggested, "will do what you can between this & our next meeting to facilitate the elections of Vicepresident & Dean. Dr. McCarthy has expressed to me his willingness to retain the chair of Sacred Scripture, in the event of his being appointed Vice-P." "I am told Dr. Thomas M'Hale," he alerted Cullen, referring to the archbishop of Tuam's nephew, who was apparently also a candidate for the vice-presidency, "is not to return to Paris. I sh^d not be surprised, if he & his friends were preparing to make a great effort to secure the Scripture Chair, in case he fails in the other object of his ambition." "It sh^d not be difficult," he added, "to keep Dr. McCarthy in possession." "It will be a matter of great & lasting importance to the College," Gillooly further maintained, "to appoint a highly qualified Dean—here again we rely mainly on the enquiries your Eminence will have made." "The selection of a mere student for the office," he insisted, "would be the continuance of a system which all admit has worked badly and is accountable for most of the abuses, which we are trying to correct."

Cullen was not able to reply for nearly a month to Gillooly's letter because he was busy on visitation in his vast diocese. "I have now to say," he finally reported to Gillooly on August 29, "that I do not know anyone that will present himself for the

---

14. Ibid., June 25–27, 1872.

vacant offices in Maynooth except a priest from Clogher who has sent me a circular. Whether he is fit or not I have no means of knowing" (G). "It is reported," he added, "that Dr. Thomas McHale will be a candidate but I have not heard the report on good authority. I have spoken to several Bishops on this matter but they seemed to have no one to propose. I think there is no one in this diocese anxious for the office." "If your Lordship," he advised, "see any of the Bishops it would be well to consult them." Cullen wrote to Gillooly again about a week later, on September 5, informing him that there were now a number of candidates for the vacant deanship. "I am happy to hear," Gillooly replied on September 6, "we are to have several Candidates for the Deanship. I hope some one of them will be found worthy of our Confidence." One of the candidates alluded to by Cullen was Thomas Carr, who was then a professor in Archbishop MacHale's diocesan seminary of St. Jarlath's, in Tuam. Carr's association with MacHale would have been enough to render Carr unfit in the eyes of Cullen, Gillooly, and their friends, if he had not also been a good friend of Francis MacCormack, the recently appointed coadjutor to the bishop of Achonry. Both Carr and MacCormack had served together as curates for several years in the parish of Westport in the diocese of Tuam, and undoubtedly, before the trustees met on September 24 to decide on the appointments of the vice-president and dean, MacCormack had both warmly endorsed Carr's candidacy for dean in Maynooth and assured Cullen and Gillooly that he was not an adherent of the archbishop of Tuam.

The day before the trustees met, Daniel McCarthy wrote to Cullen, explaining why he would like to continue to hold his professorship of sacred scripture and Hebrew if appointed vice-president. It is unfortunate that only a part of the letter survives because it gives an interesting insight into the mind of the man who was to play an influential role in the college until his appointment as bishop of Kerry some six years later. "I think it desireable," McCarthy pointed out to Cullen on September 23, "that I should still act as professor, for I have thus the very best opportunity of knowing the students."

> 1º All the Divines [the theology students] are three years in my class.
> Therefore it is reasonable to suppose that I know them and their progress
> in study better than even any professor in the College. From the reports of
> professors we can only learn who are above; and who are below the average.
> We cannot decide who come very near the low standard, and yet this knowl-
> edge seems to me most desirable in doubtful cases.
>   2º From my position as professor, I was able last year to detect a gross
> violation of rule, which could otherwise remain forever unknown. A student
> wrote two very imprudent letters without name to the Bishop of Elphin and to
> Dr. Lynch [coadjutor to the bishop of Kildare and Leighlin]. Dr. Lynch sent
> back the letter to the College, and I undertook to find out the writer. I did so
> at once when I got the written exercises in my class. The handwriting was
> decisive, and the student admitted his guilt. This is but an instance of the

opportunities which I have now of becoming acquainted with the students. (C)

The next day, September 24, the trustees appointed McCarthy vice-president and allowed him to retain his professorship, and the following day, Carr was appointed a junior dean in the college.[15] At their meeting, the trustees also resolved that the professor of humanity, who taught Latin and Greek, should teach sacred eloquence instead. The statutes approved at the June meeting were ordered to be published publicly in the college on the Feast of St. Charles Borromeo, November 4, from which date they were to be binding on all members of the college. Several modifications were also made in the statutes, the most important of which was that all cases of absence on the part of an official of the College were to be entered in the minute book of the administrative council whether the absence was authorized or not.

Finally at their next board meeting in June 1873, the trustees virtually set the seal to their reform of Maynooth by approving an elaborate set of regulations designed to fix the duties and responsibilities of the various councils—administrative, scholastic, and financial—that were entrusted with the domestic government of the college.[16] In the next several years, under the watchful eye of the visiting committee and their grand inquisitor, the bishop of Elphin, a good many of the remaining inconsistencies and anomalies were attended to, but in the process some very serious tensions among the faculty and students were created. The bishops' successful reform of Maynooth, however, also had some very important consequences for the further institutionalization of their body was concerned. The bishops had met in three successive years between 1869 and 1871 in their efforts to settle the affairs of Maynooth. By the end of 1871, it had become evident that the biannual meetings of the Maynooth board of trustees in June and October virtually had become general meetings of the episcopal body, especially when taken in conjunction with the biannual meetings of the Catholic University board, which usually took place the day after the Maynooth board met.[17] After the two special general meetings, which took place in January and February of 1873 in connection with the respective crises created by the bishops protesting the

---

15. Ibid., September 24–25, 1872.
16. Ibid., June 24–25, 1873.
17. In October 1866, the bishops of the board of the Catholic University resolved to hold regular meetings twice a year on the Tuesday during Passion week (that is, some two weeks before Easter) and on the day after the Maynooth board meeting in October. See "Minute Book of the Catholic University 1861–1879," October 24, 1866. During the 1870s, and especially after 1874, the bishops of the Catholic University board found it increasingly more convenient in the spring to meet the day after the Maynooth board met in June instead of on Passion Tuesday. In addition to the Maynooth and Catholic University boards, there were also meetings of the board of bishops that governed the Irish College in Paris, but these appear to have become largely perfunctory affairs in the 1870s.

vesting of school sites in the Board of National Education and the introduction of Gladstone's University bill, only one general meeting was held before Cullen's death in November 1878, and that was occasioned by the plenary, or national synod, held at Maynooth in August and September of 1875. This more than six-year lapse of special general meetings was made possible by the regular biannual meetings of the Maynooth and Catholic University boards, as well as by the organization of special meetings of those boards as events required.

At the same time that the Irish bishops were successfully reforming Maynooth, they were also attempting to prevent the Board of National Education from further encroaching on what the bishops believed to be their prescriptive right to control education. When the royal commission on primary education made its report in May 1870, the Irish bishops must have been pleased.[18] The majority report, endorsed by eleven of the fourteen members of the commission, in effect promoted the principal of denominational education for Ireland, and the general expectation was that Gladstone and his government would soon translate the recommendations of the commission into legislation. These expectations would not be met for nearly a decade, however, as the national board fought a stubborn rear-guard action against the Irish bishops.[19] In this period, only one of the major recommendations of the Powis commission was put into effect, not by legislation but by the administrative act of the national board itself. This was the very important decision to supplement the payment of teachers according to their students' results on examinations administered by the inspectors of the national system, and it was adopted by the national board in February 1871.[20] Payment according to results had been a prominent feature of the English system of primary education since 1862, but Irish teachers had always received a base salary, which was in 1871 to be supplemented by results' fees. This gave the Irish teachers greater security than their English counterparts, and it certainly improved their comparatively low earnings. Cullen was somewhat ambivalent about payment by results.[21] First, he did not believe that the question of how teachers were paid was a religious one. He thought payment by results would not be advantageous to the teachers in good, larger schools, but it would not be advantageous to those teachers

18. Royal Commission of Inquiry into Primary Education (Ireland), Parliamentary Papers, vol. 1, pt. 1: Report of the Commissioners (C6), H.C. 1870, 28, pt. 1.

19. Donald H. Akenson, *The Irish Education Experiment* (London, 1970), pp. 316–28.

20. Ibid., pp. 317–18.

21. "Royal Commission," vol. 4: Minutes of Evidence Taken before the Commissioners, from November 24, 1868 to May 29, 1869 (C 6-III), H.C. 1870, 28, pt. 3, p. 1184.

in poor areas, where the schools were badly attended and teachers had not the advantage of either numbers or ability. On balance, however, he thought that the results system would provide an incentive for both the teacher in terms of better instruction and for the manager in terms of encouraging attendance.

The chief adviser to the national board in their adoption of the results system was Patrick Keenan, chief of inspection in the national system and a Roman Catholic who was well connected in Irish Liberal and Whig political circles.[22] In early 1872, when Keenan succeeded Alexander Macdonnell, a Protestant, as the resident commissioner of the national board, the highest permanent paid official in the national system, the bishops were generally pleased with the appointment, though they remained very suspicious of the system in general and of the board in particular. However, when Keenan was then succeeded as chief of inspection by John E. Sheridan, also a Roman Catholic and former head inspector, the appointment was not very pleasing in Catholic clerical circles. When Woodlock, who was convalescing in Blarney, heard early in the new year the rumor that Sheridan was likely to succeed Keenan, he wrote to Moran, asking him to request Cullen to prevent it.[23] Several days later in a letter to Woodlock, the bishop of Down and Connor was indignant that the appointment had been made. "The appointment of Sheridan," Dorrian informed Woodlock on January 11, "is an outrage on all the Convents and an insult to all the Bishops & Priests of Ireland" (W). "What destroys us," Dorrian then declared, "is our association and friendship with Catholics, who are *for* the 'mixed system' to the bone, yet by us hoped to be friendly to our cause and whom we spoil by our confidence." "If you inquire into Sheridan's case," Dorrian charged, "you will see who betrays us." "I am ready to prove anytime that John Lentaigne," he further maintained, referring to a commissioner of the national board who was the inspector-general of prisons in Ireland and a Roman Catholic, "said to an M.D. 'the Bishops would spoil all education in Ireland' and to a Nun in Cavan 'the Bishops cant be satisfied on Education, and we must drive a coach and six through them.' Know well that he is doing his *best* to eliminate Denominationalism from the Industrial Schools Act." "I fear," Dorrian added, "we are too passive with these people."

When David B. Dunne, professor of logic and metaphysics in the Catholic University, wrote Woodlock two days later, he was also very disappointed. "So Sheridan has been appointed to succeed Keenan," he observed grimly on January 13. "It would be hard to find a worse appointment from a Catholic point of view" (W). There was, however, from a Catholic point of view, even worse to follow in the wake of Keenan's promotion. "The National Board," Dunne informed Woodlock some six weeks later, on February 23, "has just appointed to the office of

22. Akenson, p. 37.
23. C, Woodlock to Moran, January 7, 1872.

Catholic Head Inspector, Mr. Malloy, a gentleman who had the special qualification of having two sons at the Belfast Queen's College. A second Catholic Head Inspectorship has just become vacant. The person most spoken of for the vacancy is, I hear, a Mr. MacSheehy (of Bray District) who is a Free Mason" (W). "There is a rumour," Dunne further reported, referring to the position of the joint-secretaries to the national board, "that a vacancy will shortly occur in the Catholic Secretaryship, and this Mr. McSheehy [sic] is chiefly spoken of. (Of course, in referring to these matters you will not quote *me*)." "I also hear," Dunne added, finally exhausting his store of gossip on education, "that Government has decided not to make any change of an important character in the National System—not even to the extent of the changes recommended by the R. Commission."

A short time later, Cullen was further annoyed by a number of the ten Catholic commissioners on the twenty-member board who acted in what he believed to be an unwarranted way. In March, the venerable bishop of Ossory, through his coadjutor, Partrick Moran, had requested the board to transfer the managership of the national schools in Callan to a priest whom he had appointed to replace the celebrated Robert O'Keeffe. O'Keeffe was the former parish priest of Callan and had been suspended by the bishop because he had sued the bishop for libel before a lay tribunal. The board considered the case on April 23 and decided both to receive and to act on the bishop's suspension. O'Keeffe was then dismissed by the board as manager of the Callan schools, but several of the Catholic commissioners voted against the decision, and Cullen reported the conduct of some of the Catholics on the board to a number of the bishops. "The conduct of some of the Catholic Commissioners," the bishop of Galway commiserated in reply on May 2, "in Dr. Moran's case is very extraordinary. It is the *Barabbas* scene to some extent re-enacted" (C). "I could not expect," MacEvilly further pointed out, referring to several of the Catholic commissioners, "Morris would go right nor would I expect much from Waldron. But Judge Monahan completely surprises me." "The conduct of the Catholic representatives," he added, drawing a very interesting political moral from the situation, "shows the utter dishonesty of those who appoint men bearing the name of Catholic on our Board. Why not appoint Catholics of a representative character having the confidence of the Catholic body? The Protestants & Presbyterians will have as their representatives real representative men staunch unflinching supporters of their principles and we will have as Catholic representatives men in whom neither the Catholics nor their Pastors confide." "It is a manifest delusion," MacEvilly maintained, "to say Catholics have such a number of their body on several Boards when these members are repudiated by the body they are said to represent." "I fear," he concluded sadly, "the same course would be pursued in any Education Board yet to be constructed."

Some ten days later Cullen wrote to Kirby, alerting him to a more serious problem with the board that had resulted in a difference of opinion among the bishops in the body. "I wrote to Propag," Cullen reported on May 13, "about a dispute which has arisen among the Bishops" (K). "Dr. Moriarty, Dr. Butler and Dr. Donnelly," he explained, referring respectively to the bishops of Kerry, Limerick, and Clogher, "take grants for building schools from Government or the national Board, and mortgage the schools for the amount. All the other Bishops are against this way of acting which would give great power to the state over the schools." "I think the whole case," Cullen noted, referring to the national synod that had taken place in 1850, "is in the Council of Thurles. Would you show the chapter De Scholis Nation[alibus] to the Card. and he will see what ought to be done."[24] "In my opinion," he maintained, "it is very dangerous to put our neck in the halter, just at a moment when everything is done to destroy Catholic education. If the Government get mortgages of £400 or £500 on any of our schools, they will be able to do as they wish with them." "The Bishops," he advised Kirby, pointing to the approaching Maynooth board, "will meet at the end of June in Maynooth. It wd. be well to have an answer before then. It is desirable that the Pope should sanction it."

Cullen had written Barnabò a long and interesting letter on May 7, explaining the situation and asking him to take appropriate action. "On January 16, 1841," Cullen pointed out, "a letter was written by Propaganda to the Irish bishops about the national system of education, and some rules were proposed to the same to be observed in regard to that system. Among those rules, number four reads: '*Illud quoque perutile forecenset S. Congregation, si loca ipsa scholarum in episcoporum vel parochorum potestate et proprio jure permaneant*' [That the Sacred Congregation also thinks that it would be useful if the site of the said schools be under the authority and permanent legal control of the bishops or parish priests]."[25] "This rule," Cullen further noted, "was generally observed, and thus now the premises of a large part of the national schools are the property of the bishops or the parish priests, so that if the national system of education become openly hostile to the church, they are able to separate themselves from the actual system, and to declare their schools totally free of every influence of the government. This is a great advantage in these times when so many attempts are made to introduce harmful systems of instruction in the public schools." "This independence of the Catholic schools," Cullen further explained,

> is not pleasing to the government, and there have been various attempts to destroy it. First it was proposed that the titles of the school be given to the commissioners of public education, and to induce the parish priests to make this concession, the government promised to indemnify the costs of the school,

24. *Decreta, Synodi Nationalis Totius Hiberiae Thurlesiae Habitae Anno MDCCCL* (Dublin, 1851), pp. 55-59.

25. S.R.C., vol. 36, fols. 1295-96.

and to agree to other advantages. Seeing that this project did not succeed, another proposal was made, namely that the authority in the schools would remain in the hands of the clergy, but that the government would give a loan to the parish priests for the money necessary to indemnify or enlarge the schools, or for building them anew, on the condition however that the sites of the schools and the buildings were subject to a mortgage for which the parish priests would be obligated to repay to the government the money taken as loan if the schools ceased to be connected with the national system.

"At the last meeting [October 1871] of our bishops," Cullen reported,

> this question was dealt with, and almost all the bishops were agreed that the schools ought to be free of the authority of the government, and that subsidies ought not to be accepted from the same for building new schools, so that in this way the recommendation of the Sacred Congregation was maintained, and the government not be given any pretext for appropriating the schools. After a long discussion, the following resolution was proposed, namely
>
> That we will not accept subsidies for the building of schools from the commissioners of public education, and that we will not permit our priests to receive them until the circumstances will be so changed that the bishops as a body (*La Radunaza de' vescovi*) will be of opinion that it is possible to accept such subsidies.

"This resolution," Cullen observed, "was adopted by all the bishops, except the bishops of Limerick, Monsignor Butler, of Clogher, Monsignor Donnelly, and of Kerry, Monsignor Moriarty. These three bishops declared that they had received subsidies for the building of their schools and that they would continue to receive them." "In order to avoid," Cullen added, "public discussions and dissensions on this affair, I promised to mention the controversy to Your Eminence and to ask that it be decided by the Sacred Congregation."

> It is not necessary to say much on this matter. It is enough to observe that in the past the priests have made collections and built the parochial schools without any help from the government, that this way of acting has served well enough for maintaining the freedom of education, and that there is not any reason why the government should be given a new influence by the acceptance of gifts.
>
> In the diocese of Dublin, there are about two hundred and forty national schools, which nearly all were built by the parish priests without help from the government, and this state of things gives great freedom to the clergy in the managing of the schools, while on the other hand prevents the government from undertaking things against religion, because it knows that the parish priests are the owners of the schools, and that they are able when they wish to break every connection with the government. The same state of things prevails in almost all the dioceses and it does not seem reasonable that innovations ought to be introduced, which certainly will have the effect of diminishing the influence of the clergy.

"A letter from the Sacred Congregation," Cullen finally suggested to Barnabò, "enjoining the bishops to observe what was prescribed for them, as I have said, on January 16, 1841, on the principle of this line, will have the effect of putting an end to the present controversy, and preventing dissensions that would do great harm in the times in which we live when so many efforts are made to deprive the bishops of their rights over the education of the people."

When Kirby received Cullen's letter of May 13, he submitted a memorandum concerning it to Propaganda, and Barnabò then apparently informed Kirby that he would write a letter embodying Cullen's advice to the four archbishops before the bishops were scheduled to meet in Maynooth at the end of June.[26] Kirby then conveyed the good news to Cullen, for he informed the Propaganda again that Cullen had written on May 30 to express his satisfaction that Barnabò had consented to write about the national schools and that Cullen hoped the letter would do much good.[27] Barnabò wrote the four archbishops on June 13, enjoining them to make it clear to their suffragans that they were not to accept mortgages from the national board for their schools (L). The three dissident Irish bishops apparently submitted to the injunction of the cardinal prefect, for the question was not raised again either in Cullen's letters or in the Roman correspondence.

The bishops continued to be deeply suspicious of the national board and maintained an unceasing vigilance over it. In October 1872, for example, while Cullen was in Rome seeking reassurance from the pope and the authorities about Father O'Keeffe and the Callan imbroglio, the bishop of Ardagh wrote to warn him that the board was once again plotting against them. "I met Drs. MacEvilly, Dorrian and Conaty this week," Conroy reported on October 17, referring respectively to the bishops of Galway, Down and Connor, and Kilmore, "and they are all of opinion that the conditions which the Board seeks to impose on managers who may wish to have the payment by the result system in their schools, are very insidious and dangerous" (C). "These conditions," he explained, "have not yet been forwarded to the managers of the schools, and it would be well if all the Bishops could agree to act with unison in the matter." Shortly after Cullen returned from Rome, Conroy wrote him again both to welcome him home and to warn him of impending danger. "It would be quite necessary," he advised Cullen on November 8, "to have a line inserted in the *Freeman* to warn managers of schools against signing the contract which the N. Board has proposed as the condition of gaining payment by results in the national schools. Many priests will not understand the danger, and unless the action of the ecclesiastical managers be

26. Ibid., 1302
27. Ibid., 1304.

uniform much harm will result" (C). "I am writing to Fr. Daniel," Conroy reported, referring to Cullen's clerical factotum in journalistic matters, "by this post to insert a line in this sense; but a short letter from Y.E. to your priests would be invaluable."

The following day, the bishop of Elphin also wrote Cullen to welcome him home and to alert him to the national board's plot. "As soon as your Eminence will get a quiet moment," Gillooly suggested on November 9, "I beg you will get a copy of a very important document, which has been lately sent out to the Managers of Schools from the Educ^n office in the name of the Commissioners" (C). "It is," he explained, "a proposed Agreement between Managers & Teachers of N. Schools, by which the Comm^{rs} are trying in a covert mischievous way, to establish the system of giving three months notice to Teachers before dismissal—or rather of bringing the motive of dismissal under the judgement of the Commissioners." "It is, I think," he further advised the cardinal, "of the utmost importance that the Bishops sh^d take counsel together and act in concert, on this dangerous movement of the Board of Com^{rs} and that they sh^d do so as speedily as possible. It is with a view to your securing this united action that I take the liberty of calling your Eminence's attention to the question." "I have already written," he reported, "to all my priests cautioning them against signing the document without my express permission. I believe some other bishops, Dr. Conroy amongst others have done the same." "What is all-important," Gillooly finally, and most interestingly, pointed out, "is to take such steps as would prevent certain members of our Body from sanctioning this Agreement or at least from doing so, in an assumed ignorance of the action of the rest of the Body."

Cullen decided to take Conroy's more modest advice, to write a public letter to his clergy to forestall the latest machinations of the board, rather than Gillooly's suggestion that he convene a meeting of the bishops. Cullen's letter, which was dated November 10, read:

> Rev. and Dear Sir—It has been reported to me that a printed memorandum of agreement between managers and teachers of national schools has been widely circulated in this diocese and that inspectors of the National Board have invited the managers to sign it, and to bind themselves to the conditions laid down therein.
>
> Having been consulted by several Catholic managers as to the best course to be adopted in this case, I have recommended them not to sign the document in question until it shall have been maturely examined, and its objects and tendency fully explained.
>
> My reason for giving this advice is that at present our education question is surrounded with difficulties and dangers, and that were we to sign agreements which we do not perfectly understand we might perhaps sanction principles hostile to our interests, or calculated to throw too much authority in educational matters into the hands of men in power, some of whom may be anxious

to banish the influence of religion from the school, and to rear up youth in ignorance of, or indifference to, the true faith.

The experience of late years cannot leave the least doubt as to the fatal results of this Godless policy; for, indeed, where children have been let grow up without religion an abundant harvest of Communists, incendiaries, and murderers has been produced; and where, as in France, the State has usurped all authority in educational matters, to the unjust exclusion of the parents and the Church, a revolutionary spirit has been fostered, and the rising generations have been given in charge in the Lyceums and universities to professors whose teaching poisons the mind with error and infidelity, and corrupts the heart.

The evil thus produced should make us most cautious and watchful in regard to every step we take in matters connected with the education of youth.

Hence, whether the memorandum we treat of be harmless or dangerous, in my humble opinion our proper course is to reserve judgement on it, until after due consultation we shall have come to a resolution on its merits, in which all may agree. Undoubtedly it is desirable that if this proposed agreement be calculated to do good we should offer it no resistance, but at the same time it is our duty, if we find that its tendencies are dangerous, that it insinuates false principles, its conditions are calculated to weaken the proper authorities of the school—it is our duty, I say, to unite in opposing it, even though it may be accompanied with the promise of temporal advantages.

In conclusion I beg of you to examine the memorandum now before us most closely, and to consult others about it, so that after some short time, we may communicate our views to each other, and adopt some line of conduct in which all may agree without any danger of dissension, which at the present moment would be most fatal to true Christian education, and retard the proper settlement of the important question which now occupies the public mind.[28]

Shortly after this letter was distributed, Cullen apparently asked Gillooly to draw up two circulars—one from the managers and the other from the teachers—to the national board protesting the new three months' agreement which they were to be asked to sign. Gillooly completed his assignment and came up to Dublin the following week to secure Cullen's approval of the circulars and to have them printed for distribution to all the bishops. "I left a printed copy of the Circulars," Gillooly reported to Cullen on Thursday, November 21, "for your Eminence before starting from Dublin on Wednesday. I now forward some sixty copies more correctly printed and hope your Eminence will have the satisfaction of seeing the movement swiftly pervade your entire diocese" (C). "I am sending both Circulars today," he further reported, "to each of our Clerical Managers, with a request that they shall be signed in each parish as speedily as possible and forwarded to the Commiss[rs]. I have also written to nearly all the Bishops, enclosing copies of draft letters—with your Eminence's *Imprimatur.* The Archbishops I

<hr>

28. *Freeman's Journal,* November 12, 1872.

leave to your Eminence." "I have every hope," Gillooly added, "that the work of this day will have the blessing & protection of her whom we this day honour & invoke." "I think the Teachers," he finally pointed out, "should, if possible, be got to sign their memorial—it will be more telling & effectual than that of the Managers. It will have the best effect on the Teachers themselves to get them to sign it—it will prevent their future agitation against us and make them feel the value of our good will & protection."

Cullen had, in fact, written the archbishop of Cashel several days before he received Gillooly's letter to alert him to the crisis. "I had seen that Three Months' Notice paper," Leahy informed Cullen on November 20, "and forbidden any Priest to sign it before receiving your letter" (C). "It is a dangerous and premeditated encroachment," he maintained, "having for object ultimately to make the Nat¹ Teachers independent of the Catholic Bishops & Clergy & dependent on the Government." "Your Eminence's letter to the Clergy," Leahy added, "which appeared in the public Papers, was most timely. I hope that many of the clerical managers through the country have not been surprised into the signing of this paper." Indeed, as the archbishop was soon to learn, a considerable number of the clergy in his own province had not only signed the new agreement, but had done so with the approval of their bishops. "Before I received your letter," the bishop of Limerick informed Gillooly on November 25, "the great body of the Clerical Managers here, had signed the 'New Agreement,' and had done so with my full concurrence" (C). "Your Lordship's letter," Butler assured Gillooly, "as a matter of course, made me reconsider the subject with great care; and this additional consideration, has, I must say, convinced me more & more that it is right & expedient for us to accept this *new rule*."

"The agitation got up," Butler explained, "and carried on so long so vigorously by the Nat¹ Teachers against the irresponsible powers of Managers had produced its effect on Public opinion, and several Members of Parliament—some of them Cabinet Ministers—had taken up the Teachers' cause, and were anxious, as much from hostility to us as from favour to the Teachers, to liberate them entirely from our control."

> Various modes of managing Nat¹ schools were mooted—such as "local school boards"—direct management by the Nat¹ Board itself &c. &c; and when the time came for broaching the subject in the House of Commons, many were apprehensive—myself amongst the number—that some measure wholly subversive of Managerial control, and therefore inadmissable by us, would be carried. Finally this rule of "3 months notice" was adopted, not without difficulty by the Cabinet; and when Lord Hartington proposed it in the House, it was at once acceded to, without complaint or objection that I ever heard of, by all the Irish members & all our friends in Parliament.

"For myself," Butler confessed, "I rejoiced exceedingly at the result for I considered that we had, thro' the friendly action of the Government, escaped a grave danger, and that an agitation which demanded the surrender of all our Managerial power was set at rest by a concession which practically deprived us of none—at least of any that we need value or ever care to exercise."

> But here your Lordship takes issue with me holding (and it is the only objection mentioned either in your letter or in the printed forms accompanying it) that the "3 months rule" will necessarily "weaken & undermine our Managerial authority." You do not explain how this very evil result would arise; but it could arise only on one supposition—namely—that a considerable number of cases would occur where his duty to faith & morals would oblige a Manager to dismiss a Teacher summarily, and where, from the difficulty of stating or proving the case against the Teacher the Board could not be expected to sanction the dismissal. I say it is only in cases like these that any inconveniences could arise: for it is no inconvenience to lose the power of summary dismissal, when the Teacher does not deserve such a punishment and when it would be, therefore, wrong & cruel to inflict it: nor is it any detriment to our real power as Managers to be obliged to ask the sanction of the Board in cases that can be stated & proved, and when such sanction is then sure to be given. Now it seems plain to me that the cases in which the Managers would feel obliged to dismiss summarily, tho' he could not give his reasons, or prove his case to the Board should be exceedingly few—not one in a thousand—so few that they would practically come to nothing. I am managing schools for the last thirty years, and for the last eleven I have acquaintance with all the schools of the Diocese, and I never knew or heard of such a case. And then if a case so unusual, so exceptional should ever arise, the difficulty could be at once met, and faith & morals saved by the payment of £10, that being the highest quarterly payment of any of our Nat^l Teachers.

"Now if under all these circumstances," Butler warned Gillooly, "the Bishops and Priests should refuse to acquiesce in this 'new rule,' it seems to me that very bad, if not fatal results, must follow."

Gillooly forwarded Butler's letter to Cullen, who undoubtedly was very annoyed by it. Cullen was, however, even more upset a week later, when he received a reply, dated December 5, from the archbishop of Cashel in reply to one of his own letters. Leahy thanked Cullen for forwarding Gillooly's printed circulars and explained that the bishops of the province of Cashel had just met the day before, in Thurles, to report to Propaganda on the *terna* commended by the clergy of Waterford for a coadjutor to their ailing bishop. Leahy then explained that there was a serious difference of opinion among his suffragans about the new agreement proposed by the board. "The bishops of Cork, Kerry, and Limerick," he reported, "were for the Agreement, and have in their respective Dioceses given their sanction to their Clerical Managers entering into this Agreement" (C). "The matter has now," Leahy then sadly explained, "become one of very great gravity, on account of the division once more planted in the heart of the Episcopate."

"Those good Bishops & others, I suppose," he added, "will cut the ground from under the feet of the rest of us who may oppose the change in the National System." "Would it not be right," Leahy suggested, "to call together a Meeting of the Bishops of Ireland with the least possible delay, in the hope of all the Bishops being brought to adopt one & the same line of action in this most important matter?" "This division among the Bishops," he further observed, referring to the fact that Gladstone would introduce his University bill when Parliament convened in February, "comes at a most unfortunate time, just on the eve of what we expect to be the final discussion & settlement of one great branch of the Education question in Parliament." "I pray your Eminence at once," Leahy urged in conclusion, "to consider when & how the meeting of the Bishops may be held."

Cullen obviously was perplexed about how to proceed, and he wrote the bishop of Elphin to ask for his advice. "I believe in this province," he explained to Gillooly on December 6, "we are all unanimous about the agreement" (G). "I have written to Dr. McGettigan," he reported, referring to the archbishop of Armagh, "and he states in reply that he himself and all his suffragans are opposed to that document. From the province of Cashel the accounts are not so cheering. Dr. Delany, Dr. Butler, and Dr. Moriarty have decidedly declared themselves in favour of the agreement. I suppose you are all right in the West. The declaration of the three southern Bishops will do great mischief. The Commissioners were well inclined to yield but they will now say that the most influential Bishops are on their side." "I suppose," he admitted, "there is now no remedy but to get a meeting of bishops to settle the matter." "But when," he asked, "can the meeting be held? Probably the University question will also require a meeting, but we cannot know anything in that matter for a long time. What is to be done?" "I have put in the hands of the publisher," he assured Gillooly, "a statement of the case regarding managers, with all the necessary quotations from rules, reports and parliamentary evidence on the matter. As soon as I can get it out I will send your Lordship a copy." "It is a sad thing," Cullen concluded, "that the division now introduced should weaken the episcopal body. In every part of the world the Bishops are fighting gloriously for Catholic education. It is a pity that we should give a bad example in Ireland."

On that same day, Cullen also wrote the archbishop of Cashel to explain that it would be difficult to hold a meeting of the bishops before Christmas. "This matter of the *Three Months' Notice Agreement*," Leahy replied insistently the next day, December 7, "is urgent. It cannot without great detriment to religion be allowed to stand over till the beginning of next year when a Meeting of the Bishops might be called together. If, as your Eminence says, the *great bulk of the Prelates* are against the Agreement, we ought to take immediate action by issuing an Address expressing our opinions" (C). "Your Eminence," Leahy suggested, "could get one printed & send a copy to each of the Prelates, asking his opinion, & his signature in case of his approval of it." "I send a paper," he added, "I have drawn up hurriedly—not that I would have this one adopted, but to indicate to your Eminence (excuse the liberty) *the grounds which I think we ought to take,* in order to put the saddle on the right horse." Also on December 7, Gillooly replied to Cullen's letter asking his advice. "A general Meeting of the Bishops," Gillooly advised, "is most desirable, or rather necessary, and should be convened as soon as possible. The 19th Inst. would be a convenient day enough. At that Meeting a certain number of the body might be chosen as delegates, to consider the Educⁿ Measures that may be proposed by the Govᵐᵗ and to act for the Body with reference to such measures" (C). "Some Committee of the kind," he maintained, "will be absolutely necessary for our security. If the Meeting is to be held for this latter purpose as well as for consideration of the New Rules, it would be well I suppose to mention both objects in the notice."

"I wrote to your Eminence on Saturday," Gillooly apologized on Monday, December 9, "in a great hurry and forgot to say, that in this Province we are all unanimous in our opposition to the 'Agreement' and that the Letters from Managers and Memorials from Teachers have been forwarded to the Commʳˢ from Galway, Achonry & Killala as well as from this diocese" (C). "Only one Teacher," he assured Cullen, "in this Diocese declined to sign the Memorial. Cards like the enclosed were sent to them and I presume to N. Teachers generally in other dioceses. It is clear that the Teachers' Memorial is feared by our opponents—which is the best proof of its timely influence."

> The opposition of the three southern Bps will come to nought at our Meeting—and if the Meeting be convened at once, the evil example will not have time to effect any harm. The Commʳˢ who rely on them will, like themselves, see at once, that the Resolution of our Meeting will be confirmed by the Holy See, and that the minority will be obliged to act in conformity with the Body. I shᵈ therefore think it extremely important to prove *as soon as possible, to all concerned,* that there is an immoveable determination to provide for & to enforce unity of action in those mixed questions—both by our own Meetings & by the authority of the Holy See. I have been long anxiously desiring, that the Holy See shᵈ be got to rule for our Meetings, that the Resolutions of the Majority shᵈ be strictly obligatory on all, until the Holy See shᵈ otherwise decide.

"Would not," Gillooly suggested, "our next Meeting be a most convenient one for adopting a Petition to the H. See to that effect?" "I am sure," he noted in conclusion, "the great majority of the Bps would joyfully sign it, and would feel grateful to your Eminence for proposing it."

When Cullen replied to this most interesting letter, however, he chose to ignore nearly all of Gillooly's suggestions, except one, which he vetoed. "Dr. Leahy of Cashel," Cullen pointed out on December 11, "suggests that all the Bishops should sign the declaration which he had drawn up and which I send. I think it would produce a good effect. Any changes considered necessary may still be made as it is not struck off as yet" (G). "I also send," he added, "a proof of some observations I got printed regarding the power of managers, proving that the Board always admitted that that power was supreme in the dismissal of masters. I have about ten or eleven pages more giving an analysis of all the changes made to our detriment by the Board. It is desirable to keep before us the fact that the Board has made many encroachments on us and that some day or other we must resist." "It would be impossible," Cullen maintained, touching on Gillooly's chief suggestion, "to get the bishops to meet before Christmas." "We can talk over these matters," he concluded more gently, referring to the recent appointment of John F. P. Leonard, a Dublin priest, as the vicar apostolic of the western district of the Cape of Good Hope, "when you come up for the consecration."

That Cullen decided not to convene a meeting of the bishops before Christmas raises some very interesting questions. Before Cullen had returned to Ireland in 1850 as the pope's apostolic delegate and archbishop of Armagh, the informal, regular, annual meetings of the Irish bishops had become a serious concern to the Roman authorities because of their increasingly contentious and divisive nature. To the Roman authorities, these meetings had become a good example of the very great danger in allowing bishops to assemble without observing the proper synodical forms. For a meeting to be synodical, it must be convened only on the authority of the Holy See and presided over by someone delegated to do so by the pope, its proceedings must be both canonical and subject to the rule of secrecy, and the agenda before, as well as the acts and decrees after, the meeting must be approved formally by the Holy See in order to be binding. During the 1850s Cullen finally was able to impose the synodical forms on Irish episcopal meetings, though by the end of the decade the resolutions passed at such meetings were no longer submitted for formal Roman approval. The other forms, however, were still being observed up until the crisis precipitated by the national board's memorandum of agreement in November 1872. Cullen was naturally, therefore, reluctant to convene or preside at a general meeting of the bishops without having first secured the permission of the Roman authorities. He was also very much concerned, without such a permission, that he would be unable to control the agenda of such a meeting. Though he was morally sure that the great majority of the bishops would agree to condemn the board's latest encroachment, he was less sure that other issues would not also be introduced and pronounced upon by the bishops. Undoubtedly Cullen's greatest concern, given the bad temper of some of the bishops toward the board as evidenced in Gillooly's and Leahy's letters, was that when assembled the bishops would insist on issuing a statement that would place the

Irish-Liberal alliance in jeopardy and thereby wreck any hope of Gladstone and his party's satisfactory settlement of the University question in the next session of Parliament.

Apparently Cullen raised the issue to Leahy of which tactics should be pursued given the delicate nature of the political situation and suggested that it might be more prudent for the bishops, in the interests of their educational objectives overall, to remonstrate with the board privately before taking the drastic step of denouncing them publicly. "If there is any chance," Leahy agreed in his reply on December 13, "that within a reasonable time the Commissioners may give in and withdraw this obnoxious Agreement, it would be better not at once to publish anything but wait awhile, because once we come before the public with our Protest, there is open war between us & them" (C). "If we could," he added, "better not push them to the wall. Yet, every one is expecting, and impatiently expecting, something from us." "Does not the part taken by those few Bishops," Leahy added in a less conciliatory postscript, "call imperatively for a strong prohibition by the Holy See against any Priest or Bishop taking on himself to accept & practically to adopt any changes or modifications in the National System without the concurrence of the body of the Bishops?" "They should not be allowed," he maintained, "to break away from the body of the bishops & act for themselves. Apart from other great evils, it is the worst example to the body of the Priests of Ireland." Two days later, Leahy had some further thoughts about how they should proceed in the present crisis. "Concurring as I do," he again assured Cullen, on December 15, "with your Eminence in thinking it would be only prudent not all at once to come out with our Protest against the *New Agreement,* I am at the same time of the opinion that copies of it ought without delay be sent to all the Bishops for their signatures so that it might be published without loss of time after its becoming known, should it become known, that the Commissioners would not recede from the ground they have taken" (C). "Copies would, of course," he added, "be sent to the Bishops of Cork, Kerry, and Limerick, to give them an opportunity of getting if so minded, out of the exceptional awkward position they have taken, and to put it out of their power to say they had been passed over when, if only asked, they would have given their names."

By the time Cullen received Leahy's letter, on Monday, December 16, he had already asked a number of the bishops, who had come up to Dublin the previous day for the consecration of the new vicar apostolic of the western district of the Cape of Good Hope, to meet informally with him to decide upon the best course in the present crisis.[29] At their meeting on Monday, Cullen as usual left little to

29. Ibid., December 16, 1872. The bishops who assisted at Leonard's consecration were Moran (Ossory), Conroy (Ardagh), Gillooly (Elphin), Dorrian (Down and Connor), and Lynch (Coadjutor to Kildare and Leighlin).

chance. He distributed copies of his statement about the board's various encroachments over the previous forty years that had been detrimental to Catholic interests, as well as a memorandum concerning the control managers had exercised and which the board had admitted as legitimate. He also apparently had drawn up for the approval of the bishops a form of amended agreement to be presented to the board.[30] In this way, apparently, Cullen hoped that by not cornering the board, the bishops could reach some accommodation and thereby avoid a break with either the board or the government. It was also agreed at this meeting, apparently, that Cullen should convene a general meeting of the bishops early in the new year. Within the week, Cullen decided on how he was going to proceed and wrote to all the bishops.

"I beg to send your Lordship," Cullen informed the bishop of Kerry on December 22, "some observations upon the changes hitherto made in the system of National Education and also upon the change lately proposed. I send another paper suggesting means calculated to remove or prevent disputes with the National Board without compromising Catholic principles."[31] "These papers," Cullen explained, "have not been published; they are destined for the use of the bishops." "Several of the prelates," he added, "are anxious to hold a meeting to prevent further encroachments on our rights." "Will your Lordship," he asked, "approve of there being a meeting on the 21st of January here in Dublin to deliberate on what is best to be done? One line in reply will oblige." Moriarty replied in his own inimitable way on Christmas Day. "I can not sign their protest," he explained to Cullen. "I consider the new arrangement a most substantial improvement in the Nat. System."

> 1. It gives some protection—though a scant measure of it—to the poor teachers against capricious eviction.
>
> 2. It will bind them better to the Managers by improving their position. We need this very much for it is not easy to get teachers to stay with us.
>
> 3. I consider the new arrangement the surest safeguard of our Managerial authority. If we do not accept it, the Parliament will transfer education to the care of School Boards. To throw the people of this part of the country on their own resources for education is out of the question.

"I have many other reasons," he assured Cullen, "but, on the whole, I wish to give my teachers the rights that the law gives to my servant man." "I agree with the protest," Moriarty added, "in thinking the Board an inconvenient court of appeal. The Manager and teacher could not easily appear in *propria persona* [in his own person]. The Board would always accept the reasons of the Manager, and the teacher would only have a sham protection." "But with an arbitrary power,"

---

30. C, Conroy to Cullen, December 19, 1872.
31. Peadar MacSuibhne, *Paul Cullen and His Contemporaries* (Naas, 1977), 5:195.

Moriarty pointed out, "of dismissal at three Months Notice an appeal is never necessary, or if needed in some most improbable case, a £10 note will settle the question, leaving faith and morals *in tuto* [safe]." "Finally, My dear Lord," Moriarty then shrewdly observed, "I do not wish a meeting of the Bishops. From the Manifestos that have appeared and from opinions I have gathered, I am sure that many of the Bishops would be in favor of a strong protest. If so, the Education question will be settled." "The secularist party," he warned, "will declaim against the exorbitant demand of clerical despotism. We shall raise the opposition which the ministry dare not confront." "It will be," he concluded, "the story of Tantalus told again."

It should be observed at this point that Cullen's letter to Moriarty and the other Irish bishops was a most interesting production. First, he was not convening a meeting. He was only asking the bishops, in fact, if they approved the convening of a meeting, and he was in no way, therefore, preempting the right of the Holy See in such matters. The date which Cullen set for the proposed meeting was yet another example of Cullen's very fine sense of timing. It would not only allow him enough time to find out through Kirby what the Roman authorities' disposition was with regard to convening such a meeting, but also it was far enough away to prevent any precipitate public action on the part of the bishops against the board that might endanger the University bill, which Gladstone was expected to introduce in Parliament about the middle of February. Indeed, Cullen had begun to lay the necessary groundwork in Rome by alerting Kirby to the crisis several days before he wrote to the bishops. "We have got," he explained on December 19, "a bone of contention at present among us. The National Board has passed a law lessening the power of the priests who manage the schools. Dr. Delany, Dr. Moriarty, and Dr. Butler have submitted. All the other Bishops resist" (K). "It will be necessary," he warned, "to hold a meeting, or to do something else to prevent a split. I will send you the papers regarding the matter." "If we could meet in January," he suggested, "and discuss the question we might keep united."

When Cullen then received the replies of the bishops, which indicated that besides Moriarty only two other bishops, MacHale and Butler, disapproved of holding a meeting, he decided to write Barnabò. "It seems," he explained to the cardinal prefect on December 27, "that in every country there are discussions now in regard to public education, and it is not to be wondered at that there are also among us controversies on this important matter. The question that occupies us presently is connected with the system of national education which was introduced in Ireland about forty years ago."

> This system was founded to bring children of every religion together from which the practice and teaching of religion was obliged to be excluded in the hours in which Catholics and Protestants are found together in the school. On principle the Protestants were opposed to this system, and because of the

> opposition the Catholic priests were able to convert the parochial schools into national schools retaining for themselves the ownership of the buildings and the right to nominate to remove the teachers. In recent months the commissioners who manage the system have introduced a rule that limits the power of the parish priests to remove teachers, and thus remove a right that served to protect the faith from wicked teachers if ever they were to be found in the schools. This rule had been hardly made when many of the bishops protested against it, but unfortunately the bishops of Cork, Killarney [correctly, Kerry], and Limerick have approved it, and exhorted their parish priests to adopt it. In this way being divided we lose all power, and the clergy will be by this deprived of a right that gave them great authority over the teachers.[32]

"To put an end to this dissension," Cullen suggested, "and to reestablish unanimity, it seems that it would be very useful to hold a meeting of the bishops to decide a question that concerns all the parishes of the Kingdom." "Almost all the bishops," he assured Barnabò, "are anxious to meet, and I have suggested that all might come to Dublin to deal with this business on January 21 next. I hope therefore that the prelates, after having examined the rule already mentioned, will be able to adopt a unanimous mode of acting." "Many seem certain," Cullen further reported, "that Mr. Gladstone will soon propose a law on the teaching of the superior sciences by introducing a University in Ireland, and on this occasion it will be very opportune that the bishops make some united effort to obtain a University that will not be hostile to the Catholic Church." "If, before the proposed meeting," Cullen advised Barnabò, "your Eminence wrote some few words in the name of the Sacred Congregation and the Holy Father expecting union and recommending the maintaining of the rights of the Church in regard to education, I am convinced that great profit would result from them." "It will be necessary also," Cullen formally suggested in conclusion, "to add that if the bishops were not able to agree among themselves, they should refer the whole business to the Holy See, and await the decision on it without carrying their differences before the public. This manner of acting was prescribed in the last chapter of the Synod of Thurles, and it may be said from that time till the present there has not been any dissension of any importance among the bishops of Ireland."

Also on December 27, Cullen wrote to Kirby in order that he might put the necessary verbal gloss on his letter to Barnabò. "I have written to all our Bishops," he reported, "about holding a meeting on the 21st January next to try to prevent the National Board from curtailing the rights of the managers of national schools" (K). "The managers of the Catholic schools," Cullen explained, "are generally the priests, who heretofore have the right of appointing and dismissing the teachers."

> By a late rule the Board requires that the teachers shall not be dismissed without three months notice (which in itself is fair enough) and that if in a

---

32. S.R.C., vol. 36, fols. 1400–1401.

sudden emergency the priest dismiss his teacher without notice he is obliged to prove to the Board that he had just cause for dismissing him. The priests very seldom dismiss the teachers without notice. They do so only when a teacher is detected in some gross offence which requires his immediate removal. For instance if the priest find that the teacher is trying to corrupt a young female or has privately corrupted her, his remedy was to dismiss that teacher. Now he must go to the Board, and reveal the misfortune of a poor girl, a resolution to which she and her family would not consent. Or, if the master had been found teaching heresy or enrolling young men as Freemasons or Fenians, the manager is now obliged to refer the matter to the Board or if he dismiss the teacher without three months notice, he must pay the said teacher three months salary out of his own pocket. This curtailment of the powers of the priest has excited great indignation—and it is calculated to give more power to the Board.

"All the Bishops," Cullen assured Kirby, "condemn the innovation except Dr. Delany, Dr. Moriarty, and Dr. Butler." "This division," he observed in conclusion, will weaken the body. To avert this, the Bishops nearly all wish to have a meeting."

Two days later, after receiving a reply to his letter of December 19 from Kirby, enclosing a recent allocution by the pope, and the assurance that Barnabò was well disposed to the proposed meeting, Cullen wrote Kirby a long letter in Italian, which was undoubtedly meant to be read to the Roman authorities. "I have read with great pleasure," he assured Kirby on December 29, "the magnificent allocution of His Holiness in which he defends the Holy See and the Church against all their enemies. I hope that it will make a great impression on the souls of all Catholics" (K). "Among other things," Cullen further observed, "the Holy Father recommends to the Bishops to meet among themselves in these difficult times and take together measures in defence of religion. We are here determined to act without delay in conformity with this advice." "Tomorrow," he informed Kirby, "I will invite all the bishops of Ireland to meet in Dublin on January 21, and then we will be able to show what we feel about the insults offered to the Church and to her Supreme Head. I have already written to all the bishops to learn if they believed it was opportune to meet in this [next] month, and two archbishops and twenty-three bishops have answered me that it was very much their desire that all should come together to take counsel with each other in these times of persecution. The only dissidents were the archbishop of Tuam, the bishop of Kerry, and the bishop of Limerick, who believed it was useless & more than useless to have a conference of Prelates." "Monsignor McHale," Cullen then added, "probably will not come but the other two that think with him do not wish, I think, to separate from their colleagues. I hope that good will come of the proposed meeting."

"I believe," Cullen pointed out, "that the powers of Apostolic Delegate to put in execution the decrees of the Synod of Thurles that were given me when I was translated to Dublin, are still in force. If this be so, I should have some right to make the bishops come, but as they come voluntarily, it is better not to talk of rights." "It will be necessary however," Cullen suggested, as he had to Barnabò two days before, "that the Sacred Congregation, in the name of the Pope, instill Union among the bishops." "In the question of education," he further explained, "the bishops of Kerry and Limerick go with the government. Monsignor MacHale goes in an opposite direction, and says, that it is necessary to resist everything that the government proposes. The difficulty in adopting his proposal derives from the fact that the government gives nearly annually £500,000 in Ireland to schools that are in great part Catholic, and thus rather than being in perpetual battle with them, it seems better to treat this question peacefully, and to defend our rights without openly breaking with those that would be able to take away the subsidy that we now have." "But when the bishops meet," he concluded, "we will see what ought to be done."

As the day of the bishops' meeting approached, its agenda apparently continued to grow. "I think," Cullen reported to Kirby on January 7, 1873, "we shall address the people on the persecution of the Church, and write a letter to His Holiness. We shall also send a letter to the Bishops of Germany in conformity with the Pope's allocution" (K). "Nearly all," he assured Kirby, "will agree on the education question—except on the part of Dr. Moriarty there will be little opposition. Please God everything will go on well." Two days before the meeting, writing again to Kirby, Cullen reported that all was in good order. "We have a very fine pastoral letter written by Dr. Conroy already in type," he explained on January 19.[33] "If the Bishops adopt it, we have put in a long paragraph dedicating all our dioceses to the S. Heart. I hope there will be no opposition. We have a long letter prepared for the Pope, and an address to the Bishops of Germany. In the pastoral to the people we treat of the liberty of the Church, the Pope, the Persecution, education, and wind up with the Sacred Heart" (K). "I think," he added, most interestingly, "I will ask the Bishops to hold another synod *like* that of Thurles next August. Of course we must get leave from Rome." "I have got," he noted in conclusion, "an excellent letter from the Propaganda about our meeting."

The day before the bishops' meeting, the bishop of Kerry wrote Cullen to explain that he was not well and his doctor had forbidden him to make the journey to Dublin. "With regard to the proposed 'agreement,'" Moriarty assured Cullen on January 20, "I am of the same opinion still—that to refuse three months notice to our poor teachers is a scandalous piece of oppression" (C). "If to require this," Moriarty further maintained, "argues distrust of managers, to refuse it argues distrust of teachers who are a most exemplary and obedient body. It is our interest to make them, and keep them, friends." "The appeal to the Board," he admitted, "is a clumsy way of settling a disputed case of dismissal. It were better

33. Patrick Francis Moran, *The Pastoral Letters and Other Writings of Cardinal Cullen* (Dublin, 1882), 3:477–96.

to leave out all question of appeal or arbitration—thus throwing on the dismissed teacher both the onus appellandi [the burden of appeal] and the onus probandi [the burden of proof]. He will be slow to go before a sessions court without a clear case." "It is much harder," Moriarty finally advised Cullen, "to keep teachers than to get rid of them." Cullen, however, had already anticipated all.

"We have finished our meeting splendidly," Cullen reported to Kirby on January 22, "—everything harmonious—we adopted a beautiful pastoral address written by Dr. Conroy, in which we spoke of the Pope, the persecutions in Italy, Germany, and Switzerland. We laid down good principles on education, and in the end we determined to consecrate the whole country to the *Sacred Heart. Evviva* Jesus, *Evviva* Maria" (K). "Dr. McHale," he then observed, "was not at our meeting, but 24 Bishops were present. We all signed a long letter to the Pope which I will send you and a letter to the Bishops of Germany. I will write tomorrow if I can to the Propaganda." "The Bishops all expressed a wish," Cullen added, "to have another national council. We can do so now with a good prospect of success and I will send a petition to get the Pope's permission for that purpose." Though Cullen undoubtedly wrote to Barnabò either the following day, as he promised Kirby, or within the next few days, his letter has not survived in the Propaganda's *scritture,* or general correspondence. The bishops exact decision regarding the national board's memorandum of agreement, therefore, is not entirely clear. What does emerge, however, is that before the meeting Cullen decided not to deal directly with the board, but rather to go over their heads and deal directly with the government.

Cullen apparently made his overture through the Irish lord chancellor, Thomas O'Hagan, to the lord lieutenant, the Earl Spencer, and the chief secretary of Ireland, the marquis of Hartington. "Ld. Spencer & I," Hartington informed O'Hagan on January 18, "have discussed with the Law Officers, and other advisors the suggested alterations in the new Rule & agreements between Managers & Teachers" (C). "On the whole," he explained encouragingly, "we are disposed to think that there is no substantial objection to the omission of the National Board as a court of appeal, and to leaving both parties to their remedy before the civil tribunals." "I shall be prepared," Hartington promised, "to recommend this alteration to the Government; but I think it is a question whether the National Board should not take the initiative in calling our attention officially to the state of things, and whether they should not express their opinion upon it." "At all events," he further explained, "the whole matter was so much discussed in the Cabinet, (though I do not recollect that this particular point was much considered) that I should not be justified in making any alteration without their consent; & this I shall not be able to obtain before the end of next week or the week after."

O'Hagan forwarded this letter to Cullen, and when the bishops met on January 21, Cullen must have informed them that because the whole matter was to be brought before the cabinet it would be best to defer the publication of their resolutions on the agreement until they learned the government's decision. From Cullen's point of view, however, the real purpose of the meeting was less to confront the government than to persuade the minority among the bishops to conform to the will of the majority. In this respect the meeting was eminently successful. Even before he had circularized the bishops about convening the meeting, Cullen had known that the bishops of both Cork and Limerick were likely to conform to the will of the majority.[34] The only likely dissident, therefore, was the bishop of Kerry, and when he fell ill shortly before the meeting, the occasion for any confrontation between him and his colleagues was fortuitously obviated. Even if Moriarty had been able to attend the meeting, however, Cullen had arranged that there really would be nothing for the bishops to decide. In the pastoral, written by Conroy at the behest of Cullen and approved by all the bishops except Moriarty, the bishops had little to say about the board's recent memorandum of agreement regarding the education question. "It is chiefly," they explained, "for the consideration of difficulties arising on this all-important subject of Education, that we are now assembled; but we reserve for a future occasion the resolutions we have adopted, confining ourselves at present to express our deep regret that the generous grants lately made by the Legislature on behalf of Education, have been accompanied by conditions which have, up to the present time, deprived many meritorious teachers of the long expected rewards of their labours—rewards which should have been made dependent on their certified efficiency."[35] Two weeks later, Moran reported to Kirby what had shaped the bishops' thinking at the meeting. "The Government," he explained on February 5, "very much feared that we would attack them on the subject of the National schools. However, it was deemed better to see what the Gov^t could be induced to do by quiet means" (K). "There is no doubt," Moran added, laying down Cullen's line, "the National System would require a great many improvements, and I think if we remain united and are vigilant we can obtain everything by degrees."

In reserving their resolutions "for a future occasion," the bishops had neatly placed the educational ball in the government's court, and the question now was how they would respond. If Hartington correctly explained his timetable to O'Hagan, then the cabinet discussed their reply to the bishops before the end of January, and they decided, in effect, to accept the bishops' amended version of the agreement. The timing of their acquiescence, however, posed another problem for the cabinet. Given the fact that Gladstone was scheduled to introduce his University bill in the House of Commons on February 13, they shrewdly decided to inform

34. C, see Patrick Leahy to Cullen, December 19, 1872, for the attitude of William Delany, the bishop of Cork; and George Butler, the bishop of Limerick, to Cullen, December 27, 1872, for his (Butler's) view.
35. Moran, 3:488.

Cullen, through O'Hagan, on February 18, of their decision (C). They thus hoped to maximize the effect on the bishops of this significant mark of their good will at the very moment the prelates were to examine Gladstone's measure. Cullen conveyed the good news of the cabinet's decision to overrule the board to the bishops in a circular letter of February 20, in which he also informed them that many of the bishops were anxious to meet to discuss Gladstone's bill and asked them if they could meet a week from that day on February 27, in Dublin.[36] "His Eminence," Cullen's secretary, P. J. Tynan reported to Kirby on February 24, ". . . is in great spirits because of the victory gained over the Education Board in making them withdraw a most insidious proposal by which they wd not only restrict the power & control of Managers, but make themselves the *final* tribunal in deciding questions between teachers & Managers" (K).

Indeed Cullen had every reason to be pleased with himself. He had virtually single-handedly engineered this very significant victory over the national board. Though there was a great deal to be said in favor of the three bishops' minority point of view, in terms of the equity and fairness of the agreement regarding the teachers, Cullen's genius was that he discerned immediately, and correctly, that the real issue was not justice but power. The problem was not that this particular encroachment in itself was very serious, but rather that it was the culmination of a long series of violations that had led the bishops as a body to the conclusion that they had to take their stand or worse was sure to follow. Certainly Cullen understood that the "three months' notice" issue involved a perception of the motives of the board based on only an instance. That is the reason he drew up and distributed among the bishops his historical sketch of the encroachments of the board since the inception of the system, which both heightened the cumulative effect on the bishops of these encroachments and indicated that the bishops really did need to be concerned about the way the primary system of education was being administered.

Cullen's genius, however, was not simply that he understood the real nature of the issue, but also that he appreciated the serious consequences that were likely to follow upon the bishops' efforts to protect their interests. The argument made by the three bishops in the minority—that it was neither prudent nor expedient to confront the government at that moment because all Catholic legislative hopes in regard to educational reform were dependent on the Irish-Liberal alliance, and the disruption of that alliance would mean the end of those hopes—had very great weight with Cullen. He realized almost immediately that there were two distinct priorities at stake. There was a short-term one that involved preventing the bishops from publicly denouncing the national board, and thus avoiding a confrontation that would jeopardize the Irish-Liberal alliance, and a long-term one that

36. MacSuibhne, 5:198. Cullen to Moriarty, February 20, 1873.

involved preserving the unity of the body by persuading the minority to conform to the views of the majority or, failing that, by invoking the authority of Rome through an appeal to Propaganda. The great difficulty with these priorities was that Cullen could avoid a confrontation by not allowing a meeting of the bishops to be called, but at the same time he also needed to have a meeting in order to persuade the three bishops to accept the view of the majority. He resolved the dilemma by not allowing a meeting to be called before he had made sure the bishops would hold their collective hand as far as the national board was concerned. Through his letters, memoranda, caucusing, and timing, Cullen kept the initiative, in effect, in his own hands, and he was able thereby to avoid the confrontation with the board he so dreaded, as well as to preserve the unity among the bishops he so desired.

The confrontation with the government that Cullen had worked so hard and so skillfully to avoid for some three months, however, was not to be long delayed. The story of the bishops' rejection of Gladstone's proposed University bill on February 28, the narrow defeat of the ministry on March 12, and the consequent disruption of the Irish-Liberal alliance, has already been told. Though the bishops in general, and Cullen in particular, had deliberately brought on that crisis, in the first flush of their victory over the government, they did not appear to realize that they might have to pay a very significant price for their triumph. Cullen, at least, was soon made aware of the consequences, when he received a letter, the day after the ministry resigned, from the rector of the Catholic University, who had been acting as his emissary in London during the recent crisis. "I have had long conversations with Major O'Reilly, Mr. Dease, and The O'Conor Don," Woodlock reported on March 14, referring to the members for the counties Longford, Queen's, and Roscommon respectively. "All seem to think the present position of the Univ^y question very disastrous; they say there is no use in my staying here, as we can do positively nothing just now."

> Neither party will touch us, and this state of things may continue for years. The Liberals are enraged with our party for having defeated Gladstone; and it would be ruinous for the Conservatives at the approaching Elections, whether they come off now or (as is more probable) in 3 or 4 months hence, if it were known, they were in communication with the Irish Catholics. However when man is weakest, God is strongest: & I trust, He will help us.
>
> Humanly speaking, the position is so bad, that it would seem, as if nothing could do us any good or bring English parties to their senses, except another out-break of Fenianism, or a second Clerkenwell outrage. Even a wholesale

return in Ireland of Home-Rulers or Repealers to Parliament, these M.P.'s say—(and they are among our truest friends)—would seem powerless to put our case into a good position.

"I do not like," Woodlock then concluded, "being in this modern Babylon, & I am glad to get out of it as soon as I can."

Shortly after he returned to Dublin from London, Woodlock wrote the members of the episcopal board of the Catholic University in an attempt to arrange a meeting to decide what was to be done in the present crisis. Though the archbishop of Armagh replied on March 19 that he would be ready to attend in Dublin on April 1, the bishop of Elphin, who wrote that same day, thought that the meeting should be deferred (W). "I don't think," Gillooly explained, "you could succeed in getting the Members of your Univ^y Board to meet in Passion Week. Better, I think, to wait till we see what the Gov^mt proposes to do on the Educ^l Question and also with reference to a General Election." "Meanwhile," he advised, "you must agitate and raise the wind as best you can. We'll make John Bull open the purse strings before long." The other members of the board apparently thought as Gillooly did and preferred to wait upon events. The Catholic University meanwhile was in desperate straits with regard to money and students. The annual collection in November 1872 had produced only some £4,000, and there were virtually no students in the faculty of arts, though the medical school had succeeded fairly well in maintaining its enrollment.

In desperation, Woodlock wrote a long letter to the archbishop of Cashel, explaining the situation and asking his advice. The archbishop, who before his promotion had served as vice-rector of the University under Newman and who was, therefore, both conversant with and sympathetic to the difficulties faced by Woodlock, attempted to respond positively. "Two things," Leahy advised on March 26, "must be done. You must, somehow, get money—and you must get students. But first, you must get money. Without getting the money and placing the University financially on a stable footing, you will not get students" (W). "A great effort," he insisted, "must be made." "It will be very well," he explained, referring to the national synod that the bishops had agreed at their recent meeting in January to hold sometime later that year, "to lay a Tax upon Bishops & Priests at the National Synod. But that won't do—that alone won't do. There must be a great effort made to get together a large sum of money." "There ought certainly," Leahy agreed, "to be a simultaneous collection through all Ireland. And, I think, the Bishops of Ireland, or the Cardinal in their name ought to ask the Bishops of England, Scotland, America, and Australia, to grant a Sunday for a simultaneous collection for the University in their respective Dioceses." "We should," he then maintained, "set the example ourselves in Ireland. It only remains to be considered whether we should initiate this movement at once, striking the iron while it is hot,—or wait for the National Council."

The consensus among the bishops appeared to be to wait for the national synod to be convened, and, in the meantime, matters appeared to go from bad to worse in regard to the University. The most immediate and serious threat was that Henry Fawcett, the radical member for Brighton, had introduced once again his bill to open Trinity College to all religious denominations, which would, in effect, establish a fourth Queen's College in Dublin. Woodlock had written his brother-in-law, Sir Dominic Corrigan, the junior member for Dublin City, asking him to do what he could to prevent the passage of Fawcett's bill. "Unless something has occurred," Corrigan replied candidly on March 23, "since I was last in London of which I am not aware, I see no chance of stopping Fawcett's Bill" (W). "Gladstone is, I think," he then pointed out, "pledged to support the Bill failing to carry his own. The Tories will support it and who are to oppose it? About 20 Irish Members." "If I hear any news in London worth sending," Corrigan then promised, "I will write to you." As April 2, the day for the second reading of Fawcett's bill, approached, Woodlock became more and more anxious. On March 28, he wrote to Mitchell Henry, the senior member for county Galway and a prominent Home Ruler, asking him to use his best efforts to oppose the second reading and, failing that, to have the bill appropriately amended in the committee stage. "Of course," Henry assured Woodlock in his reply from the House of Commons on March 31, "if Fawcett's Bill should ever pass the second reading we must do our best to improve it—or to obstruct it" (W). "I see more and more plainly," Henry then added, pointing out the political moral in the lesson, "we should get nothing satisfactory out of an English Parliament. If Home Rule had no other advantage it will at any rate have this one—it will enable and indeed *compel* Irish Members to go *straight* & that is really the great defect—& English & Scotch Members know it & trade upon it."

The day after he wrote Henry, Woodlock wrote also to Cullen. "Even if Fawcett's Bill," Woodlock explained on March 29, "is restricted to the abolition of Tests [religious], it is, I think a bad Bill; for it opens Trinity College to Catholics, and thus offers them a strong temptation to enter a College where their faith will be exposed to the greatest danger, at the same time that in the opinion of English Liberals every just cause of complaint will be taken from us and every sufficient ground for demanding Catholic University Education" (C). "Therefore," he maintained, "I think the Bill ought to be opposed on the second reading, no matter in what form it is presented; and if the Irish Members cannot muster a respectable number to divide against it, they ought, in my humble judgement, to walk out of the House." In the event, Fawcett's bill eventually did pass its second reading on April 21, after a spirited debate and after an amendment proposed by Mitchell Henry to establish a royal commission to investigate the whole matter of higher education, an amendment which he finally withdrew. When the bill was then considered in committee after the Easter recess, at the end of April, Woodlock returned to London to encourage the Irish members in their efforts to have the bill amended so that it would be less of a threat to Catholic interests.

"I had a long conversation to-day," Woodlock reported to Cullen from London on April 29, referring to the members for counties Kildare and Westmeath, "with Mr. Cogan about Mr. Smyth's motion on Fawcett's Bill. Several of the other Irish M.P.s came up while we were talking, they seem to care very little for the Catholic University" (C).[37] "Cogan himself," Woodlock noted, "& The O'Conor Don seem the best of the lot. Sir R. Blennerhassett, Butt, Mitchell Henry, & Smyth himself are the only persons, who think anything good can come of Smyth's motion." "Perhaps Sir John Gray," he added, "takes somewhat the same view. But the others make a great outcry against it, and say, that, as the Bishops have rejected Gladstone's Bill, nothing can be done now; in fact, that we must let things take their course; that Fawcett's Bill will pass, and that Trinity College being thus opened to all, we ought to be satisfied, so the House of Commons will say, with being put on an equality with Protestants." "I forgot to say," Woodlock then pointed out in a postscript, referring to the junior member for county Wexford, "I saw Mr. D'Arcy to-day along with the other M.P.s. He joins the others in saying we can expect nothing, as the Bishops rejected Gladstone's Bill. It was useless for me to say in reply to him & the others, that the Bishops had no alternative, as the Bill was so bad and confirmed & extended Mixed Education."

Several days later, Woodlock reported to Cullen that his brother-in-law, Sir Dominic Corrigan, the junior member for Dublin City, was urging him to have nothing to do with Smyth's motion regarding Fawcett's bill. "There is," Woodlock explained on May 2, referring to Smyth, "a very strong feeling against him and his motion. But it seems to me if we can force Trinity College to come to some terms now, it is our best chance, otherwise the question may be deferred, as far as Parliament is concerned, for ten years. And Smyth's amendment distinctly states: that the new arrangement must be such as to meet the views of the heads of the Catholic University, that is, of the Bishops" (C). On the following Monday, May 5, Woodlock finally reported to Cullen that Fawcett's bill would be discussed that evening (C). "It is the first business," he assured Cullen, "on the list. I am going to get a bit of dinner, & then to set off for the House, and stay there till the end." "I was," he informed Cullen the next day, May 6, "at the House of Commons last night till eleven o'Clock. The result, as your Eminence will have seen by the newspapers was most unsatisfactory."

No union among the Irish Members; and all their shortcomings proceeding

---

37. P. J. Smyth, the junior member for Westmeath had moved, "That it be an Instruction to the Committee [i.e., of the whole House], that they have the power to provide for the establishment, as a College of the University of Dublin, of the institution known as The Catholic University." *Hansard's Parliamentary Debates,* 3d series, 215:1525 (May 5, 1873).

from want of organisation, for there was no substantial difference of opinion expressed; although I fear, there exists among the greater number great coldness, if not opposition to the Univy. I breakfasted with Mitchell Henry this morning. He remarked, I think very well, that among our Cath. Members there is in general great ignorance of the question, except those who have studied in Trinity College, and they are all prejudiced in favor of that Univy. I am afraid even our best men, O'Conor Don & Major O'Reilly are influenced too much by English party feeling, and like the Chancellor [Lord O'Hagan], are too timid.

"I had nearly forgotten," Woodlock then added, "to tell your Eminence that Mitchell Henry & some of our other friends tell me, there will be a great debate on the Univy when Fawcett's Bill goes to the Lords. He thinks I ought to see some of our Cath. Peers, Lord Denbigh &c; I will ask Dr. Manning to introduce me to them." "Mr. Henry thinks," he further reported, "I ought to write to Lord Granard or to some other Peer, saying that the Bishops demand supreme control only in *rebus fidei & morum* [in matters of faith and morals]; but that they do not object to the laity sharing the management of the Univy in other respects." "What would your Eminence," Woodlock asked, "think of this?" "I would," he assured Cullen in conclusion, "show your Eminence the letter before sending it."

In his reply the next day, May 7, Cullen studiously ignored Woodlock's question about whether the laity should be allowed to share in the governing of the Catholic University, but he did endorse Woodlock's suggestion that he attempt to organize an opposition to Fawcett's bill in the House of Lords, and he urged Woodlock to see as many Catholic and Liberal peers as he could (W). "This morning," Woodlock informed Cullen by return on May 8, "I duly received your Eminence's letter. I have seen Lord Denbigh & he will speak against Fawcett's Bill. There is no hope of it being thrown out: but Ld Denbigh & I hope others will protest against it being supposed to do anything for Irish Catholics, & will urge Govt not to delay to redress the admitted grievance" (C). "We had," Woodlock reported to Cullen again, nearly a week later, on May 14, "a very excellent little debate last evening in the Lord's on Fawcett's Bill. Lord Denbigh mad [*sic*] a very good short speech in which he declared that the bill was no concession to Catholics. He wound up by saying, that he had lately had a private audience of the Pope, and that His Holiness said to him: that he had always opposed mixed Education & would do so to the end" (C). "This announcement," he assured Cullen, "was listened to with the greatest attention, and without the least mark of disrespect—very different, I am sure, from the way in which it would have been received by the House of Commons." On the evening before Fawcett's bill was to be read for the third time in the House of Lords, Woodlock wrote Cullen a final letter on the subject. "I spoke to Lord Granard," he explained on May 16, "about the advisability of protesting against Fawcett's Bill in the 3rd Reading, which is to take place to-night in the

House of Lords" (C). "But neither he nor Lord Howard," Woodlock concluded, referring to the duke of Norfolk's uncle, "whom I also saw this morning, thought it desirable." Shortly after the passage of Fawcett's bill, Woodlock returned to Dublin to resume his duties as rector of the Catholic University.

In the meantime, Woodlock's very serious difficulties with regard to finances and students in the Catholic University had been compounded by the problems and embarrassments he was having with his faculty. While Woodlock was in London, in early March, dealing with the crisis produced by the bishops' rejection of Gladstone's University bill, David B. Dunne, professor of logic and metaphysics in the University, who had for some time been in serious financial difficulties, wrote to Woodlock, on March 12, explaining that he had been finally obliged to declare his bankruptcy (W). Shortly after this acute embarrassment, upon his return to Dublin, Woodlock decided to relieve his dean of students, Father A. O'Loughlin, of his responsibility for St. Patrick's, a house of residence in the University. Before taking action, however, Woodlock, on March 28, broached the subject with both Cullen and Leahy of transferring responsibility for St. Patrick's house to the Jesuit fathers. Apparently Cullen took the matter under advisement, but the archbishop of Cashel was adamantly opposed to turning the house over to the Society of Jesus. "I love the Jesuits," Leahy protested to Woodlock on March 29, "believing them to be the choicest portion of the Priesthood of the Catholic Church" (W). "Holding these sentiments," he maintained, "I am entitled to be credited with sincerity when I say St. Patrick's House ought not to be committed to their care and for a simple reason—the insane prejudices against Jesuits might hereafter prove a serious difficulty in the way of University arrangements into which St. Patrick's might enter."

Though Woodlock prudently allowed the matter to drop for a time, he must have been even more convinced that O'Loughlin must go when, in the midst of his efforts in London to rally opposition in the House of Lords to Fawcett's bill, he received a long letter from O'Louglin that testifed to both the dean's lack of judgment and to his general ineptness. "The day before yesterday," O'Loughlin reported to Woodlock on May 8, "I had rather a mysterious letter. The writer was (and is) a woman we all know very well. An audience '*in the Church*' with a view to her unfolding a matter which she felt herself bound in conscience to unfold & as soon as might be."

> Well—this, & the fact that her husband was ready at hand to treat with me on any subject, in *foro Externo* [i.e., outside the confessional], as she was, did not please him, made me rather cautious. So I resolved to see the husband, & I did—who w^d say nothing, & then the wife at her own house, who told me she knew of a house of ill-fame adjoining the School of Medicine, & that the C.U. Students were the maintaining of it!! And then she bound me to the strictest secrecy as to her name—but gave me all the power to act in the matter as I

thought fit to act! Well—this house I have seen. It is in Cecelia street on the right hand as you go to the quay, (Wellington, I believe) & three doors from the quay. It is the lowest kind of eating house. The abominable look of the whole place, I could not describe to you. My informant alleges that our students frequent this den of after-noons & are not unfrequently seen in the company of the wretched denizens. One of the women was seen at the *Medical School,* not long ago—I *mean on the premises*—& a student on another occasion was seen *drunk* there & was with another. Can all this be true? I do my best to tell you the weary, weary story as I heard it myself (W).

"Well—" O'Loughlin finally asked, "what action you will ask have I taken in the matter?" "Very little—save to mention it to Dr. McSwiney, Scratton, and Mc-Devitt. McS. made light of it," he replied, referring respectively to the professor of medical jurisprudence, the bursar, and the librarian in the University. "McSwiney promised," he then noted, "to have an eye on the premises."

One thing—one feature of this bad case—was put forward forcibly that this filthy establishment was maintains [*sic*] by *the C.U. Students.* Of the interns, I can speak as to their being indoors at the hour regulated by the rule—of course afternoon abominations are beyond my Ken—of externs I know next to nothing of their conduct but [illegible]. Now you have the distressing episode. Don't be uneasy about it. I won't do anything rash—nor shall I make light of the matter. No use either (it seems to me) in concealing my informants name if you wish to have it. I don't think she meant to bind me to secrecy in your regard. How could she? The whole thing must be looked into when you come home.

"I have not," he assured Woodlock in concluding, "spoken to any one of the medical people, except McS. about the matter nor have I moved, I may say at all but as I have said." Woodlock's anxieties were not much relieved when he received within the week a letter from the secretary and bursar of the University, Thomas Scratton. "People outside," Scratton reported gloomily on May 13, "are asking if we have *shut up*" (W). "The position of the University," he then explained, "is bad as bad can be. Inside and out there are most serious complications and difficulties. Last week there was scarcely anyone here but myself. Stewart absent—Dunne ill—Kavanagh irregular, more scio [nature I know]. Besides this Dean O.L. will have informed you of something even graver." "I begin to fear," he further observed, "that the stigma of the Queen's colleges, that they are dangerous to faith & morals, will soon more truly apply to ourselves."

Scratton was apparently alluding in his final remark to yet another case among the faculty that had just been brought to the attention of Woodlock. Though the details are not entirely clear, it appears that Henry Hennessy, the professor of natural philosophy in the University, had married a Protestant in a civil ceremony, and when she was later received into the Catholic Church, they had had their marriage solemnized according to the rites of the Church. What made the situation awkward was that before their marriage was duly solemnized Hennessy had introduced the lady as his wife to at least one of his colleagues—J. B. Robertson, the professor of history—indicating that he (Hennessy), as a Catholic, had been living, in effect, with the lady in sin. When Woodlock learned the facts, presumably through Robertson, he was so scandalized that he decided, while in London, to write Hennessy, who was convalescing from a recent and serious illness, and to suspend him from his duties in the University. "I am happy to hear you are so far recovered," Woodlock explained on May 10, "as to be able to drive out. I regret that my absence from home has rendered it impossible for me to see you before now, as I want to do, on important business. I expect to be home in about a week or ten days, and I must request you not to resume your duties at the University before my return" (W).

The reason for Woodlock's great caution in this letter and for his failure to give any reason for the suspension was that he realized that, in the event that Hennessy was not inclined to resign, the legal action which would have to be taken to deprive Hennessy of his tenure might be gravely compromised by the motives for Woodlock's action. In fact, Hennessy, in replying to Woodlock's letter, cleverly chose to take his suspension from his duties as a sign of the rector's solicitude for his health rather that as an indication of any moral turpitude on his part. "Although I am advised by the Doctors," he explained on May 14, "not to write any letters or indeed to occupy my mind I cannot refrain from thanking you for your very kind letter as well as for your visit when I was most dangerously ill" (W). "Had I seen you before your departure for London," he added, "I would have had the pleasure of telling you of my marriage which has been duly solemnized according to the rites of the Church not long after the reception of my wife as a Catholic in the parish Church of this district." "I am still delicate," he noted in conclusion, "and was consulting the Doctors only two days since, but I hope on your return to have the pleasure of introducing you to Mrs. Hennessy." When Woodlock returned to Dublin, he and Hennessy apparently discussed the complications arising out of his marriage, but Hennessy persisted in assuming that he had not been suspended, and he obviously had no intention of resigning. "I heard," Woodlock informed Hennessy on July 4, "you were here yesterday and you were making inquiries about the day fixed for the oral examinations at the end of the Session" (W). "Permit me to say," Woodlock added, "that for many reasons I think it better that you would not come to the University in the present unsettled state of your business. Should you wish to see me, I shall be happy to meet you anywhere else." Hennessy replied the next day. "I called at the University," he explained to Woodlock on July 5, "on business of a private nature, and you ought to be moreover perfectly aware that I firmly deny that I am in a position to forego my rights as a professor and a member of the Council. The positive injunctions of my physician prevented me from discharging as usual the duties of my office but, I am at a loss to understand what reason you could have for not wishing to see me (if the occasion arose) at the University on University business" (W). "As I am still only convalescent," he concluded, "I go on business anywhere as little as possible, and this is as far as I know the only valid reason why I should not be at the University every day." Woodlock was undoubtedly counseled by his legal advisers to proceed very cautiously in the case and informed that his suspension of Hennessy, moreover, was not a sufficient ground for depriving Hennessy of his salary. Woodlock, therefore, wrote to Scratton, informing him of the legal complications and asking him as bursar to forward a cheque for Hennessy's salary that quarter. "Your letter has just duly reached me," Scratton replied on July 11, "and I hasten to send you the draft for Mr. Hennessy. Of course I say nothing about his case to anyone" (W). "Whether there be sufficient reason or not," he observed grimly, "for acting with vigour in his circumstances, it is quite evident that if the lawyers make out that a man cannot be dismissed for past immorality the University had better never been founded, and to carry it on is an impossibility."

Meanwhile, morale was at such a low ebb among the faculty, that the professor of history, J. B. Robertson, wrote the archbishop of Cashel asking for some words of encouragement. "I received this morning," Robertson informed Woodlock on June 6, "a very important letter from Archbishop Leahy, which I enclose, and when you have read it, I will beg you to return it. I requested his grace to send me a word of consolation, which I might communicate to my colleagues; for they were much discouraged."

> I suggested to Archbishop Leahy, whether it would not be well, if the Bishops were to give exhibitions to a certain number of students by their own authority, and independently of competition. They would of course, as in the first years of the University be obliged to pass the matriculation examination. My object in making this suggestion was to underscore the number of our students. The paucity of their numbers is the most discouraging feature in our University. When I am addressing the meetings of students, it is so painful to me to see none, but those following the study of Medicine. What do you think of the suggestion I have made?
>
> Dr. Leahy's letter is hopeful as showing that so influential a prelate is determined to uphold in every way our University; that he solicits suggestions from our Professorial body as to reforms in the mode of the collections; and lastly, by his declaration, that in the approaching Synod, the affairs of the University, and especially its financial organisation will claim the earnest attention of the assembled prelates (W).

"I think it would be well," Robertson advised Woodlock, turning to another aspect of the rector's responsibility, "if you were to see what subjects the Historical Society choose for their debates." "Last Friday," he explained, "I was in the Chair, and the subject of the Debate was the four Stuart Kings." "Would you believe," he asked, "that Mr. Michael Coxe justified the judicial murder of Charles I?" "I called him to order," Robertson confessed, "but I was on the whole too lenient towards him. And the reason was that he is singularly courteous and docile to the Chairman. But his whole speech was very intemperate, and abounded in gross exaggerations and invectives." "I endeavoured," he assured Woodlock, "at the conclusion of the Debate to refute some of his statements, and to vindicate certain truths, which he had impugned." "The Cardinal and the Holy Father," he maintained, somewhat naively, "would be dreadfully shocked, if they heard that a student of the Catholic University had justified the execution of Charles I!!" "Pray say nothing," Robertson further advised, "to Coxe of this business; but I will write to him myself on the subject; for I did not on the occasion discharge my duty with sufficient energy. There is not a good spirit among some of those medical students; for they backed Coxe in many of his assertions." "A paper," he warned in concluding, "is to be read this evening by young Meagher on Lord Edward Fitzgerald. This is a very ticklish subject."

What was most remarkable in the face of all this, especially in the light of his breakdown the year before, was Woodlock's tenacity and perseverance. He simply refused to give up, and on June 13, he again wrote the archbishop of Armagh, explaining the serious nature of the crisis. Apparently Woodlock suggested that an episcopal commission similar to the one set up for the reform of Maynooth in August 1869 now be constituted for the Catholic University. In his reply the next day, June 14, McGettigan agreed that the University had not received enough attention of late and assured Woodlock that his suggestion was certainly a step in the right direction (W). He also promised that, if at all possible, he would call to see Woodlock at the University on Monday, June 23, before he went on to Maynooth that evening, for the meeting of the board of that college the next day. In any case, when the bishops discussed the problem of the University on June 25, they decided that a meeting of the board of the University should be called for July 23, in Dublin, to recommend what action should be taken.

In preparation for the meeting, Woodlock drew up a long report, which he had printed on July 16 and distributed to all the bishops. The "Report on the Present Condition of the Catholic University," which ran to twenty-six pages and some seventy-five hundred words and which was marked "private and confidential," was a candid attempt not only to assess the current grim situation but also to provide a solution for it by making a large number of recommendations. "It is admitted on all hands," Woodlock explained to the bishops, "that the University, owing to the great difficulties with which it had to contend for over twenty years, has not had the success which was anticipated, and is desirable. On the other hand, it is possible, with God's blessing, to give it that development; and there seems to be no reasonable medium between doing so and closing the institution altogether, by winding it up or allowing it to die out" (C). "Now, I believe," Woodlock maintained, "no one would deem it expedient to give up the battle for higher Catholic education; and therefore it is quite a matter of necessity that the University should be placed on a new and more efficient footing than heretofore." "There is, it seems to me," Woodlock then pointed out, referring to the lack of a charter from the state, which prevented the University from granting degrees, "one chief cause operating to the prejudice of the University; I mean our inability to obtain legal recognition for the institution as a University or University College." "The remedy, as far as it depends on us," he maintained, "seems to be no other than to continue our efforts to obtain that recognition, repeating our demands on every available occasion, by petitions, at public meetings, etc., and especially at elections for Members of Parliament." In a more practical vein, Woodlock then suggested that a University bill should be drafted and introduced in parliament at the beginning of the next session, in early 1874. "Such a Bill," he advised, "ought to take into account both the requirements of Catholic principles and the concessions made by Mr. Gladstone, in his speeches made last spring; and without emanating from your Lordships, ought to be brought forward by some member enjoying your confidence, while it would be generally known that you deemed its principles not antagonistic to Catholic teaching."

After raising the unrealistic question of whether it might not also be expedient to appeal, over the heads of the members of parliament, to the queen to grant a charter to the Catholic University, Woodlock turned to a candid discussion of the "shortcomings and drawbacks of the University," which he thought could be reduced to four.

> First, it has not succeeded in attracting students in such numbers as might have been expected; secondly it has not benefitted Catholic Schools and Colleges as much as was intended; thirdly, it has not gained the confidence of the people generally, and especially of those classes which ought to be immediately interested in it, and benefitted by it; and fourthly, the mass of our people, and especially of our clergy, do not recognize the necessity, or even the advantage of its existence; and hence the difficulty of maintaining it by annual collections increases every year.

In regard to the first of these shortcomings, attracting students, Woodlock pointed out, the means to do so could be divided into the moral, intellectual, and material. As far as moral means were concerned, Woodlock suggested three things: first, that one or more good halls or houses of residence be set up near, but not in, the University; second, to have in the several houses a graduated rate of pensions to meet the financial needs of the various classes of students; and third, that the management of the various houses should be in the hands of religious bodies, such as the Jesuits, Carmelites, or others. As for the intellectual means, Woodlock had two recommendations. The first was that the vacancies in the administrative and professorial staff be filled. There was at that moment no vice-rector and no professors of higher mathematics, classical literature, Irish, ancient history, modern languages, geology, natural history, or botany. He also pointed out that the reason that many of the professors had left was the relatively low scale of salaries in the Catholic University compared to other institutions. Woodlock's second recommendation was that the problem of granting degrees be resolved by conferring such degrees with the authority of the Holy See. Finally, as for the material means, Woodlock suggested that an "imposing building," such as the "Sapienza" in Rome or the "Halles" in Louvain should be erected in Stephen's Green. "Besides attracting students," he argued, "a material building would also have the effect at this moment of convincing the enemies of Catholic Education that we are determined not to give up the battle, but, if necessary, to hand it on to future generations."

In regard to the second type of shortcoming of the University, namely, it not being sufficiently advantageous to Catholic schools and colleges, Woodlock attempted to make it clear that the interests of Catholic intermediate and university education were complementary, not antagonistic. He then proposed that the Catholic University should no longer consist, in effect, only of the one institution in Dublin, but that it should be constituted in the future of all those colleges that might desire to be incorporated with it, if they fulfilled conditions that the University, with the approval of the bishops, would fix. Maynooth, for example, might be made a college of the University, and that college might even be ranked in the University before the college in Dublin. Indeed, Maynooth's theological faculty should be the theological faculty of the University. Turning to the third heading, the want of confidence in the University by the priests and people, and especially by those middle classes for whom it was designed to benefit, Woodlock suggested that laymen should be given a share in the governing of the University, especially in financial matters. Finally, in discussing the fourth general heading, that neither priests nor people recognized either the necessity or the usefulness of the University and hence the increasing difficulty in maintaining the annual collections, Woodlock recommended that a graduate course of studies for ecclesiastics, who were destined to teach in local seminaries and classical schools, as well as a training school, or teachers college, for primary school teachers, be set up in the University. In order to regularize and augment the annual collections, Woodlock advised, the collections "should be made obligatory on every parish in Ireland, either by a decree from the Holy See, or in such other way as to the Bishops may seem desirable" and that, in order to provide a nucleus for a sufficient and permanent endowment for the University, every priest enjoying faculties should be obliged to contribute a fixed minimum sum.

In concluding this long report, Woodlock recapitulated those recommendations he thought to be essential for the bishops' consideration.

Firstly—The establishment of one or more University Houses, near, but not in, the University Buildings, under some of the religious bodies which devote themselves to teaching, and which may be encouraged to set up such houses by pecuniary and other helps, and by appointments in the University.

Secondly—The appointment of a full staff of University professors, and also of a certain number of younger men or tutors to assist the students with extra professorial help.

Thirdly—The erection of suitable and imposing University buildings in Stephen's Green, to be exclusively devoted to teaching purposes, as the Sapienza in Rome, the Queen's Colleges, etc.

Fourthly—The extension of the University to certain other colleges besides the one in Dublin, on conditions to be carefully fixed and well defined, and which would include regulations respecting age, studies, discipline, and professional teaching; also representation on University Council or Senate, and, consequently, voice in fixing courses of studies, examinations, examiner, etc.; and, perhaps, payments by results.

Fifthly—Association of laymen with the Bishops as a Board of Control over the University, especially in financial matters, so that there might be a University Council nominated by the Bishops, in some measure as Mr. Gladstone's Bill proposed to constitute a University Council to be named by Government.

Sixthly—Addition to the University of practical departments, such as an Ecclesiastical House of higher literary and scientific study; a training house for young ecclesiastics to be employed by the Bishops in conducting classical schools; preparatory classes for higher branches of civil and military service; a training school for schoolmasters for primary schools, etc.

Seventhly—The annual collection for the University to be made of [sic] obligation in every parish; certain parish priests or the members of the University Council to be the agents in the various dioceses; and the clergy to be required to contribute a fixed sum every year.

Woodlock finally concluded,

We have in Catholic Intermediate Schools and Colleges at least from five thousand to six thousand boys and young men, who desire, and whose parents ardently desire, Higher Education on Catholic principles; we have a University under the immediate direction of your Lordship, which can be moulded in any way you please; and there seems no reason why, with such materials, a great system of Catholic Education may not be constructed, which our enemies will respect and fear, to which Irish Catholics abroad as well as at home, will give their sympathy and active support, and to which God and his Vicar will give that blessing that is always fruitful.

The reaction of those few bishops who even bothered to respond to Woodlock's report was not encouraging. It should be noted, however, that the last two weeks in July were usually designated by the Irish bishops as the period in which they held their annual retreats for clergy, and they attempted to allow as little to intrude on this time of spiritual reflection as possible. The bishop of Elphin, who was on retreat with his clergy and could not be in Dublin for the meeting on July 23, explained on July 18, "I have carefully read over your Report and find much in it that I consider useful & practical" (W). "Of course," Gillooly added, "I do not approve of your proposal of new Buildings &c. The remnant of our Funds should be husbanded and all unnecessary expenditures avoided. The material development of the University sh^d come last and follow naturally from its organisation in the Country." "Beyond this observation," he noted, "I will not venture as I cannot have the advantage of discussing with the other prelates the several propositions of your Report." "I will only add," Gillooly concluded, "that I will gladly cooperate to the best of my power in any scheme that may be adopted at your meeting next week, for the sustainment & improvement of the University Schools." The day before the meeting of the University board, the bishop of Dromore also wrote to Woodlock about his report. "I steal a moment," John Pius Leahy explained on July 22, "from our spiritual exercises which are going on this week to acknowledge the receipt of your Pamphlet. It is indeed a very able document" (W). "I fear however," he added, "from what has taken place hitherto that there will not be any satisfactory reply to your appeal. But if the Catholic University be doomed to fail, assuredly the failure cannot be laid to your charge. No man could possibly have done more than you have done to uphold it."

"On my return last evening from Waterford," the bishop of Galway, who had been assisting at the month's mind mass for the late bishop of Waterford, reported to Woodlock that same day, July 22, "I found your letter before me, in which you refer to the statement you were so good to forward to me a few days ago, and desire the expression of my views regarding it" (W). "I would consider it a great misfortune," MacEvilly explained, "regards [correctly, regarding] the prospects of the successful issue of the question of higher Catholic Education if the Catholic University were closed, and hence every effort should be made to keep it open. But the mode of doing so is the question." "I presume the non Members of Board," he observed, "will not attend your meeting on tomorrow without your invitation to do so. So the important question to be submitted by you tomorrow must be decided by the Members of the Board who may attend. This is throwing on them a very heavy responsibility, and a question of this kind should be reserved for the assembled Bishops." "Now what occurs to me," MacEvilly advised, "is this. I suppose it is likely there may be [a] National Synod held in the course of the coming year, and it would seems [sic] very fitting that as the Catholic University was organised under the Superior Authority of the H. See by a National Council, the work, indeed, I may say the necessary work of its reorganisation should be reserved for the same."

At their meeting the next day, July 23, the bishops of the University board, probably on Woodlock's suggestion, decided to set up an episcopal commission to determine the best means of sustaining the Catholic University and to report to the bishops before their scheduled general meeting, in the second week of October, in Dublin. The commission met for several days at the end of August and instructed its secretary, the bishop of Elphin, to write the bishops, giving them an epitome of the report they would submit to the body in October. "It is only this evening," Gillooly confessed to Cullen on September 23, "I have had a few minutes to write the circular to the Bishops, relative to our inquiry about the Cath. University. I enclose it herewith to your Eminence, that you may make in it any correction you think desirable and then get your good Secretary to put it in the printer's hands and forward it to each of the Archbishops & bishops" (C). "It w^d be well," he suggested, "the Commission w^d meet a couple of days before the Bishops to prepare their report. If I can find time I will make a draft of it." "I suppose," he added, "your Eminence will have a grand address prepared to be issued by the Bishops to their flocks."

Cullen had Gillooly's circular corrected and printed, and he distributed it to the bishops on September 27. "I have been requested," Gillooly had explained, "to inform your Lordship that the Episcopal Commission appointed in July to consider the best means of sustaining our Catholic University, met on several days towards the end of last month, in the University House, Stephen's-green, under the presidency of His Eminence Cardinal Cullen; and that, after having examined most of the University Officers and Professors, and several Superiors of Religious Houses, they agreed to the heads of Report, which they will be prepared to submit next month to the General Meeting of the Bishops."

> Meanwhile, obeying their instruction, I beg leave to give your Lordship an outline of the recommendations which they will propose to the meeting.
>
> 1.—A better provision for certain important Offices and Chairs, hitherto inefficiently filled.
>
> 2.—Appointment of Lecturers and Professors to important Chairs now vacant.
>
> 3.—A better organisation of the Medical School—the erection of new buildings for its accommodation in Stephen's green—and the maintenance of suitable and separate boarding-houses for the medical students.
>
> 4.—Placing the boarding-houses, present and future, of the University, that of medical students excepted, under the care and management of competent members of religious houses.
>
> 5.—Connecting with the University, on a plan to be submitted, all our Catholic Colleges and High Schools, lay and clerical.
>
> 6.—Establishing, in connection with the University, an agricultural College, under the care of the Benedictine Fathers.
>
> 7.—Collation by the University of degrees in Arts, as well as in Philosophy and Theology, according to a scheme to be submitted.
>
> 8.—Establishment of a Finance Committee to supervise and control the expenditure of University funds; and to watch over the financial interests of the University.

9.—Better organisation of parochial and other collections for the support and development of the University.

10.—Political action and organisation for the enforcement of our education rights and claims in Parliament.

In a postscript to this circular, Cullen asked the members of the commission to meet in Dublin, at the University, on October 12 and 13, in order to prepare their report for the general meeting.

Before the bishops could meet, however, the University suffered yet another serious blow to its already badly impaired public image. Some ten days before Cullen distributed Gillooly's circular to the bishops, Woodlock wrote to Thomas Hayden, professor of anatomy and physiology in the medical school of the University, inquiring if there were any substance to the rumours that their professor of chemistry, William K. Sullivan, was about to accept the presidency of the Queen's College in Cork. "I am astonished," Hayden replied on September 17, "to find your [*sic*] were not aware of the rumours in regard to Pr. Sullivan's probable appointment to the presidency in Cork. The air has been full of them here for the last few weeks & from the fact of his not coming to our Meeting last Saturday, or sent [*sic*] any intention in reply to the notice he received of the object of our Meeting, viz. to propose our new prospectus, I am disposed to *infer the worst*" (W). "The loss to the U.," Hayden then maintained, "would be very great, so great indeed that it seems to me, if I may take the liberty of offering a suggestion, some effort should *be at once made* to avert the evil." "Would it be possible," he asked, "to have him appointed Vice Rector, with some increase in salary?" "I am sure," Hayden added, "he would make a sacrifice to remain with us, but the present condition of the Univ^ty, the uncertainty of its future, & the necessities of a young & in part grown family, must be allowed its legitimate weight." "I would have written to you," Hayden finally assured Woodlock, "long since on this subject, had I not thought you were in full possession of what was passing, & most probably in communication with Sullivan on the subject. If I hear anything definite I will let you know." Indeed, Sullivan had begun to consider the Cork appointment some four months before, when he first heard that Sir Robert Kane had retired from the presidency. "My position here," Sullivan had confided on May 15 to his good friend William Monsell, the senior member for county Limerick and undersecretary for the colonies, "is now so precarious that I am forced to look about to see what I can do."[38] "The University," he explained, "is all but defunct, and I do not believe enough will be collected this year to pay the salaries of the

---

38. M, 8318/5. For the career and work of William Kirby Sullivan (1823–90), see "Some Notable Cork Scientists," *Journal of the Cork Historical and Archeological Society,* 2d series, 10, no. 64 (October–December 1904): 236–41. T. S. Wheeler, "Life and Work of William K. Sullivan," *Studies: An Irish Quarterly of Letters, Philosophy and Science* 34 (March 1945): 21–36.

professors who are still attached to it. I believe too that it is the desire of the Authorities to get rid of the lay professors, at least that is the only solution that seems to me to explain the state they have reduced the Institute to." "There is some talk," Sullivan then reported, referring to another of his teaching appointments, "of closing the College of Science next year when the seven years for which it was established should have expired. I know that I was appointed before 1859, but from the manner in which I have been treated by the Department of Science and Art I am sure the law would be rigidly applied in my case." "This state of things and the altered aspect of the University Question," he added, "which seems to me to be set at rest for this generation—at least so far as the Catholic University is concerned, is so serious that when I saw the announcement in this morning's Freeman's Journal that Sir Robert Kane had resigned the presidentship of Queen's College, Cork it occurred to me to ask you:"

    1. Whether the place had been given away.
    2. Whether in the event of my applying for it, I would have any chance of getting it—and
    3. What would you think of my applying for it?

"Would you do me the great service," Sullivan requested, "of ascertaining whether any appointment has been made,—the other two questions are so delicate, that I must leave it altogether to yourself whether you can give me an answer." "Need I say," he concluded, "how grateful I shall be if you feel in a position to do so."

Monsell apparently replied to this letter, judging from Sullivan's response, that the place had not been given away, that Sullivan's chances if he applied for it would be very good, and that he did not approve of Sullivan applying for it. "I would have sooner thanked you," Sullivan responded on June 16, in what would prove to be his swan song about the Catholic University, "for your opinion, so candidly given, but that I was anxious to send you a few cuttings from newspapers to show how differently my position is viewed at this side from which it appears to you."[39] "I think," Sullivan then pointed out, "you have taken too flattering a view of my position. The conspicuous leadership with which you have invested me is a brevet rank and that not even acknowledged by the ruling powers, who as you will know would not bestow the humblest educational office on a layman for which they could find an ecclesiastic fitted." "I fully admit," he agreed, "that your conclusion from the premises as laid down by you is just and legitimate. But what about the Premises themselves?"

> Surely if they are correct I ought not to remain a day in the mixed Royal College of Science, in the mixed Agricultural Training Department or on the Senate of the Queen's University, of which I am an acting member. Indeed the

39. Ibid.

Agricultural Training Department is more objectionable than any Queen's College inasmuch as it is a *Boarding Establishment*. Before I joined the Catholic University I was connected with the College of Science and with the Glasnevin institution [i.e., the Agricultural Training Department]. During the seventeen years that I have been professor of the former I have taken a prominent part in the work of the latter. Is this compatible with the conspicuous leadership which you have assigned me? The truth is I joined the Catholic University not because I was an opponent of mixed education, for as I was at the time, as I informed Dr. Newman, in favour of the principle in theory, but because I believe that all progress must emanate from within a people and cannot be impressed upon them by external means, and consequently that a great Liberal Catholic University could do more for the advancement of learning and the intellectual and political training of Irish Catholics than any number of Government Institutions, I believed that such a University was possible in the hands of Newman.

"I think," Sullivan maintained, "though I am obliged to say it myself, that no one has worked harder or given more of his time to assist in the founding of such an Institution, than I have for sixteen years."

"Even after the departure of Dr. Newman," he confessed, "I did not despair of seeing a Catholic University in which the ideas and idiosyncracies of the Irish people would find a genial nursery. That hope has alas! vanished."

If during the time I have been connected with the University I have appeared to anyone as a leader, it was not on account of any abstract opinions or discussions of education principles, but in Academic Work. If you go back to my pamphlet published nearly ten years ago you will find that the chief objection I urged against the Queen's Colleges was the exclusion of Catholics from its chairs. I stated then if the premises of Lord Clarendon had been fulfilled and the Catholics given that share in them to which they were entitled we should perhaps never have heard of the claim for a Catholic University.

But even had I taken a more decided view of the denominational side of the Education Question than I have done, the present position of the University is so wholly different from what it was when I joined it that I would be released from all ties which might be considered to transcend my freedom to accept the office of president of a Queen's College

The bishops ideal of a University is certainly not mine. I feel everyday more and more the hopelessness of labouring to establish a free Catholic University. The bishops want a Seminary or rather a number of Diocesan Seminaries under their absolute control. With them Science and secular learning are naturally secondary objects, and while on the one hand the supposed dangers to faith which are believed to arise from the cultivation of Sciences tend to make them suspicious of it, they are not from their education [on the other hand] alive to its importance as an element of secular education.

"They wish besides," he charged, "to impose upon University Students the discipline which in my opinion is even unsuited to a Seminary."

"Without suitable buildings, museums &c.," Sullivan further observed, "without endowment to pay the professors, without prestige, without the facility of giving degrees, with the common sense of the majority in opposition to their system of discipline, with the apathy of a large number of the clergy and bishops and the unconcealed hostility of a considerable number of priests, it is not possible to maintain a central Catholic University in Dublin." "The bishops," he shrewdly added, "I have no doubt prefer an examining University, and this affords the simplest solution to the Government. I assume that if any step be taken next year to meet the wants of the bishops, it will be in this direction."

> As a scientific man I cannot consent to see young Catholics—my own sons—deprived of the means of competing in knowledge with their Protestant fellow countrymen. As a layman I cannot consent to allow the office of teacher to become among Catholics the exclusive privilege of priests. In no sense then can I be considered to be in the camp of the bishops any more than in the opposite one.
>
> I have carefully weighed your conclusion. I have consulted several friends here and although there is not one whose opinion I would defer to more than you own, I have come to the conclusion that though I may not become a candidate for Cork, my antecedents and present position would not be a bar to my doing so. I am further strengthened in this view by the remarkable unanimity with which public opinion—the opinion of all parties in T.C.D. [Trinity College Dublin], the Academy [Royal Irish Academy] &c. have bestowed the office upon me.

"If I could," Sullivan confessed, "I would have detached myself long since from the Catholic University. I made two attempts already."

"But," he further insisted, "after the sacrifices I had made of time and labour, which if devoted to scientific or professional pursuits would have been more profitable to me in reputation or money, I cannot be expected, where there is no vital principle at stake to plunge into certain ruin." "On the other hand," he added, "although my chance of Cork would in any case be very slender judging by my previous experience, I am bound in the interests of my family to look for legitimate promotion. The only promotion open to me is a Queen's College. Even though the Catholic University were to be richly endowed tomorrow there is no opening there. Even a Pro Vice Rectorship can only be filled by a priest." "But mere promotion," Sullivan assured Monsell in concluding this very long letter, "is not my only or even my secondary motive—I see my position growing day by day more precarious, at the same time that the two ideas for which I laboured—a great technological Institute, and a great free Liberal Catholic University are further from realisation than ever."

Sullivan did decide to become a candidate, and when he was asked by the lord lieutenant to become president of Queen's College, Cork, he wrote Woodlock on September 19, explaining that he had decided to accept, and Woodlock forwarded his letter to the archbishop of Cashel. "The appointment of Sullivan," Leahy replied on September 21, "is a great blow to the Catholic University, to Catholic Education, to the Catholic Church of Ireland" (W). "It is announced," he reported, referring to a Dublin evening paper, "in the Mail in Capital Letters, because the Mail knows it is a heavy blow to us." "I send the Letter," he added, referring to Sullivan's resignation, "to the Cardinal." "At the desire of Mgr. Woodlock," Leahy informed Cullen that same day, "I forward to your Eminence Dr. Sullivan's letter to him. His appointment to the Presidentship of Cork College is undoubtedly a great blow to the Catholic University & to the cause of Catholic Education. It is one other instance of the deserter going over to the enemy for filthy lucre" (C). "I thank your Eminence," he added, referring to the papal briefs authorizing a national synod, "for the papers relating to holding of the Plenary Synod. After what Rome says we could not think of abandoning the Catholic University, though rumour has been saying that the Bishops, or some of them, are for winding up the University."

Indeed, Sullivan's accepting the presidency of the Queen's College, Cork, appears to have stiffened the resolve of the bishops as a body to sustain the University at any cost. "We had the Maynooth Board meeting on the 14th and the University meeting on the 15th and 16th," Cullen reported to Kirby on October 19, "all the Bishops were present excepting Dr. Power [Waterford] who was suffering from bronchitis, and Dr. Keane of Cloyne who, it is said, is suffering from the brain and loss of memory, dangerous symptoms if they really exist—Dr. McHale was present at the Maynooth Board, but went home immediately and took no part in matters connected with the University" (K). "Now," Cullen then explained, "having been taught by Mr. Gladstone's bill that we must be guided by scripture authority *Nolite confidere in principibus in filiis hominum in quibus non est salus* [Place not your confidence in princes who are the sons of men in whom there is no salvation]. We have determined to put our trust in God, and the blessing of the Holy See, and to make united efforts to encourage the University and to make it flourish. You will see from the resolutions what we have done—but we did a great deal more than we published. I hope God will bless what has been done." "We have however," Cullen confessed, "great difficulties to contend with. Mr. Sullivan one of our most distinguished Professors (he is celebrated in Chemistry) left us and was made President of the Queens' College in Cork." "Another," he added, referring to Henry Hennessy and David B. Dunne respectively, "who had a great name was also discovered to have led for some years an improper life. We called on him to resign but I think he will bring his case into a law court, and defy us. Another has been in the court of bankruptcy." "You see," he pointed out, "what troubles there are in managing laymen. Sullivan was receiving from the University as salary three hundred pounds per annum and an equal sum in fees from the students. He will get something more from the Queen's College. The second had three hundred per annum and the third two hundred pounds." "The first," Cullen further observed, referring to Sullivan, "was very good at teaching, the other two let their classes dwindle away, and in the end did very little or nothing for their salaries. I trust things will now take another turn. I dare say the Jesuits will keep good discipline in the residence house." "The priest who was therefore [sic] before [O'Loughlin]," Cullen noted finally, "utterly failed."

The resolutions published by the bishops after their meeting in regard to the Catholic University included:

Resolution No. 1—That, with a view to the improvement of Catholic Education, and in order to make our University a great centre of Catholic Education throughout Ireland, we will take immediate steps to affiliate to it the several Colleges, Seminaries, and higher schools of our respective dioceses; that we approve and adopt the scheme proposed to our meeting relative to examinations for Matriculation and Degrees in Arts, Philosophy and Theology; and that we sanction the arrangements for the creation of Bourses and Exhibitions, and authorise the University Council to complete and carry out this scheme in all its details.

Resolution No. 2—That we pledge ourselves to have the prescribed collection for the Catholic University made every year on the third Sunday of November, in every parish in our respective dioceses, giving it precedence of all local claims.

Resolution No. 3—That, whilst earnestly exhorting our flocks to support the Catholic University by their generous contributions, and to sustain by their influence our Catholic Educational Institutions, we renew our most solemn admonitions to Catholic parents to keep their children far away from all condemned colleges and schools.

Resolution No.4—That, whilst we sympathise with our people in every legitimate effort to ameliorate the condition and promote the temporal welfare of our common country, we, as Bishops, call upon them to use all constitutional means to uphold the cause of Catholic Education, and we pledge ourselves to support and exhort our people to support as candidates for Parliamentary honours only those who will, in Parliament and out of Parliament, strenuously sustain our Educational Rights, which are inseparably bound up with the best interests of religion.

Resolution No.5—That the administration, financial and disciplinary, of St. Patrick's House of Residence, Stephen's-green, be confided to the Jesuit Fathers.

Resolution No. 6—That the erection of a new School of Medicine and University Hall, on the University site of Stephen's-green, shall be commenced without delay, the plans to be previously approved by the University Council; and that a Committee be organised by the Rector to aid in collecting funds for that purpose.

Resolution No.7—That the Rector be authorised to engage the services of competent gentlemen as lecturers on the following subjects for the present year, eight lectures to be delivered on each subject, viz—English Language,

English Literature and Poetry, Fine Arts, Geology, Irish Antiquities, Evidences
of Christian Religion, Modern Irish History.

Resolution No. 8—That we will use our best efforts to establish and
maintain Classical Schools in the principle towns of our dioceses.[40]

Though no list of the resolutions that the bishops preferred not to publish appears
to have survived in the Cullen correspondence, they may be deduced, in part at
least, from the bishops' further correspondence with Woodlock.

Whatever was resolved by the bishops, publicly or privately, however, the crucial question was whether they would be able to raise enough money to make their
resolutions effective. Thus, all depended immediately upon the result of the annual collections that were scheduled in most Irish dioceses for the third Sunday in
November. "We had our collections," Cullen reported to Kirby on Wednesday,
November 19, referring to the diocese of Dublin, "for the University last Sunday. I
think we shall get fourteen hundred pounds. All the Bishops promised to collect
except Dr. McHale—but several Bishops never collect" (K). "It is very hard,"
Cullen explained again, "to manage the professors who are nearly all laymen, and
it is also difficult to get students." "We had a famous professor of mathematics Mr.
Casey," he added, by way of example, "We pay him three hundred pounds per
annum. Trinity College offered him within the last few days four hundred pounds
per annum if he would go to them, and they would require him to give only fifty-
two lessons in the year. They would also provide apartments, and firing. However, he has not consented to go." "See how difficult," Cullen then concluded, "for
a poor people to fight with a rich government."

The collection in Dublin, however, exceeded even Cullen's expectations. In the
end it amounted to nearly nineteen hundred pounds, the largest annual sum ever
collected in that diocese for the University. Indeed, Dublin, which usually contributed about one-fifth of any national collection made in Ireland, proved once again
to be an accurate barometer as some ninety-eight hundred pounds was eventually
collected for the year 1873–74.[41] The figure would have been even larger if the
collection had been made in all the dioceses. Neither the archbishop of Tuam nor
the bishop of Meath authorized collections in their dioceses. Needless to say,
Woodlock was delighted by the opportunity provided by the increase in funds to
fill the vacant offices and chairs in the University and to reduce the University's
debt of some forty-five hundred pounds. In his report of the previous July, it will
be recalled, Woodlock had pointed out to the bishops that the office of vice-rector
and some half dozen chairs in the arts and science faculties needed to be filled.
This difficulty, moreover, had been compounded by the resignations of Hennessy,
who was finally persuaded to resign, and Sullivan. The bishops then filled two

---

40. *Freeman's Journal,* October 18, 1873.
41. See the Catholic University balance sheet on p. 264.

positions inexpensively by appointing Gerald Molloy, professor of theology in Maynooth and a geologist of some note, as vice-rector as well as professor of natural philosophy (replacing Hennessy).[42] John Campbell was appointed professor of chemistry to replace Sullivan, and two priests, George Polin and Robert Ormsby, were appointed to the vacant chairs of modern languages and ancient history. The chair of higher mathematics, as Cullen pointed out to Kirby, had been filled earlier by the appointment of John Casey, and the chair of Irish was in time offered to and accepted by Bryan O'Looney. Two more appointments were eventually made in the faculty of law: Hugh H. McDermott and R. P. Carton, both distinguished barristers, were appointed professors of constitutional and common law, and of equity and conveyancing.[43]

An effort was also made to revitalize and reform the student body.[44] There are apparently no figures for the academic year 1872–73, which is in itself telling, of the number of students enrolled in the University. In the academic year 1871–72, however, there was a total of ninety-seven students enrolled, of whom fourteen were in the arts faculty and eighty-three in medicine. Apparently in 1872–73, the number of arts students had diminished virtually to zero, while the number in medicine remained at about eighty. At the opening of the academic year 1873–74, which began on the second Monday in October, the number of arts students had increased to twenty-five and the number in medicine was seventy-five, for a total of one hundred students. Fifteen of the arts students, moreover, lived in St. Patrick's House, which was entrusted to the supervision of two fathers of the Society of Jesus. Father O'Loughlin, the former dean of discipline in charge of the house was relieved of his duties. He did, however, retain his title as dean of the University church. A house of residence was also opened for the medical students and placed under the supervision of Christopher Nixon, a demonstrator in anatomy on the medical faculty. Because the house was opened late in the term and Nixon then fell ill, however, it failed to attract any of the seventy-five medical students, who chose instead to live off campus.

The bishops' achievement in providing the necessary funds, refurbishing the faculty, and revitalizing the student body, especially in the arts faculty, was very impressive. Even more important to the future of the University, however, was the decision, which was not published by the bishops, to give the laity a voice in the governing of the University, by setting up an academic council to include them. Because at the general meeting of the bishops in October, the bishops had been unable to make arrangements to implement their resolutions, the bishops of the

42. On resigning his chair in Maynooth in June 1874, Molloy was indemnified to the extent that he did not receive his salary as a professor in the Catholic University; he was entitled to receive two-thirds at his former Maynooth salary, or some £175.
43. See "Registry of Colleges" section in I.C.D., 1874.
44. W, see undated memorandum on student numbers and salaries of faculty.

University board were asked to convene again on December 2. Woodlock, therefore, wrote the archbishop of Cashel about the vital issue of lay participation and its consideration at the forthcoming meeting. "Quite right," Leahy replied on November 11, "that the powers & attributions of the Lay members of the Council should be clearly defined before they begin to act" (W). "Therefore," he advised, "it might be better not to invite them to the Meeting of the 2.nd Dec. but to have the Bishops devote [a] good part of that Meeting to the consideration & determination of the question. A good excuse for not inviting the Lay Gentlemen just now is that they will not have been all elected by that time, as they certainly will not, nor the Council consequently be fully constituted." "As to the power they should enjoy," Leahy then explained, turning to the crucial question, "it will be for the Bishops to settle that. The Bishops ought to settle it before the Lay Gentlemen are called on to act." "To speak my own individual opinion," he assured Woodlock, "I certainly think they ought not be asked to take part in the deliberations of the Council without allowing them a definitive voice—power to speak & act in every respect all the same as the Bishops, except of course questions touching faith & morals." "The acts of the Council could, of course," Leahy added for good measure, "be liable to be revised & overhauled by the *Coetus Episcoporum* [the body of the bishops]."

At their meeting on December 2, 1873, however, the bishops deferred a consideration of the powers and attributes of the proposed council until their next meeting, in March 1874.[45] Before that March 3 meeting, John O'Hagan, a prominent Catholic barrister and queen's counsel, advised the bishops that a legal instrument was necessary for the admission of laymen to the council of the University. The bishops of the board, therefore, instructed Woodlock to have the instrument prepared in order that it might be submitted to the general meeting of the bishops scheduled for their adoption in June, at Maynooth.[46] When the bishops met on June 25, Woodlock submitted the required legal instrument, but upon considering it, the bishops resolved to defer the matter again "to the October meeting of the prelates so as to afford the Bishops an opportunity of examining the constitution of the senate in the English Cath. University, and, the documents concerning the organization of the governing body of the C.U. of Louvain."[47] In October, the matter was, in effect, again deferred, and it continued to be deferred repeatedly as long as the bishops were responsible for the governing of the University.[48]

The bishops' refusal to allow any lay participation in the governing body of the University, in spite of the continued recommendation of such by Woodlock year

---

45. W, "Minute Book of Board of Catholic University 1861–1879."
46. Ibid.
47. Ibid.
48. Ibid.

after year in his annual reports as rector, was the real reason that the University was doomed, in the long run, to fail. The student body, though increased in the next several years, remained small in comparison to Trinity College and the Queen's Colleges. The students continued to be relatively few in number, especially in the arts faculty, despite the efforts of the bishops and clergy to recruit and even to subsidize them because the University could not grant degrees. Without a degree, a graduate of the Catholic University, no matter how able or proficient he had been in his studies, labored under a crushing disadvantage in any kind of professional endeavor that required educational credentials. In this regard, as has already been pointed out, the medical students in the Catholic University were the exception that proved the rule. In order to grant degrees the University needed a charter from the state, but as long as the bishops insisted on retaining absolute control in the governance of the University no English government would dare to grant a charter that defied the adverse public opinion both inside and outside of Parliament. To all appearances, therefore, the bishops' attitude had foreclosed on any University education under their auspices for those five to six thousand boys and young men in Catholic intermediate schools and colleges who, Woodlock maintained, desired such an education.

On the other hand, in light of the bishops' recent, formidable, and successful effort to save the University from extinction, their position was defensible. They had argued for years that only because of their collective efforts had the University survived as long as it had. They had succeeded in keeping the University running in spite of the government, in spite of the Catholic upper middle class, and in spite, even, of some of their colleagues and a considerable number of their own clergy. Their recent revival of the virtually defunct University had not been simply a matter of redeeming Irish-Catholic honor. It had also been yet another proof that the only counter they had in the great game for Catholic higher education was their collective will and energy. The ministry of the day, whether Whig or Tory, Liberal or Conservative, remained their unremitting enemy, and the Catholic upper middle class, as represented by Sir Dominic Corrigan and William K. Sullivan, at least from the bishops' point of view had proven to be not only false friends but also deserters and traitors. To the bishops, therefore, the request that they give the laity, which in effect meant Sir Dominic, Sullivan, and their class, a voice in the governance of the University, without the quid pro quo of legislation promising a charter and an endowment, was only to add insult to injuries already sustained. The bishops certainly understood that without a charter and an endowment they would always be chained to the annual Sisyphian task of collecting the necessary money. If, moreover, the price for securing the charter was that the laity be given a determinant voice in governing the University, the situation would be tantamount to their having to pay the piper without even being able to request a tune. If, however, the state was willing both to charter and to endow the University, then they were willing to negotiate the role of the laity. In the meantime, it was absolutely necessary that the laity be excluded from the governance of the University until it was certain that the University was legally and financially secure.

Given the fact, therefore, that Gladstone had made it clear that an endowment was politically impossible, the bishops' continued refusal to relinquish their only bargaining counter made sense. But how, it may well be asked, were the bishops able to persuade the Irish laity to defer for so long in a matter that so vitally concerned them? In fact the upper-middle-class Catholics did not defer. They continued to send their sons to Trinity or the Queen's Colleges, or abroad if necessary. They did not support the Catholic University in proportion to their incomes as did the rest of the Catholic laity, except inasmuch as they were required to by social and political pressure. This was also the reason that the great majority of the Irish-Catholic M.P.'s, who were largely drawn from this same class, were lukewarm or indifferent to the needs of the Catholic University; it was also the reason Woodlock complained so bitterly about them to Cullen while Woodlock was in London and attempting to mobilize them for political action. That the bishops, therefore, continued to ignore the demands that this class be given a share in the governing of the University will cause little surprise. However, the Catholic upper middle class constituted only a small part of the laity. What was the effect on the higher educational needs of that part of the laity that was so fundamentally important to Catholic interests—the more than 100,000 Catholic tenant farmers, who held between thirty and two hundred acres, and their cousinhood of shopkeepers in the towns, who numbered perhaps between forty and fifty thousand. This was the class from which most of the bishops and the greatest part of the clergy were recruited, and it was the class that the bishops and priests euphemistically liked to refer to as "the people," or the "bone and sinew" of the nation. The higher educational needs of the most aspiring members of this class were generally met because the traditional professions of priest, doctor, solicitor, and even barrister, were available to them without a university degree. This was well illustrated in a letter from the bishop of Ossory to Woodlock, shortly after the bishops' strenuous effort, at their October 1873 meeting, to revitalize the University. "Mr. Healy, a shopkeeper of this town," Moran reported from Kilkenny on November 5, "called on me today to say that he was in correspondence with you about sending his son to study at the Cecelia Street school of Medicine. He requested me to write to you to say that he has always been a contributor to the Catholic University and to ask you whether you would accept payment in ready cash of £100 for fees &c. instead of the £150 spread over [torn] years which you mentioned in your note. He states that in the programme of the R.C. [Royal College] of surgeons which he has rec^d a great reduction is made for payments such as he proposes" (W).[49]

---

49. See also M, 8269 (10) for a letter from W. K. Sullivan to William Monsell, no date. "The real difficulty of Ireland is not want of Capital, or *incapacity* for skilled work on the part of the

The bishops' achievement between 1869 and 1874 with regard to all levels of Catholic education was, to say the least, very impressive. They had not only reformed the national seminary at Maynooth to their satisfaction and broken the power over primary education of their archenemy, the national board, but also they had pulled themselves together as a body to put new life and energy into the Catholic University. In the process, and under the masterful guidance of Cullen, moreover, they had maintained their unity as a body. And in not allowing themselves to be divided, they had not only sustained but also increased their already considerable power and influence in educational matters.

workmen—of course they have not in their present condition much trained skill—it is rather financial and social. Our banks do not encourage manufactures, and our middle classes do not give a practical education to their children. Even a moderate farmer who has from £500 to £1000 laid by never thinks of educating his son for trade—his only idea is to make a lawer [sic], a priest or a doctor."

Epilogue

This has been the story of the Roman Catholic Church's part in the initial stage of the emergence of the modern Irish political system. Though the story has been told largely in terms of the constituent elements—the leader, the party, and the bishops as a body—of the system, there was little doubt that between 1870 and 1874 the bishops were the most vital and dominant element in that emerging system. The early ascendancy of the bishops was a result of the fact that they were virtually full grown as a body by 1870, while the leader and the party had still a good way to go before they would realize their full political potential as constituent elements in the emerging system. The early ascendancy of the bishops also had some very important and unanticipated consequences as far as the development of the system was concerned. The most important of these was that their early dominance provoked a reaction that, ironically, made the Irish political system a good deal more radical, when it finally did emerge, than it might otherwise have been.

Crucial, therefore, to any understanding of the bishops' part in relation to the leader and the party during this period is a proper appreciation of the significance of the Gladstonian Irish-Liberal alliance in this political complex. The Irish-Liberal alliance was, in fact, subversive of any attempt to realize an Irish political system, and the reaction of virtually all advanced Irish Nationalists, whether revolutionary or constitutional, was that the alliance must be broken up if the Irish people were not to be transformed, over the long run, into mere West Britons. The commitment of the Irish bishops as a body to the Irish-Liberal alliance, in the general election of 1868, and the very great enthusiasm they exhibited in promoting it in the constituencies, provoked a profound reaction among all shades of advanced Nationalists, who instinctively realized that it was really a question of whether the identity of the people as a nation would live or die. The real problem, however, in the midst of this political delirium, was one of rallying all the advanced Nationalists in the national interest when they were so deeply divided among themselves about appropriate means and ends. Both the occasion and the focus for this rally were provided by the founding of the Amnesty Committee, in Dublin on November 12, 1868, at the very height of the general election.[1]

The committee, which demanded that the government release all the Fenian

---

1. Emmet Larkin, *The Consolidation of the Roman Catholic Church in Ireland, 1860–1870* (Chapel Hill, 1987), pp. 640–45.

prisoners, provided the common denominator for nearly every shade of Nationalist opinion, from the Fenians on the extreme left to those with more moderate and reformist views on the right. The immediate aim of the committee, of course, was to secure the release of the imprisoned Fenians, but the ulterior purpose of the more radical elements was to embarrass, and perhaps even undermine, the Irish-Liberal alliance by adding an ultra-Nationalist dimension to the Gladstonian program of legislative reform in the constituencies. Indeed, when Gladstone met Parliament in February 1869, he announced that the government would unconditionally release about half of the approximately eighty Fenian prisoners, but he would not release either the leaders of the conspiracy or those who had been serving in the British army when convicted. The Amnesty Committee, by arranging banquets, receptions, and church-door collections for those who had been released, attempted to mobilize public opinion on behalf of those who were still in prison, but Gladstone refused to be moved. In a further effort to rouse public opinion, the Fenian and the more advanced constitutional Nationalists on the committee proposed, in late May 1869, that a series of monster meetings be launched during the summer and carried into the fall all over Ireland. The more moderate members of the committee refused to countenance the proposal, and the radical elements withdrew and, at the end of May, formed the Amnesty Association.

Some forty monster meetings were held between June and October, climaxing on Sunday, October 10, in Dublin, when some 200,000 people were reported to have attended. Gladstone, however, remained adamant, and a week after the Dublin meeting, he announced that in the interest of public safety he could not release any more prisoners. The Fenians in the Amnesty Association were so furious over his decision that they decided to break up every meeting in Ireland that gave any countenance to Gladstone or to his program of reform. As the Fenians began to break up league meetings all over the country, the brunt of their actions, ironically, fell on the recently formed Tenant League, which advocated a much more radical measure of land reform than either Gladstone or his party were prepared to introduce in the House of Commons. The sad result was that at the end of 1869, the advanced Nationalists, revolutionary and constitutional, were in greater disarray than they had ever been, and the Irish-Liberal alliance, with the bishops and clergy as its guarantors in Ireland, appeared to be even more formidable.

Then, in January 1870, when the bishops as a body, exasperated by Fenian violence and intimidation, secured the formal condemnation of the Brotherhood at Rome, no one could have anticipated the long-term political consequences of their action. In condemning the Brotherhood, the bishops unwittingly initiated a profound shift to the left in the Irish political spectrum. The immediate reaction of the Fenians to their condemnation was to increase the level of violence, but that escalation was met with even more severe coercive measures on the part of the government and increased episcopal and clerical denunciations of the Fenians as a prohibited secret society. Therefore, when Isaac Butt founded the Home Government Association in May 1870, many of the more thoughtful Fenians were much more amenable to the necessity of accommodating the advanced constitutional Nationalists, in order to break up the detested Irish-Liberal alliance and at the same time teach the bishops and their clergy a salutary political lesson.

Consequently, between 1870 and 1874 the Fenian Brotherhood gradually gave up revolutionary politics for constitutional politics, and the Irish political spectrum quickly was radicalized. This Fenian conversion to constitutional methods not only would have an immediate impact in the constituencies, but also it would have a serious effect on the power and influence of the clergy and, by extension, on the vitality of the Irish-Liberal alliance. The Fenians' immediate influence in the constituencies actually had less to do with their voting strength than with their organizing power. Though they made up perhaps between 10 and 20 percent of the vote in the constituencies, it was more importantly their great energy and determination, as well as their willingness to resort to intimidation if necessary, that soon made them a force to be reckoned with in local politics. Ironically, these very qualities long had been the source of the power and influence of the clergy in the constituencies, and the Fenians wasted little time in taking the whole page out of the clergy's book. In a word, now that the Fenians had adopted constitutional politics, the clergy were faced with an alternative organizing power in the constituencies, where they had long exercised a virtual monopoly. As it soon became evident, moreover, in by-election after by-election, that the voters had set their hearts on Home Rule, it also became clear that the days of the Irish-Liberal alliance were numbered.

When that alliance unexpectedly collapsed in the aftermath of the defeat of Gladstone's University bill, in February 1873, and the anticipated political rapprochement between the bishops as a body and the Home Rulers as a movement still failed to come to pass, the movement was thrown into a severe political crisis, the resolution of which required calling a national conference for November 1873. The Nationalist consensus effected by Butt at the conference, and his emergence as leader, were confirmed in the general election of early 1874, as the Home Rulers swept the constituencies. Still the bishops refused as a body to come to terms with the apparent consensus. The real question, of course, was how Cullen and the bishops as a body were able to remain aloof in the aftermath of the collapse of the Irish-Liberal alliance, especially in the face of the Home Rule victory in the general election. Cullen's intransigence with regard to both the Home Rule movement and its leader certainly facilitated this aloofness, but he could not have sustained his position by his will alone. Indeed, if he had not been able to sustain his point of view in rational and practical terms, the bishops could not really be described as an autonomous body. Thus, in addition to his argument that the Home Rule movement was at once too Fenian and too Protestant, as well as led by a man whose personal life was morally suspect, Cullen also argued, with even greater effect, that as far as the bishops' main priority was concerned—Catholic education—the Home Rule movement had little to offer after the March 1873 collapse of the Irish-Liberal alliance, or even after the Home Rule victory in the general election a year later.

In March 1873, for example, Butt could not count on much more than a dozen of the sixty-four Irish Liberal members in the House of Commons, and Cullen could plausibly argue that the appropriate time for the bishops as a body to come to terms with the Home Rule movement, as distinguished from their individual accommodations with Home Rule candidates in the constituencies, was, not before, but after the next general election, when the Home Rulers would perhaps hold the balance of power in the new House of Commons and would thus be able to prove their mettle as a party in the interests of both Home Rule and the education question. After the general election, and in spite of the Home Rule victory, Cullen could still argue that, given Disraeli's overall Conservative majority of fifty in the House of Commons, the appropriate moment for the bishops to commit themselves as a body still had not arrived because the Home Rule party was powerless to force the pace of consideration on either Home Rule or the education question. In a word, Cullen and the bishops well understood that the real issue was power, for that was what politics was all about, and it was the Conservative government rather than the Home Rule party with which they would have to deal if they ever hoped to secure a satisfactory solution to the education question in the next Parliament.

Indeed, the crucial development for the bishops as a body during this period was that their politics became increasingly identified with the education question. As the architect of that policy, Cullen for some time had made the education question his chief political priority, much to the chagrin of those, both clerical and lay, whose priority was more nationalist or agrarian than educational. Cullen had always displayed very great caution in dealing with the national and land questions because he believed that they were potentially and dangerously divisive as far as the Catholic body was concerned. He understood, perhaps earlier and better than any of his episcopal colleagues, that effective Catholic power was a function of the unity of the body and that the education question was the one issue on which Catholics in general, and bishops and clergy in particular, could be relied upon to present a united front to the enemy, however defined. By early 1874, therefore, the refusal of the bishops as a body, with Cullen at their head, to come to terms with the Home Rule movement, because the bishops were determined to play out their hand on the education question in spite of the efforts of the reemergent leader and party to set a national agenda, was not only realistic and consistent but also it was fortunate for the emerging Irish political system. Given the relative strength, in early 1874, of the bishops vis à vis the leader and the party, any consensus achieved would have resulted not only in the bishops' domination of the system but also in their consequent and inevitable effort to modify the national agenda in the interests of the education question. This would, in fact, have been as subversive of the emerging system as the Irish-Liberal alliance had been earlier. Though it was not yet time, therefore, the time was fast approaching, and that will be the story of the emergence of the modern Irish political system.

Bibliographical Note

The sources of this study were mainly archival, and the printed materials used were few in number. I have not listed the books, articles, and newspapers in a formal bibliography because the reader will easily find what is pertinent in the footnotes. A number of works that have been liberally used in the writing of this volume, however, deserve especial mention. They are Patrick J. Corish's "Political Problems, 1860–1878," in *A History of Irish Catholicism,* gen. ed. Patrick J. Corish (Dublin, 1967), 5:1–59; E. R. Norman's *The Catholic Church and Ireland in the Age of Rebellion, 1859–1873* (London, 1965); David Thornley's *Isaac Butt and Home Rule* (London, 1964); L. J. McCaffrey's *Irish Federalism in the 1870's: A Study in Conservative Nationalism* (Philadelphia, 1962); volumes 4 and 5 of Peadar MacSuibhne's *Paul Cullen and His Contemporaries* (Naas, 1965, 1974, 1977); and Sean Cannon's, "Irish Episcopal Meetings, 1788–1882: A Juridico-Historical Study," *Annuarium Historiae Conciliorum: Internationale Zeitschrift für Konziliengeschictsforschung,* vol. 13 (1981), pp. 270–422. Monsignor Corish's essay and Norman's, Thornley's, and McCaffrey's books are really basic works, which no scholar or student of the period can fail to profit by. The late Father MacSuibhne's volumes contain a considerable number of Cullen letters, which, though some lack designation as to location, some are not quoted in full, and some are unfortunately paraphrased, are, taken all together, very valuable. Father Cannon's illuminating study of Irish episcopal meetings is one of the most original pieces of work to appear on the modern Irish Church in recent years. The exhaustiveness of the research and the fine handling of the conceptual framework make this book a significant contribution not only to knowledge but to inter-disciplinary studies as well. The archival materials consulted are to be found mainly in Dublin, London, and Rome.

In Dublin the main bodies of material consulted were:

1. The papers of Isaac Butt. National Library of Ireland.
2. The papers of Paul Cullen. Dublin Diocesan Archives.
3. The papers of William O'Neill Daunt. National Library of Ireland.
4. The papers of Laurence Gillooly, C. M. Elphin Diocesan Archives, Sligo. They have been microfilmed and are on deposit in the National Library of Ireland.
5. The papers of Patrick Leahy. Cashel Diocesan Archives. These are also available on microfilm in the National Library of Ireland.
6. The papers of William Monsell, first Baron Emly. National Library of Ireland.

7. The papers of Bartholomew Woodlock. Dublin Diocesan Archives.

In London the main bodies of material consulted were:

1. Foreign Office Papers for Italy and Rome. Public Record Office, Chancery Lane.
2. The papers of Henry Edward Manning. Westminster Diocesan Archives.

In Rome the main bodies of material consulted were:

1. The papers of Tobias Kirby. Archives of the Irish College.
2. The Irish correspondence in the Archives of the Sacred Congregation for the Evangelization of the People, formerly the Society for the Propagation of the Faith. Piazza di Spagna, Rome.

Index